Henryk Grossman Works, Volume 2

Historical Materialism Book Series

The Historical Materialism Book Series is a major publishing initiative of the radical left. The capitalist crisis of the twenty-first century has been met by a resurgence of interest in critical Marxist theory. At the same time, the publishing institutions committed to Marxism have contracted markedly since the high point of the 1970s. The Historical Materialism Book Series is dedicated to addressing this situation by making available important works of Marxist theory. The aim of the series is to publish important theoretical contributions as the basis for vigorous intellectual debate and exchange on the left.

The peer-reviewed series publishes original monographs, translated texts, and reprints of classics across the bounds of academic disciplinary agendas and across the divisions of the left. The series is particularly concerned to encourage the internationalization of Marxist debate and aims to translate significant studies from beyond the English-speaking world.

For a full list of titles in the Historical Materialism Book Series
available in paperback from Haymarket Books, visit:
https://www.haymarketbooks.org/series_collections/1-historical-materialism

Henryk Grossman Works, Volume 2

Political Writings

Henryk Grossman

Edited and Introduced by
Rick Kuhn

Translated by
Dominika Balwin, Ben Fowkes, Joseph Fraccia, Floris
Kalman, Rick Kuhn, Ken Todd, and Frank Wolff

Haymarket Books
Chicago, IL

First published in 2020 by Brill Academic Publishers, The Netherlands
© 2020 Koninklijke Brill NV, Leiden, The Netherlands

Published in paperback in 2021 by
Haymarket Books
P.O. Box 180165
Chicago, IL 60618
773-583-7884
www.haymarketbooks.org

ISBN: 978-1-64259-598-7

Distributed to the trade in the US through Consortium Book Sales and
Distribution (www.cbsd.com) and internationally through Ingram
Publisher Services International (www.ingramcontent.com).

This book was published with the generous support of Lannan
Foundation and Wallace Action Fund.

Special discounts are available for bulk purchases by organizations and
institutions. Please call 773-583-7884 or email info@haymarketbooks.org
for more information.

Cover art and design by David Mabb. Cover art is a detail of *Variant 4,
Morris, Garden Tulip / Popova, Untitled textile design* (2006).

Printed in the United States.

10 9 8 7 6 5 4 3 2 1

Library of Congress Cataloging-in-Publication data is available.

Contents

Acknowledgements

Tom O'Lincoln and Ben Hillier offered valuable comments on or advice for drafts of the introduction to this volume. I am grateful to the staff of the YIVO Archive in New York, particularly Leo Greenbaum, who provided access to manuscript and published material associated with the Jewish Social Democratic Party of Galicia; Angus Cameron and Jürgen Braunstein obtained material that was difficult for me to access. The Australian National University provided funding and other support for the project of which this book forms a part. My partner Mary Gorman as well as close friends and Socialist Alternative comrades encouraged, indulged and supported my Grossmania.

Introduction

Rick Kuhn

From the start, Henryk Grossman's writings were pervaded by a Marxist under-standing of society that necessarily transgressed the boundaries of conven-tional academic disciplines. Many of the essays and letters mainly concerned with economic questions, in the first volume of his works,[1] included political analyses and comments. These were also present in his best-known public-ation, *The Law of Accumulation and Breakdown of the Capitalist System*. The first full English translation will be the third volume of this series. Grossman's political perspectives were also implicitly articulated by studies in economic history that will be included in the fourth volume. While his framework was consistently Marxist – characterised by internationalism and the promotion of working-class revolution through the political intervention of socialists – the positions he took on some issues changed. That is particularly apparent in this, the second volume, which brings together the first English translations of primarily political publications and correspondence. Those written before the First World War were inspired and informed by the activities and perspect-ives of the Bund (the General Union of Jewish Workers of Lithuania, Poland and Russia), and Grossman's own involvement with the workers movement in Galicia, the Austrian-occupied province of partitioned Poland. They were mainly devoted to advocating Bundist positions on the 'national question', in relation to the structures of socialist organisations and, later, states. After the War, his approach to these and many other issues was Leninist. The discussion below provides context for the writings in this volume and offers brief assess-ments of their value; their titles are **bolded**.

The Galicia of Grossman's youth was undergoing rapid political and eco-nomic change. The province had gained considerable autonomy after 1866 and was ruled by ethnically Polish, aristocratic landowners through the Sejm (parliament), elected on a thoroughly undemocratic franchise. The peasants on their land were predominantly Polish in the west of the province, where Kraków was the cultural capital of partitioned Poland. L'viv, the province's largest city and seat of the Sejm, was in the less developed east, where the Polish nobility exploited and oppressed a predominately 'Ruthenian' (Ukrain-ian) peasantry. The third largest ethnic group, about ten percent of the pop-

---

1 Grossman 2017a.

ulation, were Jews whose mother tongue was overwhelmingly Yiddish. Like Ukrainians, Jews were subject to systematic discrimination, although they were mainly artisans, small commercial businesspeople or, increasingly, workers, rather than peasants. The slow pace of industrialisation in Galicia was not sufficient to employ the expanding population and emigration increasingly took on mass proportions from the 1880s.

From the much smaller town of Tarnów, Herz Grossman and Sara Kurz moved up and out to Kraków. He changed professions, from the traditional Jewish occupation of running a bar, to become a small industrialist and mine owner. The couple was Jewish but assimilating to Polish high culture. They were known by more Polish versions of their very Yiddish names, Henryk and Salome. For the purposes of the Austrian state, they only married three years after the birth of the last of their five children. Chaskel, always known as Henryk, the fourth, was born in 1881. Eventually, in 1915, he formally changed his name to Henryk, probably one of the few fruits of his legal training.[2]

Bundism

Young Henryk did not have a traditional Jewish education. He attended an academic high school, where the language of instruction was Polish. He never learnt to write confidently in Yiddish. While at school, Grossman became involved in the socialist movement and helped produce a socialist magazine. He continued to support radical secondary students after entering Kraków's Jagiellonian University, in 1900. There, he joined Ruch,[3] the organisation of university students associated not only with the Polish Social Democratic Party of Galicia (PPSD) but also the Social Democracy of the Kingdom of Poland and Lithuania (SDKPiL), the Party of Rosa Luxemburg, and the more nationalist Polish Socialist Party (PPS), with which the PPSD was aligned, in the Russian-occupied Congress Kingdom of Poland. Grossman helped smuggle literature for the SDKPiL into the Russian Empire and joined its front, the Fund for the Assistance of Political Prisoners and Exiles. But his principal political reference point was the Bund. Both the SDKPiL and the Bund were parts of the internationalist, Marxist wing of the world labour movement.

The October–November 1904 Congress of the PPSD took place in the context of rising strike levels in the Austro-Hungarian Empire. There was a major

---

2   Unless otherwise indicated, the sources of all information about Grossman's life can be found in Kuhn 2007.
3   'Ruch' means 'Movement'.

debate between the leadership, which wanted to consolidate the Party's nationalist orientation and the internationalist left. The leadership prioritised achieving Polish independence over the pursuit of working-class interests and moved to formalise the PPSD's relationship with the PPS. It also opposed the activists seeking greater autonomy for the Jewish workers' organisations they had built, despite the leadership's malign neglect. The leaders around Ignacy Daszyński defeated the internationalists of the Party's left and the young Bundists.

All of Grossman's publications before 1911 were interventions into political controversies. They cast light not only on his own positions, as a Bundist on the left wing of international social democracy, but also on the history of the left in Galicia, particularly struggles against Polish nationalism and the efforts of Jewish workers to establish effective organisations.

Student critics of the PPSD's leadership established the journal *Zjednoczenie*, a left split from the established student publication *Promień* which followed the PPS line.[4] *Zjednoczenie's* first issue, whose editor in chief and publisher was Grossman, appeared in February 1905. It began a series of articles on the different socialist organisations in Russia, where the social crisis associated with the Russo-Japanese War and Russia's defeat led to the outbreak of the 1905 revolution. The first article in the series outlined the politics of the Russian Social Democratic Labour Party (RSDLP) and quoted at length from a 1903 essay on the national question by Vladimir Ilych Lenin, notably his negative assessment of the PPS.[5]

The message 'From the editors' explaining the appearance of *Zjednoczenie*, promised a more open approach to socialist thought and, in contrast with the PPS's nationalism, stressed: 'We will not just "tolerate" the Ruthenians, or deny Jews the right to determine their nationality'.[6] At this time, Grossman was particularly concerned with the national question. He and other Jewish members of the Party, both students and workers, were critical of its dismissive and assimilationist attitude to the Jewish working class, which they had been drawing into socialist trade unions and associations.

From 1897, the Bund had successfully recruited Jewish workers into its own ranks and trade unions under its leadership. In 1902, Grossman initiated similar efforts to organise Jewish workers in Kraków into the Postęp association,[7] affiliated with the PPSD, and then into PPSD-oriented unions. Grossman and the other socialist students building Jewish workers associations, together with

---

4 *'Zjednoczenie'* means *'Unification'. 'Promień'* means *'The Ray'.*
5 Lenin 1964, p. 460.
6 Grossman 1905c, 'From the editors', see below, p. 65.
7 *'Postęp'* means *'Progress'.*

the young workers they had drawn into politics, transformed themselves into organic intellectuals of the working class. Similar processes were occurring in L'viv and, to a limited extent, some smaller cities in Galicia.

The PPSD leadership, pre-eminently Daszyński but also Herman Diamand and Max Zetterbaum, both Jews, argued that the Jewish population was embracing higher Polish culture and language. The faster this took place, the better, they argued. So devoting resources specifically to Jewish workers, outside election campaigns, was a waste. Labour Zionists were making efforts to organise Jewish workers, in competition with the Social Democrats. Daszyński and other leaders nevertheless regarded the successes of Grossman and his comrades, together with their call for arrangements through which Jewish socialists could co-ordinate their activities across Galicia, as a threat to their control of the Party and its Polish nationalist outlook. Given the PPSD's hostility, covert preparations for the establishment of a separate Jewish socialist workers party began as early as August 1904. The PPSD's leaders learnt about this activity and the Party's 1904 Congress condemned the notion of a separate party for Jewish workers. Two weeks later, the PPSD dissolved the Jewish Agitation Committee in L'viv.

Grossman wrote a pamphlet, *The Proletariat Faced with the Jewish Question*, published in January 1905, to make the case for a Jewish social democratic party. It was couched as a response to articles on the Jewish question in the prominent left political-cultural journal *Krytyka*.[8] Tobiasz Aschkenaze, a Jew, advocated Jewish assimilation to Polish culture. Under the pseudonym Henryk Biro-Jakubowicz, the Bundist theoretician Bronisław Grosser, who Grossman knew personally, provided a sober and favourable account of his organisation's history and policies. But the target of Grossman's polemic was the initial contribution to the discussion, by prominent PPS theorist Kazimierz Kelles-Krauz, writing under the pseudonym Michał Luśnia. In making a case for the recognition of eastern European Jews as a nation, against the dominant view in his Party, Kelles-Krauz was attempting to win the Bund over to the PPS's primary goal of Polish independence.[9]

On the basis of the rise of Zionism, which Grossman identified as a bourgeois movement, Luśnia concluded that the Jews had achieved national consciousness and become a nation. Luśnia did relate the rise of nationalism to

---

8 '*Krytyka*' means '*Critique*'.

9 For more detailed discussions of Kelles-Krauz's position on the Jewish question, including more extensive quotations from his article in English, see Sobelman 1990 and Snyder 1997 particularly pp. 191–201.

the development of capitalism. But, the pamphlet maintained, his approach was idealist rather than materialist and ignored class divisions in Jewish society. Grossman insisted that there were two Jewish questions. The bourgeois Jewish question concerned the Polish capitalist class's oppression of Jewish workers and competition with Jewish capitalists. These consequences of capitalism would be eliminated by socialism. The Jewish working class's Jewish question concerned its own effective organisation. This analysis, although it reproduced the rationale for Austrian Social Democracy's adoption of a federal structure in 1896 and 1897, ignored the racism that affected all Jews, if in different ways. Jewish workers were not only disadvantaged by their lack of a social democratic organisation of their own; antisemitism profoundly affected many aspects of their lives. There were parallels between Grossman's position on this issue in his polemical pamphlet and the way Rosa Luxemburg and the SDKPiL, in their justified hostility to PPS's nationalism, failed to grasp the significance of national oppression.[10]

Grossman's perspective embodied a far more consistent class orientation than Luśnia's. While Luśnia sought to win the Bund over to the view that the pursuit of Polish independence was the priority in the current stage of the struggle for socialism, for Grossman independent working-class organisation and the struggle between capital and labour were fundamental.

In his argument for the establishment in Galicia of an independent Jewish social democratic party, like the Bund, Grossman engaged in exaggeration, in an effort to straighten out socialist opinion. Both Luśnia and Vinitisky – a pseudonym of Vladimir Medem, an influential Bundist leader and theoretician – were unsure whether the Jews in Eastern Europe would eventually assimilate or not. According to Grossman, they were wrong: with industrialisation, as more and more Jewish artisans became workers in enterprises run by Jewish capitalists, the main tendency was a decline in the need to learn Polish. Furthermore, Yiddish literature and culture was expanding in scope and quality. It was possible and simpler to make a much stronger case for establishing specific organisational forms for Jewish workers by demonstrating, in these terms, that they were a distinct section of the Polish (and Russian) proletariat, with their own language and customs which they would not abandon in the space of a few years. Such an approach was quite compatible with Grossman's insight that 'It is not the Jew who subsides into capitalist society but modern capitalism that encroaches upon Jewry!'[11]

---

10   See Luxemburg 1976.

11   Grossman 1905a, *The Proletariat Faced with the Jewish Question*, see below p. 58.

In the socialist camp, Grossman argued more persuasively, the 'legend' of the superiority of Polish culture and the need for Jews to assimilate to it ghettoised Jewish workers and hindered their participation in the struggle against capitalism. Given the PPSD's legitimate outrage at assimilationist policies that discriminated against Poles in Germany's Polish provinces, its attitude to Jews in Galicia was hypocritical. The pamphlet concluded that the establishment of a Jewish party, alongside the other national organisations in the general Austrian Social Democratic Workers Party would destroy the vestiges of the ghetto *within* the working class.

With its lapses into breathlessness, florid prose and show-off references, *The Proletariat Faced with the Jewish Question* was Grossman's first known work. He was capable of a more direct and effective political style: these deficiencies were not apparent in his writings published a few months later. A brief reference to the methodology of considering a tendency and its counter-tendencies, in relation to the process of Jewish assimilation, on the other hand, foreshadowed his identification of its significance in Marx's discussion of movements in the rate of profit.[12]

The appearance of *Zjednoczenie* provided PPSD leaders with the opportunity to purge Grossman, a severe irritant because of his activities among Jewish workers and efforts to spread ideas critical of the Party's broader nationalist politics. When he refused to renounce his association with *Zjednoczenie*, he was expelled. Three weeks later, he reversed his position and was readmitted. The PPSD Executive was compelled by pressure from hundreds of Party members and Jewish workers, which it had not expected, to welcome Grossman back. He returned to organise the impending split in the PPSD that created the Jewish Social Democratic Party of Galicia (JSDP). Forced to choose between the two projects he had been pursuing in parallel, the Bundist organisation of Jewish workers and the effort to build a cross-national radical socialist current in Galicia around *Zjednoczenie*, Grossman opted for the one that had already won a significant working-class following. Meanwhile, *Zjednoczenie* continued to appear under a new editor in chief. But a Galician rival to the PPSD, like the SDKPiL in competition with the PPS in the Congress Kingdom, never emerged.

In early April, as secretary of the 'Temporary (Secret) Committee of Jewish Workers in Galicia' Grossman sent a **letter** to the Foreign Committee of

---

12   Grossman 1905a, *The Proletariat Faced with the Jewish Question*, see below p. 61; Grossman 2017c; Grossmann 1992, pp. 130–4.

the Bund, which foreshadowed the split and sought assistance in the form of Yiddish literature and letters and articles for the new Party's journal, because 'we lack strength in writing in Yiddish'. Grossman's own communications with the Bund were written in Polish. Another letter to the Foreign Committee concerned the smuggling of literature into the Russian Empire. On 27 July Grossman, then the JSDP's secretary, explained his Party's situation to Bundists in Russian-occupied Poland, possibly the Bund's Warsaw Committee, asking them to send a competent person to edit the weekly newspaper which the JSDP planned to publish in the near future.

In late March, inspired by the PPSD, the Galician Trade Union Conference decided that its local associations and unions for Jewish workers would be dissolved. The Jewish socialists accelerated their plans. They announced the existence of their new Party and distributed its manifesto on May Day 1905. In Kraków, 2,000 people attended the JSDP's May Day demonstration, which marched to join the PPSD's rally in a display of working-class solidarity. Across Galicia, the JSDP soon had about 2,000 members.

Grossman, not only the new Party's founding secretary but also its principal theorist, was the main author of its manifesto, *What Do We Want?* This and his subsequent justifications for the JSDP's existence recapitulated or expanded on themes in *The Proletariat Faced with the Jewish Question*, in different registers, to different audiences, emphasising different aspects of the case for the Party. The manifesto was primarily addressed to Jewish social democrats and highlighted the PPSD's failure to organise Jewish workers effectively and to combat Zionism. It was not, however, only published in Yiddish but was also widely distributed in Polish, so that Polish members of the PPSD could have direct knowledge of the new Party's purposes. The JSDP finally ensured that Jewish workers could participate as equals in the struggle for socialism, around the General Party's programme, and disavowed any desire for a national programme that set out specific demands concerning the Jews of Galicia. But the PPSD immediately launched a campaign of slander and, in some places, intimidation against the new organisation. The dominant axis in the organised General Austrian Social Democratic Workers Party (SDAPÖ), between the PPSD and the German-Austrian Party, ensured that the JSDP was not admitted to the federal organisation, alongside the Czech, Italian, South-Slav and Ukrainian Parties.

At this time, no effective left currents existed in the SDAPÖ and its constituent parties. While there had been some opposition to the decision at the PPSD's 1904 Congress to consolidate the Party's nationalist politics, the concessions to Austrian imperialism of the German-Austrian Party's leaders went essentially unchallenged until the emergence of the small 'Reichenberg left' later in the decade.[13] So an alliance between the Jewish militants in Galicia and other revolutionaries for common struggle in pursuit of internationalist organisational structures and policies, including more serious efforts to combat antisemitism, was impossible. In contrast to the situation in Russia, where the Bolsheviks had built a militant left current, there was in Galicia even less of a plausible alternative to Bundism, i.e. the establishment of a separate party of the Yiddish-speaking proletariat.

The Jewish Party's 'Reply to the Polish Social Democratic Party of Galicia' answered the arguments and calumnies of the PPSD, in a special publication before the JSDP's founding Congress in June 1905. It was probably written by Grossman, who had participated in a delegation which had put the case for the JSDP directly to the Executive of the General Party in Vienna. The reply, also issued in Polish as well as Yiddish, demonstrated that the leadership of the Polish Party had been opportunistic and untrustworthy in its dealings with Jewish activists, and was ignorant about the history of and rationale for the General Austrian Party's shift to a federal, national structure, which could readily accommodate the Party of the Jewish proletariat. Daszyński's own argument for the autonomy of the PPS in Germany's Polish provinces from the Social Democratic Party of Germany (SPD) was equally valid for Jewish social democrats in Galicia.

Between 1905 and 1907, there were intense working-class struggles over economic and political demands across the Empire. The movement in Austria-Hungary paralleled and was stimulated by developments across the border in Russia, which culminated in the revolution of 1905–7. The JSDP grew rapidly, despite the hostility of the PPSD and the General Party. It organised many workers into Vienna-based social democratic trade unions for the first time, mobilised them in strikes, boycotts and political demonstrations, particularly in the Empire-wide campaign for universal male suffrage, and undertook extensive educational and propaganda work. On 5 October it began to publish the weekly *Sotsial-Demokrat*.

The JSDP's growth (to a membership of 2,500) and activity strengthened its appeal to the October 1905 Congress of the General Social Democratic Workers Party of Austria (SDAPÖ) in Vienna, against the General Party Executive's condemnation of the Jewish organisation and refusal to admit it to the Austrian social democratic federation. Grossman prepared two large broadsheets in German to make the JSDP's case for recognition. *Report to the Congress of the General Austrian Social Democratic Party* elaborated on the analysis in

---

13   The current was based in Reichenberg, now Liberec in the Czech Republic, around Josef
       Strasser. See Hautmann 1970 and Strasser 1982.

What Do We Want?, providing an account of the political economy of the Jewish working class in Galicia and detailed information about the JSDP's growth and activities. Most of *To the Social Democrats of Austria* recycled material from the 'Reply to the Polish Social Democratic Party'. It emphasised the JSDP's orthodoxy, hostility to Zionism, right to a place in the federal Austrian Party and the PPSD's execrable record of relations with the Jewish working class.

In the face of the revolutionary movement in Russia and the activities of the St Petersburg Soviet, the Tsar promised a constitution and a parliament on the day the Austrian General Party Congress opened. In the climate of rising working-class self-confidence and activity, the Congress was preoccupied with the campaign for universal male suffrage in Austria. The JSDP's representatives, including Grossman, agreed that discussion of their appeal could be postponed. But the appeal never made it back onto a Congress agenda and the JSDP remained outside the General Party. There was, however, some sympathy for the Jewish Party among Czech social democrats. Grossman repackaged material from earlier explanations of his organisation's existence for an article, 'The Jewish Social Democratic Party of Galicia', published in the Czech Party's theoretical journal, in early 1906. In *The Proletariat in the Face of the Jewish Question*, he had argued that Marx's comments about the fate of the Jews, in his very early work *On the Jewish Question*, had been superseded by later developments. The point was now bolstered by a comparison with Engels's 1852 observation (then still attributed to Marx) that the Czech nation was dying out.

While admission to the General Austrian Party had been ruled out, at least for the time being, the Bund encouraged the Jewish Party. One of the Bund's founders, Shmuel Gozhansky, addressed the JSDP's second Congress, at the end of May 1906. The two organisations' political affinity was apparent in a successful motion, moved by Grossman, to demand national cultural autonomy. The motion constituted a major, formal shift away from his and the JSDP's earlier contention that, for the working class, the Jewish question was just a matter of Jewish workers' right to their own organisation. The proposal for national cultural autonomy was formulated by the prominent SDAPÖ theorist Karl Renner in 1899 and adopted by the Bund in 1901, although only raised as one of its *immediate* demands in 1905. National cultural autonomy meant the devolution of responsibility for educational and cultural matters to democratic, national bodies which would administer the affairs of their nations, wherever in the state its members lived.[14] For the Bund and JSDP, though not Renner, the Jews were a non-territorial nation, equally entitled to national cultural autonomy.

---

14   See Synopticus (i.e. Renner) 1899; Tobias 1972, pp. 331–2; Gechtman 2005, p. 66.

With considerable oratorical skill, Grossman's report to the Congress 'Our Position on Electoral Reform' outlined the struggle for universal male suffrage in Austria and the importance of not fetishising legal, as opposed to illegal, revolutionary forms of struggle. He moved that the Party commit itself to participate in any general, mass strike called by the SDAPÖ over the demand. Enthusiastically received, his speech also discussed rival proposals for the reform of the Austrian state and made the case for establishing institutions for national cultural autonomy.

The argument that none of the proposals for electoral reform – proportional representation, national curia, nationally uniform electorates and strictly geographical electorates with universal, equal male suffrage, which he favoured – would eliminate the national struggles which paralysed the parliament and hindered the class struggle, was convincing. On the other hand, assigning responsibility for education and other national matters to cultural national institutions, he declared like Medem in 1904, could disarm national conflicts.[15] Although such arrangements might reduce, it was an illusion to think that they could eliminate entrenched, systemic, if informal racism in employment, for example, or the discriminatory possibilities of many economic and other policies, let alone in any formula for the allocation of resources to national cultural institutions.

Implementing national cultural autonomy would also, Grossman maintained, contribute to the preservation of a democratised multi-national Austrian state. He shared this positive attitude to the Austrian state with the German-Austrian Social Democratic Workers Party. Its stance was in sharp contrast to the more consistent opposition to national oppression expressed in the support of Russian social democrats, both Bolsheviks and Mensheviks, for the right of nations to self-determination, including secession from the Russian state. National oppression was a feature of both Empires. In Russia, however, it was particularly stark. Local ruling classes had some influence over Austria's provincial administrations, which had responsibilities exercised with a degree of autonomy from the central government.

A few months after the JSDP's second Congress, Grossman ambitiously proposed that the Party could hegemonise Jewish opposition in Galicia to the conservative regimes in L'viv and Vienna. His two-part article in the *Sotsial-Demokrat*, 'On Our Agitation and Propaganda', outlined the Party's achievements and suggested that it could go on to win over petty-bourgeois and even bourgeois Jews, and stand candidates in elections. This would require an expan-

---

15   Medem 1943, p. 216.

sion of its agitation and propaganda beyond the current preoccupation with internal party and trade union affairs to include the politics in the municipal governments and local Jewish councils, and the activities of Galician politicians in the Sejm and the lower house of the imperial parliament, the Reichsrat. Karol Einäugler, a JSDP founder and leader in L'viv, counselled against this. The Party was still vulnerable to PPSD attacks on the trade union branches associated with it, while the prospects for electoral success were very slim.[16] This sober judgement proved more accurate. While it did not experience any major setbacks, the JSDP's rapid early growth was not sustained, as the level of class struggle subsided. The Party did not stand a candidate in the first elections under universal male suffrage to the Reichsrat, in 1907.

There was no controversy over Grossman's article, '**Polish Club, Jewish Club and Zionist Charlatanry**', later in September 1906. In response to the announcement that Adolf Stand was to be the Zionist candidate for Kraków in a Reichsrat by-election, it expressed the JSDP's firmly established hostility to Zionism. Stand's goal of setting up a Jewish Club, i.e. caucus, in the Reichsrat, as opposed to the conservative Polish Club, would not serve the interests of Jewish workers. A Zionist Jewish Club would simply be the Jewish equivalent of the Polish Club, attempting to unite Jews under the leadership of the dominant classes.

On 11 April 1907, Grossman addressed a large public meeting of voters, called by the JSDP, in mainly Jewish Kazimierz on the question of '**Who Should the Kazimierz Electorate Vote for?**', in the first elections under universal male suffrage to the Reichsrat on 14 May. The candidates were the conservative architect, deputy mayor of Kraków and recipient of public construction contracts Józef Sare and Adolf Gross, a very successful left liberal lawyer and member of the Kraków municipal council. Both had been invited to attend. Gross did, Sare did not.

Grossman criticised Sare's conservative, clerical politics, backed by the *kahal*, the council of the local Jewish community, dominated by bosses, and his commitment to join the Polish Club in the Reichsrat if he was elected. That was a commitment to the ruling, antisemitic clique which was responsible for the misery of Jews in Galicia. He also attacked the Zionists, who were standing candidates in other predominantly Jewish electorates, had entirely neglected Austrian politics until recently and were proposing to set up a Jewish national caucus in the Reichsrat. The JSDP demanded recognition of Yiddish in public administration and the introduction of Yiddish instruction into primary

---

16   Eyneygler 1906.

schools, and identified the rulers of Galicia as the main obstacles to Jewish workers' cultural and political development. The successful motion Grossman moved supported Gross. It called on him not to join the Polish or the Jewish Club, to vote with the social democrats on labour questions, and endorsed the principle of national cultural autonomy as the means to resolve the national and Jewish questions.

The indictment of the idea of a Jewish Club suggested a more precise analysis of Zionism as a petty-bourgeois rather than a bourgeois movement. While Zionism certainly had capitalist sponsors, most Jewish members of the capitalist class, in Austria and elsewhere, were more comfortable with liberal or even conservative political parties. Grossman's characterisation of Zionism as petty-bourgeois was explored further in his pamphlet *Bundism in Galicia* published early in 1908.[17] The study outlined and drew lessons from the experience of the Jewish socialist movement in Galicia, including a tacit repudiation of his and the JSDP's justification for the Party's existence as a purely organisational expedient, as Grossman was withdrawing from intimate involvement with its struggles.

Having handed over the post of JSDP secretary in May 1906, in October he ceased to be the legally responsible editor and publisher of the *Sotsial-Democrat*. Grossman attended the seminars of the first Marxist professor at a German-speaking university, the economic historian Carl Grünberg, during the winter semester of 1906–7 at the University of Vienna. As the pace of class struggle declined, particularly after the first Reichsrat elections under universal male suffrage in May 1907, he started taking the final exams for his law degree in Kraków and then embarked on an academic career by moving to Vienna, where he undertook postgraduate research under Grünberg. The move was also associated with his relationship with Janina Reicher, a painter from a wealthy Jewish family in Congress Poland. He and Janina married there in late 1908.

Grossman's continued authority in the JSDP was indicated by the prominent role he played at the JSDP's third Congress in October 1908. Despite the imminence of his departure from Galicia, he was re-elected to the Executive. He was again returned to the executive at the Party's fourth Congress in 1910. Only from October 1911 did JSDP Congresses elect Executives without him.

Bundism in Galicia made a more persuasive case for the JSDP than Grossman's previous publications. It argued that the existence of the JSDP was far from being the consequence of Zionist influences, as both Zionists and mem-

---

17   Although the year on its title page was 1907, and it originally appeared as an article series from September to November 1907 in the *Sotsial-Demokrat*.

bers of the PPSD contended. Jewish workers in Galicia had in fact been a vanguard of the Austrian social democratic movement when they argued in 1892 for a federation of national parties, even though their own organisation rapidly collapsed.

Furthermore, Grossman now asserted, federalism was not simply a technical means to advance the class struggle, as he and the PPSD had previously maintained. Now he regarded the achievement of such an organisation as an aspect of the wider struggle for equal national rights in the Austrian *state*. He endorsed the SDAPÖ's federalist approach to socialist organisation and its German-Austrian Party's position on the way in which the state should accommodate different nations. Grossman did not recognise that the first relieved the parties of different nations of responsibility to whole-heartedly participate in each other's struggles against national oppression and weakened the scope for coherent assaults on the state. For the German-Austrian Party, the second, in the form of national cultural autonomy, was an excuse for supporting the preservation of the Austrian state in its current borders.

The situation in the Russian Empire was different. From 1903, the programme of the RSDLP and its Bolshevik and Menshevik factions, mainly made up of members of the dominant nationality, included the right of oppressed nations to secede from the Empire and affirmed the right of minorities to education and dealings with state institutions in their own languages. When the Bund reaffiliated to the RSDLP in 1906, neither organisation regarded the Bund's policy of national cultural autonomy as an obstacle.

The PPSD's and Zionists' approaches to the struggle against antisemitism were fundamentally defective. They abstained from engaging in it seriously, because they held that full Jewish emancipation would only occur in the indefinite future with, respectively, the achievement of socialism or a Jewish state in Palestine. In the meantime, the PPSD preached Jewish assimilation to Polish culture and the Polish language. In an insightful analysis of the failure of assimilation in Galicia, Grossman pointed out that it had been a possibility for a substantial layer of educated Jews, as the newly established autonomous government in Galicia from the late 1860s recruited personnel into its rapidly expanding local administration and schools. That process was concluded by the end of the 1880s. From then on, it was much more difficult for Jews to find such jobs. The response of the Jewish petty bourgeoisie was Zionism. Jewish workers began to set up their own social democratic associations. But the increasingly nationalist PPSD blocked their path to an autonomous Jewish social democratic party, beside those of other nations in Austria. The Zionists therefore faced weak competition in their efforts to win over workers. Jewish workers themselves were the crucial 'subjective' factor in the struggles to achieve equal rights for Jews, in accord with the Marxist principle that 'the emancipation of the working class must be the act of the working class itself'.[18]

Grossman's broad argument, that the PPSD's failure to allow Jewish workers to establish their own Galician organisation was responsible for the disappearance of their local associations during the late 1890s, carries weight. His account of the specific mechanism, the Polish Party's softness on both Jewish and Christian clericalism, is flimsier. In the absence of other evidence, the examples he used to justify this accusation look more like sensible concessions to workers' religious beliefs, in order to reinforce their involvement in strike action, than a general policy of capitulation to reactionary ideas. The local Jewish workers associations had to deal with increasingly adverse conditions, beyond the PPSD's control, from the late 1890s. There was a wave of state repression of social democratic activity, across Galicia, following antisemitic pogroms provoked by a populist peasant leader in 1898, and a serious economic recession from 1899 until 1902. But the PPSD was responsible for the absence of an effective mechanism through which Jewish social democrats in local workers associations could support each other across Galicia and this certainly played a role in the collapse of the associations.

It was not Zionism, directly or through the Bund, Grossman contented, but rather objective circumstances that led Jewish socialists to set up their own independent party. The influence of the Bund clarified and helped accelerate the process. Given the reality of Austrian Social Democracy's federal structure and the PPSD's indifference to their situation, only a separate social democratic party of Yiddish-speaking, Jewish workers could facilitate their participation in struggles for socialism and arrangements to end national oppression. *Bundism in Galicia* can therefore also be regarded as a response to Otto Bauer's influential *The Question of Nationalities and Social Democracy*, which denied that Jews were a nation and attacked JSDP.[19]

From Bundism to Communism

After taking up residence in Vienna, Grossman remained a Bundist social democrat. In 1910, he delivered a lecture for his Party's small Viennese organisation, on the economic history of Jews in Galicia. But there is currently little evidence of the specifics of Grossman's political views from his re-election to

---

18   Engels 1990a, p. 517.
19   Bauer 2000, pp. 291–308.

the JSDP's Executive in 1910 until after his discharge from the Austro-Hungarian Army in 1919. His two longer publications on the early economic history of Galicia, in Polish and German were, however, informed by a diplomatically phrased historical materialism. They punctured the nationalist myth that Galicia's economic backwardness was due to the policies of the Habsburg Empire, as opposed to the attitudes and power of the local, Polish nobility. The Polish study sympathetically compared Joseph II's mercantilist efforts to transform relations of production in Austria with the programme of contemporary socialism.[20] And in 1912 and 1913 he helped to clear Karl Radek's name.

On 21 August 1912, Radek had been expelled from the Social Democracy of the Kingdom of Poland and Lithuania, on spurious grounds relating to activities many years before. Radek was a leading member of an opposition faction in the SDKPiL, allied with the Bolsheviks, and a leftist in the Social Democratic Party of Germany, living and working as a journalist on social democratic newspapers in Germany. The SDKPiL set up an inquiry into Radek which assembled material but dissolved before delivering a verdict and before his expulsion. The left-dominated Bremen SPD inaugurated its own inquiry to establish the justice of Radek's expulsion from the SDKPiL, shortly after it took place. That inquiry cleared him, but the SPD right used the expulsion as an excuse to exclude Radek from the German Party, as well, in 1913. He was eventually cleared in 1914, by a third inquiry established by the Russian Social Democratic Labour Party, to which the SDKPiL was affiliated.

Grossman had been a member of Ruch's executive and the investigative committee which, in 1904, had exonerated Radek of some of the charges that were later resuscitated. His testimony, in 'Letters about the Radek Affair' and other, later documents which have not survived, Grossman declared that Ruch's arbitration court had settled the matters and they should not have been raised again. In signing the very formal letter he wrote to the Bremen Inquiry into the accusations, Grossman referred to and emphasised his law degree. Although clearly motivated by a sense of justice, in doing so he also gave political comfort to dissidents in the SDKPiL, particularly strong inside Russian-occupied Poland, sections of the SPD's left and the Bolsheviks, against the leadership of the SDKPiL and the right wing of the SPD. At this time, Grossman was clearly on friendly terms with both Radek and Feliks Dzierżinski, who were on opposite sides in the SDKPiL faction fight.[21] Both were later leaders of the Communist Party of the Soviet Union (CPSU).

20 Grossman 1911; and Grossmann 1914. English translations of these studies will be included in the fourth volume of this series.
21 See Untersuchungskommission 1914, pp. 14–21; Strobel 1974, pp. 371–7; Radek 1913.

In Vienna, Grossman's studies under Grünberg resulted in several publications on Habsburg economic policy in Galicia during the eighteenth century and the history of statistical collections in the Empire. His book on Habsburg trade policy in Galicia was recognised as his higher doctoral thesis by the University of Frankfurt am Main in 1927. Janina and Henryk were in Paris, where her work appeared in at least two exhibitions, for a period during 1910 and 1911. Their first son was born there in 1910, their second in Vienna in 1914.

Before the First World War, Grossman's views on the relationship between working-class consciousness and organisation placed him on the left wing of the socialist movement like others, including Lenin and Luxemburg as well as Jules Guesde and Henry Hyndman, pioneering Marxists in France and England, who thought of themselves as orthodox social democrats. Their responses to the War and the Russian Revolutions of 1917 indicated the extent of their leftism and commitment to the politics of working-class self-emancipation. Conscripted in 1915, Grossman served on the eastern front, before a transfer in 1916 to undertake research for the recently established Scientific Committee for the War Economy of the War Ministry, in Lublin, the administrative centre of the Austrian-occupied sector of the Congress Kingdom of Poland.

During the War, Grossman was able to write studies of the history of census collections in Austria and, more closely related to his military post, on the organisation of credit in the Congress Kingdom. The Russian Revolutions of February and November 1917 took place while he was stationed in Lublin. In December 1917 a transfer relocated him in Vienna to work on economic aspects of the peace negotiations with Russia, in the War Economy Section of the War Ministry. This position provided better opportunities than those available to most inhabitants of the Austro-Hungarian Empire to gain an understanding of what was going on in Russia. Like Lenin and Luxemburg and in contrast to Victor Adler, Jules Guesde, Henry Hyndman and Georgii Plekhanov, Grossman maintained his commitment to workers revolution by breaking with social democracy and becoming a Communist.

The racist policies of the new, rump Austrian state, under social democratic leadership, led to the lapse of a preliminary offer of a post in the Austrian Statistical Commission to Grossman. Deemed a citizen of the new Polish Republic, he moved to Warsaw in 1919. Even before taking up a senior position at the Polish Central Statistical Office in December, he delivered a paper on the theory of economic crises in Kraków, which became his first attributed publication on Marxist economic theory. An aspect of his revolutionary politics, he regarded capitalism as inherently crisis prone.[22]

---

22   See Grossman 2017d.

At the Statistical Office, Grossman was soon in charge of designing new Polish Republic's first population census. While there, he published several articles related to this work.

In 1920 he joined the Communist Workers Party of Poland (KPRP). Grossman's writings and behaviour until his death in 1950 were informed by a Communist outlook. That also made his loyalty as a servant of the Polish state suspect. Appointment to a full professorship in economic policy at the private Free University of Poland in 1922 provided more secure employment. But he was arrested five times and did prison stretches of up to eight months because of his political activity, particularly in the illegal Communist Party's front organisations.

At the Free University, Grossman published several studies of economic theory and economic history, and worked on the first part of a new translation of the first volume of Marx's *Capital*, eventually published by the publishing house Książa, controlled by the KPRP, in 1926.[23] The same publisher had already issued a volume of Marx's writings – his *Critique of the Gotha Program* and related letters to Ludwig Kugelmann – translated, edited and introduced by Grossman, shortly before the fortieth anniversary of Marx's death, in March 1923. The introduction, 'Notes on the History of Socialism in Poland Forty Years Ago', was a pioneering survey of a dramatic shift in early Polish receptions of socialist ideas and particularly Marx's analyses.

In 1874, an initial, clear-sighted and even sympathetic account by a Catholic priest and professor at the Jagiellonian University in Kraków was published. Stefan Pawlicki wrote from a conservative perspective highly critical of capitalism, before a Polish socialist movement had emerged. Just a few years later, other prominent intellectuals responded to the establishment of the first socialist organisation in Poland, in 1878, with rabid hostility, distortion and lies. Grossman, who as an undergraduate attended six of Pawlicki's university courses, seems to have had a soft spot for the old priest. He also used the opportunity to mock Leon Biliński's outrageous lies about socialists in an address to students in 1882, when he was the rector of the University in L'viv. Biliński, an economist, was later the Austro-Hungarian Minister of Finance and had been the first Finance Minister of independent Poland, in 1919.

The final section of Grossman's introduction outlined the background to the *Critique of the Gotha Program* and the history of its publication. It also offered criticism, from a Communist perspective, of bourgeois Marx experts; the leadership of the SPD; its preeminent theoretician Karl Kautsky; and, by implica-

---

23   'Książa' means 'Book'.

tion, their successors and cothinkers who had attempted to 'adapt Marxism to the opportunistic practices of everyday life'.[24]

Repression for his Communist affiliation and activities, and the offer of a well-paid post at the Institute for Social Research, whose director was Carl Grünberg, led Grossman into qualified exile in Germany: so long as he was not involved in Polish politics, he was allowed to visit Poland. The Institute was associated with the University of Frankfurt am Main, and Grossman received an appointment there. He is best known for his work on economic theory, published during his period in Frankfurt, between 1925 and 1933: a series of essays and *The Law of Accumulation and Breakdown of the Capitalist System, Being Also a Theory of Crisis*.[25]

Leninism, Stalinism and Marxist Economic Theory

Grossman's 'Notes on the History of Socialism' included a communist critique of social democracy. Works he published when he lived in Frankfurt dealt with a much broader range of political issues. His conception of revolutionary politics should be readily apparent to disinterested readers of *The Law of Accumulation*, let alone those who bother to look at works which preceded and followed it, where his Leninist approach is explicit.[26] That did not prevent reformist and Stalinist critics, and their equally deluded successors to the present, from accusing him of having a mechanical theory of capitalist breakdown, which left no place for political action.[27] From the early 1930s, this misrepresentation also required blindness to Grossman's explicit or, more accurately, blatant expressions of his political views in substantial entries in Ludwig Elster's *Dictionary of Economics*.

These embodied a commitment to interventionist Marxist politics, elaborated by Lenin, that are very far from the mechanical approach often attributed to Grossman. The Bolshevik leader's '"keen practicality", his rare ability to foresee future developments in the essential features of the circumstances of the moment, is just the result of his theoretical superiority in assessing the total

---

24   Grossman 1923, 'On the History of Socialism in Poland', see below, p. 206.
25   See Grossman 2017a; and Grossmann 1992 (an abridged translation. A full translation will appear as the third volume in this series).
26   Grossmann 1992, pp. 33, 95; Grossman 2017e, p. 143; Grossman 2017b, p. 385.
27   For example, Helene Bauer 1929; Braunthal 1929; Varga 1930; Sweezy 1942, pp. 211, 214; Foster and McChesney 2010, pp. 52–5.

process of capitalism'.[28] So Grossman endorsed Lenin's far from mechanical conception of the transition from capitalism to socialism and, crucially, the role of a Marxist party in a revolution. The entry on the Communist International referred favourably to its statutes, adopted at its second Congress in 1920, paraphrasing them: 'The Party ... must not simply be the masses' advocate; as their leader, it must be ahead of them and show them the way forward'.[29] In his discussion of the German Communist Party's failed revolutionary uprising in 1921, Grossman also argued that a revolutionary party cannot substitute itself for the working class, the only force capable of making the socialist revolution. The success of the revolution depends on the party winning the class to follow its lead: 'The conquest of power can, however, only be achieved by the masses and not by the struggles of their vanguard'.[30]

The degeneration and recent defeat of the Russian Revolution, in other words Stalinism, distorted Grossman's understanding of political developments in Russia and the history of Marxist currents there, before and after the Revolution, as it did the views of the vast majority of those who were Communists at the time.

When Grünberg was incapacitated by a stroke in 1930, Grossman took over his task of writing entries on very diverse socialist topics, requiring familiarity with extensive literatures, for the expanded fourth edition of Elster's *Dictionary*. Its three volumes were published in 1931, 1932 and 1933. The *Dictionary* was a standard reference work on economics, broadly understood, including entries on theories, institutions, movements and individuals. Grossman updated Grünberg's 'Social Democracy' in the previous, 1911 edition, for 'Social Democratic and Communist Parties'. He rewrote or expanded others: the 'Second International' section of 'The Internationals'; 'Anarchism', which incorporated substantial passages by Grünberg; and 'Christian and religious socialism', attributed to both Grünberg and Grossman.

Grossman also wrote new entries related to socialism: 'Bolshevism'; the 'Third International' section of 'The Internationals'; 'Lenin, Vladimir Ilyich', his longest biographical essay; and accounts of 12 other deceased Marxists and leftists. He was a contemporary of all these individuals, apart from Alexander Herzen and Olinde Rodrigues. The length of his contributions, an indicator of Grossman's political views, ranged from a couple of hundred words, on Rodrig-

---

28 Grossmann 1932h, 'Lenin (pseudnym for Ulyanov), Vladimir Ilyitsch', see below, p. 417.
29 Grossmann 1932e, 'The Third International', see below, p. 383.
30 Grossmann 1932e, 'The Third International', see below, p. 392.

ues, to over 20,000 words, on Bolshevism.[31] One entry was included in the first volume of Grossman's works.[32] 'The Further Development of Marxism to the Present', which he appended to Grünberg's entry on 'Socialist Ideas and Theories: I Socialism and Communism', included extensive discussions of the history of Marxist political practice, as well as Marxist economic theory.

These entries provided useful information, with qualifications, about their subjects. They also demonstrated Grossman's own revolutionary Marxist outlook. Together they can be regarded as components of a single, partisan narrative about the history of socialism. Their presence in a mainstream reference work is remarkable. Grossman contrasted Marxist politics, oriented to mass working-class organisation, struggle and revolution, with rival currents within the working class, principally reformism and anarchism. He used the attitudes of individuals and organisations to imperialism, war and the Bolshevik revolution as indices of the adequacy of their politics.

Grossman's closeness to the Communist Party of Germany (KPD) and support for the Soviet Union are readily apparent in the entries on the Second and Third Internationals, Bolshevism, Lenin, and social democratic and Communist parties.[33] These tended to reproduce early 1930s official Communist interpretations and misportrayals of events. It is not at all surprising, as Grossman later recalled, that KPD leaders were grateful for his essay on Bolshevism.[34]

Overall and particularly in the Soviet Union, Stalinism was counter-revolutionary both as practical politics and ideology that falsified history to justify its policy zigzags.[35] The unexpected form of the counter-revolution in Russia nevertheless meant that many dedicated Communists elsewhere still regarded their movement and themselves as revolutionary, and engaged in some activities which advanced workers' interests. This was certainly the case for Grossman. Furthermore, his acceptance of Stalinist positions on some issues did *not* lead him to give up his concept, dating back at least three decades, of Marxism as a theory of working-class self-emancipation; belief in the need for a party, along the lines of the Bolsheviks, as a necessary precondition for successful workers' revolution; or continued advocacy of his own pioneering elaboration

31 Grossmann's and Grünberg's longer contributions were republished in Grossmann and Grünberg 1971.

32 See Grossman 2017b.

33 It was also explicit in his correspondence, see Grossman 2017f; Grossman 2017g; Grossman 2017h.

34 Grossman 1948.

35 See Trotsky 1972.

of Marxist economic theory that had been explicitly denounced by official mouthpieces of the Stalinised Communist movement inside and outside Russia.

It is also notable that, in contrast to his fulsome treatment of Lenin, Grossman did not take advantage of the numerous opportunities his narratives offered to express praise, even in passing, for Stalin's personal contributions to Marxist theory or leadership of the Soviet Union, as opposed to simply acknowledging the victory of the 'Stalin-tendency' in the CPSU and the validity of its policies. Another indicator that Grossman's acceptance of Stalinism was not unqualified was his recognition of Trotsky's contributions between 1917 and 1923 and inclusion of his works in bibliographies at the end of entries. Among these was *The Permanent Revolution*, particularly anathematised by Stalin and his acolytes, and *The Third International after Lenin*, which provided devastating criticisms of the International's policies.

'**The Second International**' noted that organisation's hostility to anarchism and its inclusion of elements hostile to revolutionary Marxism from its foundation in 1889. Grossman nevertheless argued that its politics were predominantly revolutionary until around 1905. His indices were the resolutions on imperialism of its Congresses and the related issue of national self-determination, militarism and war, and collaboration with bourgeois parties. Even during its revolutionary period, he made clear, issues were fudged, particularly to accommodate the International's largest party, the Social Democratic Party of Germany (SPD).

A centre current, between the reformist right and revolutionary left, emerged in the International around the turn of the century. At the 1900 Congress, Kautsky's resolution, which did not rule out socialists participating in bourgeois governments, was adopted. While the International's position was strengthened in 1904, in line with a shift to the left in the SPD, the reformists continued to gain strength and there was an emphasis on unity. This contrasted with the organisational separation, Grossman pointed out, between Mensheviks and Bolsheviks that resulted from the 1903 Congress of the RSDLP. It should be noted, however, that this split was not and was not understood at the time as a definitive organisational division between reformists and revolutionaries.[36] In the spirit of Engels's and Lenin's assertions about an aristocracy of labour, Grossman attributed the rise of reformism to the emergence of a layer of workers bought off from class struggle by a share in wealth derived from imperialist exploitation of colonies. More concretely and accurately, he noted that union

---

36   See Harding 1983, Volume 1, pp. 189–96; Cliff 1975, pp. 118–27.

bureaucrats, keen to avoid sharp class confrontations which might endanger their jobs and organisations, were the driving force of reformism in Germany.[37]

On the basis of the alleged capitulation by Bebel, Kautsky and the SPD Executive to the right of the Party and the trade union bureaucracy, in 1906 at the Party's Mannheim Congress, Grossman argued that the International was dominated by reformism from its 1907 Congress. This conclusion was problematic for several reasons.

The leadership of the SPD had shifted decisively to the right. On the floor of the Congress, however, Kautsky had not so much capitulated; rather, he was outmanoeuvred. Unlike Bebel, he remained a centrist for several years afterwards.[38]

Grossman's account of the development of the International's position on the colonial question was also inaccurate. The congress resolution in 1900 did not maintain the categorical rejection of colonialism enunciated in 1896; it only condemned 'bourgeois' colonial policy.[39] The resolution in 1904, which Grossman regarded as a turning point, did not constitute a dramatic change, only consolidating the 1900 position. In 1907, an effort to shift the International's stance further to the right, by explicitly allowing the possibility of colonial policy under a socialist government, was in fact defeated, when the motion of the right-wing majority of the commission on the colonial question was amended.[40] The final resolution in 1907 did explicitly reconfirm those of 1900 and 1904. The spokesperson for the commissions on the colonial question behind the successful motions of 1900, 1904 and the unsuccessful proposal in 1907 was Henri van Kol, on the quiet, the owner of a coffee plantation in the Dutch East Indies.[41]

On the issue of militarism and war in 1907 at Stuttgart, a radical amendment, proposed by Luxemburg, Lenin and, not mentioned by Grossman, the Menshevik Julius Martov, was incorporated into Bebel's motion, which avoided the issue of mass action. The resolution was then passed unanimously and constituted a victory for the left rather than a rightward shift.[42] So, while the discussions at the Stuttgart Congress registered the German Party's deepening reformism, its impact on the International's formal positions was still muted.

---

37   See Cliff 1957; Post 2010; Bramble 2012.
38   Sozialdemokratische Partei Deutschlands 1906, p. 303; Schorske 1983, p. 51. See Kautsky 1909 for his continued centrism.
39   Second International 1896, p. 18; Second International 1900, pp. 25–6.
40   Second International 1904, pp. 23–4; Second International 1907, pp. 24–5.
41   Buschman and Pollmann 1987.
42   Congress 1907, pp. 64–6, 102, 104–5.

One reason was that, as Grossman pointed out, the International's resolutions were not binding on its affiliates.

Revolutionaries, including Lenin, had a better appreciation of the 1907 Congress's outcome,[43] even if, without the benefit of Grossman's hindsight, they were less aware of the pace at which the influence of reformism was expanding in the international movement. The founder and outstanding leader of German Social Democracy, the entry '**Bebel, August**' in Elster's *Dictionary* explained, obscured contradictions in the theory and practice of the social democratic movement and was even prepared to vote for Germany's military budget in 1913.

Later Congresses of the International provided further evidence for the weaknesses of most of its affiliates' commitment to revolutionary working-class politics. The support of German-Austrian social democrats for the survival of the Austrian Empire and opposition to the right of its oppressed nations to national independence had prompted the Czech social democrats to split the central Austrian union movement in 1909. In line with his own earlier move away from Bundism to a Communist stance on the national question, in '**Adler, Victor**', Grossman criticised the father of Austrian socialism, condemning Austrian Social Democracy's nationality programme, which did not call for the right of nations to self-determination. The Copenhagen Congress of the International, in 1910, placed unity above political clarity and principle, by condemning the Czech 'Separatists' without declaring for the right of nations to self-determination. The same Congress supported the bourgeois fantasy of international arbitration as a means to avoid war.

The Second International collapsed on the outbreak of the First World War. In his entries 'Adler, Victor', '**Hyndman, Henry Mayers**', '**Guesde, Jules**' and '**Plekhanov, Georgii Valentinovich**', Grossman outlined his subjects' important roles in building Marxist organisations, popularising Marxist theory and, particularly in Plekhanov's case, creatively applying and developing Marxism. He also identified the capitulation of these self-proclaimed orthodox Marxists, along with open reformists, to Austrian, British, French and Russian nationalism, respectively.

The behaviour of the prominent US union organiser and left-wing socialist, described in '**Debs, Eugene**', was a dramatic contrast. Debs was an opponent of business unionism and reformism in the Socialist Party of America. He was gaoled for his opposition to the First World War. '**De Leon, Daniel**' also dealt with a prominent figure in the socialist movement in the United States. It acknowledged De Leon's revolutionary Marxist politics, while noting his failure

---

43   See Lenin 1962f.

to formulate an effective strategy for a Marxist party. Like De Leon, the French socialist leader Jean Jaurès died shortly before the outbreak of the War but, unlike him, was a reformist and not a Marxist. 'Jaurès, Jean', nevertheless and in contrast with the standard Communist view, expressed considerable sympathy for its subject's capacities as an organiser and a principled socialist opponent of war and imperialism, committed to class struggle and political intervention. This was in contrast to Guesde's abstention from engagement with various contemporary controversies, including the campaign against antisemitic persecution of the Jewish army captain, Alfred Dreyfus, in which Jaurès was very active. Grossman also expressed sympathy for the commitment to working-class struggle, critique of mainstream social democracy, opposition to the War and support for the Bolshevik revolution of a syndicalist and unorthodox Marxist, in 'Sorel, Georges'. The entry did not mention Sorel's association, from 1909 until 1914, with the proto-fascist Action française or his antisemitism. Later, Grossman was highly critical of Sorel's theory of political myths and inability to grasp Marx's economic theory.[44]

The historical background in the entry on 'Bolshevism' included valuable material on pivotal economic and political developments in Russia back to the seventeenth century, intellectual antecedents and the pioneering activities of the Bund and Social Democracy of the Kingdom of Poland and Lithuania. It paid particular attention to Lenin's leadership of the social democratic movement and then the Bolshevik faction and Party. Grossman's shift from Bundism to Communism was apparent in his recapitulation of Lenin's critique of the Bund's federalism, without comment. The complementary entry 'Lenin, Vladimir Ilyich' provided further information on Lenin's political activities. It mentioned Lenin's 1899 critique of the way the Russian Narodniks had used Simonde de Sismondi's contention that capitalism depended on the existence of non-capitalist markets and Luxemburg's later development of the theory. Grossman had previously dismissed the underconsumptionist idea that foreign markets were a prerequisite for capitalism in several publications and had also written a monograph on Sismondi.[45]

Stalinist distortions of history are apparent in Grossman's account of Bolshevism's development after 1902, particularly the immediate implications of the split at the RSDLP's second Congress, in 1903, which refounded the Party;

---

44   See Grossmann 1929, p. 33.
45   For Grossman's criticisms of the error of regarding capitalism as dependent on non-capitalist markets, implicitly or explicitly directed against Luxemburg, see Grossman 2017d; Grossmann 1992, p. 41. Also see the later assessment, Grossman 2017k, which tackled Sismondi's underconsumptionism.

the portrayal of Lenin's ideas about the coming Russian revolution as unchanging between 1905 and 1917; the distinctiveness of Lenin's attitude to the First World War; what was at stake in the factional disputes in the Soviet Communist Party during the 1920s; and the significance of Soviet 'planning' from 1928.

The factional divide between Bolsheviks and Mensheviks only emerged *during* the RSDLP's 1903 Congress, when Lenin still lacked a critique of the SPD's centrist leadership. Bolsheviks, unlike the Mensheviks, regarded the working class as the leading force in the 1905 revolution and the struggle against the autocracy. Nevertheless, on the basis of a swing to the left by the Menshevik faction and especially its working-class base, during the high point of the revolution from October until December 1905, Lenin favoured reunifying the RSDLP and this took place at its fourth Congress in April–May 1906. Subsequently differences deepened and, as Grossman noted in 'Lenin', the split was finalised by the establishment of a separate Bolshevik Party in 1912, after the period of reaction and intense faction fighting within Russian Social Democracy – involving numerous currents, inside the Bolsheviks, in the Menshevik camp and outside both – that lasted until 1910.[46] The assertion that Lenin already recognised soviets as the embryo of a *workers* state, as opposed to a 'provisional revolutionary government', in 1905 foreshortened developments by almost a dozen years.[47]

While Grossman mentioned Lenin's discussion of the 'revolutionary democratic dictatorship of the proletariat and peasantry', which would modernise Russian society and encroach on the power of capital in order to establish the preconditions for socialism – the dictatorship of the proletariat – he did not explain the shift from this conception to the one that informed the successful pursuit of the immediate establishment of workers' power, with the support of the peasantry, in 1917. Grossman did indicate that the Bolsheviks extended their 'revolutionary goals', but misleadingly implied that this took place well before 1917.[48] He therefore avoided a systematic discussion and explanation of

---

46   For a brief, tabular presentation of the changes in relations between the Bolsheviks and Mensheviks, see Cliff 1989, p. 65.

47   Grossmann 1932h, 'Lenin (pseudnym for Ulyanov), Vladimir Ilyitsch', see below pp. 413.

48   See Lenin 1962g, pp. 28, 82; and Lenin 1964i, p. 341. For the timing of the shift in Lenin's position, see Cliff 1975, p. 200. In a letter to the editor of *Novaya Zhizn*, written in early 1905 but unpublished until 1940, Lenin did argue that the Saint Petersburg Soviet 'should be regarded as the embryo of a provisional revolutionary government', Lenin 1962h, p. 21. In 1906, he used a similar formulation, 'rudiments of revolutionary authority', in published texts, e.g. Lenin 1962i, pp. 155, 156. But from 1905 through to 1917, his conception of such a regime, elaborated in Lenin 1962g, was 'the revolutionary dictatorship of the proletariat and peasantry'.

the shift in the Party's perspectives for the coming revolution that would have contradicted Stalinist orthodoxy[49] and acknowledged that Lenin's tactics that year accorded better with Trotsky's theory of permanent revolution than his own previous analysis. On the other hand, Grossman's account of the revolutionary process during 1917, with its emphasis on the issue of dual power, was superior to the Stalinist orthodoxy which identified the February revolution as bourgeois and a distinct stage from the proletarian revolution of October, rather than part of a single process.[50]

After the workers movement experienced setbacks, with the defeat of the 1905 revolution and the onset of a period of deep reaction in 1907, Lenin insisted on taking advantage of opportunities for legal activity among workers – in trade unions, newspapers, insurance organisations and elections to the Duma – while continuing to build the still illegal Party and propagating its revolutionary politics. He recognised that the First World War constituted a crisis for capitalism and a revolutionary opportunity, and could be transformed into civil wars between capital and labour within the belligerent countries. This was particularly true in Russia, where the Tsarist state was brittle and had a very narrow base of support. The prospects for revolution were especially favourable in Russia, the 'weakest link' in the chain of imperialist powers. It was not the case, however, as Lenin and Grossman asserted, that Trotsky and Luxemburg advocated the pacifist slogan of 'neither victory nor defeat'. Like Lenin, both Trotsky and Luxemburg favoured turning the imperialist war into a revolutionary class war, although they did not use his formula: 'revolutionary defeatism'.[51] Grossman celebrated Lenin's successful tactics in 1917. After returning to Russia in April 1917, 'In scarcely four weeks, he succeeds in completing the struggle for the *intellectual rearmament of his Party* with the path to the revolutionary seizure of power'.[52] He also noted Trotsky's important role in the Bolshevik Revolution, creation of the Red Army and prominence in the early Communist International (Comintern).

Grossman's accounts of economic policy and conflicts inside the CPSU in post-revolutionary Russia, after the phases of War Communism and the New Economic Policy (NEP), however, essentially reproduced, with some gaps, prevailing Stalinist arguments. These asserted that Lenin endorsed the policy of 'socialism in one country' – the idea that Russia could quickly industrialise while preserving workers' power indefinitely in the absence of revolu-

49   Stalin 1952a, pp. 40–3.
50   Stalin 1952a, pp. 60–1.
51   For a discussion of this issue, see Draper 1953–54, pp. 340–2.
52   Grossmann 1932h, 'Lenin (pseudonym for Ulyanov), Vladimir Ilyitsch', see below, p. 415.

tions in the west, without engaging in extensive economic relations with more developed countries – which Trotsky criticised.[53]

The only evidence Grossman provided was tenuous: Lenin's brief comments about the desirability of providing material incentives to encourage peasants to join cooperatives. He did not mention Stalin's defeat of Bukharin and other proponents of the NEP, in 1928–9. Yet this was the prerequisite for Stalin's total political dominance and implementation of coercive, arbitrary, centralised decision-making in economic affairs, labelled 'planning', which consolidated his regime. The implementation of the first Five Year Plan from 1928 was therefore not, as Grossman portrayed it, an advance towards socialism but the final destruction of the gains made by workers and peasants in 1917 and the consolidation of a bureaucratic state capitalist regime.[54]

The thin layer at the top of the CPSU, Russian state and industries exercised collective control over the means of production, excluding working-class influence as effectively as private capitalists did. The increasingly harsh measures pursued under the Five Year Plan led to dramatic declines in agricultural productivity, even as a greater surplus was coerced from the peasantry, as it was herded into collective and state farms. After Grossman wrote his entry on Bolshevism, the continuation and intensification of these policies led to mass starvation in the countryside. Grossman regurgitated Stalinist criticisms of 'Trotskyism's' (the Left Opposition's) proposals in 1926–7 as 'super-industrialisation', which endangered the proletariat's alliance with the peasantry. He did not see hypocrisy in the contrast between this accusation and the reality of the Five Year Plan, which led to a flood of former peasants into the cities. That influx and the imposition of draconian workplace discipline undercut the proletariat's living standards and conditions of work. Repression of peasants and workers was the basis for rapid industrialisation, to sustain state capitalist Russia's military competition with private capitalist states. The problems experienced by the new economic system were not fundamentally due, as Grossman asserted, to 'inexperience' and 'lack of any data'. Genuine, countrywide planning was impossible in the absence of democratic structures within enterprises and the state, the only real basis for reliable statistics. In their absence, the distrust and fear experienced by central 'planners', all levels of factory managers, not to mention workers, meant that no-one had a clear measure of industrial capacity, labour productivity or the quality of products. The official Russian economic statistics Grossman quoted at length were essen-

53   On the debates over economic policy in the USSR during the 1920s, see Day 1972.
54   See Cliff 1974; and Reiman 1987.

tially fictional. A study trip to Russia in August–September 1932 only seems to have confirmed his illusions.[55]

Distortions, derived from the current official Communist line, were also apparent at places in the treatment of the Communist movement in the entries on 'The Third (Communist) International' and 'Socialist and Communist Parties'. There were also gaps in these accounts. But they do provide quite reliable information about social democracy after the First World War, the Third International until 1921 and the electoral fortunes of both currents.[56]

The discussion of developments in Germany, where the prospects for workers' revolution were favourable several times between the War and 1924, was particularly poor. Paul Levi was denounced for going over from the KPD to reformism in 1921–2. But there was no mention of his earlier role in consolidating the Party, after the murder of Rosa Luxemburg, Karl Liebknecht and Leo Jogiches; winning over the majority of the Independent Social Democratic Party (USPD), which transformed the KPD into a mass party; and pioneering the united front tactic.

Grossman referred to two major setbacks the Communist movement experienced in 1923, without commenting on the Comintern's role in them. Its misleadership was important in the faulty handling of events by the Bulgarian and Germany Parties. The Bulgarian Communist Party, on its own initiative, decided not to take sides in a right-wing coup against the elected government of the Peasant Union Party in June. Then, encouraged by the Comintern, it launched an ill-fated insurrection in September when workers' and peasants' organisations had not yet recovered from repression. The occupation of the Ruhr by French and Belgian troops, and hyperinflation gave rise to a revolutionary crisis in Germany, which peaked in October. The Communist International and KPD leaderships responded irresolutely, placing excessive emphasis on participation in the state governments of Sächsen and Thuringen, led by left Social Democrats. An insurrection was called off at the last moment. Heinrich Brandler and August Thalheimer, leaders of the German Party copped all the blame in Grossman's entry, as they had in the Comintern.

The interpretation of the united front tactic in 'The Third International' is that of the 'Third Period' Comintern, not its original conception. In January 1921, the KPD issued an 'open letter' to the SPD, rump USPD and the social democratic trade unions, appealing for joint action around concrete demands. This was an effective political wedge. Agreement would provide much improved

---

55   Kuhn 2007, p. 155.
56   See Hallas 1985 for an excellent, brief account of the Comintern's evolution and the events discussed below.

opportunities to win workers in these reformist organisations over to revolutionary politics, by demonstrating the greater effectiveness of the KPD in struggle. Refusal by social democratic leaders to participate would raise questions about their commitment to fighting in workers' interests.

The sixth Congress of the Comintern, in 1928, whose programme Grossman effusively praised, proposed that a new, 'Third Period' since the First World War had begun. This phase would be characterised by wars and profound crises. Worried by the prospect of war with private capitalist countries and conducting a fight against the 'right' around Bukharin inside the Communist Party of the Soviet Union, the Stalinist machine replaced the Comintern's most recent right zag with a left zig of even greater sectarian hostility to social democratic parties and trade unions than the earlier left zig of 1924–5. The 'united front from below' involved appealing for joint action not to reformist organisations as a whole but only to their working-class members. It was not a wedge and amounted to the unpersuasive demand that they simply abandon their leaders. Given these shifts, it was no wonder that the tactic 'led to major misunderstandings [about the united front] in the Communist Parties of some countries'.[57] Contrary to Grossman, this tactic was the opposite of a success.

His outline of the sixth Congress also seemed to endorse the theory of stages, the Stalinist return to the Menshevik notion that countries had to pass through a bourgeois revolution and stage before socialism could be on the agenda. Although Trotsky's theory of permanent revolution, counterposed to this stagism and anathema to Stalinists, was not mentioned in the main text of the essay, *Permanent Revolution* was listed among Trotsky's works in the bibliography at the end of the entry on Bolshevism.

The Comintern's right zag of 1925–8 had led to the Communist Party of Great Britain's accommodation to the trade union bureaucracy, during the 1926 General Strike. In the same period, the theory of stages had justified subordinating the Communist Party of China (CPC) to the bourgeois Kuomintang. While Grossman noted both the strike and the Chinese revolution of 1926–7, he failed to acknowledge that both had been defeated, let alone the Comintern's culpability. The CPC, formerly a mass workers party, was subject to vicious repression by the Kuomintang and virtually ceased to exist. Neither it nor any other party outside Europe and the United States of America were considered in the entry on Social Democratic and Communist Parties. The Communist Party of Poland, to which Grossman had belonged, was not mentioned either. This may have been related to his deal with the Polish authorities, which allowed him to visit

---

57   Grossmann 1932e, 'The Internationals: The Third International', below, pp. 377–402.

the country for two weeks a year in return for abstention from involvement in Polish politics, or to aspects of the factional conflicts which, thanks to the intervention of the Comintern, had disrupted the Party.

Grossman offered insights into currents outside the mainstream of the modern socialist movement, in short entries on 'Herzen, Alexander' and 'Rodrigues, Olinde', who belonged to earlier socialist traditions, and much longer essays on anarchism and Christian socialism.

Herzen was a significant figure in the history of the left in Russia and the antecedents of the Bolsheviks. It seems likely that, on the basis of preparation for his entries on 'Bolshevism' and 'Lenin, Vladimir Ilyich', Grossman made a case for a much longer entry on Herzen than Grünberg's perfunctory observations in the previous edition of Elster's *Dictionary*.[58] Lenin's appreciation of Herzen as a pioneering Russian revolutionary democrat featured in the revised entry's bibliography, as well as a longer study by the leading Bolshevik (and later Communist) Lev Borisovich Kamenev.[59] Rodrigues, not present in earlier editions, was a follower and successor of the French utopian socialist Henri de Saint-Simon, in whose thought Grossman later identified a precursor of Marx's conception of modes of production.[60]

The insightful survey of 'Anarchism' made use of Grünberg's discussion of Max Stirner and Pierre-Joseph Proudhon in the third edition of Elster's *Dictionary*.[61] Grossman, unlike Grünberg, characterised anarchist ideas as an extreme form of bourgeois individualism which sought to eliminate all constraint on individual freedom. Anarchism went beyond classical political economy's advocacy of restricted state activity to call for the abolition of the state and religion. In a more thoroughly materialist account than Grünberg's, he also pointed out that the work of Stirner and Proudhon reflected the class position of the petty bourgeoisie, faced with increased competition from big capital. The revolutionary collectivist anarchism of Bakunin, the communist anarchism of Kropotkin and related movements self-identified as anarchist arose later in the nineteenth century.

Grossman highlighted Bakunin's rejection of struggles for short-term improvements and identified his method as putschism, intended to spur the masses into action. The entry on 'Kropotkin, Peter' identified the Russian anarchist's critique of parliamentary institutions as his only original theoretical contribution. Grossman's categorisation of William Morris, after 1885, as

---

58   Grünberg 1911d.
59   Lenin 1963; Kamenev 1916.
60   See Grossman 2017l.
61   Grünberg 1911a.

a communist anarchist was mistaken.[62] In revolutionary syndicalism, theorised in particular by Georges Sorel and entailing a critique of reformist social democracy, he recognised a movement committed to working-class struggle, in contrast to the individualism of anarchism. The centrality of the Russian Revolution in Grossman's political perspectives was expressed in the space he devoted to the anarchists in Russia. After the defeat of the 1905 Revolution, they played a mainly disruptive role in the opposition to Tsarism. Kropotkin supported the provisional government and opposed the October Revolution. Most other anarchists were also hostile to the Soviet regime.

The entry '**Christian and Religious Socialism**' examined efforts to combat the rise of social democracy with a political mixture of Christianity and mild social reform, and later Christian theological efforts to justify the abolition of capitalism. Most of the material on France, Germany and Austria before the First World War came from Grünberg's equivalent contribution to the third edition of Elster's *Dictionary*. Grossman added theoretical precision and accounts of post-War developments. He associated the emergence of genuinely socialist Christian currents with 'the present stage of the transition from capitalism to socialism',[63] revealing his own Communist politics in passing. There were increases in religiosity, he observed, after the defeats of the 1905 Revolution in Russia and the German Revolution of 1918–19. A small Jewish social reform current in Poland was noted but other, much more significant non-Christian movements, which combined Islam with socialist ideas in Central Asia and the Dutch East Indies (now Indonesia), were not mentioned at all.

After the Nazis were handed power in Germany, Grossman was in Parisian exile from 1933 until 1936. For a while, he moved away from Stalinism and associated with dissident German Communist leaders of the Socialist Workers' Party of Germany. In May 1933 he wrote of the failure of the Communist Party of Germany (KPD) to respond effectively to the rise of the Nazis:

> I am convinced that the KPD was not destroyed by individual policy errors. Every party makes mistakes – one only learns through one's own mistakes – which can be corrected. The 'Nazis' made many, many mistakes

---

62   Two of Grossman's references mischaracterised Morris: as 'closer to communist anarchism than Marxism', Diehl 1922, p. 281; and as an anarchist communist, Fritsche 1966. While Morris remained a member of the Socialist League after it came under anarchist domination, unlike the other Marxists Eleanor Marx, Belfort Bax and Edward Aveling, he was explicit and consistent about *not* being an anarchist and resigned from the League in 1890, see Thompson 1976, pp. 549–53, 570.

63   Grünberg and Grossman 1931, 'Christian and religious socialism', see below p. 309.

and yet they were finally victorious. But the fundamental mistake of the
KPD was that at its head stood figures without responsibility, who were
not capable of taking independent decisions at the decisive moments.
All the independent ones, who were capable of thinking for themselves,
were thrown out of the Party. What remained was a bureaucracy, which
submitted slavishly to the Muscovites. But a revolution cannot be made
on command from Moscow.[64]

Just over a month later, he recommended Trotsky's analysis of 'the German
catastrophe', which drew attention to the disastrous, sectarian policies of the
Communist International.[65]

In Paris, he wrote a study of the relationship between the emergence of
capitalism and of the modern scientific world view, which prompted his later
and long unpublished monograph on René Descartes.[66] He moved to London and then, in 1937, to New York. In exile, Grossman also wrote studies of
French and English antecedents which highlighted distinctive and important
aspects of Marx's economic theories, and offered a critique of bourgeois economics' fundamental assumptions, from Adam Smith to the still dominant
neo-classical school.[67] These studies drew on the framework and analyses of
his work in Warsaw and Frankfurt, developed before the terminal Stalinisation
of the international Communist movement. A subjective commitment to workers' revolution and his self-confidence, not to say self-regard, meant that he did
not modify these views, even when his identification with the Stalinist Soviet
Union led him to political positions that contradicted working-class interests.
Grossman's illusions in the Soviet Union and its leadership from the end of the
1920s until 1933 were rekindled around 1936, apparently by the Soviet Union's
whole-hearted, verbal but highly qualified practical support for the Republican
side in the Spanish Civil War.

There was a break between Grossman and Max Horkheimer, Grünberg's
successor as director of the Institute for Social Research and then its US incarn-
ation, in the early 1940s. Horkheimer's abandonment of historical materialism
and increasingly conservative outlook, as well as Grossman's apologetic attitude to the Soviet Union, personal frictions and pay cuts were factors.

In early 1949, Grossman took up a professorial chair in Leipzig, at the oldest University in the Soviet Occupation Zone of Germany. He enthusiastic-

---

64   Grossman 2017i, p. 245.
65   Grossman 2017j, p. 247; Trotsky 1975.
66   Grossmann 2009a; and Grossmann 2009b.
67   Grossman 2017m; Grossman 2017l.

ally joined the Society for German-Soviet Friendship and the Socialist Unity
(i.e. Communist) Party. He died the following year. Despite his efforts, none of
Grossman's works was ever republished in East Germany.

Structure and Conventions

The order of the works below follows their dates of publication. Original texts
quoted by Grossman have been modified to comply with this book's citation
and stylistic conventions. Minor errors in his quotations, spelling of names,
references and the consistency of tense have been corrected without comment. It has been possible to hunt down and provide specific sources for the
vast majority of the quotations in this volume, for which Grossman provided
no reference. Due to lack of wit and/or access to obscure publications, a few
escaped capture by the editor, who has modified most of the initial translations
in many places, after comparing them with the original texts. Where they exist,
published English translations are used in quotations and references. Other
things being equal, editions available free on websites, such as www.archive
.org, www.books.google.com and the Bibliothèque nationale de France, have
been preferred for references. Words in square brackets in quotations stem
from Grossman, unless otherwise indicated; elsewhere they are the editor's or
translator's. Emphasis in quotations is the original author's, unless otherwise
indicated. Translations of foreign-language texts in the body of the book are
provided inside inverted commas in footnotes. Places, apart from those with
very commonly used English names (such as countries, capital cities, large
rivers and historical provinces), are generally designated by the names used
in the countries within whose borders they currently lie. Grossman generally
referred to Great Britain as England and the Netherlands as Holland, and sometimes, the United States of America as America. Explanations of abbreviations
and basic biographical information about people mentioned in the body of the
book are provided in the index.

The Proletariat Faced with the Jewish Question Arising from the Undiscussed Discussion in Krytyka*

Translated from Polish by Halina Zobel and Dominika Balwin

Dedicated to my dear friend Janek Bross

∴

From the Publisher

In order to explain the character of this work I will cite an excerpt from a letter from the author to me, in which he writes:

> You must be aware that there was a discussion, over more than a year, of the Jewish question in *Krytyka* in Kraków in which [Michał] Luśnia, Dr [Tobiasz] Aschkenaze and [Henryk] Biro-Jakubowicz participated in turn.[1] An interesting aspect of this discussion was that its participants did not argue with each other. I take part in this discussion as, for the time being, the final participant.
>
> Will I be the last?
>
> I may meet with a 'bold rebuff' from Mr Luśnia but it is equally possible that this rebuff will assume the form of silence.[2]
>
> Time will tell ...

---

* [Originally published as Grossman 1905a; and, abridged, Grossman 1905b. 'Krytyka' means 'Critique'.]
1 [Michał Luśnia was a pseudonym of Kazimierz Kelles-Krauz; Luśnia 1904; Aschkenaze 1904; Henryk Biro-Jakubowicz was pseudonym of Bronisław Grosser, Biro-Jakubowicz 1905.]
2 [Luśnia/Kelles-Krauz, did not reply. He died a few months after the appearance of Grossman's pamphlet.]

Preface

The reader must forgive me for having, at times, interspersed my positive views with polemical arguments.

I adopted this form as better suited to the expression of my own views and to emphasise contentious points. Moreover, I considered it my duty to expose the real nature of people like Mr Luśnia, who smuggle in their reactionary, idealist-organic whims under the guise of the 'scientific method', thus increasing the already considerable confusion in the heads of ignorant Galicians.

∴

Under the capitalist mode of production, the pace of development rapidly accelerated. The ursine immobility of past periods of production was replaced by the constant revolutionising of all spheres of social life.

Unceasing upheavals in production are answered by convulsions in all social relations. Former gods fall and immutable authorities are questioned.

The feverish pace of material production also affects intellectual production. Capitalist development repeatedly throws up social problems which it cannot solve:

> Now there are more and more of these sphinxes!
> The mysteries ...
> As grains of sand, or flowers in the field
> – *KORDIAN*[3]

This incompetence of bourgeois society will only accelerate its fall.

The proletariat inherits an important task!

The Formulation of the Problem

> To know means to distinguish.
> – [ARTHUR] SCHOPENHAUER

The nineteenth century was, as we know, *the creator* of nations. A number of social groups became nations in the course of the century. This means that a group of people speaking one language or several dialects

---

3 [Słowacki 2010, p. 24.]

so closely related and mutually intelligible that they could be considered a single language, and having a lot in common but which had previously *not concluded* from this linguistic and historical commonality, even if it was aware of the latter, that it constituted a single separate and *organic whole*, now *suddenly* comes to this conclusion. Moreover it becomes conscious that it possesses a worth and dignity equal to those of other nations and should determine independently or at least on the principle of voluntarily adopted and mutual dependency *all forms* of its existence and its fate, precisely as an indivisible, *organic whole*. If we further emphasise what is already implicit in the above formulation, namely that *such consciousness involves not one stratum but all*, however diverse the strata of a nation may be, then we will have, it seems, a succinct yet comprehensive formulation of the great historical fact: '*the creation* of modern nations'.[4]

Classic.

Mr Luśnia wants to explain the formation of a nation. As a proponent of the materialist conception of history, he is entitled to take the supra-historical viewpoint of the classless consciousness of a classless nation, which as '*precisely ... an organic whole*' wants 'to decide for itself'. It is therefore easy to understand the misfortune which befell him. That is, in considering the Jewish question he has mistaken the Jewish bourgeoisie for the Jewish nation and, with a narrow Zionist focus, has somehow completely forgotten about the Jewish proletariat.

Thus witty Mr Luśnia, by means of the simple logical operation of omitting the proletariat, has also avoided the issue of class struggle and, achieving this abstraction from reality, arrived at a complete abstraction, that is, the harmonious regulation of '*all forms of its existence*' of 'each stratum in the nation', as 'precisely ... an organic whole'. Beyond 'all the forms of its existence' a nation may, 'after all' (!) be differentiated.

> A group of people ... having a lot in common but which had previously not concluded that it constituted an organic whole, now suddenly comes to this conclusion.

We can see that Mr Luśnia reduces the historical development of a nation to a certain kind of inference: *how* does a particular nation arise? It simply 'comes to this conclusion', suddenly. The profundity of this method is apparent.

---

4 Luśnia 1905, p. 57. [Grossman's emphasis.]

Instead of expressing his own opinions and *explaining* to the reader the process of formation of a nation and of national consciousness, Mr Luśnia prefers to order a group to speak and come to its own conclusion.

Let us apply Mr Luśnia's logic elsewhere.

How can one, for example, explain the formation of class consciousness? Applying the method of Mr Luśnia, it is very simple.

'A group of people, having a lot in common, but which had not previously concluded that it constitutes a class, now suddenly comes to this conclusion.' The reader will note that at the end of this explanation, the process of formation of class or national consciousness is as clear as it was at the beginning. It must be acknowledged, however, that by means of Mr Luśnia's method it is possible to explain everything very easily, one need only require a particular group to suddenly come to the appropriate conclusion.

This argument 'seems to him' to be 'a comprehensive formulation of the great historical fact of the formation of modern nations'.

No Mr Luśnia!

To explain a particular fact means defining the conditions of its existence. To explain the emergence of a particular fact (which is what you have in mind) means defining the conditions under which this fact was created, arose or, to use old-fashioned philosophical language, defining the factors which called forth the fact.

How did you fulfil this task, that is how did you explain the fact of the emergence of a nation? Very simply. By a certain group coming to a conclusion. Instead of historical factors, we infer.

Thus a group of people 'having a lot in common' but not as yet having a national consciousness, 'suddenly comes to the conclusion' that it constitutes a nation. Mr Luśnia evidently takes the previously unknown position (against all common sense), that it is possible to draw conclusions despite the absence of consciousness.

We are thus presented with Mr Luśnia's unconscious inference.

What is more, to explain the formation of national consciousness not only is it essential for a group to conclude that it constitutes a nation but 'moreover' that 'it possesses a worth equal to that of other nations'.

Thus a condition of the *formation* of a particular nation, is the *existence* of another nation. That is, Mr Luśnia, having closed historical development in a vicious circle of his own inferences, cannot extricate himself from it. So he has to skip over it. He is saved by 'suddenly'. Suddenly a group comes to the conclusion that it constitutes an organic whole, that it is a nation.

Even accepting all Mr Luśnia's mistakes as proven, it still remains to be explained how and why a particular group, at the very moment of the violent *destruction* of traditional forms of relatively undifferentiated life, at a time of intensifying class antagonisms, why at *this* very moment it suddenly comes to the conclusion that it constitutes an organic *whole*!!

If the formation of nations was something more than a matter of inference for Mr Luśnia, he would know that national consciousness is the result of a long historical process, a product of economic and social as well as cultural, climatic and anthropological causes. So, neither was the nineteenth century the sole creator of nations nor can a nation be formed as the result of a 'sudden' conclusion. Quite the opposite, nations are created in the course of centuries, historically, and capitalist development accelerates this process, as it does many others. He would know that nations, as the products of historical conditions, change and develop in different historical epochs in accordance with these conditions. Thus the French nation was not the same in the period of the troubadours as under Louis XIV; and the French nation of the Encyclopaedists was not the nation of [Louis] Napoléon III.[5] In other words, particular socio-economic conditions, with their legal, political, religious and emotional expressions, also determine the meaning of what constitutes a nation. He would also know that, as class differentiation develops in capitalist society and class antagonisms emerge, previously homogenous national consciousness, which was nothing more than the national consciousness of a small ruling class, also *disappears*. Now, *beside* those small ruling minorities which previously constituted the 'nation' within particular social groups, there emerges for the first time, as a *new* nation, the conscious proletariat, the oppressed majority. In other words, in capitalist society *there is no uniform national consciousness* and the working class's national consciousness, within a certain social group, has nothing in common with the bourgeoisie's national consciousness but is *hostile* to it. What binds these two classes together is, on the one hand, a formal factor: the common language, in which the two different class consciousnesses, hostile to each other in terms of their content, express themselves. On the other hand they are bound by a functional link, conditioned by the given economic system, the mode of social production. The functional relationship between the bourgeoisie and proletariat, capital and labour, is like the functional relationship between an anvil and a hammer, which cannot and do not have anything in common beyond the function which links them. The functional relationship between the bourgeoisie and proletariat not only does not constitute a homogenous nation, on the contrary the relationship between these two classes gen-

---

5   [The reign of Loius XIV was 1643–1715. The Encyclopedists contributed to the *Encyclopedia* edited by Denis Diderot and Jean le Rond d'Alembert between 1751 and 1765.]

erates two hostile class consciousnesses. He would know that man as such, the purely abstract man of German philosophy's pure reason, does not exist. There is only man as the product of history, that is as a member of a certain social class – a bourgeois or a proletarian. Likewise, beyond the form of language, there is no abstract, homogenous national consciousness. Rather, the Polish nobleman and the Polish worker alike represent two mutually hostile nations.[6]

He would also have known that this entire classical process of the 'disintegration' of homogenous national consciousness, for the first time in English society, was already described sixty years ago by Frederick Engels. In his work on the condition of the working class in England, Engels succinctly demonstrated that the national consciousness of the English bourgeoisie could not be that of the emerging proletariat, which fiercely 'rejected' it and did not want to know anything about it.[7] Engels argued that the English worker was escaping from emasculated bourgeois knowledge, which was adapted to the bourgeoisie's narrow-minded, hypocritical morality, and preferred to look for different knowledge without a bourgeois admixture. In other words the bourgeoisie's ideals and way of looking at things were not those of the proletariat. On the contrary, the proletariat creates new ideals and new art, new morality and culture and a new way of looking at things. Engels showed that, in contrast to the propertied class, 'working-men ... form a separate class, with separate interests and principles, with a separate way of looking at things ... and that in this class reposes the strength and the capacity of development of the nation'.[8]

Enough! The reader has seen that the fiction of a nation as an organic whole, i.e. organic sociology, still has its proponents; that it is even possible to *profess* the fiction of the organic unity of the nation while acknowledging the reality of class struggle; and that Mr Luśnia, who as we will see later is able do a lot of other things, has even managed to combine these two extremes into one organic whole!

6　'Est-il des grands qui revêtus d'un pourvoir sans bornes, n'ont du moin pour le moment rien à craindre ou à espérer de la haine ou de l'amour de leurs inférieurs; alors sous un même nom ces deux ordres de citoyens composent deux Nations rivales'. Hélvetius 1773, 135. ['If there be statesmen invested with unlimited power and that have not, at least for the present, anything to hope or fear from the love or hatred of their inferiors, then ... these two orders of citizens, under the same name will compose two rival antagonistic nations' Hélvetius 1969, p. 90.] Formulating this opinion, I do not doubt for a moment that this position will be met with charges of extremism, exaggeration, narrowness and one-sidedness etc. I would, however, prefer to provoke discussion!

7　Engels 1975, p. 502.

8　Engels 1975, p. 529.

The conclusion of all this is that when approaching the 'Jewish question' one cannot discuss, as Mr Luśnia *does*, the Jewish question in general but must specify which Jewish question one is talking about, something that Mr Luśnia *does not do*. The Jewish question of the Jewish bourgeoisie is not the Jewish question of the Jewish proletariat. This again is the consequence of the simple fact that there is no Jew as such but that, beside the Jewish bourgeoisie, the Jewish proletariat also exists!

Questions

[T]he high and formal discussions of learned men end oftentimes in disputes about words and names; with which (according to the use and wisdom of the mathematicians) it would be more prudent to begin, and so by means of definitions reduce them to order.

– FRANCIS BACON[9]

'An oppressed class', Marx wrote, 'is the condition of every society based on class antagonism'.[10] In the course of historical development, which was at the same time the history of class struggles, Jews have not had the fortune, until modern times, of belonging to the ruling class. So they had, of necessity, to belong to the oppressed class, together with the Roman slave or medieval serf.

This explanation of 'eternal' oppression of Jews and the ominous fact that 'antisemitism is older than capitalism' is all too trivial (as indeed every scientific explanation is trivial). It is too trivial, in particular, where it concerns a chosen people; the whole sinister meaning of being a Jew, the 'eternal exile', disappears instantly and the mysterious veil falls from its dismal destiny. The striking scenery, the actors and the whole tragic scenario in which the chosen people can at last be rescued by the chosen ones – the Zionist knights, our home-grown Jewish bourgeoisie – all disappear!

This 'eternal' oppression took on such complicated forms under the capitalist system that it broke down into two elements, as did the very Jewish community against which it is directed. Just as the oppression of the Jewish proletariat by the non-Jewish bourgeoisie is the oppression, disguised in national terms, of the ruled by the ruling class, of the proletariat by the bourgeoisie, the

---

9   Bacon 1905, p. 81.
10   [This passage echoes the *Manifesto of the Communist Party*, 'every form of society has been
      based ... on the antagonism of oppressing and oppressed classes' Marx and Engels 1976,
      p. 495.]

struggle of the non-Jewish bourgeoisie against the Jewish bourgeoisie is nothing other than a specific competition of bourgeoisies against each other within
a national framework.

Thus the struggle against the Jews is not a specific feature of the capitalist
era. It existed both in ancient Rome and in the medieval ghetto. Only its form
has changed. The forms of this conflict and the nature of its weapons depended
on the law that oppression follows the line of least resistance, in accordance
with the way of the thinking prevailing at a given time.

As long as theological views ruled over human minds, ruling classes were
able to cloak their interests in religious disguise, only to replace it later with
national disguise.[11]

While, however, this Jewish question, created as a result of the class character of past societies, has existed in Europe for as long as Jews were a part of
these societies, it was never as loud as it is today. It is becoming so loud because
it is not now limited to the Jewish proletariat, the Jewish masses, but also concerns the Jewish bourgeoisie. And the latter can fill the whole world with its
clamour, and drown out everything else with is shrill voice.[12]

Thus the fight against Jews, despite its specific anti-Jewish form, is only a part
of a general campaign in a class society and the oppression of Jews is a part of
general oppression.

For the *proletariat*, the Jewish question has ceased to be an issue. This does
not prevent petty bourgeois socialism, however, from locating the Jewish question precisely there. 'By the Jewish question, strictly speaking, we understand
a *mutual* internal *relationship* between Christian communities [!] and the Jews
living among them'. 'The solution to the Jewish question is a *just arrangement
of relations* between the Christian and Jewish parts of society'.[13]

The petty bourgeois consider everything from the angle of a harmonious
'society' and mutual understanding. They do not see the bourgeoisie and the
proletariat but, on the contrary, in their fantasy there exist homogeneous Jewish and Christian 'societies', which they counterpose, in order to bring them
into a harmonious 'mutual relationship', a 'just arrangement of relations'.

---

11   Wherever this disguise is missing, the class struggle between the Jewish bourgeoisie and
     the Jewish proletariat comes to surface in all its ruthlessness and violence.
12   In the specific language of the Jewish bourgeoisie this is called 'posing the Jewish question'.
     Mephisto, ich kenne dich! [Mephisto, I know you!]
        It should surprise no-one that our various local scholars discussing the Jewish question
     have only Zionism on their minds. They notice only those phenomena which attract their
     attention through vulgar noisiness. These men do not even suspect that the real problem
     lies somewhere else entirely.
13   Wileński 1904, pp. 1, 30. [Grossman's emphasis.]

This harmonious ideology forgets, however, that the harmony of Jewish society (read the bourgeoisie) with Christian society (i.e. the bourgeoisie) in capitalist society – if the Jewish bourgeoisie is quite numerous – is a utopia, or at least is not and cannot be an objective or a task of the proletariat. On the contrary, as far as the proletariat is concerned, the Jewish question cannot and does not consist, is not based on a 'mutual, just internal relationship' between the Jewish and the Christian proletariats, *since the interests of the proletariat are one*, they are not and cannot be contradictory. If one understands the Jewish question in terms of a 'mutual, internal, just relationship' etc., etc., then one gives an irrefutable and telling proof that one does not represent the class position of workers, whose interests are one and are consistent and do not have to be brought into agreement, that is, into a 'mutual, just relationship'. One stands, at best, in the position of petty bourgeois socialism which resembles genuine socialism in name only!

Mr Luśnia goes even further. He openly stands on the side of the Polish-gentry bourgeoisie when he sentimentally shouts: '*Our* long-standing, centuries old Jewish question has revived for *us*'.[14]

Until now, as history tells us, the issue was long-standing, centuries-old; 'ours' only for the Polish gentry and bourgeoisie!

The proletariat, however, as I have stated, does not see a *question* here but has only a *task*: in so far as the struggle within the bourgeoisie is of no concern to it, the oppression of the Jewish proletariat as Jews will disappear when class society, of which it is a manifestation, also disappears.

The victorious proletariat, having destroyed the class form of society, will abolish *every* oppression, as it removes the *need* for oppression and its tools!

$$\cdot \; \cdot$$
$$\cdot$$

The Jewish question for the proletariat consists in something entirely different.

If one Jewish question was the result of class contradictions and conflicts then, since the latter do not exist within the proletariat, they cannot generate the other Jewish question.

The *only* Jewish question that can exist within the proletariat is the question which the proletariat itself, considering the Jews, encounters on the road to its great objective – the abolition of class society. That is, the Jewish question can only be comprehended as a *question about the choice of the means* leading most rapidly to the goal of proletarian power.

---

14   Luśnia 1904, p. 53. [Grossman's emphasis.]

While for the Polish bourgeoisie 'the presence of such unassimilated (Jewish) masses in our province is undesirable and dangerous for national reasons',[15] on the contrary for the proletariat, whose main criterion is the class struggle, *national considerations* are not an aim in themselves. At most, they are one of many *conditions* under which the proletariat develops, which it has to take into account and to which, in the struggle against the bourgeoisie and the existing order, it necessarily has to adapt, whether it wants to or not, *in the interest of the class struggle.* 'Men make their own history, but they do not make it just as they please; they do not make it under circumstances chosen by themselves, but under circumstances directly encountered, given and transmitted from the past. The tradition of all the dead generations weighs like a nightmare on the brain of the living'.[16]

The proletariat, *taking into account* the fact that nations exist, draws various conclusions from this.[17] *Even if it regards the Jews as a nation*, the proletariat encounters a new issue because of the specific position of the Jewish masses and has to consider how they are involved in the powerful cycle of capitalism. Does capitalist development, destroying the present conditions of their existence and replacing them with new forms of life, not lead perhaps to the *decline* of this national consciousness? Or are there, on the contrary, factors at work which mould and intensify the consciousness of the Jewish proletariat as a collective actor!

This is the 'foremost question' which the *proletariat* has to answer in order to ensure the proper conduct of the class struggle. This is a precondition for the answer to the question. When the proletariat understands the course of development, it can adjust and adapt its activities in accord with the direction shown by development. Resolving the issue of whether the Jews – the Jewish proletariat – constitute a nation does not, in itself, explain anything.

As we can see, the proletariat's Jewish question differs fundamentally from the bourgeoisie's Jewish question.

Whereas the latter is the result of *genuinely contradictory* interests, either between the bourgeoisie and the Jewish proletariat or within the bourgeoisie itself, the proletariat's Jewish question, which excludes really contradictory interests, is only a *theoretical* problem for the proletariat.

---

15   Luśnia 1904, p. 56.
16   Marx 1979, p. 193.
17   Under different socio-political conditions [these conclusions] *cannot be identical.* For example, they differ between Russia and Austria. The conclusions the proletariat drew from these conditions here in Austria are generally known (i.e. the statutes of the Social Democratic Party of Austria).

The proletariat's Jewish question therefore has as much to do with the bourgeoisie's Jewish question as, to use Spinoza's example, a dog on earth with the dog constellation in the sky.[18]

If the first [the bourgeoisie's Jewish] question is solved by the *future, genuinely revolutionary action* of the proletariat, which abolishes class antagonisms, then this [the proletariat's Jewish] question can be solved by the proletariat *now*, by a *theoretical* assessment of whether or not present social trends are to assimilation and by drawing the appropriate practical conclusions.

The answer to the first [Jewish question] is the ultimate objective of the proletariat, the answer to the second only the means to that end.

This is my way of stating the question!

Evolutionary Trends

... Time,
Revealing what is hidden, then shrouding what appears.
Anything can happen; nothing is beyond belief.
  – SOPHOCLES[19]

We have seen that Mr Luśnia, who regards himself as a socialist, has adopted the premise of an organic national whole. Let us see how Mr Luśnia understands the materialist method (of which he is a proponent and a 'defender').

It is generally known that the filthy, overcrowded Jewish *khederim*[20] with filthy floors and rooms filled with foul air, once or twice a year present an unusually festive sight. Given a sign of an impending inspection, the horrified *melamed*[21] suddenly locks up the children at a helpful neighbour's house, or even in the stinking toilet; the floors are swept in the meantime by his enlightened spouse; there is fresh air and only three or four children are seated in the class (depending on the regulations).

For the sake of appearances this *school* has to disguise the filthy poverty of everyday reality.

Mr Luśnia's behaviour is similar. For the sake of appearances, on special occasions he too has a scientific method and historical materialism, social

---

18   [Spinoza 1954, p. 58.]
19   [Sophocles 2007 p. 30.]
20   [A *kheder*, plural *khederim*, was an elementary Jewish school which taught Hebrew and religion.]
21   ['Melamed' means 'Jewish religious schoolteacher'.]

development and economic factors. In practice, however, this scientific burden, which is entirely obscure to Mr Luśnia, gives way to something else, something which is not historical idealism only because there is absolutely nothing ideal in it!

A nation is, according to Mr Luśnia, the result of an ordinary act of reasoning, and the solution to the Jewish question occurs by means of the 'broadening of a concept'.[22] By the same logic, according to Mr Luśnia (who is a proponent and 'defender' of historical materialism), social movements owe their existence, owe their existence – we repeat – to this or that *idea*.

> Anyone who cares to look, must notice that neither backwardness, nor Palestine or Uganda, exhausts the historical substance of Zionism. There is something else inherent in this concept, something *fundamental*[!], quite independent of the faults and virtues of successive leaders of the movement, something which promises, in this or that form, a permanent, new and significant element in our public life. This something is the *idea* of Jewish nation.[23]

If the idea underlying this idealistic prattle was true and correct, if the 'fundamental essence' of Zionism was nothing else than the 'idea of a Jewish nation', assuming 'this or that form', the proletariat would do absolutely nothing to combat it. It fights against Zionism not because it sees in Zionism this or that 'idea' but as an enemy of its tangible, class interests!

Instead of explaining this or that idea, with which this movement adorns itself, in terms of the substance of social movements, Mr Luśnia prefers (as a proponent and 'defender' of historical materialism) to explain the movement in terms of this or that idea.

---

22   Reader, please do not die laughing! 'What is the solution to this problem [that the Jews cannot migrate and that it is impossible for them to assimilate if they stay]?' asks Mr Luśnia. 'It is very simple. We *should broaden* the concept of equal rights for Jewish citizens to include the *right to possess* [!] their own nationality.' (Luśnia 1904, p. 128) What historical materialism! Mr Luśnia! Mr Luśnia! If the Jews can neither leave, nor assimilate, then the 'solution' is that they do not leave and do not assimilate! What this has in common with the 'broadening of the concept' will remain a mystery forever, a mystery about which Goethe once wrote that it is 'gleich geheimnisvoll für Kluge wie für Thoren'. [Grossman substituted 'Weise' for 'Kluge' ('clever'), Goethe 1869, p. 86; 'to the wise as much a mystery as to the fool', Goethe 2014, p. 65.]

23   Luśnia 1904, p. 57.

In the formation of a Jewish nation, a key role is played not by the *economic factor* but by other factors ... ideological and cultural. Above all perhaps the *idea of equality*; if other nations are nations [!] ... why should we Jews be worse off? Such is their entirely natural reasoning.[24]

⁙

Let us summarise Mr Luśnia's reasoning.

What is the essence of Zionism? The idea of a nation.

What produced this idea? The idea of equality and an 'entirely natural' reasoning on that basis!

⁙

Poor society, poor Galician proletariat! You had to make so many sacrifices, you had to fight so many battles, just to rouse yourself from the suffocating sleep of thoughtlessness and apathy. Where, however, are your ideas, where are your thinkers? Today various Luśnias feed you intellectual swill with impunity and you don't wince!

Your enemies can be happy: their work was not in vain.

Our 'theoreticians' know how to repeat Marx's words. They thoughtlessly defend this or that of his theories. Where, however, a *new* phenomenon occurs, where one has to look with one's own eyes, if only because Marx could not write anything about this phenomenon, in those cases, where Marx's tools and methods should be applied to add another to his earlier magnificent efforts, in those very cases our 'theoreticians' demonstrate their lack of intelligence. The method defended by them proves to be a useless, incomprehensible tool!

Anyway, Mr Luśnia is only a representative of this type.

A number of people, too 'scientific' not to *recognise* the superiority of this method, have, however, nothing in common with the contemporary revolutionary movement which is able to *apply* it in reality.

The entire work of these 'scholars' therefore reduces itself to restating Marx, either in an attempt to reconcile scientific German theory to their non-scientific, idealist prattle, or to the assimilation of this German theory, while still adhering to their idealist positions.

I will now attempt to explain the Jewish question by means of Marx's method.

---

24   Luśnia 1904, p. 60.

To engage in polemics in the defence of this method against Mr Luśnia's idealist muddle would give too much credibility to the latter. I will, therefore, address only the assumption of the mantle of the German scientific theory by this idealist prattle.

∴

What do Mr Luśnia and his Marxist method represent?
- It is not a theory or a well thought out scientific system; ideas cannot constitute the essence of social movements.
- It is not, however, a dogma either. Every dogma requires the power of emotions or faith. Mr Luśnia does not have any power, apart from the power of mediocrity.
- It is not eclecticism. That also requires an intellectual effort, at least an apparent unity and consistency of a few elements taken from different wholes.
- It is not a superficial philosophy, which also has its own logic. Mr Luśnia is a living anathema to every logic, his shallowness has produced not philosophy but merely satire.

What then do Mr Luśnia and his method represent?

Mr Luśnia's position is a catechism; a collection of mechanically assembled forms and formulations, sentences and statements of different sizes, measures and kinds, which can serve any purpose![25]

∴

According to [Franz] Mehring, Marx solved the Jewish question in theory, as early as 1843.

Yet life did not stand still, it moved forward. The Jew of 1843, apart from a handful of assimilated members of the bourgeoisie and intelligentsia, was the Jew of the ghetto, with a slave's soul, a bent neck and a rabbit's heart. That Jew has disappeared. In the new generation, the Jewish proletariat is the revolutionary vanguard of socialism, striding forward with head held high!

Life did not stand still. It *in fact revised* the Jewish question and theory was overtaken by practice.

---

25 We will devote a special work to Mr Luśnia's 'sociological' views on the approaching anniversary of his literary activities.

The present task of theory is not only to catch up with this revolutionary practice, to understand and to explain this factual revision but at the same time to point out the course of its future development!

The only objective of science can be the unequivocal explanation of our social circumstances and, since these undergo changes, at the same time to point out the direction of change, that is, the trends in their development.

One does not have to *prove* that the Jewish masses, unlike the assimilated intelligentsia, constitute a separate, unassimilated collective group. Only a Poloniser, who cannot distinguish between his desires and reality, could contradict this.

> The Jewish population of Galicia still displays today many distinctive features compared to the rest of society, in relation to its ideas, customs, occupations and way of life. This is the case *despite* attempts, deserving recognition, to draw the Jewish population closer[26] to the rest of the province's society and despite changes in this direction which have already taken place, in particular among the educated strata of the population. The significance of this persistent separateness is enhanced by the fact that the Jewish population *constitutes a very significant part of the local population.*[27] We do not recognise the linguistic and religious differences and different customs of the masses of the Jewish proletariat in our society ...[28]

The historical factors which give rise to this situation are well known.

The problem arises when we want to determine the direction of the changes that are taking place.

∴

If Comrade Vinitsky states[29] that he does not know whether the Jews are assimilating or not, he is completely consistent when he concludes that the proletariat's task is to fight against artificial influences of any kind on the spontaneous evolution of the Jewish proletariat. So he is not an enemy of *spontaneous*

---

26   The Poloniser, like the petty bourgeois, enjoys being intoxicated with words. He prefers to
      replace 'Polonise', which is too frank, with 'draw closer', which sounds nobler.
27   Pilat 1893. [Grossman's emphasis.]
28   Declaration of the ninth Congress of the Polish Social Democratic Party of Galicia and
      Silesia (Polska Partia Socjalno-Demokratyczna 1904).
29   See Medem 1943, p. 189. [Vinitsky was a pseudonym of Vladimir Medem.]

assimilation, he is only against those who encourage assimilation. Comrade Vinitsky forgets only that ignorance cannot be a permanent programme for the proletariat but only a temporary necessity. Therefore if *someone proves* that the current tendency *is* to the assimilation of the Jewish proletariat, they would also have the right to *shorten this development* and accelerate it, and thus also *simplify* and facilitate the conditions of the proletariat's emancipatory struggle. So if Comrade Vinitsky has the right to fight assimilationists, others also have the right to fight those who are not assimilationists. They, knowing why they are fighting those opposed to assimilation would, however, have an advantage over Comrade Vinitsky, who is fighting assimilationists because ... he does not know!

Will the Jews be assimilated or not? 'In the final analysis nobody can solve this mystery of the future with any certainty. It is certain that today there are powerful factors at work in both directions'.[30]

Because the *future* will solve this question, Mr Luśnia, a 'sociologist of the Marxist school', has the right to assert that science cannot at present resolve the issue in theory, with certainty. So he prefers to guess.

There are different kinds of certainty. The highest form of certainty is mathematical (logical) certainty, based on arbitrary assumptions, known in logic as 'definitions of name'.[31] In this context, [Immanuel] Kant stated that the extent to which knowledge can be considered really scientific depends on how much mathematics it contains. In shifting from the sphere of internal phenomena (ideas) to the sphere of external things, we can say with [Wilhelm Maximilien] Wundt that 'direct certainty is possible only in relation to that which is [subjectively] accessible to us'. 'All *objective* certainty is of an indirect kind, and is developed from facts subjectively given to us'.[32]

If all objective certainty with regard to *contemporary* phenomena is of 'an indirect kind', then this is all the more the case with phenomena in the *future*. Thus, although the certainty attained by various sciences in their respective areas is not of a mathematical kind, it does not cease to be certainty of a particular kind which is achievable by those given sciences.

In the social sciences, mathematical certainty is also impossible. Despite this, one need not resort, as Mr Luśnia does, to conjecture. On the contrary, by evaluating various factors (economic, legal, psychological etc.) in accordance with their importance one can, even if they operate in contradictory ways,

---

30 Luśnia 1904, p. 127.
31 See Pascal 1869, p. 527.
32 Wundt 1889, p. 153. [As opposed to the Polish translation Grossman referred to, the phrasing and emphasis is different in the second German edition, Wundt 1893, p. 423.]

determine the overall direction of their development. And that can be done with *sociological certainty*.

Scientific socialism as a whole and the sociology of Marx's school proves precisely that!

∴

Modern industry transforms the small workshop of the patriarchal master into a modern manufactory run on capitalist principles, only to transform it again into the large factory of the industrial capitalist.

The scattered working population in the workshops of individual masters *unites* in large manufacturing workshops or factories.

Due to specific, historically conditioned circumstances, Jewish workers do not disperse in the course of this transformation process among their non-Jewish comrades but, on the contrary, separate and form their own clusters, constituting in this way a number of 'Jewish professions'. This distinctive phenomenon, observed incidentally not only in Galicia but elsewhere too,[33] is explained on the one hand by the *requirements of productive technology*. While non-Jewish workers celebrate Sundays and Catholic holidays, Jewish workers celebrate Saturdays and Jewish holidays. There is also a need for easy and *uniform* communications within workshops, since Jewish workers originally only spoke Yiddish. On the other hand Jewish workers only very unwillingly abandon Jewish workshops, since doing so disrupts many aspects of their lives; their surroundings, customs, ideas and traditions.[34]

Please do not misunderstand me. I am not trying to argue how things should be or the opposite. I am only *explaining* phenomena and the conditions which gave rise to them.

There are two consequences of the transformation of the craft workshop into the capitalist manufactory.

First, the direct relationships which previously linked Jewish masters with their workers, and workers with consumers, disappears. A modern manufacturer does not produce to order but produces on a mass scale and sells products to capitalists: wholesalers or exporters. Formerly a Jewish master or his workers had daily, continuous contact with the Polish clients on whose orders they worked. They necessarily succumbed to the influences of their Polish surroundings and had to learn Polish, if only for the sake of business. Now that direct

---

33   See Lonu 1903, p. 64. [Lonu was a pseudonym of Shmuel Gozhansky.]
34   See a mediocre article: M R 1905, p. 14.

contact between Jewish workers and the Polish environment has ceased, the need to learn and use Polish has also disappeared. Jewish workers in big workshops, cut off from external influences, speak only Yiddish among themselves or to their Jewish boss or supervisor.

Thus not only do *assimilative influences cease* but the capitalist transformation of industry increases the Yiddish 'backwardness' of Jewish workers. This also explains the incredible growth of Yiddish literature.

Secondly, the Jewish workers are now part of a *mass*, both in the workshop and in political life. The necessary consequence of this situation is a change in their self-perception. Previously isolated, individual Jewish workers could not regard as purely coincidental the dissimilarities they perceived between themselves and Polish workers, which were not different from those he perceived between themselves and other Jewish workers. Now, as part of a mass, they are forced to notice what characterises them as a part of a mass, a collective whole. Individual differences recede into the background. 'The larger, however, the number of similar phenomena which one observes', wrote [Karl] Kautsky, 'the more, as already mentioned, does the universal, the normal, assert itself, the more do the individual and the accidental recede to the background'.[35]

Such is the explanation of a phenomenon in the face of which [Polish] social patriotism has proved completely powerless. Hiding its ostrich head under the wings of ignorance, it deceives itself that since *it* does not notice a phenomenon, the phenomenon itself will disappear.

A numerous stratum of small traders and stall-holders, finding clients only amongst Jewish workers, are entirely dependent on them and yield to their influence. This stratum, by uniting with the Jewish proletariat, accelerates the previously described development.

The transformation of craft workshops into capitalist manufactories gives rise not only to an appropriate class consciousness but to a national consciousness as well. Here these two phenomena merge. It is not an accident that the *least* class conscious groups of workers (shop assistants, hairdressers etc.) and especially workers employed in craft production, in short the *least* proletarianised elements, show the *greatest* progress in assimilation! This is irrefutable proof of the correctness of the propositions above. This sense of nationality will not disappear but, on the contrary, will increase greatly as capitalist development, of which it is a consequence, engulfs increasing numbers of workers.

One should add something here. The economic relations of the Jewish community, backward and until recently not very differentiated in contrast to its

---

35   [Kautsky 1903, p. 15.]

surroundings, found expression in the view that Jews do not constitute a nation and should assimilate and disappear.

Class struggle, this most normal manifestation of contemporary life and developments, was until recently hardly visible in the Jewish community. Jews appeared to constitute a fragmented and anachronistic organ in the contemporary capitalist system, unfit for contemporary life and struggle, alien to it. Their gradual disappearance therefore seemed an inevitable, logical necessity.

When the progressive march of capitalism swept aside the fantasies of the Jewish bourgeoisie about Jewish unity and the class struggle emerged with unprecedented persistence and power, the Polonising perspective on the Jewish people – as a fragmented organism – also had to disappear and give way to new ideas.

If Jews did not previously live normal lives then the enormous strength and revolutionary force with which they have entered the class struggle are signs of an almost complete return to health. Nearly ten years of the Bund's socialist activities among Jewish workers is rapidly closing the chasm of dozens of years which until recently separated the Jewish proletariat from its non-Jewish surroundings. *It was never closer to contemporary ideals and today's great tasks than precisely when it became 'separate' and 'itself'*, and placed its hot, passionate, southern character onto the revolutionary side of the scales.

The Jewish proletariat became aware of its strength and its existence and will not allow this existence to be torn away!

∴

Polonisation (assimilation) has played an extremely reactionary role in the history of the proletariat.

By repeatedly separating the most intellectual individuals from the masses, it lowered and hindered the development of class consciousness. Polonising the most intellectual individuals means nothing other than leaving the unassimilated Jewish masses to the mercy of the bourgeoisie, rendering them intellectually and thus politically dependent on it.

Cold reality has unmercifully frustrated the tender dreams of the Polish bourgeoisie about Jewish-Poles. For the Jewish proletariat the lofty ideal of Polonisation is only a bourgeoisie fallacy, protecting the interests of Polish capitalists.

Polonisation, as the programme of the *bourgeoisie*, has long been bankrupt. When the influence of the bourgeoisie over the proletariat completely disappeared, it lost all practical significance.

Polonisation remains the slogan of a part of the Polish *proletariat.*

THE PROLETARIAT FACED WITH THE JEWISH QUESTION

It has two faces. It appears as a programme: the Jews must be Polonised. It also appears as an opinion: the Jews are becoming Polonised.

1) *Programmatic assimilation* does not differ from the Polish bourgeoisie's programme for assimilation, which I have already discussed. Programmatic Polonisation as a slogan of a part of the Polish proletariat is understandable, especially here in Galicia. In fact it would be rather surprising if it did not exist.

The primarily petty bourgeois and craft character of our workers movement, in this backward province, had to leave its mark. Many arguments and bourgeois slogans have struck a chord and found support amongst workers. Programmatic Polonisation was inherited from the Polish bourgeoisie by the petty bourgeois Polish proletariat. This once again confirms the general truth that no people, groups or parties are exempt from the influence of the society of which they are a part.

2) *Polonisation as an opinion* is, however, as we saw when analysing developmental trends of the Jewish proletariat, a theoretical formulation of Polonisation actually taking place during the period of craft production. Capitalist development, in destroying the social conditions of the petty bourgeoisie, also demands the revision of corresponding theories. If twenty five years ago Polonisation took as its starting point real petty bourgeois social conditions, contemporary Polonisation takes as its starting point its own fantasy. If, twenty five years ago the ideas of this theoretical Polonisation were reflections of reality, the present desire to Polonise is nothing but an attempt to make reality conform with ideas. The only amusing aspect of this entire situation is the use of old petty bourgeois theory as a magic wand to redeem the future.

The desire to Polonise is – if one is consistent – nothing other than a desire to restore all the petty bourgeois social conditions which gave rise to Polonisation. Complaints that Jewish 'separatism' and 'separateness' are on the rise and that assimilation has not 'yet' produced the expected results, as well as pious sighs of hope that it will occur, only amount to a reactionary petty bourgeois jeremiad. It has the lofty intention of coercing the world into outmoded social conditions. The course of events is, however, arrogant enough to ignore these whims!

∴

How, in a word, does the Poloniser resolve the Jewish question?

The Jews must assimilate, that is, disappear. This solution of the Jewish question according to the logic of Polonising wisdom is a splendid notion. The Jews need only be *removed*, and inexorable logic will lead to an astounding result: there will be no Jewish question!

The Jewish question is caused by the Jews themselves!

There were once visionaries who dreamt of eliminating the so-called social question, that is oppression and poverty. A wise man, whom they met, gave them brilliant advice: 'I tell you truely, there will be no human misery if there are no people'.

Indeed, the Jewish question is caused by the Jews themselves!

The Legend

Il y a des folies, qui se prennent comme les maladies contagieuses.[36]
    – [FRANÇOIS] DE LA ROCHEFOUCAULT

Who does not know it?

The legend: mighty, sinister, with a hundred limbs like boa constrictors.

The bourgeoisie its mother, darkness feeds it.

Wherever life awakens and an idea grows, thence the legend hastens, kills. Terrifying the philistine, disgusting in its gruesomeness, the legend, slithering in the silence, the bourgeois legend being able to unite with the proletariat, slanders and defiles it.

The legend does not rest but undergoes constant change. Elusive but omnipresent, a hundred times suppressed but resurrected again and again – eternal.

A philistine, an intimidated Galician philistine, trusts it because it terrifies him. It makes the proletarian tremble. Fainting from fear he falls at the feet of the bourgeoisie ...

The murderous legend! It triumphs in the graveyard of human ideas.

As swamps have their will-o'-the-wisps and wars their plagues, Night and Ignorance have their legend.

It is a sad nocturne!

Polonisers do not scorn this legend, their legend!

A Jewish socialist or a Zionist – is it worth the effort to make the distinction? Do bourgeois make an effort to make a distinction between a socialist and an anarchist? Even if they could make the distinction, do they prefer to pretend that they can't? Don't they prefer to attack both indiscriminately? Won't they find eager listeners?[37]

---

36   'Folly is as contagious as certain diseases', La Rochefoucauld 2003, p. 60.

37   ['The Polonisers' in question are the leadership of the Polish Social Democratic Party of Galicia who were hostile to the aspirations of Jewish workers in the party to have their own independent, province-wide organisation.]

The Polonisers, being unable to convince, prefer to terrify with a legend. Jewish socialists or Zionists, ah, is it worth distinguishing between them? Jewish 'exclusiveness', 'separatism', 'return to the ghetto', cultural backwardness – the Polonisers rend their wretched garments. Since they do not have the courage to say 'Polonise', they whisper 'make them citizens, make them a part of the province, draw the backward masses closer'.

On the subject of the Jewish question, socialist-Polonisers are in agreement with the various other parties. *Together* they defend the superiority of Polish culture against Jewish backwardness and separatism, and the return to the ghetto.

The Polonising slogans of the Polish bourgeoisie have become so common, so widespread, so much an integral part of society's ideas! Doesn't fighting this legacy of Polish philistinism amount to cutting into its dearest possessions, to national treason?

Polonisers will not do this. They prefer to adapt to prevailing prejudices. After all, they have suffered so much and made so many efforts to gain the right to call themselves patriots!

If the tendency of development moves in the opposite direction to their dreams, Polonisers tries to check its progress. Not, indeed, a small task! And this great task finds the means appropriate to its magnitude. The legend! ...

The same legend about 'unscrupulous agitators', which the bourgeoisie directed a thousand times against them, *they* direct today against the spontaneous movement of the Jewish proletariat. Do they believe that social trends can be generated by individuals?

The same legend of cultural inferiority which he resisted with such indignation when it was expressed by the Hakata,[38] he today takes pleasure in deploying against the Jewish proletariat.

So they were not interested in destroying the legend but only regretted that they could not use it themselves!

The Polonising legend has been lent authority: Marx wrote this and Engels or [Wilhelm] Liebknecht that. Marx allegedly decided the Jewish question in favour of assimilation. This is apparently why Marx's 'On the Jewish Question' was translated into Polish. Marx has been invoked a thousand times in this spirit.[39] Didn't Marx write clearly that struggling for Jewish emancipation means 'to liberate humanity from Jewry?' (Is it not so, Comrade [Herman] Diamand?)

---

38   [The Hakata was a German chauvinist organisation formed in 1894 to eradicate Polish influence in the German-occupied provinces of partitioned Poland.]

39   For example, at the conference of Jewish socialists in L'viv in May 1903.

It is common knowledge that Aristotle was distorted and misunderstood more by medieval Scholasticism, which proclaimed him the only knowledgeable authority, than by anybody else. Nor did anyone conceal their shallow competence more by reference to authority.

Polonisers, when referring to Marx's views on the Jewish question, add this extreme shallowness to their legend.

∴

When Kant published his historic *Critique of Pure Reason*,[40] various critics and scholars, for whom erudition and the history of philosophy can replace philosophy itself, threw themselves on the new work with the scalpel of criticism and looked in the cellars of their philosophical knowledge for the appropriate heading under which it could be categorised. Oh, they declared, this is a system of transcendental, super idealism! Having attached the relevant label, they could easily wheel out pertinent polemical guns. They felt satisfied.

Kant's sharp retort to these experts in categorising and sorting, in the *Prolegomena*,[41] was superfluous. People such as they, whose entire work consists in searching for labels and headings for phenomena, never notice or understand any *new* phenomena. For them Euclidean geometry will never be anything other than a systematic manual for drawing!

∴

One of the most terrifying and astounding developments for contemporary Polonisers, which they still unsuccessfully attempt to combat, is the emergence of the Jewish proletariat as an independent, collective personality, i.e. the process which transformed the Jews of the ghetto into a conscious and fearless revolutionary vanguard.

Polonisers do not understand this process. They prefer to search for the appropriate label in the rummage shops of history. In this way a question can be simplified and it is easy to find the appropriate arguments. This process is for them Jewish 'separatism', return to the ghetto.

Yes, for you experts in categorising, Euclidean geometry will always be a manual for drawing.

---

40   [Kant 1998.]
41   [Kant 2004.]

This idiotic retrospection, which sees all new phenomena only through the grimy lenses of half-learned history, has the noble aim of using the legend of the ghetto, the curse of the past, to frighten the present away from realising its contemporary goals. It forgets, however, that ghosts cannot murder the living!

The revolutionary movement of the Jewish proletariat destroys the Polonisers' prattle every day with a thousand proofs and will not rest until the legend of the ghetto and separatism, unworthy of the proletariat, disappears, and until all the ghosts risen from the dead disappear, leaving behind nothing but a legend of this legend!

• •
•

At the end the eighteenth and beginning of the nineteenth century, the modern, big bourgeoisie mounted the stage, raising the banner of rebellion and revolution against the exclusive rule of the feudal aristocracy and the absolute power of the central state, aiming to create conditions that corresponded with the trend of the time. This movement also attracted other social strata: the intelligentsia, the petty bourgeoisie, workers, artisans and the peasantry. In the course of the triumphant destruction of feudal institutions and the unfettering of newly formed social forces, the townspeople, intoxicated by victory, proclaimed the slogans of liberty, equality and fraternity for the 'nation'. They also abolished the ghetto's boundaries, established in the middle ages.

'Die Ghetto mauern wurden gesprengt ...',[42] [Heinrich] Graetz was moved to cry in a quavering voice ...

These boundaries were, however, abolished in a bourgeois way, i.e. only to the extent required by the interests of bourgeois society. The ghetto was abolished only in law.

One has, however, to be childishly naive in the extreme to believe that it is possible, at a moment's notice, to abolish by means of decrees relations that took centuries to form.

The universal freedom and equality before the law that abolished the ghetto, were fundamentally the ruling class's freedom and equality, created by it and for it. That is, they were freedom and equality in so far as they suited the interests of the bourgeoisie.

The ghetto, which had been formally abolished, still continued to exist as a specific totality of socio-economic conditions, a totality which was a coherent

---

42   ['The walls of the ghetto walls were burst open ...', Graetz 1895, p. 459.]

whole, cut off and different from the rest of society. Abolished in law, it continued to exist as a socio-economic, religious, political, cultural and social ghetto.

We have seen earlier that the bourgeoisie can and does take advantage of this state of affairs.

The factor which actually destroyed and is still destroying the ghetto is a hundred years of capitalist development. Capitalism accomplished this astonishing revolution in the course of only one hundred years of domination.

Modern capitalism does not, however, destroy the ghetto by expelling Jews from the world, as various Polonising sages think. On the contrary, modern capitalism constantly creates the Jew anew. This is confirmed by ordinary observation and statistics, for which I tried to account theoretically above. The ghetto does not disappear because of Polonisation or assimilation, that is, when the social environment absorbs the Jews. On the contrary, it disappears because the Jews absorb and assimilate contemporary developments.

It is not the ghetto which disappears in the modern world but the modern world which decomposes the medieval ghetto. It is not the Jew who subsides into capitalist society but modern capitalism that encroaches upon Jewry!

∴

So the Jews do not disappear. On the contrary the Jewish proletariat, as a class, develops a consciousness of itself as a collective individual precisely as the ghetto disintegrates and becomes a site of class struggle. The Jewish proletariat now seeks and creates new forms for the free development of its individuality in the external world.

The Jewish workers associations in Galicia were at first local, then there was a gradual trend to centralisation of committees transcending local boundaries. Finally there was an effort to establish an independent organisation for the whole Jewish proletariat. These forms of organisation corresponded to stages in the development of the Jewish proletariat's class consciousness.[43]

---

43   Polonisers do not like to mention the fact that such associations *have existed across the whole province for many years* and that they themselves were often forced by circumstances to set them up. Where was Jewish 'separatism' then? An independent Jewish organisation is only a *consequence* of this fact. If Polonisers now fight so ruthlessly against the trend to an independent organisation of the Jewish proletariat (which would only be a *small part* of the general Austrian party and share its common programme), this proves only that they are unable to understand the *implications of their own assumptions.* An independent organisation is allegedly a betrayal of the 'idea of solidarity'. In that case, it is worth remembering that in Austria the Social Democratic Party consists of six independent organisations of this kind. Did they also betray the 'idea' of solidarity? The Polish Social

This whole process, presented above, is the result of the *disintegration of the ghetto* and the encroachment of capitalism. This does not stop Polonisers, who see things upside down, from regarding the process as a *return to the ghetto* and the betrayal of the 'idea of solidarity'.

With equal justification they could see modern industrial or commercial courts as a transgression of the principle of equality before the law and a return to the judicial system of the estates of the middle ages. They could also see a return to medieval communal particularism in the current tendency to administrative decentralisation. Here too they could see a breach of the 'idea of solidarity' by 'isolated' and 'separate' communes or provinces. After all, the 'idea of solidarity' is here also breached by delegating some functions and means of coercion from the authority of the central state and its officials to the communes and provinces, which are given autonomous administrative power.

As Kautsky stated,

> diese Selbstverwaltung bedeutet nicht *Wiederherstellung* des mittelalterlichen Particularismus. Die Gemeinde wird dadurch nicht wieder das selbstständige Ganze, das sie ehedem gewesen. *Sie bleibt* ein Glied des grossen Ganzen, der Nation, hat in ihrem Rahmen und für sie zu wirken. Die Rechte und Pflichten der einzelnen Gemeinden dem Staate gegenüber werden nicht mehr durch besondere Verträge festgesetzt. Sie sind ein Produkt der *für Alle in gleicher Weise geltenden Gesetzgebung* der staatlichen Zentralgewalt;[44] sie werden bestimmt durch die Interessen des gesammten Staates oder der Nation, nicht durch die der einzelnen Gemeinden.[45]

This statement is too important not to be cited in the original.

Democratic Party of Galicia and Silesia is not the *only* such organisation, as one is led to believe, but *one* of six!

44   It must be remembered that the same French National Assembly which destroyed feudal particularism, created, by the decree of 14 December 1790, no fewer than 44,828 new municipalities (municipalités).

45   ['This self-administration does not imply the *reconstruction* of medieval particularism. The commune does not again become the autonomous entity that it once was. It remains a part of the greater entity, the nation and has to operate within its framework. The rights and obligations of the individual communes in relation to the state are no longer ruled by particular agreements. They are a product of the legislation of the central state authority which *applies to all in the same way*. They are determined by the interests of the whole state or nation and not by those of the individual communes.' (Kautsky 1893, p. 48) Grossman's emphasis.]

Those who believe in idiotic retrospection, ranting about return to ghetto, should read it with care!

. .
.

The legend in our ranks represents opportunism. However, not even the kind of opportunism that exists in Western Europe but our own Galician opportunism. The principal common feature of both forms of opportunism is *capitulation*: the renuciation of the direct path of the revolutionary proletariat. In the west this is in favour of reforms. And in our province? Our 'society' has not yet produced any reforms; it produces ignorance and prejudice.

Opportunism in our province is capitulation in the face of prejudice and patriotic traditions. Capitulation even before the struggle has begun ...

Its motto is thus not the struggle against prejudice but conformity.

The legend!

I judge it to be impossible to describe the events of one's own times, without offending many.[46]
– [NICCOLÒ] MACCHIAVELLI

It was my desire to hurt.

I was not writing a history of events but a critique of views in our very own ranks. The statement of the Italian philosopher, the judge of human souls, expresses an even greater truth.

In the section on trends of development, I discussed only those factors resulting in the transformation of the Jewish masses into a Jewish proletariat conscious of its national identity. I left out *countertendencies* operating in the opposite direction.

I did this for several reasons.

First, because these counter-tendencies include general capitalist tendencies to assimilation, to uniformity, which affect *all nations* to the same extent, making them all resemble one type we may call 'the average European'. So they could be disregarded as having no particular bearing on Jews and not affecting the Jewish question, relating in general to the existence of independent nations in the future.

If we disregard these general capitalist assimilatory tendencies, which are tantamount to progress and culture, and concern ourselves with assimilation

---

46   [Machiavelli 1882, p. 5.]

in a narrower sense, not that of a general type but relating to a single nation, we come to the second reason. For many years, in the discussion of Polonisation, factors that were actually or apparently leading to assimilation were misapprehended and overemphasised, while counterposed factors were disregarded. It would be redundant to go over this again here. My task has been to point out *new* phenomena, not to reiterate old assertions.

Finally and most importantly, examining the conditions under which the Jewish proletariat wages the class struggle, we are faced with a fact which casts doubt on the efficacy of assimilationist tendencies and demands explanation. We are faced with the concrete and undeniable fact, which imposes itself on us with unyielding strength, that Yiddish 'backwardness' is spreading amongst the Jewish proletariat. Popular Yiddish literature, dealing with physics, anatomy, biology, zoology, mineralogy, botany, mathematics and astronomy, geology, economics, sociology and history, is spreading in working class communities. Socio-political literature is expanding, from popular pamphlets to serious works like Marx's *Capital*. The number of publications and journals, primarily fiction, folk poetry and Jewish short stories, is growing. Shakespeare and Dante, [Émile] Zola and [Maxim] Gorky, [Lev] Tolstoy and [Marya] Konopnicka, [Herman] Heijermans and [Gerhard] Hauptmann are introduced to the Jewish worker in Yiddish translations. Proletarian theatres, educational institutions, libraries and reading rooms are being set up spontaneously from humble beginnings. There are thousands of such attempts and efforts within the proletariat.

The masses read this literature and take it seriously and each pamphlet that is read generates demand for another. Working-class members of the Jewish intelligentsia are not ashamed of their language, no longer look for knowledge in foreign, Polish or Russian, publications. Popular and more serious Yiddish literature is more than sufficient to satisfy their needs. These workers do not therefore become *separated from the masses*, do not become strangers; they work among and for them.

Where does this lead and what does it mean?

Old, Polonising slogans have lost their significance and paled. The Jewish proletariat has a new life and experiences new ideas.

Reality contradicts and subordinates assimilationist tendencies. I could, therefore, safely ignore them.

What strikes us today and deserves attention is the new direction of ideas amongst the masses. It was necessary to *explain* this development and its causes. Its consequences, on the other hand, are inexorable.

The Jewish proletariat will not stop half way. It follows the path of the revolutionary proletariat and its interests are the interests of the whole revolutionary proletariat.

This path is neither spun out of fantasy nor based on tradition. It is the inevitable result of the Jewish proletariat's material and social circumstances, and pushes it in this direction.

The Jewish question, as presented above, is the only Jewish question that can exist *within the proletariat*. This is the only way it can be conceived by the *proletariat*; the Jewish question within the proletariat does not otherwise exist.

Everything else is petty bourgeois simpering about social harmony or bourgeois fear, disguised in national phraseology, or the problem of national minorities in general. But for the *proletariat* this is not and cannot be the Jewish question.

With the achievement of an independent Jewish organisation, which is the practical goal of the Jewish proletariat in its historic struggle for emancipation, the last visible vestiges of the ghetto will also disappear, to the extent that the *proletariat* can get rid of them under capitalism. Only in this way will the Jewish proletariat achieve *equality with the proletariats of other nations* in the Austrian social democratic movement. In previous centuries the ghetto meant that the Jews were in an exceptional situation. The establishment of an independent Jewish organisation is essential for the Jewish proletariat as a class movement. Abolishing the Jewish proletariat's exceptional situation in the Austrian social democratic movement, means the real destruction of the ghetto, at least in the proletariat's own ranks!

When the proletariat's final liberation and victory arrives, it will also finally liberate the Jewish proletariat and be its victory.

Consciousness of the path that the proletariat has to follow to achieve its great goal, also provides the theoretical solution to the Jewish question. Our greatest task at present is to identify this path.

> The sparks I strike today – will light tomorrow.[47]
>
> – [MARYA] KONOPNICKA

January 1905

---

47   [Konopnicka 1915, p. 246. The Jewish Social Democratic Party of Galicia was established within months of the publication of Grossman's pamphlet, on May Day 1905.]

CHAPTER 2

From the Editors*

Translated from Polish by Dominika Balwin

When initiating the publication of a new organ, intended for students, we must justify its emergence and provide a short statement of the beliefs of its editors, in at least a few words.

Over recent years, young people in Galicia[1] have become immensely political; not only university students but also students in high schools make peremptory judgements without appeal on the most complicated political and social problems in Galicia and Austria, as well as neighbouring states, extolling one current to the skies, spitting on others, acknowledging certain activists as infallible leaders of the nation, condemning others.

The very fact that young people are keenly interested in politics is a very positive phenomenon; the evil resides in the way in which a considerable proportion of our youth approaches solving political problems.

We are aware that social phenomena are the most complicated of all those known to us; we are also aware that investigating them objectively is unusually difficult because social position, class interests, national interests, traditions and intellectual sympathies have a great, unintentional influence that colours our understanding of them.

If we pass now from social phenomena in general to contemporary political life, we can readily observe that accurate assessments pose even greater difficulties.

To overcome them, we must, above all, master as much knowledge as possible in the area of social-political phenomena. Further, in judgements about these phenomena, we have to consciously avoid emotional criteria.

On matters concerning the future, it is necessary to be guided above all by realism, to strictly distinguish between what is relatively possible from what is desired. We write 'relatively', because it is not possible to predict the future

---

* [Originally published as Grossman 1905c. Grossman was the principal editor of *Zjednoczenie: Organ Młodzieży Socyalistycznej, Union: Organ of Socialist Youth.*]

1 [Between 1795 and 1918 there was no independent Polish state. Predominantly Polish-speaking territories were in provinces of the Russian Empire (the Congress Kingdom of Poland), the German Empire (Posen, Silesia, East Prussia) and the Habsburg/Austro-Hungarian Empire (Galicia).]

when dealing with socio-political issues, with the same accuracy as physical phenomena; we cannot quantitatively measure the former, as we can the latter. In Galicia recently, despite what we have written above, discussions in young people's circles and the journal particularly intended for them, *Promień*, have been guided by different principles: not the serious education of young people, awakening them to criticism and independent judgement; but only adherence to the programme of the PPS.[2]

That this has indeed been the case is apparent in *Promień*'s avoidance of reviews of books from different tendencies. The literature of other parties has been boycotted; and discussions of programmes have either uncritically invoked authorities or primarily relied on emotional arguments.

On the question of Poland's independence, the decisive arguments have been that Marx, Engels and Liebknecht once said that Poland is necessary or that every nation has the right to freedom. Whether a right to something can always be realised in the short term has not been discussed.

We will not be concerned with gaining uncritical followers, who would only be our followers because they do not know anything of other tendencies, but rather with teaching young people to think independently and about how they can defend their views against a variety of opponents.

We are socialists because only socialism provides a complete solution to all burning social questions. We will also strive to comprehensively introduce our readers to the doctrines of socialism.

Being sincere socialists, however, we will carefully investigate non-socialist literature, to extract the greatest possible benefit for socialism; we will also look the truth boldly in the eye, not silently overlooking the mistakes of socialist parties.

Facts and logical reasoning, rather than invocations of Marx and Engels, will be decisive for us.

We will set aside the question of Polish Independence in the future, for today we want to achieve as much as possible for the Polish nation within the borders of the states of the partition.

We will also always defend the rights of all nations, whether long recognised, strong and highly civilised or those whose right to exist others dispute, for one reason or another. For us, the opinion of its members is decisive in determining whether or not a social group constitutes a nation.

---

2 [The Polska Partia Socjalistyczna (Polish Socialist Party) was the name of the nationalist, socialist organisations in the German- and Russian-occupied provinces of Poland with which the leadership of the PPSD sympathised. '*Promień*' means '*The Ray*'.]

We will not just 'tolerate' Ruthenians[3] or deny Jews the right to determine their nationality.

People who consider themselves to be a nation are indeed one. This is the only just principle.

We will not spend too long describing the character of our publication.

It will contain scientific, literary, political and informative articles and translations.

The fact that we are socialists will not lead us to occupy ourselves exclusively, in the fields of politics and social issues, with socialism. On the contrary, all problems related to democracy in the broad meaning of the word will be of great concern for us.

We would like our publication to be in close contact with young people; we will therefore carry extensive correspondence from different localities about the lives of young people and we ask our readers to inform us about the issues, whether scientific or socio-political, ethical or philosophical, which concern them most.

Such is our programme. Its achievement will depend not on us alone but also on the support which we find.

---

3   [I.e. Ukrainians.]

CHAPTER 3

Letters to the Bund*

Translated from Polish by Dominika Balwin

Kraków 8 April 1905

Dear Comrades,

In what is a decisive moment for us, we turn to you with a request. As you know, a movement for the creation of an independent Jewish organisation has existed in Galicia for a few years: in recent times this movement has broadened and deepened to include all the larger towns. In the context of Galicia, this is a serious matter. Due to a great number of circumstances and events, workers in Kraków, L'viv, Przemyśl and Tarnów have decided that the time has come to establish a Jewish social democratic party; the timing of its appearance has been set for the first days in May. We have resolved to celebrate May Day *together* [with the Polish Social Democratic Party] as a visible sign that our demand to establish an independent organisation does not mean, as the Polish socialists claim, destroying solidarity and fraternity.

The publication issued by us, the *Jüdische Socialdemokrat* whose first issue will appear on 1 May, will include our programmatic article 'Vos viln mir', in which we demand a Jewish organisation and call on workers to form it.[1] The Party[2] will expel the editor of this publication – at that time we will voluntarily leave the Party *en masse*.[3] Though we know the Polish Party will not treat us delicately, *we do not want this to lead to a fratricidal war*, we want to maintain good will.

Comrades! In this moment which is such a decisive one for us, we turn to you for help. The socio-political circumstances in which we fight are not the same but, on the other hand, our struggle is based on the same and common theoretical foundations: the Jewish proletariat must have an independent organisation adapted to the environment of the Jewish masses. We know that only such an organisation can make of today's backward, impoverished Jewish workers,

---

* [Grossman 1905d, published here for the first time.]
1 [Organizatsions Komite fun der Yudisher Sotsial-Demokratisher Partey in Galitsien 1905, see *What Do We Want?*, below, pp. 73–82. '*Jüdische Socialdemokrat*' means '*Jewish Social Democrat*'.]
2 [I.e. the PPSD.]
3 [In fact the new Party was announced on May Day.]

oppressed by their poverty, what you have already made them: a conscious and courageous revolutionary vanguard!

Thus you are and will be the role model for a whole new generation of Jewish workers and intellectuals. Every one of us was educated by your literature.

The struggle which we are leading is a difficult one. The assimilated intelligentsia, torn away from the masses, is unable to provide materials in Yiddish which the mass movement demands for its agitation and press. We know, however, that the movement itself will create and produce the means it needs.

For the time being, however, we are struggling with obstacles and count on your help. We know that at the moment you are not in a position to send us any sum of money so we are asking you for help in a different form. We are unable to publish any scientific pamphlets in the field of socialism, so perhaps you would be in a position to give us a certain amount of your scientific literature, which we could sell and thus gain a double benefit – we would spread socialist thought and earn money from the sales. This literature could be varied in content, serious and also popular – for example now, before Passover, the *Haggada shel Pesach*.[4] These publications can be sent to *Maurycy Fast, Przemyśl, ul. Mickiewieza l.ii*, who will be our main administrator, responsible to our Congress.

Naturally we will keep separate accounts and make payments for the publications which we have previously received from you in various cities around Galicia.

In addition I am sending you Sławka Gr's[5] letter – he knows of our request to you and endorses it.

Regarding the request for pamphlets which you could send us, we intend to distribute them free of charge at our discretion.

We ask you for regular letters or articles about the revolutionary movement in Russia, both in general and especially about the Jewish movement; perhaps, *even this week*, you could send us such an article or letters about the revolutionary movement in Russia in *Yiddish*, so that it can be published in the first issue of the *Jüdische Sozialdemokrat*, or for example an article about 'May Day in Russia'. As we lack strength in writing in Yiddish, every article written in Yiddish is an immense help.

Comrades! The step which we are now taking, a definitive step forward, is decisive for the future of the social democratic movement here, among the Jewish masses. We are therefore also counting on your help, as also on the help of

---

4   [The text of the domestic Jewish Passover service, which was often adapted to refer to circumstances of contemporary oppression.]
5   [Presumably Bronisław Grosser, who was in Galicia around this time and one of whose pseudonyms was Sławek.]

other social democrats. In a month we will be able to make this request openly; at present still secretly as

> the Temporary (Secret) Committee of Jewish Workers in Galicia,
> we send you our fraternal greetings.
> On behalf of the Committee,
> Henryk Grossman
> (Secretary)
> PS. My address
> Henryk Gr. Kraków ul. Sebastyana 36

Our founding Congress will probably be held in Przemyśl on 27 and 28 May – unless extraordinary obstacles arise which cannot be foreseen.[6]

From the literature which you have we need: *Zionism, Haggadah shel pesach, History of the Jewish Labour Movement, History of the Jewish Movement*,[7] and your publications on Marx, Engels and Lassalle which we want to distribute *en masse*.

Kraków 3 July 1905

Respected Comrades!

I have just received your letter and I will pass it on immediately; you can send the blotting paper[8] to *my* address.

At the same time, should you need our services more often in the future, please contact me directly, without prior notice and I will gladly try to take care of the matter. Please include only the appropriate indications.

As in the past, I will give the literature to the person who says he has come on your behalf.

If for some reason or other my address is not convenient for you, please send the papers to the Ferdinand Purisch's address, ul. Sw. Sebastyana 19.

With soc-dem greetings,

Henryk Grossman

PS. I will shortly send a more extensive report about the state of our work and Party in Galicia.

---

6 [The Congress actually took place on 9–10 June 1905, the third anniversary of the execution of the Bundist hero Hirsh Lekert.]

7 [Lonu 1903; a Bundist version of the *Haggadah shel pesach*, the text of a Passover service; Anonymous 1900; probably Anonymous 1902.]

8 [This was a common expression for illegal, underground publications.]

Kraków 27 July 1905

Respected Comrades!

On 1 May this year the Jewish Social Democratic Party of Galicia was established – as you surely know. Over 9–10 June the first, founding Congress of our Party was held in L'viv, attended by 53 delegates from around the province, representing about 2,000 organised workers, that is nearly a third of all those who are organised in Galicia!

A letter from the Committee of Bund Abroad was sent to the Congress, and expressed warm regards and best wishes.

At present I turn to you with a request to find us an editor for the *Yiddish weekly, which we intend to publish soon, as well as to provide support*, to the extent you can manage, in terms of literature or writing periodic letters for our publication.

However, before I come to my precise request, I will just briefly describe our position so that you know the situation. I attach our publications *What We Want* and *Before the Congress*,[9] which explain the matter in more detail. I will send you the minutes of the Congress shortly.

In Galicia – inhabited by three nationalities (Poles, Ruthenians[10] and Jews), Jews comprise about 13 percent of the population. In spite of this, as the Jewish population is mainly concentrated in the cities, the proportion to the rest of the population there amounts to 30–40 percent.

As social democrats, we take a position of conscious, uncompromising class struggle, which is our guiding principle. In the name of the class interests of the whole proletariat, we – as Jews – consider it imperative, however, to adapt our struggle to the circumstances of our surroundings, to the circumstances of the masses of the Jewish proletariat. This is the theoretical position of the Bund, with which in theoretical principle we are therefore in agreement. If this position of the Bund has been questioned from various angles in Russia, then in Austria this principle is officially recognised by Austria's Social Democrats (see *Before the Congress*).[11] It is stranger here, that Austrian Social Democracy does 'not recognise' us as a party. If, therefore, Jewish socialists in Russia, where it is

---

9   [Organizatsions Komite fun der Yudisher Sotsial-Demokratisher Partey in Galitsien 1905, see *What Do We Want?*, above, pp. 73–82; Żydowska Partya Socyalno-Demokratyczna Galicyi 1905, see *Before the Congress*, above, pp. 83–102.]

10   [I.e. Ukrainian.]

11   [Żydowska Partya Socyalno-Demokratyczna Galicyi 1905, see *Before the Congress*, below, pp. 83–102.]

completely rejected, are the exception to the rule, then in Austria, on the contrary, it is the exception to the exception. When the Austrian Party accepted the *principle of national organisation* and brought it to life, it broke into six officially recognised national organisations. In spite of this, they do not want to recognise a seventh, Jewish, organisation.

First and foremost, we are hampered by the Polish Social Democratic Party of Galicia which is under the strong influence of the PPS[12] of the Kingdom of Poland. It is characteristic that, when the antisemitic organ of the all-Polish National Democrats (*Słowo Polskie*) in its issue of 8 May this year called on all 'patriotic' elements to crusade against the 'separatists' (that is, us) and therefore stood on the side of the Polish Social Democratic Party, one of the most honest democratic publications in Galicia, the organ of the populists (*Kurjer Lwówski*) writes in its issue of 30 June: 'With the existence of the Czech, German, Ruthenian etc., Social Democratic Parties in Austria, there is no logical reason why a *Jewish* organisation should not exist'.[13]

At our Congress we adopted the programme of Austrian Social Democracy in full and without any limitations and, despite 'not being recognised' as an official part of it, *we consider ourselves* part of the General Party and act on the basis of a common programme and common tactics.

Achieving 'recognition' will depend on our strength and, we are convinced, that it will soon occur, as it must as matters stand.

That we have right on our side is clear, not only in theory but also in accord with the entire *history of the workers movement* among Jews in Galicia. Our newly formed Party is just the last link in this chain of organisational development. I cannot write further here but just want to note that the battle to form a Jewish workers party in Galicia has been going on since 1897 and its more important stages were the first conference of Jewish socialists in L'viv in 1899, the second conference in L'viv in 1903, the ninth Congress of the Polish Social Democratic Party in Kraków in 1904 and the Trade Union Conference in Przemyśl in 1905 and, finally, the proclamation of the Jewish Social Democratic Party on 1 May 1905.

Our opponents from the Polish Party *did not reply* to our arguments in *Before the Congress* (!), by which they condemned themselves in public opinion. On the other hand there is almost no day on which they do not attack us in

---

12   [The PPS, Polska Partia Socjalistyczna (Polish Socialist Party) was the name of the nationalist, socialist organisations in the German- and Russian-occupied provinces of Poland.]

13   [*Słowo Polskie* 1905. '*Słowo Polskie*' ('*Polish Word*') was a twice daily newspaper in L'viv, associated with the antisemitic National Democratic Party. *Kurjer Lwówski* 1905. '*Kurjer Lwówski*' ('*Lwów Courier*') was a daily newspaper in L'viv, associated with the Polish Peasant Party.]

Naprzód[14] or their other publications in a manner that is dirty and unworthy of social democrats, just as, in its time, the PPS attacked the Bund

Despite this, our movement is growing and continues to garner wider mass support. Today we can pride ourselves on the figure of about 3,000 [members] organised in trade unions!

Our work and the growth of our influence progresses so rapidly that we simply do not have an adequate agitational strength, especially since the PPSD did not fulfil its responsibilities in this regard at all and we have to begin building from the ground up ourselves.

Above all we feel the *lack of a press*. The PPSD practised the politics of assimilation regarding the Jews. While workers yielded to it only partially, this policy totally tore the intelligentsia away from the masses and it did not even know their language, Yiddish.

The first new generation of the intelligentsia which sought out paths to return to the masses nevertheless carries the mark of assimilationist influences and either knows little or no Yiddish at all.

So, as well as difficulties of a general kind and financial difficulties (Jewish workers here are very poor), we are dealing with a seemingly strange difficulty: the lack of an appropriate editorial strength.[15] We therefore ask you to match us with an intelligent person, knowledgeable about socialist theory and workers' struggles. I add that an important part of our struggle is the *struggle with Zionism* and Poale Zionism.[16]

An intelligent person will easily become familiar with our situation, especially as there are eager helpers here.

As to payment, we will come to an understanding with the person. Poverty stricken as we are in Galicia, we cannot afford much.

Finally we ask you to provide us with extensive and regular *letters*, about various events in your life, work and struggle. Actually the Foreign Committee of the Bund promised to send us such letters but we would prefer to have direct relations with you.

Please forgive us for turning to you at such a difficult time for you. However we know that we are turning to our closest friends. In different political and social circumstances, we are struggling for the same ideals, the liberation of the Jewish proletariat.

Long live the international workers movement!

---

14   [*Naprzód* (*Forwards*) was the PPSD's daily newspaper in Kraków.]
15   The Yiddish weekly published by the PPSD is edited not by a Galician but a PPS Jew from Lithuania.
16   The Poale Zion organisation attempted to combine socialism with Zionism.

With fraternal greetings,
Henryk Grossman
Secretary
Address: Kraków
ul. Sw Sebastyana 36

What Do We Want?[*]

Translated from Polish by Dominika Balwin, from Yiddish by Rick Kuhn

We want to spread social democratic thought, the idea of class struggle, to carry it into the ranks of the Jewish proletariat. We want to show Jewish proletarians the great goal and the path to that goal; a better future and a brighter tomorrow for those who today are so oppressed and ignorant, pariahs among the nations.

We want to awaken the Jewish masses from sleep; the time for sleep has already passed without return. Life inevitably throws up burning problems and the wave of history will wash over those who have not solved them. So rise up, you, who have previously bowed down; awaken, you, who slept; speak, you who have previously been silent. Today you must not be silent!

The proletariat is growing daily, the workers movement is becoming powerful. It has already encompassed a hundred countries and speaks a hundred languages. Jewish proletariat of Galicia, awaken. Do not sleep while others fight, do not be silent when others call to the class war.

Join the huge, rising wave, join the international workers movement. Let the foundations of palaces shudder from your united assault, let capitalism tremble until the final blow knocks it off its feet.

We want to give you consciousness and power, we want to raise you from poverty and despair, to demolish your social and religious prejudices and to crush soulless structures. We want to rouse you to the class struggle, to fight for your immediate and longer term interests. So awaken!

1

Over the past two decades Jewish society has changed immeasurably. Capitalism's mighty circle is beginning to embrace the Jews. Capitalism has intruded

---

[*] [Originally published as Komitet Organizacyjny Żydowskiej Partyi Socyalno-demokraticycz-ney w Galicyi 1905; and Organizatsions Komite fun der Yudisher Sotsial-Demokratisher Partey in Galitsien 1905 and also a pamphlet in Yiddish. The language in the Polish version is more literary than that in the Yiddish. Grossman wrote this manifesto, according to Feyner 1948, p. 18; also see Reyzen 1927, column 616. As Grossman probably wrote the manifesto in Polish, that version has been preferred in matters of detail. Where there are significant differences between the versions, they are noted.]

into the moribund Jewish ghetto, revolutionised and divided it into new classes and created new relations between them. The Jewish proletariat has emerged and is emerging in greater numbers every day, a wage-earning Jewish working class, which until recently did not exist ...

The transformations in economic relations are accompanied by the corresponding responses of political parties which are beginning to appear among the Jews.

These transformations are happening here extremely slowly. That is also why the transitional period in which we find ourselves claims more victims, undermines living conditions and destroys the previous sources of income of numerous strata without creating new ones.

General gloom and fear, the prevailing insecurity, the poverty of the broad masses and their terribly low living standard, and the consequent illness and mass emigration of thousands of families – these are the tracks that mark capitalism's progress as it encroaches into Jewish society.

In these circumstances the rising Jewish workers movement has had an immensely difficult and important task. The politically and culturally backward Jewish masses were and are different from the surrounding Polish population in various ways. Apart from a handful of the assimilated intellectuals and a few individual workers, the Jewish proletariat lives in specific, historically created circumstances. It is significantly different culturally in terms of customs, religion and language.

As long as the socialist movement did not draw in the masses, these differences were not so obtrusive and did not come to light as strongly as at present.

During its first years, the social democratic movement among Jewish workers barely managed to involve those individuals who were assimilated, detached from the masses and on its periphery. The agitation and work conducted among *these* workers was the same as among Polish proletarians. The socialist movement initiated among Jews by Polish socialists – which we willingly acknowledge and do not think to deny – was not a mass movement and barely reached a few assimilated workers. It is no wonder that, in spite of the fact that it was conducted among Jews, it was a *Polish* movement. This entire movement considered itself an appendage of the Polish movement and, deprived of all independence, expected everything from the Polish movement.

When this movement subsequently began to penetrate the masses – unassimilated masses in such a different environment from that of the Polish proletariat, and possessing their own language and specific culture and customs – it was necessary to change the forms and ways of agitating immediately, if the work was to be effective. *It was necessary to take into account the circumstances of the new environment.* It was necessary to adjust to the needs and life of the Jewish masses. Jewish workers must not only be addressed in another language [i.e. Yiddish], their psychology must be understood; their souls have to be addressed, they have to be fired up, revolutionised and swept up!

Alas! Polish socialists did not do this. Without understanding the Jewish masses and their needs they could not do this and the majority of them did not even want to. For these and other reasons (which we discuss elsewhere) they did not take the special circumstances and needs of the Jewish masses into account. Convinced that sooner or later Jews would be assimilated and wishing that this would finally happen, they were unable to distinguish their desires and will froms harsh reality. They mistook their desire for actual reality. Thus they did not take the needs of the Jewish proletariat into account and, instead of adapting their forms of agitation and work to these circumstances, preferred in their blindness, on the contrary, [to try] to bend the social circumstances to their wishes and to their forms or agitation.

Is it any wonder that under these circumstances the Polish forms of agitation had to become a kind of Polonisation? Is it any wonder that a socialist movement conducted *in this way* did not embrace the Jewish proletariat?

The entire work of the Polish socialists in relation to the Jewish workers movement was based on the consistent neglect of its needs. While the specific environmental circumstances of the Jewish masses demanded consideration, Polish socialists at the time preached 'drawing closer' (read Polonisation) and the disappearance of Yiddish.[1] The Polish socialists made no effort to demonstrate to the Jewish masses the actual nature and goals of Zionism, to unmask Zionist demagogy. They suspected Zionism in all the independent actions of the Jewish proletariat. Not to mention that an alien, Polish ideology, which could neither win it over nor fire it up, was imposed on the Jewish masses and that a psychology of suffering was drummed into Jewish workers. Instead of arousing a sense of their own power and health, and a sense of the dignity of Jewish workers as Jews, they were mournfully told: Jew, you are doomed; you will disappear. In a word, instead of awakening their pride, everything was done to shake and weaken their dignity. People like Hirsh Lekert do not emerge in such an atmosphere! Sadder still: invoking assumptions accepted from the outset, the most vital interests of the Jewish proletariat were sacrificed. The Jewish proletariat was neglected. Over a period of more than 10 years the Jewish proletariat was not given the press it needed nor supplied with the agitators the

---

1 [The Yiddish version of this sentence is: 'At a time when the special circumstances of the Jewish masses demanded consideration, the Polish socialists preached "drawing closer" (read Polonisation), wanted to prove that the Yiddish language was disappearing'.]

movement demanded. Neither its agitational nor its organisational needs were taken into account or they were pushed into the last place ...

On the contrary, the assimilationist Party policy tore away from the masses those most able to work amongst them.

So, while others fought, the Jewish proletariat slept. While in Russia the Jewish proletariat, persecuted and oppressed under Tsarist rule, rose up to fight and moved to the forefront of the revolution; when it threw off the slavish soul of the ghetto and transformed itself into a hero, when its heroic struggle resounded throughout the world, winning it respect and acknowledgement – here, in far better political circumstances, the Jewish masses remained passive and quiet. Where a gigantic flame could have been ignited, only ashes smouldered ... And miserable Jewish life in the province of Galicia dragged on: handfuls of Jewish workers, scattered in cities and towns, not fighting, because they lacked consciousness and enthusiasm: not living, because they were nurtured in a foreign hothouse ...

2

What was done for the Jewish proletariat with regard to agitation and organisation was not according to the policies of the Polish socialists but *contrary to* their policies. There was a battle for [the establishment of] every Jewish workers association, it was necessary to fight and plead with the Party for every Jewish meeting, to argue and justify its necessity ... To argue over the wording of every declaration ... How much energy, which could have been put to better use, was wasted on this!

Yet that which has the right to live, will live and must live! So, despite obstacles, the life of the Jewish worker would not let itself be fettered by imposed formulas and was able to break the bonds choking it. Through the force of internal necessity, over several years 'separate' Jewish Briderlekhkeyt and Postęp[2] associations arose in Galicia; 'separate' meetings were arranged and 'separate' declarations made. As the movement grew, again with the force of the same internal necessity, the tendency to centralise the Jewish workers movement appeared, to unify dispersed efforts, to create an *independent* institution which could lead the Jewish movement independently. Indeed, the conference of Jewish workers in May 1903 in L'viv passed a resolution in favour of

---

2 [The associations of Jewish workers, affiliated with the Polish Social Democratic Party of Galicia were called either 'Postęp', 'Progress' in Polish; or 'Briderlekhkeyt', 'Brotherhood' in Yiddish.]

such an institution. *A Jewish Agitation Committee for Galicia was set up*. The significance of this fact for the Jewish workers movement in Galicia was epochal; it is not that [a motion for] the establishment of a Jewish social democratic party failed to pass at this conference. The epochal meaning of this resolution is based on the fact that in creating a Jewish agitation committee, Jewish workers acknowledged, unanimously and without reservations, *the principle* that the Jewish movement must be led and run independently, that an independent institution, which understands the life of the Jewish proletariat and is adapted to that life, *has to* exist; that only such an institution can effectively lead the work *among the Jewish masses*. Just as the fifth curia in Austria,[3] initially welcomed, could not satisfy the proletariat, since the *principle* of universal suffrage, once recognised, cannot be made to wait for its full realisation, so the Jewish Agitation Committee, even though it was a half-measure, was *the acknowledgement of a principle* whose full realisation was not far off.

The Jewish workers, whom half-measures could not satisfy, were able to draw final conclusions from the conference, all the more because life itself and the circumstances of the environment in which they lived were pushing them all the more forcefully in this direction. So, since May 1903, the movement for a Jewish party has been growing and broadening. Ever greater masses are becoming conscious of the need for it, as the socialist movement embraces ever greater masses.

Indeed, only an independent organisation can organise the Jewish proletariat. Only an organisation that takes into account the environmental circumstances in which it functions, that is suited to the needs and lives of the Jewish masses and to their ways of thinking, is able to spread socialist ideas among them, to produce the press they need, to educate agitators. Only an organisation which understands the life of the Jewish masses is able to awaken the currently passive and detached masses, to draw them into the vortex of struggle, to make them conscious!

Organisation is not something intangible and unchanging. Organisation is not a goal in itself. Organisation is a means to an end, a tool. One may have been good yesterday, today perhaps it is already obsolete and worn out. Organisation has to be subject to change, to adapt to circumstances. Yet the circumstances of the Jewish masses are distinct. A single organisation of the Jewish and Polish

---

3 [In 1896, a fifth electoral group, which encompassed those not in one of the four groups for landowners, chambers of commerce, and those who paid substantial taxes in rural communities and cities, was constituted. The fifth curia, which included the vast bulk of the male population, peasants and workers, elected less than a fifth of the deputies to the lower house of Austrian parliament.]

proletariats is not sufficient, just as a single organisation is not sufficient for the proletariats of all the other nations in Austria. Just as each of these nations possesses its own organisation, so too the Jewish proletariat should have such an organisation. The entire past of the social democratic movement among Jewish workers in Galicia points to the need for a Jewish social democratic party. The class interests not only of the Jewish but of the whole proletariat in Austria demand such an organisation. A Jewish social democratic party is not the idea of this or that individual; the circumstances of life are themselves pushing the Jewish proletariat in its direction. Under the socio-historical circumstances in which we live, a Jewish *social democratic party is an historical necessity!*

Not only the previously mentioned development of relations in the past, not only the needs of the present moment speak for us; not least the similar organisations of other nations in Austria – but the so-called Brno Program[4] most clearly concedes to us this fundamental and basic right, acknowledging the right of the proletariats of *all* nations to independently decide their own fates. Thus it should not be the Polish proletariat which decides this! The Jewish workers are already mature enough to decide their own fate!

3

And you would have thought that if Jewish workers in Galicia raised the demand for a Jewish social democratic party – a demand justified from the point of view of the social democratic movement throughout Austria – not only would nobody oppose this demand but everybody would, on the contrary, applaud it. The opposite occurred, however. The demand was opposed; the Jewish proletariat was denied the right to such an organisation. Polish socialists in Galicia did this.

The essential and elementary condition for all effective work, an organisation adapted to the environment, which is understood as the point of departure for all work among the proletariats of other nations, for this the Jewish proletariat still has to struggle!

These same Polish socialists, who with such effort struggle for the freedom of their own nation, do not understand that the Jewish proletariat also wants the same rights as the others. They do not understand that there is no friendship between master and servant, between someone with full rights and someone

---

4   [On the General Austrian Social Democratic Workers Party's federal organisational statute see Żydowska Partya Socyalno-Demokratyczna Galicyi 1905b, 'Reply to the Polish Social Democratic Party of Galicia', below, p. 93–94.]

deprived of rights, that only the free can forge brotherhood with the free, only equals with equals.

So, in their blindness, they ruthlessly fight the tendency to set up a Jewish social democratic party. They fight [the step] that will place the Jewish proletariat on an equal footing with the proletariats of other nations, and they do this despite the fact that such a party is the result of the entire previous movement among Jewish workers. They are scared of this consequence which they do not have the courage to deal with, so they want to avoid it, even though they cannot remove the circumstances which give rise to it!

A sad phenomenon is playing out before our eyes!

They risked doing what only a mad person would do. It was resolved to destroy what life itself was creating, which they themselves – the Polish socialists – with the force of ruthless necessity, willingly or unwillingly, helped to create. So the deliberate and systematic march of destruction began.

If the march of life created the 'separate' Jewish workers associations, if this same life forced even Polish socialists to establish and acknowledge the Jewish Agitation Committee, if finally life gave rise to the consequent fact – a Jewish workers party – the progressive march of life was opposed by a counter and backwards march, a march of destruction.

So the right to a Jewish workers party was denied. Matters went even further: the same people who, at the L'viv conference, had agreed to the Jewish Agitation Committee and even proposed it themselves, a year later at the Kraków Congress[5] spoke against their own proposal. Despite the protests of Jewish comrades, the Jewish Agitation Committee was abolished. The resolution of the Jewish conference in L'viv was ignored in a contemptible manner. And not because such a committee is unnecessary (**they** managed to justify it) – but only because such a committee could lead to a Jewish workers party.

When the movement created by life could not be stifled, when the 'squabbling Bundists' developed and grew, they struck a final, crazed blow! At the Trade Union Conference in Przemyśl[6] it was resolved to abolish the Briderlekhkeyt and Postęp associations as seats of 'Jewish' agitation. No attempt was even made to use a fig leaf.

If the Polish socialists were half-hearted in creativity, when the Jewish workers movement was being built, they did not shy away from the consequences when it came to its destruction!

---

5   [The ninth Congress of the PPSD, 30 October to 1 November 1904.]
6   [The third Galician Trade Union Conference, 26–27 March 1905.]

We stand at the end. Less than a year is left until the dissolution of the Briderlekhkeyt and Postęp associations, we have been given a year of slow death. Political scores were settled at the Trade Union Congress without regard for the usefulness of trade union organisations, and despite their usefulness!

4

Comrades! Jewish workers! Recent events should convince even those who have previously had doubts. The blindness of the Polish comrades cannot continue. The Przemyśl Conference should not remain unanswered and it will not go unanswered. We can no longer stay in the Polish Social Democratic Party. We will not willingly allow our throats to be cut. Comrades, we must respond!

The formation of a Jewish Social Democratic Party is a historical necessity, its formation is rapidly approaching. Comrades, to we have to act!

Two paths lead to the Jewish party: *with* the will of the Polish comrades, or *against* their will. We tried the first. We did not want battles and fights and we still do not want them! At the Kraków Congress, Comrade Bross cried out to our Polish comrades: 'We want to convince you of the correctness of our demands, we want to explain to you the need for a Jewish party, and we are convinced that you will sooner or later yourselves put forward your own proposal for the formation of a Jewish party'. Recent events and resolutions shattered our illusions. Regardless of the harm that may ensue, it was decided to kill off the 'Jewish movement'.

The Polish comrades themselves cut off the first path and are pushing us to 'split'. We have no option left but to embark on the second path. And we will not retreat!

We will not be frightened by charges that we are Zionists, we will not be shaken by the accusations that we are chauvinists, that we want ghettoes and splits, backwardness and superstition.

We are not nationalists, we are not chauvinists and no-one has enforced the *class* character of our struggle more strongly than we have. Nobody has fought Zionism as a class movement of the Jewish bourgeoisie more ruthlessly than we have. We do not want national *programmes*, we only demand a national *organisation*. It is, in the end, necessary to distinguish between these. We want the same sort of national organisation that the Germans, Poles and Czechs, Slovenians, and even the Ruthenians[7] already have in Austria, which only the Jews do not have!

---

7   [I.e. Ukrainians.]

Just as proletariats of various nations are members of the international workers movement and do not cease to be even though they have national organisations so we Jewish social democrats are also international socialists, fighting for the liberation of the whole proletariat.

The programme of the whole proletariat in Austria is our programme too; its fight will be our fight! Indeed our goals are common, our economic demands and political slogans are the same!

So a Jewish Party is not a split and separatism but an equal right. Only it can elevate the Jewish proletariat to a higher economic level and higher intellectual life.

A Jewish social democratic party is a necessity and a Jewish social democratic party does not exist!

Jewish proletarians! An historical moment is approaching, a great moment arrives. The moment is coming when you will be equal to the proletariats of other nations, when you will be accepted on the same terms into the great family of nations.

The Jewish Social Democratic Party of Galicia arises! Do not sleep at this time! Show that you are mature enough to lead yourselves, that you have understood your historical role and will not retreat from it!

Polish comrades deny you this right. But even they will have to acknowledge the accomplished fact. We do not want a fratricidal fight and eagerly hold out our hand in brotherly peace. And it is impossible that they will not accept it. After all, we fight for common goals and we must fight for them together!

Jewish proletarians! Throw off your fears and doubts! Join the ranks of the new organisation and help to build it. It will lead you to the proletariat's goals. To battle and to victory! To action! To work!

Great events require great souls. So cast off the soul of the ghetto which you have born. Leave the ghetto streets where you were enclosed. Forward to battle and to victory!

Long live the Jewish Social Democratic Party of Galicia!

Long live the international workers movement!

Proletarians of all countries unite!

For the Organising Committee of the Jewish Social Democratic Party of Galicia

J[akób] Bierfass, Rubin Birnbaum, Abraham Blasbalg, Jonas Blum, Jakób Bros, J. Dorfmann, Z[achariah] Dutki, Karol Einäugler, Franciszka Fargel, Maks Felsenfeld, Szymon Glückstein, Henryk Grossman, N. Grundleger, Ozyasz Landau, Landesberg, Helena Metzger, M[oyshe] Papier, Abraham Wassermann, Abraham Poch, Uscher Schapira, Adolf Spanlang, Leopold Wechsberg, Dawid Winnitz, J. Antman.

30 April 1905
All information from Secretary Henryk Grossman, Kraków ul. Sebastyana 36.
Address for payments: Adolf Spanlang, Kraków, ul. Estery 13.

∴

Declaration

We, supporters of an independent Jewish social democratic organisation in Galicia, resign from the Polish Social Democratic Party of Galicia and Silesia on 1 May this year.

We will inform you shortly of further action with the goal of forming the Jewish Social Democratic Party of Galicia, specifically about the founding Congress and the manner of its convocation.

Organising Committee of the Jewish Social Democratic Party of Galicia

CHAPTER 5

Reply to the Polish Social Democratic Party of Galicia*

Translated from Polish and German by Dominika Balwin and Rick Kuhn

On 1 May the formation of the independent Jewish Social Democratic Party was proclaimed across Galicia, at a numerous series of mass meetings.

The movement, which has been growing in size and strength for nearly seven years, reached its final conclusion; the goal, which has been a beacon for Jewish workers in Galicia since 1899, was finally realised.

The newly formed Party impatiently awaited the attitude which the Polish Social Democratic Party would take to it. When, on 1 May in Kraków, a procession of close to 2,000 Jewish workers, organised by the 'separatists', entered the mass meeting in the Riding School they were greeted with applause from the Polish comrades, among them Comrade [Ignacy] Daszyński ... The *joint* demonstration gave rise to the hope that the Jewish Party, an accomplished fact, would be recognised by the Polish comrades as an equal and that there would be fraternal relations between the two parties.

In the course of the twenty or so days that have passed since then, a series of occurrences and events have occurred which have shattered such illusions, and require consideration and a response.

On 2 May an open letter to Jewish workers from Comrade Daszyński appeared in *Naprzód* (later also posted on walls in Kraków and L'viv[1] in Yiddish and Polish), followed on 8 May by the resolution of the Executive of the Polish Party and subsequently the resolution of the Executive of the Austrian Party on 13 May, and finally a series of vicious 'articles' in the form of correspondence from the provinces and chronicles that were attacks directed against us. Although these attacks are the *only* arguments which are currently used against us, we will answer Comrade Daszyński's letter and the resolutions of the Polish and Austrian executives calmly and rationally, without polemicising against the Polish Party (the Executive of the Polish Party does not like arguments). We will, rather, elucidate the matter for those who are interested and facilitate the orientation of public opinion which *Naprzód* is now urgently trying to per-

---

* [Originally published as Żydowska Partya Socyalno-Demokratyczna Galicyi 1905b, pp. 1–6.]
1 [*'Naprzód'* means *'Forwards'. Naprzód* was the daily newspaper of the PPSD in Kraków.]

suade that we are a gang of wreckers, proof of which is immediately provided by a correspondent-slanderer, who does not even hesitate to fling the equally vile and absurd insinuations that we talk about 'Polish chauvinists sucking the blood of the Jewish proletariat' or the 'schmutzige Adlerpartei'.[2]

Of this, however, more later!

• •
•

Comrade Daszyński is not, indeed, to blame but the very letter that was directed against the 'separatists' contains a serious accusation against the Polish Social Democratic Party.

News of the formation of an independent Jewish organisation caught Comrade Daszyński and the Polish comrades unawares. Yet the formation of a Jewish party was not a surprise for anyone else, since it was a fact with a history of several years behind it. Every resolution of the Polish Social Democratic Party over the past three years was preparation for the Jewish party. Supporters of a Jewish party warned publicly and openly against such behaviour. Discontent spread wide throughout Galicia, flaming up overtly, here and there. Yet what the whole world knew and what the Polish Party ought to have known, was for it a 'conspiracy' and a secret.

In truth, it is hard to find a stronger accusation against the Polish Party than the words of Comrade Daszyński. The Party wants to lead the work among the Jewish masses, yet does not know how they think and feel, or what plans and intentions they have.

It is hard to suppress a smile at the sight of Comrade Daszyński – just as Jewish workers in all the larger centres of Galicia left the Polish Party – calling after them: wait, it's a conspiracy, we did not expect this, did not know that this is what you really think!

The Jewish workers did not wait. The withdrawal of Jewish workers from the Polish Party is today an accomplished fact.

There was no question of any 'deception'. That is only a tale circulated to explain the accomplished fact of withdrawal, which cannot be concealed. The evidence of this is the series of Jewish gatherings at which the Polish comrades sustained a complete defeat. We will mention only the gathering in Kraków where, *after a 6 hour discussion* and despite heated appeals by *members of the*

---

2   ['Schmutzige Adlerpartei' is German for 'filthy Adler party'. Victor Adler was a founder and the preeminent leader of Austrian Social Democracy.]

Polish Executive, over 400 of those gathered declared themselves for the Jewish party, with only 12 (!) against!

It is not we who are afraid of discussion and run from it! So do not tell us that we 'surprised' you, the Polish Party!

After all, Marx already observed that in matters of grave import it is not enough to explain that one was caught unawares. 'A nation and a woman' and still less, let us add, political parties, 'are not forgiven the unguarded hour in which the first adventurer that came along could violate them'.[3]

The statement that you were surprised, Comrade Daszyński, does not solve the problem, only formulates it in a different way. How did it come to this, that you let yourselves be surprised? And there are not two answers; in this case both sides are in agreement. Comrade Daszyński unintentionally *endorses in full our accusations against the* PPSD. The Jewish proletariat took the PPSD by surprise; an evident admission that you, Polish comrades, are incapable of leading the Jewish masses, *you do not have your finger on the pulse of its life*, you stand far removed from all that agitates the life of these masses and troubles them!

When these masses demand an independent organisation, in which they could develop appropriately, when they also demand it because they wish to decide on an equal footing with the Polish and Ruthenian[4] proletariats on local administrative and province-wide[5] matters, Comrade Daszyński, passing over our arguments in silence, cannot come up with a better answer than a personal observation: 'Here am I, your trusted envoy, while there is a handful of thoughtless youngsters. Here am I, with your best interests at heart, while they want to tear you apart ...'

Comrade Daszyński! It may not be pleasant for you, nonetheless you must come to terms with the fact that Jewish workers *demand arguments*. A warm hearted response may be very pleasing to them, certainly, but will not in the least influence their steps and actions ...

.·.

We are happy about the fact that the Executive of the Polish Party has at last been convinced about differences arising 'from the linguistic and cultural separateness of the Jewish working population, *demanding the accommodation of certain different forms of organisation* and agitation'. We have always asserted

---

3   Marx 1979, p. 108.
4   [I.e. Ukrainian.]
5   [I.e. Galician.]

this, and the Jewish Social Democratic Party represents precisely such a 'different form of organisation'!

If the Executive of the Polish Party determines that such a different form of organisation of the 'Jewish proletariat' should not be independent; that it cannot be a *direct* part of the Austrian Party; that this would be a tragedy for the Jewish proletariat; that such a tragedy can only be avoided in one way; that this 'separate form of organisation of the Jewish proletariat' will only be a part of the General Party indirectly; that is, if it is part of the *Polish* Party and only through its mediation a part of the General Party – then the Executive of the Polish Party should have *proved* this!

How can this be! So it will be a tragedy if the Jewish proletariat ceases to be inferior and becomes an equal part? So an *independent* organisation will be a tragedy, even though it is federated with the other social democratic organisations in Austria?! So it will be a tragedy for it to receive the same treatment as the proletariats of other nations?

Never! The Executive of the Polish Party has not and could not prove this and no social democrat would believe this! *Baseless* accusations, not backed up by any arguments, that an independent Jewish organisation would be dangerous and reactionary will convince no-one. And, if the Executive of the Polish Party could not prove that an independent organisation would be bad and harmful, we, on the contrary, have continuously proved, are proving and will continue to prove that the Jewish proletariat could not and cannot develop adequately within the Polish Party and that the needs of this proletariat were put in last place by the Polish Party!

The task of a social democratic party is to fight for the realisation of its programme. On what is this struggle and activity based, how does it manifest itself?

Above all in certain organisational forms, secondly in agitation and finally in the press. Organisation, agitators and press, these are the means by which a socialist party fights.

Let us discuss these questions in turn and see what the Polish Party has achieved.

The resolution of the Executive of the Polish Party of 8 May promises and undertakes that if the Jewish proletariat demands separate forms of organisation and agitation, the Polish Party is ready to create a national agitation committee for Jews (within the Polish Party).[6] Now let us cast a glance back to the past. Until May 1903 they did not want to know about any such committee. When in May 1903 a motion for the formation of a Jewish social democratic

6   [Zarząd polskiej partyi socyalno-demokratycznej w Austryi 1905.]

party arose; *under this pressure* the Polish Party formed a Jewish agitation committee for Galicia.[7]

After the May conference in 1903, once the 'danger' of a separate Jewish party had passed, the committee was not established. The Kraków Congress in 1904 went further and even formally abolished it, claiming that a national committee for Jews was not needed and fought and condemned those who demanded and defended the committee. Now that a Jewish social democratic party is emerging, *the Polish Party again promises* to form a national agitation committee. The deciding factor here is *not the agitational needs* of the Jewish proletariat but pressure, the danger of the moment. One creates the committee in order to take it away again later! Commentary is superfluous.

Comrade Daszyński, we await your reply!

Further. Jewish conferences were held in 1899[8] and 1903. At the time the Polish Party apparently still acknowledged that the Jewish proletariat should make its own decisions, that it best knows its own needs. In L'viv, forty Jewish delegates from around the province voted for a national committee and then the Kraków Congress dealt brutally with the agenda of the resolutions of the Jewish conference.[9] (The Jewish committee was abolished.) The just principle, upheld in May 1903, that the Jewish proletariat can make its own decisions, was brutally trampled in October 1904! Comrade Daszyński, we await your reply!

And further. The Executive of the Polish Party now promises to set up branch associations and separate local committees. Yet how long ago did the Trade Union Conference in Przemyśl resolve to abolish separate Postęp and Briderlikhkeyt associations?![10]

And this is supposed to be the possibility for development which you announce?! And is not the Executive of the Polish Party mocking the seriousness of the entire Przemyśl Conference, if it now promises what the Conference condemned a month earlier? And you have the temerity to say that you are adequately satisfying the needs of the Jewish proletariat, when you change your line on the most vital questions every month and risk destroying the whole movement among the Jewish masses by closing down the Postęp and Briderlikhkeit associations?

---

7   [At the conference of Jewish socialists in L'viv in May 1903.]

8   [A conference of Jewish members of the PPSD, on 25 December 1899, in L'viv.]

9   [Ninth Congress of the PPSD, in Kraków, 30 October to 1 November 1904.]

10   [The third Galician Trade Union Conference, 26–27 March 1905. The associations of Jewish workers, initially affiliated with the Polish Social Democratic Party of Galicia, were called either 'Postęp', 'Progress' in Polish, or 'Briderlekhkeyt', 'Brotherhood' in Yiddish.]

This is how one takes into account the need for 'separate forms of organisation' in practice. This is how one treats Jewish committees, Jewish associations and Jewish conferences! Let us move on to agitation. The most important centres of the Jewish movement are neglected, the most important centres do not have Jewish agitators. The Polish Party itself admits this. As a result of the complaints and demands of Jewish workers at almost every Congress, it is resolved that the Party should try to recruit Jewish agitators. So for 15 years the need for agitators has been satisfied with resolutions! We know the Polish Party looked for such agitators. Think about it, comrades, the Party which for 15 years looked for agitators and could not find them, wants to lead the work among the Jewish masses! Comrade Daszyński, we await your reply!

We are just beginning our work; come to our meetings; listen to our Jewish speakers, whom we have already created and whose numbers grow from day to day! And the press? Polish comrades! What did you do for 15 years? Where are the publications for the Jewish masses, the newspapers and pamphlets?

While *Naprzód, Głos robotniczy* and *Robotnik śląski, Prawo ludu* and *Latarnia*,[11] workers calendars and May Day specials and even newspapers for children are published in Polish, for this Jewish mass, which represents such a numerous element in the Party, for this mass, among which there are nearly no illiterates, for them it was not even the Party but a private individual who published a single Yiddish weekly, which goes bankrupt every few months and then vegetates again for a period. Naturally, the Executive of the Polish Party then claims in the congress report that the newspaper is going under because there are no subscribers, that evidently the workers do not know Yiddish! Polish comrades! No-one will believe this, you do not believe it yourselves – why would the Kraków Congress (the same one which claimed that Yiddish was disappearing) resolve to publish a Yiddish newspaper?! Such is the result of years of work. Such is the relation between Polish and Jewish work. Comrade Daszyński, we await your reply!

Have you printed even a single pamphlet in Yiddish? Oh, yes ... one can be found and it is a pamphlet directed against us! Thus we can humbly claim credit for this: that if we 'separatists' did not exist the Jewish proletariat would not even possess this pamphlet ... How then do you propose to educate the Jewish masses, whose ignorance you so bemoan? We await your reply!

---

11   [*Naprzód, Głos robotniczy* (*Workers' Voice*) and *Robotnik śląski* (*Silesian Worker*) were the
        newspapers of the PPSD in Kraków, L'viv and Silesia. *Prawo ludu* (*People's Right*) and *Latarnia* (*Lantern*) were PPSD journals.]

Have you, who call us Zionists, published even a single pamphlet against Zionism, have you done anything to explain the reality of Zionism to the wide mass of the Jewish proletariat? We await your reply!

Where are the libraries for Jewish workers, where they can educate and develop themselves? Has even a single one been created through your efforts?

So where is the possibility for our development, of which you speak?

No, it did not and does not exist!

We do not claim that the Polish Party did nothing; even the worst organisation, least adapted to circumstances can do *something*. It often happens that Social Democratic Parties change their organisations. Does that mean that the old one did nothing, that it was completely useless?

No-one would say that. One throws off the old form of organisation when a new one better satisfies needs and better assists the class struggle, leading faster to the goal. No-one wants to walk when one can take a train! Organisational questions are not points of programme and principle which can only express a single substance (*Principielle Fragen*);[12] the question of organisation is a question of practicalities, a question of worse or better adaptation to circumstances (*Zweckmässigkeitsfrage*).[13]

So when we can speed ahead by rail, do not point out that one can also move forward on foot. Do not order us to vegetate when we want plenty of movement and fresh air. Look at what the Bund accomplished among the Jewish masses in a few short years. It has revolutionised the backward and passive masses, made conscious the ignorant and unconscious masses, roused them to the struggle, pushed them to the forefront of the struggle. It made heroes of the children of the ghetto, washed away the mark of ages, which was visible on our foreheads ... If today we can walk with our heads held high, if we can repulse every insult about the speculating Jew and the cowardly Jew with dignity and disdain, pointing to the Jewish blood spilt for freedom, pointing to the Jewish heroes dying for freedom, it is thanks to the Bund. It rehabilitated us, gave us gravity and pride, gave us human dignity! ...

Do not rush into the argument that the Bund in Russia and a separate Jewish party in Galicia are two quite different things. We understand and remember well the tremendous difference between the political circumstances in which we and the Bund operate, *and that our struggle in Galicia must be different from the Bund's in Russia.*

---

12   [*'Principielle Fragen'* means 'principal questions'.]

13   [*'Zweckmässigkeitsfrage'* means 'question of fitness for purpose'.]

However, the very fact of the Bund's existence, the reasons for its creation and existence are the same there and here. The same fundamental socio-cultural circumstances; the same external national difference in relation to the environment, the same internal class stratification, the same bourgeoisie with the same ideology, the same language and customs, even the same superstitions and prejudices, in a word the same forces of light and darkness.

We have arisen for the same reasons the Bund arose. Despite the different political circumstances, we have the same socio-cultural environment, which leads to the same consequences.

∴

We are influenced not only by this consideration, however, by the need to adapt organisational forms to the environment over which they are to spread. We are not only socialists but also democrats, we are social democrats and that is why we fight and must fight for genuinely equal rights for the Jewish proletariat. 'Socialdemakraten, die der Classenherrschaft den Krieg predigen, *dürfen* nicht die Verweigerung des Selbstbestimmungsrechtes billigen.'[14]

We social democrats, who alone fight for real equal rights for all at the level of local government, the province and the Empire, must above all lead by example, practicing this equality in our own party, so that the Jewish proletariat which is today oppressed and persecuted everywhere, feels equal and becomes equal here in the ranks of social democracy! This is a great psychological and educational moment, a great agitational moment which you, Polish comrades, disregard!

You write in the resolution of the Executive that you want to realise 'complete equality for Jewish workers'. So give them the right they demand, to make their own decisions independently, the right which you extend to all other nationalities, the right which you have acknowledged as fundamental and inalienable and which – as we will demonstrate in the documentation below – all of social democratic Austria acknowledged as fundamental. Show that you are not merely paying lip service to the notion of equality, that the rights you extend to others you extend to Jews as well!

This is what you do not do. You prefer to point to a few Jewish individuals who occupy leading positions in Party institutions. But we are not concerned with this, we are not concerned with these few Jews – chairpeople and Jewish

---

14   Daszyński 1902, p. 735. ['Social democrats who preach war on class rule *should not* approve
       the denial of the right to self-determination.']

leaders – we are not concerned with these few titles and posts. We are not concerned with *individuals* but want the masses as a whole, as a group, to be able to decide about itself and for this group to become equal to others! We want to decide about local and provincial matters on an equal footing with the Polish and Ruthenian proletariats. We do not want to be second class citizens; we demand equal rights!

So why should we deny ourselves an independent organisation; why should we deny ourselves the right to decide independently about ourselves? Is it because you think that the unity of the Party will be disturbed?

Do you really believe that? When Austrian Social Democracy abandoned central organisation and *divided* itself into national organisations, did not the entire bourgeois press howl with delight over the disintegration of Social Democracy in Austria? The minutes of the Brno Congress most clearly confirm this (official speaker, Comrade [Josef] Krapka): 'Als auf dem Wiener Parteitag zum Ausbau der Selbständigkeit der nationalen Organisationen weitere Schritte gethan wurden haben die bürgerlichen Parteien *mit grossem Jubel hinausposaunt*, dass die sozialdemokratische Partei zerfranst ist, und ihr nahes Ende wurde bis auf das Datum Festgestellt.' And yet Comrade Krapka could say 'Ich bin aber heute in der Lage zu konstatieren, dass die Partei durch die Autonomie gestärkt und womöglich noch mehr *geeinigt* dasteht als ehedem'.[15]

And today you quote these same bourgeois publications as critical evidence against us? Are you not ashamed of this? And could we not use the same weapon against you, pointing out that the socialist *Naprzód* and the all-Polish, antisemitic *Słowo Polskie call in chorus for* a crusade against 'separatists'?[16]

But we do not want to fight by these means and we will not! The needs of the Jewish proletariat are decisive for us, not the whining of the bourgeoisie.

Did Comrade Krapka, quoted above, not clearly conclude that the *division* of the Party into national organisations *united* it all the more? Was this not confirmed by numerous other speakers at the Austrian congress? So which unity will be damaged?

---

15   [Sozialdemokratische Arbeiterpartei Österreichs 1899, p. 63. [Grossman's emphasis. 'As further steps were taken at the Vienna Congress to extend the independence of the national organisations, the bourgeois parties *with great jubilation trumpeted* that the Social Democratic Party was fraying and specified to the day its imminent end'. 'I am, however, today in the position to state that the Party has been strengthened and, if anything is more *united* than previously thanks to this autonomy'.]

16   *Słowo Polskie* 1905. [*Słowo Polskie* (*Polish Word*) was a twice daily newspaper in L'viv, associated with the antisemitic National Democratic Party.]

Did you, Comrade Daszyński, not voice another opinion? How long ago did you write the article 'Nationality and Social Democracy?'[17]

We do not want to interfere in the internal affairs of the Prussian province [of partitioned Poland] and just quote your statement.

Defending the party autonomy of the PPS[18] in Prussia, you wrote about normalising relations between the Polish and German parties: 'Und diese Regelung kann nur auf der Grundlage der *formellen Gleichheit* zwischen beiden Parteien geschehen: *eine andere giebt es für Socialdemokraten nicht*, und kein logisch denkender Genosse kann die formelle Abhängigkeit ... wünschen'.[19] So there, when Polish relations were at issue, even formal dependence annoyed you, yet where Jews are concerned you accept both *formal* and *actual* dependence?

We do not allege insincerity; we ask only: how do these two positions coexist in one breast?! Does the logic which you mention apply only in relation to Poles? So the complete independence of the PPS in Germany does not threaten the unity of the Party, yet the Jewish Party (despite the fact that it wants to be *part of* the General Party) would destroy this unity? Answer! What then is this unity of yours? Did not [Zygmunt] Krasiński foresee all this in *Iridion*:

Eutychian: What are thy principles, what gods dost thou profess? ...
Philosopher: My god is unity conceived in unity by unity, of necessarity the opposite of all nonunities, and itself contained in itself ...
Eutychian: Satis est – with thy teaching thou wilt not overturn the Empire.[20]

Comrade Daszyński! The independence of national organisations and international unity – this is the slogan of Austrian Social Democracy! We are not a threat to *real* party unity: 'Sind denn die praktischen Fragen der Wahlkämpfe der organisatorischen Technik so schwierig, so unlösbar, wenn man die pol-

---

17   [Although Grossman referred to 'Nationalität und Socialdemokratie', the article's title was 'Nationality and Socialism', Daszyński 1902.]
18   [The Polska Partia Socjalistyczna (Polish Socialist Party) was the name of the nationalist, socialist organisations in the German- and Russian-occupied provinces of Poland with which the leadership of the PPSD sympathised.]
19   Daszyński 1902, p. 736. [The second emphasis is Grossman's. 'And this arrangement can only occur on the basis of the *formal equality* between the two parties. *For social democrats* there can be no other basis and no comrade who thinks logically can desire formal dependence ...']
20   [Krasiński 1975, pp. 83–4. 'Satis est' means 'that is enough'.]

nische socialdemokratische Partei als vollständig gleichberechtigt betrachten will?'!²¹ Apply your words to us too!

Do you want unity and solidarity between the two parties? We do too! The coexistence of our parties can be achieved on the same principles on which it was established in Austria where two or three parties work side by side in solidarity (as in Bohemia and Moravia).²²

When the demand for solidarity is fulfilled, only then will the words of Comrade Daszyński be realised: 'Ich bin sicher, dass auf dem Boden der Gleichheit auch die Solidarität wachsen wird, und dass man sich gegenseitig leicht versteht, wenn der Stachel der Demütigung beseitigt ist.'²³

We demand nothing else!

Now to the final matter. The resolution of the Executive of the PPSD states: 'The organisation of Social Democracy in Austria is based on the programme unanimously approved at the Congress in Brno in 1899.'

In truth, this is an incredible fact, unique in the history of political parties. We state here emphatically and categorically and immediately prove, using documentary evidence, that the Polish Social Democratic Party of Galicia does not know when its organisational statute was formulated and approved!!

For it is not true that the *organisational statute* of Austrian Social Democracy was adopted in Brno in 1899. What was approved there and what the PPSD quotes, and what is summarised in the so-called Brno Programme (*Nationalitätenprogramm*)²⁴ is not an organisational statute and does not concern the organisation of the Social Democratic **Party** but the Austrian **state** and its future, and describes the possible national state of the future (*nationalen Zukunftstaat*).

However the General Social Democratic Party of Austria (*Gesammtorganisation der Socialdemokratie in Österreich*) had already, in part, adopted its organisational statue, which is binding today, at the fifth Congress (Prague 1896)²⁵

---

21   [Daszyński 1902, p. 736. 'Are the practical questions of electoral campaigns, of organisational technique then so difficult, so irresolvable if the Polish Social Democratic Party is regarded as having completely equal rights.']

22   [Both the Czech and German Austrian Social Democratic Parties operated in mixed Czech-German areas of Bohemia and Moravia, the territory that is now the Czech Republic.]

23   [Daszyński 1902, pp. 736–7. 'I am sure that, on the basis of equality, solidarity will also grow and that mutual understanding will be easy once the thorn of humiliation has been eliminated.']

24   ['*Nationalitätenprogramm*' means 'nationality programme'.]

25   See Sozialdemokratische Arbeiterpartei Österreichs 1896, pp. 93–104, 111–30 and 157–64.

and definitively at the sixth Congress in Vienna in 1897.[26] In Brno, the statute
which had previously been passed (and not at the point, quoted by the PPDS,
which deals with the state) was merely finalised.

Let us ascertain this immediately.

In 1897 Comrade Dr [Victor] Adler stated: 'Je mehr es aber nothwendig war,
jedem einzelnen Theile volle Selbständigkeit zu geben, umso nothwendiger war
es auf der anderen Seite, die Einheitlichkelt trotz dieser Autonomie aufrecht
zu erhalten'.[27]

Such was the guiding idea, which illuminated the construction of the Austrian organisation and was realised at this Congress.

Comrade [Antonín] Němec stated: 'Die einzig richtige Lösung dieser Schwi-
erigen Frage wird die sein: Keine gemeinsame [i.e. central] oesterreichische
socialdemokratische Partei, sondern eine *geeinigte* Partei der oesterreichischen
Socialdemokratie, *welche aus den verschiedenen Nationalitäten zusammenge-
setzt ist*'.[28]

Comrade Adler embodied these ideas in concrete *organisational proposals*, which are summarised in the statement: 'Die Hauptschwierigkeit unserer
Organisation ist die Verbindung von *selbständigen nationalen Organisationen*,
mit einer vereinigten internationalen Executive.' Then he declared: 'Die vom
Prager Parteitag [1896] ausgebaute und vom sechsten [1897] Parteitag *durchge-
führte Organisation der oesterreichischen Socialdemokratie nach selbstständi-
gen nationalen Gruppen* hat ...'[29]

Here, then, the organisational statute binding us was created! I assume
clearer proof is not required.

On the contrary. In 1899 (Brno) the organisational statute, in so far as national organisations are concerned, was not adopted, since it had already been
in existence for two years. The Congress in Brno obviously cites the national

---

26   Sozialdemokratische Arbeiterpartei Österreichs 1897 pp. 110–36, 164–72 and 210.

27   Sozialdemokratische Arbeiterpartei Österreichs 1897, p. 114. [Grossman's emphasis. 'The
     more it was necessary, however, *to give full independence to every single part*, the more
     necessary it was, on the other hand, to maintain unity despite this autonomy.']

28   Sozialdemokratische Arbeiterpartei Österreichs 1897, p. 125. [Grossman's emphasis. 'The
     only correct solution to this difficult question would not be a common [i.e. central] Aus-
     trian Social Democratic Party but rather a *united* Party of Austrian Social Democracy,
     which is composed of the different nationalities.']

29   Sozialdemokratische Arbeiterpartei Österreichs 1897 pp. 164–7, 169. [Grossman's empha-
     sis. 'The principal difficulty in our organisation is the connection between *autonomous
     national organisations* and a united international executive.' 'The organisation of Austrian
     Social Democracy *in autonomous national groups*, initiated by the Prague Party Congress
     [1896] and *completed* by the Sixth Party Congress [1897], has ...']

organisation adopted in 1897: 'Durch die vom Wiener Parteitag 1897 beschlossene Gliederung der socialdemokratischen Partei nach nationalen Gruppen wurden vollständig neue Formen in der Organisation geschaffen, die deren weiteren Ausbau dringend nothwendig machen, um ... ein gemeinsames Vorgehen zu sichern',[30] and only established the institution of the General Austrian Executive and improved the resolutions of the earlier Congress to enable the united advance of these different national organisations (which had existed since 1897, in line with the organisational statute).

So we see that division into national organisations was already completed in 1897 and, on the contrary, there were no resolutions along these lines passed in 1899.

The material quoted by the Executive of the PPSD is not mentioned under the agenda item 'Organisation' but appears in the discussion on the 'Austrian nationality program', which – as we have mentioned – concerns the Austrian state in the future (compare the words of the official spokesperson, Comrade [Josef] Seliger, 'nationaler Zukunftstaat').[31]

Without mentioning the actual content of that programme (that Austria (!) should be transformed) or the reasoning of other speakers, we will only quote the words of Comrade Daszyński: 'Vor zwei jahren haben wir den Weg gefunden mit der nationalen Frage im *Innern der Partei* fertig zu werden. Es handelt sich jetzt auch darum, ob wir *für das ganze Reich* dasselbe Programm aufzustellen im Stande sind.'[32] From this, we have to conclude that at the time (1899) Comrade Daszyński knew that the organisational statute of the *Party* was adopted 'two years previously', that is in 1897, and that in 1899 it was the programme for the *state* that was adopted. What he knew at that time, he and other members of the PPSD Executive alike in signing the resolution of 8 May, for reasons incomprehensible to us, have today forgotten!

In truth it is an incomprehensible puzzle that the Executive in Vienna adopted such an 'authoritative' resolution!

---

30 Sozialdemokratische Arbeiterpartei Österreichs 1899, p. 74. ['The arrangement of the Social Democratic Party into national groups, decided by the Vienna Congress of 1897, created completely new forms in the organisation which make further development urgently necessary in order ... to secure joint action.'] Sozialdemokratische Arbeiterpartei Österreichs 1899, p. 72.

31 ['National state of the future.'].

32 [Sozialdemokratische Arbeiterpartei Österreichs 1899, p. 83. Grossman's emphasis. 'Two years ago we found the way to solve the national question *within the Party*. What we must do now is find out whether we are capable of advancing the same programme *for the entire Empire*.']

In any case we have clearly and unequivocally proved that the Executive of the PPSD had no right, in the organisational dispute under discussion, to invoke the organisational statute passed by the Brno Congress; that this Congress did not pass any such statute; that the organisational statute of Austrian Social Democracy was created in 1896 and 1897; and that the whole resolution of the PPSD, so far as it refers to the 'Brno organisational statute', is laughable and nonsensical.

The PPSD does not know, or does not want to know, when its organisational statute, binding it today, was adopted!

∴

It is not surprising that the Executive of the PPSD, not knowing when the organisational statute of Austrian Social Democracy was adopted, also does not know for *what reasons* it was approved or why the division of the Party into national organisations was carried out. The PPSD writes: 'To cite tactics used to oppose Zionists and Jewish chauvinists cannot be a serious basis for the formation of a separate Jewish party.' Why? Because 'such a party, not founded on positive national demands, would be a demagogic evasion, unworthy of social democrats'. Once again we will prove with documentation that *it was not, in fact, national factors* which were decisive here but, on the one hand, purely practical ones, improving agitation among the proletarian masses speaking different languages, the struggle of each nationality against its *own* bourgeoisie (or, as the PPDS puts it, 'tactical reasons'); and [on the other hand] the need for the independence of and independent decision making by the proletariats of different nations. In other words the arguments and reasons which we have cited and which force us to demand an independent party.

Let us listen. At the Prague Congress in 1896, Comrade Němec (as the official spokesperson for the Czech organisation) said

> Die gesammte oesterreichische Socialdemokratie befolgt dieselben Prinzipien und dieselbe Taktik. Die Czechen haben jedoch eine selbstständige Organisation und diese ist nothwendig ... Wir müssen eine selbständige Organisation haben, weil wir die deutschen Genossen, die schneller vorwärts kommen, unnützer Weise hemmen würden.[33]

---

33   Sozialdemokratische Arbeiterpartei Österreichs 1896, p. 103. ['The whole of Austrian Social Democracy adheres to the same principles and the same tactics. The Czechs have, however, an independent organisation and this is necessary ... We have to have an inde-

What then is the motivation for a separate party? The need for better agitation! Further. Comrade Němec demands that the Party Executive comprise representatives of every nationality. How did he justify this?

> Mit dem grösseren Wachsen der verschiedenen Agenden ist es nothwendig, *dass die Deutschen ihre Angelegenheiten selbst besorgen*, weil sie die czechischen Genossen nicht übersehen können ... Es handelt sich hier nicht etwa um einen chauvinistischen Standpunk, um keine Trennung der Partei [evidently, already at that time there was talk of 'splitting' the Party], sondern wir sagen uns, die bisherige Parteivertretung hat uns nicht sonderlich genützt.[34]

And when Comrade [Anton] Hüber concluded that national organisations are not needed, that 'Wir haben keine Ursache, separate czechische, italienische und polnische Organisationen zu bilden, sondern wir brauchen *eine* socialdemokratische Organisation ... es ist eine stramme, zentralistische Organisation unbedingt nothwendig',[35] how did Comrade Dr Adler reply?

> Solche Dinge sind in der Theorie sehr schön und vielleicht in einem anderen Lande möglich. In der oesterreichischen Praxis sind sie absolut unmöglich und wir sind daher den Weg gegangen, welcher in Oesterreich allein möglich ist: die gemeinsame Vereinbarung über die Taktik und *die Selbständigkeit in der Organisation*. Fur uns gibt es *nur eine volle Autonomie* in der politischen Organisation
>
> Die Selbststandigkeit der Organisation *liegt so sehr in der Natur unserer Verhältnisse*, dass eigentlich niemals ein Zweifel daruber war, dass sie nothwendig ist.[36]

---

pendent organisation because otherwise we would unnecessarily hinder the German comrades, who are going ahead faster.']

34 Sozialdemokratische Arbeiterpartei Österreichs 1896, p. 103. [Grossman's emphasis. 'With the more rapid growth of their different agendas, it is necessary *that the Germans take care of their affairs themselves*, because the Czech comrades cannot have an over view of these ... Here it is not a matter of a chauvinist viewpoint, of a division of the Party [evidently, already at that time there was talk of "splitting" the party], rather we say that the previous form of representation within the Party was not especially useful for us.']

35 Sozialdemokratische Arbeiterpartei Österreichs 1896, p. 125. [Grossman's emphasis. 'We have no reason to establish separate Czech, Italian and Polish organisations, rather we need *one* social democratic organisation ... a tight, centralised organisation is absolutely necessary.']

36 Sozialdemokratische Arbeiterpartei Österreichs 1896, p. 127. [Grossman's emphasis. 'Such matters are in theory very attractive and perhaps possible in other countries. In Austrian

How did Dr Adler justify the need for separate organisations? His best argument at the time (1896) was the argument that arguments are completely unnecessary since the matter was self-explanatory!

Recently deceased Comrade Joachim Fraenkel stated:

> Uns Polen hat es gefreut, dass die czechischen Genossen angeregt haben, die Leitung der Gesammtpartei *auf föderalistischer* Grundlage aufzubauen ... Da sich die Partei in den letzten Jahren stark entwickelt hat, und sich noch weiter entwickeln wird, so ist es nothig, *dass schon jetzt nationalen Streitigkeiten vorgebeugt wird.*[37]

Why did he say this? So ... that there would be no disputes! Today it is presented as the opposite: that the formation of separate parties will result in disputes.

And once again Comrade Němec:

> Als wir den Antrag einbrachten, dass die Parteivertretung den gegebenen *Verhältnissen entsprechend* in ihrer Zusammensetzung geändert werde, habe ich ausdrücklich erklärt, **ich verwahre mich dagegen, dass dies aus nationalen Gründen gewünscht werde** ... Ich habe gesagt, es handelt sich hier um die *praktische* Durchführung unserer Beschlüsse, es handelt sich darum, ein *besseres vorgehen* zu ermöglichen.[38]

So not national factors but practical organisational requirements! And what has the Executive of the PPSD to say about this? Is this also 'a demagogic evasion, not worthy of social democrats'?! We await an answer! So much for 1896; now to 1897. Dr Adler said:

---

practice they are absolutely impossible and we have therefore gone along the only path that is possible in Austria: mutual agreement about tactics and *organisational independence*. For us there is only full autonomy in political organisation. Organisational independence *is so much a feature of our relations* that actually there was never a doubt that it was necessary.']

37   Sozialdemokratische Arbeiterpartei Österreichs 1896, p. 129. [Grossman's emphasis. 'We Poles were happy that the Czech comrades proposed that the Executive of the General Party be constructed on a *federal* basis ... As the Party has developed strongly in recent years and will develop further, it is necessary that *national conflicts are guarded against right now*.']

38   Sozialdemokratische Arbeiterpartei Österreichs 1896, p. 162. [Grossman's emphasis. 'When we raised the proposal that representation within the Party be altered to *express existing relations*, I explicitly declared that I was **defending myself against any suggestion that this is desired for national reasons** ... I said that it was a matter here of the *practical* implementation of our decisions, of making *improved action* possible.']

Wir gehen mit dem vollen Bewusstsein darauf los, ein festes Gefüge der ganzen österreichischen Arbeiterschaft, das zwar sprachlich nicht einheitlich sondern verschieden ist, aber darum nicht minder fest herzustellen, und wir sind *durch Erfahrung belehrt*, dass wir dieses feste Gefüge nicht dadurch herstellen können, dass wir *Alles über einen Leisten* schlagen, sondern nur dadurch, dass wir den praktischen Bedürfnissen in der ehrlichsten Weise Rechnung tragen.[39]

How does he justify the need for separate organisations? In terms of *experience gained*. Of what that consists, he did not say.

Delegate Comrade [Josef] Hybeš: 'Wir Tschechen, mussten, *um unsere Macht auszunützen*, eine spezielle nationale Organisation konstruiren'.[40]

So once again not national considerations but purely practical needs!

Comrade [František] Soukup:

Die ganze Entwicklung der oesterr. Sozialdemokratie muss zu einer Dezentralisation der Organisation führen. Es handelt sich heute nur darum, *dem faktischen* Zustand eine Sanktion zu geben.

Jedes Volk – das ist eine Thatsache, mit der gerechnet werden muss – ist ein geschlossenes Ganze, mit anderen Traditionen, anderer Geschtichte, kultur- und politischer Entwicklung ... Wenn auch das Programm gemeinsam ist [so there are *no* national programmes, rather the programme is shared!] die *Organisation jeder Nation in Oesterreich muss selbständig sein*; ... Diese Selbstständigkeit fordern wir hauptsächlich *aus dem Grunde*, weil jede Nation selbst am besten wissen muss, was *ihr passt*.[41]

---

39   Sozialdemokratische Arbeiterpartei Österreichs 1897, p. 79. [Grossman's emphasis. 'We set out, fully consciously, to build a solid structure for the entire Austrian working class, which is indeed not linguistically uniform and is, on the contrary, diverse but can nonetheless be solid. And *experience has taught* us that we cannot build this solid structure by *measuring everything by the same yardstick* but only by taking practical requirements into account in the most honest way.']

40   Sozialdemokratische Arbeiterpartei Österreichs 1897, pp. 118. [Grossman's emphasis. '*In order to fully exercise our power*, we Czechs had to construct our own special organisation.']

41   Sozialdemokratische Arbeiterpartei Österreichs 1897, pp. 118–19. [Grossman's emphasis. 'The entire development of Austrian Social Democracy had to lead to the decentralisation of the organisation. Today, it is only a matter of formally recognising the *actual situation*. Every people – this is a fact that must be acknowledged – is a self-contained whole with distinct traditions, a distinct history, culture and political development ... While the Programme is common [so there are *no* national programmes, rather the programme is

So once again not national considerations but purely practical needs!

Similarly, Comrade Radimsky who even quoted the *Communist Manifesto* by Marx and Engels: 'Die Komunisten unterscheiden sich von den übrigen Parteien nur dadurch dass sie in den verschiedenen nationalen Kämpfen der Proletarier die gemeinsamen, *von der Nationalität unabhängigen Interessen* des gesamten Proletariats hervorheben.'[42] In other words socialists (communists) of a particular nation, *although they have national needs* which they can seek to satisfy on an equal basis with other (non-socialist) parties, as socialists take into account and emphasise the common interests of the whole proletariat independently of national interests!

Yet again Comrade Dr Adler: 'Darüber wollen wir gar keinen Zweifel aufkommen lassen, dass wir diese Organisation in nationalen Gruppen *blos zu dem Zwecke machen,* **um den Klassenkampf desto schärfer** *international zu führen.*'[43] And finally the statement in 'The Report on the Justification for the Newly Founded [1897] Organisation':

> Erklärung. Die vom Prager Parteitag angebahnte und vom sechsten Parteitag [1897] durchgeführte Organisation der oesterr. Sozialdemokratie nach selbstständigen nationalen Gruppen *hat den Zweck,* für die Arbeit der Organisation des vielsprachigen Proletariats in Oesterreich **die besten praktischen Bedingungen zu bieten,** *die praktischen Schwierigkeiten der Sprachverschiedenheit zu überwinden.* Indem wir so **die Nützlichkeit der vollen Selbstständigkeit** für die Organisation *jeder Zunge* anerkennen, schaffen wir ... [etc.] ... wir erklären, dass diese Organisation **ausschliesslich** [!] bestimmt ist, die wirksamste Form zu schaffen, in der ... die Sozialdemokraten aller Zungen den Kampf führen gegen die Ausbeuterklassen *in ihr eigenen Nation* und gegen die Ausbeuterklassen aller Nationen.[44]

---

shared!], the *organisation of each nation in Austria must be autonomous* ... We demand this autonomy principally *on the basis* that each nation knows best *what suits it.*']

42   Sozialdemokratische Arbeiterpartei Österreichs 1897, p. 169. [Grossman's emphasis. 'The communists are distinguished from the other working-class parties by this only: In the national struggles of the proletarians of the different countries, they point out and bring to the front *the common interests of the entire proletariat, independently of all nationality*. Marx and Engels 1976, Grossman's emphasis.] Sozialdemokratische Arbeiterpartei Österreichs 1897, p. 139.

43   ['We do not want there to be any doubt about this, that we adopt this organisation in national groups only *for the purpose of conducting the international class* **struggle the more keenly.**']

44   Sozialdemokratische Arbeiterpartei Österreichs 1897, p. 169. [Grossman's emphasis, except for **'usefulness of full autonomy'.** The original emphasised *'in autonomous national groups'.* 'Explanation. The organisation of Austrian Social Democracy in autonomous

There is not a word about national considerations, only and solely considerations concerning the appropriate means of conducting the class struggle!

And, in the closing speech, Comrade Němec again stated: 'Wir haben uns
diese Organisation gegeben, nicht um uns gegenseitig zu bekämpfen, sondern
nur darum, damit wir, *jede Nation für sich* ihre Bourgeoisie besser zu bekämpfen können'[45] Cannot this 'tactical consideration' be a serious basis for a separate organisation?

Again, two years later in the Brno Congress Report signed by Comrade
Ferdinand Skaret we read: 'Der sechste sozialdem. Parteitag [1897] hatte den
Beschluss gefasst, die Organisation in selbstständige nationale Gruppen zu
theilen, um so bei der Vielsprachigkeit des oesterr. Proletariats *für Organisation und Agitation günstigere Bedingungen zu schaffen*'.[46]

We think we have provided thorough evidence.

Does the Executive of the PPSD think that the Czech or German comrades
do not have national needs and do not attempt to satisfy them?

**Yet despite all this, when Czech and German social democrats were form-
ing national organisations, they did not plead national considerations!**

We have refuted various objections, not missing a single one. These have
burst like bubbles in the light of facts and evidence, as has the conclusion based
on them.

We wish to make one more point. Lacking arguments, the PPSD fights us in a
manner unworthy of social democrats. If – as we claim – the contentions of the
Executive of the PPSD have turned out to be incompatible with the facts, if this
has occurred here, where everyone can immediately correct them on the basis
of shorthand minutes, what is the situation where checking is not so easy? We

---

national groups, initiated by Prague Congress and completed by the sixth Congress [1897]
has the purpose of **providing the best practical conditions** for the work of the organising
the Austrian proletariat, with its many languages, in order to overcome the *practical difficulties of linguistic diversity*. In affirming **the usefulness of full autonomy** for the organisations *of each language* ... we create [etc.] ... we declare that this organisation is **exclusively**
[!] designed to create the most effective form in which Social Democrats of all languages
can conduct the struggle against the exploiting classes *of their own nations* and against the
exploiting classes of all nations.']

45   Sozialdemokratische Arbeiterpartei Österreichs 1897, p. 210. [Grossman's emphasis. 'We
       organised this way not in order to fight among ourselves but only so that we, *each nation
       itself*, could better fight its own bourgeoisie.'

46   Sozialdemokratische Arbeiterpartei Österreichs 1899, p. 11. [Grossman's emphasis. 'The
       sixth Social Democratic Congress [1897] resolved to divide the organisation into inde-
       pendent national groups, in order to *establish more favourable conditions for organisation
       and agitation*, given that the Austrian proletariat speaks many languages.']

refer to the various letters from the provinces, where mud is ruthlessly thrown on past Party comrades.

We hereby categorically state that correspondence referring to the 'filthy Adler Party' and about letters from Comrades Dr Adler and [Engelbert] Pernerstorfer allegedly shown to workers etc. etc. are lies and untrue. We condemn them as common slander, and *must protest most emphatically against this method of fighting*, tearing our reputation to shreds and serving only to discredit us in public opinion.

Furthermore we declare that we have *never and nowhere hurled insults at the Polish or the Austrian Party; on the contrary, we were always concerned to maintain fraternal relations*.

We are extremely surprised that the Austrian Executive could adopt such a resolution from the PPSD Executive; the accusation that we want to preserve *Jewish clerical traditions* confirms only complete ignorance about the character of our work and organisation.

What consoles us is that when *the truth is confirmed*, when the Austrian Executive possesses better information and comes to know the character of our work better, it will withdraw its resolution, which harms the broad masses of the Jewish proletariat, and give us the recognition we seek.

We know how the Bund fought for recognition and we know what sacrifices it made ...

So we will not retreat!

We will determinedly follow the path which we judge correct, fully convinced that only an independent Jewish organisation can raise the Jewish proletariat to a higher level of material and intellectual life; only a Jewish organisation that is the equal of other organisations can create out of today's passive Jewish masses a political force conscious of its goals. Difficulties and resistance will be dashed against the granite foundations of our movement. Through difficulty and sacrifice we will go unwaveringly forward – to victory!

Our means is the Jewish Social Democratic Party, our aim: the realisation of socialist ideals!

CHAPTER 6

Report to the Congress of the General Austrian Social Democratic Party in Vienna, 1905[*]
(1 May–23 October 1905)

Translated from German by Ben Fowkes

The same grounds and circumstances which played a decisive role in the estab-lishment of Social Democracy in Austria on the basis of national autonomy also led to the organisation of Jewish Social Democracy of Galicia on the same basis.

The process through which the other nations have already passed is only now starting to stamp its mark on Jewish society, which has undergone fun-damental changes in the last two decades. The powerful impulse of capital-ist development is also beginning to seize hold of the Jews. Capitalism has penetrated into the declining Jewish ghetto, revolutionising and undermin-ing it, dividing it into new classes. In other words, it has established entirely new class relations. A Jewish proletariat emerged and is still emerging, daily becoming more numerous. The class of Jewish wage-workers did not exist at all until very recently. These economic transformations have been accom-panied by the emergence of corresponding constellations of political parties, which are increasingly crystallising out in Jewish society. The clique of Jewish careerists, which is the curious starting-point for the Party of Jewish Conser-vatives, corresponds to the Polish Conservative Party; the raucous All-Polish Party finds an analogy in the reactionary Zionists, the new Party of Jewish Independents corresponds to the Polish Democrats, while the organisation of the Jewish proletariat, finally, most vehemently opposes all these other parties.

Recent, well-known events have caused the Polish Social Democratic Party to start a disgraceful struggle against the new Jewish proletarian organisation, instead of supporting it. Thanks to this, our organisation has had to conduct an extra struggle, over and above its struggle with the class enemy, the Jewish bourgeoisie and in particular Zionism. This struggle has been imposed on us against our will by members of the Polish organisation, who are supposed to be our brothers.

---

[*] [Originally published as Jüdishe sozial-demokratishe Partei in Galitsien 1905a.]

Despite the variety and multiplicity of the difficulties with which we are confronted, our Party is not only developing in a gratifying manner but the pace of its development has also accelerated so much that we are only able to satisfy the new requirements that have arisen in part, owing to the relatively small number of agitators at our disposal and a lack of adequate financial resources.

The schools we have set up to train agitators are properly run and guarantee the continuous and orderly development of our movement. It is easy to understand that our main tasks have been and continue to be organisational in nature.

In this respect we are in the fortunate situation that we are a nation which does not have any special agrarian questions to solve. The Jewish population of Galicia lives for the most part in towns both large and small. Jews make up 30 to 40 percent of the urban population, and it is this situation which calls for a particular kind of agitation. Since both capitals[1] and the largest towns in the province were under our influence (so far as the Jewish proletariat is concerned) before the establishment of our Party, it is now important to win over the smaller towns. Socialist ideas have not penetrated these regions of Galicia, with their artisanal character. The miserable economic relations there have not changed in thirty years, the working day is 18 hours long and wages scarcely purchase the most meagre necessities. Jewish workers live under these circumstances without protest or feeling that they are being taken advantage of. They are often supported by their parents and when they marry they become masters and exploit others. Two factors have recently been bringing about changes in these antiquated circumstances. With the extension of the railways and roads and the emergence of many markets, the artisanal products of small masters are more and more undermined. They no longer work on orders from individuals. In the larger towns production is for large department stores, intermediaries or exporters. Here the small masters increasingly become dependent wage workers producing shoddy goods for the local market.

Clothing manufacture and shoe-making have been the industries most transformed in this way. Non-metropolitan Galicia is increasingly becoming the location of so-called shoddy work. Increasingly the figure of the merchant, the dealer (exporter) steps between the direct producers and consumers. They anticipate the emergence of capitalist factory owners and a higher stage of capitalist development. The process of change has not been completed and occasionally has not even begun. Even though it has become apparent in the poverty of the masses, the reduction of consumption and the shattering of long

---

1   [I.e. Kraków and L'viv.]

undisturbed social layers, its assault on existing relationships has revolutionary consequences. It has made the initial entry of a second modern and revolutionary factor, represented by the modern labour movement, possible. To the extent that this movement demands better conditions of work and wages, it leads to the concentration and capitalisation of production, which can better afford these higher expenses. The transition to industrialism and to factory production, however, encounters its most significant obstacle from the start: the lack of any protection for outworkers. In short, this labour has not, so far, been covered by the legal provisions that protect industrial labour. To the extent that merchant-entrepreneurs have free and unlimited scope for exploitation, they cling desperately to this antiquated form of production, which does not require a larger capital, as is the case with the factory system, and gives rise to the extraction of more surplus value.

So the Jewish proletariat enthusiastically welcomes Comrade [Johann] Smitka's proposals, which he presented to the Labour Advisory Council[2] and will protect outworkers. They have particular significance for Galicia with its extensive out-work. They will not only, finally, restrict the excessive exploitation of the physical and intellectual capacities of the workers; they will not only call a halt to the swindle of the Jewish 'philanthropists', who want to give 'many Jewish families the opportunity to exist', by extending out-work. The realisation of these proposals will also become one of the most important factors setting Galicia onto the path of industrialisation. And we know that the proletarian labour movement can only develop through and against capitalism.

1 **The political struggle.** Any kind of political work is difficult under these circumstances of economic backwardness and the retarded character of rural relations has also stamped its mark on the workers movement. Despite all these obstacles, the Jewish proletariat in Galicia has actively participated in all the important events that have taken place since the establishment of our Party.

May Day: 1 May was preceded by lively agitation in support of the celebration of May Day, during which the significance of this date was discussed. On this day, which was also the day when our Party proclaimed its existence, a series of celebratory meetings took place across the whole province. Wherever it was possible we demonstrated together with the Polish workers. Thus, after Jewish workers held their meeting [in Kraków], they marched in a 2,000 strong procession to the Polish meeting, after which we continued to demonstrate together on the street.

---

2 [A consultative body in the Austrian Ministry of Commerce.]

The movement for universal suffrage: Our organisations unleashed a variety of activities in this area, whether in the press and through public appeals or by holding both public and closed meetings over the whole province, at which we demonstrated against the outrageous measures of Baron [Paul] Gautsch and in favour of universal suffrage. The movement became more widespread and, for the first time, we succeeded in involving the small towns of Galicia in it; they had previously lain in a deep sleep. We must also stress the solidarity between Jewish and Polish workers, as was shown by the events in Kraków and the general strike in L'viv.

2 The number of organised workers and the form of organisation. In view of the low level of development of economic relations,[3] the pulse of political life has only recently begun to beat more strongly. There are still many strata for which the political struggle is too abstract and too far removed from daily life and needs. This increases the significance of trade union organisation, which is a way to lead the indifferent masses towards the modern workers movement. And someone who has been enlightened about their economic oppression by a trade union will also understand how to make use of their experience elsewhere, in *political life*!

It will be understood that it is difficult to establish the precise number of organised workers, given that we are only in the process of constructing our organisation and are constantly setting up branches in new locations. The real situation will therefore outstrip the following data, restricted as they are to what can be solidly verified.

The members of our Party are mainly organised in branches of the central industrial unions, in educational and general trade union associations. The number of male and female workers organised comes to more than 2,500. If we bear in mind both the total number of organised workers in contemporary Galicia and, on the other hand, the short period of our activity, in our situation this is an impressive figure.

It goes without saying that our political influence on the masses is much greater than that and more than 2,000 people participated in our demonstrations in Kraków and L'viv. We can note with satisfaction that almost all the organised Jewish workers are in our ranks.

Party affairs are conducted by an *Executive Committee* located in Kraków, elected at the first, founding Congress in L'viv (9 and 10 June 1905, 52 del-

---

3   Galicia accounted for 5,915 out of the total of 189,121 organised workers in Austria at the end of 1904, which is 3.13 percent, while the total number of industrial workers in Galicia who would be susceptible to organisation is only 113,000.

egates) and by four *District Committees* (Kraków, L'viv, Tarnów and Tarnopol). In other towns there are *Local Committees* or individual representatives. Our general associations are usually called Brotherhood or Forwards.[4] Associations with the latter name have been established across the whole province and new ones are continuously being set up.

Our activities extend to Oświęcim (25 [members]), Wadowice (30), Chrzanów (35, a branch of the Kraków Forwards), Podgórze (150), and Kraków (over 600: shoemakers 70, painters 60, tailors 120, leather workers 12, bakers 30, metalworkers 40, commercial employees 80, general women's association 120, butchers 15, Forwards 100). In addition to these, in Kraków we have a cultural institution, Education, a non-Party association under the influence of members of our Party with the purpose of spreading culture among the Jewish masses. It does this by putting on performances of the best Yiddish and foreign dramatic works, organising lectures, a library etc. Our reading room, currently for members only, is about to be made available to the general public. The association intends to extend its activities over the whole of Galicia in the near future. Tarnów (300: tailors 120, commercial employees 90, shoemakers 10, hatters 10, Forwards 70), (90 commercial employees and others), Przemyśl (80 [in] Forwards), Sanok (60), L'viv (over 400, bakers 130, tailors 80, cabinet makers 100, Brotherhood 90), Brody (*Zgoda*: brush-makers 30, tailors 10, women feather pluckers 20, horsehair workers 10 etc.), Buczacz (300: cabinet makers, bakers, tailors and commercial employees etc. in Brotherhood), Tarnopol (120 [in] four groups shoemakers, tailors, cabinet makers and bakers), Podwołoczyska (40), Złoczów (60 [in] *Brotherhood*), Ivano-Frankivsk (80). For the moment in Kolomyia we only have a connection through our organ, *Sozialdemokrat*, 40 copies of which circulate there. In other small towns, such as Dębica, Brzesko, Skałat and many others, where socialism has only just made an entry through our agitators, we have not yet succeeded in establishing solid links. Work in the smaller towns meets with difficulties, mainly because of a lack of skilled agitators on the spot. In view of this problem, we had to appoint a permanent agitator based in Tarnów to deal with the towns of this kind in Western Galicia. Our Party Executive has resolved to appoint an agitator based in Tarnopol, for the small towns of Eastern Galicia, and this decision will be put into effect in the near future. In almost all cases, our organisations contain *working women*. For the present, a special association for women only exists in Kraków but we have already applied to the political

---

4 [The associations were called 'Briderlekhkeyt' ('Brotherhood', in Yiddish); and 'Postęp', ('Forwards', in Polish).]

authorities for permission to establish new associations of this kind in L'viv, Tarnów and Podgórze.

• •
•

We have set up the Association of Young Workers in Galicia for *young workers*. This now has more than 1,000 members (400 in Kraków, 60 in Tarnów, 300 in L'viv and so on). It is developing well and intends to issue a monthly journal fairly soon.

• •
•

The internal life of our organisations is particularly well developed. We have held at least 600 closed and 200 public meetings and, in addition, have organised *celebratory evenings* to commemorate Engels, [Ferdinand] Lassalle and the Jewish revolutionary Hirsch Lekert. The lectures and discussions conducted at least once a week by our associations (on Friday evenings or Saturday afternoons) have dealt with the programme of Austrian Social Democracy, the general strike, historical materialism, the revolution in Russia etc., in addition, natural scientific themes, literacy courses etc.

3 **Economic struggles.** In view of the end of the crisis and the rise in economic activity, this year has been favourable for the struggle to improve working conditions and wages. In Kraków we successfully led strikes by painters, metalworkers, butchers and washerwomen. In Tarnów there were two boycotts and two strikes by tailors, one of which brought out almost 300 workers and lasted for ten days. In L'viv there were strikes by the cabinet makers and the matchbox makers and eight boycotts in the baking trade. During the great *strikes by Polish building workers*, led by the Polish Party, the Jewish workers observed their duty of solidarity, in spite of the infuriating tactics of the Polish socialist leaders, whose unscrupulous behaviour could well have sparked off conflicts between Polish and Jewish workers. The organisation of the Jewish proletariat declared that it would participate in a general strike if this came about and, in addition, gave material support to the Polish strikers. In Buczacz a strike of cabinet makers has now entered its fourth week. The small-scale exploiters of Galicia have proved that in brutality and obstinacy nothing distinguishes them from their big masters in Berlin or Crimmitschau.[5]

---

5 [There was a bitter strike and lockout in Berlin's electricity industry in September–October

4 Literature and press. We have published 6,000 copies of *What We Want* in Yiddish and 5,000 in Polish,[6] 2,500 copies of *Before the Congress*[7] in the Jewish language and 1,500 in Polish, many thousands of copies of revolutionary songs (Yiddish) and a pamphlet by Comrade Henryk Grossman in Polish, entitled *The Proletariat Faced with the Jewish Question*.[8] The first five issues of the popular scientific monthly journal *Der Yudisher Sotsial-Demokrat* came out in L'viv in 5,000 copies altogether. For the present, we have replaced it with our Party organ, the weekly *Der Sozialdemokrat*, which is published in Kraków. Print run: number 1, 1,400 copies; number 2, 1,600 copies; number 3 and subsequent issues, 2,000 copies. In reaction to various important events our Executive Committee and the Local Committees have issued manifestos in Yiddish and Polish in more than 10,000 copies.

In addition to this, we have made use of the scientific and other literature issued in Yiddish by the General Union of Jewish Workers in Lithuania, Poland and Russia (the Bund), which includes the most valuable socialist treatises, such as those of Marx, Engels, [Karl] Kautsky, Lassalle, [Max] Schippel, [Gustav] Jäckh and [Georgii] Plekhanov. We are distributing these books in many thousands of copies. There is a most urgent need for a popular scientific monthly in Yiddish. To fulfil this will be a task for the future.

5 Support for deserters. One important and difficult task for our organisations has been to provide assistance to Russian deserters, who entered the province in large numbers because of the well-known events in Russia. They almost always lacked any financial means and were often forced into sweated labour. In view of this, it was important to acquire from the political authorities appropriate labour books, place them in employment and draw them into our organisation. We often had to intervene with the police to prevent them from harassing deserters. If one takes into account the miserable situation of the whole Jewish proletariat in Galicia, the material assistance our organisations provided to them – from their own resources – was quite considerable, amounting to almost 1,500 crowns. Deserters who traveled westwards received from our committees a railway ticket to the next town and a certain amount of money for

---

1905. For five months in 1903–4 thousands of textile workers struck in Crimmitschau, in the German state of Saxony.

6 [Komitet Organizacyjny Żydowskiej Partyi Socyalno-demokraticyczney w Galicyi 1905, see *What Do We Want?*, above, pp. 73–82.]

7 [Żydowska Partya Socyalno-Demokratyczna Galicyi 1905a, including Żydowska Partya socyalno-demokratyczna Galicyi 1905b, see *Before the Congress*, above, pp. 83–102.]

8 [Grossman 1905a, see *The Proletariat Faced with the Jewish Question*, above, pp. 34–62.]

the necessities of life. Kraków found itself in a particularly difficult situation as it is at the western end of Galicia and thus had to bear the expense of travel to Vienna, which was much greater. The *Jewish community councils* (*kahals*) took a shockingly brutal attitude to this emigration, refusing to help in any way at all.

6 The fight against Zionism, against Jewish nationalism, the representative of the Jewish bourgeoisie, is self-evident. We have conducted this with success everywhere, in the sense of the resolution of our first Congress, which proclaims that 'the Congress considers it necessary to fight against Zionism in all its tendencies and forms'.

The existence of (various forms of) Zionism, leaving aside its own internal differentiations, can be explained by the fact that, whereas in Western Europe the bourgeoisie as a rule has long abandoned the hope of winning the proletariat over to its side, these most recent epigones of the bourgeoisie are still under the illusion that they may succeed in this endeavour. In order to achieve this, they deck themselves out with various more or less radical formulae about 'democracy' or 'socialism', without abandoning their [ideology's] reactionary content.

The organisation of the Jewish proletariat in a specific social democratic party has contributed not a little to clearing our field of combat against Zionism, which hides behind the veil of nationalism. The struggle increasingly takes on the character of a pure *class struggle* of the Jewish proletariat against the Jewish bourgeoisie, which nothing can disguise.

7 **Repression.** Three people were prosecuted because of a demonstration in Tarnów against night-work. One was found not guilty, one was sentenced to three days and the third, Comrade *Sommermann*, was sentenced to *one month of incarceration*. In L'viv a strike of bakers resulted in the prosecution of some comrades for public disorder. In Tarnopol Comrade *Goldstein* will be faced with a trial by jury because he was denounced by a Zionist for a meeting he held in Podwołoczyska. In Przemyśl, Comrade *Wolf* has been condemned to four months' imprisonment for insulting his majesty the Emperor and an additional six weeks for public disorder. In Kraków, comrades *Feldstein* and [Jonas] *Blum* have been prosecuted for various 'crimes' committed during a demonstration for universal suffrage. A brief mention should also be made of such acts of harassment as the dispersal of a mass meeting called by us in Brody, because of the slogan 'Down with Gautsch'; the prohibition of a meeting in Tarnów, because the street number of the meeting place was not accurately provided; and the utterly ridiculous obstacles put in our way by the chief administrator of the Wadowice district and other people.

8 Our relationship with the Polish and Ruthenian Social Democratic Parties of Galicia.

a) After 1 May, we approached the Polish Party by letter with a proposal for an *agreed and harmonious regulation* of our mutual relations. The Polish Party preferred a struggle, however, and dared to spread defamatory allegations about the Jewish workers movement of a kind even the worst antisemitic scoundrels writing in the *Słowo polskie* or the *Głos narodu*[9] would not have ventured to utter. With these disgraceful slanders it sought to undermine the existence of our organisation by misleading public opinion. In view of all this, our Congress *condemned* the tactics of defamation engaged in by the leaders of the Polish Party. It is the Polish Party alone that bears the responsibility for this struggle, which we are conducting unwillingly, and it is also responsible for the *consequences*.

b) Our relationship to the Ruthenian Party can only be theoretical. We have expressed the wish to be on friendly terms. In practice there can be no question of a relationship with this Party because it only exists ... on paper.[10] This did not, however, prevent the representative of this Party, who represents nothing, from boldly proclaiming its official refusal to recognise the existence of thousands of organised Jewish proletarians!

9 The Party Congress of the General Austrian Social Democratic Party. After the decision of the General Austrian Executive, which refused to recognise us officially, we turned to the General Party Congress to achieve our objective, by *proposing motions in these terms.* This step was prepared by holding numerous Party meetings across the whole of Galicia, at which our attitude to the General Austrian Party was discussed. In every meeting, a resolution was unanimously adopted to the following effect: our activities are based on the programme and the general tactics of Austrian Social Democracy; and our organisation arose on the same basis and with the same motives as were expressed by Comrade [Victor] Adler in his 'Report on the guiding Principles of the Organisation Newly Created in Austria [1897]'.[11] Our resolution went on to declare:

---

9   ['*Słowo Polskie*', ('*Polish Word*'), was a twice daily newspaper in L'viv, associated with the antisemitic National Democratic Party, '*Głos narodu*' ('*Voice of the People*') was a right-wing and antisemitic daily newspaper in Kraków.]

10   [The Ukrainian Social Democratic Party at this stage functioned as a skeletal section of the Polish Social Democratic Party of Galicia.]

11   Sozialdemokratische Arbeiterpartei Österreichs 1897, p. 169.

The organised Jewish workers therefore expect from this year's General Austrian Party Congress that it officially acknowledge the Jewish Social Democratic Party and in this way guarantee to the Jewish proletariat within Social Democracy the same rights, self-determination and the freedom to develop on the basis of equal rights.

If the General Party Congress fails to recognise the application to the Jewish organisation of the guiding principles expressed in the above-mentioned report to the Congress and fails to concede equal rights to it, the organisation of the Jewish proletariat, the Jewish Social Democratic Party of Galicia, will *proceed further along the path to autonomy*, in the name of the class interests of the Jewish proletariat and in the name of international socialism! Nevertheless, we shall still entirely and completely fulfil our duty in the proletarian struggle against our common enemy ...

CHAPTER 7

To the Social Democrats of Austria*

Translated from German by Ben Fowkes

The question of the organisation of the Jewish proletariat in Galicia has already been on the agenda for many years and continues to await a successful solution.

In the statement that follows we would like to present the most important factual information to provide points of orientation for discussions about the question at this year's Congress of the General Austrian Party.

The Jewish Social Democratic Party of Galicia proclaimed its existence on 1 May 1905 and constituted itself at its first Congress on 9 and 10 June 1905 in L'viv. 52 delegates participated in the Congress, among them three women. Many organisations sent letters of greeting to the Congress but we stress in particular the letter received from the General Jewish Workers Union in Lithuania, Poland and Russia (the Bund). They start by expressing their regret that they were unable to send a guest, for technical reasons. They continue their letter as follows:

> As you know, we as an organisation, which limits its activities to the pro-
> motion of the interests of the Jewish proletariat in Russia, have always
> regarded it as out of the question to intervene in any way in the organ-
> isational questions of Galician Social Democracy. But you will be aware
> that our sympathy lies entirely with the cause for which you are stepping
> forward as pioneers. We have always upheld the view, and have based the
> whole of our activity on it, that only an organisation which has arisen
> organically from the struggles of the Jewish working masses and is harmo-
> niously entwined with them can become the genuine and real leader of
> these masses in their struggle for political and social emancipation. One
> cannot fail to note that your activity constitutes the starting point and
> basis for a *broad* mass movement which will finally lead the Jewish pro-
> letariat in Galicia out of its oppressed and passive condition and place
> it alongside the workers of all other nationalities, who have previously
> stepped forth on the road to active struggle and have already succeeded in
> establishing their own social democratic organisations. We send you our

---

* [Originally published as Jüdische sozial-demokratishe Partei in Galitsien 1905b.]

hearty greetings and wish success to your first Congress, which should lay a firm foundation for the social democratic movement of Jewish workers in Galicia. We hope that you will successfully overcome all the obstacles standing in your way and that you will succeed in establishing a strong fighting organisation, which will form a mighty part of the united and fraternal family of all the social democratic organisations of Austria and thus also of the worldwide socialist proletariat.

The most important decisions of principle taken by the first Congress are:

Attitude to the General Austrian Social Democratic Party
Although the Jewish Social Democratic Party has not been recognised by the General Executive of the Austrian Party, the Jewish Party regards itself as a part of Austrian Social Democracy and regards *acting on the basis of the general programme and tactics of the Party* as its obligation.[1]

Attitude to the Polish Social Democratic Party
Considering that the Jewish Social Democratic Party is necessary for the development of the class consciousness of the Jewish proletariat in Galicia; considering further that joint action by the Jewish and the Polish parties is in the interests of the proletariat of both nations, the Jewish nation and the Polish, the Congress resolves as follows:
1. The struggle which is now taking place between ourselves and the Polish Party was forced on us against our wishes and it is in the interests of the social democratic movement that a reconciliation between the two organisations should be brought about as quickly as possible.
2. Because the Polish Party, through various unworthy means, has tried to undermine the significance and the existence of the Jewish Social Democratic Party, these tactics are hereby condemned.[2]

The struggle against Zionism
Considering that Zionism, the movement of the Jewish bourgeois class – dressed in the hypocritical cloak of Poale-Zion ('socialist Zionism') – is trying to lure the Jewish proletariat into its lair and to arouse in it sentiments of nationalism and chauvinism; and standing as we do on the

---

1 [See *Yudisher Sotsial-Demokrat* 1905, p. 2. Grossman's emphasis.]
2 [See *Yudisher Sotsial-Demokrat* 1905, pp. 3–4.]

ground of the class interests of the Jewish proletariat, we hereby resolve
to combat Zionism in all its tendencies and forms in the strongest way
possible.[3]

∴

Earlier attempts to bring the numerous Jewish proletarians who live in extremely oppressed and miserable conditions into the social democratic movement have unfortunately had little success. The reason for this failure, apart
from the difficulty of the overall situation, was that the *previous ways of organising the Jewish proletariat were completely insufficient* and excluded the possibility of vigorous and all embracing agitation. The fact that the system whereby
the Yiddish-speaking proletariat was supposed to be organised within the
framework of the Polish organisation was inadequate is something which *actually does not even need demonstrating to an Austrian social democrat*. All the
social democratic organisations in Austria were established precisely on a basis
of national autonomy in order to adapt *their agitation to proletarians who spoke
different languages*, and it was recognised that each nation must decide for
itself on matters of organisation and agitation.

And for that reason, the same yardstick should be applied to the Jewish proletariat, since the Jewish proletarian masses have their own language and their
own specific cultural and social milieu, and they have their own special task of
fighting the Jewish bourgeoisie. We are not concerned here, however, merely
with a violation of abstract justice. Our point is rather that practical life itself
and the whole history of the Jewish workers movement in Galicia has led up
to the creation of an autonomous Jewish party, as its logical result. Let us give
examples of this previous history. The Polish and Jewish workers initially organised together in joint associations but separate Jewish ones started as early as
1892. This first 'sin' was followed by others but the 'guilt' lies with life itself,
because it was life that created this situation. The Polish Party, or, to put it more
correctly, what was still the Galician Party, is not to be blamed for this. It took
account of the needs of life, and in practice it created special Jewish associations. This process of 'spreading out' lasted until 1897. At a certain stage of
development, however, the fragmented movement in the province had to be
centralised. This was unconditionally necessary for further development. It was
exactly then that a certain degree of consciousness began to arise in the Jewish

---

3   [See *Yudisher Sotsial-Demokrat* 1905, p. 3.]

proletariat, though it was not yet very strong. We could see this at the Congress of the Galician Party held in Przemyśl in 1897.

At just that time, the Party in the whole of Austria was finally constituted as a federation of national organisations. Thus the Galician Party was now converted into a Polish Party. Comrade [Jan] Kozakiewicz (who was a deputy in the Austrian parliament at the time) drew the logical conclusion from this, calling at the Przemyśl Congress[4] for the Jews and the Ruthenians[5] to set up their own autonomous organisations. (The Ruthenians did this two years later.) Only six delegates voted with Kozakiewicz. The question was not, however, settled; a failure with disastrous consequences for the movement, which underwent a serious decline in the years between 1897 and 1899. The Jewish workers associations lost members during this period and the Yiddish newspaper (the *Folkstsaytung*) had to cease publication. It resurfaced and became an organ of agitation ... during elections. After the elections ... it disappeared again. Thus the penalty was paid for the inadequacy of the leaders of that time. The movement, which had a future before it, came to grief thanks to a failure to recognise the needs created by life itself. This sad situation led in 1899 to the *first conference* of Jewish workers in Galicia, which was intended to remedy the deficiency. It ended without achieving anything, because Dr [Samuel Łazarz] Schorr, who was supposed to move the motion for an autonomous party at the conference did not do so, as a result of political manoeuvring behind the scenes. When, in a word, there was no change in the way the Jewish proletariat was organised, the disappointed Jewish workers in Galicia understood for the first time that the only way of bringing about a radical improvement was to constitute a Jewish Social Democratic Party. Ever wider layers of the proletariat became aware of the need for such an organisation and this movement finally led to the second conference, which also had the task of creating an autonomous Jewish organisation. Like the first conference, however, it ended without achieving this.

The significance of these two conferences, it should be said, lies not in their results but in the very fact that they were held. The results of both conferences were negative but there were many positive aspects as well: the fact that all the Jewish workers associations of the province had a *separate* discussion of *their own* affairs and the unconditional confirmation of the need for centralisation, the need to combine fragmented forces and the need to create an independent

---

4   [The Przemyśl Congress of the Social Democratic Party of Galicia in 1897. The Party changed its name to the Polish Social Democratic Party of Galicia in 1899, after the establishment of the Ukrainian Social Democratic Party.]

5   [I.e. Ukrainians.]

institution which would autonomously direct the Jewish workers movement. The mere decision to summon these conferences was a victory for the *principle*!

The second conference, indeed, went one step further. Although it provisionally rejected the proposal for an autonomous party, it had to give some satisfaction to the dissatisfied opposition: it resolved to set up a (central) *Jewish Agitation Committee for Galicia*. What happened then, however, was that the Polish social democratic leaders *prevented* this committee from *being established*, because that, in their view, would be a significant step to an autonomous Jewish party, which was a 'danger' to them. Even so, the establishment of this Committee (if only on paper) confirmed to a still greater degree the movement's need for centralisation.

We can therefore see that *life itself authoritatively and unconditionally points in the direction of the organisational autonomy of the Jewish movement*, just as life has created the autonomous workers organisations of the Germans, Czechs, Italians and so on. Never, perhaps, has a development 'emerged from within in such an organic way' (Dr [Victor] Adler's words).

It was disastrous that the Polish Party leaders were not only unaware of this tendency of development but, on the contrary, endeavoured to enforce their wishes, which tended in the opposite direction. At that time, when life itself was pushing towards autonomy, when life required that the particular cultural and psychological characteristics of the Jewish proletariat be taken into account, when even the Polish leaders themselves had to make 'concessions' (on paper) which were required by the needs of practical activity (like, for example, calling the conferences and the creation of the aforementioned 'Committee'), they simultaneously proclaimed an unqualified and brutal *theory of Polonisation* – a theory of which even the *most violent of Germanisers (the Hakatists)*[6] would not need to be ashamed ...

At the second conference, the Polish leader Dr [Herman] Diamand, who was one of the people who called the conference and who drew up the proposal for the so-called 'Jewish Agitation Committee for Galicia', made the following statement:

There are no distinctive Jewish qualities which need to be preserved [!] ... Any attempt to maintain distinctive Jewish features is harmful ... *Hard as it may be for us to get rid of our habits, we have to adopt new forms of behaviour* and we should not allow the difficulties [!] we often encounter

---

6   [The Hakata was a German chauvinist organisation formed in 1894 to eradicate Polish influence in the German-occupied provinces of partitioned Poland.]

in Polish society to deter us from doing that. We must bend all our efforts *to achieving the disappearance of all peculiarities*.[7]

According to Diamand's theory (the theory of the Polish Party's official spokesperson!) whether someone belongs to the Jewish, Czech or Polish nation is merely a question of 'habit'. A Jew must therefore wean himself from this 'habit' or, to put it in a less cowardly fashion, he must be forced to become a Pole ('adopt a new form').

So this is how the Polish (Social Democratic!) Party views the 'right of each nationality to national existence and national development'!![8] Let us point out here that it is characteristic of the Polish Party that in translating the Brno nationality programme it has *simply suppressed the whole of the concluding section*, which contains the passage we have just quoted! ...[9]

Is it really true that there are no distinctive Jewish peculiarities which have to be 'preserved'?

Karl Kautsky can give the best answer to this question:

> There is no doubt that, owing to their *distinctive* moral and intellectual *qualities* and unique social position, the Jews play an important part in the socialist movement.
>
> ... It is enough to point out that the Jewish race does possess its own spiritual physiognomy, which finds its expression in a splendid power of abstraction and a keen critical intellect.[10]

It is no wonder that such a brutal and callous presentation of the policy of Polonisation as Dr Diamand's, at the precise moment when life itself was exerting pressure in the opposite direction, provoked a reaction from the Jewish proletariat, which called in ever greater numbers and determination for an autonomous Jewish organisation!

The last Congress of the Polish Party, held in Kraków in October 1904, was attended by roughly 40 Jewish delegates, and 18 of them declared themselves

---

7   *Naprzód* 1903, p. 3. [Grossman's emphasis.]
8   [Sozialdemokratische Arbeiterpartei Österreichs 1899, p. 8.]
9   [The position of the General Austrian Social Democratic Workers Party, itself a federation of national Social Democratic Parties, on the national question was adopted at its Congress in Brno, in 1899. It called for Austria to be transformed into a federation of self-administered national states and foreshadowed the protection of national minorities by an eventual law, whose content was not specified.]
10 Kautsky 1904.

in favour of a Jewish party. It is safe to say that the majority of the Jewish proletariat *already* supported us *at that time*.

The Polish Party was taken aback by the rapid growth of the movement and
after the Congress wanted to choke it off at any cost. But the Jewish workers
could not be indifferent to these attempts. The class interests of the Jewish proletariat were much more important for them than the Polonising appetites of
the Polish Party leaders.

On May Day 1905 the autonomous Jewish Party of Galicia proclaimed its
existence. It is easy to understand that under such circumstances the *overwhelming majority of the organised Jewish proletariat immediately entered its
ranks.*

The present conflict, therefore, is of a purely *organisational* nature. We stand
fully **on the basis of the Party programme and the overall tactics of Austrian
Social Democracy.** Even so, despite the fact that this question has nothing to
do with the programme or the tactics of Social Democracy, they have ventured
to cast doubt on our socialism!

In our manifesto *What Do We Want?*, issued on 1 May 1905, we point out the
specific circumstances under which the Jewish proletariat lives, and we continue as follows:

> ... only an independent organisation can organise the Jewish proletariat.
> Only an organisation that takes into account the environmental circum-
> stances in which it functions, that is suited to the needs and lives of the
> Jewish masses and to their ways of thinking, is able to spread socialist
> ideas among them, to produce the press they need, to educate agitators.
> Only an organisation which understands the life of the Jewish masses is
> able to awaken the currently passive and detached masses, to draw them
> into the vortex of struggle, to make them conscious!
>
> Organisation is not something intangible and unchanging. Organisa-
> tion is not a goal in itself. Organisation is a means to an end, a tool. One
> may have been good yesterday, today perhaps it is already obsolete and
> worn out. Organisation has to be subject to change, to adapt to circum-
> stances. Yet the circumstances of the Jewish masses are distinct. A single
> organisation of the Jewish and Polish proletariats is not sufficient, just as
> a single organisation is not enough for the proletariats of all the other
> nations in Austria. Just as each of these nations possesses its own organ-
> isation, so too the Jewish proletariat should have such an organisation.
> The entire past of the social democratic movement among Jewish work-
> ers in Galicia points to the need for a Jewish social democratic party. The
> class interests not only of the Jewish but of the whole proletariat in Aus-

tria demand such an organisation. A Jewish social democratic party is not the idea of this or that individual; the circumstances of life themselves are pushing the Jewish proletariat in its direction. Under the socio-historical circumstances in which we live, a Jewish *social democratic party is an historical necessity!*[11]

And further, we read in the manifesto *What We Want?*:

> The programme of the whole proletariat in Austria is our programme too; its fight will be our fight! Indeed our goals are common, our economic demands and political slogans are the same!
>
> So a Jewish Party is not a split and separatism but an equal right. Only it can elevate the Jewish proletariat to a higher economic level and higher intellectual life.
>
> A Jewish social democratic party is a necessity and a Jewish social democratic party does not exist!
>
> Jewish proletarians! An historical moment is approaching, a great moment arrives. The moment is coming when you will be equal to the proletariats of other nations, when you will be accepted on the same terms into the great family of nations.
>
> The Jewish Social Democratic Party of Galicia arises! Do not sleep at this time! Show that you are mature enough to lead yourselves, that you have understood your historical role and will not retreat from it!
>
> Polish comrades deny you this right. But even they will have to acknowledge the accomplished fact. We do not want a fratricidal fight and eagerly hold out our hand in brotherly peace. And it is impossible that they will not accept it. After all, we fight for common goals and we must fight for them together!
>
> Jewish proletarians! Throw off your fears and doubts! Join the ranks of the new organisation and help to build it. It will lead you to proletariat's goals. To battle and to victory! To action! To work!
>
> Great events require great souls. So cast off the soul of the ghetto which you have born. Leave the ghetto streets where you were inclosed. Forward to battle and to victory!
>
> Long live the Jewish Social Democratic Party of Galicia!
>
> Long live the international workers movement!

---

11   [Komitet Organizacyjny Żydowskiej Partyi Socyalno-demokraticyczney w Galicyi 1905, see *What Do We Want?*, above, p. 77.]

Proletarians of all countries unite!
[…] the Organising Committee of the Jewish Social Democratic Party[12]

The Polish Party Executive, however, did not recognise the logic of the facts, even after the Jewish Party had proclaimed its existence. In its resolution of 8 May 1905, it shortsightedly opened a struggle against the Jewish Social Democratic Party, although it is unable to adduce any arguments, capable of withstanding serious criticism, against the existence of the new organisation.[13] The Executive of the Polish Party still wants to save what is for it a lost cause and this involves it in the most glaring self-contradictions … It has had to admit, to its embarrassment, that distinctive forms of organisation and agitation are necessary for the Jewish proletariat and it now promises to recognise Jewish workers associations (branches), a Jewish provincial committee, Jewish local committees etc. – but all within the framework of the Polish Party (!!). At this point one can only ask, in astonishment, why, if it is prepared to recognise 'a particular form of organisation', this should not be *autonomous?*

What does this mean? Would it be an unfortunate surrender to Jewish clericalism and separatism etc. if the Jewish proletariat ceased to be a subordinate group and instead formed an autonomous organisation enjoying equal rights? Would it therefore be a misfortune if this autonomous organisation was in a federal union with the other social democratic organisations? Would it be a misfortune if the Jewish proletariat were treated according to the principle of *equal rights*, along with the proletariats of other nations?

The Polish Party Executive has not proved this, it will never be able to prove this and no social democrat will believe this is so.

Nobody will be persuaded by empty accusations, which are not backed up any argument, about the harmfulness and the reactionary nature of a Jewish Social Democratic Party. And, while the Polish Party Executive has been unable to prove that autonomous Jewish organisation is bad and harmful, we, on the contrary, have always maintained and proved, and will substantiate again that the Jewish proletariat did not properly develop and could not develop within the framework of the Polish Social Democratic Party, and that the needs of this proletariat were only 'satisfied' as an afterthought, at the last possible moment!

It is the task of Social Democracy to fight for the realisation of its programme. Its activity, and its struggle, is expressed first and foremost in certain organisational forms.

---

12   [Komitet Organizacyjny Żydowskiej Partyi Socyalno-demokraticyczney w Galicyi 1905, see *What Do We Want?*, above, pp. 81–81. Editor's ellipsis.]

13   [Zarząd Polskiej Partyi Socyalno-Demokratycznej w Austryi 1905.]

The Polish Party Executive's resolution of 8 May 1905 promises, among other things, that because the Jewish proletariat in Galicia demands particular conditions for organisation and agitation, the Polish Party is prepared to create a Jewish agitation committee for the *province* within the framework of the above-mentioned Party (!).

We shall now place on record, with the greatest possible emphasis, some aspects of the background to this decision. Until May 1903, the Polish Party did not wish to know anything about setting up a Jewish agitation committee for the province. When a proposal was put forward at that time, urging the creation of a Jewish social democratic party, the Polish Party, acting *under this pressure*, conceded a provincial committee for the whole of Galicia, which was also called for by the Jewish conference of May 1903 in L'viv.[14]

After the conference, when the 'danger' of an autonomous Jewish party seemed to have passed, this Provincial Committee failed to take practical form. Its controlling majority, represented by Dr Diamand, allowed it to lead a shadow existence. The most recent Congress of the Polish Party, held in Kraków in 1904, has gone still further, and even abolished the 'Jewish Provincial Agitation Committee' in formal terms. This happened because the Party majority, which has only the barest knowledge of the life and needs of the Jewish workers, bases its actions on the conviction that a provincial committee for Jews is unnecessary, and attacks and reviles the people who consider that it is actually needed. It should also be noted in passing that in May 1903 it was the Polish Party leaders who proposed the 'expedient' of a provincial committee. And now, after 1 May 1905, when the existence of the Jewish Social Democratic Party was proclaimed, the Polish Party Executive has again promised to create a Jewish provincial committee within the Polish framework. It is therefore pressure from outside, the fear of the consequences of doing nothing, which is the decisive factor, and not the needs of the Jewish proletariat! They want to 'concede' a provincial committee in order to be able to take it away again later.

There were Jewish conferences in 1899 and 1903. The Polish Party appeared at that time to recognise that the Jewish proletariat needed to make its own decisions and that it was the best judge of its own needs. Forty Jewish participants resolved to set up a Jewish provincial committee but the last Polish Party Congress in Kraków passed over the resolutions of the Jewish conference and went straight to its own agenda! (The Provincial Committee was set aside.) The principle that the Jewish proletariat has to make its own decisions, recognised in May 1903, was brutally trampled underfoot in October 1904! The Polish

---

14   [The PPSD convened this conference of its Jewish members.]

resolution of 8 May 1905 recognises special requirements and local committees. How long is it, however, since the Galician Trade Union Conference, held in Przemyśl in March 1905, going beyond its sphere of competence, for political reasons 'resolved' to dissolve the separate Jewish workers educational associations? Is *that* the free development of the Jewish proletariat about which the Polish Party Executive has been declaiming? When the Polish Party Executive now promises to allow something whose condemnation it arranged a month earlier, is it not deriding and undermining the dignity of the Przemyśl Trade Union Conference and its own last Party Congress? And, in addition, the Polish Party Executive has the temerity to assert that the Polish Party has now satisfied the needs of the Jewish proletariat – the same Party which changes its mind almost every month about those needs and previously wanted to destroy the nucleus of the Jewish workers movement by closing the Jewish workers educational associations. This was how the 'particular forms of organisation' *looked in practice*, this was how they treated Jewish associations, Jewish committees and Jewish conferences!

The Polish Party has not said a word in reply to these serious accusations, already raised in our publication *Before the Congress*, in Yiddish and in Polish.[15] It has thereby admitted its **complete moral defeat!** ...

It is not, however, just these factors which require the adaptation of the form of organisation to the circumstances of the Jewish proletariat. We are not just socialists but also democrats: we are social democrats, and we therefore fight and must fight for equal rights for the Jewish proletariat. 'Social democrats who preach war on class rule *should not* endorse the denial of the right to self-determination'.[16] So, when the Polish resolution of 8 May 1905 waffles about 'complete equal rights for the Jewish workers', it should also 'not approve the refusal' of the right of self-determination of the Jewish proletariat within Social Democracy, in the sense of the organisational principle of Austrian Social Democracy, which guarantees every nation its autonomy ...

We demand equal rights regardless of the howls of the bourgeois newspapers, which the Polish Party has played off against us. When Austrian Social Democracy was reconstructed on a federal basis according to nationality, the bourgeois press expressed its delight: 'As further steps were taken at the Vienna Congress to extend the independence of the national organisations, the bourgeois parties *with great jubilation* trumpeted that the Social Democratic Party

15   Żydowska Partya Socyalno-Demokratyczna Galicyi 1905a, including Żydowska Partya So-
      cyalno-Demokratyczna Galicyi 1905b, see *Reply to the Polish Social Democratic Party of
      Galicia*, above, pp. 83–102.
16   Daszyński 1902, p. 735.

was fraying and specified to the day its imminent end'. But this is how Comrade [Josef] Krapka continued his speech: 'I am, however, today in the position to state that the Party has been strengthened and, if anything is more united than previously thanks to this autonomy'.[17]

Today the Polish Party appeals in justification to the same bourgeois press. We could use the same method and refer to both antisemitic and Zionist newspapers which have joined the chorus supporting the Polish Party in its fight against us (see for example *Słowo polskie*).[18] We do not, however, fight with such methods and we never will. It is not the groans of the bourgeoisie but the class interests of the Jewish proletariat which are decisive for us!

What then did [Ignacy] Daszyński, the same person who is responsible for the 'struggle' of the Polish socialists against our workers organisation, write in his article on 'Nationality and Social Democracy',[19] mentioned above? We have no wish to interfere in the organisational arrangements in the Polish parts of Prussia but let us hear what Daszyński wrote when it was a question of Poles and not of ordinary Jewish workers: 'This arrangement can only occur on the basis of formal equality between the two parties. For Social Democrats [!] there can be no other basis and no comrade who thinks logically can desire formal dependence ...'[20]

So where Polish workers are concerned, he regards even 'formal' dependency as harmful. But where 'his' Jews are concerned, he and his Party want to hamper the satisfaction of even their practical needs. *Where does this peculiar contradiction come from? ... Moreover, we must point out here in the most emphatic manner that we want to be* **a part** *of the General Austrian Social Democratic Party, as a member with equal rights, whereas the Polish Socialist Party (PPS)[21] in Prussia wishes to be independent of the Social Democratic Party of Germany. So we see that the Polish socialists are the last to have the right and reason to talk about Jewish 'separatism'.*

In the Polish Party Executive's resolution of 8 May 1905, already repeatedly mentioned, the following can be read: 'The Social Democratic organisation in Austria is based on the programme which was unanimously adopted in 1899

---

17   Sozialdemokratische Arbeiterpartei Österreichs 1899, p. 63. [Grossman's emphasis.]
18   *Słowo Polskie* 1905. '*Słowo Polskie*' means 'Polish Word'.]
19   [Grossman referred to 'Nationalität und Socialdemokratie', the article's title was 'Nationality and Socialism', Daszyński 1902.]
20   [Daszyński 1902, p. 736. Daszyński emphasised '*formal equality*'.]
21   [The Polska Partia Socjalistyczna (Polish Socialist Party) was the name of the nationalist, socialist organisations in the German and Russian-occupied provinces of Poland with which the leadership of the PPSD sympathised.]

at the Brno Party Congress'.[22] **We can categorically state here that the Polish Social Democratic Party of Galicia does not know when its own organisational statute was adopted and we are ready at any time to corroborate with documentary evidence this unprecedented fact in the history of political parties.** It is not true that the Austrian organisation was created in 1899. It was created in 1897 at the Vienna Party Congress. The Brno programme relates to the 'nationalities in the Austrian state of the future' (Seeliger), the 1897 Party Congress (two years earlier!) regulated the *organisation of the Party*. Certain details, which the Brno Party Congress added to the organisational statute, were dealt with independently of the nationality debate *at a completely different point on the agenda*. Deputy Daszyński was well aware of this in 1899! This is what he said in Brno: 'Two years ago we found the way to deal with the national question within the Party. What we must do now is find out whether we are capable of advancing the same programme for the entire Empire'.[23]

By 8 May 1905, when he appended his signature to the Polish executive's resolution, he had incomprehensibly forgotten about this ...

The only authoritative statement on Austrian social democratic organisation is the official 'The Report on the Justification for the Newly Founded [1897] Organisation', read by Comrade Dr Victor Adler, in which he declares:

> *The organisation of Austrian Social Democracy in autonomous national groups, initiated by the Prague Congress and completed by the sixth Congress [1897] has the purpose of providing the best practical conditions for the work of the organising the multi-lingual Austrian proletariat, in order to overcome the practical difficulties of linguistic diversity. In affirming the usefulness of full autonomy for the organisations of each language ... we create [etc.] ... we declare that this organisation is exclusively designed to create the most effective form in which ... the Social Democrats of all languages can conduct the struggle against the exploiting classes of their own nations and against the exploiting classes of all nations.*[24]

It is very characteristic of the Polish Party Executive that it made use of the Brno programme (leaving aside its ignorance of the material facts, which we have just demonstrated) to justify its denial of the right to exist of our autonomous organisation of the Jewish proletariat. We already pointed out above how

---

22 [Zarząd polskiej partyi socyalno-demokratycznej w Austryi 1905.]
23 Sozialdemokratische Arbeiterpartei Österreichs 1899, p. 836.
24 Sozialdemokratische Arbeiterpartei Österreichs 1897, p. 169. [Grossman's emphasis, apart from '*in autonomous national groups*' and '*usefulness of full autonomy*'.]

the Brno programme has been used in practice by our (socialist) opponents and how, in addition, an important section of that programme was simply suppressed ...

Because we have not set out a *separate* national programme but have a programme (a general programme and a Brno nationality programme) in common with Austrian Social Democracy, we are simultaneously suspected of separatism and accused of 'demagogic evasion'. And yet we stand strictly on the basis of the principles of *Austrian* Social Democracy, exactly as they are stated in the 1897 report on organisation. Comrade [Antonín] Němec also said on that occasion:

> I explicitly declare that I was defending myself against any suggestion that this [national organisation] is desired for national reasons ... I said that it was a matter here of the *practical* implementation of our decisions, of making improved action possible.[25]

The mode of struggle adopted by the Polish Social Democratic Party and their theory are in complete correspondence with each other. It would require a very long treatise to cover even a fraction of the accomplishments of their leaders and various 'organs' in fitting theory to practice. Their central organ (*Naprzód*) has set in motion a systematic campaign of defamation against us. The most hair-raisingly fabricated reports about knife fights, denunciations, 'independents'[26] and so on are served up, without mentioning any names, of course. The Polish socialist leaders also find time to slander Jewish trade unionists to the central trade union executives,[27] so that the latter act against Jewish workers in their trade union organisations on the basis of this false 'information'. The Polish socialists want to compel Jewish workers in the trade unions to pay party taxes to the Polish Party, although those workers do not want to belong to that Party (this is how these socialists view freedom). As a result of these circumstances, Jewish workers are then deprived of their right to be in a trade union. Two strikes, by Jewish painters and metalworkers, were brought to a successful conclusion but the Polish socialists instructed one of their 'organs' to write that we had called the strikes frivolously, for purposes of self-advertisement (!), despite the fact that the central trade union offices had approved of them.

25   Sozialdemokratische Arbeiterpartei Österreichs 1896, 162. [Grossman mistook the year of the Congress at which Němec made this statement. Grossman's emphasis.]
26   [Possibly a reference to the liberal Party of Independent Jews, based in Kraków.]
27   [JSDP members in Galicia led Jewish workers in local branches of the central trade unions, based in Vienna and associated with the Austrian Social Democratic Workers Party.]

We would prefer to spare our readers any further examples of this mode of struggle. All it does is demonstrate the moral bankruptcy of the slanderers who are attacking us; it is they alone who are thereby compromised and damaged!

Our activity so far (see our *Report to the Congress of the General Austrian Social Democratic Party in Vienna*)[28] is the best evidence not only that we have a right to an organisation, in line with 'The Report on the Justification',[29] in 1897, but also that our organisation is viable and worthy of preservation. We will not let ourselves be prevented by any obstacles whatever from continuing to work in the way we have chosen for the benefit of international socialism. We expect, however, that all the Austrian comrades who prefer not to give a hearing to the slanders 'unworthy of social democracy' that are thrown at us, will not fail to give our organisation recognition and equal rights.

∴

The report of the General Executive of Austrian Social Democracy contains the remark that the Jewish Social Democratic Party of Galicia has placed itself outside the General Austrian Party.[30] We find that this accusation contradicts the practice of Austrian Social Democracy. For example, the Ruthenian Social Democratic Party established itself in 1899 and on this view would also have stood 'outside' the list of national organisations within Austrian Social Democracy, as set out in the text of the 1897 statute. This did not prevent the [General Austrian] Party from taking note of its existence without any problem. We too, therefore, expect that we will not be deprived of our most basic requirements, contrary to the demands of justice and equity, on the basis of so-called formal pretexts.

---

28   [Jüdishe sozial-demokratishe Partei in Galitsien 1905a, see *Report to the Congress of the General Austrian Social Democratic Party in Vienna, 1905*, above, pp. 103–112.]

29   [Sozialdemokratische Arbeiterpartei Österreichs 1897, pp. 169–70.]

30   See Gesamtparteivertretung 1905, p. 9.

CHAPTER 8

The Jewish Social Democratic Party of Galicia*

Translated from Czech by Ben Fowkes

The Jewish Social Democratic Party of Galicia proclaimed its existence on 1 May 1905 and immediately instituted a series of festive May Day meetings, as well as a number of demonstrations held jointly with the Polish comrades, as a token of its solidarity with them. In Kraków, for example, up to 2,000 Jewish comrades took part in a demonstration. The Party was actually founded at a congress held in L'viv on 9 and 10 June 1905, attended by 52 delegates, three of them women.

The Congress was greeted by a cordial message from the Russian Union of Jewish Workers (the Bund), and *unanimously adopted as its programme the programme adopted* by Austrian Social Democracy at its Vienna Congress held in 1901, as well as the national programme of the Brno Congress of 1899. The [L'viv] Congress undertook to work on the basis of the general tactical line of Austrian Social Democracy, regardless of whether the latter officially recognised the Jewish Party or not. The Executive Committee was mandated to call for the recognition of the Party at the joint Congress of Austrian Social Democracy. The Congress condemned the manner in which the Polish Party was carrying on its fight against the new Party but affirmed the wish of the Jewish Party to co-exist with the Polish Party in an atmosphere of peace and cooperation. The new Party regards Zionism as a movement of the Jewish bourgeoisie aimed at stirring up chauvinistic feelings in the working class and obscuring its class consciousness; and for these reasons it will also fight with the utmost energy against Zionism in its 'socialist' guise.

By proclaiming the programme of the Party in this way the L'viv Congress also laid the foundations for the new organisation.

Why has the new Party been set up?

It is an undeniable fact that a Jewish nation exists in Austria alongside the German, Czech, Polish nations and so on. Social Democracy has always been able to come to terms with reality. Even if it did not initially take the existence of the different nations sufficiently into account, it soon made a thorough correc-

---

* As yet we have received only fragmentary news about this new organisation from the press of our Polish comrades. We are therefore publishing this informative article by the Secretary of the new Party, so that the Czech organisations do not have to rely on one-sided information – the Editorial Board. [The article was originally published as Grossman 1906.]

tion of this mistake. In 1897 Comrade [Victor] Adler used the following words to describe the way things had changed:

> If today you [read] the old pamphlets ... from the 1860s and 1870s you will find that the concepts 'international' and 'anational' are treated as the same. *The prevailing notion was that people could divest themselves of their history, their national identity*, and that the nation could be absorbed into a purely abstract concept of humanity ... What emerged from that approach is incidentally nothing other than the old bourgeois humanism and cosmopolitanism.[1]

This changed point of view found expression both in socialist theory and socialist practice. Its practical effect was the change in the organisation of Social Democracy in Austria which we experienced between 1889 and 1897 and which, taking account of national identities, culminated in the *transition from the centralised to the federal* form of organisation. This allowed the Party to adapt its agitation to national identities. We too proceeded from this practical viewpoint but the Polish Party declared that the division into national organisations did not arise out of practical needs, the interests of the class, but for national reasons, which we were unwilling to place in the forefront.

The change in the [General Austrian] Party's viewpoint nevertheless emerges plainly from the *new ideology*, of which the federation of autonomous national organisations is the exact expression. Its definitive formulation is contained in the following words spoken by [Engelbert] Pernerstorfer: 'In this sense of a real and genuine internationalism the idea will finally come into its own that one can be a good German, an excellent Slav, an enthusiastic Italian and, even so, a passionate, international social democrat.'[2]

Jewish nationality is a reality for us, not arrived at in a metaphysical way through speculations but was imposed upon us by our lived experience; *we therefore want this identity of ours to be taken into consideration in the same way as those of other nations* and, indeed, for the same practical reasons, which are required by the class interests of the Austrian proletariat. That is why we do not want to set up our own organisation in Bohemia or elsewhere in Austria, where the Jews only form a small percentage of the population or where they have become denationalised, but we do want an organisation where the *Jewish*

---

1 [Sozialdemokratische Arbeiterpartei Österreichs 1897, p. 78. Grossman's emphasis.]
2 *Arbeiter-Zeitung* 1897, p. 3.

proletariat constitutes a compact, unassimilated mass, as in Galicia where Jews form between 30 and 40 percent of the urban population.

This line of argument is so natural and so entirely consistent with the principles of the whole workers movement in Austria, which guarantee the *same* rights to all nations – for Social Democrats this is something that goes without saying – that it is inconceivable that what is regarded as correct for others is condemned as soon as Jews are involved. Yet that is what happened!

When the question of national organisations began to be discussed, between 1895 and 1897, it was pointed out in various quarters that this form of organisation was *not being created for national reasons* but on *practical* grounds.[3]

The same grounds have led to the creation of the Jewish Party: *we want to achieve better conditions for agitation by taking into account the Yiddish language*, we want to fight against the bourgeoisie of our own nation and against Jewish chauvinism and clericalism, we want to demand the right of self-determination, the better to be able to conduct our own class struggle.[4]

---

3   Adler said: 'We do not want there to be any doubt about the fact that our purpose in dividing this organisation into national groups is to be able to conduct the class struggle more vigorously because more internationally.' Moreover, the detailed justification of the change, submitted by Adler stated: '... the organisation of Austrian Social Democracy in autonomous national groups has the purpose of providing the *best practical conditions* for the work of the organising the multi-lingual Austrian proletariat, in order to overcome the practical difficulties of linguistic diversity. In affirming the usefulness of full autonomy for the organisations of every each *language* ... we also declare that this organisation is *exclusively* designed to create the most effective form in which the internationally minded and fraternally combined Social Democrats of all languages can conduct the struggle against the exploiting classes of *their own nations* and against the exploiting classes of all nations.'
     [Antonín] Němec said: 'When we submitted the proposal to alter the composition of the party's representative bodies so as to bring them into correspondence with existing conditions, I explicitly declared that I protest *against the assumption that this was happening for national reasons.* I said that what we were interested in was the practical implementation of our decisions, that we were aiming to make improved action in the future possible ... We should adopt this form of organisation so that *every nation may itself* be able to fight against its own bourgeoisie.'
     [František] Soukup: 'Our main reason for endeavouring to achieve this autonomy is that every nation must itself know best what is appropriate for it.'
     [Cf. the relevant passages in the German minutes of the 1897 Congress, which are not identical, Sozialdemokratische Arbeiterpartei Österreichs 1897, respectively pp. 169, 119, 124–5, Żydowska Partya Socyalno-Demokratyczna Galicyi 1905b, 'Reply to the Polish Social Democratic Party of Galicia', above, pp. 99, 101, 125. Grossman's emphasis.]
4   See our pamphlets Komitet Organizacyjny Żydowskiej Partyi Socyalno-demokraticyczney w Galicyi 1905, *What Do We Want*, above, pp. 73–82; and Żydowska Partya Socyalno-Demokratyczna Galicyi 1905a, which includes Żydowska Partya Socyalno-Demokratyczna Galicyi 1905b 'Reply to the Polish Social Democratic Party of Galicia', above, pp. 83–102.

But these reasons are not sufficient, as soon as Jews are involved! The Jews are required to provide in addition a special national program!

The Polish comrades maintain that the organisation of Social Democracy which was unanimously accepted at the Brno Congress (!) allegedly depends on a programme according to which every nation must have its own territory! But, as anyone who has even a rough idea of the history of the workers movement in Austria knows, the issue at stake in Prague in 1896 and in Vienna in 1897 was not the *territorial principle* but the language principle. We have also made this point clear to the Polish comrades: in our pamphlet *Before the Congress*[5] we cited a whole series of statements made at these Party Congresses, to which the representatives of the Polish Party were unable to give an answer.

When Comrade Daszyński wrote, in *Sozialistische Monatshefte*, about the conflict between the German and Polish Social Democrats in the Polish Empire[6] he expressed the following opinion: 'And this arrangement can only occur on the basis of formal equality between the two parties. *For social democrats there can be no other basis* and no comrade who thinks logically can desire formal dependence, e.g. of the Poles on the Germans'.[7] At that time, of course, it was a matter of equality for the Poles. In dealing with the Jews, in contrast, Daszyński permits not only a formal dependency on the Polish Party but a factual one as well.

Why then does the Polish Party so stubbornly oppose the Jewish Party, if our fundamental viewpoint is so clear and so much in line with the point of view of the other Social Democratic Parties in Austria?

I have already stated above that we regard the Jews as a nation, which, as such, must have the right to lay claim to independent and free development. And a social democrat ought not doubt the fact that the decision as to whether a group is a nation and should be regarded as a nation can only be made by that group itself. When, at a conference held in London between 10 and 12 September of this year, the Jewish workers associations which belonged to the Social Democratic Federation constituted themselves as a 'union of all Jewish social democratic groups in England', establishing as their party newspaper the London *Neue Zeit*,[8] the English workers placed no obstacles in the way of the Jewish workers' decision.

---

5 [Żydowska Partya Socyalno-Demokratyczna Galicyi 1905a, which includes 'Reply to the Polish Social Democratic Party of Galici', see above, pp. 83–102.]
6 [Here, 'the Polish Empire' means 'the Polish provinces of the German Empire'.]
7 [Daszyński 1902, p. 736. Grossman's emphasis. Daszyński emphasised *'formal equality'*.]
8 [*'Neue Zeit'* means *'New Times'*.]

But the Jewish proletarians in Galicia must have guardians, who think and speak for them. The Polish Party disputes the right of the Jews to develop themselves. *The Jews in Galicia have to be Poles*! The Polish Party denies that it has any appetite for domination and asserts that it has always satisfied the needs of the Jewish masses. That is, in fact, untrue but, even if it were true, would this be a reason not to allow the Jewish proletariat to determine its own fate? What would the Czech workers say if the German organisations wanted to busy themselves with agitation among the Czechs and claiming the Czechs did not need their own organisations?

The Jewish social democrats greeted the decisions of the Vienna and Prague Congresses with enthusiasm, because they hoped that the main obstacle to the development of the socialist movement among the Jewish proletariat would now be removed. Jewish conferences were held in 1899 and 1903, at which it was pointed out that organisationally no improvement had taken place in the Jewish situation, *since the movement had not received the autonomy* it requested. These efforts did not meet with success. For the Polish comrades characterised as 'Jewish separatism' what the Party programme called 'national identity' in dealing with the Germans, Czechs, Italians and so on. That is their name for *our wish to profess our membership of our own nation*. The Jews are not allowed to retain their nationality; they must abandon it at any cost. 'The preservation of Jewish peculiarities [!] is harmful', cried the official spokesperson Dr [Herman] Diamand. 'We must adopt new forms. The difficulties we sometimes encounter in Polish society cannot prevent us from doing this. We must work with all the means at our disposal for the disappearance of all aspects of strangeness. There are no distinctive Jewish qualities which need to be preserved'.[9]

According to the words of this Polish socialist, therefore, the Jews must give up their identity. Adler commented: 'As if a person could get rid of their history or national identity'. And why should this happen?

> There is no doubt that, owing to their *distinctive* moral and intellectual *qualities* and unique social position, the Jews play an important part in the socialist movement.
>
> ... It is enough to point out that the Jewish race does possess its own spiritual physiognomy, which finds its expression in a splendid power of abstraction and a keen critical intellect.

---

9 [*Naprzód* 1903, p. 3. There are some differences between this Czech and the German version of this originally Polish text, see *To the Social Democrats of Austria*, above, p. 117–118.]

It is owing to this that the Jews, since the time they entered into European civilisation, in proportion to their numbers, have given the world more great thinkers than, perhaps any other nation and the names of [Baruch] Spinoza, [David] Ricardo and Marx constitute epochs in the history of human thought.[10]

This is what [Karl] Kautsky wrote to the editorial board of the London *Neue Zeit*. And we are being asked to make an effort to get rid of this identity as soon as possible!

The Poles also deny that what they call 'Jargon'[11] is a language, because it contains so many German, Polish and Hebrew elements! But is a tongue spoken by eight to nine million people not a language? A language in which the lofty ideas of the revolution are understood; a language into which the classical works of modern literature have been translated; a language in which it is possible to read the *Communist Manifesto*, Marx's *Capital*, the Erfurt Program, Kautsky's *The Social Revolution* and so on?[12] Isn't all this enough to make our idiom a language? Is there then any difference at all between this denial and the Germans' talk of the need to 'eradicate' the 'inferior culture' of the Poles?

Of course, the Polish comrades maintain that they are doing the Jewish workers a favour by suppressing their 'Jargon' and imposing the Polish language on them. If the Germans want to spread the German language among the Poles of Prussia and Silesia they call it 'Germanisation'. But such behaviour towards the Jews is regarded as presenting them with the Polish language as a gift. Daszyński announced that the Poles do not want to 'Polonise' the Jews but to offer them rights to the Polish language, which intelligent Jewish socialists already use. What would our Polish comrades say if the German Hakatists[13] in Prussia were to say that they do not want to Germanise them but simply to give them the right to speak German, a language intelligent Poles have long been using?

In Russia, the Bund pointed out that all over Europe reactionaries have always placed obstacles in the way of the Jews' cultural development but never opposed their assimilation; it also quoted a circular issued by the Russian government stating that the movement to prevent the Jews from assimilating with other nations is harmful to the Russian state idea.

---

10   [Kautsky 1904. Grossman's emphasis; editor's interpolations.]
11   ['Jargon' was a pejorative term for Yiddish.]
12   [Marx and Engels 1976; Marx 1976b; Sozialdemokratische Partei Deutschlands 1891; Kautsky 1916.]
13   [The Hakata was a German chauvinist organisation formed in 1894 to eradicate Polish influence in the German-occupied provinces of partitioned Poland.]

In Galicia too the cultural development of the Jewish masses is seen as harming the 'Galician state idea', as is shown by a series of prohibitions, such as the ban on speaking Yiddish in meetings and the persecution of the Yiddish press etc.

The most important trump card that is played against us is Marx's 1843 essay on the Jewish question, which is still supposed to be entirely valid in the current situation. The world has undergone half a century of development, programmes and slogans have changed, conditions and institutions have changed, industrial Europe has changed and a mighty capitalism has arisen. The organised proletariat has mounted the world stage and it too has already undergone significant changes. And the Jews have not changed in the meantime? The waves of history have passed over without touching them?

At that time, Marx wrote: 'What is the essence of Judaism? Practical need and avarice. What is the secular religion of the Jews? Profit. What does the Jew worship? Money!'[14] *These are supposed to be the characteristics of the modern Jewish proletariat?*[15] Is this the way disputes between socialists should be conducted?

We are concerned that the Jewish proletariat should not be abandoned and neglected, that it should not fall into slumber and decay, and that it should become a strong link in proletariat, as Kautsky envisaged. But the Polish Party was not capable of awakening the Jewish proletariat. It did not even try. It is not possible to mention all the details here but it will perhaps be sufficient if we report the story of the Jewish Agitation Committee for Galicia. The Jewish conference of 1903 resolved that this Committee be set up. This was admittedly only a half-measure but it marked a certain advance because the movement would have gained a degree of concentration if this Committee had actually been established. But after the conference, as soon as the 'danger' of a Jewish Party had passed, the Polish Party left the Committee on paper. And the most recent Party Congress, held in 1904 in Kraków, even dissolved it! Now, after 1 May 1905 and the proclamation of the Jewish Social Democratic Party, the

---

14   [Marx 1975, pp. 169–70. In Marx's German original, the passage is slightly different: 'What is the mundane basis of Jewishness? Practical need, self-interest. What is the mundane worship of the Jew? Haggling. What is his mundane God? Money', Marx 1982, p. 164.]

15   How even an individual such as Marx can be mistaken is shown by his views about the Czech question. In 1852 he wrote: 'the Czech nation is doomed to die out, as is shown by numerous events of the last four centuries'. [It is now known that Engels rather than Marx wrote the article from which these words came, in English: 'dying Tschechian nationality – dying according to every fact known in history for the last four hundred years', Engels 1979a, p. 46.]

Executive of the Polish Party has again promised to establish this Committee, *contradicting its own previous decision*!

The Polish Party also used another method to ensure that the world did not come to know of the existence of Jews in Galicia: it drove the Jews away from its ranks. So now, when a separate party has been set up, it has no right to complain.

Despite all this, we immediately declared, at the very moment when we came into existence, that we wanted to remain in fraternal contact with the Polish Socialist Party,[16] and that we would act together with it wherever common action was necessary. But the Polish Party greeted us with insults and insinuations, to which we could not reply as we had no Party press of our own. Since they had no other weapons, the Polish socialists were not ashamed to employ violence and pressure where they were able to, against the defenceless and economically dependent Jewish workers' trade union organisations!

Relevant material on this point will be submitted to the Congress.[17] Here we only state that *the central trade unions,[18] which were supposed to protect workers, violently attacked members of our Party because of their political convictions.*

The Jews in Galicia must become Poles. If they do not, they will not be accepted into the trade unions and will thereby be compelled, against their wishes, to engage in strike breaking and the forcing down of wages.

By using this form of struggle, which is in glaring contradiction with the fundamental principles on which the modern workers movement has been built, it is of course possible to damage us. But it also does no less damage to the people who employ it, as it shatters the previously firm and unshakeable foundations of justice between nations which have existed among us.

---

16   [I.e. the PPSD.]

17   [Grossman's article was presumably written before the Congress of the General Social Democratic Workers Party of Austria in October 1905 but was published after it.]

18   [JSDP members in Galicia led Jewish workers in local branches of the central trade unions, based in Vienna and associated with the Austrian Social Democratic Workers Party.]

CHAPTER 9

Our Position on Electoral Reform*

Translated from Yiddish by Rick Kuhn

Comrades! When we came together a year ago to discuss and decide on our tactics, we had a very easy task, because it was very difficult, i.e. we could not then accurately predict the circumstances we would live through and the forces we would have at hand, to which we would have to adapt our tactics.

We had to start with the general principles which bind together every social democrat, whether in Berlin or Kraków. And as the chief principle we decided on was that we regard ourselves as a part of Austrian Social Democracy and its tactics would also be ours. During the past year we had the chance to evaluate the situation and the Executive had, in these circumstances, to determine tactics which it regarded as necessary for the well-being of the Jewish working class. I will present and attempt to justify these tactics and ask you to take note of them. Before I do that, we have to consider what we have to do now and in the near future: tactics are not actually ours but those of the General Party. The Congresses of the individual socialist organisations in Austria, however, may discuss these tactics to determine whether and to what extent the general positions reflect the concrete circumstances in which particular organisations find themselves, in order to correct these general principles. We have to do this all the more because we have no direct influence on the determination of the general tactics.

Electoral Reform

Comrades! The past year has been a year of struggle for univeral suffrage. Our Party has conducted an enormous amount of educational agitation through meetings, proclamations and the press. You know the course of this movement, you know each of its phases and you know the current situation. So I won't repeat what we have said countless times before. All of us are aware that this necessary franchise must become a *reality*, just as it is a necessity in our *thoughts*.

---

* [Originally published as Grossman 1906b, report of Grossman's speech to the second Congress of the JSDP. The ellipses are those of the reporter.]

I will shortly explain our interest in this matter. When [Paul] Gautsch had to resign, when it became known that [Konrad] Hohenlohe, 'the red prince' would take over his post, many held their breath, thinking: finally, finally. But those who knew Austria's political history did not cease to doubt. We recall the very similar situation in Count [Eduard] Taafe's time, when electoral reform was laid on the parliamentary table and then too, it was defended by a red – indeed not a prince, but a red excellency (Dr [Emil] Steinbach).[1] The reform failed.[2] Since that time the workers movement has made collosal progress; its power and desire to struggle has grown terrifically. What do the idiotic defenders of the current order want? So long as privilege survives, the state can go to the devil – that is the practical side of their 'loyalty', which they talk about all the time. And we see that Hohenlohe resigned, more accurately he, like Gautsch, had to resign, thanks to the intrigues of the 'Polish Club' and related swindlers. The Hungarian question is given as the reason; the question of an automous tariff. There is also an element of truth in that. But there is no doubt at all that Hohenlohe *only used the opportunity to resign with honour, given the growing disturbances over the question electoral reform*, that is *in relation to the issue for which he was appointed*. Let us not be taken for fools: the reform is threatened. Now the moment approaches when the proletariat will have to intervene. If the situation does not improve *in the nearest future* – and the parliament does not preside over one of life's surprises – then the proletariat will have to take the last legal step in its struggle and this step will be

The General Mass Strike

by the *peoples of Austria* (sustained bravos), which has been discussed by us on many occasions over the past period. So my task is easier. I will only emphasise one circumstance. What is the place of the general strike amongst the weapons of the working class? An understanding of this circumstance is a warning to the ruling class – and it will suddenly illuminate the situation in which we find ourselves like lightning.

We know that, no matter how long it takes, the extent of rights corresponds exactly to the degree of strength; we know every social class has as many rights as it has the courage to use its power to conquer. This is also true of the proletariat, power is our right. (Applause) The capitalist order will be made to recognise that it has to reckon with the demand for abstract justice.

---

1 [The parliament referred to is the Reichsrat, the lower house of the Austrian legislature.
2 [In 1893.]

But the rising proletariat must first *create* this power and in doing so *prove*, by means of demonstrations, protests etc., because to exercise power is often also to create it, because its exercise has an agitational effect. Finally, at a certain stage of development, we start to *use* the accumulated power. The development of relations in Europe and most recently in Russia absolutely illustrate this.

Revolution and Legal Struggle

But the use of power takes different forms. There were times when the proletariat fought with weapons on the barricades. Then weapons gave way to ballot papers. Now we are preparing for a mass strike which is again the prelude to active revolutionary struggle. That is the dialectic of history: after a period of active revolution there is a period of legal struggle that again gives way to revolutionary struggle. We can therefore say that legal struggle prepares for illegal struggle. That is, a period of *accumulating* forces prepares the way for the moment when a revolutionary outbreak opens a period when rights are extended.

We are not therefore supporters of revolution for revolution's sake. Nor are we supporters of legality for the sake of legality. Barricades and ballot papers are, for us, equally good. They are only means to our end of gaining rights for the oppressed working class. The period of revolutionary struggle lasted up to 1848. Parliamentarism was discredited in the romance countries, Spain, France and Switzerland. But we should consider what Engels wrote in the preface to Marx's *Class Struggles in France: 1848–1850*.[3] In the period since the German proletariat achieved the right to vote, it has gone from one triumph to the next. Since then there has been a change in the form of the proletariat's struggle across the world. The period of legal struggle arrived. 'The ballot paper replaced the barricade'. But if the bourgeoisie thinks we are obsessed with legality it has made a great mistake and demonstrated, yet again, its incapacity for dialectical thought. The time is coming when we will again shake things up with the former revolutionary zeal. The mass strike, *the last step on the legal path, is the first step of the revolution!* The modern mass revolution of the proletariat has to start with the proletariat leaving the factories and the basements, in which it is confined, and going out onto the streets. Whatever forces the proletariat to leave the factories, mines, workshops and basements, whatever forces it onto the street, that pushes it into revolution. When they force us to say A, they should not be amazed that we say B. Comrades we do not make empty threats

---

3   [Engels 1990c.]

that we cannot carry out. Such threats are stupid. But we should make clear what the step before which we stand signifies and we warn the bourgeoisie about its consequences. In initiating a general strike we know what we are starting but we don't know how it will end. The person who can start and end a revolution at will has not been born. And indeed this is because a mass movement has its own laws of development independent of the desires of individuals and even of organised parties. Once the wave is set in motion, we have to ride it and that is our task, but we won't adopt this course if we don't want to be swept along. That is what we tell our enemies today. Learn while there is time! The proletariat is losing *patience*. If the electoral reform is definitely put aside, anyone who recalls the period of Count Taaffe would have to say: wouldn't things have been better if this right had been granted then? Why did this defeat and the outrage of so many forces happen? Why so many sacrifices in vain? And when the stifling political atmosphere of that time, which suffocated us, is remembered, a better cry arises like a storm: enough now! We have run out of patience. We can't think of waiting now. The reform or a life and death struggle! In the current situation, with such a mood amongst the masses and when we Social Democrats, that is the most conscious section of the proletariat, *do not want to lose our influence over them, we have to take account of this mood.* We know that we *must gain voting rights or our influence over the masses will be lost for years to come.* We say that openly. And so have to place everything on this card. And there is no sacrifice which we are not prepared to take bare. And we will not retreat until we have won. *The mass strike is a necessity.* (Bravo) And when many ask about the possibility of a strike in our agragian province, with hardly any industry and the limited strength of our trade unions, on the one hand, we will point to Russia. And we will ask: where are the large industries there? Where are the important trade unions? And yet Russia is the classic land of the mass strike! And, on the other hand, we will point to the *mood* of our masses and we say that is our power, that is the guarantee for the mass strike. It will help us to fulfil our duty, as a party and as a working class. (Ceaseless applause).

In the spirit of these remarks, I move the following resolution:

The Congress resolves
    Only the full democratisation of Austria, whose first condition is general, equal, direct and secret elections, will give the Austrian proletariat the possibility of developing its economic and social powers, and successfully conducting its proletarian class policies. For this reason and despite the various inadequacies and flaws in the regime's electoral reform proposal, we regard this proposal as the first step in eliminating antiquated

electoral privileges, which are damaging for the proletariat, and as the first attempt to democratise the state.

Therefore, in accord with the tactics of the General Austrian Social Democratic Party, the Jewish proletariat will, on the call of the Executive of the Jewish Social Democratic Party, engage in energetic struggle for the people's rights and will join the general mass strike in Austria.

Our Tactics

And now comrades, I come to the second part of my presentation. From the current situation I will turn to the past and will defend the tactics we applied over the last year. Comrades! The entire forces and power of social democracy as the vanguard of the entire working class relies on clarity about its goals and the means for achieving them. Our entire task, then, is focussed on bringing consciousness into heads. Consciousness in heads that is the greatest *revolutionary* deed we can achieve. So, the moment the electoral proposal appeared, we had to fulfil two tasks. On the one hand, we had to deal with the whole complex of questions to which the electoral reform gave rise, with the other different electoral proposals made by various parties. For example, with plural, proportional voting; national curia; representation of interests; etc. And we came out in favour of general, equal, direct and secret elections. (Bravo) On the other hand, while fighting with all our energy for this electoral reform, we have indicated its significance for the proletariat, the limits of the advantages it brings. We have underlined these limits so that *confusion*, our greatest enemy, does not arise. Particularly where a radical abolition of *national conflicts* was expected, we have demonstrated that general and equal suffrage is not a final answer to the question but its *precondition* and that it has to be supplemented with a series of institutions before peace between the peoples of Austria finally emerges.

The Executive conducted a special and extensive discussion of this question at a series of sessions and in the press, which I will try to outline in brief.

I will not mention those suggestions, whose damage to the people has been absolutely apparent and I will only consider with two prosals with which we Jewish socialists have had to deal, because they came from two Jewish parties. I have in mind

Proportional Elections

in national curia. Before I discuss this, I want to draw attention to one matter. When Dr [Adolf] Gross of Kraków raised the slogan of proportional represent-ation, *Naprzód*'s report of his speech placed a question mark in parentheses (?) after the word [proportional].[4] *Naprzód* identified proportionality as some-how a kind of creature, of whose existence in the world it had just become aware for the first time. These ignoramuses only live off the literary section of the *Arbeiter-Zeitung*; if proportional representation is explained there, then the 'learned men' of *Naprzód* also want to effuse the light of the holy spirit.[5] It is a fact that Deputy [Ignacy] Daszyński and the gentlemen of *Naprzód* have *to this day said nothing at all about the question of proportional representation*.

Now I will go on to the issue itself. I refer those who read German to the impressive explanations of the issue by Advocatus in the second volume of *Neue Zeit* of 1895.[6] Although the recent literature on the franchise has been enormous, no-one has gone further than Advocacatus or written anything new. Proportionalists are fanatical and enthusiastic about justice. In truth and vir-tue, they base themselves on Mirabeau's article 'the parliament is to the nation what a scale map to its physical extent; whether in part or as a whole, the copy must always have the same proportions as the original'.[7] Justice and truth are the slogans of the proportionalists. But I ask why do they only want justice in the *franchise* for the parliament and not in *the form* of voting in the parliament? Dr Gross says that voting for candidates in elections is somehow different from voting [in the parliament]. The speaker [i.e. Grossman] polemises against Dr Gross's statements and underlines our class standpoint in this question. It is not worth going into the technical side of this form of representation. It does not matter who votes first if it is a adopted as a means of solving the national question in the parliament! Not even the best electoral system will eliminate national conflict but only the reform of the parliament itself. But more on that later. Now on to

---

4 [*Naprzód* (*Forwards*) was the daily newspaper of the Polish Social Democratic Party, in Kraków.]

5 [*Arbeiter-Zeitung* (*Workers' Newspaper*) was the daily organ of the German-Austrian Social Democratic Party in Vienna. The sentence sarcastically portrays uninformed *Naprzód* writers' pathetic efforts to appear profound.]

6 [Advocatus (Paul Vogt) 1895. *Neue Zeit* (*New Times*) was the theoretical journal of the Social Democratic Party of Germany.]

7 [Mirabeau 1834, p. 7.]

Zionism

There is a party here, the Narodowa Demokracja,[8] a party of conjurors who switch their positions almost every day. The joke of this Party does not end there. On the contrary, all they understand is taking impertinence to the extreme and scolding: [']what, we changed our position? You moved away from and [then] approached us. That's how the optical illusion arises. We, however, have been in the same place forever!['] The Zionists play the same role in Jewish society. A party of true attention seekers and political comedians, patented saviours of the people. Today Dr Gross proposes proportional representation, they do too. Tomorrow, [Benno] Straucher proposes national curia, they do too etc. (Bravo) Initially, when we demanded rights for people, they were hostile. Both Republican France and despotic Russia oppress the Jews. What then is the point of political rights in the diaspora? And instead of strengthening the political consciousness of the Jewish masses they have weakened it and wrenched it away in a different direction ... For years they have wanted to hear nothing about a contemporary political program or about universal, equal suffrage.[9]

[']Zionism is above all other parties. All true Jews will find a place in our ranks, without regard to their political party.['] They came shamefully late to people's rights. They had no interest in the people, because they have been deprived of rights they are weak, so they had no value at all for them. So they started by proving that there is no Jewish proletariat ... it would be an interesting matter, [which happened] not so long ago, to remind the world about this and I am in favour of placing the Zionists in Galicia on the agenda of the next Congress. (Bravo)

And only when this Jewish and non-Jewish proletariat, deprived of all rights, started to win rights through struggle did it have value for the Zionists. Then it became worthwhile for them to concern themselves with it. They therefore suddenly caught up and declared themselves in favour of universal suffrage. But not for proportional representation. The speaker cites an article in *Wschód* 42, of 1905,[10] where the Zionists came out explicitly against proportional representation. In *Wschód* of 1 November 1905, they demanded proportional representation and, in number 51 of 20 December, they already criticised their earlier

---

8   [Narodowa Demokracja (National Democracy) was a nationalist, antisemitic party.]
9   [Until recently, the Austrian Zionists had argued that involvement in Austrian politics was a diversion from the project of constructing a Jewish homeland in Palestine.]
10   [*Wschód* (*East*) was a Zionist weekly in Kraków.]

position, without admitting this change. Having buried their own position of yesterday, they found a new panacea and proclaimed it anywhere and everywhere in a resounding proclamation: 'We demand the recognion of our nation. And, in accord with the idea of justice and in support of our national minorities, we demand that national curia should be established',[11] in *Wschód* number 50 of 13 December 1905. And again this comedy: whoever is against curia is a traitor to the people. But even that was not their last position. And you, comrade Meysels, defend these curia, do not forget that you even outdo the Zionists. Why, when our Party has energetically protested against a national curia for Jews and entered into the struggle against the Zionists, these gentlemen have again withdrawn these curia. For a long time 'the postulate of Jewish existence' was somehow less important than to now (number 2 of 1906) demand *in the case* (!) that the electoral reform establishes national curia or national electoral districts, the separate Jewish nation should *also* be taken into consideration – such a one for Jewry – by coincidence and finally if we have come out even more strongly against these curia and we have counterposed the national cultural autonomy of peoples to them a further phenomenon is apparent. And they already want autonomy for the Jews, why not? And the curia would be the start of autonomy! This is how they have changed their perspective six times in three months ... A perspective every two weeks! A Jewish curia will introduce autonomy. Anything that is Jewish, even if it is dirty and detestable, is good because it is autonomy. If these gentlemen are given Jewish police and Jewish commissioners, they will cry out that it is salvation, because it is Jewish autonomy ...

The speaker discussed the harmfulness of national curia. Anyone for whom our critique of national curia is not sufficient should read over the Zionists' own commentary on the idea. In *Wschód* 52 of 13 December 1905, we read 'that theory condemns professional groups on the gounds that parliament does not represent interests but is rather the expression of the sovereign power of the people, which does not depend on individuals' occupations'. So far: correct.

'But groupings of the population and [political] parties which defend particular interests or particular strata can also, for the same reason, not play any role at all'! And they bring such idiocy into the world. Political parties can play no role at all in a parliamentary institution!! And now the crowning idiocy: 'Only [!] groups which include the fabric of all social interests, which consist of all strata and efforts should be able to express themselves and they are *national groups*.'

---

11   [The curia proposed were national chambers of parliament.]

The oil has risen to the surface. This idea of national curia in its naïve frankness cannot be credited. Comrade Meysels, I congratulate you! And you ask, comrade Meysels, what would happen if the Viennese comrades came out in favour of national curia? That question is the same as saying 'what would happen if they rejected the socialist program?'

National curia are also supposed to be a means to recognise

The Jews as a People!

Don't laugh! It is sad to find someone in our ranks who allowed himself to be caught by this turn of phrase. What would happen if we were recognised *as a people*?

Until 1857 Jews were statistically recognised as a nation. Was this a period of happiness for Jewish people? But comrade Meysels I want to state, with full emphasis, that workers' time and efforts are too precisious to be used in academic games about 'recognition' even if the gentlemen of the Zionist fraternities dabble in such matters. (Bravo)

The state is not a scientific institution which can issue judgements on such matters. If we have the courage to recognise that we are a people, no-one will take that away from us. For us, abstract 'recognition' has no point at all. We struggle for real rights and the recognition of them will come soon! Next, the speaker discussed the third proposal, for

Nationally Uniform Electorates

and demonstrated that these are also not a means to solve the national question. It is not possible to talk about uniform national electorates here. Let us imagine that such electorates are granted. How is the parliament somehow changed? Why would national struggles disappear? How would majorities disappear? Again this fundamental question and again this fundamental answer. At best, national frictions can be diminished during the elections [themselves]. But even that won't happen for long, because how can life be made to comply? How can the enormous wave of population movement be stopped? Who can guarantee us that the national electorate of today will not be a conglomerate of peoples tomorrow? History teaches us much. The speaker demonstrated with statistics how [formerly] nationally homogenous countries are now inhabited by several nations.

We note that uniform or non-uniform electorates will *not* eliminate national struggles.

But we have only done half of our work if we only *criticise*. On the contrary, we point out a positive path to the solution of the national question and the elimination of national struggles, to the extent possible under the capitalist order:

Cultural Autonomy

of nations. Parliament itself therefore has to be reformed. Today a majority also has the right to decide on the sort of (national) matters that *should not* be determined by the domination of the majority. *So let us remove these matters from the central parliament's authority and hand them over to special institutions established for each people.*

Let us limit the responsibility of the central parliament in favour of the self-determination of each people in national affairs. Only in this way can fear of domination by the majority and the potential for domination by the majority be removed. Only in this way will peace betweeen the nations of Austria be a possibility. The central parliament will deal with genuinely common economic and political matters. Economic interests don't depend on whether I am a Jew, a Pole or a German. Rather, my relation to them will be determined by the class I belong to. However far this idea is from being realised, everyone knows it has to be realised if Austria is not to fall apart. Freed from national conflicts the central parliament will become, as it should be, a field *of utterly unobscured class struggle.*

The institutions thus established for cultural autonomy will deal with national needs, with schools and with everthing to do with schools.

And it has been typical, comrades, when I discussed this at a meeting with a PPSer,[12] that he said: 'What sort of affairs will this institution deal with[?] Only with educational matters[?]'

Comrades! This institution will deal 'only' with educational matters. And that is said in a province striken by poverty and illiteracy. The primary school is the basis of existence and here, in the classical land of ignorance, that is a trivial matter not worth discussing. It is forgotten that this most important social institution should be close to the children, better adapted to their psyches and consciousnesses, not to mention that its language must be intelligible to them.

---

12   ['PPSer' here refers to a member of the Polish Social Democratic Party of Galicia, although the PPS, Polska Partia Socjalistyczna (Polish Socialist Party) was the name of the national-ist, socialist organisations in the German- and Russian-occupied provinces of Poland with which the leadership of the PPSD sympathised.]

And I fear that years, long years will pass and we still won't have such schools. Only cultural autonomy can fulfil this task. We are happy with the electoral reform. It takes the people's cause a step forward. But our duty is to demonstrate that this reform will not eliminate national struggles but will be the first step on that path. We have fulfilled this duty over the past year and so I ask you to bring our tactics to mind and propose the following resolution, which clarifies our fundamental standpoint in the face of the electoral reform to the extent that it is concerns national matters.

For reasons of principle, the Congress declares

> Any attempt to put an end to damaging national struggles in Austria, which make any practical parliamentary activity impossible and obscure the class consciousness of the proletariat, will be a half-measure and remain without success, to the extent that it seeks to reduce national frictions outside the parliament (during elections) and not *in the parliament*. Not only the regime's proposal for 'nationally uniform' electoral districts but also proposals for proportional representation and national curia etc., from elsewhere, have this goal.
>
> The basis of national struggles in the parliament arises from that fact that *in the parliament* there are numerous national minorities, which fear domination by the majority in matters of their real or perceived national needs. The only way to restore the central parliament to health is to eliminate the possibility of domination by the majority on national questions. And we therefore demand that those functions which serve to satisfy national-cultural needs be removed from the central parliament and we require that they be assigned separately to each people.
>
> The central parliament, freed of purely national matters will only deal with matters which are of *common concern for all peoples*, economic, social-political affairs etc. It will become the appropriate field in which to develop the now unobscured class struggle. In a word, we require what the theory of political rights known under the name of the cultural autonomy of nations.

Instead of national dissension, which damages the class struggle, we want peace among peoples, which will create the possibility for the political class struggle of the proletariat. (Sustained, continuing applause)

CHAPTER 10

On Our Agitation and Propaganda: A New Phase in Our Movement*

Translated from Yiddish by Rick Kuhn

Hardly three months have passed since the last Congress[1] and its positive outcomes are apparent in every respect. Our organisations have grown significantly and increased in strength.

Our two Congresses have been two steps on our road. The Congress of 1905[2] was the first free movement of slaves who had freed themselves from their chains. We had to erect a house right over our heads. We therefore created an *organisation*. It was not the best and was not complete but it was what was possible under the circumstances. It had very important tasks which it completely fulfilled. We have to thank this organisation for our survival, during the *difficult period* which followed its birth, and for our success in repelling attacks from all sides. We survived the attacks of the socialist and non-socialist Zionists, the most violent attacks by the PPSers[3] in the press and in the trade unions, the oppressive and vicious 'arguments', public and private slanders. We survived all this without having *any* organ at all that could defend us, which could immediately refute the slanders hurled at us. Not one of the comrades clenched their fists in a faint and asked 'when will our monthly newpaper come out?'! And not only did we do all that, we also did our work, we held meetings, we agitated and led strikes and boycotts not only in Kraków and in L'viv but also across the province. In a word, we grew, we strode ever forward until the great political movement for electoral reform came. Our, in Galician circumstances, powerful agitation showed that we, a young party, had become a force and that in the political life of Galician Jews, as in the life of the province, we play a significant role which grows stronger every day.

And those who prophesied in their little newspapers that we would not survive so much as two months had to observe how their desires were blown away

---

* The article by Comrade Grossman which will end in the next issue concerns a *very important question* in the life of our Party and we are opening a discussion on this matter. [Originally published as Grossman 1906c.]

1   [The second Congress of the JSDP, on 30–31 May 1906, in L'viv.]

2   [On 9–10 June 1905, in L'viv.]

3   [I.e. members of the Polish Social Democratic Party, PPSD.]

like feathers in the wind and had to observe our *second Congress, in L'viv*, at which there were delegates from almost the *entire* conscious and organised Jewish proletariat in Galicia. This Congress, at which there were also delegates from the Bund and Bukovina, forced the entire bourgeois press to pay attention to us, which irritated *Naprzód*[4] intensely. We have become a *political factor* in the province. If the first Congress *built* a structure, the second *instituted* greater unity, greater coherence in the Party and achieved a degree of confidence: our belief in our own power grew and hence also our desire for and courage in struggle. The most serious political discussions, which also concerned national problems, deepened and internally united [us in our] perspectives. That also had great significance, as the Zionist-PPS alliance had long worked (each in its own and particular interest) to cause chaos in our Party. These perspectives are relevant, because they sought to divert us onto the path of nationalism. The discussion at the Congress handled them appropriately and also demonstrated, beyond what we anticipated, a significant growth in our intellectual forces among the workers.

Returning home from our Congress, we were in a stonger position, to the extent that we have not had to consider the tenth Congress of the PPS in L'viv, where the latest rescue attempt was made by giving the Jews a 'Section' ... From every corner of the province, the Executive received letters, in which enormous consciousness and the understanding of the PPSers' shameless twisting in their changes of front were apparent in our ranks. A number of these letters unanimously make an admirable comparison between the Section and the Duma! Both in relation to the way in which it was granted and its competence, and also the way in which it can be dissolved just like the latter ...[5]

In a word, it was apparent that the Executive did not need to take any action over this matter. The PPS has lost the last skerrick of trust that it previously enjoyed among the Jewish masses and it has become clear and established that *from this time on we are no longer threatened*, our movement has sent down its roots so deep that we are in general secure from danger in this period. Now we can deploy more forces in *another direction* and, in truth, after the Congress we can see a progessive but steady *growth in the breadth* [of our movement].

---

4 [*Naprzód* (*Forwards*) was the PPSD's daily newspaper in Kraków.]

5 [The PPSD attempted to regain influence among Jewish workers by setting up a Jewish section subordinate to it. 'The Executive' refers to the leadership of the JSDP. The Russian Tsar had conceded an elected but undemocratic Duma/parliament, with very limited powers and no control over the government, in 1905, in order to derail the revolutionary movement. The first Duma, from its inception in April until its dissolution by the Tsar in July 1906, achieved nothing.]

A series of new organisations are emerging; from new shtetleykh[6] we receive requests for us to take them up. That is a very pleasing and unusual development for those who know Galician passivity and somnolence and is thus proof of the *growing trust* in our Party, even among the masses which are still outside the organisation. Over the one and a half years of our existence we have gained solid ground under our feet. We have experienced the trust the masses have in us. We have won this real authority, which is not harmful, by means of continuous and conscientious work. This phase in our movement sets new tasks for us.

The Jewish workers movement in Galicia is not new and already has a good few years behind it. It was a major mistake for the Jewish workers movement that on many occasions when work among the Jews was begun it was only conducted in a few larger towns. The movement was limited to them and it did not go further. After a certain time the movement collapsed in these few towns and, after another few years, the process was restarted and so on without end. Pitiful economic relations were in part to blame and there is no question that economic developments amongst the Jews have changed a great deal, to their advantage, over the past 15 years. Primarily, however, the blame lies with the PPS alone. It never understood the the Jewish masses' life circumstances and treated them like the Polish masses. Invariably they underestimated the remoter areas: 'what, these 30 tailors in Chrzanów or the 20 people in Wieliczka or in Mostyska should be the material we work with?[7] Should we waste our efforts on them?' They did not, therefore, work in the remoter areas and when the more conscious individuals in the larger towns emigrated to America and also to the 'centres', the movement collapsed ... The movement was never able to overcome this 'vunerable point'. The falseness of this path was always apparent to us and today we have organisations in localities where no PPSer's has ever set foot. But I want to draw particular attention to this circumstance and demonstrate how great a significance it has for the entire structure of our movement.

In our *Report to the Congress of the General Austrian Party* in 1905,[8] we already demonstrated that the modern workers movement, apart from its normal consequences, is the factor which has a revolutionary influence on the economic evolution of Galicia, *drives* the general development of the province.

---

6 ['Shtetleykh' is the plural of shtetl, Yiddish for a 'small Jewish town'.]
7 [Chrzanów and Wieliczka were Jewish towns in western Galicia (today southern Poland), Mostyska in eastern Galicia (today western Ukraine).]
8 [Jüdishe sozial-demokratishe Partei in Galitsien 1905a, see *Report to the Congress of the General Austrian Social Democratic Party in Vienna, 1905*, above, pp. 103–112.]

In a province where the agrarian interests of the szlachta[9] mean that they use every method to restrict the development of industry, the only counterweight is the workers movement which revolutionises even the most remote provinces.

Perhaps no other socialist party is as dependent on economic conditions as the Jewish Party. The poverty of workers is the greatest enemy of the movement and the Jewish workers live in the *greatest* poverty. Workers in remoter areas have earned starvation wages and worked 16–20 hours a day for so long that they try, as soon as possible, to be free of this employment by becoming masters and exploiting others in the way they themselves have been exploited or by moving to a larger town. And if they can do neither and have to remain workers where they are, they have no desire to belong to an organisation because they are tired and exhausted from over-work and, even if they want to, they cannot because they do not have the time.

Only the improvement of the current situation, reduced working hours and increased wages, will make the existence of these slaves more bearable. That also affects the expansion of the extent of the Jewish working class in remoter areas. It facilitates proletariatisation and creates the very possibility of a workers movement. The conditions of existence of the Jewish masses therefore show us that, before anything else, we have to deal with the creation of a stronger *union movement.*

Given the general situation in the province we [have to] eliminate or at least limit another aspect of Galician life, which has so far undermined the Jewish workers movement almost everywhere, and that is *emigration.* So long as workers in the remoter areas earn a starvation wage for 16–20 hours of labour a day they will escape, beginning a series of movements from the smallest to the largest Galician towns. They move to them very willingly, because they find better conditions there than at home. They also *push wages down* there. And, if they are absorbed into an organisation, become conscious and fight with great effort in a strike for a better situation then others come from the remoter areas and push wages down again. That unnecessarily increases the workers' struggles. It makes the situation insecure. When they really have already become conscious and have greater cultural needs, which they did not have in the little shtetl and which they cannot now fulfil due to low earnings, they emigrate to Vienna, Germany, London, Paris and America. Like many other intelligent workers over the last 10 years, they leave Galicia! The way this has affected the organisations in the larger towns is not difficult to explain.

---

9   [The szlachta was the Polish gentry.]

There is another very important aspect of this problem. There, where one can shout and others must remain silent, only one thing can be heard. Because we do not even have an organ to spread information in Vienna, nothing has been heard about us there until recently and now not much. The slanders in *Naprzód* are believed. In the trade union organisations we have the possibility of showing the Viennese our *power*, in relation to facts which are accessible to them, and the lies of *Naprzód* that we do not exist at all etc. cannot be sustained.[10] But we cannot show them our power only when trade union organisations take action in which we participate. How often has it happened that, at a congress in which our delegates take part, the Viennese and other participants become convinced that our movement is purely social democratic and, that, at the same time, the slanders of *Naprzód* and the PPSers in general are exposed. And it is even more common that the same people who both participate in trade unions and political agitation, like our comrades [David] Winitz, [Moyshe] Papier, Schoenherz, Gruber and Mehlzak etc. are recognised in Vienna as courageous workers and social democratic trade unionists. It is to our advantage when *Naprzód*[11] throws dirt, accusing us of being 'separatists', parasites because in Vienna they know how much these slanders can be believed. The best proof of that is the most recent Congress of the Austrian tailors, where our delegates were present and the PPSers suffered a complete defeat. This Congress also showed how 'recognition' of our Party comes about. This Congress shows that in Vienna they do not take *Naprzód* so seriously, that the Viennese trade unionists will not damage trade union organisations in accordance with the PPSers' fantasies and that our real power is beginning to be taken into account. It is therefore ever more clearly apparent that we have to build trade union organisations everywhere possible. That is the basis of our movement!

But while our movement expands our difficulties also grow. Our tasks increase, agitation becomes more diverse and expensive and requires greater efforts, more agitators, literature, travel expenses etc. Where will it all come from? That is the burning practical question which requires an immediate answer.

---

10   [Grossman is contrasting the appreciation and recognition of Jewish workers' branches of the central trade unions by the leaderships of these social democratic unions in Vienna with the still hostile attitude of the leadership of the General Austrian Social Democratic Party to the JSDP.]

11   [*Naprzód* was the PPSD's daily newspaper in Kraków.]

[Part 2]

In order to fulfil all the tasks set out in the first part of this article, prayers[12] are necessary. Where will it come from, that is a question. Should we seek the philospher's stone? Should we recall those superstitious times, when the greatest scholars of the epoch, led by some indominable force, with unheard-of endurance sought virgin ground, this miraculous and mysterious means, which in the hands of a sage can transmute [matter] into glittering gold? The 'science' which rejuvenates the body and extends life? The contemporary working class is a long way from such ideas – only our bourgeoisie follows dreams about gold; the proletariat knows that its future and its good fortune are not dependent on money ... which cannot ... be its *goal* or a means to the goal.[13] Its political defence is not the National Fund[14] and also not paid up capital in banks but rather the organised *class struggle*, the successive clashes between the proletariat and the bourgeoisie, which has been more unified and coordinated, growing more and more into a gigantic power, until a gigantic, extreme struggle breaks out all along the line. Money is not significant in our movement as a political means, it is rather a simple *technical* means. As such it is necessary for us but it does not fall to us from the sky. It can, rather, only be a *result* of our struggle itself, for *which* it is indeed necessary. There is a series of causes and consequences which affect *each other* and are dependent on each other.

If Social Democracy as an organisation of the *proletariat* first of all defends its own interests, it does not follow that, at certain times, it cannot also be the *political* expression of other layers of the society, e.g. of the intelligentsia, petty bourgeoisie etc. The bourgeoisie is not homogenous; it is made up of different layers and classes, whose interests are in part contradictory, like, for example, the interests of the petty bourgeoisie and bourgeoisie. Naturally, in this struggle, the petty boureoisie is condemned to annihilation. It is a declining class and can have no independent political significance in the long term, while on the other hand the proletariat, also in struggle against the big bourgeoisie, is an indendent, growing class. The declining petty bourgeoisie is therefore forced to follow behind the growing power of the proletariat in which it sees its political protector. We have to understand this. We cannot only be a party of wage workers or only a certain number of loosely allied *associations* and organisations in different towns. While that was understood at the start of our movement's organisational life, we should not forget that our task is to be a *people's*

---

12   ['Prayers' seems to be slang for 'money'.]

13   [This sentence satirises Zionism and is not clear in the copy of the newspaper available.]

14   [I.e. the Jewish National Fund, set up in 1901 to finance Jewish colonisation in Palestine.]

movement in the broad sense of the word. Only then will we be able to have decisive political influence, *only then will we have the extensive material means about which* I have spoken. As a result of the growth of the moral influence of the Party, not only on the mass of workers but also on the petty bourgeoisie and bourgeois circles which sympathise with the workers movement, material means flow into the Party. While the power of German Social Democracy, for example, does not lie in accumulated money but in the *consciousness and the breadth* of its movement, nevertheless its material means are the touch-stone of its power, of its influence and its technical *movement.*

And precisely in this regard, we have done nothing! If you read the correspondence in the *Sotsial-Demokrat*[15] carefully, you will see that we do not take an interest in general affairs of the province or particular towns. In the correspondence, all you can read about is the *internal* affairs of our organisations, about the general economic or political relations in a particular town. Nothing or almost nothing is written about the municipal council, the kahal, local Polish or Ruthenian politicians, their policies in the Sejm or Reichsrat.[16] I draw attention to this *defective aspect* of our movement. If its bad consequences have not yet been evident then they may be deadly for us during the era of universal suffrage. A broader outlook is necessary. It can turn us into a people's movement, it can generate material means and political influence![17]

And now a second matter. The hopes for the development of our movement, which we picture, and the influence that we will win through it does not free us at all from the Party duties, which we already have to fulfil today. I will not mention the names of any particular individuals but I will emphasise that precisely those who complained most about the Executive at the last conference, as is now apparent, had the least right to do so! There is no art in demanding that *the Executive* send an agitator, folding your hands and waiting. How can

---

15   [*Sotsial-Demokrat (Social Democrat)* was the weekly newspaper of the Jewish Social Democratic Party of Galicia.]

16   [A kahal was the council regulating a Jewish community's religious, welfare and other affairs. Ukrainians were known as Ruthenians. The Sejm was the Galician parliament, the Reichsrat the lower house of the Austrian parliament.]

17   Someone may see in this a contradiction with what I stated in the first article, which draws attention to the importance of trade union work in the first instance; this is, incidentally, not so. It is to be understood that our struggle and work cannot always be the same but is becoming ever more diverse and many-sided as, for example, a river which is narrow at its source and grows broad and mighty towards its mouth. If, therefore, in remoter areas we have to *begin* our work with trade unions, in the larger towns we have to participate actively and intensively in the political movement and who knows whether we will have to stand candidates in future general elections in both capitals. [Kraków in western and L'viv in eastern Galicia.]

the Executive fulfil the wishes of eight or twelve towns which all demand an agitator at the same time? Have those who make such demands considered what they are talking about? Are they saying to the local committees, which already exist, that they should sleep and leave the entire organisational work to the agitator who they await in vain?! Comrades, a greater readiness for sacrifice and enthusiasm for work is required of you. Fewer speeches and more deeds! Reality has demonstrated that towns which speak less do the best work. We have no fear of enemies, we have already overcome so many difficulties that we can also overcome those we still have. But that is possible *only when we do not make any mistakes* and today it is an inexcusable mistake to shift the whole burden of work onto the Executive. Instead of working independently, writing a letter to the Executive: send us money and an agitator. And just that is being done. When the general elections take place and when the Executive has to receive material means from across the province in order to be able to publish a Polish newspaper, which we need so urgently, and in order to be able to begin broad political activity?[18] The Executive was not created for one town but for the *entire movement.*

But a great deal of complacency and coldness has grown among us about material support for the Party. Many comrades would prefer to go to prison or be arrested rather than sacrifice money. In part, the cause is poverty but it is also a misunderstanding of the current situation. As the general elections approach, the time when the regime and the bourgeoisie only used *repression* is disappearing. At present, the reactionary parties cannot gain mandates as they want, making do with the police and starosty.[19] Want to or not, they have to go among the people and try to win their sympathy. So they set up various associations, publish newspapers, issue leaflets and pamphlets. The *form of the struggle has changed.* The *prisons* are no longer a threat to the workers movement (a hundred thousand cannot be locked up in gaol) but the networks which the bourgeoisie set up everywhere are. We have to counterpose our broad educational agitation to these bourgeois networks. The new situation demands a new means of struggle. And I am convinced that when the broad circles of our comrades understand this situation they will support our Party materially with the same willingness and preparedness for sacrifice with which they have sacrificed their personal freedom and gone to prison!

---

18   [Grossman's optimistic and ambitious perspective of significantly expanding the influence of the JSDP beyond the working class and publishing a newspaper in Polish was not realised.]

19   ['Starosty' means 'heads of local administrations'.]

CHAPTER 11

Polish Club, Jewish Club and Zionist Charlatanry*

Translated from Yiddish by Rick Kuhn

The Polish Club is hated in this province.[1] Mr [Adolf] Stand is a candidate for parliament and makes assurances that he will not join the Polish Club.[2] And the loud trumpets of Zion announce to the whole world: 'Candidate Stand's proclamation that he will not join the Polish Club, that he will, however, try to establish a Jewish Club in the parliament is greeted with stormy applause'!

In this small and, at first glance, innocent report, the full extent of the moral and political misery of our Zionists is apparent. At the same time, it shows that the Jewish petty bourgeoisie stands absolutely on the very lowest step of political maturity because it has permitted Mr Stand in broad daylight to commit such a political swindle, in the same way. Mr Stand is a great person, a new prophet who has been sent to redeem the oppressed. If the entire province[3] hates the Polish Club, why should he, Stand, not do the same? The whole province wants to throw off the yoke of the bandits of the Polish Club. Mr Stand wants the same, only it is necessary that he makes the effort to assemble new bandits for a Jewish Club.

And he, the great prophet of 10 million Jews, wants them to shout bravo to him. This charlatan pursues his handiwork with such audacity that he cries out entirely openly to the bandits of the Polish Club: go away because I want to lie there!

Is economic and political distress caused by a *name*, in that the Club *calls itself* the Polish Club? How will our terrible distress disappear if we have a Jewish Club instead of a Polish Club? Even the biggest idiot will not argue that the plight of the entire province, that the sea of sorrows and millions of victims have their source in a *name*. A name is only an expression. Whether a Club was called Polish or Jewish or Turkish, does not change anything, so long as an

---

*   [Originally published as Grossman 1906d.]

1   [I.e. Galicia.]

2   [Stand ran unsuccessfully in a by-election for the Reichsrat electorate of Brody-Złoczów, in eastern Galicia, after its representative Emil Byk, a Jewish member of the Polish Club, had died. The Polish Club was the conservative Polish caucus in the lower house of the Reichsrat (Austrian parliament) in Vienna.]

3   [I.e. Galicia.]

institution set up like the Polish Club rules the province. So long as such an institution exists, nothing will change for the better in the province. Mr Stand assures that he will create a *Jewish Club* and openly commits himself to it, thus to one calamity he wants to add yet another! When Poles cry 'down with the Polish Club', Mr Stand shouts bravo and concedes that rubbish which Poles throw out is still good for the Jews. But in this way too, by selecting the most out-dated and stinking 'antiques' for the Jews, he is a patented defender of Jewry.

What, then, is the Polish Club? It arose thirty years ago. Before that the Galician diet[4] only sent a parliamentary 'delegation' to Vienna. When *direct* elections for the parliament were introduced in Austria, the population directly, rather than the provincial parliament, elected members of the parliament in Vienna.[5] That was when the Polish Club was established. But thirty years ago Polish society was not so class divided. The bitter class struggles of today had not emerged. At that time all layers of the people could unite in one national *Polish* Club. Once differentiation into classes and class struggles started to make greater progress in Polish society, class differences exploded the *national* framework of the Club and the leaders of the oppositional Polish classes started to group *outside* the Club. And, as a result, the Club which was once the representatives of several classes became the representative of *one* class and other classes started to establish their own representation.

Thus the anomoly that we saw and still, sadly, see among Poles is disappearing. While we see groupings according to classes and class interests in the entire Austrian parliament – so that liberals unite with liberals, conservatives with conservatives and the socialists of different nations with the socialists – the Polish Club wants to unite within it the *entire* Polish people and wants to include all classes.

That reeks of reaction, that is a futile effort to halt the modern movement in the direction of the intensification of class contradictions and class struggles, which is apparent to our readers and requires no further explanation.

Without 'solidarity', the Polish Club would not have been the Polish Club. That is, the Polish Club only exists thanks to the existence of solidarity among different classes. The significance of this solidarity, understood by the whole province, is that the representatives of oppositional classes, for example of the peasantry, petty trades etc., have not been able to vote for the interests of their classes but rather had to vote together with the majority of the Club, i.e. in the interests of the large landowners or ... they had to leave the Club!!

---

4 [I.e. the Sejm.]
5 [I.e. the Austrian Reichsrat.]

And Mr Stand and company want to establish this hated institution amongst the Jews! And, in fact, they rely on the stupidity of the broad masses. When they cry out that they combat the Polish Club and at the same time want to create a Jewish Club, Zionist charlatanry celebrates its triumph.

That *Naprzód*[6] and the Polish Socialist Party[7] have adopted an unclear position on the matter and one that is unworthy of real socialists is no mystery to us. Not for the first and not for the last time, they have demonstrated complete ignorance. That is a relevant matter for the Jewish proletariat, which we will mention at the appropriate time. The Jewish proletariat will disdain the Zionists with their political swindles. If the Polish Club was set up thirty years ago in the context of the then weak development of class contradictions and class struggles in Polish society then *today*, when class struggles seethe all along the line in Jewish society, it is no more than a fantasy. Awakened, not only does the Jewish proletariat struggle for the restriction of the economic domination of the Jewish bourgeoisie but it is also conscous enough to prevent itself from being politically chained. Shoulder to shoulder with the Polish proletariat, it will shout: down with the Polish Club, down with the Jewish Club, down with Zionist charlatanry.

H. G.

---

6   [*Naprzód* (*Forwards*).]
7   [I.e. the PPSD, whose Kraków daily newspaper was *Naprzód*.]

CHAPTER 12

Who Should the Kazimierz Electorate Vote For?[*]

Translated from Yiddish by Rick Kuhn

We called today's meeting to familiarise the broad public with the life of the
Jewish proletariat, which, for significant parts of society, is still a book locked
with seven seals. Those who accuse us of separating ourselves from Polish and
Ruthenian society,[1] the so-called Jewish bourgeoisie, are themselves more distant from Jewish society. The speaker discussed the relationships and circumstances in which the Jewish proletariat lives and demonstrated with factual
evidence that those who first stated, just four weeks before the election, that
there is a Jewish people and the people live in misery, are to blame. The kahal[2]
has always supported the ruling clique and who, if not them, are to blame
for Jewish misery. Now, just before the election, Messrs [Józef] Sare and company have become mouthy Jews. They call the kahal the only basis for Jewish
autonomy. But if they are happy with this sole Jewish autonomy, why don't they
grant universal suffrage for the election of the kahal? You understand: they do
not want any autonomy for the people. They like the autonomy of the kahal's
current favourites. Going on to criticism of the Galician Sejm,[3] the speaker
explained that the politics of the ruling clique has always been antisemitic.
Ritual murder has been talked about in the Galician Sejm and not a single
Polish deputy raised his voice against it. These politics still exist. Mr Sare may
personally be a decent human being. But he has reached out his hand to the
kahal clique for a seat in the Reichsrat.[4] He declares that he is not running but
he has already signed the manifesto of the Rada narodowa,[5] in which the socialists are attacked, with Father [Leon] Pastor. (Cries of 'shame') Today's meeting
requires a decision of him: he should not accept a seat from the clique.

Comrade Grossman subjected the Zionists' tactics to a serious critique. He
demonstrated how demagogic they are. For fifteen years they have talked about

---

[*] [Report of a speech by Grossman, originally published as Grossman 1907b.]
1 [Ukrainians were known as Ruthenians.]
2 [The kahal was the council regulating a Jewish community's religious, welfare and other
affairs.]
3 [The Sejm was the Galician parliament.]
4 [The Reichsrat was the Austrian parliament.]
5 [The Rada narodowa (National Council) was the electoral organisation of the conservative
Polish Club, i.e. caucus, in the Reichsrat.]

Palestine and now they don't say a word and their entire programme consists of the demand for more Jewish seats. But the Polish Jews of the Rada narodowa also make this demand. They don't actually have a political programme at all and, in practice, conduct clerical agitation. Whoever promotes Jewish clericalism promotes Polish clericalism at the same time. For us socialists, religion is a private matter; in the parliament meat is not salted and questions are not resolved. (Bravo) The Zionists at one time said they were democrats. Another time they declared that they were loyal to the regime. The speaker reads a letter on the characteristics of the Zionists from a comrade in Kolomya, according to which the Zionist candidate Dr [Ozjasz] Thon of Kraków once stated that he is a progressive person and on another that he is a great tsadik.[6] (Hilarity) In the best case criticise them, but criticising is not enough: demands have to be made.

The speaker then discussed the minimum demands in the socialist programme and in particular the demands of the Jewish proletariat, for example primary schools with Yiddish as the language of instruction. A certain prejudice against Yiddish has taken root among the Jewish intelligentsia but that is of little concern to us. In this language, we have taken culture into the Jewish masses. In this language, revolutionary ideas have permeated the Jewish masses in Russia! We demand what is necessary, unconcerned whether the editor of *Naprzód*,[7] Mr [Max] Hecker is happy about it or not. With conviction and clear arguments the speaker rebutted the accusation that such schools would be religious or the opposite and proved that the demand is not in the least against the interests of the Poles or Ruthenians. In Jewish schools we want to raise friends of the Poles. If they are our friends, we will be their friends. (Applause) Discussing the questions of Saturday as the day of rest, considering the use of Yiddish in public administration etc., Comrade Grossman dealt particularly with the national question, arguing that, as legal reforms are not carried out every year, we already have to clearly state our view about the way to resolve national question and thus the Jewish question in Austria today. Today, the speaker concluded, we make basic demands because, if we are to ruthlessly tear down everything that stands in the path of our cultural and political development, we will also have to bring down those who rule the province. (Stormy applause)

---

6 ['Meat is not salted' is a references to the process of making meat kosher (compliant with Jewish dietary law). 'Tsadik' means 'righteous person/Hasidic spiritual leader'.]

7 [*Naprzód* (*Forwards*), was the daily newspaper of the PPSD, which had an assimilationist attitude to Jews.]

[After a short speech by Adolf Gross, the candidate supported by Grossman and the Jewish Social Democratic Party] Comrade Grossman again spoke and moved the following motion:

1. The assembled voters of the Kazimierz electorate at the meeting of the Jewish Social Democratic Party resolve to decisively combat the candidate of the kahal clique and to support the candidature of Dr Adolf Gross with all our might.

2. They demand that the deputy from this electorate not enter the Polish Club or the Jewish Club.[8]

3. On labour questions he should vote with the socialist caucus.

4. Recognising that only national cultural autonomy, not only for Jews but for all the peoples in Austria, will fundamentally resolve the national question and end national struggles, in accord with this principle, we demand that the real demands, for the specific identity of the broad Jewish masses in cultural-linguistic respects, e.g. the acceptance of the Yiddish language (jargon) in the trades tribunals, trades inspectorate and evening and primary schools, with the conviction that the realisation of these demands, to the extent that they are necessary, does not in any way contradict the interests of Polish and Ruthenian society, and also in the belief that full and practical equality of Jews as citizens of the province can bring about friendly co-existence with Polish and Ruthenian society.

... [After the discussion,] The motion was overwhelmingly adopted. The meeting dispersed while singing the *Internationale*.

---

8   [The Jewish Club was the Zionist proposal, realised after the election, for a Jewish national caucus in the Reichsrat.]

CHAPTER 13

Bundism in Galicia: A Contribution to the History of the Jewish Workers Movement in Galicia*

Translated from Yiddish by Floris Kalman and Rick Kuhn

[1]

Several years ago, during the period of the Jewish proletariat's campaign for an independent political organisation in Galicia, accusations could be heard from both the Polish Socialist Party[1] and the Zionists, that the 'national' aspirations of the Jewish proletariat in Galicia resulted from the intellectual influence of Zionism on a section of the Jewish workers, on their 'misguided' younger generation. According to them, this influence had no relationship at all with proletarian class struggle. During the decade and a half since those aspirations, this 'younger' generation has incidentally had time to mature. In these circumstances, consequentally, the Zionists as well as the Polish socialists have also explained these 'nationalist' influences in a different way. That is, in terms of the influence in Galicia of the Jewish Bund's struggles and impact in Lithuania, Poland and Russia. They have not, however, wanted to deny the Zionist origins of the 'nationalist' aspirations of Jewish socialists in Galicia. On the contrary, they have sought to prove a deeper intellectual connection between Bundism and Zionism, a connection that deserved more attention, and to consider the extent to which it stamped the Jewish workers movement. During the period of upheaval in political relations in the province and parties over the past year, Zionism, already having 'historically' mounted Austria's parliamentary tribune, from there declared to a perplexed world that, as far as it was concerned, there was no 'Jewish question', nor a national and language question, [to be debated] in the parliament.[2] It reduced the extent of its demands to meagre 'equal economic rights' for Jews. So Jewish Social Democracy *alone* remained in the struggle for Jewish national emancipation, which some people see as a futile attempt to revive the dying ideas of 'bourgeois' Zionism on the terrain of the workers movement, in other words, a belated attempt at life after death.

---

* [Originally published as Grossman 1907a.]
1 [I.e the Polish Social Democratic Party.]
2 Ebner 1907, p. 9.

It is now high time to examine these claims; not because we, for a moment, feel the need to settle accounts with those who claim to be the intellectual fathers of the Jewish workers movement in Galicia, for the purpose of narrow party advertising or even to refute this naive conception, which seeks to explain social phenomena in terms of more or less accidental, superficial 'influences'. For we know very well that at the root of every social movement there lies a particular social need which, with the help of this movement, strives to break the bonds that bind it.

This analysis becomes necessary, however, if we want to know the Jewish proletariat's tasks, in the face of the coming constitutional struggles over the reconstruction of Austria, which will put an end to ruinous national struggles and create the conditions for the free cultural development of peoples. To understand the nature of these tasks it is necessary to explain the Bund's influence on the development of the Jewish proletariat in Galicia. The limit of its influence is apparent in the fact that it only *accelerated* the *necessary* internal evolution of this proletariat. Similarly – in Marx's words – the German revolution of 1848 would certainly have occurred even if the February Revolution in France had not accelerated it.[3] Although it is important, from an historical point of view, to consider how the struggle and ideology of the Jewish proletariat in Russia influenced the development of the Jewish working class in Galicia, it is irrelevant whether this or that pamphlet, this person or another were the means through which Bundist influence penetrated the territory of Galicia. All such detailed researches are worthless and do not in the least clarify the issue. An American who observes these movements from a great distance, for example, would not notice these details. Accidental circumstances can be of no interest to us, as opposed to the general conditions of the Jewish proletariat in Galicia, thanks to which the ideology of the Bund found a strong basis in Galicia when it came here and which brought about a decisive change in the intellectual development of the Jewish proletariat.

•   •
•

To gain an understanding of these circumstances and also of the whole naive perception which the Zionists have of historical processes, it must remembered that when the Jews stepped into Austria's national arena it was not an isolated occurrence. On the contrary, the history of Austria in the second half of the nineteenth century consists of a sequence of more and more national groups

---

3   [While published under Marx's name, the article was written by Engels, 1979b, p. 21.]

or rather of their bourgeois components reaching maturity and becoming active on Austria's historical scene, protesting against the centralisation of the
state. In 1867, through the settlement with Hungary, Austria was ruthlessly
delivered up to the German[-Austrian] bourgeoisie.

> The Polish bourgeoisie already emerged as a parliamentary equal in 1869.
> In 1871 and 1872 [Eduard] Taaffe tried to give the Czechs equality with the
> Germans. By the time [Kasimir Felix] Badeni appeared, the emergence of
> nations was complete.[4]

The appearance of the Jews was merely the latest stage in this process.

The struggle against German centralism took two forms. During the period
of constitutional struggle, 1860–74, an effort was made to replace German centralism with *territorial autonomy*. As a result of specific Austrian conditions
and considerable national mixing, however, territorial autonomy did not, even
then, serve the interests of many national groups. In Galicia, for instance, where
the Ruthenians[5] lived beside Poles, territorial autonomy could only mean the
replacement of German centralism with Polish centralism. So the Ruthenians already proposed the idea of *national autonomy*, as opposed to territorial
autonomy, at that time. When the Jewish proletariat, which was not concentrated within the boundaries of any territory, in turn made its appearance in
the nineties, it quite naturally adopted the slogan of national autonomy too.

I have indicated elsewhere the economic situation underlying the awakening of the Jewish working class's national consciousness over the past decade.[6]
It is even easier to do this with regard to the Jewish petty bourgeoisie and
the intelligentsia which was recruited from it. The emergence of the nations,
described above, with the facts which I introduce below, prove that the Jewish nation's process of development is *the consequence of preconditions deeply
embedded in Austrian relations*. The Polish bourgeoisie dreaded this consequence but was forced to acknowledge it. In 1866, during the Sejm debate
over the address to the Kaiser, the Ruthenians fought provincial autonomy and
Deputy [Stepan] Kaczala said, with the most wonderful clarity:[7]

---

4 Rudolf Springer [i.e. Karl Renner. Editor's interpolations].
5 [I.e. Ukrainians.]
6 [Grossman 1906a, see 'The Jewish Social Democratic Party of Galicia', above, pp. 128–135;
  also see Komitet Organizacyjny Żydowskiej Partyi Socyalno-demokraticyczney w Galicyi
  1905/Organizatsions Komite fun der Yudisher Sotsial-Demokratisher Partey in Galitsien 1905,
  What Do We Want?, above, pp. 73–82; and Jüdishe sozial-demokratishe Partei in Galitsien
  1905b, *To the Social Democrats of Austria*, above, 113–127.]
7 [The Sejm was the Galician parliament.]

The issue here is not *peoples* but only Crown Lands and the autonomy of provinces, which is nothing but centralism in disguise.

Gentlemen! There is a big difference between equal rights for peoples, and for provinces. Wherever there is only one nation in a province, provincial autonomy is a good thing. But where there are more it will always mean the rule of one over the others. This will be a kind of centralism worse than that of the [imperial] state.[8]

At that time, words with profound implications came from the Polish side (Deputy [Julian] Szemelowski):

The province alone is represented in the Reichsrat ... There is no party of the Ruthenian people here ... We do not have different nations; for what would happen if Mr [Maximilian] Landsberger suddenly spoke in favour of a separate nation for the half-million Jews who live in the province.[9]

This consequence was realised a quarter of a century later, at the beginning of the 1890s.

∴

The Jewish masses still slept deeply, in the depths of the sea of Austrian nations. It was only when a stronger urban life awoke that a very small ripple of so-called cultural reconciliation between the Jews and the Poles, in another words assimilation, was superficially apparent, for a time.

The bourgeois publicists are fond of explaining this phenomenon by saying that Polish culture is superior and thus attracts the more sensitive individuals among the Jews. But how can they explain the rather late rise and short duration of this current, which did not yet exist in the 1870s and after 1892 had vanished completely? In truth, this was mainly a movement of the tiny *Jewish intelligentsia*. This explains not only its assimilation during the 1880s but also its nationalisation during the 1890s and its German character in the 1870s.

The speed with which these national phases followed one another recalls similar national changes which affected the intelligentsias of other Austrian nationalities. In Austria this was a *typical* phenomenon.

---

8   [Sejm Krajowy Królestwa Galicyi 1866, p. 155. Editor's interpolation.]
9   Sejm Krajowy Królestwa Galicyi 1866, pp. 149–50. [Editor's interpolation.]

After Galicia had achieved territorial autonomy and the [provincial] government[10] had passed from the hands of the *German* to those of a *Polish* bureaucracy, Galicia had to set up its own schools, its own court system with a legal
profession, its own administration and bureaucracy, in a word it had to appoint
its own people to all the posts in various areas of public life. Thousands could
find employment and Polishness represented a force of attraction. A significant
portion of the Ruthenian and Jewish intelligentsia were assimilated in this process, although rather late, which explains the weakness and the short duration
of assimilation here.

By the end of the 1880s, the ranks of the provincial admistration were over-
full and sated. The province produced an intellectual reserve army and, since
all of them could not find employment, there had to be a *selection* process. *Native born* Poles were preferred, Jewish Poles or assimilated Ruthenians had to
wait. From a force of attraction, Polishness became one of repulsion. The rejected Jewish intelligentsia, having lost the ground from under its feet, returned to
Jewishness and became nationalist.

Under these circumstances, the assimilationist movement achieved no great
results, in spite of the great efforts of its supporters. 'A future researcher' into
social movements in Galicia, wrote one of the experienced activists in this
group,

> will be astonished at the *picture of a handful of young people* who, around
> 1880, stood out from the half-Germanised ... Jewish masses – holding the
> flag of the white eagle.[11] This little band threw itself into the work with the
> full idealism of youth and inspired older people to follow it. They set up
> a newspaper (*Ojczyzna*) and an association based on their ideals. In their
> struggle, they used the living word, oral propaganda, lectures, schools; for
> several years they spread their ideas through a Hebrew publication. They
> published several pamphlets in Polish and Yiddish. They set up scientific
> courses and public reading rooms.[12]

---

10   [Grossman's text was presumably written in Polish and then translated into Yiddish for
     publication. The word 'government' seems to have been mistranslated as 'economy' here,
     as it was in a quotation from Feldman's published Polish text on p. 166, below.]
11   [I.e. the Polish coat of arms.]
12   Feldman 1893, pp. 12–13. [Grossman's emphasis. *Ojczyzna* (*Fatherland*) was published
     between 1881 and 1892, until 1887 in Hebrew and Polish, then only in Polish.]

And the result? An unbiased and disinterested author described it this way in *Neue Zeit*:[13] 'The assimilationist associations in Galicia collapsed, in spite of great sacrifices; and we see that agitation which runs counter to real social relations is unable to achieve anything.'

> In Galicia, where the Poles form the dominant element, the assimilated Jews, for whom a special category exists of 'Poles of the Mosaic faith', number barely 0.37 percent of the total Jewish population. If we assume that this figure is incorrect and multiply it by ten, it remains evident how incapable the Poles are of assimilating the Jews.[14]

The assimilationists gave up.

> We are tired and exhausted, we give up, we read in 'Ostatnie słowo'. We believed and still believe that the Jews can only become citizens with the cooperation of indigenous Polish society[!] It seemed that Polish society would reach out to us, to work together for the common good. We were deluded. What has the province done for the moral and economic uplift of the Jewish masses over the 25 year period of autonomous government?[15]

Ojczyzna became silent.

The historical ground was cleared for new currents. And these became apparent as Jewish society differentiated, slowly pushing beyond the Polish nationalist ideology of assimilation. And the modern Jewish 'question' and 'questions' swam to the surface demanding an answer.

The answer came from two directions and in *two* forms, and expressed, as we have seen, the different social and economic content of the two camps into which Jewish society has split: in the long term, the petty bourgeoisie and, preceding it for a while, the Jewish intelligentsia on one side; on the other, the proletariat.

---

13   [*Neue Zeit* (*New Times*) was the theoretical journal of the Social Democratic Party of Germany.]

14   Rezawa 1894, p. 332. [In places Grossman's Yiddish text paraphrased rather than translated the original.]

15   [Feldman 1893, pp. 15–16. 'Ostatnie słowo', the title of an article, means 'the last word'. The final word in this quotation was mistranslated from Polish into Yiddish as 'economy'.]

2

Indeed, to properly understand and assess the current national movement among the Jews, it is necessary to avoiding thinking that somehow the 'nationalisation' of Jewish camps is embodied in a single programme. This nationalisation is, rather, the result of economic and social circumstances of two distinct classes and has only this much in common: it appears in both camps at the same time. The notion that events which occur at the same time have the same cause is an *a priori*[16] deduction, not based on empirical analysis of the actual relations of social phenomena that are not so simple and uncomplicated.

But it is not just a matter of distinct causes.

This significant fact stamped the character, the aims and the future development of both camps to some extent. When it first appeared, Jewish nationalism – a full brother of Polish nationalism and, in in this respect, having the same rights – immediately took a stance opposed in principle to the Jewish proletariat and the answer it had already given to the Jewish 'question', in other words, to an *independent Jewish workers party in Galicia*. The Jewish working class could not, as Zionism did, live in a world of misty dreams nor be satisfied with rending its garments in mourning for the oppression of the people, without drawing the appropriate conclusions. On the contrary, oppressed and poverty stricken, it wants 'the world to echo with the sound of the misery of the Jewish proletariat';[17] consequently the Jewish working class proceeded immediately to the plane of *practical political struggle*.

Jewish nationalism had to take a different attitude. In 1892, when a pamphlet, *What Should the Program of Jewish Youth Be?* which marked the beginning of the contemporary Zionist movement here, appeared in L'viv,[18] Feldman accused it of emphasising, even in its title, the Zionist goal of influencing the young, first and foremost. 'This aim is proof of weakness and of a refusal to participate in political life. Youth has not been – nor can it be – a political party'.[19] The incorrectness of this perspective lay in the fact that he assumed that the fundamental content of the programme resulted from its early weakness. In time the young grew up and found an echo in the petty bourgeoisie and, in spite of this, the movement has to the present not become *political*. Political indifference became its programme for a long time and this has been the fundamental

---

16   ['A priori' means 'deduced from given presuppositions'.]
17   *Arbeytershtime* 1892.
18   [*Anonymous* 1892.]
19   [Feldman 1892, pp. 16, 19.]

content of Jewish nationalism. It has repeatedly proved its full agreement with Polish nationalism, in whose form and likeness it was created.

From the standpoint of the Jewish proletariat, as for those of other Austrian nations, the most important and immediate issue is the relationship with a particular *government*, a particular dominant system of government policy. The nationalist viewpoint regards the issue of the relationship with a particular territorial state organisation as most important: Jewish nationalism aims to achieve an independent state; Polish or pan-Polish nationalism also included such independence in its programme.

But this has welcome consequences for both categories of supporters of independence, in that public attention *is easily drawn away from the issue of a given party's relationship with existing, real domestic politics*, which is the only test of reactionary or progressive politics. It is absolutely clear that even the greatest reactionary can demand a people's or even a 'socialist' republic in Palestine and, as a result, fail to take advantage of the existing constitution or to *struggle* for the democratisation of an existing state, thus indirectly bolstering the absolutism of the clerical-szlachta bureaucracy in Austrian.[20] That reactionary point of view found its best expression in the formula that Zionism, as a *general national* movement, cannot limit itself to any particular group or class. It must rather include people from all social strata and from the most diverse political camps, uniting east, west, north and south.

To dress up this reactionary stance, it only had to be 'nationalised', i.e. to bind together, with a bond of inner 'logical' necessity, political abdication and the national, anti-assimilationist viewpoint. Political abdication was thus made acceptable to those who might have had doubts about its reactionary content. For, while it is not the best, it is still the logical outcome of the nationalist viewpoint.

That nationalist standpoint was above doubt, for it allowed the Zionists to refute the fantasies of the assimilationists easily, with the truth, from a purely mechanical standpoint and without reference to social evolution and capitalist trends. But, in practice, daily life, with awful ridicule, itself confirmed the impotence and barrenness of those assimilationist aspirations at virtually every step.

A second answer [to the Jewish question] came from the proletariat.

From the *Jewish* working class point of view, nothing was easier than to question that 'logical bond' and remove the mask of the nationalist phrasemongers, who had turned the problem on its head. Having put it back onto

---

20   ['*Szlachta*' means the Polish 'nobility'.]

its feet, Zionism's damaging effect on the nation could be demonstrated, not because Zionism opposed assimilation but because it did not stand up to the regime's szlachta bureaucracy.

And while Zionism was still finding its way among very young people, in declarations at patriotic Maccabean evenings[21] and other nationalist festivals – without abandonning its wailing and rending of garments which had no impact on relations in the province – the Jewish proletariat organised itself in July 1892 into a *political party*, a 'Jewish workers party' with its own political organ: *Di arbeytershtime*.[22]

At a time when Austrian Social Democracy was rigidly centralist in organisation and when the gathering of Germans and Czechs, Poles and Ruthenians into the same ranks was regarded as its greatest merit, the formation of such an organisation, itself proved that the first Jewish workers organisation arose on a 'national' basis.

Such a general description, however, does not explain anything at all. The important question is, what kind of theoretical expression did this organisation give to the relationship between socialism and the national question.

Due to lack of appropriate material, I am not in a position to answer this question in detail. But an article in the third issue of *Arbeytershtime* can shed important light on the issue:

> ... It is wrong to believe that all the *nations* and languages in Galicia, i.e. the Polish, Ruthenian and Jewish/Yiddish, can be united under the Polish flag. Only a small section of the workers here would participate in such unity. The broader masses of the working class could not be drawn into such unity. If one wants to enlighten the *broad masses* of Jewish, Ruthenian and Polish workers, it is necessary for *each language and people to be separately drawn together* and enlightened. And it is necessary for the Polish associations with their newspapers in Galicia *to educate their own workers*, the Ruthenian their own and the Jewish their own; they should *manage themselves separately*. But there should also be a chief committee which should be *composed of* representatives of all these parties.
>
> This chief committee should make decisions when all these independent workers parties have to act together ... This kind of unity is called *federal unity*.

---

21   [Commemorating the Jewish revolt against the Seleucid Empire, from 167 to 160 BCE.]
22   [*'Di arbeytershtime'* means *'The Workers' Voice'*.]

It is noteworthy, that the fundamental assumption here is that Jews are a nation with their own *language*. The circumstance is that no attempt is made to prove this assumption, over which there is no discussion, as over a matter that is self-evident.

At that time, this was not extraordinary.

Just how widespread this standpoint was in the socialist camp is best illustrated by the circumstance that the PPSD,[23] which a few years later officially enthused over assimilationism and fought against the 'reactionary Zionist invention of a Jewish nation', at that time the same PPSD, on its own judgment and represented by none other than [Ignacy] Daszyński himself, ridiculed 'assimilationist humbug', 'which had finally gone bankrupt a year earlier [he may have been referring to *Ojczyzna* in 1892] and was an offspring of the Polish szlachta. Its ideal was Yankel in *Pan Tadeusz*. That good natured Yankel who could be put to any service'.[24] Or, when the same Daszyński called the first Socialist Congress in Galicia, he said that 'the theory of assimilating the Jews to the Poles must be a matter of indifference for socialists, since it is a theory that has almost nothing in common with the Jewish masses'.[25] This showed that the theory, a contrario,[26] could only be of concern to the bourgeoisie.

'Let us regard the Jews', he continued 'like any other nation, i.e. let us give them the same rights'.[27]

More important than the academic fact of 'recognising' the Jews as a nation is the question of the kind of practical conclusions Jewish socialists draw from it.

From the socialist viewpoint, the minimum programme presented by the Jewish socialists (like the socialists of Austria as a whole) starts from the standpoint of daily struggle with capitalism. So it cannot have 'national revival' as a *goal*. Socialism, which in the practice of life is class struggle, has as a goal *extending* the proletariat's *political rights* and making mass organisations possible and also raising the masses' intellectual and economic condition, for the struggle against the szlachta and the bourgeoisie as political and social classes. Or, in other words, just as every class struggle is naturally a *political* struggle,[28] so the obvious collary is that Social Democracy had to struggle first of all for the *democratisation of Austria*.

---

23   [The PPSD, was the Polish Social Democratic Party of Galicia and Silesia.]
24   *Naprzód* 1893c, p. 3. [Adam Mickiewicz's *Pan Tadeusz* was a classic Polish nationalist, epic poem, Mickiewicz 1917.]
25   [*Naprzód* 1892a, p. 2.]
26   ['A contrario' means 'on the contrary'.]
27   *Naprzód* 1892a, p. 2.
28   [A reference to Marx 1976a, p. 211.]

At that time, no account of the *scope* of this struggle and how extensive it would be had been produced. It had not been considered that, in a country such as Austria which is a conglomeration of different peoples with centrifugal national tendencies, *democratisation cannot be restricted to general political reforms, on the pattern of other western nations*; and that 'the tasks of Social Democracy in Austria are significantly *different* from those in other European countries'. Despite the centrifugal tendencies of the nations living in Austria and despite the totally unbearable situation, Austria 'exists and *constitutes the terrain* on which Social Democracy must conduct its activity'. So Social Democracy's struggle against the state[29] is at the same time a struggle to maintain this state. This is only possible in Austria if those centrifugal tendencies are eliminated though an 'upheaval in the whole state structure' and a 'radical, ruthless abolition of the institution of the feudal Crown Lands. Only *when they have ceased to exist* can *the autonomy of nations* develop'.[30] These words, taken from the 1903 report of the Austrian Social Democratic Party, are the latest lesson about the important and difficult task in Austria, of formulating the minimum programme or, more precisely, of formulating socialists' *political activity*, which is complicated by the national question.

The adoption and application of these principles in Austria, however, required many years and much experience, which the Jewish socialists did not have in 1892. They did not, therefore, arrive at *political conclusions* about the restructuring the state but, as can be seen from the quotation above, they limited their conclusions to organisational questions, to calling for the *restructuring of the Party*.

They did understand the need for nationally organised parties in general and for a Jewish one in particular, in order to make agitation and organisation on a large scale possible and to conquer the broad masses. It is, however, worth noting the one-sided, superficial and formalistic assessment of such parties as *exclusively technical means of assisting* socialist activity to win over the *working masses*.

The objective, *historical* aspect of this form of organisation in the Austrian national conglomeration, as a necessary stage in the development of the proletariat itself which also struggles for equal national rights, was not considered at all.

Such a narrow formulation of the perspective, which then became the *general* property of Austrian Social Democracy, its first formulation on Galician

---

29   I.e. the struggle to democratise the Austrian state.
30   [Sozialdemokratische Arbeiterpartei Österreichs 1903, pp. 11–12. Grossman's emphasis.]

terrain, is without doubt one of the sources of the organisational frictions during the first years of the Austrian Party's existence, in general, and of the Jewish organisation, in particular.

The logical conclusion had not been reached because national organisation was regarded as *only* an external tool for more easily winning over the masses, a given form of organisation, in the historical and political circumstances here, as no more than a necessary and unavoidable starting point for the working class in the proletariat's struggle, that in these conditions, was only an unpleasant concession which complicates the situation. These national centres were regarded as an *obstacle* to unified action by the Austrian working class and the formation of separate national organisations suited to specific circumstances was considered a malum necessarium (a bad thing that is, however, necessary), as a concession which, however, could not be entirely rejected but had to be avoided as much as possible.

Thus the transition from a centralised to a federal party organisation in Austria was *not a unified* and *simultaneous outcome* of a change of opinion in Party ranks about organisational forms. Instead, each national component of the Austrian working class formed its own national organisation, one by one over a few years, according to the degree of its maturity. In this way they manifestly demonstrated, in each particular case, how necessary this concession was for them. And the theoretical concession, 'recognition', came quietly after it had been accomplished in fact, again separately in each single case. The adoption of the federal form of organisation in 1897, was merely a formal confirmation of the restructuring of the Party, which had already been implemented in practice.

This explains a phenomenon that initially seemed inexplicable. The national components of the Austrian proletariat, which had not organised themselves along national lines for long, did not show sufficient understanding of the need for this kind of organisation for other components, which they even opposed. The formation of national organisations within Austrian Social Democracy was, therefore, *not regarded as a principle*, to be applied, for the sake of 'justice', to *all* national components of the Austrian proletariat. On the contrary, each of them was obliged to prove its need for such an organisational concession separately. The Jewish proletariat also had to undertake this task.

∴

At that time, however, the first Jewish workers organisation collapsed, although the slogan it raised undoubtedly expressed the needs of the whole Austrian proletariat and thus it finally achieved victory a few years later.

It collapsed not only because of the opposition it encountered from the then still centralised, general Austrian social democratic organisation, not only because of the unfortunate *personal composition of the movement's leadership*. But, more importantly, it collapsed because of the immaturity of the Jewish proletariat itself.

Generally speaking, the social circumstances of the Jews in Galicia at the beginning of the 1890s were not an entirely appropriate basis for a mass movement, in the European sense of the word. There was, in general, no large-scale industry in Galicia and even less among the Jews. In the towns, with the exception of a few larger ones, obvious, modern class differences were not apparent. The tiny industrial proletariat was little differentiated from the petty bourgeoisie, which fills our towns and shtetleykh.[31] So its *social significance*, which is now apparent to all and will be greater in the future, was only apparent to a few.

3

We find very small traces of the struggle which the first Jewish organisation conducted with the Galician Party of that time and later with the PPSD.[32] They are sufficient, however, to convincingly demonstrate that in this struggle the PPSD proceeded from *theoretical premises* very *different* from those it employed fifteen years later. Daszyński then poured pitch and sulfur onto 'assimilationist humbug'[33] and *Naprzód* called on Jewish workers 'not to let themselves be led astray by nationalist deceit, which drains the strength of the proletariat under the guise of Polish [or Jewish-Palestinian] patriotism ...'[34]

The PPSD not only had a negative attitude to assimilationist humbug and 'Polish patriotism', it also had positive position, which complemented its attitude to assimilation. The Jews are a nation which, it is true, has been oppressed and persecuted up to the present, in the interests of ruling classes. But its proletarian component is fraternally bound together with the Polish proletariat. The proletariats of the two nations have no cause to fight one another. On the contrary: 'The ice has been broken, the very ancient *hatred of the two nations*

---

31 ['Shtetleykh' is the plural of 'shtetl', 'small Jewish town'.]
32 [The Social Democratic Party of Galicia became the PPSD in 1897, when the weak shell of a Ukrainian Party, which was dependent on the Polish organisation, was set up.]
33 [*Naprzód* 1893c, p. 3.]
34 *Naprzód* 1893b.

begins to weaken from below, i.e. within the proletariat which, united by the strong bond of common interests, will be victorious.'[35]

The Jewish Socialist Party[36] was not, in fact, attacked in the name of assimilation because Jews were not a nation, but on the basis of the perspectives on organisational affairs of that time, in the name of one centralised, *general party*, which should encompass the proletariats of every nation. While the separate Jewish organisation was combatted, Jewish nationality was not. On the contrary, it was recognised, not only theoretically but also in practice in the confines, it was understood, of the centralised organisational form, i.e. *separate associations* for Jews were set up and, in the first instance, the organisation of the Jewish proletariat was left to Jewish workers themselves. 'For some time now', we were told,

> *Jewish workers* have been busy organising the Jargon[37] speaking proletariat of Galicia. This began in L'viv and, after the inadvisable attempt to set up their own party, took the correct path. And so Jewish workers *associations* came into being in L'viv, Ivano-Frankivsk, and Kolomyia.[38] These did not form a separate *party*; they were subordinated to the general *provincial* Social Democratic Party. This *separate organisation of associations* ... had no connection whatsoever with a separate *party*. It was simply a requirement of pragmatic politics. *There was a conviction that, on the road to a collective society, the social democratic movement had not spread itself sufficiently among the Jewish workers.* Age-old antagonism, mutual prejudice and, to some extent, difficult *conditions of existence* [!] – these were the factors which brought about *separate Jewish workers organisation in Galicia*, without at all setting up a separate party. *During their short period of existence they have been under the wing of the experienced guardians* of the general Social Democratic Party of Galicia.[39]

Very soon, however, the situation changed completely. The Austrian Social Democratic Party and with it the Galician Party changed their form of organisation and in 1897 finally organised themselves along national lines, already formulated by the Jewish socialists back in 1892.

---

35 [*Naprzód* 1893b. Grossman's emphasis.]
36 [I.e. the 'Jewish workers party' set up in 1892.]
37 ['Jargon' was a pejorative term for 'Yiddish'.]
38 [Ivano-Frankivsk, now in Ukraine, is known as Stanisławów in Polish and Stanisloy in Yiddish. Kolomyia in Ukraine is known as Kolomea in Polish and Yiddish.]
39 *Naprzód* 1893b. [Grossman's emphasis.]

Note: in order to extend this picture, the following two examples serve to illustrate the organisational techniques of the PPSD, at that time, and the *ideological* aspect of its *agitation*. In the context of the PPSD's *theoretical* standpoint, discussed above, they throw light on its relationship with Jews at that time and explain *why* the Jewish workers movement grew over the next five years and also the character of the movement. It grew, therefore, in breadth. The PPSD was not capable of giving it depth and turning the mass of Jewish *workers*, scattered across the towns, into an enlightened *working class*. By adapting to the masses' clericalism, more than anything it clouded their class consciousness. This unworthy opportunism soon reaped its revenge. After 1897 the Jewish workers movement fell apart.

First example: correspondence from Ivano-Frankivsk.

> Quite important changes have recently taken place in the party system here. Until now the only association has been Praca ... Now members have decided to establish two new workers associations to replace Praca. This is mainly in the interests of those who only speak Jewish Jargon and do not understand Polish and have thus been unable to benefit from talks and lectures in Polish. One will be called Siła, for *Christian workers* and the other Yad Khazaka, for *Jewish workers*. The two associations have the same constitution. After the formation of the two associations, *Praca will be disbanded*, and its property will be divided equally between between Siła and Yad Khazaka.[40]

Second example: 'From Kolomyia. A strike of 400 Jewish weavers, *tallit* ... makers, has broken out. Unity is general, the poverty terrible.'[41]

> The Jewish weavers' strike. The unavoidable class war has broken out amongst the Jews ... Who would have thought that these destitute people, debilitated by scrofula and consumption would rise to up strike. The strictly orthodox Jews were forced to strike by their no less observant exploiters. The poverty of the Silesian weavers[42] was a trifle compared

---

40 *Naprzód* 1892c. ['Praca', Polish, means 'Labour'. 'Siła', Polish, means 'Stength'. 'Yad Khazaka', Hebrew, means 'Strong Hand'. Grossman's emphasis.]

41 *Naprzód* 1892b. [In the Polish original 'strike', '400' and 'weavers' were emphasised. A *tallit* is a Jewish prayer shawl.]

42 [Weavers in Silesia rose up against appalling wages and conditions in 1844. Engels and Marx both wrote about the uprising and Engels later translated and quoted Heinrich Heine's famous poem 'The song of the Silesian weavers', Engels 1975b, p. 323.]

with the poverty here. They earn one to three guilders per week for a sixteen hour day.

On 24 July *about 200 of them assembled with the rabbi*. In an hour-long speech, *Comrade* [Max] *Zetterbaum* described the pitiful situation of those assembled ... Trembling and emaciated old men *agreed with him*, declaring that they too would beat the strike breakers, even if this meant months in prison.

... To ensure that workers employed in smaller factories did not go to work before all their demands were met, the gathering asked them to *take an oath on the Holy Torah*. Then a committee was formed to carry out the meeting's resolutions ...[43]

The ... weavers' strike ... The favourable course [of the strike] is due mainly to the local *rabbinate*, which made all the workers take an *oath* that, under threat of a curse, they would not return to work until notice was taken of their demands.[44]

Kolomyia. The strike has been broken. Ten Hasidim, mainly family men with 5 or 6 children, broke their *oaths on the Holy Torah* with the excuse that at 2 guilders and 50 kreutzer, they are doomed to starvation and that during the holidays they had to go into debt and that they went back to work, thanks to Heller's urgings. The pleas, struggles and threats of the other workers were in vain. Police guarded the factory by day. They stayed there overnight. The rabbi's *demand* made no impression whatsoever on the *pious hypocrits* [!!] ... Three months of struggle and hunger exhausted the workers ... In this whole affair, Heller proved that he tramples on the laws of the Jewish religion [!!] when he is concerned about the interests of his capital.[45]

And finally the epilogue. At the second Congress of the Social Democratic Party of Galicia, in March 1893, Luwisz discussed the defeated strike and said 'The strike collapsed *because* [!] several older family men broke their oaths.'[46]

---

43   *Naprzód* 1892d. [Grossman's emphasis, apart from 'week'. Editor's interpolation. The *Torah* is the five books of the Hebrew *Bible*.]
44   *Naprzód* 1892e. [Grossman's emphasis.]
45   *Naprzód* 1892f. [Grossman emphasised '*demand*'. Hasidim, plural of Hasid, are members of Jewish sects.]
46   *Naprzód* 1893a, p. 3. [Grossman's emphasis.]

This was the consciousness that the PPSD carried into the ranks of the Jewish workers. Nor was this an unusual accident or an exception. That is confirmed by a further incident, which proves the stubbornness with which the PPSD has clung to its clerical opportunism. In *Naprzód* of 5 May 1907, we read:

> Sanok. Despite the rabid agitation of Plinkiewicz and his supporters, the workers gathered in groups in the early morning in front of their organ-isation's premises. From there they followed their unfurled banner with placards and music, across the town into the Orthodox church to mass. Here we must note that, although a majority of workers in the factory were Poles, they were nevertheless prevented from worshipping in the Polish [i.e. Catholic] church by the canon, father Staszicki. Thus, in order to pray in a church, the workers went to the Orthodox church. After the prayers, the workers went to the gardens in Olchowce where there was a very large gathering, addressed by Comrade *Kaczanowska*, from Kraków.[47]

The struggle against attempts to create a Jewish workers party, however, con-tinued and actually started up again, after a few years. The *justification for the struggle, however, changed.*

The PPSD, having now set itself up on a national basis, could no longer use the same weapons in this struggle, the argument for a general and centralised party had been voided by historical development.

But in accord with the general patriotic and nationalist course which finally triumphed in the PPSD and, after 1897, increasingly shaped the character of the Party, the PPSD changed the theoretical foundations of its relationship with Jews. From the Polish-Jewish intelligentsia, it inherited the assimilationist viewpoint and transplanted it into the workers' domain. The struggle against a Jewish workers organisation, which had earlier been fought in the name of a unified centralised organisation, turned into a struggle in the name of 'non-recognition' of the *Jewish nation* and Polonisation.

We would be straying too far if we examined the literary and 'scientific' aspects of PPS[48] assimilationism in Galicia. It is enough to know that the thread which connected the PPSD's assimilationism with the earlier assimilationism was very weak; and the similarities between them was only apparent and not real. All these phenomena were actually an expression of petty bourgeois influ-

---

47   *Naprzód* 1907. [Editor's interpolation.]
48   [The PPS, Polska Partia Socjalistyczna (Polish Socialist Party) was the name of the nation-alist, socialist organisations in the German- and Russian-occupied provinces of Poland with which the leadership of the PPSD sympathised but here the reference is to the PPSD's assimilationism.]

ences on the Polish workers movement, just as assimilationism until 1892 was expressed by the petty bourgeoisie itself. But the PPSD's assimilationism differs from the earlier version which was a *natural current, in tune* with Jewish society, that was not yet deeply differentiated. And there was, besides, a certain idealistic fire in the strong faith of the movement's leaders. This should be especially noted with regard to the *Ojczyzna* group but does not apply at all to the assimilationism of the PPSD, which *opposed* the Jewish masses and was an artificial burden placed on the them and against their will, by the leaders of the PPSD. 'Any attempt to maintain distinctive Jewish features', declared Dr [Herman] Diamand in 1903 'is harmful ... Hard as it may be for us to rid ourselves of our habits, we have to adopt new forms of behaviour and we should not allow *the difficulties we often encounter in Polish society* to deter us from doing that ...'[49]

These are, moreover, very significant ideological characteristics of our assimilationism, which demonstrate its complete artificiality and at the same time illustrate the transformation of *Ojczyzna's* idealism into the cynical sobriety of the new assimilationists, who are devoid of self-respect.

We are not concerned, however, with matters apart from the issues that interest us. We are not concerned with the evolution of the PPSD, only with Daszyński's 'assimilationist humbug' of 1893 into Diamand's assimilationist 'panacea' of 1903 but also the evolution of the *Ojczyzna's* assimilationism, supported by Polish society, into the imposition of Diamand's, which was *against* the will of the Polish environment. But what is important to us is that 'cultural' reconciliation, in its old and new forms, began with literature and education, and ended with political abdication. In 1901, for instance, Polish socialism in Galicia, already faced with the Jewish question, could only say that the daily struggle of the Jewish proletariat against capitalism *brings* the Jews *closer*, culturally and politically, to the non-Jews. Apart from this brilliant discovery, it took no further steps forward. On the contrary, it confined itself to a series of observations and 'freely admitted' that the culturally distinctive features of the Jews irritate non-Jews and leave much to be desired, not only the long coats, sidelocks and the filth of shtetl Jews but even those of the 'Europeanised' Jews: a certain mawkish nervousness, exaggeration, one-sided touchiness, which even characterise Jewish 'intellectuals'. It took comfort, however, in the hope that 'these defects will disappear over the years'[50] and that

---

49   *Naprzód* 1903. [Grossman's emphasis.]
50   Młot 1901, p. 533.

the solution to the Jewish question lies in the *cultural* development of Jewish society. Only *then*, after the khederim,[51] the ghettos, long coats and the fanatical Hasidic masses have disappeared will the differences in customs and civilisation decrease to a minimum. *Then* the class struggle of Jewish society will emerge [!] clearly and the result [!] of this struggle will be differentiation between capitalists and proletarians.

The social struggle and *the victory of socialist ideas* will *then* solve the Jewish question.[52]

Although its own awareness of the character, circumstances and tasks of the proletarian class struggle was not distinguished – as we saw in the quotation above – by its high level of development and Polish socialism in Galicia did not satisfy the most elementary requirements of scientific socialism, we see that it began to make Jewish workers class conscious.

In applying general criticisms of capitalism to Jewish relations, Polish socialism also regarded the appearance of the Jewish question as belonging to the set of problems associated with the social question. It did not regard the Jewish question as somehow *an exception* to capitalism's *general laws* of motion (as the Zionists did). On the contrary, it *also applied the laws of capitalist development to the Jewish question.*

To this extent that Polish socialists' perspectives transpanted the most elementary and general principles of the *Communist Manifesto*[53] onto Jewish terrain. This led to an important consequence, compared to the Zionists. Rejecting the idea of mass migration to Palestine, they acknowledged existing historical circumstances and living conditions as facts and tied the ultimate goal and future of the Jewish proletariat to those of the proletariats of different extractions in the whole [Austrian] state.[54] In so far as their arguments were against the reactionary emergence of Zionism, they had progressive significance.

---

51   [A kheder, plural khederim was an elementary Jewish school which taught Hebrew and religion.]

52   Młot 1901, p. 533.

53   [Marx and Engels 1976.]

54   Although such a view can be *inferred* from the practice of the PPSD and, to a lesser extent, from the reflection of its activity in its literaure, it must nevertheless be remembered that it never had a complete and unified perspective on the Jewish question which explained developments. Theoretical chaos has been and still is its preferred characteristic. We find, moreover, next to the above interpretation, perspectives which seriously break with it. This is what Dr Zetterbaum, the 'theoretician' of the PPSD in Galicia, wrote in January 1901: '*in principle, socialists have no objection* [!] *to the ultimate goal of Zionism – the establishment of a Jewish state in Palestine*'. It was only that he 'has strong and justified doubts as to whether this idea can be realised in the near or distant future.' (Zetterbaum 1901, 1, p. 8; also Zetterbaum 1900 p. 326).

But this general critique of capitalism does not, in itself, provide an immediate answer to the Jewish question nor the appropriate political programme and tactics in relation to it. There is a vast abyss between the recognition of the general principles of socialism to be applied to the Jewish question and drawing satisfactory conclusions from these for party activities and tasks. In other words, the difference between general socialist theory and Social Democracy's immediate programme and practice. Polish socialism has never bridged this abyss nor has it ever even realised that it exists!

Consequently the [PPSD's] programme for immediate action amongst Jews is extremely nebulous. Apart from general economic and political agitation, which could be used in Moravia, Tyrol and Bohemia, it has retained a quite mysterious desire for 'cultural reconciliation', which will result from the 'cultural development of Jewish society', consisting of the disappearance of khederim, of ghettos and Hasidic fanaticism. How the Party should act, however, in regard to this expected development, whether and how to perhaps assist or passively await it, is *nowhere stated*. The Jewish question will be resolved after cultural reconciliation, when the socialist idea triumphs, i.e. at the moment when the maximum socialist programme is realised. There is no clarification, however, of why this reconciliation and the triumph of socialism will necessarily coincide in time.

But we find there absolutely no *political* demands, calls for any immediate, contemporary action or any struggle for equal social and national rights for the Jews. In fact, up to the moment of the triumph of socialism, the only role assigned to the Jewish masses in relation to the Jewish question is *totally passivity*.

The Jewish workers are called upon to struggle, moreover, for the same universal political freedoms and economic gains for which the Polish proletariat, into whose ranks the Jewish workers are supposed to dissolve, has fought. But the need for a specific and day to day struggle, first and foremost of the Jewish workers themselves, for their own emancipation has not been understood. An illusion has arisen that equal rights for the Jews will be a gift, which will fall into their laps like ripe fruit from a tree, at the moment of socialism's final victory, instead of being the result of a *struggle* for equal rights and the final link in that struggle.

This stance does not accordingly distinguish, in a programatic sense, the Jewish question in Galicia, Lithuania or the Kingdom of Poland. The slogan of 'cultural reconciliation' is a *universal* prescription for the Jewish question, whether in Galicia, England or Holland.[55] Since, in relation to the Jewish ques-

---

55   The slogan is enough for the PPSD to publicly oppose the independent organisation of the

tion, Polish socialists do not propose any programme of immediate action appropriate to the specific circumstances of its terrain of struggle, for them there are no differences between socio-political conditions in Holland and Galicia. And the article from the *Calendar*,[56] cited above, was just as applicable to Kraków as Warsaw.

And this is proof of Polish and Jewish nationalism's extensive and profound community of ideas. In both their principles and conclusions, the viewpoints of Polish socialism and Zionism express political abstention with regard to the Jewish question, thereby *cutting themselves off* from the real circumstances in which a solution is required. As a consequence, they arrive at a *universal standpoint*, which is independent of place and time. Their solutions have a further and logical consequence. On the one hand Palestine, on the other 'cultural reconciliation': equally universal and worldwide measures, making a mockery of historical circumstances of time and place.

By cutting themselves off from the real movements which constitute the basis of the Jewish question, both tendencies have unequivocally shown that *the organic connection between the Jewish question* (like any other social issue) and *the given socio-political system of the Empire*, is a mystery to them. So too is the corollary that the Jewish question which has arisen on a particular socio-political basis, cannot be solved in isolation from that basis and its circumstances. This can only occur *through the conduct of struggle on the basis of these circumstances and against them.*

And the results of this position did not take long to appear. The PPSD, positing equal rights for the Jews as an outcome of socialist victory without *day to day struggle for these equal rights* and assigning to the Jewish working class, up to that moment, a totally *passive* role in this regard, quite naturally could not take advantage of the specific features of the Jewish masses' daily life. That, naturally had consequences for the Party's practical activity. It almost never came into contact with the Jewish *masses*. This outcome, reached deductively from the PPSD's theoretical viewpoint on the Jewish question, was fully confirmed by the facts. And in truth, the period from 1897 to 1899, saw the complete disappearance of the emergent mass movement of the Jewish proletariat.

This is how the PPSD, thanks to its negative, destructive activity or rather practical inactivity, prepared the soil for the seeds of Jewish nationalism and allowed Zionism to fight for the souls of Jewish workers.

Jewish workers of Galicia, 'In no constitutional country in the *world* [!], where the Jewish working masses are included in the socialist class movement (America, England, Holland, Austria) is the Jewish proletariat organised into a separate political party.' (*Naprzód* 1905). [Grossman's emphasis.]

56   [Młot 1901.]

The pessimism with which Zionism has distanced itself from the possibility of achieving equal civil and national rights for Jews here, the lack of faith in the *struggle* for equal rights and the consequent poison of despair with which it has contaminated the political atmosphere are only the subjective side of an objective fact: the Jewish masses have not constituted an independent factor in the province's politics at all. Both these phenomena are a logical consequence of the universalist viewpoint which stands outside the struggle taking place within the framework of real, concrete socio-political conditions. As for the PPSD, it failed to fight Zionist ideology; on the contrary, as we have seen, it made strenuous efforts to accustom the Jewish masses to understanding the Jewish question from its own mystical viewpoint of cultural reconciliation, which stands 'above' considerations of time and place.

This formula, which has long since eliminated the *struggle with capitalist society on its own political ground*, is the principal expression of the content of the PPSD's political assimilationism. Its double political effect was finally the material bankrupcy of the Jewish workers movement and its intellectual degeneration. In other words, through its material neglect of the Jewish workers movement, the PPSD helped to deliver the Jewish working class to the swindle of Zionist ideology.[57]

---

57   Soon after the first [Zionist] Congress in Basel, this ideology was popularised in Galicia thus:

'The Jews are not only an economic, but also a racial proletariat. What should they wait for? For the universal deliverance of mankind by Social Democracy, in whose ranks the workers of Skhidnytsia and Khodoriv fight? And when the great bust up comes, and when the dream of nationalisation of the means of production is realised, will this by itself cause racial hatred towards the Jews to disappear? "The racial proletariat", according to Ludwig Stein ... "is much worse off than the economic one. Economic barriers can be breached, *but not racial ones*."' (Landau 1897, p. 294 [quoting Stein 1897, p. 390]). [Grossman's emphasis. Skhidnytsia and Khodoriv, now in Ukraine, were known as Schodnica and Chodorów in Polish.]

The theory that it is impossible to break through racial barriers and consequently that the struggle for equal rights here and for a better lot for the Jews in this place is futile, was merely a fragment of a greater theoretical whole, namely the 'historiosophical analysis' of the development of contemporary capitalist states. This analysis was made at the Basel Congress by Max Nordau. Its significance can only be compared to the achievements of Copernicus and Newton. Nordau posed the question of why European nations emancipated us. And his answer was 'that, just as France gave us the metric system of weights and measures, so it created intellectual parameters, of a kind, which other countries took up, either willingly or reluctantly, as a standard of behaviour. *Every country which wanted to be considered civilised, had to possess certain institutions*, which were set up, developed or reformed by the revolution: a parliament, freedom of the press, jury trials etc. The emancipation of the Jews was a necessary part of the institutions of a civilised state, *like a piano*

This does not, in the least, mean that the PPSD did not fight *Zionism*. On the contrary. But this fight, and the Party's negative attitude to Zionism had their origin in [the idea of] socialism as the *final goal* and not in the minimum programme, i.e. social democratic political activity (which the PPSD did not conduct over the Jewish question). Secondly, the PPSD's *starting point* was Polish society, i.e. it fought Zionism in the name of interests whose basis was Polish relations. So the struggle against Zionism hung in mid-air and, due to the untenability of its theories and its false starting point, arbitrarily concealed from the Jewish proletariat the *real* horizons of the world in which it lived, that is, Jewish capitalist society. It caused this struggle to be for the Jewish proletariat, what it was for the PPSD itself: an *external* struggle between Polish and Jewish nationalism; a struggle which had no organic connection at all with the daily struggle of the Jewish proletariat against the Jewish bourgeoisie. When this struggle turned against Zionism as something external and alien, it naturally lost its Jewish capitalist ground from under its feet and was placed onto Polish nationalist ground. In a word, the PPSD turned the class struggle of the Jewish proletariat into a chauvinist fight between *two nationalisms*.

---

which must stand in the living room, although not a single member of the family can play the instrument. This was, in fact, how the Jews of western Europe were emancipated, not from any feeling of *necessity*, only *to imitate the political fashion*. Not because nations decided to extend a fraternal hand to the Jews, only because the leading intellects accepted a certain ideal of European civilisation, which required *that there should be a paragraph on the emancipation of the Jews, in the legal code.'* [quoted in Landau 1897, p. 298. Grossman's emphasis.]

It is superfluous to add that this 'psychological' theory of political fashion does not have the least scientific value; not to say that it is poorly supported sophistry. But it is a method of great moral and political value for the Zionist petty bourgeoisie. By means of this 'method', Zionism is easily able to secure its own *ideology* and the predominance of its *interests* in Jewish society. As the *Communist Manifesto* already showed, Kant's German philosophy of the eighteenth century was unable to understand France of that time. In the demands of the French Revolution, it only saw demands for 'practical undertanding' [presumably, Kant's 'practical reason']; and, in the phenomenon of the revolutionary will of the French bourgeoisie, it sought the law of pure will [Kant's 'pure reason'] as such. In a word, Kantian philosophy understood the revolution according to its own image. It now becomes so much easier to understand that Nordau's explanation of French revolutionary will and the original 'need to imitate' is in reality *his* need to imitate originality. And the difference between the error of German philosophy and that of Zionist historiosophy is only the difference between Kant and – Nordau.

4

The role which the PPSD assigned to the Jewish masses could not, however, satisfy their practical and intellectual needs. It did not satisfy their *practical* needs
because, as they were now feeling social and national pressure at every step of
their daily struggle, they could not agree to a passive and a waiting role. At best,
only Jewish intellectuals, who carry on fantastic politics and could boldly wait
for national and social liberation until we have Palestine, could agree with this.
The Polish socialists could agree with this. For they were so cut off from the Jewish masses that they could not feel its needs and postponed their satisfaction
until the Jewish question is solved with the triumph of socialism in the future.

But the Jewish working class, for whom waiting and passivity meant prolonging the social and economic pressures from which it suffered, that Jewish
working class, for whom a passive stance was equivalent to political suicide,
could not wait.

It is clear that, in so far as the Jewish proletariat had freed itself from the
bond which tied it to petty bourgeois elements, historically doomed to extinc-
tion, it had attached itself to the most diverse trends and political camps,
because of its own feelings of powerlessness. This newborn Jewish proletariat
now *showed tendencies to break away from the politics* of seeking its salvation
in any movement that it could fasten onto, whether assimilation, independent Poland or the Polish workers movement. [But] it was not yet confident of
its own strength and was neither able nor willing to create the conditions for
modern development.

These tendencies found a wonderful example and an extremely powerful
psychological image in the Bund's activity in Lithuania, Poland and Russia. This
example was rich both in moral encouragement and in the political education
for its own struggle.

Nor did this [passive] role satisfy *intellectual* needs. Socialism, which for Jews
meant the PPSD, was therefore deprived of any real basis in Jewish society.
Consequently, as it did not possess any theoretical arguments to justify itself,
the PPSD appropriated socialist phraseology as an historical justification for its
existence. The only content of this phraseology was impracticality developed
to an extraordinary degree, a howl, a hollow bluff, which turned socialism on
Jewish terrain into a caricature.

Marxism in Galicia was never blessed with superflous depth. However much
can be said in general about this, given the intellectual chaos in the Polish workers movement in Galicia, Marxism *had to* remain a poor abstraction
amongst Jews, a dry doctrine brought into the Jewish workers movement from
outside, from the Polish environment, without organic connection to the life

in the Jewish world. The socialist theory which the Poles introduced to Jews was appropriate only for Polish relations. Polish socialism used it to explain the development of Polish society and only demonstrated its correctness on the basis of the economic development of Polish society. In a word, Polish socialism introduced Jews to nothing but general and abstract socialist slogans. It could, at the same time, have researched and become familiar with the relations in and development of Jewish society, on the basis of socialist theory. But it did not do this. In the sphere of Jewish relations, the PPSD generated intellectual deadness, passivity and inertia, as a consequence of political passivity. These are the reasons for our somewhat distorted socialist mode of thinking and the dramatic spread of Zionist ideology. The struggle against this ideology from the standpoint of the Jewish working class was entirely neglected but should have been the most important task of the Jewish proletariat.

Just as Social Democracy had to raise the proletariat's class conscious and organise it in every other province and among every other people, as well as settle accounts with given social ideologies, so Jewish socialism had to struggle to free the spirit of the Jewish proletariat from the shackles of *the traditional ghetto world view* of the past. This was especially so when Zionism held fast to the ghetto world view, as we have seen above, and when Zionist ideology, as summed up earlier, deserted the struggle for rights and created intellectual slaves to the society against which it had supposedly declared war. The question of establishing the Jewish workers movement on the basis of Marxism was, at the same time, a question of the *intellectual and moral revival* of the broad Jewish masses.

But the soul of the proletariat as a class cannot be formed over night. For such a historical change to occur it is necessary to do more than revile Zionism and the bourgeoisie. The PPSD, however, was incapable of doing more.

Socialism acquires strength in a given country or people only *when it applies its theory to the specific development and problems of that country or people*. It cannot remain an abstract doctrine, which raises itself above life. It cannot confine itself to demonstrating the economic exploitation of the proletariat by the possessing classes or the need for and necessity of economic and polit-ical struggle. Socialism, taken as a world view which has penetrated the flesh and blood of the workers movement, must slowly widen the class perspective of the proletariat in all aspects of social life. It must subject every important phenomenon of this social life to critical analysis from the perspective of the interests of the proletariat. In brief, at every step and at every opportunity it has to conduct a *struggle for minds* and modes of thought against hostile ideologies.

So the task of Jewish socialism should not only have consisted of propagat-ing general principles of socialism but also in clarifying *all* the Jewish workers movement's *practical interests* and all the important phenomena of Jewish social life, on the basis of these principles, revealing causal relations and their place in our general economic, political and cultural process.

It has long been apparent that the fulfilment of these tasks depended on capacities which the PPSD did not and could not have. It was thus incapable of carrying them out.

It had been clear, for a long time, that an individual's way of thinking is not a matter of choice or chance. On the one hand, individuals depend on the environment in which they live and which constitutes *the object* of their thought. On the other hand, the form of our individual thought depends on *our physical organisation*, i.e. our adjustment to the *environment*, which enables us to interpret it. That *physical organisation* bears a direct relationship to our psychological functions.

If we transfer the concept of thought from the world of individual speculation onto the field of social life, we can, in some respects, say the same about forms of collective thought, in the case of the Jewish working class's theoretical views and the theoretical tasks (just mentioned) which it has to fulfil.

Recognition, based on scientific socialism, that all forms of social consciousness are to be explained in terms of class and group interests is of great practical significance in the assessment of a proletarian party, i.e. Social Democracy. It is also significant to the extent that it remains true *in reverse*. The class interests of the proletariat find their expression in the consciousness of the party (in a programme) or when this party consciousness is the multifaceted expression of the proletariat's class interests and the most far-reaching conception of the implications drawn from the objective trends of previous social development. Workers parties do not always fulfil this requirement (as evidenced by the PPSD). Both the character and the content of collective party thought remain *directly dependent on the particular party's adjustment to the very working class* whose expression it should be.

The establishment of the Jewish workers movement on the basis of Marxism (i.e. fulfilling the above mentioned tasks of making abstract socialist theory into the flesh and blood of the workers movement; in other words of adjusting it to the development of Jewish society and its specific problems) could therefore only, we repeat, be a result of the closest possible adjustment of party organisation to the historical forms of the Jewish proletatiat's circumstances. It could only result from the mutual organic growth of party organisation and the workers movement itself, just as the latter has grown out of capitalist society.

Such an adjustment of organisational form and the historical way of life of the proletariat, in the context of Austrian capitalist society, meant the adoption and implementation of *nationality* as an organisational principle within the framework of the Austrian state. This meant, in other words, constituting the workers movement not in separation from existing historical, national and state circumstances but, on the contrary, on the basis of these circumstances.

Putting the question this way was simultaneously an historical and logical consequence of the policy towards Zionist and PPSD conceptions of the Jewish question, which the Jewish working class had made into a principle.

We have seen that both sides broke with the real circumstances which, for us, constitute the foundation of the Jewish question. This is why the 'solution' they arrived at remained up in the air, losing the ground from under its feet, it turned into unplanned experiments and worthless utopias.

Placing itself *on the ground of these circumstances* in Galicia, not Palestine, as the basis for its day to day struggles, the Jewish workers movement had to be consistent by going further in the direction it had chosen. That is, it could not limit itself to considering the circumstances of its activity constituted by the state and ignore other, national circumstances. It could not define the limits of its activity at will. On the contrary, its task was to consciously adjust itself to the historical, national and state conditions which it confronted. And the result of that adjustment is the principle of national organisation.

To the extent that the objective conditions of the *common Empire* and the centralising tendency of bourgeois society found expression in the general organisation of Social Democracy on the level of the whole state, the historical *national* circumstances found expression in the national form of organisation, within that framework of the general organisation. At the same time, this response to the proletariat's conditions of existence, the conditions of existence of nations and the common state, is not a mechanical admixture of two opposing tendencies in capitalist society. On the contrary, it results from the harmonisation of the historical and very complex forms of existence of the proletariat and its social thought.

The creation of a national organisation of the Jewish proletariat in Galicia introduced the organisational apparatus objectively necessary for the realisation of the objectives we discussed above. The task consisted of adjusting the isolated, cosmopolitan theory of socialism to the specific circumstances of capitalist development among the Jews and the cultivation of a corresponding consciousness in the Jewish proletariat.

But the adjustment of theory could only result from adjustment to circumstances and of organisation. Similarly, in physiology the form and structure of an organ is intimately related to its function and performance.

The separate organisation of the Jewish proletariat is nothing other than an objective, necessary, material element which constitutes the objective condition for the Jewish proletariat's consciousness.

In this way the Jewish proletariat infuses a deeper content and significance into the national organisational form. It goes beyond the formalistic and narrow assessment of such an organisation as a set of exclusively *technical* conditions to facilitate mass organisation. It reveals the objective, *historical* significance of this form of organisation as an indispensable stage in the *intellectual development* of the proletariat.

If the Jewish proletariat in Austria imposed precisely this deep historical content on the national form of organisation, this was entirely thanks to the Bund and its literature. Today, on the tenth anniversary of its creation, we can say that without the Bund we would not be what we are. And we are grateful because the Jewish working class found in the Bund's literature not only what the working class needed in general but also what the Jewish working class here specifically required intellectually. The Bund, with its literature and practice, taught [the Galician, Jewish working class] how to adjust general socialist theory to the specific circumstances of the Jewish society. And, thanks to this, the 'solution' to the Jewish question here was transferred from the sphere of the maximum socialist program's misty past,[58] to which it had been consigned, to the terrain of practical action and political struggle for the social and national liberation of the Jewish working class.

Ideologically speaking, the PPSD did not really withdraw from the struggle for Jewish masses' equal rights; in practice, it did nothing. It did not shape the Jewish proletariat into a *separate political force*. Ideological struggle combined with its actual abstention from action, amounted to an empty form without content.

So, as far as the Jews are concerned, the words of the *Communist Manifesto* 'the emancipation of the working class must be the act of the working class itself ...'[59] mean that their liberation can only be the product of their own political struggle.

And really, equal national rights for the Jewish proletariat are not at all an exotic blossom, ripening somewhere outside the sphere of the day to day struggle, that will somehow bring the Jews good fortune on the victory of socialism. This result, equal rights, can only be the *realisation of the consequences* of an inner development of both the *subjective* factor, i.e. the Jewish working class

---

58   [This sentence makes more sense if 'past' is regarded as having been mistakenly substituted for 'future'.]

59   [The words are not from the *Communist Manifesto* itself. Engels quoted them in his 1888 preface to the first authorised English edition, Engels 1990a, p. 517, paraphrasing the 'Provisional rules' of the International Working Men's Association, drafted by Marx, Marx 1985, p. 14.]

which puts this development into practice, and the *objective* factor, i.e. the rest of the capitalist society.

The Jewish working class, as a component of the general workers movement, strives to free itself from the yoke of capitalism. To realise this task, it also needs a corresponding consciousness.

But it cannot become consciousness in the broad mass without its own democratic, cultural institutions and without equal national rights. On the other hand, to win such state cultural institutions itself requires that the mass of Jewish workers achieve equal national rights, which is impossible at this historical point without an active struggle by a class conscious Jewish proletariat.

The resolution of this apparent contradiction will be achieved through *the very class struggle* of the Jewish proletariat, which achieves its national and cultural requirements in the state through its political struggle and, at the same time, through the struggle itself becomes both class and nationally conscious. To the extent that it becomes nationally conscious and develops itself, by achieving class consciousness through political struggle, the Jewish proletariat requires its opponent to make concessions and thus both transforms its environment, capitalist society, and makes that environment ready to take its national cultural needs into account.

The subjective and objective implications of the conditions for achieving equal national rights for Jews, mentioned above, are bound together and influence each other. The means of implementing this struggle and the whole evolutionary process is precisely the autonomous organisation of the Jewish working class. That is why the struggle for the 'recognition' of this autonomy extends far beyond the boundaries of ordinary organisational disputes and becomes an issue of the greatest importance for the Jewish proletariat. Its aims are indeed more far-reaching and extensive: the struggle for equal rights in the Party is only a small aspect of the great struggle for equal rights in society. But the first struggle is a precondition for the second.

∵

If we want to express what the Bund has achieved for the contemporary Jewish workers movement here in a few words, we could say that it discovered, so to speak, the Jewish working class as an independent factor in the general workers movement; a factor with specific historical circumstances and with characteristic forms of development.

Before the rise of the Bundist movement in Galicia, the reality was a mass of Jewish wage slaves, who searched blindly for the solution to the so-called Jewish question. In this regard, the PPSD, by pinning their hopes on the moment of socialism's victory, artificially partitioned off equal rights for the Jewish masses from their other activities and socialist struggle. The basic precondition for this position was the utopian relationship between the PPSD and the Jewish worker masses, in that it *did not accurately assess the political significance* of the independence of these masses. On the one hand, there were the Jewish worker masses who had to be treated like children and should not, for their own good, be given full freedom. On the other hand, there were the experienced PPS politicians who, as far-sighted statespeople and according to their own grand plans, were creating the temple of the future out of the unenlightened and unfortunate Jewish masses. That was the PPS's way of thinking.

The development of life in Galicia improved on this view. The Jewish masses began to search for other solutions. Into this situation, the practical and theoretical activity of the Bund cast a ray of light. It brought a consciousness and understanding into these elementary efforts and raised the Jewish working class to the status of a conscious political factor. This awareness and its fifteen years of development enabled the Jewish workers movement to ideologically eliminate the assimilationist tendencies of the PPSD.

CHAPTER 14

Letters about the Radek Affair*

Translated from German by Rick Kuhn

11 May 1911 to Karl Radek

Kraków

Valued Comrade!

Comrade Joseph (Domański)[1] turned to me as one of the arbitrators in your matter with the request that I make a statement, in possible recollection of the content of the determination at that time. I am happy to do this and affirmed, *insofar as memory does not fail me,* **that the decision concerning the negative determination of the accusation that your behaved dishonourably** (the sale of books which belonged to Comrade Zembaty)[2] *was acquittal.* The court also stated that Comrade Zembaty, when he raised the allegation, did so in good faith. At the same time, the court made you aware that, in future, you must avoid situations that can provide third persons gounds to raise accusations against you. *I do not remember exactly* when the Zembaty affair occurred. I believe it was either in the winter of 1902 or 1903.

With greetings
Dr Heinrich Großmann
Currently in Kraków

17 September 1912 to Józef Dománski

Vienna

As I learnt from *Vorwärts* of 14 September that in Bremen a nine-person Commission of Inquiry has been selected to consider the Radek matter and as I, on

---

*   [Originally published as Grossmann 1913.]
1   [Possibly Radek's interpolation. Joseph/Józef Dománski was a pseudonym of Feliks Dzierżinski.]
2   [Possibly Radek's interpolation.]

the other hand, know that one of the members of the Party Executive of the SDKPiL[3] has raised accusations against Radek, including Zembaty's accusation of 1904 concerning the theft of books, I regard it as my duty to send the Bremen Commission of Inquiry the following

Declaration

I dealt with Zembaty's accusation that Radek had stolen several books from him, as a member of the executive of the socialist university students' association Ruch in Kraków and then as a member of the court of arbitration on this matter.

1.   Two members of this court, the late Rudolf Moszoro and I, were given the task of examining the facts and, on the basis of our report, the court unanimously pronounced the accused *Radek not guilty on all counts*.

2.   Now, in order to protect the accuser, Zembaty, from the charge of slander, the second part of the judgement, whose exact wording, however, I no longer remember, stated that the accuser had acted bona fide[4] and similar but that this can and could not have any implications for the deeds and person of Radek.

3.   For a long time after this affair, in Ruch, we had friendly relations with Radek *as with a citizen and colleague with full rights*. Radek played an active role in the life of Kraków's associations and also wrote for the Kraków Party organ *Naprzód*, although people were well aware of the case of Zembaty contra[5] Radek. All this, on these grounds: because the affair was regarded as having been resolved and Radek was viewed as innocent.

4.   If, in view of these facts, the accusation of the theft of books in 1904 is continuously raised against Radek, it can only be construed as an unheard of and malicious violation of all moral and legal concepts.

The only forum called upon to examine this affair was the collegial court of arbitration of 1904. This fulfilled its duty without encountering contradiction from any side. Res judicata[6] must be fully recognised and, as a member of the court of 1904, as a citizen and as a human being I must raise my decisive protest against the challenge to the judgement of 1904, which was *not contested at the time*.

---

3   [The SDKPiL was the Socjaldemokracja Królestwa Polskiego i Litwy, Social Democracy of the Kingdom of Poland and Lithuania.]
4   ['Bona fide' means 'in good faith'.]
5   ['Contra' means 'against'.]
6   ['Res judicata' means 'a matter already judged'.]

The affair of the theft of books in 1904 has been dead for 8 years and it should finally disappear from the world.

Dr jur. Henryk Grossman, writer in Vienna

Member of the arbitration court of 1904

Vienna 17/IX 1912, XIII Neue Weltgasse 19.

CHAPTER 15

Notes on the History of Socialism in Poland Forty Years Ago*

Translated from Polish by Dominika Balwin

The appearance in Polish of previously unpublished, shorter works by Marx does not require any special justification. A detailed discussion of their significance for economic theory and socialism is not so much pointless as premature today, before Marx's basic and monumental work, *Capital*,[1] is better understood in the Polish literature. For the time being, these works can speak for themselves!

The publication of these shorter works, at a time when the worlds of labour and science are preparing to celebrate the fortieth anniversary of the death of this scholar of genius and immortal warrior in the cause of working class liberation, encourages us to cast a glance back to the origins of the socialist movement here and its impact on contemporary economic science.

The fact that for almost half a century the workers movement in Poland was unable to publish a single serious, independent work on socialist theory or the workers movement in general illustrates most eloquently the intellectual immaturity of the Polish working class. This, in turn, is merely an indication of the broader situation: of the extremely low level, the infancy of economic theory in general in Poland. There are deeper historical reasons for this. What Marx wrote about Germany in 1873 was also true of contemporary Poland, 'Political economy remains a foreign science ... up to this very moment'.[2] In Poland the delay in the process of giving land to the peasants and removing the remnants of feudalism held back the development of capitalist production, so that the real basis for political economy was lacking. It was therefore a commodity imported from England, France and Germany and the theoretical reflection of a foreign reality. Under these circumstances there was no place for the workers movement and it could only be a foreign, exotic plant. If one can speak at all

---

* [Originally published as Grossman 1923, the introduction to a volume of letters from Karl Marx to Ludwig Kugelmann; and Marx 1989.]
1 [Marx 1976b. At this time, Grossman was also involved in the preparation of a new translation of *Capital*, into Polish, for Książka, the same Communist-controlled publishing house which issued the book in which this introductory essay appeared.]
2 [Marx 1976b, p. 95.]

of Polish socialism at that time, it was an émigré socialism which hardly found an echo in the country. This is apparent when we look at Polish opinions about the character of these [socialist] movements.

In 1850, [Kazimierz Jaksa] Komornicki wrote with reference to the views of foreign economists, in [Józef Ignace] Kraszewski's *Athenaeum,*

> I think that the French utopians find little sympathy among us ... [Char-les] Fourier's dreams whose realisation [Louis Auguste] Blanqui does not dare to doubt, [Robert] Owen's experiments, in which neither he nor his imitators succeeded, [Pierre-Joseph] Proudhon's crazy hypotheses, which we listen to like ancient tales about giants storming the heavens or fant-astic fairy tales ...[3]

Only after the emancipation of the peasantry in the 1870s did capitalist produc-tion develop rapidly in Poland, during the period of 'organic work',[4] the period of the pioneer's idealisation of the new system[5] and removal of the representat-ives of the old order. The blades of emerging capitalism were not turned down against the proletariat emerging from the swaddling clothes of craft production but up against the representatives of feudal relations, the church and nobil-ity. The emerging bourgeoisie dreamt (although quietly and carefully) about transforming the country and its relations in accordance with its needs, along foreign lines. Hence the weakness of Polish liberalism, progressive criticism of the church and religion ...

At that time, when the Polish bourgeoisie was in statu nascendi,[6] Polish soci-ety, which was still predominantly anti-liberal and clerical, must have listened sympathetically to the echoes from abroad of the proletariat's battle against the liberal bourgeoisie. In this situation, the priest, Stefan Pawlicki, a mem-ber of the Congregation of the Resurrection of our Lord and a professor at the Jagiellonian University, undertook the first study of socialism, *Lassalle and the Future of Socialism*, which is unusual, at least here, and serious in form and con-tent.[7] Because of general hostility to the liberal bourgeoisie, Father Pawlicki was not an uncritical admirer of the golden calf of capitalism and its theor-

---

3 Komornicki 1850, p. 110. [Editor's interpolations.]
4 [The strategy of promoting education and economic development advocated by Polish posit-ivist intellectuals as the means to strengthen Poland, as opposed to the revolutionary strategy embodied in the uprisings against the occupying powers, Russia, Germany and Poland.]
5 [I.e. capitalism.]
6 ['In statu nascendi' means 'in the process of being born'.]
7 [As a student at the Jagiellonian University in Kraków, Grossman took six courses offered by Pawlicki.]

etical reflex, free competition, so he was able to examine it with open eyes and to see not only the fat dividends for stockholders but also the *other* side of the coin, 'the negative side of the social structure' based on the free market.[8] That is why he unreservedly admired the *scientific achievements* of the new socialists, particularly Marx's profound analysis of the working class's economic situation.[9] Socialism was the consequence of the economic situation of the working class and the whole contemporary social system. 'Unfortunately, ... most European countries today contend with the social question, that is, social disorder, though hardly anyone sees this and even they can do nothing about it, since even these few *are deprived of the ability to reason soberly, by the madness of civilization.*'[10] With bitter irony he wrote of the 'obverse side' of this civilisation, which 'is as important as or even more important than its reverse. If it leads to immense poverty and upheavals in property relations, what then will this bright new culture be worth?'[11]

> Our golden civilisation is celebrating on top of a sleeping Vesuvius. Yet the indications of an eruption are so visible, so numerous![12]

'The pressure of *poverty* and the affluent classes' *selfish* displays, arouse ever greater bitterness and hatred in the masses towards the authorities *which neither know how nor want to redress social distress.*' At the same time we see

> the wealth of whole provinces accumulated in the hands of a few capitalists. This glaring antithesis between the idleness of the rich and bloody work for daily bread, great wealth and naked poverty, awakens hatred of all kinds of property, without which socialism cannot exist.[13]

These facts gave rise to socialism and the social question. They were not the work of subversive individuals but the inevitable consequence of existing conditions.

> Does this stubborn persistence, this constant growth and increased boldness not *demonstrate some profound truth or partial truth*, demanding life and real expression ever more loudly? Let us not close our eyes to the sight

---

8   Pawlicki 1874, pp. 91–101.
9   Pawlicki 1874, p. 92.
10   Pawlicki 1874, p. 5. [Grossman's emphasis.]
11   Pawlicki 1874, p. 7.
12   Pawlicki 1874, pp. 5–6.
13   Pawlicki 1874, p. 8. [Grossman's emphasis.]

... let us examine it well and *become fully acquainted* with it, because an encounter with it is inevitable and much is to be gained from knowing one's enemy before meeting him.[14]

'Before meeting' the modern working class movement which did not exist at that time in Poland.

The real socialist movement in Poland begins in 1877 ... before 1877 practical socialism did not strike deep roots in the country. For some time, circles of *émigré* socialists organised and repeatedly attempted to agitate in Poznań, Galicia and the Kingdom from *the outside*, without achieving any success.[15]

In circumstances where there was no immediate threat from a workers movement and the issue of socialism arose not from the society's local, economic experience but came from the outside world, as a reflection of distant social conflicts, it is possible to speak of the golden age of scientific discussion of socialism in Poland. Undisturbed by practical anxiety about its own material future, there was still had and could be the *desire to study* phenomena and *uncover the truth*. It was at this point that an independent book on the workers movement and socialism appeared, advancing an *objective* view, typical of those scholars who, while they stood on the opposite side to the [socialist] movement socially and regarded it as a threat to the material well-being their [own] class, could nevertheless see that the movement embodied 'a profound truth or partial truth'. Instead of condemning it with blind hatred, they wanted above all to 'understand it well and completely'. Pawlicki analysed the economic situation and poverty of the working class, and argued against those who asserted that it is impossible to eliminate this poverty. Alongside the system of *capitalist production*, he regarded the *modern state and militarism*, entailing ever greater financial burdens, as an additional cause of poverty.[16]

He understood its leaders no differently from the workers movement itself. 'Praising all the positive aspects [of Marx's and Lassalle's] spirit, I speak of them sometimes with evident sympathy'. For him, Lassalle is not a run of the mill demagogue.

---

14   Pawlicki 1874, p. 10. [Grossman's emphasis.]
15   Estreicher 1896, p. 5. [Poznań was a Polish province occupied by Germany, Galicia the Polish province occupied by the Austro-Hungarian Empire, the Congress Kingdom of Poland occupied by Russia.]
16   Pawlicki 1874, pp. 113, 115.

He *conceptualises the idea* which, while false in its totality, because it is one-sided, nonetheless contains a *kernel of truth* and will sooner or later germinate and grow. This is Lassalle's historical significance and the power of his name.

Venerating his mission, he devoted himself entirely to it ... On this rests his fame and his deserved recognition.[17]

Three years after the collapse of the Paris Commune and one year after the International's Hague Congress, Father Pawlicki wrote of Karl Marx, who as founder and leader of the International[18] was hated by the bourgeoisie of the entire world, with the same objectivity and defended him from unjust slander. 'Thanks to liberal newspapers there is a completely false image of Marx and the International; they are accused of the most monstrous crimes.' Pawlicki sees in these accusations only slanders. Marx, for him, was a 'profoundly and comprehensively educated philosopher, always ready to sacrifice his personal interests to his theoretical convictions.' Marx's most important literary achievement, *Capital*, is 'a brilliant work'. Marx and Engels are 'men whose great knowledge cannot be disputed', because they helped demonstrate the negative side of the present social system. 'The new socialists, especially Marx, rendered many services, by raising [the issue of] this poverty and placing its shocking image before the eyes of the affluent classes.'[19]

At that time, from his conservative position, Pawlicki already saw and noted the *bankruptcy of official liberal economics* in comparison to scientific socialism. 'In the daily press of different political tendencies and from university *lecterns* alike, a formal crusade against the emerging enemy was announced.'[20] Liberalism

> nevertheless gained no laurels and even lost some credibility. If governments allied with it gained some *material* advantages over the social movement, at least temporarily, *theoretical* liberalism recorded only defeats over the last few decades ... Within its ranks, it could not find a *single exceptional figure* who could seriously take up the fight against the leaders of the social movement. To me, the liberal opponents of Lassalle and Marx seem to be *Lilliputians* throwing themselves upon giants. This indicates their great weakness and *great lack of spirit* ... These dwarves do not

---

17   Pawlicki 1874, p. 10. [Grossman's emphasis.]
18   [The International Working Men's Association existed between 1864 and 1876.]
19   Pawlicki 1874, pp. 48, 50, 58, 92. [Editor's interpolation.]
20   Pawlicki 1874, pp. 142–3. [Grossman's emphasis.]

even have suitable weapons to substitute for their lack of talent, *they do not have a system* in which to believe ... political economy entirely slipped from their hands and fell into those of their opponents, once Lassalle demonstrated that political economy must fall from the heights to which Ricardo had raised it into the abyss of socialism.[21]

'Against an idea, one should fight with a different idea and not physical force', he concluded idealistically. He was right, from a scientific point of view, when he argued that 'to effectively combat a *theory* one needs to confront it with a *better one*. Liberalism could not do this for the simple reason that it does not have an alternative'.[22] Bankrupt as a *science*, it put all its hope in the *authorities*. Hence the call for police and legal repression.

Father Pawlicki, however, warned against this method of countering the movement, which had a serious base in economic conditions and a superior scientific theory to that of its opponents. Socialism would not exist if its *causes in 'social unrest' were removed*. However, a decaying plutocracy, controlling stock exchanges, banks and parliaments, whose only aim was to accumulate wealth at all costs, was incapable of this [removal]. So Pawlicki warned that 'physical persecution of socialists is useless'. 'Governments have been involved in combating socialism for thirty years and cannot boast about a single serious success, despite legal proceedings, shackles and exile being used against the representatives of the new movement. Not only has this movement not disappeared, it grows stronger every year'. 'An idea cannot be bayoneted or jailed'.[23]

The above presentation is not intended to analyse and criticise Father Pawlicki's ideas but to underline his attitude to the working class movement and its theoretical representatives. It was a unique picture. He based his argument entirely on foreign sources dealing with economic and social issues. The very fact that there was no workers movement in the country and that it could not yet pose a threat facilitated his objectivity. Marx was right about our writers on the social question:

At the time when they were able to deal with political economy in an unprejudiced way, modern economic conditions were absent from the reality of [Poland]. And as soon as these conditions did come into existence, it was under circumstances that no longer permitted their impartial

---

21 Pawlicki 1874, p. 143. [Grossman's emphasis. Lilliput, in Swift 1894, was inhabited by tiny people.]

22 Pawlicki 1874, p. 143. [Grossman's emphasis.]

23 Pawlicki 1874, pp. 115, 142.

investigation within the bounds of the bourgeois horizon. In so far as
political economy is bourgeois, i.e. in so far as it views the capitalist order
as the absolute and ultimate form of social production, instead of as a
historically transient stage of development, it can only remain a science
while the class struggle remains latent or manifests itself only in isolated
and sporadic phenomena.[24]

The idyll reflected in Pawlicki's book was soon disrupted by the *emergence of the
Polish socialist movement*, from 1878 and 1879: the activities of Ludwik Waryński and his comrades in the Kingdom, the great jury trial of 1880 in Kraków,
the foundation of the First Proletariat, the Poznań trial of 1882 and two trials
in Warsaw.[25] Suddenly, the idyll of bourgeois economics in Poland burst like
a soap bubble. The birth of the new class movement finished off the weak
plant of so-called independent economic science. Voices like Pawlicki's disappeared for ever, as if by magic. His work was isolated, forgotten and not
subsequently consulted. After 1877, studies of socialism like Pawlicki's were
no longer possible. As soon as the first nuclei of the workers movement in
Poland emerged, the middle class camp moved into battle against the proletariat. Since then, no serious work has appeared analysing the practice or
theory of the workers movement. The desire to conduct *scientific research and
study* died once and for all and gave way to the trivial defence of interests:
apologetics.

The Warsaw progressives declare themselves against socialism in an 1878 article in *Nowiny*, by [Aleksander] Świętochowski,[26] aided by liberal university
economics, in the person of the rector of the University of Lwów, Professor
Leon Biliński. Impressed by 'the memorable socialist agitation of 1878–9', Biliński decided to offer a picture of the 'terrible effects of socialist efforts on the
fatherland, church, family and social order', of course 'on the basis of sober
and just science', from the university rector's lectern in an inaugural address to
students in October 1882.[27] In fact, this particular lecture by the distinguished

---

24   Marx 1976b, p. 96. [Grossman replaced 'Germany' with 'Poland'.]
25   [Waryński was arrested in Kraków, in Galicia, in 1879. He was acquitted of all major charges
       by the jury the following year. In 1882 Polish and German socialist agitators were tried in
       Poznań. In 1882, Waryński and others founded the Proletariat organisation in Warsaw, the
       capital of the Congress Kingdom of Poland, known as the First Proletariat to distinguish it
       from later groups with the same name. In 1885 its leading members, including Waryński,
       were put on trial.]
26   ['*Nowiny*' means '*News*'. Świętochowski 1878, Grossman mistook the year for 1879.]
27   Biliński 1883.

'Member of the Academy'[28] was indeed 'sober': for the first time in the history of Poland and other western countries a mass class of free wage labourers emerged as a phenomenon. They organised themselves in national and international associations and aim to fundamentally change the social system. 'Sober' science regarded neither this broad social movement nor its socialist theory as *problems* worthy of research. 'Above all', Biliński naively confided, 'I wanted to *caution* university students loudly against disastrous socialist currents'. At the university, which should be a source of the light of science and learning, he called for a murderous crusade against socialists and, at the same time, as is normal for 'sober and just science', he clearly demonstrated that, while combating socialists and socialism, he had read *not a single* work by a distinguished literary representative of socialism of the past or present. In the sixty pages of his speech, overloaded with erudite quotations and the titles of scholarly works, there is not a single reference to any work by the socialists against whom he polemicised. With the skill of an ignoramus and compiler, he drew his wisdom and information about socialism second and even third hand, from questionable sources such as [Landelin] Winterer, [Heinrich] Semler, [Émile] Laveley, [Rudolf] Meyer and Bernhard Becker, as befits 'sober' science.[29] Thus, according to the worthy Member of the Academy, in his biography of [Gracchus] Babeuf, [Philippe] Buonarroti[30] 'in 1837 already explicitly decreed that regicide, assassination and murder were means to achieve communism'.[31]

At this time, when western economic theory was forced to pay attention to scientific socialism, its most famous representative [Eugen] Böhm-Bawerk admitted (1884) that Marx is 'the greatest theoretician of socialism, indisputably original and consistent' and devoted a long chapter to the presentation and critique of Marx's *scientific theory*.[32] In the same way, a number of other well-known economists in the bourgeois camp regarded Marx as 'the most significant event in contemporary socialist literature'.[33] Yet the honourable Professor

---

28   [I.e. the Polska Akademia Umiejętności (Polish Academy of Arts and Sciences) based in Kraków.]

29   [The references are presumably to Winterer 1891; Semler 1880; Laveley 1881; Meyer 1873; and Becker 1875.]

30   [Buonarroti 1836.]

31   Biliński 1883, p. 18.

32   [Böhm-Bawerk, whose seminars Grossman had attended in Vienna, was not quite as effusive about Marx as Grossman's (mis)quotation suggests:
      '... Karl Marx is pre-eminently a theorist, and indeed, after Rodbertus, the most distinguished theorist of socialism. Although his doctrine coincides in many respects with the pioneering research of Rodbertus, he displayed undeniable originality and a high degree of keen logic in developing his doctrine ...' (Böhm-Bawerk 1959a, p. 248).]

33   Knies 1883, p. 301. Thirty years later, even Aleksander Świętochowski, although his critique

and Member of the Academy, the pride of our economic science, had nothing more to say about Marx to young people than that 'murder, robbery and arson with the ultimate aim of confiscating all property and transferring it to the cosmopolitan workers republic was already Marx's programme in 1850'. He blamed Marx for the 'terrible growth of socialism in France', as well as the 'black gang', which 'desecrates churches, tears down crosses and steals gold and silver from churches', prowling there at the time; finally recalling that 'assassinations using dynamite were probably [!] decided on at a congress in Roanne'. Admittedly, he said, there is doubt about the link between assassination attempts and socialism. 'These facts, however, are incontestable for anyone familiar with the socialists' programme since 1848 and especially the international programme since 1863'. Matters were similar in Germany and Hungary. In Germany there were calls for violent explosions with the aim of destroying 'everything that stands in the way of socialism'. 'Let all the castles, buildings and monuments perish in flames ... let fire be our watchword.' He diligently repeated the police press in saying that 'the antisemitic unrest in Hungary is the result of the careful planning of the socialists who burn down Jewish factories under the cover of antisemitism. They want, by this means, to deprive the workers of bread in order to win them over to their cause.' He accused socialists of 'drugging the owners of factories and stealing their money' because they needed funds for agitational purposes. Finally, he asked 'how is it possible to ward off the spectre of socialism which is a danger to the whole civilised world?' As a cure for socialism he recommended, depending on the circumstances of particular countries, normal criminal laws or *special*, more severe *laws*. We have seen Father Pawlicki's argument that 'to effectively combat a theory one needs to confront it with a *better one*'. It could be assumed that this was especially the duty of a professor who addressed university students with words of science and explanation. Biliński understood science differently; he regarded idealistic fantasies of this type as unnecessary: he referred not to theory but to *prisons* and gallows! He looked approvingly in the direction of Russia, where the government 'responds with a state of siege and the gallows'. Similarly in France and Germany, 'where socialism is almost in power, normal laws are considered inadequate'. He listed the provisions of special criminal laws: in France in 1872 and in Germany in 1878. In other countries no special laws exist, since in Austria, for example, 'our penal system is severe enough ... even without special laws'.[34]

---

of Marxism was not profound, admitted 'it would be impudent and ineffective to diminish the significance and power of this mighty current, which emerges from Marx's theory. His *Capital* was a monumental work.' (Świętochowski 1910, p. 220).

34   Biliński 1883, pp. 28, 34, 35, 37, 39, 41–42.

The above examples from Biliński's work illustrate the nature of official, economic science at universities in Poland and its relationship with socialism, in theory and practice, at the end of the 1880s and start of the 1890s. It appeared that economics in our country in the late nineteenth century was still literally at the level of Germany at the beginning of the eighteenth century, as indicated by what the early German cameralists called it: '*eine Polizeywissenschaft*'.[35]

How did this science and its relationship to socialism develop over the next forty years?

I will devote a separate study to the characteristics of this development. It is, however, very significant that when the police, in their blind crudeness, now confiscate such a monumental work as Marx's *Communist Manifesto*, the representatives of science and the press are silent.

• •
•

The letters to Dr [Ludwig] Kugelmann are related to Marx's *Critique of the Draft Program of the Social Democratic Party*, dated 5 May 1875 and written during the same period, that is, before the unity Congress of 22 to 27 May 1875, in Gotha. They concerned the draft programme, drawn up in the middle of February of that year, as a compromise by delegates from the two factions of the German workers movement, the so-called Lassallians and Eisenachers.[36]

The so-called Eisenach Programme of August 1869, of the recently established German Social Democratic Workers Party to which [Wilhelm] Liebknecht and [August] Bebel belonged, was not strictly socialist but a mixture of Marxist, Lassallian and bourgeois democratic demands and positions.

In addition to Marx's demands for 'the abolition of class rule' and 'abolition of the current mode of production (the wages system)' and, furthermore, the [assertion that] class struggle for liberation on an international scale is necessary, it contained Lassallian demands, 'workers to receive the undiminished proceeds of labour' and 'state loans for free producers' cooperatives' and finally, the legacy of bourgeois democratic ideology, phrases about a 'free people's state', 'free administration of justice' etc.[37]

---

35   [Cameralism, *Kameralwissenschaft*, was the eighteenth-century German university discipline of public policy within which '*eine Polizeywissenschaft*', literally 'a police science', dealt with economic policy.]

36   [The Lassallians were the members of the German General Workers Association, which Ferdinand Lassalle had founded in 1863, a year before his death.]

37   [Social Democratic Workers Party 1869.]

The draft repeated these positions and demands, embellishing them with other Lassallian phrases about the iron law of wages and the political formula that in relation to the working class all the other social classes form 'one reactionary mass'.[38]

Marx's criticised these views and was intended for a small group of influential people. It was written with absolute sincerity in an attempt to expose the truth, without taking extraneous personal or tactical considerations into account.

Marx criticised the Gotha Program ruthlessly, arguing that it was regressive compared with the level of theoretical development previously achieved. The settlement of the fundamental disputes dividing the two factions in the workers movement through a compromise and the unification of the proletarian movement on that basis would be a short-term success that demoralised the Party, achieved at too high a cost. Two years later, in a letter to Engels of 23 July 1877, Marx wrote 'that fusion has degraded the Party, both in theory and in practice'.[39] That was obvious. Historically conditioned contradictions within the working class cannot be overcome by means of deals and compromises but must be fought through to the end, as long as they are not removed by the very dialectic of the real historical process.

Marx's criticism undoubtedly influenced the ideas of other prominent contemporary activists about socialism, as we see in Liebknecht's pamphlet on the agrarian question, where he interpreted particular points of the Eisenach programme entirely in the spirit of Marx's criticism.[40] His criticism, however, had almost no influence on the character of the Party's decisions in general, as was apparent when the original draft, in the letter published here, is compared with the final version, as amended at the unity Congress in Gotha. In part, this was an expression of the immaturity of the contemporary workers movement in Germany, which was still entirely incapable of raising itself to the level of Marx's theory, as recently expressed in *Capital* (1867) and refined in practice by the titanic struggles of the first 'International' (1864–2). It was also a consequence of the systematic persecution that started after 1874 and the impending Exceptional Law.[41] That early period of repression by the Prussian prosecutor and the police, the so-called 'Tessendorf era',[42] forced the workers movement to

---

38   [Marx 1989, pp. 88, 91.]
39   [Marx 1991, p. 246.]
40   [Liebknecht 1876, pp. 181–2.]
41   [Marx 1976b. From 1878 until 1890, the 'Exceptional Law', also known as the 'Socialist Law' or 'Anti-socialist Law', banned socialist organisations in Germany.]
42   [Hermann Ernst Christian Tessendorf was a German public prosecutor and eventually the chief public prosecutor.]

concentrate all its efforts on the practical struggle against repression and on keeping its repressed organisation alive. What the internal development of the workers movement did not achieve, brutal outside pressure brought about in the form of the *organisational need to merge the two factions of the workers movement* despite their programmatic differences, whose significance was marginalised for the time being by circumstances, and despite the increasingly widespread conviction in the Party that the newly formulated Gotha Program was inadequate. In this context, Marx's 'Gotha letter' fell into oblivion.

Only after the Exceptional Law ended and the creation of a new party organisation at the Halle Congress (1890) could the workers movement in Germany begin to think about formulating a new programme, which would express the theoretical views prevalent in the Party.

The forgotten 'Gotha letter' was brought to light between the Halle Congress and the Erfurt Congress [1891], during discussions about the new programme with the aim of deepening them. But this was not done by those to whom the letter was addressed but by Friedrich Engels who drew it from Marx's literary estate and published it in *Neue Zeit*.[43]

I am publishing this letter in Polish now because its extraordinary content and skilful critical analysis make it an important milestone in the development of the theory of scientific socialism. When the workers movement is going through a critically significant period, it can deepen understanding of crucial problems of the proletarian class struggle, which were so glaringly apparent in the tactics of 4 August 1914 and whose origins go back to the end of previous century.[44]

The critique of the Gotha Program is unknown not only here but also more widely. It is no mere coincidence that after its publication by Engels in 1891, to the horror of certain circles in the German Party, this exceptionally important historical document was not republished for a period of thirty years, preventing the masses from reading it. Meanwhile, the Party's publishing houses spent tens of thousands on worthless local screeds of unknown extent!

Everyone will understand the reasons for this extraordinary course of events when they read the 'Gotha letter', especially part four, on 'the democratic section' [of the program]. During the period when Marx's work was condemned to oblivion and in the confusion brought about by the Party's Executive, a 'new spirit' arose and, influenced by Kautsky's popularisation [of Marxism], over-

---

43   Marx 1989. [*'Neue Zeit'* means *'New Times'*.]
44   [I.e. the capitulation of socialist organisations in most countries to the politics of their ruling classes, on the outbreak of World War I, and the revisionist controversy inside German Social Democracy in 1896–1900.]

whelmed the German Party after 1891. This was the first link in a systematic and unbroken chain of attempts to adapt Marxism to the opportunistic practices of everyday life.

Is it any surprise that Marx's analysis is not only forgotten and concealed by his own camp but that his opponents all failed to understand it? Indeed, not only professional persecutors of Marxists, like our own Erazm Majewski, but even the best 'experts' on Marxism among the representatives of official wisdom, demonstrate astonishing and disarming ignorance. In 1891, the same year that the devastating critique of the Gotha Program appeared, Georg Adler, a professor at the University of Freiburg, wrote: 'the new Gotha program bears almost exclusively Marx's communist imprint and only a few and insignificant concessions have been made to the Lasallians'. 'In general, the Gotha program is imbued with the spirit of Marxist theory.'[45] Emil Hammacher, author of another voluminous critique of Marx and a professor in Bonn, exhibited similar remarkable ignorance of the 'Gotha letter'.

Marx distinguished two stages in the distribution of goods in his analysis of the communist system. At the point of its emergence from capitalist society, it will bear the birthmarks of the old, maternal society and so, for the present, distribution would be according the principal of *equal right*, the principal of *equivalence*. But this formal equality, inherited from capitalist society, will in fact be unequal given that individuals and their needs are unequal. Only in the more advanced stage of communist society, when labour productivity has increased dramatically and notions of law and morality taken over from bourgeois society have disappeared, when people work not only in order to survive but because they feel a need to work, only then could the distribution of goods be based on the principle: to each according to their needs. This is Marx's position. What did Hammacher make of this? He explained 'that what is meant is the following':

> Originally, the effect of an equal law operates unjustly, because individuals are *still* (!) different ... Only once all the dross of the bourgeois state has fallen away is absolute *equality*, because it is *absolute perfection realised*. It apportions needs and capacities equally to all. Not only social but also *mental inequality* between people is, in Marx's clear (!) formulation, a 'bourgeois limitation'.[46]

---

45   Adler 1891, pp. 219, 223.
46   Hammacher, 1909, p. 377.

So, with the short word 'still', the learned Professor attempted to 'explain' that, according to Marx's critique of the Gotha Program, individuals 'still' un-equal in capitalist society will in time be liberated from this human, psycholo-gical inequality and brought into the domain of equal abilities. According to the assurances of the learned Professor, Marx himself supposedly made this 'clear'. This is the very same Hammacher who, elsewhere in his book, stated that 'per-haps the most beautiful [words] that Marx wrote' was precisely this passage, where Marx mentioned that true freedom and the *all-round development of the individual* will only be possible under the system of the future, when the mater-ial existence of every individual is assured and they have enough time at their disposal.[47] But a certain kind of 'knowledge', which long ago ceased to strive to obtain the truth and to explain phenomena, is only apologetics for the existing form of ownership. 'Do not understand' is its motto but, as Du Pont de Nemours wrote to Jean-Baptiste Say over a hundred years ago, accusing him of *obfusca-tion*: 'Dupez votre peuple, afin de lui prendre plus aisement son argent!'[48]

---

47   Hammacher 1909, p. 385. [The italicised words are from Marx 1989, p. 87: the passage that
      Hammacher quotes is from Marx 1981b, pp. 958–9.]
48   ['Fool your people in order to take their money more easily', Nemours 1833, p. 34.]

CHAPTER 16

Adler, Victor*

Translated from German by Ken Todd

Born 24 June 1852 in Prague, completed medical studies in Vienna. Originally German nationalist in political orientation, he began to draw closer to the workers movement in 1881. From 1886 his life story cannot be separated from the history of Austrian Social Democracy. Adler exerted himself to unite the workers movement, which was suffering from fierce struggles and internal divisions, founded the weekly publication *Gleichheit*, later called the *Wiener Arbeiter-Zeitung*[1] (from 1895, a daily). At the Party Congress in Hainfeld (1889), he succeeded in uniting the Party and giving it a programme and solid organisation. The nationalities programme adopted in Brno (1899), however, brought the national struggles raging in the bourgeois camp into the workers movement. Nor did the conquest of universal [male] suffrage (1907) succeed, as Bismarck's electoral law in Germany had, in creating unity or preventing the ultimate break up of Austria. As the creator of the tactics of Austrian Social Democracy and also at the Congresses of the Second International, Adler was less concerned with clarifying contradictions than he was with conciliating them through compromises, in reality, that is, with obscuring them. After the outbreak of the World War, he espoused the theory that it was the duty of socialists in all countries – in order to prevent the defeat of their own country – to fight on the side of their governments, with 'the will to victory' in defence of the fatherland, and to stay the course. After the breakup of the Austro-Hungarian Empire he became Foreign Affairs Minister of German-Austria. He died in Vienna on 11 November 1918.

Writings

See Victor Adler's collected works, 1922–29, *Aufsätze, Reden und Briefe*, 11 volumes, Wien: Verlag der Wiener Volksbuchhandlung.

---

* [Originally published as Grossmann 1931a.]
1 ['*Gleichheit*' means '*Equality*'. '*Wiener Arbeiter-Zeitung*' means '*Viennese Workers' Newspaper*'.]

Literature

Austerlitz, Friedrich 1919, 'Der tote Führer', *Der Kampf*, 12, 32: 725–6.

Brügel, Ludwig 1922, *Geschichte der österreichischen Sozialdemokratie. Band 3*, Wien: Verlag der Wiener Volksbuchhandlung, pp. 272 et seq.

Hartmann, Ludo Moritz 1918, 'Victor Adler', *Der Kampf*, 11, 12: 773–6.

CHAPTER 17

Anarchism*

Translated from German by Joseph Fracchia

1   The Essence of Anarchism and Its Currents

Anarchism (the word '*an-archie*', without domination, first used in the year 1840 by [Pierre-Joseph] Proudhon) is both a theory and also a movement. In theory, anarchism strives for the abolition of contemporary social ills that, from the anarchist viewpoint, consist of all round (political, economic, legal, religious etc.) dependence and coercion – in absolutist or democratic form – exercised on people. It studies the circumstances under which human groups can possibly live together without any authoritarian coercion, thus with the greatest freedom of all individuals. Anarchism draws the most extreme conclusions from the individualist perspective of bourgeois – political and economic – liberalism on innate human rights: the theory that regards the full development of the *individuals'* powers as the highest goal of society, which can only be realised through complete freedom of individuals from any external social interference. This notion found its most acute expression in the Physiocratic formula: 'Laissez faire, laissez aller, le monde va de lui-même'.[1]

Bourgeois liberalism – the Manchester doctrine[2] – is in theory anti-statist but on the contrary, because of the class contradictions and conflicts that arise from private ownership, in practice needs the state to protect property from the propertyless. It does not draw the ultimate conclusions from its own theory, namely the abolition of the state, but rather concedes its influence, even if the least possible, on economic life. Anarchism, on the contrary, demands the complete abolition of the state and, what is more, the elimination of all coercion in every sphere of social life. In this respect, anarchism is in funda-

---

* [Originally published as Grossmann 1931b. Grossman included some passages from Grünberg 1911a.]
1 ['Laissez faire, laissez aller, le monde va de lui-même' means 'leave it to itself, let it go, the world goes on by itself', a free trade injunction against government intervention. The similar slogan, 'Laissez faire et laissez passer, le monde va de lui même', 'leave it to itself and let it pass, the world goes on by itself' has been attributed to Vincent de Gournay, a French Physiocrat.]
2 [There was a reference here to a non-existent entry in in Elster's *Dictionary* on 'Manchester-lehre' ('Manchester theory'). The issue of Adam Smith's and more broadly classical political economy's attitude to the state was, however, discussed in Elster 1933, p. 216.]

mental and unbridgeable contradiction with socialism, which does not have an atomistic conception of individuals but an organic conception of classes as its starting point and accepts firm obligations on individuals and also the limitation of their sphere of freedom as well. Anarchism's anti-statist attitude results, further, in its anti-parliamentarism. Anarchism combats all state apparatuses and all coercion, even if they have a democratic form, because here a minority also remains dependent on the decisions of a majority.

In the realisation of its goal, anarchism renounces all legal coercion. It does not seek a situation of disorder. It wants to maintain organisation in human society and only to change the kind of organisation: it wants to replace today's coerced organisation with purely contractual organisation. All the requirements of social life: production, commerce and consumption, buying and selling, tenancy and rent, marriage and family should be fulfilled through voluntary and cancellable contracts of affected members or uncoerced, associated groups and not by legal means. For every law implies rights and duties and consequently an authoritarian organisation to control the fulfilment of these duties and to guarantee the exercise of these rights. The current order cannot, therefore, be combatted by means of laws, because that would only mean affirming the current condition of all round dependence. The view that the anarchists want to attain their goals through violence is, in this general conception, erroneous.

The core of anarchism is the *theory of the state* common to all its currents, while two currents can be distinguished in the sphere of *economics*. The most consistent current is the individualist anarchists ([Max] Stirner, Proudhon) who – in contrast to socialists – are determined supporters of private property. This perspective is grounded in the essence of anarchism. A theory that wants to confer on individual people spheres of freedom to the greatest extent must give them the possibility of exerting this freedom by means of private property. Private property only needs to be liberated from certain injustices which now afflict it. But then it will constitute the basis of the order of economic rights to a still greater degree than under the capitalist social order. Communist anarchism ([Mikhail] Bakunin, [Pyotr] Kropotkin), which demands a certain community of goods, wanting to abolish not only the state but also private property, is less consistent. As, however, majority rule is a practical necessity in large, centralised societies while anarchism rejects any kind of dependence of the minority on the majority, communist anarchism is opposed to all forms of centralisation and is for the greatest decentralisation of economic life, into small autonomous groups based on the voluntary decisions of the participants.

In understanding anarchism, it is useful to distinguish its essence sharply from different, only apparently related tendencies. Earlier and recent philosophies of rights and the state are often, erroneously counted as anarchist; these exhibit a certain relation to anarchist ideas, to the extent that they too proceed on an individualist basis. For example, Jean-Jacques Rousseau, who in his *Contrat social* was a champion of political liberalism but never advocated anarchism.[3] He wanted rights to issue from everyone's individual wills, the volonté générale,[4] and then for the order of rights that emerged in this way to be *binding* on all members of the national community. In individual matters, for example of child rearing and religion, Rousseau actually conceded the state a very extensive coercive power.

Just as little can Wilhelm von Humboldt, Herbert Spencer, and Friedrich Nietzsche be counted as anarchists. They all did combat the state in many areas of its activity, from the viewpoint of their liberal individualism, without negating the right of coercion as such. They just demanded *very narrow limits* on that right.

Still less can a religious or Christian anarchism be spoken of. It was precisely against religion that the anarchists developed their greatest activity. For, according to the anarchist conception, religion demands the strongest moral subordination of people to dogmas, resignation to divine will. Further, all authority has faith as its precondition and resignation creates the most favourable atmosphere for tyranny. Anarchism's opposition to all authority and dependence also includes the struggle against dependence on dogmas and church organisations. The doctrine of Lev Nikolayevich Tolstoy (1828–1910) is, indeed, called 'Christian anarchism'. It has, however, nothing to do with the Christian religion and is much more a theory of love that refuses all authority: law, state, property and church dogma.

2   Early Individualist Anarchism: Godwin, Stirner, Proudhon

As individual flashes of ideas, anarchist thoughts are, like those of ethical socialism, as old as the philosophy of rights itself and are consequences of particular principles of natural law: consideration of whether and how the coercive power of law, that is law itself, is justified. In this sense one can speak of anarchist ideas in antiquity (in the doctrines of Zeno and Carpocrates) and in the Middle Ages (the doctrines of Christian sects and heretics as protests against the accumulation of church injunctions and decrees, against making Christianity mechanical, through the church's apparatus of domination) and

---

3   [Rousseau 1923.]
4   ['Volontê gênêrale' means 'general will'.]

one can glimpse precursors of anarchism in natural law and individualist currents of the sixteenth to the eighteenth century. Wherever it was a matter of overthrowing outmoded authorities, antiquated laws and regulations, atomising old social conditions or dissolving sclerotic ideologies. Especially during the struggle of the advancing bourgeoisie against feudal domination at the start of the bourgeois revolution in England (1642–8) and the French Revolution of 1789, natural law slogans about innate human rights arose. Anarchism was first presented as a *political theory* with immediate application to practical life by William Godwin, in his *Enquiry Concerning Political Justice* (1793).[5] Starting from the natural law perspective that people are more admirable the more they can express themselves in their individuality, Godwin drew the ultimate conclusions, namely that all governments and laws are evil and the cause of all vices. Nevertheless, anarchism will not be a state of disorder but rather a state of *mutual forbearance*. For Godwin, the ideal is a state of society without government, with neither coercive nor state power, but in which property, liberated from the defects with which it is afflicted, will be retained in principle. The differences between rich and poor, however, will abolished, goods will be equally distributed among members, and each will voluntarily renounce their property in favour of the pressing need of the other. Property will only be abolished if it arises from the labour others. Small communities (parishes), that reach agreements with each other about the extradition of criminals, will suffice for the regulation of property disputes. No written laws will be required for small parishes; justice can be determined case by case.

The idea of denying the need for any order of rights, as embodied in the historically developed state, first became really significant and widespread with the development of the capitalist mode of production and the decline of the smaller producers that accompanied it. They felt oppressed by the state that imposed taxes on them, did not sufficiently protect their property against the competition of superior, large industrialists, passed laws strengthening loan and finance capital, and delivered the petty bourgeoisie to the former. They were therefore anti-statist in orientation. Anarchism is thus a phenomenon accompanying the incipient workers movement, likewise in economically backward states if the working class is still strongly permeated with petty bourgeois elements, robbed of their earlier economic autonomy. In this regard, anarchism goes back to Max Stirner (the pseudonym of Johann Kaspar Schmidt 1806–56) and especially to Pierre-Joseph Proudhon (1809–65), whose direct influence on the workers movement, during its youthful phase both in and outside France, was very significant.

---

5   See Grünberg 1932a. [Godwin 1842.]

In his *The Ego and His Own*, which appeared in 1845, Stirner,[6] developing
Ludwig Feuerbach's theory further, rejected all institutions and ideas – God,
humankind, society, people and state, truth, freedom, humanity, justice – as
unreal, abstract, fictional assumptions, created by human imagination.[7] Only
individuals with their needs and their wills are real. Therefore, only the 'ego', the
individual, is to be taken as the starting point and everything that constitutes
a constraint on living absolutely freely is to be combated and eliminated. Religion, conscience, morality, rights, law, family, state are just yokes and oppressors, imposed on individuals in the name of an abstraction and which individuals must combat. There is no other right than actual might. 'He who has power
has right'.[8] ... Consequently every state is a despotism, whether of one or of
many despots. Therefore every state, even a democratic one, is to be combatted.
Stirner rejected every sort of subsumption of an 'ego' by others, out of which
any obligations (that are social or concerning rights) could grow. Entirely consistently, he mocked bourgeois radicalism and liberalism, as well as socialism,
'free competition', as well as the 'the principle of ragamuffin society – partition'.[9] However, it is clear that no 'ego' can exist *alone*. If the collective disintegrates into mere 'egos', for each of whom others only have significance as objects
and who simply use them but is not willing to sacrifice anything for them, will
not then every human connection cease? Stirner denied this. Individuals will
seek one another *because* and *if* they need one another. Stirner preached his
'unions of egoists',[10] i.e. free associations into which each 'ego' enters and in
which it remains *when and so long* as it serves *its* interests. In short, it is not
the union which possesses and makes use of the 'individual', as is the case for
the state and society, but rather the 'individual' possesses and makes use of the
union. The absolute exercise of self will and self interest replaces attachment.
Stirner is the first theoretician of absolute egoism. If rich and poor exist then
it is only because the poor patiently bear their oppressed condition. In order
to change it, they only need to rebel against the rich; as soon as they seriously
want to, they will be stronger and the domination of wealth will come to an
end. Salvation lies in struggle, not in fruitless appeals to the magnanimity of the
oppressors. 'Take hold, and take what you require'.[11] In fact, however, Stirner did
not demand the abolition of private property. He was only against state or com-

---

6   See Grünberg 1933a.
7   [Stirner 1907.]
8   [Stirner 1907, p. 132.]
9   [Stirner 1907, p. 350. Stirner emphasised 'partition'.]
10   [Stirner 1907, p. 234.]
11   [Stirner 1907, p. 18.]

munal property, against legally guaranteed property in any form whatsoever; but for the ego, he demanded ownership of 'everything' which the 'ego' requires and can obtain. '[T]he egoist behaves as proprietor'.[12] Stirner's 'union of egoists' is therefore nothing but an association of real petty bourgeois proprietors.

Proudhon[13] was above all a moralist and his theory can only be understood from the perspective of ethics; for Proudhon morality dominates all other problems. The social question, according to Proudhon, is a question of justice. The existing capitalist order is unethical and, therefore, also unfree and leads to the poverty for the majority of society. Consequently, it should be replaced by another social order in which justice prevails. Poverty is the result of the immoral mechanism of exchange that currently exists and in which individuals receive less value for the products of their labour than they have an economic right to. The value of a product is nothing other than the amount of labour time required for its production. If exchange relations among people were regulated by justice then everyone would give and receive equal values in exchange. At present, however, exchange is unjust, because the value of products does not express the labour expended in making them. Under just exchange, there will be no income without labour. It actually exists because of the institution of private property. For it alone enables the owners of capital and land to take advantage of circulation, because commodities, in exchange, are sold at *prices* above their values. Property thus enables owners to tax the proceeds of social production, i.e. to seize a part of the proceeds for themselves, without payment of a counter value. As the propertyless are not free, because they cannot produce without means of production, they have to accept these deductions. A lack of balance in social distribution results. On the one hand, there are those who do not work, the ruling bourgeois class, whose income flows to it solely from property: the new industrial feudalism that lives on interest from its capital, rents and sharecropping leases on landholdings, on rents from houses, share dividends, profits from entrepreneurial activities, stipends, sinecures and pensions etc. It lives, in short, from the labour of others. In this sense, according to Proudhon, property = theft (La propriété c'est le vol). On the other hand, there is an entire class of people who possess no property other than their labour, are disadvantaged in exchange and suffer deprivation. The cause of the deprivation and dependence of the great majority of people accordingly lies not in the sphere of the production of goods but in the *sphere of circulation*. The state is only necessary in such a society, built on unjust exchange and deprivation, only as long, namely, as economic justice and the maxims of

---

12   [Stirner 1907, p. 342.]
13   See Grünberg 1932c.

reciprocity (mutualisme) do not hold sway. The sole function of government actually consists in suppressing revolts by the oppressed majority against economic inequities. It follows from this analysis that only the fixation, the constitution of value based on labour, through an economic organisation which abolishes existing competition and monopoly, can create the guarantee that the law of value, according to which all receive the full value of the products of their labour, i.e. value in proportion to labour performed, will be realised. In this way, the disturbed balance of distribution and social harmony will be restored, and a new society can arise on the ruins of the dominant economic anarchy. In such a society, based on economic justice in exchange, the state loses all justification.

Proudhon now wanted to investigate the conditions under which his postulate of proportional or constituted commodity value can be realised. The improvement of the situation of the oppressed classes cannot be expected from direction by the *state*, from reformism of any kind. The state is by nature always conservative. Situated between hostile parties – a majority deprived of rights, on one side, and a powerful privileged minority, in whose hands all social all are concentrated, on the other – it, even in form of a democratic majority, always acts as the servant and defender of the propertied. To the rule of legal despotism, Proudhon counterposed the rule of the *contract of exchange* (le contrat d'échange); not the contract in Rousseau's sense, which is an ideological construct that only masks the tyranny of the majority with the fiction of the volonté générale, but a system of voluntary, real, direct contracts among the participants, without any representation. Proudhon rejected all coercion of the individual by an authority. Only a general contract, under which all commit to pay only the *just price* i.e. the *cost value* without any additions, profits etc., in all sales and purchases, will put an end to all the working class's disadvantages. For social inequality only arises because commodities are sold at prices above their values. The *contractual industrial organisation*, encompassing all spheres of the economy, will replace the authority of government – and all coercive domination in general: 'the producer deals with the consumer, member with his [workers'] association, the peasant his community; the community with the district; the district with the department'.[14] In this way economic rights, economic justice will be restored, interest on capital abolished, on the basis of the reciprocal services, and equilibrium in distribution realised. Worker will receive the full value of their products. In exchange, all receive only their cost values,

---

14   [Proudhon 1851, p. 310. Editor's interpolation. The published English translation is unsatisfactory.]

i.e. values proportional to their contribution, so that every parasitical interme-diation, which requires excessive compensation, disappears. The *free contract* thus simultaneously becomes a *just contract*, which encompasses the *entire structure of society*. *Large landholdings* will be divided and mobilised. For, with the application of the principles of contractual justice, every payment of a sharecropper's rent creates a right of participation in ownership and in a relat-ively short time large landholders will disappear, while small sharecroppers will become direct proprietors. Proudhon regarded this system, corresponding to the 'property instincts' of peasants, as better than the nationalisation projects of socialists. Small peasants remain on their plots of land, free and independ-ent.

In the industrial sphere, Proudhon's suggested solution was of a different kind, for here the producer, unlike the peasant, cannot remain free and inde-pendent. The necessity of using a combination of numerous workers with different specialisations is inherent in the nature of every industrial under-taking. For that reason, 'workers associations' are the necessary cells of indus-trial organisation. Through them, by virtue of contractual justice, workers also become their own capitalists and the entrepreneurs disappear. Far from being an opponent of private property, Proudhon saw the natural right to the products of their own labour as the expression of individuals' personalities. Proudhon therefore did not want to *abolish* it but to make it, purified of cur-rent abuses, accessible to all and to *generalise* it, i.e. to tear it from the hands of the small number of current owners – the state that accumulates it in its domains, the church that immobilises it in its dead hand, the bankocracy that increasingly concentrates it – in order to raise all to the status of property own-ers. In so doing, property must, in view of its social effects, not be a means of subjugation but rather become a means of furthering personal freedom. Just as little will *competition* be abolished. It is a vital force that enlivens society. Here too only its abuses are to be abolished and competition is to be perfec-ted, by means of the higher *principle of reciprocity* (le principe mutuelliste). Freedom will be preserved through the preservation of individual property and competition, thus modified. In this way property, in the system of newly cre-ated guarantees of just contracts and reciprocity, will have *equitable* effects: a harmonising principle will emerge from a formation that had previously been antisocial. If the abolition of property, which socialists desire, means the gen-eralisation of wage labour, generalising property means the abolition of wage labour, that is, of both capital and the proletariat.

According to Proudhon's conception mentioned above, the view that expro-priation is the cure for the social problem is an anachronism, as property only acquires its meaning from and through circulation and also because expropriation would allow the functions of the state to grow and restrict individual freedom. A decisive transformation and improvement of social organisation is to be attained above all through the *reform of the mechanism of circulation* and, indeed, by means of interest free credit (le crédit gratuit). The principal evil lies in transaction fees, in duties on circulation, levied on goods by trade and all who participate in exchange without working themselves. So precisely these transaction fees are to be abolished, through reform. This can be achieved through the institution of interest free credit, which has the further advantage of not curtailing individuals' freedom and activity and, indeed, because *exchange among the producers* takes place *directly*, i.e. excluding intermediaries. In direct exchange all the charges levied by intermediaries – in the form of interest exacted by money lenders, yields by owners of state bonds, dividends by shareholders, rents by landlords – automatically disappear. The exclusion of mediation will be identical to the end of interest on loans and thus to credit without charge, with universal access to capital. Cheaper production of all commodities, houses etc. will be the consequence. All monopolies, all special rights will disappear; general economic equality will ensue. Proudhon's suggestions for bringing about free credit culminated in the establishment of a 'Bank of Exchange or People's Bank' (Banque de échange, Banque du peuple) founded on direct exchange among producers, excluding of all kind of mediation so that producers' obligations to pay tribute to intermediaries will be eliminated.

Instead of money, producers who want to sell their commodities will receive vouchers, issued by the bank, from purchasers. The vouchers will not be convertible into cash but will rather represent orders for the bank to pay members [of the bank] in return for benefits in goods and services, up to a definite amount. These orders could be realised at any time, as vouchers in the hands of buyers represent only goods they previously delivered.

Joining the People's Bank should be open to all producers and entitle them to the right to exchange their products against vouchers – however, only on the condition that the prices set excluded profit and are simply determined by the amount of the labour time applied and expenditures. In essence, the bons de circulation,[15] which bring about the elimination money, constitute bank notes that cannot be exchanged for cash at a mandatory rate; the *legal mandatory exchange rate* seems to be replaced by a *contractual obligation* on participants to accept the vouchers. In contrast, conversion into commodities or services is always assured. On the other hand, although it carries on its operations without remuneration or capital, the bank will not be endangered

---

15   ['Bons de circulation' means 'circulation vouchers'.]

if its members respect their obligation to reciprocally accept payment in its vouchers. Proudhon hoped that the People's Bank will finally unite all producers and consumers – economic freedom and equality of all will be achieved and the exploitation of people by people will be ended. Once humans live together according natural law, there will no longer be a need for government in *whatever form*. For it has always had and still only has the purpose of maintaining the privileges of the propertied against the propertyless classes. With these privileges, the justification for the existence of political constitutions themselves will therefore disappear. Into their place will step the organisation of economic powers through free contracts between individuals and groups, who identify and administer their own affairs. Therefore: 'No parties! No more authority! Absolute freedom of people and citizens!' 'Whoever lays a hand on me to rule me is a usurper and tyrant; I declare him my enemy!'[16] Even if Proudhon remained true to his anarchist ideals – that in their still embryonic development in his text on property already received great applause on German soil and whose influence was visible in several writings by Moses Hess (1812–1875) and Karl Grün (1813–1887) – in time, he modified many points in the works of his second creative period.[17] His dream of a world in which *integral justice and unlimited freedom* will be achieved spontaneously, without external coercion simply through the progress of science and economic rights, gave way to the conviction that justice and freedom cannot exist side by side, without limiting each other, that governmental coercion can, indeed, be limited but not completely eliminated. The realisation of the new society seemed to him less imminent and more difficult to achieve. It is merely an ideal, which humanity progressively approaches, without ever reaching. This conception necessarily gave rise to the search for means to make waiting during the *transitional period* more bearable. Instead of unconditional freedom and the absolute negation of all authority, the federative system, 'federalism', emerged as a transitional state between the old world of authority and the free society of the future and, at the same time, as a compromise between the two principles. Through the *decentralisation of the state* – understood by Proudhon as the organisation of society into small political groups, united by a federal contract that establishes a central power, to which falls 'the simple role of the general initiative, mutual guarantee and oversight, whose decrees are only executed with the agreement of all the federated governments'[18] – a number of state functions will be passed

---

16   [Proudhon 1851b, pp. 34, 31.]
17   Proudhon 1851a; Proudhon 1861; above all, Proudhon 1921; finally, his posthumous work
      Proudhon 1865.
18   [Proudhon 1921, p. 122.]

to subordinate units and the freedom of individuals will grow. In the course of history, the significance of authority will become steadily smaller and that of freedom progressively greater.

Proudhon was the typical representative of the petty bourgeois conception of property, of small-scale industry and small landholding. His ideal was the initial phase of a development which in the later period of urban-industrial expansion and its consequences, the large city, large-scale industry and the large state, has long since been superceded.

3   More Recent Anarcho-communism and Its Tactics; The
     'Propaganda of the Deed': Bakunin, Kropotkin, William Morris

The origins of revolutionary anarcho-communism stretch back – if one excludes the ephemeral groups that gathered in 1841 around the periodical *L'Humanitaire*,[19] under the intellectual leadership of Jean Joseph May – to the period of disappointment, social bitterness and hopelessness that followed the proletariat's defeat in the June Days of 1848. A pale, impotent socialism vegetated in emigration and the working class milieu in France became the playground of ultra-moderate elements, which hoped to entirely win over the Empire. Joseph Déjacque (born around 1821, died 1864 or 1867 in Paris) and Ernest Coeurderoy (born 1825, died 1862 in the environs of Geneva) were among the first representatives of this anarchist current. Their ideas and writings had already slipped into complete oblivion well before the anarchist movement's upswing during the 1860s. The seeds of the ideas which were later developed further by Bakunin and others can be found in their writings.

Michael Bakunin (1814–76) characterised his theory of rights, the state and property as anarchism.[20]

> In a word, we reject all legislation, all authority, and all privileged, licensed, official, and legal influence, even though arising from universal suffrage, convinced that it can turn only to the advantage of a dominant minority of exploiters against the interests of the immense majority in subjection to them.
>
> This is the sense it which we are all anarchists.[21]

---

19   [*'L'Humanitaire'* means *'The Humanitarian'.*]
20   Grünberg 1931a.
21   [Bakunin 1971c, p. 231.]

No legislation has ever had any purpose other than to secure the exploitation of working people by ruling classes. The established law is tied to the state, which regulates the life of the people from top to bottom through legislation. 'Every government is necessarily based on exploitation on the one hand, and on the other hand has exploitation for its goal and bestows upon exploitation protection and legality.'[22] Private property is at once the consequence and the foundation of the state. Political equality, in so far as it is does not have social and economic equality as its basis, is a fiction. The main reason for this is the ignorance of the masses, which arises from their unfavourable situation. It follows that the educated minority will always rule over the uneducated masses. The state bestows on the privileged representatives of mental labour all wealth, all culture, the pleasantries of family life, the exclusive enjoyment of political freedom, as also the possibility of exploiting millions of workers and ruling them in their own interests. This is not because they have greater understanding but because they were born into the privileged class. The millions of proletarians, the representatives of manual labour, live in misery and ignorance. The point is to find a method of making it impossible for anyone to exploit the labour of others and to allow everyone to share in the social stock of goods, produced by labour, in so far as they have contributed directly to the production of this stock, through their labour. The method is to permit private property only in means of consumption, during the next stage in humanity's development. In contrast, means of production, i.e. 'land, instruments of labour, like all other capital, on becoming the collective property of the entire society, may be used only by the workers, that is, by agricultural and industrial associations'.[23] In this manner all workers will be assured of the fruit of their labour. 'I am not a communist,' wrote Bakunin, 'rather a collectivist'.[24] The collectivism of the future society, wrote Bakunin contradicting Marxism, does not in any way require the erection of any kind of central power. The state is, indeed, an historically necessary evil; it is, however, a transitory form of society. Bakunin struggled not only against the state but also against the principle of authority itself; for the state, like religion, is built on the idea of authority. The established law of the jurists will also fall along with the state and be replaced with free contracts. 'I want society and collective or social property to be organised from the bottom to the top, through the vote of the free association, not

---

22   [Quoted from a rather free translation in Eltzbacher 1908, p. 128, cf. the original French, Bakounine 1895, p. 324.]

23   [Marx 1986b, p. 208, includes the programme written by Bakunin from which the quotation is taken.]

24   [Bakounine 1873, p. 37.]

from the top to the bottom by means of some *authority*.[25] Eternal obligations are not compatible with freedom and justice. 'The right of free union and of equally free secession is the first, the most important, of all political rights.'[26]

Bakunin also extended his demand for absolute freedom and self-determination to nations and took the principle of self-determination to its most extreme logical conclusion. Every nation has the right to join together freely with and likewise to separate itself from other nations. Along with the right of association, mentioned above, the right of the nation to freely determine its destiny is among the most important of rights. The ambition of constructing larger state units threatens freedom which can only be realised through the destruction of all large and small political centralisations and through the principle of federalism, of the voluntary association of free nations.

If Bakunin's ideal was anarchy, his method for realising it was putschism. Bakunin dismissed every political action of the proletariat, whose objective is not the *immediate* and definitive economic emancipation of workers, as 'social liquidation',[27] as a bourgeois movement. The real economic emancipation of workers will result from a social revolution, i.e. forcible overthrow, whose acceleration and facilitation are the task of those who foresee the course of development. It is necessary to destroy all existing institutions: the state, the church, the judiciary, banks, the university, administration, the army, the police. And it is not sufficient to destroy them in *one* state; they must be annihilated in all countries. For, given the interdependence of all the privileged interests and all the reactionary powers of Europe, no revolution can count on success if it does not become international. Even though, according to Bakunin, profound causes are slowly ripening the revolution and it cannot be manufactured, he nevertheless rejected the notion of revolutionary spontaneity. It must always be prepared by a small group of professional revolutionaries, who form a kind of revolutionary general staff, whose task consists of unleashing the peasants and workers ('the sole real power of the century')[28] and their slumbering revolutionary fervour, through revolutionary deeds. Every insurrection, however unsuccessful it may be in the short run, is useful: the people only learns to develop its powers and energies through struggle. The victorious revolution will arise out of many small, unsuccessful uprisings. For the people, especially peasants, only understand ideas in concrete form. They can-

---

25   [Bakounine 1873, p. 28. Grossman's emphasis.]
26   [Bakunin 1971a, p. 105.]
27   [Bakunin 1971b, p. 168.]
28   [It has not been possible to identify the source of this quotation. Bakunin did refer to the 'idea of humanity' as the 'invisible power of the century', Bakunin 1953, p. 140.]

not be revolutionised through scientific principles or dictatorial decrees but solely through revolutionary deeds, i.e. through the effect of the cessation of burdensome political and economic pressure on the people, through the cessation of tax paying, the dissolution of courts, the army, police and accordingly the elimination of debt payments, property titles, court records etc. Only after the thorough destruction of property and of its unavoidable consequence, the state, can reorganisation take place. It too must be accomplished from the bottom to the top, through the free and recallable revolutionary representatives of individual streets, quarters, communes and provinces.

The 'anarcho-communist' current, whose principal theoretician – in so far as one can speak of theory here – can be regarded as the Russian Prince Pyotr Kropotkin (1842–1921),[29] built on Bakunin. There is in Kropotkin's critique of the existing social order, especially the state, law and private property, not a single thought that could be considered new and signifying a theoretical extension or deepening of the train of thought which is fundamental to anarchism. Further development of the theory can only be seen in Kropotkin's expansion of the critique of the state to include the state in its democratic, *parliamentary* form. 'Parliamentarianism inspires only disgust in those who see it close at hand'. Where the interests of the ruling classes are concerned, the 'anonymous beast with six hundred heads' of parliamentarianism is just as unyielding as any other despot. '[I]t has become everywhere an instrument of intrigue, of personal enrichment.'[30] It serves only to provide the possibility for the peaceful settlement of disagreements within the bourgeois class itself and for the creation of equilibrium among diverse, antagonistic interest groups. Advantages for the dominated majority will never be exacted, however, by means of legislation. The name 'parliament' originates from 'speak', parler; they are tribunes for talk, which always seek to delay decisions favourable to the people and only retreat in the face of the resolute will of the masses, in the best of cases, legalising improvements after they have been won on the 'street'. 'It took forty years of agitation, which sometimes carried fire through the countryside, before the English parliament decided to guarantee to the farmer the benefit of improvements he made on land he held by lease.' All constitutional 'freedoms' – the freedom of the press, the right of association and assembly, the privacy of correspondence and the inviolability of the home – are likewise so many illusions and apparent rights, which 'are only respected if the people do not make use of them against the privileged classes'.[31] But, on the day the people begin to

---

29   See Grossmann 1932b, 'Kropotkin, Petr Alekseevich', below, pp. 407–9.

30   [Kropotkin 1992, pp. 130, 127, 121.]

31   [Kropotkin 1992, pp. 126, 42. Kropotkin emphasised the words after 'respected'.]

use these freedoms to undermine the privileges of the ruling class, all of these celebrated, guaranteed 'rights' are thrown overboard.

Kropotkin's opinions about the ways and means of bringing about the ideal social order deserve attention. The anticipated transformation of the established order will not be achieved peacefully but only through forceful overthrow. The social revolution will not be an uprising that only lasts a few days, rather a longer revolutionary period of several years will have to be experienced, until the economic and legal transformation is completed. The social revolution will indeed begin in a single state but its spread throughout Europe will be necessary to assure its success. The task of preparing the revolution rests with professional revolutionaries united in secret societies and revolutionary organisations. These are indeed still a minority. But, on the eve of the revolution and through correct revolutionary tactics, they will win over the masses and become a majority. Before the great revolution in France, the number of those who thought about abolishing the monarchy and feudalism was small; this minority began the revolution and in a few years succeeded in carrying the masses along with it. The means by which the masses can be won for the cause of revolution are courageous action, insurrectionary deeds. In revolutionary times, declarations of war by the oppressed and their acts of revenge against contemporary society multiply and make more propaganda than a thousand pamphlets. Government persecution drives rebels to valour. Opponents join the uprising; the government becomes disunited; concessions come too late; the revolution breaks out. Taking the example of the French Revolution, Kropotkin showed how the rebels of that time accustomed the people to defy police, troops and cavalry. People were educated by daily life to undertake active assaults on the ruling class: burning barns in the villages, refusing to pay rent to the landlords and taxes to the state, breaking into granaries, destroying the landlords' harvests, burning account ledgers – and so the revolution broke out everywhere. The so-called 'propaganda of the deed' of more recent anarchism is thus by no means the perpetration of senseless crimes against individual representatives of the ruling order for propaganda purposes, as pursued, for the first time in Russia from 1869, by Bakunin's desciple, [Sergey] Nechayev, and recommended from 1878 by the German Johann Most (1846–1906), a former Social Democratic representative in the Reichstag.[32] It was actually much practiced in France, Germany etc. and led, in consequence, to most severe government repression, which affected the entire working class. It is rather a revolutionary tactic in *an immediately revolutionary situation*,

---

32   [The Reichstag was the lower house of the German imperial parliament.]

with the purpose of drawing the broadest masses into active daily struggle against all of the ruling class's positions of power, in order to destroy class domination.

William Morris (born 1834 in Walthamstow near London, died 1896 in Hammersmith), who reorganised applied arts in England and strongly influenced the English public through his novels, is also to be reckoned an anarcho-communist. Initially a social reformer, then one of the leaders of the socialist movement in England. After 1885, swayed by Pyotr Kropotkin, he ultimately modified his socialist views which had been particularly influenced by Charles Fourier's ideas and especially the theories of Marx and Engels. He propagated his new views in the Socialist League that he founded in 1885 and its organ, *The Commonweal: [Revolutionary] Journal of Anarchist Communism*.[33] From then on, he no longer regarded the socialist social order as the final goal but rather merely as a necessary transitional stage. During that period, in the novel *News from Nowhere, or an Epoch of Rest*, which appeared in 1890, and in other essays Morris looked forward to the abolition of the state, with its legal coercion and centralised government, and its replacement by a federation of free communities without government and without legalised force.[34] Every community regulates its social affairs on the basis of the voluntary agreement of its members and, indeed, not through elected representatives but directly through the 'meeting of the neighbours',[35] i.e. of those directly concerned. On the other hand, Morris decisively rejected the *tactics* of anarchism.

In contrast to 'communist' anarchism, more recent 'individualist' anarchism is, in its essentials, founded on the basis created by Stirner. Its most notable recent representatives are Benjamin R. Tucker (born 1854), the editor of the periodical *Liberty*, which was founded in 1881 in Boston and has appeared in New York as a weekly since 1892, and the Scot John Henry Mackay (born 1864), the author of *The Anarchists: A Cultural Portrait from the End of the Nineteenth Century*,[36] which appeared in 1891 and which, not without reason, attracted significant attention.

---

33   [Morris was never an anarchist of any kind. *Commonweal* did not proclaim itself 'A Revolutionary Journal of Anarchist Communism' until after Morris had lost the editorship and left the Socialist League after it was dominated by anarchists. See Thompson 1976, p. 588.]

34   Morris 1892; Morris 1893; Morris 1896.

35   [Morris 1892, p. 126.]

36   Mackay 1891.

4   Anarchism and Revolutionary Syndicalism

Modern revolutionary syndicalism, just like anarchism, had its origins and
expanded in the Romance countries, especially France. Among its theoretical representatives, the French, Georges Sorel (1847–1922),[37] [Hubert] Lagardelle, [Édouard] Berth and [Victor] Griffuelhes, and the Italian Arturo Labriola
should be mentioned. At several points, it built on anarchist ideas, principally those of Proudhon; in particular, it is anti-statist and rejects all political-
parliamentary activity. Political reformism is for it a chimera. The goal is not
the conquest of state power, for which the socialists strive, but its destruction.
All parliamentary activity delays the achievement of the final revolutionary
goal and leads to concessions to and compromises with bourgeois parties and
classes, within the framework of the dominant economic order, consequently
to the bourgeoisification of the workers movement and to the corruption of its
representatives. The state is by its nature always the representative of the pos-
sessors and the oppressor of the dispossessed. The expectation that it can contribute to the improvement in the working class's situation is therefore utopian.
Revolutionary syndicalism therefore distrusts all legislation and emphasises
that the great upheavals in history were never a product of legislation but rather
of the spontaneous and direct action of the popular masses. Instead of indirect action by the politicians, it demands direct action by unions in their daily
struggles, independent of all existing political parties. In contrast to political
parties, which, in addition to workers also encompass neighbouring petty bourgeois and intellectual elements, the syndicate is limited to workers employed
in factories. To a *party* – an organ of political society modelled on the state
and constituted as a mechanical and administrative unit only held together
by a common ideology – it counterposes the *class* – people who exercise the
same function in production and constitute a real unity of those with the same
interests – modelled on the masterless workshop, as a natural formation of
economic society. The spontaneous daily struggles of the working masses will
awaken the spirit of revolutionary struggle, the energy and the revolutionary
initiative of the working class and prepare it for revolutionary actions on a larger scale. The path on which the great social upheaval can be accomplished
is not fatalistically waiting for the coming upheaval, to which the parliamentary activity pursued by social democracy actually leads and through which
the broad masses are degraded into a passive body without its own will, com-
manded by a powerless general staff. It is rather continual combat against the

---

37   See Grossmann 1933b, 'Sorel, Georges', below, pp. 450–454.]

ruling state power and the entrepreneurs, by the living organism of the workers, always ready to go onto the offensive.

Although the syndicalist movement is attached to certain anarchist ideas, on the other hand many of its leaders (Berth) decisively deny the anarchist character of syndicalism. Actually there are unmistakably large differences between anarchism and revolutionary syndicalism, in their starting points and goals, as also in their means. This is why there have also been fierce conflicts between anarchists and revolutionary syndicalists. While anarchism is atomistic and starts from the individual as the sole reality, revolutionary syndicalism is a proletarian, *class* movement and is attached, in many respects, to the Marxist theory of class struggle, which it regards as the most valuable component of the Marxist system, even if, as a matter of fact, it severely deforms the pure theory of class struggle. Although every class struggle actually always is and also must be a struggle for political power, revolutionary syndicalism withdraws from political struggle and limits class struggle solely to trade union action. Precisely because of this class character of syndicalism, it encounters powerful criticism in anarchist circles. The anarchists, like for example the Italian [Errico] Malatesta, insist that anarchy cannot identify itself with the workers movement. This is not the goal but only a means to the realisation of anarchism. 'The anarchist revolution that we want goes far beyond the interests of one class: what is proposed is the complete liberation of humanity, which is currently in a state of servitude, from an economic, political and mental point of view.'[38] The chasm between the means the two movements employ is just as great as that between their goals. A resolution was adopted at the international congress in Amsterdam in 1907, which stated that anarchists do regard the syndicalist movement and the general strike as important means of struggle but not as a substitute for social revolution. If a political general strike is proclaimed, they recommended supporting it but this means can never allow the direct struggle against the military power of the government to be forgotten. The anarchists are convinced that the destruction of capitalist society can only be brought about by armed insurrection and forceful expropriation.

---

38   [Federazione dei Comunisti Anarchici 2007, p. 54.]

5   The Anarchist Movement

Anarchism, in contrast to socialism, is not proletarian but rather a general freedom movement, i.e. a liberal, essentially bourgeois current, even if it does include certain proletarian elements. It seeks to enlighten individuals, to educate individual people. Anarchism has no party organised in permanent form, bound together by party organisation, party congresses, party programmes, monetary contributions and discipline. That is why anarchism, in its practical politics, is far from exercising influence comparable with that of socialism. On the other hand, the view that anarchism is incompatible with organisation is mistaken. Rather, it was established by a resolution at the international anarchist conference in Amsterdam in 1907 that a free organisation of anarchists, without, by the way, executive power, is necessary for both peaceful anarchist propaganda and purposes of struggle in revolutionary periods.

It would go too far to treat the history of the anarchist movement in detail. Here only a general overview will be provided.

a *The international movement.* Proudhon's ideas had already led to the formation of political groups during the 1840s in France and Germany (Moses Hess, Karl Grün among others) but these quickly disintegrated after the revolutionary period of 1848. In the 1860s too, the anarchist movement was not autonomous but participated in the International Working Men's Association (IWMA) founded by Marx in London on 28 September 1864, as the common organisation of the workers movement in all countries. Because of their support for decentralisation and anti-political views, members of the International from Romance countries, influenced by Proudhon, were diametrically opposed to Marx's views. So the internal history of the IWMA, during its first phase from 1865 to 1867 is the history of the struggle between these two currents. While Marx's followers demanded the collectivisation of the means of production and regarded the conquest of political power as the sole means to emancipate the working class, the Proudhonists only wanted to take the path of social reform and to raise the demand of mutualism, for the establishment of voluntary exchange and credit cooperatives.

The authentic anarchist movement dates only from Bakunin's appearance in the First International. With the entry of various Bakuninist sections of the Alliance de la démocratie socialiste,[39] which he established in Switzerland, Spain, France, Italy etc., as members of the IWMA (the incorporation of the Alliance as a whole was rejected by the General Council of the IWMA, in London),

---

39   ['Alliance de la democratie socialiste' means 'Alliance for Socialist Democracy'.]

the influence of the Proudhonist current was set back and that of anarcho-communism strengthened. As a result, the demand for the socialisation of land, removed from the agenda at the Lausanne Congress in 1867 because of the influence of Proudhonist adherents of individual property, was adopted at the Congress in Brussels in 1868 and upheld the next year, 1869, at the Congress in Basel. On the other hand, as the anarchists, unlike the Marxists who sought to conquer it, had the destruction of political power as their goal and rejected the class struggle, the contradictions between the two currents at Congress in the Hague in 1872 led to the expulsion of Bakunin's followers from the International. After the emigration of the General Council of the IWMA to New York, the anarchist wing, which had previously organised itself as the 'Jura Federation', presented itself as the successor of the entire International and held an anti-authoritarian conference in St Imier in 1872. The Jura Federation repeatedly called Congresses: in Geneva (1873), Brussels (1874) and Bern (1876). The last anarchist Congress took place in Verviers in 1877. After an earlier attempt in London in 1881, a new anarchist international was only founded in 1907 with the Amsterdam Congress, at which delegates from fourteen countries were present. The new International, however, was only able to exercise very limited influence on the anarchist movements in individual countries. With the revival of the Socialist International in 1889 (the so-called Second International), the final divorce between the anarchist and socialist movements was completed by decisions against admitting anarchists, energetically adopted at several International Socialist Congresses (Brussels 1891, Zürich 1893, London, 1896).

b Anarchist movements in the Soviet Union.[40] There is no purpose here in following in detail the history of the anarchist movement in individual countries: it was the same, constantly repeated picture of anarchist oral and written propaganda, as well as the history of the formation of loose individual organisations and journals, which quickly disappeared, after a short-lived existence; the history of the fluctuations in their strength and their social roots, as they blossomed and decayed. In this regard, we direct the reader to the specialist literature cited below. Here it is worth examining relations in the Soviet Union, because they demonstrated the practical conduct of anarchist organisations toward the proletarian revolutionary movement for the first time. The earlier Russian anarchism of the 1870s was an expression of the backward state of a country with an overwhelmingly peasant population and a weak, under-

---

40 [More precisely, the Russian Socialist Federal Soviet Republic, which became part of the newly constituted Soviet Union in 1922.]

developed proletariat, at a time when the declassed intelligentsia found no employment opportunities either in the service of the absolutist state or in still underdeveloped industry. The movement was anti-statist and under Bakunin's influence. The later well known leaders of Russian Social Democracy – Plekhanov, Axelrod, and Deutsch – were at that time very close to his line of thought.

With the emergence of industry and the industrial proletariat in Russia, a second, proletarian stage of Russian anarchism, whose spokesperson after 1904 was Kropotkin, began. The influence of anarchism on the working class was only small, particularly during the period of the rising revolutionary wave to 1905. Only after the defeat of the revolution of 1905–6 did it grow, as an expression of the weakened class movement of the proletariat: from now on, the anarchist movement occupied itself with individual expropriations and assassination attempts and finally degenerated, with the decomposition of the movement into criminal and provocative elements, into pure banditry. In the years 1907–8, the anarchist movement disappears entirely from view. A third stage of the anarchist movement began in February 1917, in the wake of the general revolutionary uprising. The anarchists participated in the first revolution against tsarism, and no repressive measures of any kind were taken against them by Kerensky's government. Similarly, the anarchists participated in the Bolshevik October Revolution and even entered into the soviets as members. During this period of transformation there were seldom confrontations between the anarchists and the new power. The relationship between anarchists and the dictatorship changed, however, with the consolidation of the Soviet regime: from 1918, the anarchists struggle against the new authorities – for example, the partisan leader [Nestor] Makhno, a village teacher[41] – and attempted to introduce an anarchist order in the localities that they controlled. As a result of this stance, the Soviet government in April 1918 took measures for the liquidation of anarchist organisations. In response, a secret, all-Russian organisation of anarchists was established in 1919 and there was a series of assassination attempts: on 25 November 1919, a dynamite bomb was thrown at the Moscow Committee of the Russian Communist Party; subsequently an unsuccessful assassination attempt at the Kremlin took place. The state political police, then the Cheka, shot the arrested anarchist leaders, liquidated their organisations and by 1921 the movement in the Soviet Union had almost entirely disappeared. Anarchist leaders ([Aleksandr] Schapiro among others)

---

41   [Makhno was not a schoolteacher; he came from a peasant background and was a worker before being imprisoned between 1909 and 1917.]

emigrated. The centre of the new Russian movement is the Berlin Anarcho-Syndicalist International.[42]

Literature

Apart from the literature that is mentioned in Karl Diehl, 1923, 'Anarchismus', in *Handwörterbuch der Staatswissenschaften. Erste Band*, edited by Ludwig Elster, Adolf Weber and Friedrich Wieser, fourth edition, Jena: Fischer, pp. 276–92, reference is made to the following fundamental writings.

1   *General*

Adler, Georg 1909, 'Anarchismus' in *Handwörterbuch der Staatswissenschaften*, edited by Johannes Conrad, Ludwig Elster, Wilhelm Lexis and Edgar Loening, third edition, Jena: Fischer, pp. 444–69.

Almanach des ennemis de l'autorité, 1913, Paris: L' Idée libre.

Andrieux, Louis 1885, *Souvenirs d'un préfet de police*, Paris: Rouff.

Anonymous 2007 [1907], *The International Anarchist Congress: Amsterdam, 1907*, Federazione dei Comunisti Anarchici, http://www.fdca.it/fdcaen/press/pamphlets/sla-5/sla-5.pdf, accessed 3 October 2016.

Almandos, Luis Reyna 1919, *Hacia la Anarquia*, second edition, Buenos Aires: Casa editora 'El Ateneo' de P. García y cía.

Armand, Emile 2014 [1926], *L'initiation individualiste anarchiste*, Paris: La Lenteur, Le Ravin bleu.

Berkmann, Albert 1929, *What Is Communist Anarchism?*, New York: Vanguard Press.

Cornelissen, Christiaan, 1908, 'Ueber die Evolution des Anarchismus', *Archiv für Sozialwissenschaft und Sozialpolitik*, 26, 2: 343–61.

Courtois, Alphonse 1885, *Anarchisme théorique et collectivisme practique*, Paris: Guillaumin.

Diehl, Karl 1923, 'Anarchismus', in *Handwörterbuch der Staatswissenschaften. Erste Band*, edited by Ludwig Elster, Adolf Weber and Friedrich Wieser, fourth edition, Jena: Fischer, pp. 276–92 (with extensive accounts of anarchist movements in indivual countries).

Diehl, Karl 1925, *Ueber Sozialismus, Kommunismus und Anarchismus*, fifth edition, Jena: Fischer.

---

42   [The anarcho-syndicalist International Workers Association was established in December 1922 in opposition to the Communist supported Red International of Labour Unions as well as the social democratic International Federation of Trade Unions.]

Domela Nieuwenhuis, Ferdinand 1897, *Le socialisme en danger*, Paris: Stock.

Fabbri, Luigi 1908, 'Die historischen und sachlichen Zusammenhänge zwischen Marxismus und Anarchismus', *Archiv für Sozialwissenschaft und Sozialpolitik*, 26: 559–605.

Faure, Sébastien (ed.) 1925–34, *L'Encyclopédie anarchiste*, five volumes, Paris: La Librairie internationale.

Fiorentini, Lucio 1895, *Socialismo ed anarchia*, Roma: Fratelli Bocca.

Franz, J., 1878, 'Der doktrinäre philosophische Idealismus in der sozialen Frage', *Neue Gesellschaft*, 1, 9: 458–74.

Garin, Joseph 1885, *L'anarchie et les anarchistes*, Paris: Guillaumin.

Golovin, Ivan 1880, *Der russische Nihilismus: Meine Beziehungen zu Herzen und Bakunin nebst einer Einleitung über die Dekabristen*, Leipzig: Senf.

Gorev, Boris Isaakovich 1926, 'Anarkhizm', in Otto Yulyevich Schmidt (ed.), *Bolschaya sovetskaya entsiklopediya. Tom 2*, Moskva: Sovetskaya Entsiklopediya.

Grünberg, Carl 1911, 'Anarchismus', in *Wörterbuch der Volkswirtschaftslehre. Erste Band*, edited by Ludwig Elster, third edition, Jena: Fischer, pp. 92–7.

Hamon, Augustin Frédéric 1895, *Psychologie de l'anarchiste-socialiste*, Paris: Stock.

Hamon, Augustin Frédéric 1897, *Le socialisme et le congrès de Londres*, Paris: Stock.

Lagardelle, Hubert 1908, 'Die Syndikalistische Bewegung in Frankreich', *Archiv für Sozialwissenschaft und Sozialpolitik*, 26: 96–143, 606–48.

Lenin, Vladimir Ilyich 1964 [1918], *The State and Revolution*, in Vladimir Ilyich Lenin, *Collected Works. Volume 25*, Moscow: Progress, pp. 385–498.

Lombroso, Cesare 2009 [1894], *Gli anarchici*, Milano: La vita felice.

Lorulot, Aandré 1913, *Les théories anarchists*, Paris: Giard & Brière.

Malato, Charles 1894, *De la commune à l'anarchie*, Paris: Stock.

Malato, Charles 1897, *Philosophie de l'anarchie: 1888–1897*, second edition, Paris: Stock.

Malato, Charles 1898, *L'homme nouveau*, Paris: Stock.

Malogodi, Olindo 1894, 'Genesi economica dell' anarchismo', *Critica sociale*, 4, 16, August: 235–6.

Mühler-Lehning, Arthur 1976 [1927], *Anarcho-Syndicalisme*, Amsterdam: Anarchistiese Uitgaven.

Nin, Andrès 1923, *Les anarchistes et le mouvemenent syndical*, Paris: Librairie du travail.

Oppenheimer, Ludwig 1924, *Die geistigen Grundlagen des Anarchismus*, München: Meyer & Jessen.

Rabani, Emile 1926, *Le devoir anarchiste*, Paris: Giard.

Ruge, Arnold 1846, 'Der teutsche Kommunismus', *Die Opposition*: 96–122.

Stieklow, Georg 1913, *Marx und die Anarchisten*, Dresden: Kaden.

2 Specific

Barazov, Vladimir Aleksandrovich 1906, *Anarkhicheskii kommunizm i Marksizm*, Saint Petersburg: Narodnaya Polza.

Coeurderoy, Ernest 1852, *De la révolution dans l'homme et dans la société*, Bruxelles: Tarride.

Coeurderoy, Ernest 1854, *Hurrah!!! Ou la révolution par les cosaques*, Londres: Ernest Coeurderoy.

Coeurderoy, Ernest 1910–11 [1854–55], *Oeuvres*, three volumes, Paris: Stock.

Déjacque, Joseph 1857, *De l'être-humain, mâle et femelle, Lettre à P. J. Proudhon*, Nouvelle-Orleans: Lamarre; https://fr.wikisource.org/wiki/De_l%E2%80%99%C3%8Atre-Humain_m%C3%A2le_et_femelle_-_Lettre_%C3%A0o_P._J._Proudhon, accessed 11 October 2016.

Déjacque, Joseph 1912 [1859], *À bas les chefs*, Paris: Temps nouveaux.

Déjacque, Joseph 1970 [1854], *La question révolutionnaire*, Paris: Champ libre.

Déjacque, Joseph 2016 [1858–59], 'The Humanisphere', in *The Humanisphere: Four French Utopian Fantasies*, edited by Brian Stableford, Encino: Black Coat Press.

Drahn, Ernst 1925, *Johann Most: Eine Bio-Bibliographie*, Berlin: Prager.

François, Albert 1905, *Elisée Reclus et l'anarchie*, Silly: Gand, société coopérative 'Volksdrukkerij'.

Fritsche, Gustav 1966 [1927], *William Morris' Sozialismus und anarchistischer Kommunismus*, Leipzig: Tauchnitz.

Ghio, O. 1903, *L'anarchisme aux Etats-Unis*, Paris: Colin.

Gorev, Boris Isaakovich 1918, *Anarkhisty, maksimalisty i makhaevcy: Anarkhistskye techeniya v pervoy russkoy revolyutsii*, Petrograd: Kniga.

Grave, Jean 1893 [1882], *La société au lendemain de la révolution*, third edition, Paris: La Révolte.

Grave, Jean 1897, *L'individu et la société*, second edition, Paris: Stock.

Grave, Jean 1899 [1893], *Moribund Society and Anarchy*, translated by Voltairine de Clere, San Francisco: Isaak.

Grave, Jean 1907 [1895], *La société future*, ninth edition, Paris: Stock.

Grave, Jean 1910, *Réformes, révolution*, second edition, Paris: Stock.

Grave, Jean 1911, *La conquête de pouvoirs publics*, Paris: Temps nouveaux.

Grave, Jean 1924 [1899], *L'anarchie, son but, ses moyens*, second edition, Paris: Stock.

Kulczycki, Ludwig 1910–14 [1909, 1910], *Geschichte der russischen Revolution*, translated by Anna Schapire-Neurath and Rosa Schapire, three volumes, Gotha: Perthes.

Landauer, Gustav 1978 [1911], *For Socialism*, translated by David J. Parent, St. Louis: Telos Press.

Langhard, J. 1909 [1903], *Die anarchistische Bewegung in der Schweiz von ihren Anfängen bis zur Gegenwart und die internationalen Führer*, second edition, Bern: Stämpfli.

Mackail, John William 1922, *The Life of William Morris*, two volumes, second edition, London: Longmans Green.

Mondolgo, Rodolfo 1929, 'Die Anfänge der Arbeiterbewegung in Italian bis 1872 und der Konflikt zwischen Mazzini und Bakunin', *Archiv für die Geschichte des Sozialismus und der Arbeiterbewegung*, 14: 339–65.

Morris, William 1910–15, *Collected Works*, London: Longmans Green.

Most, Johann 1903–07, *Memoiren*, four volumes, New York: John Most.

Most, Johann 1891 [1884], *The Free Society: Tract on Communism and Anarchy*, New York: Müller.

Nettlau, Max 1929 [1911], 'Ernest Coerderoy', *Archiv für die Geschichte des Sozialismus und der Arbeiterbewegung*, 1: 316–33.

Nettlau, Max 1912, 'Bakunin und die Internationale in Italien bis zum Herbst 1872', *Archiv für die Geschichte des Sozialismus und der Arbeiterbewegung*, 2: 275–330.

Nettlau, Max 1914, 'Bakunin und die Internationale in Spanien 1868–1873', *Archiv für die Geschichte des Sozialismus und der Arbeiterbewegung*, 4: 243–333.

Nettlau, Max 1922, *Enrico Malatesta*, Berlin: Der Syndikalist.

Nettlau, Max 1925, *Der Vorfrühling der Anarchie*, Berlin: Der Syndikalist.

Nettlau, Max 1929–30, 'Zur Geschichte der spanischen Internationale und Landesföderation 1868–1889', *Archiv für die Geschichte des Sozialismus und der Arbeiterbewegung*, 14: 1–66, 15: 73–125.

Owen, William C. 1908, *Anarchy versus Socialism*, New York: Mother Earth Publishing Association.

Ramus, Pierre (pseudonym of Rudolf Großmann) 1923, *Neuschöpfung der Gesellschaft durch den kommunistischen Anarchismus*, second edition, Wien: Erkenntnis u. Befreiung.

Réclus, Élisée 1896, *L'anarchie*, Paris: Temps nouveaux.

Réclus, Élisée 1911 and 1925, *Correspondance*, three volumes, Paris: Schleicher frères; Costes.

Réclus, Élisée 1925 [1899], *À mon frére le paysan*, Conflans-Sainte-Honorine: Idée libre.

Réclus, Élisée and Elie Réclus 1927, *Elisée and Elie Réclus in Memoriam*, Berkeley Heights: Oriole Press.

Rocker, Rudolf 1973 [1924], *Johann Most: Das Leben eines Rebellen*, Glashütten im Taunus: Auvermann.

Rocker, Rudolf 1920 [1905], *Sozialdemokratie und Anarchismus*, Berlin: Der freie Arbeiter.

Rocker, Rudolf 1979 [1923], *Über das Wesen des Föderalismus im Gegensatz zum Zentralismus*, Frankfurt: Freie Gesellschaft.

Rocker, Rudolf 1980 [1927], *Die Rationalisierung der Wirtschaft und die Arbeiterklasse*, Frankfurt: Freie Gesellschaft.

Scheu, Andreas 1923, *Umsturzkeime: Erlebnisse eines Kämpfers*, three volumes, Wien: Wiener Volksbuchhandlung.

Serge, Victor 1997 [1923], 'The Anarchists and the Experience of the Russian Revolution', in Victor Serge, *Revolution in Danger*, translated by Ian Birchall, London: Redwords, pp. 115–62.

Tucker, Benjamin Ricketson 1897 [1893], *Instead of a Book, by a Man too Busy to Write One: A Fragmentary Exposition of Anarchism*, second edition, New York: Benjamin R. Tucker.

Tucker, Benjamin Ricketson 1911 [1888], *State Socialism and Anarchism: How Far They Agree and Where They Differ*, sixth edition, London: Fifield.

Tucker, Benjamin Ricketson 1903 [1899], *The Attitude of Anarchism towards Industrial Combinations*, New York: Benjamin R. Tucker.

CHAPTER 18

Bebel, August*

Translated from German by Ken Todd

Leading Social Democrat, born 22 February 1840 in Cologne on the Rhine as son of a Prussian non-commissioned officer; became a wood turner; from 1860 lived in Leipzig as a journeyman, then as a master craftsperson; joined the liberal Leipzig Educational Association for Workers. At that time, he was against workers engaging in political activity because of their lack of political maturity in exercising the right to vote. He was initially motivated to read Lassalle's writings by Lasalle's appearance in Leipzig in 1863 and foundation of the General German Workers Association, and as a consequence of his antagonism to liberal workers associations. His contact with Wilhelm Liebknecht from 1865 and his reading of Marx's *Inaugural Address* of the International Working Men's Association[1] accelerated his development as a socialist. During his years in prison, 1872–5, he familiarised himself with the first volume of Marx's *Capital*.[2] In 1866, Bebel joined the International. On the introduction of universal suffrage in 1867, he was elected in Saxony to the Constituent Parliament and later to the North German Parliament. With short interruptions, his parliamentary career spanned forty years. His effectiveness was particularly enhanced by his talent as a public speaker. In August 1869 in Eisenach, with Liebknecht, he founded the Social Democratic Workers Party. In July 1870, after the outbreak of the Franco-German War, Bebel and Liebknecht in opposition to Bismarck's war policy abstained from voting for [war] credits. In 1872 Bebel and Liebknecht were sentenced to two years in prison for their protest against the annexation of Alsace-Lorraine. Scarcely out of prison, Bebel participated in the unification of the Eisenachers and the Lassalleans at the Congress in Gotha, in May 1875.

Henceforth, Bebel was also German Social Democracy's most outstanding organiser and agitator, and formulated its tactics. The distinctive feature of these tactics was that, in the person of Bebel, they acknowledged the unconditional class struggle *against* the ruling state, in theory, but, in practice, weakened this struggle through concessions, without being clearly conscious

---

* [Originally published as Grossmann 1931c.]
1 [The International Working Men's Association, founded in 1864, later known as the First International.]
2 [Marx 1876b.]

of this contradiction. Thus, in 1870 at the Stuttgart Congress of the Eisenachers, Bebel declared himself in agreement with the resolution that approved participation in parliamentary elections on agitational grounds only and otherwise demanded a negative orientation to parliament. In parliamentary practice, on the other hand, he often lapsed into the purest reformist positivism. Under the so-called 'Socialist Law', Bebel advocated illegal Party activity alongside legal activity, as an answer to Bismarck's exceptional legislation, but in relation to the 'normal' state he was for the maintenance of legality. During 1878–80 he turned sharply against Karl Höchberg's attempt to transform Social Democracy into a social reform party. His struggle against the revisionist campaign for Social Democracy to abandon its principled, oppositional stance and to make it fit to participate in government was equally sharp at the Party Congresses in Stuttgart (1898), Hannover (1899), Lubeck (1901) and Dresden (1903). Nonetheless, in 1877 he already espoused the defence of the fatherland and in 1913 declared, in the Reichtag's[3] Budget Committee, that he supported the approval of credits to arm the country for a defensive war. Likewise, the Party Executive resolved, without any opposition on Bebel's part, to enter into an electoral alliance with bourgeois democrats for the parliamentary elections of 1912. Bebel participated in all the International Congresses of the Second International and was one of its most respected and popular figures. He died on 13 August 1913 in Zurich.

Writings

1872 [1870], *Unsere Ziele. Eine Streitschrift gegen die 'Demokratische Korrespondenz'*, Leipzig: Verlag der Expedition des Volksstaat.

1876, *Der deutsche Bauernkrieg mit Berücksichtigung der hauptsächlichsten sozialen Bedingungen des Mittelalters*, Braunschweig: Bracke.

1904 [1879], *Woman under Socialism*, translated from 33rd edition by Daniel De Leon, New York: New York Labor News Press.

1921 [1888], *Charles Fourier: Sein Leben und seine Theorien*, Stuttgart: Dietz.

1884, *Die mohammedanisch-arabische Kulturperiode*, third edition, Leipzig: Verlag der Expedition des Volksstaat.

1890, *Zur Lage der Arbeiter in den Bäckereien*, Stuttgart: Dietz.

1922 [1910–4], *Aus meinem Leben*, seventh edition, Stuttgart: Dietz.

1926, *August Bebel: Auswahl aus seinen Reden*, Berlin: Neuer Deutscher Verlag.

---

3   [The Reichtag was the lower house of the German parliament.]

Literature

Anonymous 1913, *August Bebel: Zur Erinnerung an die am 17. August 1913 erfolgte Bestattung*, Zürich: Art. Institut Orell Füssli.

Bernstein, Eduard 1913, 'August Bebel', *Sozialististische Monatshefte*, 19 (16–17), 21 August, pp. 957–9.

Gerlach, Hellmut von 1909, *August Bebel*, München: Langen.

Kluehs, Franz 1923, *August Bebel, Der Mann und sein Werk*, Berlin: Dietz Nachfolger.

Liebknecht, Wilhelm (ed.) 1874, *Leipziger Hochverratsprozess. Ausführlicher Bericht über die Verhandlungen des Schwurgerichts zu Leipzig in dem Prozeß gegen Liebknecht, Bebel und Hepner wegen Vorbereitung zum Hochverrat vom 11.–26. März 1872*, Leipzig: Genossenschaftsbuchdruckerei.

Mehring, Franz, 1914, 'August Bebel: Persönliche Erinnerungen', *Archiv für die Geschichte des Sozialismus und der Arbeiterbewegung*, 4: 304–12.

Mehring, Franz, 1921, *Geschichte der deutschen Sozialdemokratie. Band 3* and *4*, 11th edition, Berlin: Buchhandlung Vorwärts.

Michels, Robert, 1913, 'August Bebel', *Archiv für Sozialwissenschaft und Sozialpolitik*, 37: 671–700.

Wendel, Hermann 1913, *August Bebel, ein Lebensbild für deutsche Arbeiter*, third edition, Berlin: Buchhandlung *Vorwärts*.

CHAPTER 19

Bolshevism*

Translated from German by Ben Fowkes

1   The Concept Defined

Bolshevism is a current within the Russian socialist workers movement, founded by Vladimir Ilyich Ulyanov (Lenin)[1] (1870–1924) which was expressed in
successive organisational forms, as follows: initially in 1903 in the Bolshevik
faction within the Russian Social Democratic Labour Party (RSDLP), then, after
1912, in the separate Social Democratic Party of the Bolsheviks, and finally, after
the victory of the October Revolution of 1917 and the Bolsheviks' takeover of
power, in the Communist Party of the Soviet Union (CPSU).[2] Bolshevism as a
theory – Leninism – considers itself to be a continuation and development of
Marxism in the period of capitalism's decline. At the same time, it constitutes
the theoretical foundation of the economic and state policy of the Soviet Union
and, furthermore, of the policy of the Communist (Third) International.[3]

2   The Genesis of the Revolutionary Movement and the Start of the
Workers Movement in Russia

Bolshevism stands at the end of the long historical development of the revolutionary movement in Russia. Hence, in order to comprehend it, a brief look
back over the most important stages in the revolutionary movement's development is necessary.

Isolated uprisings have occurred repeatedly in Russia since the seventeenth
century, whether by economically oppressed peasants and Cossacks bound to
the soil, troop detachments subjected to mistreatment or different religious
sects against the Tsar, as the head of the official church. The peasant and Cos-

---

* [Originally published as Grossmann 1931d.]
1 See Grossmann 1932h, 'Lenin, Vladimir Ilyich', below, pp. 410–418.
2 [More precisely, the Russian Socialist Federal Soviet Republic, which became part of the
newly constituted Soviet Union in 1922 and the Bolsheviks became the All-Russian Communist Party (Bolsheviks) in 1918, renamed the All-Union Communist Party (Bolsheviks) in 1925.]
3 See Grossmann 1932e, 'The Internationals: The Third International', below, pp. 377–402.

sack uprising under Stenka Razin in 1670–1 and the rebellion of 1773–4, led by [Emelian Ivanovich] Pugachev during the reign of Catherine II, are both well known. But the history of specifically political attempts at revolution against Tsarism as an absolutist form of rule did not begin until the twenties of the last century (the Decembrist uprising of 1825). The belief that the Russian revolutionary movement can be explained on the basis of the peculiar way of thinking and the character of Russia's intellectual strata is wrong. Conspiratorial, illegal and revolutionary struggle against autocracy is not an inherent characteristic of Russia but rather the product of particular circumstances corresponding to a particular phase of social and political development. Wherever freedom has been restricted by despotic and reactionary power holders and the intellectual and economic level of the broad popular masses (the peasants) has been very low, so these masses have been politically passive while the thin stratum of the emergent bourgeoisie and members of the liberal professions has been economically and politically too weak, the only possible form of political and social struggle against the existing order has been conspiracies by small, illegal and secret organisations – principally groups of intellectuals – under strictly centralised leadership. Philosophically speaking, the leaders of such conspiracies regard individual personalities and ideas as the driving forces of history and see the masses as having no historical mission or impact. State power can therefore only be conquered and its social content altered by the actions of a small but determined minority (Blanquism).[4] [Gracchus] Babeuf's[5] 'Conspiracy of Equals' against the Directory in 1795–6, military conspiracies in Spain during the nineteenth century, the conspiracy of the Carbonari in Italy against the Bourbons and the Habsburgs, the activities of the French Charbonnerie against the restoration from 1821 to 1830 and French secret societies under Louis Philippe from 1831 to 1839 all had this character.[6]

This point also applies to all revolutionary movements in Russia, from the Decembrists to the terrorist group Narodnaya Volya (the People's Will) at the end of the 1870s. They were the product of a predominantly agrarian country, in which millions and millions of peasants were not free, i.e. bound to the soil

---

4   [Blanquism was the voluntarist doctrine of the French revolutionary socialist Louis Auguste Blanqui and his followers.]

5   See Grünberg 1931d.

6   [The Directory, 1795–9, was the conservative regime that succeeded the radical, Jacobin phase of the Great French Revolution. The Carbonari were revolutionary nationalists fighting foreign rule and conservative monarchies in Italy during the early nineteenth century. The Charbonnerie, modelled on the Carbonari, conspired against the restored, conservative Bourbon monarchy in France.]

and politically passive, while, on the other hand, a modern bourgeoisie and a proletariat were absent.

It took a series of great, fruitless sacrifices and defeats before the ideology referred to above was shaken and the conviction arose that state power has deeper *social roots*, and that changing the form of the state and its social content cannot be the work of a few conspirators but is the product of a historical process in which the mutual relations between classes are transformed.

The peasantry was the class to which the revolutionaries in Russia attached all their hopes, up to the 1880s. The Tsarist regime was driven to peasant reform, i.e. the abolition of serfdom (1861), by the disturbances which followed military defeat in the Crimean War (1854–6). This began Russia's transition from a natural to a money economy and thus first created the conditions for capitalist industrial development, based on free wage labour. As it extended, capitalism destroyed the old, native forms of life in production and transportion and evoked anti-capitalist movements, as happened in other places under similar circumstances. These did not, however, aim to achieve a different future but rather idealised the past and clung to its remnants, in the shape of the rural commune (mir). The question of the necessity or avoidability of capitalism in Russia, already raised in the 1850s by [Alexander] Herzen,[7] was taken up again by the Narodniks,[8] in the period from 1860 to 1890. According to them, western European capitalism was a phenomenon of decay rather than an historical necessity. It was not necessary for Russia to pass through capitalism in order to achieve socialism. The mir was the germ cell of socialism. The Russian peasant had socialist instincts as a result of the mir system and had the strength to create socialism in Russia and thereby rejuvenate the world. The practical task, accordingly, was to 'go to the people' (narod) and to arouse them. This was what the Populists, organised from 1876 in Zemlya i Volya (Land and Freedom) endeavoured to do.

But, as a political force, the peasantry proved to be incapable of overthrowing Tsarism. Despair over this outcome led the Narodnaya Volya party, which had emerged from a split in Zemlya i Volya in 1879, to adopt terrorist tactics as the sole means appropriate for compelling reform (murder of Tsar Aleksandr II on 1 March 1881, by the bomb thrown by [Ignacy] Hryniewiecki). At the same time, however, a new force came into existence which gradually took over leadership in the struggle against Tsarism, after the 1870s: the modern proletariat. During the 1870s and still more the 1880s, a rapid proletarianisation of the peas-

---

7   See Grossmann 1932b, 'Herzen, Alexander', below, pp. 354–357.
8   [The Narodniks were populists who oriented to the peasantry.]

antry took place, as a result of the unfavourable regulation of redemption payments under the 1861 peasant reform that swallowed up as much as 200 percent of the harvest. For this and for other reasons, Russia experienced tumultuous capitalist development and, as a consequence, rapid growth of the industrial proletariat. From the beginning, the proletariat fought against unusually bad working conditions with many spontaneous strikes and itself created its first political organisations, in the form of illegal workers circles: the 'South Russian Workers Union' set up in 1875 by [Evgeny Osipovich] Zaslavsky, and the 'North Russian Workers Union' set up in 1878 by [Stepan Nikolayevich] Khalturin and [Viktor Pavlovich] Obnorsky.

Historical development proved Marxism right in the dispute over whether capitalism could be avoided in Russia. It was therefore not only accepted as the theoretical basis for understanding the development of Russia by its socialist, proletarian adherents but even met with enthusiastic agreement in bourgeois circles, who regarded the theory of capitalism's historical necessity as a theoretical justification for the practical capitalist activities in which they were engaged.

The first socialist organisation with a Marxist programme, the 'Emancipation of Labour' (Osvobozhdenie Truda) group, was founded abroad (Geneva) in 1883 by Pavel Borisovich Akselrod, Vera Ivanovna Zasulich, Lev Grigorievich Deutsch, Vasily Nikolaevich Ignatov and Georgii Valentinovich Plekhanov.[9] Its founders came from the Narodnik movement. They had belonged to its non-terrorist wing, Chernyi Peredel (Black Repartition) and they had become social democrats under the influence of Marx's and Engels's writings. With the perspective of the inevitable development of capitalism in Russia and demanding political struggle for democracy and socialism, with the help of the working class, politically organised on the model of the social democratic workers parties of western Europe, they completed the final break with their Narodnik past. The break was expressed most clearly in the proclamation issued by Plekhanov at the founding Congress of the Second International in 1889, which has become a classic: 'The Russian revolutionary movement will be victorious as a *movement of the workers* or it will not win at all.'[10] But no *mass political agitation* took place in Russia until almost the middle of the 1890s. In 1895, the Saint Petersburg League of Struggle for the Emancipation of the Working Class, in which Lenin played a leading role, clearly demonstrated that the Russian workers movement had attained a new and higher level of organisation. The

---

9   See Grossmann 1932i, 'Plekhanov, Georgii Valentinovich', below, pp. 419–422.
10   [Plekhanov 1974b, p. 454.]

mass strikes of the 1890s brought the circles, which had previously confined themselves to purely theoretical propaganda, into contact with the practical economic struggle waged by workers. Lenin's essay *Explanation of the Law on Fines Imposed on Factory Workers*[11] (1895) – which dealt with the very arbitrary punishments imposed on workers by employers – demonstrated how the political intelligentsia sought to awaken the workers' interest in the political context and in political organisation, by linking their agitation to the workers' most comprehensible economic demands of the day.

In general, however, political demands were not raised and effort was only put into making economic demands that made sense to the broad masses of workers. This was the thrust of the pamphlet *On Agitation*,[12] issued in hectographed form by the later Bundist Arkady Kremer with the assistance of Julius Martov, the later Menshevik. It called for the transition from propaganda carried out by secret educational circles to mass work.

The so-called 'Kingdom of Poland'[13] occupied a special position in this context, as a result of its higher degree of industrial development. The socialist movement already began there between 1876 and 1878, among the intelligentsia and factory workers, under the leadership of Ludwik Waryński, the most outstanding member of the *Proletariat* party. The Social Democratic Parties which arose at the start of the 1890s recognised the importance of *political* struggle very early on and placed the overthrow of absolutism and the fight for a democratic constitution in the forefront of their activity, as can be seen from 'Report on the Social Democracy of the Kingdom of Poland' written by Rosa Luxemburg[14] for the third Congress of the Second International in Zürich, in 1893, as well as from the program adopted by that Party's first Congress, in Warsaw on 10 March 1894. At the same time, the Party's newspaper *Sprawa Robotnicza* (*The Workers Cause*) emphasised the need for the closest possible cooperation between the Polish and Russian proletariats and the combination of the various centres of the Russian workers movement into a *unified* party (May 1894). In fact, the needs of the growing workers movement in Russia also called forth the demand for a united socialist party, as Lenin's *Draft and Explanation of a Programme for the Social Democratic Party*[15] (1896) demonstrated. He was not able to participate in realising it, as a result of his exile in Siberia (1897–1900).

---

11   [Lenin 1960a.]
12   [Kremer and Martov 1983.]
13   [The Congress Kingdom of Poland was the Russian-occupied territory of partitioned Poland.]
14   See Redaktion 1932b. [Luxemburg 1893.]
15   [Lenin 1960b.]

Two significant milestones can be observed on the path to achievement of this proposal: the establishment of the Bund (General Jewish Workers Union of Lithuania, Poland and Russia) in 1897, out of local circles of Jewish workers; further, the formation of the ephemeral Russian Social Democratic Labour Party (RSDLP) on 14 March 1898 in Minsk, which placed political freedom at the forefront of its efforts.

These first steps on the way to a united, Marxist political party had, however, almost no practical effect. On the contrary, they introduced a period of collapse and theoretical confusion. Quite apart from the mass arrests of Social Democrats immediately after the [Minsk] Congress, including all nine of the delegates, the facts that all social democratic groups were not represented at the Congress and that there was opposition within the newly formed Party to political demands demonstrated that all Social Democrats in Russia had not grasped the necessity of *political* struggle against absolutism and of achieving a free constitution. At the turn of the century, a current of thought emerged within the workers movement which, although it recognised the necessity of political liberty for the proletariat in principle, regarded it as more advisable on tactical grounds to postpone the direct struggle for political freedom to a later time (the 'theory of stages'). What was significant about the conception of the right wing, the so-called 'legal Marxists' – this was the name commonly applied to the Social Democrats who wrote books and journal articles which were published legally – was that this group, represented by Petr Berngardovich Struve and Mikhail Ivanivich Tugan-Baranowski, which in any case soon shifted to liberalism, engaged in a general revision of Marx's conceptions, along the lines of the German Bernsteinism (Struvism).[16] It left little scope for working-class political activity. The current, however, which consciously opposed political activity by workers was 'Economism'. It regarded the tasks of the workers movement as being defined by their economic interests, which were the only ones workers could understand, as opposed to political demands, which had no bearing on workers in their practical life. Imposing political struggle on the currently immature Russian proletariat was therefore an impermissible transposition of western European assumptions to Russia.

The programme of the 'Economists', who in Saint Petersburg and many other cities had brought the local organisations of the 'League of Struggle for the Emancipation of the Working Class' fully under their influence, was expressed particularly in the 'Credo' of the socialist [Yekaterina] Kuskova in 1898 and

---

16   [Bernsteinism was the revisionist approach of Eduard Bernstein.]

the 'Profession de foi'[17] of the Kiev Committee (early 1899).[18] Although isolated beginnings of this current were now and then apparent earlier, 1892–6, it first won serious influence on the workers movement between 1898 and 1901.

3 Lenin's Struggle against Economism and for a Unitary Party of Professional Revolutionaries

This is the point at which Lenin started to have a direct impact on the Russian workers movement, as expressed in the struggle against lack of theoretical clarity, and practical and organisational fragmentation. Although he subscribed to Struve's critique of Narodnism, in his essay 'The economic content of Narodism and the criticism of it in Mr. Struve's book'[19] (1895), he fiercely attacked the undialectical affirmation of capitalism by Struve, in the spirit of revisionism, because it did not consider the other side of capitalism's development: rising class struggle and the increasing need for the proletariat to conduct a revolutionary political struggle. Even fiercer was his attack on Economism, against which a group of exiled Social Democrats, headed by Lenin, drew up the 'Protest of the seventeen' (1899).[20]

With this, a new epoch in the history of the revolutionary workers movement in Russia began. Following Lenin's return from exile [inside Russia] in 1900, the newspaper *Iskra* (*The Spark*) was established, appearing under the editorship of Lenin, Plekhanov, Martov, Akselrod, [Aleksandr Nikolayevich] Potresov and Zasulich, initially in Stuttgart, then in Munich, London and Geneva. It provided a new focal point for the Marxist revolutionary movement and succeeded in dominating the intellectual development of a whole generation. At the same time, it effectively made preparations for the, at that time, new and grandiose idea of a centralised, unitary All-Russian political party of the proletariat. Among the main tasks which Lenin and the other editors of *Iskra* proposed to the workers movement were, as before, the elimination of the autocracy and the achievement of political liberties; this is why *Iskra* continued its unrelenting struggle against Economism. A central organisation, as the prerequisite for the success of the revolution, signified a break with organisational 'small-scale production' – propaganda carried out by circles – and the transition to 'large-scale production', i.e. to a mass movement. The Party should be an organ-

---

17   ['Profession de foi' means 'Profession of Faith'.]
18   [Kuskova 1960.]
19   [Lenin 1960c.]
20   [Lenin 1960d.]

isation of *professional revolutionaries*, who exclusively devoted their energies to the revolution. For only such a party was capable of fulfilling its task: creating an excellent party apparatus with a far-reaching division of labour (sections devoted to the education of propagandists, the daily press, scientific and popular party literature, procurement of financial resources and meeting-places, smuggling of literature and other transport from abroad etc.). Only such a cadre organisation, which constituted the political leadership, was capable of gathering hundreds of thousands of people around itself at the moment of revolution. Lenin developed this conception at length in *What Is To Be Done?*,[21] which appeared in the spring of 1902. At that time Lenin's leading idea, which he presented in *What Is To Be Done?* as well as *Iskra* was already that the Party should not be a revolutionary 'people's party' in the sense of uniting all the discontented – alongside workers, also bourgeois liberals, students and peasants. *The proletariat is the main revolutionary force.* So the *hegemony of the proletariat* had to be secured, i.e. the proletariat had to aspire to the leading role in the revolution, determine the programme, the goals and the tactics of the revolutionary movement and not merely be an auxiliary troop for the liberal revolutionary movement. For only this leading role during the (bourgeois) revolution would secure a favourable position in the further struggle for socialism for the proletariat. So the Party of the proletariat – Social Democracy – had to be an irreconcilably workers party, driving the bourgeois revolution forward, through its criticism of the liberals, at the same time exposing the Socialist Revolutionaries as representatives of the village bourgeoisie and demonstrating the non-proletarian character of their agrarian reform, which they misleadingly labelled 'socialisation'. These conceptions were in sharp contrast to those expressed by the other currents in the workers movement, abroad as well as within Russia, outside and inside Social Democracy. The degree of disagreement within Social Democracy was soon demonstrated very plainly at the second Congress of the RSDLP which, in the summer of 1903, initially meeting in Brussels, then moving to London, owing to difficulties with the authorities. It was extremely historically significant and had a decisive impact on developments over subsequent decades.

---

21   [Lenin 2008.]

4   The Second Congress of the RSDLP

Two camps already took shape within the Party before the Congress; both camps were already aware that they differed on all the most important questions. These differences finally led the Party to split into two groups over the composition of *Iskra*'s editorial board: a majority group (Bolsheviki) and a minority (Mensheviki), which gave rise to their names. The factional struggle over specific questions at the Congress, whether the draft programme published by *Iskra* and mainly composed by Plekhanov and Lenin, or questions of tactics and organisation boiled down to a central problem: should the Russian workers movement develop into a party of parliamentary reform, on the model of the Social Democratic Parties of western Europe, or did it have quite different – revolutionary – tasks to fulfil? According to Lenin – and Plekhanov also had this point of view at the time – the goal of the Party was the conquest of power and the *dictatorship of the proletariat*, a demand which featured neither in the programme of German Social Democracy nor any other social democratic party in western Europe (if we leave aside the reference in the 1881 programme of the Parti ouvrier français (the Guesdists) to the '*political* and economic *expropriation* of the capitalist class').[22] For revolutionaries, proclaimed Plekhanov at the Congress, democracy (universal suffrage, parliamentarism) is not a goal in itself, not a fetish, but a means to the objective of liberating the working class; under certain circumstances (when the working class actually achieved power) it would be entirely justifiable to deprive the class enemy – the bourgeoisie – of rights. From this fundamental conception of the role and tasks of the proletariat, a series of further consequences flowed, in questions of organisation and tactics, e.g. in the dispute with the Jewish Bund over the relationship of the Party to the national question. Lenin, who, just like the other Russian Social Democrats, absolutely recognised the right of nations to self-determination, up to and including their right to separate completely from the state that ruled over them, nevertheless rejected the demand of the Bund that the Party organisation should be federally structured in individual national sections, or curiae, (which led the Bund to walk out of the Congress and leave the General Party). Lenin regarded a strictly centralised party organisation, on a territorial basis, as the only guarantee for the success of the revolution.

But the most heated discussions at the Congress did not concern matters of principle in relation to the programme or tactics but rather questions of

---

22   ['Parti Ouvrier Français' means 'French Workers Party'. Guesde and Lafargue 1899, p. 8. Grossman's emphasis.]

organisation and they deepened the chasm between the two factions. Despite subsequent attempts at reconciliation by both sides, they were never able to reunite and they finally became two mutually hostile political organisations in very sharp conflict with each other. Lenin (*What Is To Be Done?*) emphatically opposed the worship of the 'elemental' aspect of the movement: the conception that the class conflict could lead to the emergence of a spontaneously revolutionary mass movement. The spontaneous struggle of the proletariat will never become a real class struggle as long as this struggle is not led by an organisation of revolutionaries. Admittedly, revolution cannot simply be 'made'; its growth is an organic process of maturation; when the harvest is ripe, however, it can also only be brought in by 'revolutionary reapers'.[23] To the Menshevik 'tactics as process', i.e. tactics emerging spontaneously, Lenin counterposed 'tactics as plan', as conscious leadership.[24] The task of the Party as the vanguard of the proletariat should not be to hobble behind the spontaneous course of events; the Party must rather actively support all spontaneous expressions of protest against the existing regime, take on their organisation and, finally, proceed to the preparation and conduct of the armed uprising. During the whole period the Party therefore has the function of being a collective organiser and leader; the position of a supreme commander in wartime is not dissimilar. As Lenin, from the outset, regarded the conquest of power by the proletariat as the most important task, *organisational questions* had decisive significance for him. The frontal assault – the revolution – can only be the work of 'a regular army' – the professional revolutionaries – not an '[elemental] explosion by the crowd' (*What Is To Be Done?*).[25] The sharpest struggle at the second Congress therefore developed around the first paragraph of the Party statutes, which defined the character and duties of a Party member. According to Lenin, it was not sufficient to regard those who accepted the Party programme and gave material support to the Party as Party members, on the model of the German and other western European Social Democratic parties. A Party member is rather obliged to engage in 'personal participation *in one of its organisations*'.[26] According to Martov, Akselrod and others, in contrast, a person who 'renders it regular personal assistance under the direction of one of its organisations' was to be regarded as a Party member.[27] Lenin saw the Party as a fighting detachment, an

23   [Lenin 1962a, p. 156.]
24   [Lenin 1962a, pp. 148.]
25   [Lenin 2008, pp. 831, 833. Editor's interpolation; in other translations the word 'spontaneous' is used.]
26   [Lenin 1961b, p. 474. Grossman's emphasis.]
27   [Russian Social Democratic Labour Party 1978.]

association of people unconditionally devoted to the Party's goals and bound by absolute discipline. This was the appropriate weapon for the achievement of the Party's goals. His definition of a Party member excluded all the peripheral strata, which 'sympathised' with the Party, from actively influencing it and prevented these fellow-travellers – who were essentially members of the petty bourgeoisie and the petty bourgeois intelligentsia – from acting as a ballast weighing down the Party at critical moments, i.e. diluting its *proletarian* revolutionary character (as was later shown by the fate of German Social Democracy on the outbreak of the World War).[28] Martov, on the other hand, allowed a looser Party organisation, from which sympathisers would not be barred. Differences over what was apparently an insignificant organisational question were thus only an expression of deeper principled differences between the two factions of the RSDLP, over the goals and tasks of a proletarian party. Only once the delegates from the Bund had left the Congress did Lenin and Plekhanov succeed; Martov, Akselrod, Potresov among others were in the minority.

The Bolsheviks soon lost their original majority in the Party leadership, on the Central Committee and the editorial board of *Iskra*, achieved by their majority at the Congress, when some of their representatives were arrested and Plekhanov switched to the side of the Mensheviks. As a counterbalance, Lenin created an All-Russian organisation for his faction. In 1904 the 'Bureau of the Majority Committees' was established and at the beginning of 1905 he launched the newspaper *Vperyod* (*Forward*), which continued the ideas of the old *Iskra*. In the fire of the historic events that followed, he was able to lay the foundations of Bolshevik tactics, in opposition to and struggle against the Mensheviks.

5   The Revolutionary Period of 1905

Since the start of the new century, the working class had displayed a heightened degree of activity: the strikes of 1902 in Nizhni-Novgorod and Rostov bore a revolutionary character; the student movement reached its high point; the war of 1904; finally on 22 (9) January 1905,[29] when a peaceful demonstration of unemployed workers, who did not belong to a Party, led by the priest [Georgii] Gapon and carrying sacred icons, marched to the Tsar's Winter Palace and were shot down. These were all signs of the approaching revolution. The chasm

---

28   [The German Social Democratic Party voted for war credits in the parliament.]
29   [The date in the Julian Calendar, which the Russian state used at the time, is in brackets.]

between the two factions of the RSDLP, which had appeared at the second Congress, deepened more and more under the influence of the historic events of the following years: the Russo-Japanese war of 1904 and the revolution of 1905. As before, disagreements with the Mensheviks continued to revolve around the cardinal question of the relationship between the working class and the bourgeoisie. While this had previously had more of a *theoretical* character, now, however, in the course of the great historic events of the 1905 revolution, it became a burning *practical* question. The Mensheviks – described by Lenin as the 'Girondists of socialism'[30] – imagined that the revolution would follow the course typical of earlier bourgeois revolutions in western Europe. They expected it to result, in the best case, in a liberal bourgeois constitution. On the basis of the conviction that the working class, fragmented and weak, was incapable of independent action, the Mensheviks (in [Aleksandr] Martynov's *Two Dictatorships*[31] and in articles in the new *Iskra*) advocated the tactic of supporting the bourgeoisie and an alliance with it. They warned the proletariat against scaring it off and driving it into the arms of the reaction by raising excessive demands. The Bolsheviks, on the other hand, regarded the working class not only as the driving force but the leader of the coming revolution, which would, as a result, become a new type of revolution – a proletarian revolution (Lenin's 1905 articles in *Vperyod*).[32] Lenin was certainly aware at the time, 1905, that a socialist revolution was not possible in Russia and that the coming revolution, carried out by the proletariat and the peasantry, would initially strengthen the rule of the bourgeoisie, i.e. that it would be a *bourgeois* revolution 'because the objective logic of historical development confronts them at the present time with the tasks, not of a socialist, but of a democratic revolution'.[33] The working class would not, however, be a mere appendage of the liberal bourgeoisie in this revolution. Instead, resting on the strata intermediate between itself and the bourgeoisie, it would play an independent role and have its own tasks to fulfil. Its natural ally was therefore, according to Lenin, not to be found in the camp of the bourgeoisie but rather that of the poor peasantry, in opposition to the bourgeoisie and the big landowners. What Lenin aimed for was a 'revolutionary-*democratic* dictatorship of the proletariat and the peasantry', i.e. an alliance between the urban and rural poor (although not yet a *socialist* dictatorship of the working class with the purpose of carrying

---

30   [Lenin 1962d, p. 173. The Girondists/Girondins were the main moderate faction in the
        French parliaments between 1791 and 1793, during the revolution.]
31   [Martynov 1905.]
32   [Lenin 1962b.]
33   [Lenin 1962c, p. 292.]

out the socialist revolution). Only a dictatorship of this kind, which encompassed the overwhelming majority of the people and roused 'the vast mass ... to
heroic endeavours' would be stable and create the space for a great revolution,
recalling the years 1789–93 and not 1848–50.[34] Only it would ultimately offer
a guarantee for the consistent conclusion of the bourgeois revolution, i.e. for
the complete realisation of Social Democracy's whole minimum programme,
on the basis of bourgeois society, for decisive economic reforms and for the
democratic republic as the last form of bourgeois rule and the best framework
for the proletariat's class struggle for socialism.

In pursuit of this alliance of workers and peasants, the demand for the
nationalisation of the land and the establishment of *revolutionary peasant
committees* (in which the *independently organised rural proletariat* would be
represented), whose task would be to administer the land that had been confiscated, was included in the agrarian programme adopted at the Third Party
Congress (May 1905 in London). The differences between the two factions' conceptions of the coming revolution also gave rise to divergences over tactics
during the revolution. The Mensheviks schematically transferred the parliamentary tactics of western European social democracy, which was fighting for
a socialist revolution, i.e. for their maximum programme, to the revolutionary
situation in a backward country like Russia, where the fight was initially for the
achievement of the minimum programme. From the viewpoint of misunderstood 'class unity' and based on the decisions of Congresses of the International
in Paris (1900) and Amsterdam (1904), they declared themselves against any
participation in a revolutionary government, because they could only conceive
of it on the lines of the bourgeois governments of western Europe. This tactic would therefore, in practice, deprive the working class of its leading role
and deliver power to the bourgeoisie, from the outset. This corresponded to the
Menshevik theory of stages, according to which the liberal bourgeoisie would
take the helm in the immediate future which, however, constituted in their
view a necessary stage and precondition for the *later* success of the proletariat
in the next stage of development.

The Bolsheviks, on the other hand, sought to achieve a *shift in power in
favour of the working class* through its active intervention. They therefore concentrated on the slogan of the planned organisation and leadership of the
armed workers' uprising in connection with a *political general strike*, which
the later experience of the Russian Revolution demonstrated was a power-

---

34   [Lenin 1962c, p. 292. Lenin counterposed the Great French Revolution to the European
      revolutions of 1848.]

ful weapon, despite its rejection by western European social democracy. The Bolsheviks' goal was the seizure of power by a provisional revolutionary government, in which Social Democracy would fight relentlessly against all counter-revolutionary endeavours *by using the constant pressure of the armed proletariat under its leadership* and would struggle for the consolidation and extension of the revolution's achievements and the working class's independent interests. The political revolution in Russia would not be a 'single act', not even a movement limited to a few months. On the contrary, it would last many years and be the prelude to the socialist revolution in Europe.

The tactics of the two groupings differed in other ways as well. When Tsarism, forced to make concessions, summoned a merely *consultative* State Duma, the 'Bulygin Duma',[35] which did not encroach on the powers of the autocracy in any way, the Mensheviks were at first inclined to regard this as the start of parliamentarism and to participate in the elections (declaration in *Nachalo*).[36] The Bolsheviks, on the other hand, did not demand concessions from absolutism but its overthrow and therefore called for a *boycott of the Duma*, bearing in mind that the purpose of this sham constitutionalism was to betray the people, cripple its revolutionary activity even before genuine freedom had been won and to prevent the revolution 'from proceeding consistently to its goal', by means of a counter-revolutionary agreement between the old regime and the liberal bourgeoisie (the secret negotiations of Peter Struve with Count [Sergei Yulyevich] Witte). The boycott tactics of the Bolsheviks were likewise adopted by the Social Democrats of the borderlands and eventually by the Mensheviks as well.

For the moment, the Bolsheviks did not succeed in their efforts directed toward the seizure of power. The liberal opposition continued to be very weak, even during the 'days of freedom',[37] and soon after the great economic strikes of November 1905 swung over into the camp of reaction. The political movement of the peasants, grew too slowly, isolating the proletariat in its advanced revolutionary outposts. The members of the Council[38] of Workers Deputies were arrested, the left press suppressed. The armed uprising [in Moscow] in Decem-

---

35   [The purely consultative parliament, designed by Minister of the Interior Alexander Bulygin in August 1905. It never met and was superceded by the legislative First Duma, which was announced in the Tsar's October Manifesto. The Bolsheviks, Mensheviks and Socialist Revolutionaries boycotted the indirect elections, on an unequal franchise, for the First Duma, in 1906.]

36   ['*Nachalo*' means '*The Beginning*'.]

37   [The 'days of freedom' were a period from 17 October until December 1905, during which the regime relaxed its repression and censorship.]

38   ['The Council' was the Saint Peterburg Soviet.]

ber, led by the Bolsheviks, was brutally put down. It was, nevertheless of great historical significance. It showed that the working class had already become a tremendous force, which was not prepared to abandon its independent role in the revolution. The arbitrary dissolution of the Second Duma by the government, on 3 July 1907, apparently completed the liquidation of the revolution's achievements.

6 The Period of Reaction, from 1906 to 1910

During the years of the Stolypin reaction, from 1906 to 1910,[39] the Russian workers movement came to a complete standstill. The proletariat was totally exhausted by the bloodletting of 1905. As always after a severe defeat, decay could be observed in all areas – in the political movement, science and literature. That induced a blossoming of mysticism and religiosity in the workers movement. Demoralisation was apparent everywhere. Provocateurs crept into workers' organisations and people no longer trusted one another. Fierce factional struggles raged within Social Democracy, leading to an unbelievable degree of fragmentation into factions, groups and grouplets: the Party ceased to exist as a whole. The process by which the Bolshevik Party crystallised out and separated, externally and internally, began in this period of decline. The Party as a whole was illegal, underground, its newspaper prohibited, its parliamentary representatives condemned to harsh prison terms, the Party's best forces were compelled to emigrate. Only isolated legal places of refuge remained: some trade unions, workers clubs and the Third State Duma. What path should be followed in the future?

Lenin continued to insist on the maintenance of the illegal character of the Party and fought against the 'liquidationist' and reformist current, led by the extreme Mensheviks [Yuri] Larin and Potresov, grouped around the journals *Vozrozhdenie* (*Rebirth*) and later *Nasha Zarya* (*Our Dawn*). This current regarded the revolution as over and therefore called for adaptation to the meagre legal opportunities available under Tsarism, curtailment of the Party programme, which was as a whole unrealisable, liquidation of the Party's illegal apparatus and striking out on a path of *reform within* the monarchical system, on the model of western European social democracy. The liberal bourgeoisie (the Constitutional Democrats = Cadet Party) supported the Menshev-

---

39   [While it peaked in late 1905, the revolutionary movement continued until it was thoroughly repressed in mid-1907. Pyotr Stolypin was the Russian Prime Minister from April 1906 until 1911.]

iks' liquidationism in its daily newspaper (*Rech*),[40] in the hope that they could thwart revolutionary efforts with its help. The Liquidators were also deliberately tolerated by the Stolypin government, as a result of which the Leninist tendency gave them the not very complimentary nickname of the 'Stolypin Workers Party'.

But there were also further splits and the establishment of new groups within the Bolshevik faction. Lenin, concerned to maintain the mass character of the movement, in spite of his insistence on maintaining the Party's illegality, advanced the viewpoint in *Proletary*[41] (together with [Grigorii] Zinoviev and [Lev] Kamenev) that the Party should be active whereever there were masses of workers and therefore favoured the utilisation of *every legal opportunity*, in order to avoid losing contact with the masses. But a seemingly radical tendency emerged within the Bolshevik faction the 'Otzovists' (Recallers), also known as the '*Vperyod* Tendency' after the title of their newspaper.[42] It called for a boycott of the Duma and other legal institutions (trade unions and workers clubs). As a result, the risk arose that the Party would slip back from being a mass movement to a series of small propaganda circles. At a conference in 1907 to discuss their attitude to the Third Duma almost all the leading Bolsheviks, with the exception of Lenin, and all the leading figures of Polish Social Democracy, spoke in favour of a boycott. Lenin was only able to secure a decision in favour of participation in the Duma elections, against his own supporters, with the votes of the Mensheviks and the representatives of the Jewish Bund. With the same severity, he fought another group of sham radicals, the 'Ultimatists' ([Aleksandr] Bogdanov, [Anatoly Vasilyevich] Lunacharsky and [Mikhail Nikolayevich] Pokrovsky), who accused him of opportunism. They represented a tendency closely related to the Otzovists. With a third group, led by Plekhanov, the Leninist Bolsheviks finally formed an alliance. This group in general did support the Menshevik viewpoint but energetically supported Lenin in his struggle against the 'legalism' and the 'constitutionalist illusions' of the 'liquidators'. This alliance was also based on the Plekhanov's and Lenin's philosophical struggle for Marxist materialism against the Machism[43] of Bogdanov, which was widespread at that time. Since the Bogdanovites, and particularly the Ultimatists, were able to exert an extraordinary influence within the Bolshevik faction, which reached as far as the Central Committee, long and

---

40   ['*Rech*' means '*Discussion*'.]
41   ['*Proletary*' means '*The Proletarian*'.]
42   ['*Vperyod*' means '*Forwards*'.]
43   [Machism was the philosophical approach of the German physicist and philosopher Ernst Mach.]

desperate struggle against the left had to be waged, until finally Bolshevism, after repeated splits, emerged, steeled, from the struggle, with its final form and intellectual imprint. The history of the struggle against all these 'left' tendencies provided a particularly valuable insight into the theoretical foundations of Bolshevism. It showed that Bolshevism never believed that it had to be 'furthest to the left'; after all, the Otzovists and Ultimatists characterised Leninist Bolshevism as 'right wing'. Lenin always opposed the slogan that Social Democracy must be 'more revolutionary than anyone else' (*Vperyod*, 1905).[44] But even during the period of the most severe factional conflicts, the Bolsheviks never made any theoretical or political concessions to their opponents and, as a result, gave their Party the organisational and intellectual shape which later enabled it to play a great historical role.

7   The Tactics of Bolshevism during the World War up to the Fall of
         Tsarism. Lenin's Theory of Imperialism.

Lenin evaluated the renewed advance of the Russian economy, which began in 1910, and was accompanied by a new wave of economic and political strikes, as an indication that revolutionary, working class activity would soon revive. The consolidation of the Party's organisation was an urgent necessity in this situation. But an attempt to reunite the contending factions in January 1910, at a plenum of the Party's Central Committee failed. The mutual antagonisms were too deep and soon Lenin entirely abandoned the idea of a possible reunification. The Bolshevik Conference of January 1912 in Prague constituted itself as the *founding Congress of an independent Bolshevik Party* and marked the definitive organisational separation from the Mensheviks. It was soon followed by an analogous split in the group of social democratic Duma deputies (October 1913) and, finally, by the establishment of a daily newspaper, published in Saint Petersburg (*Pravda*,[45] which is at present the central organ of the Russian Communist Party). The Mensheviks, for their part, in August 1912 organised a conference in Vienna which led to the unification of the contending Menshevik groups (the 'August Bloc'). Among them were the *Vperyod* (*Forwards*) group, less political than literary and philosophical, to which Maxim Gorky and [Anatoly Vasilyevich] Lunacharsky belonged; the 'Liquidators'; the Jewish Bund; and above all the group around Leon Davidovich Trotsky, the 'Unifiers',

---

44   [Lenin 1962c, pp. 290–1.]
45   ['*Pravda*' means '*Truth*'.]

who regarded 'unity at any price' as essential, both in the Party and in the
impending election campaign for the Fourth Duma. The antagonism between
Trotsky's group and the Liquidators over internal Party matters introduced further fragmentation into the ranks of Lenin's opponents and thereby contributed to his success.

The revolution of 1905 had not performed its historic task. The old goals
still remained to be achieved. But now, with intimation of the great events
that were approaching – the sharpening of the conflicts among the capitalist
great powers which was to lead to the World War – an evolution of Bolshevik
policy on the *extension of its revolutionary goals* began. The organisational
split in Russian Social Democracy accelerated the programmatic differentiation between the two parties even more. The Mensheviks were prepared to
make do with partial demands and reforms 'on the basis of practical work',
within the framework of autocratic rule. All they demanded was freedom of
expression, the rights to strike, organise and to assemble. To this end they led a
'petition campaign' and a 'very promising' campaign for workers' sickness and
accident insurance. The Bolsheviks regarded this as an attempt to divert the
attention of the working class away from its revolutionary struggle and towards
questions of secondary importance. They disrupted both the campaigns for the
right to organise and for insurance. Their main demands remained the same:
politically, the overthrow of autocracy and the establishment of a democratic
republic, and economically the confiscation of large-scale landed property. But,
in addition, they saw that far-reaching revolutionary possibilities would result
from the approaching war. At the Party Conference in Poronin (near Kraków)
from 23 September to 1 October 1913, Lenin predicted that war was now inevitable and would last a long time. The immense convulsions that resulted would
objectively ripen the conditions for social revolution everywhere and soonest
of all in Russia, where the political system was most antiquated and therefore
ripest for liquidation. This theoretical understanding allowed the Bolsheviks to
work to accelerate the revolution and provided a guiding thread for their tactics during the World War that soon followed. Their attitude to the War followed
from their attitude to the conquest of power. They had already sought to use the
Russo-Japanese War (1904) in the interests of workers' emancipation; they had
therefore called for the *defeat of their own government* and worked to achieve
this in both the army and the navy. They followed the same tactic during the
World War.

The majority of the leaders of the Second International ([Jules] Guesde,
[Édouard] Vaillant, [Marcel] Sembat and [Gustave] Hervé in France; [Arthur]
Henderson and [Henry] Hyndman in Britain; [Philipp] Scheidemann, [Eduard]
David and [Carl] Legien in Germany; Victor Adler in Austria; and [Leonida]

Bissolati in Italy) decided to support the defence of the fatherland, at their governments' sides, in stark contradiction with the clear decisions of the International Socialist Congress held in Basel (1912). Lenin saw this reversal not as the result of an accidental constellation of political forces but as the inevitable product of the opportunism and reformism which the Second International had pursued for decades and had turned it into a prisoner of the bourgeoisie. Lenin sought to explain this phenomenon from the standpoint of his theory of imperialism.[46]

The victory of opportunism had a necessary inner connection with structural changes in world capitalism, which between 1898 and 1900 had entered a specific historical stage, its *imperialist phase*. Its fundamental economic feature was the displacement of free competition by monopoly and the economic division of the world among international, monopolist associations of capitalists, dominated by the financial oligarchy. The bourgeoisies of the four to six great capitalist powers received billions of super profits from every quarter of the earth, through the export of capital, the domination and exploitation of immense colonial regions and territories in Asia and Africa, supplying raw materials. This turned them into leaches on the bodies of other nations ('parasitic capitalism'). In addition, this gave them the opportunity to win over, by economic means, the upper strata of 'their' workers together with the petty bourgeois fellow-travellers of the socialist parties, interest them in colonial exploitation and to corrupt them politically, with a substantial part of the colonial superprofits, in the form of higher wages for a layer of skilled workers, comfortable sinecures in ministries and public offices, in trade unions, mass circulation newspapers etc. The bourgeoisies concluded a kind of alliance with these groups against the mass of the people and against other countries. These upper strata were the channel for bourgeois influence in the proletariat. The emergence of a labour aristocracy, 'a "*bourgeois labour party*" was inevitable and typical in *all* imperialist countries' and found political expression in the opportunism of the Second International. 'The mechanics of political democracy works in the same direction'.[47] The opportunists of the Second International could only dominate the working class movement during the relatively peaceful period between 1871 and 1914 by accepting revolutionary goals and revolutionary tactics in words and reassuring that their 'peaceful' activities – their opportunist *deeds* – were merely *preparation* for the proletarian revolution. Only the attitude of the Social Democratic majority at the outbreak of

---

46   [Lenin 1964a.]
47   [Lenin 1964c, pp. 116, 117.]

War made the masses aware of the contradiction between socialist words and chauvinist deeds. The collapse of the Second International was at the same time a collapse of reformism. In Russia too Menshevik leaders such as [Pyotr Pavlovich] Maslov, Plekhanov, Potresov, [Nikolai Semyonovich] Chkheidze and [Matvey Ivanovich] Skobelev (with the exception of Menshevik Internationalists like Martov and Akselrod etc.) adopted a social imperialist position. Plekhanov demanded that settling accounts with tsarism and the Russian bourgeoisie should be postponed until after the War, in the interest of the victory of the Entente and of 'European democracy'; that the social democratic group in the Duma should vote for war credits and that workers should refrain from strike action.

The Bolsheviks formulated their opposing viewpoint as early as the 'Theses' of 6 to 8 September 1914 and the 'Manifesto of the Central Committee' of 1 November 1914.[48] According to Lenin, the World War was not an accident but a product of imperialism, i.e. an unavoidable consequence of the antagonisms of the period of capitalist decline, which would be followed by further wars, in the same way as the World War itself was only a continuation of an epoch of wars that began with the Spanish-American War (1898), the Boer War (1900) and the Russo-Japanese War (1904). In contrast to the wars of national liberation among capitalist powers in the phase of progressive, rising capitalism, the wars of great great powers in the imperialist phase are against economically less developed nations and states. They are predatory wars over the division of the spoils and this characteristic makes the formal distinction between offense and defensive wars misleading and deprives it of any meaning. Under capitalism, draft resistance and similar, *bourgeois* pacifist methods are just as naïve and harmful dreams of combatting the armed bourgeoisie without weapons as the expression the 'last' war. Their purpose is to lull the proletariat to sleep and harness it to the wagon of the bourgeoisie. But another, equally harmful misdirection of the working class is the *socialist* pacifist slogan 'neither victory nor defeat' of the Menshevik Internationalists, Trotsky and, later in Germany, Rosa Luxemburg. As a demand directed at *capitalist* governments it is utopian and arouses false faith in the humanity of capitalism. Anyone who does no more than make such 'demands' for the conclusion of a 'democratic, non-violent peace' and does not call on the masses to engage in revolutionary actions against the bourgeoisie in fact deviates towards the opportunists. Equally harmful are expressions that the war can be ended by 'reconciliation' among the socialists of different countries, by 'demonstrating that the people desire peace'. '[A]s long as capitalist

---

48   [Lenin 1964d; Lenin 1964e.]

rule lasts there can be no really democratic, non-coercive peace.'[49] Lenin counterposed the slogan of an immediate end of the war to the ideology of the bourgeoisie: class harmony (civil truce), 'national' war, defence of the fatherland, defence of democracy and the granting of war credits. Referring to the Paris Commune of 1871 and objective conditions, already ripe for revolution, he called for the transformation of the imperialist war among nations into a civil war, the overthrow of imperialism, the proletariat's social revolution against its own bourgeoisie, the conquest of political power with the objective of the socialist reorganisation of society. Both restricted legal forms of struggle and illegal forms should be used and all elements opposed to the war should be supported. Just as during the Russo-Japanese War, during the World War Lenin also stood for 'defeatism': the proletariat should work for the defeat of its own government in all imperialist countries, soldiers of the belligerent nations should fraternise in the trenches and colonies should be free to separate from oppressive mother countries. Every defeat of the government facilitated the revolution and the overthrow of the bourgeoisie. Consequently, not only ideological separation from opportunism but also *organisational* splits in the Social Democratic Parties were necessary: ruthless struggle, not only against the 'governmental socialists' who openly supported the 'civil truce', abandoned the class struggle and delivered the proletariat to imperialism. These open social chauvinists no longer had the support of the masses. The so-called *'centre'*, the veiled defenders of social chauvinism ('Kautskyism'[50] and analogous groupings in other countries, e.g. the Menshevik Internationalists in Russia) were the most dangerous. Using the ideology of the past, they were concerned to reconcile the proletariat with the bourgeois workers parties, instead of executing a sharp break with the whole past of the Second International. The task of Marxists in the struggle against opportunism was not to rely on the labour aristocracy but instead 'to go down lower and deeper, to the real masses',[51] and finally to replace the collapsed Second International with a new, Third International of revolutionary social democracy, cleansed of opportunism. Lenin soon advocated these ideas at the Conference of Bolshevik Groups Abroad in Bern in March 1915, at the first international conference of oppositional social democrats during the war in Zimmerwald (5 to 8 September 1915) and then at their conference in Kienthal (23 to 20 April 1916).[52] The pacifist majority at these conferences did speak out against granting further war credits but, at the same

---

49   [Lenin 1964i, p. 188.]
50   [The position of Karl Kautsky.]
51   [Lenin 1964c, p. 120.]
52   [See Lenin 1964f; Lenin 1964g; Lenin 1964h.]

time, they did not believe in proletarian revolution and civil war. The so-called Zimmerwald Left formed a weak minority and became the initial core of the Third International.[53]

The unexpected collapse of tsarism in February 1917, the abdication of Tsar Nicholas II, the last representative of the Romanov dynasty which had ruled the Russian people for over three hundred years, on 2 March, and the formation of a provisional government headed by Prince [Georgii] Lvov, [Pavel] Miliukov, [Aleksandr] Guchkov and [Aleksandr] Kerensky, which continued to pursue bourgeois imperialist and annexationist aims and did not wish either to end the War or to proclaim a Russian republic, posed fresh problems for the Bolsheviks.

8   From the February Revolution to the October Revolution.[54] Lenin's Conception of the State and Theory of the Dictatorship of the Proletariat

The socialists who, in defending the fatherland, placed themselves on the side of the bourgeoisie and their governments at the start of the World War, spent years combatting revolutionaries' 'illusions' and their 'insanity' in wanting to transform the imperialist war into a civil war. Lenin regarded the outbreak of the Russian Revolution as a confirmation of his diagnosis. It was natural that the revolution did not break out first in the highly developed capitalist countries of western Europe but in Russia. Precisely because of its backwardness, Russia's powers of resistance were the most limited; it was the weakest link in the chain of capitalist states. The Provisional Government and its parties now declared the end of the revolution and asserted that Russia had in fact achieved all the goals a bourgeois revolution could win and, at a stroke, the most reactionary state in Europe had turned into the most free. At this time, Lenin was already calling for the sharpest possible opposition to the Provisional Government in the first of his 'Letters from Afar', while he was still in Switzerland (March 1917). He regarded the March Revolution as simply the beginning of the transformation of the War into a civil war, 'the *first stage* of the first revolution', which would by no means be the last.[55] He therefore regarded the transition from the first to the second stage of the revolution as the most important tactical task of the Bolsheviks. The March Revolution had

---

53   See Grossmann 1932e, 'The Internationals: The Third International', below, pp. 377–402.
54   [The revolutions took place in February and October 1917, according to the old, Julian calendar, March and November according to the modern, Gregorian calendar.]
55   [Lenin 1964i p. 297. Grossman's emphasis.]

in fact come about as a result of the alliance between workers and peasants (in soldiers' uniforms). As in 1905, *soviets* (councils) *of workers' and soldiers' deputies* were established in all cities and towns. But one extremely important peculiarity of the Russian Revolution of March 1917 was that, although it had gone beyond the typical model of previous bourgeois democratic revolutions, because there was no longer any power over the toiling masses, it had still not resulted in a pure dictatorship of the proletariat and the peasantry. For the first time in history, the phenomenon of *dual power* had appeared: two powers, an intermingling of two *dictatorships*; the dictatorship of the bourgeoisie and that of the proletariat, existed side by side. The Soviet of Workers' and Soldiers' Deputies in Petrograd,[56] which in fact possessed revolutionary power, represented the interests of the poorest masses, i.e. nine-tenths of the total population. Although weak, it was the *embryonic form of workers govern-ment.* But (owing to a lack of organisation and the proletariat's insufficient class consciousness) it *voluntarily* handed over its power to the class enemy, the bourgeoisie and its 'Provisional Government', satisfying itself with exerting 'control' over the government, with playing the role of a supplementary parallel government until the Constituent Assembly was summoned. In this way, the whole power of the Tsarist monarchy, its basis in the feudal landowners, the old bureaucracy and generals, was transferred to bourgeois Russia, i.e. to the capitalist landowners and the big bourgeoisie. These people, who already ruled *economically* before 1917, now took hold of all responsible organs, the whole state apparatus (bureaucracy, police, army), to staff them with bourgeois elements from the middle class and petty bourgeoisie. In this sense, the first stage of the revolution had been completed (although the Provisional Government left the immense landed property of the nobility untouched), since revolution always signifies the transfer of power into the hands of a new class. But this new Guchkov-Miliukov government, representing the Russian bourgeoisie and the Anglo-French capitalists behind it, was not capable of solving the vital problems of either internal or external policy, which kept the broad popular masses in a state of breathless tension. It did not implement agrarian reform and it did not set a date for the Constituent Assembly. It had to delay both, to avoid stirring up 'confusion' in the country, in the interest of bringing the war to 'a victorious conclusion'. Although the government did not abandon its annexationist aims, it was supported by the Mensheviks, who had a de facto majority and the leadership in the soviets in their hands. In the programme of the Provisional Government, which was adopted with the agreement of the Petrograd

---

56   [Saint Petersburg was renamed Petrograd in 1914.]

Council of Workers and Soldiers, the question of the War was at first passed over in complete silence, then postponed to an indefinite future with the utopian watchword of a 'universal democratic peace'. This gave the Mensheviks and the Socialist Revolutionaries[57] the opportunity to advocate 'revolutionary national defence' until such a peace had been concluded. In practice this meant prolonging the war for an indefinite period. Lenin opposed this policy of the government and the proletarian parties that supported it. Having arrived in Petrograd on the night of 3 April 1917, he already formulated his famous 'theses' on 4 April 1917, in a speech to an assembly of [Bolshevik and Menshevik] delegates to the All-Russian Conference of Soviets of Workers' and Soldiers' Deputies (published in *Pravda* on 7 April).[58] Initially they met with misgivings even within the ranks of the Bolsheviks themselves and only gradually proved to be capable of mobilising the majority of the popular masses around Bolshevik slogans. According to Lenin, there could be no question of any 'revolutionary national defence'. So long as power had not passed from the bourgeoisie to the proletariat, to the soviets of workers' and peasants' deputies, the War would remain an imperialist war, waged for the sake of capitalists' profits. The social character of the War did not depend on whether the form of state was monarchical or republican but on the class character of the government and the interests it represented. The people's sharpest possible mistrust of the Provisional Government was therefore required. To 'demand' that the government of capitalists cease to be capitalist, i.e. imperialist, was to indulge in impermissible illusions. The people should not trust the government's promises but their own strength. Since two governments cannot exist in a single state in the long run, either the soviets of workers and peasants have to take sole power or the bourgeoisie has to abolish the parallel government of the workers and soldiers councils. Dual power can only be a transitional phase. The Provisional Government had, in fact, already started to place every possible obstacle in the way of a seizure of power from below. The people therefore had to consolidate and extend their own positions of power. The *arming of the proletariat* was indispensable. Lenin advanced the programme of *concentrating state power in the hands of the soviets*, even though the Bolsheviks were a weak minority in most of them at the time, compared with the bloc of petty bourgeois opportunists (the Mensheviks and Socialist Revolutionaries) who tailed behind the bourgeoisie. In all previous revolutions the ruling classes were able to achieve victory only by drawing the great mass of the petty bourgeoisie over to their side. The pro-

---

57   [The Socialist Revolutionary Party was based on the peasantry.]

58   [Lenin 1964j, pp. 21–4.]

letariat's task was to win over and organise these middle strata. So long as the Bolsheviks were in the minority, their task was confined to criticism: they had to persistently enlighten the masses about the inseparable link between capital and the imperialist war, expose the mendacious promises of the government, systematically demonstrate its errors, with reference to the facts and thus make the masses conscious of the need to transfer all state power into the hands of the soviets of workers' and peasants' deputies. Return to a parliamentary republic would be a step backwards; the most important task was to construct a republic of soviets covering the whole country, from top to bottom. The immediate task was not to 'introduce' socialism but to 'bring social production and the distribution of products at once under the control of the soviets of workers' deputies';[59] likewise, control over the whole centralised banking system, to facilitate the *transition* to socialism. In order to gain allies for the proletariat among the peasants, all the land in the country should be nationalised. The main emphasis in the agrarian programme should be placed on the soviets of rural workers' deputies and the right to dispose of the land should be handed over to the local soviets of rural workers' and peasants' deputies. The mass of working people had to be mobilised around this programme, around the slogans of 'Peace', 'Land', 'Control over production', 'All power to the soviets'. But this would be impossible so long as the old name of the Party facilitated further misleading of the masses. To make a clean break from 'social democracy', whose official leaders had gone over to the bourgeoisie, the name of the Party had to be changed to the 'Communist Party'.

The programme of action outlined here foresaw the course of future events with great perspicacity. The Bolsheviks, whose influence was still inconsiderable in July 1917, won the sympathies of the mass of workers and troops as the failure of the Galician offensive revealed the pointlessness of prolonging the war. The country's severe economic crisis, the general discontent and disappointment of the workers over the development of the revolution, the land hunger of the peasants, which burst forth in numerous spontaneous peasant movements, the persecution of the Bolsheviks by the Provisional Government during July and August and finally [Irakli] Tsereteli's admission that the government supported by the Mensheviks and Socialist Revolutionaries intended to disarm the Petrograd workers, all worked in the same direction. The Kornilov rising[60] was followed by a radicalisation of the masses and the army, who wanted a uniformly working class government with the exclusion

---

59   [Lenin 1964j, p. 24.]
60   [The coup attempt by General Lavr Kornilov during August–September 1917.]

of all bourgeois elements. 'Revolutionary democracy', i.e. the bloc of Mensheviks and Socialist Revolutionaries, failed to comprehend the real situation and repeatedly tried to form a coalition with the bourgeois parties. This was bound to undermine their reputations among the masses. On 11 September Leon Trotsky (who had returned from an American prisoner of war camp[61] in April and joined the Bolshevik Party in May), at a full assembly of the Petrograd Soviet, told the Mensheviks and Socialist Revolutionaries: 'People from both sides are offering you their hand. Now you must decide who you are with. Are you with the working class or its enemies?'[62] At the 'Democratic Conference' of September 1917, the bloc came out in support of a coalition with the Cadet Party. The bloc's indecisive, vacillating position between left and right, the policy which consisted of 'demanding', out of fear of taking power and its own responsibility, that others, who rejected the programme of revolutionary democracy, actually implement it, constituted revolutionary democracy's declaration of bankruptcy. Peace, land and workers control were now no longer the demands of just the Bolshevik Party but of the whole nation. A government which did not conform to these demands was doomed to destruction. In September the Bolsheviks became the leading Party in Petrograd. On 25 September, Trotsky became chairperson of the Petrograd Soviet, the stronghold of the Russian Revolution, in which the Mensheviks and Socialist Revolutionaries had now become a minority, as they had in the Moscow Soviet too. On 7 October (new style) the Duma was dissolved, after five years of existence, and on 7 November 1917 the Provisional Government of Kerensky, which had already become an anachronism, and the bloc that supported him was overthrown by the Bolsheviks, forcibly but almost without bloodshed. All power was transferred to a government of the workers' and peasants' soviets, headed by Lenin. For the first time in history a proletarian movement had become the ruling state power, in a gigantic country of 140 million inhabitants (a twelfth of the world's population) and 22 million square kilometres (a sixth of the world's land surface). Power was assumed by people whose historical destiny was to erect a state structure never seen before, upon the ruins of the old Empire.

The general elections for the Constituent Assembly, conducted in December 1917, resulted in a peasant-petty bourgeois majority of Socialist Revolutionaries and Mensheviks, thanks to delegates from the provinces. When it met, on 18 January 1918, it was dispersed by sailors and soldiers. Bourgeois parliamentary democracy was replaced by proletarian democracy, i.e. by the dictatorship

---

61   [On his way from New York to Russia, Trotsky was intercepted and incarcerated in a camp
      for German prisoners of war, in Amerherst Canada.]
62   [Trotsky 1924, p. 285. The 'quotation' is a paraphrase.]

of the proletariat in its soviet form. The rapid conclusion of the Treaty of Brest-Litovsk with Germany (February 1918) finally returned the millions exhausted by three and a half years of war to the peaceful work of construction.

To understand the new state structure set up by the Bolsheviks it is necessary to briefly examine Lenin's theory of the state, which performed 'the undoubted service of restoring the genuine theory of the state held by Marx and Engels' ([Hans] Kelsen).[63] The *theory of the dictatorship of the proletariat* is the essence of this theory. The dispersal the Constituent Assembly was not the result of an accidental constellation of events, namely that it had a Menshevik-Socialist Revolutionary majority but rather the inevitable outcome of the programmatic approach of the Bolsheviks. We saw that the demand for the dictatorship of the proletariat was incorporated into the programme of the RSDLP in 1903. In his theoretical justification of this position, Lenin sought to differentiate his conception of the state from both those of social democrats and anarchists.

Everywhere in western Europe, social democracy was the political executor of the inheritance of bourgeois democrats of 1848. It never went beyond their intellectual horizon. Its conception of the state thus represented an opportunist distortion of Marx's theory of the state. Despite its employment of 'Marxist' terminology, it represented the fundamentally radical-democratic conception of the state and revolution. It adopted Lassalle's belief in the state as the embodiment of the ethical idea, his belief in universal suffrage as the means to emancipate the working class, finally the belief that in a state with full political liberty (in a parliamentary republic), a 'free people's state',[64] the conquest of power, the victory of the working class, i.e. of the majority of the 'working people', would automatically be achieved by the peaceful means of parliamentary democracy, through a majority decision.

Lenin combated this ideology, because he considered that it directly contradicted the actual character of the state, as taught by experience. It also stood in contradiction to the line of reasoning which Marx and Engels set down in a series of writings over forty years. In the *Communist Manifesto* (1847), *The Eighteenth Brumaire of Louis Bonaparte* (1852), *The Civil War in France* (1871), the *Critique of the Gotha Program* (1875), and finally Engels's critique of the Erfurt Program (1891),[65] the creators of modern socialism demonstrated the need for forcible revolution and a dictatorship of the proletariat. The experiences of the Paris Commune in particular proved that the working class cannot

---

63   [Lenin 1964b; the 'quotation' seems to be a paraphrase, Kelsen 1965, p. 107.]
64   [For Marx's critique of this conception see Marx 1989.]
65   [Marx and Engels 1976; Marx 1979; Marx 1986a; Marx 1989; Engels 1990b.]

simply take hold of the existing state machine but must destroy it, the instrument of class rule. The official theoreticians of social democracy 'forgot' Marx's theory of revolution and did not mention the proletarian party's task of preparing the working class for revolution. But it was not only open reformists, like Bernstein who held fast to Lassalle's conception of the state but also such Marxists such as Kautsky and Plekhanov, who decried any criticism of the state, especially the democratic state, as 'anarchism' and even applied the notion of 'defence of the fatherland' to this class state. Kautsky did recognise Marx's conception of the dictatorship of the proletariat in words but interpreted Engels's expression, the 'withering away' of the state, as suggesting that the state could gradually change, under the influence of the proletariat, and lose its oppressive character. This interpretation necessarily obscured the unavoidability of revolution and destruction of the state apparatus. Engels's expression, however, concerned the surviving remnants of the *proletarian* state after the socialist revolution: after the complete abolition of classes, the state becomes superfluous. The entire difference between Kautskyism and Lassalle is the greater stress laid [by Kautsky] on the *class struggle*. But Lenin regarded that conception, which saw the essence of Marxism in the theory of class struggle, as an opportunist distortion of Marxism; for this theory was also acceptable to the bourgeoisie. It did not originate with Marx at all but had already been created before him by bourgeois scholars (such as, for example, Lorenz von Stein). Accordingly, only someone who develops the theory of class struggle to its ultimate conclusion, the *dictatorship of the proletariat*, can be regarded as a Marxist, i.e. a representative of proletarian politics. The democratic form does not change the essential character of the state. A democracy is also a state, hence an organ of (capitalist) class rule, yes, even 'the best possible political shell for capitalism' (Marx).[66] Universal suffrage is an *instrument* of bourgeois rule; for the proletariat it merely has formal significance as an index of its maturity. So the democratic state must also be destroyed by the proletarian revolution. The bourgeoisie will never voluntarily give up power; on the contrary, its desperate resistance must be reckoned with.

According to Lenin, the class struggle has been undergoing constant intensification during the period of early and mature capitalism, until finally, increasing further in the period of the capitalist system's decline, i.e. in the period of the transition from capitalism to communism, it burst forth in *civil war* against the bourgeoisie and the state. The state, a *product* of objectively irreconcilable class antagonisms that arose in the midst of class conflict, is the organ of *class*

---

66   [Lenin 1964b, p. 398.]

rule created by the economically dominant class for the political oppression of the exploited. It follows from its character that the task of the proletariat does not consist in trying to achieve a parliamentary majority. The liberation of the enslaved class can, rather, only happen through a forceful revolution through which the previously oppressed – the proletariat – take power, i.e. raise themselves to the position of ruling class, destroy the old state apparatus and forcibly suppress the resistance of the expropriated bourgeoisie. The dictatorship of the proletariat therefore represents nothing but the class struggle of the transitional period, intensified to its uttermost degree, conducted until the bourgeoisie has been completely annihilated. Only then will the complete disappearance, the 'withering away' of the state, become possible. According to Marx and Engels, force plays a revolutionary role. It is the midwife of every old society that is pregnant with a new one. And it will also play this role in the consolidation of socialist rule. Nevertheless, the dictatorship of the proletariat is a democracy: proletarian democracy, which will replace bourgeois democracy. It is 'democratic in a new way', for proletarians and the propertyless; dictatorial against the bourgeoisie.[67] For the first time in history, the majority and not the minority of the population will be the organ of oppression. And, according to Lenin, this theory of the dictatorship of the proletariat is the most significant distinction between Marxism and all petty bourgeois elements in the working class, on the one hand, and anarchism,[68] on the other. Marxists do agree with the latter on the question of the abolition of the state as the ultimate goal. While anarchism demands the immediate destruction of the state as the first act of the revolution, Lenin, in accord with Marx, took the view that in order to achieve this goal, a temporary dictatorship of the proletariat is needed for the overthrow of the oppressors or, what is the same thing, a 'temporary' form of proletarian state.

The state apparatus which had been destroyed had to be replaced by positive institutions which consist of a 'a working ... body, *executive and legislative at the same time*' (Marx),[69] on the model of the Paris Commune of 1871, instead of the three-way division of power (legislative, executive and judicial) of bourgeois parliamentarism, in which the dictatorship of the bourgeoisie was anchored. Fiercely rejecting all utopian intellectual constructions as he did, Lenin did not want to work out the positive features of the new state in theory but to derive them from the practical experience of previous proletarian uprisings. In the

---

67   [Lenin 1964b, p. 417.]
68   See Grossmann 1931b, 'Anarchism', above, pp. 210–235.
69   [Marx 1986a, p. 331. Grossman's emphasis.]

soviets of workers' and peasants' deputies, which were set up everywhere during the Russian Revolutions of 1905 and 1917, Lenin saw a further development
of the *embryonic forms of a new type of state*, which Marx had already identified during the Paris Commune of 1871. They arose spontaneously, through the
initiative of millions of people and not according to legislative proposals. They
will be characteristic of every future proletarian uprising. They will replace parliaments, which call the mass of the people to the ballot box every three or six
years, while otherwise excluding them from all political activity. Parliaments
are 'talking shops' where speeches are only made to engage the attention of
the people while the real work of 'states' is performed behind the scenes, by
the departments, chancelleries and staffs, and the contribution of parliamentary deputies consists in trying to place themselves and their friends 'near the
"pie"'.[70] In the soviets, Lenin saw political institutions that were, in principle, of
a different kind. The privileged position of parliamentary deputies, independent of any control, disappeared; they were replaced by delegates who could
be recalled at any time. The overwhelming majority of the functions of state
power were simplified and made accessible to all, *breaking the power of the bureaucracy*. The reduction of official salaries to the level of the average wage of a
skilled worker operated in the same direction. What emerged in 1871 with the
Paris Commune, in only an embryonic form, was continued and extended by
the Russian Revolutions of 1905 and 1917, on a larger historical scale through
the creation of the soviets of workers' and peasants' deputies.

9   The State Economic Policy of Bolshevism

A   *The Transition Phase*
The October Revolution was accomplished with unusual rapidity: the fight
aginst [Pyotr] Krasnov, the fight for Petrograd, lasted only a week. Three months
after the November uprising almost the whole of Russia, from Homel to Siberia
and from Arkhangelsk to Simferopol, was in the hands of the soviets. The initial
period of the revolution was used for the political and organisational consolidation of the new Soviet power. In economic terms, the presence of two revolutionary forces, the urban proletariat and the peasantry, and the alliance (smychka) between them, meant that in Russia two revolutions coincided historically and accomplished their tasks together. They were the peasants' belated
bourgeois anti-feudal agrarian revolution, against the big landowners, and the

---

70   [Lenin 1964b, p. 428.]

urban proletariat's anti-capitalist revolution, against the industrial entrepreneurs. They could accomplish their work together. The first could be carried out with impetuous *élan* and lightning fast thoroughness, because it was belated, confronted with overripe conditions and drew on ready models from western European experience. On the second day after the revolution, all the land cultivated by the peasantry was already handed over to them for their own use, without compensation and without any kind of open or hidden redemption payment. Thus a principal slogan of the revolution was made a reality. Everyone, without distinction of nationality, status or gender had a right to land to the extent that they (with family) cultivated it personally. This already set limits on the size of the portion of land to be allotted. It was not permitted to hire wage-labourers or to lease out land. Every trace of manorial lordship disappeared and the peasants were freed from numerous, onerous taxes and rents, amounting to hundreds of millions of rubles (Decree on the Socialisation of Land, 8 November 1917; Basic Law on Land, 27 January 1918). Furthermore, the revolution abolished all the legal provisions upholding the feudal state system (deprivation of the peasant estate of various rights; legal inequality between men and women, etc.). It also separated the church from the state and the school from the church etc.

This was, of course, not a proletarian but peasant (petty bourgeois) agrarian reform – a concession by the proletariat to the peasants in the interest of the military-political alliance with them, in order to conquer and consolidate *political* power. Economically, it signified narrowing the social foundations of the revolution: more than two million agricultural workers disappeared and turned into small landed proprietors.

Previous experience provided no guidance for the second, anti-capitalist revolution, which proceeded carefully and tentatively. The October Revolution had taken place at a time when Russia was exhausted and devastated by the war. The initial, transitional phase of Bolshevik policy is characterised by the need to safeguard the achievements of the revolution and, in the first place to set the economic mechanism into motion again. No-one initially thought of expropriating the major part of industrial and commercial capital and it was only applied in a few cases, as a punishment for sabotage by capitalists. The eight hour day for the workers was announced and expropriations were limited to the nerve centres of capitalism, i.e. the State Bank (7 November 1917), the organisation of credit (the nationalisation of private banks, 27 December 1917) and transport (nationalisation of the waterways 26 January 1918; the railways were already in state hands before the revolution). The decree introducing a monopoly of foreign trade (22 April 1918) cut Russian capital off from any connection with world capital. As these three measures turned the proletarian state into the monopoly controller of credit, transport, and all raw materials and commodities imported from abroad, it could direct the rest of capitalist industry and subject it to planned regulation (Law on Workers Control, 27 November 1917.) The decree annulling all foreign debts (10 February 1918) expressed the refusal to pay any kind of tribute (in the form of interest or principal repayments) to international capital.

B   *War Communism*
As well as the expropriation of foreign enterprises, the annullment of foreign debts was among the most important reasons for the stubborn intervention of international, particularly French capital. The resistance of the counter-revolution, already moribund, was re-ignited by *foreign intervention* in favour of the expropriated classes and for fully three years (1918–1) the *most bitter civil war* raged. This was a war of *extermination*, just as the World War had been. The main objective was not to defeat the opponent's army but to weaken its forces, to destroy its economy. The allies endeavoured to bind the cordon sanitaire[71] ever tighter around the Bolsheviks. British and American troops invaded in the north (Arkhangelsk), the counter-revolution in the east began in May 1918 with the action of the Czechoslovak Legion, inspired by the Entente. This led to the establishment of [Aleksandr] Kolchak's Government (in Omsk). There were British and Japanese troops in the Pacific port of Vladivostok. In the south, English, French, Italian, Greek and Romanian troops and the navies of all the Entente powers fought against Soviet power. The German army offensive (February 1918) liquidated Soviet power in Ukraine, turned it into the theatre of a fierce civil war (between 1917 and 1920 Kiev changed hands 16 times; Soviet power was established there three times, and in Odessa four times) and gave the Cossack counter-revolution the opportunity to consolidate (Don and Kuban regions). Piłsudski's Polish troops penetrated from the west, with French support. The counter-revolution in the western borderlands of Russia, supported by western European capitalism, led to the establishment of a series of new states, so the class character of this counter-revolution was obscured by struggles for 'national liberation'.

Already economically exhausted by the World War, this intervention by world capital completely crippled Russia's economic organism: the loss of the Donets region deprived Soviet Russia of coal, the loss of the Caucasus (Baku and Grozny) deprived it of oil; the Czechoslovak Legion's uprising cut it off from the Volga region, the Urals, Siberia and Turkestan and robbed it of the whole of

---

71   ['Cordon sanitaire' means 'an enforced boundary to prevent the spread of infection'.]

its mining industry, its cotton production, the rest of its iron and steel industry, Siberian butter, the most important wheat-producing districts and agricultural raw materials. The Russian economic organism broke up, torn into two separate pieces: Soviet Russia and White Guard Russia. The former retained roughly two thirds of the population, the metallurgical and textile industries but lacked the necessary raw materials: it had only 45 percent of the wheat, 37 percent of the barley, 8 percent of the sugar, 10 percent of the coal, 23 percent of the raw iron, and 33 percent of other metals. The reduction in the cultivated area, combined with a fall in fertility led to a 1920 harvest 37 percent below the pre-war figure. The same period saw a fall of 56 percent in the output of intensive agriculture (hemp, flax, peas and sugar beet). Production for the market declined still more, as the peasants went over to cultivation for their own needs. Agriculture ceased to form the basis for feeding the cities and delivering raw materials to industry. The decline in production by small-scale industry amounted to 56–62 percent in 1920, compared with the pre-war period, and the decline in large-scale industry was even greater, 60–98 percent. The extraction of mineral fuels and the production of metal ceased almost completely. By 1920, 80 percent of the railway network was in the hands of the Whites. The transport of goods had fallen to 20 percent of the 1913 level and was almost exclusively devoted to military purposes. A serious food crisis, severe fuel and raw material crises, a transport crisis arose. These led to a catastrophic fall in the urban population. The size of the urban proletariat fell by 60 percent in comparison with the pre-war figure (the fall was 49 percent in Moscow, and 66 percent in Petrograd). Wages fell by almost 55 percent.

In the Russia of the Whites, these crises were alleviated by material support from capitalist countries. In contrast, the Allies imposed the *severest of blockades* against Soviet Russia until 16 January 1920: imports fell from 935 million poods[72] in 1913 to 178 million poods in 1917 and 500,000 poods in 1919. And a disproportionately large share of the small quantity of products available for distribution went to the Red Army, newly created by Trotsky, which was fighting at the front. As a result of this economically unproductive consumption, necessary consumption was still more restricted and the economy was distorted.

Under these circumstances, the Bolsheviks felt compelled to go beyond the previously limits of the economic policy initially followed and introduced a *compulsory system of rationing* all important products, to secure the products that were unconditionally necessary for the maintenance and preservation

---

72   [A pood is 16.38 kilograms.]

of the revolution, independently of *accidental market conditions*. The *second stage of expropriation*, now *extended to cover the majority of capital* ('War Communism') only followed the factory owners' sabotage of necessary production during the Civil War and as an answer to the actions of owners protecting capitalist property. *Large-scale industrial capital* was expropriated and nationalised (26 June 1918), *small-scale industrial capital* (29 November 1918), (domestic) *commercial capital* (29 November 1920) and the cooperatives (30 November 1918), finally, on the land, at the same time the capital of kulaks (large peasants) was expropriated and Committees of Poor Peasants were set up (11 June 1918).

The actual extent to which industrial capital was expropriated was immense. According to the census of 1920, there were over 37,000 state industrial enterprises, employing almost two million workers. Capitalist management of the factories was gradually replaced by proletarian management. As the *market* was the source from which capital constantly drew new strength, during the Civil War the Bolsheviks were compelled to cut capital off completely from its invigorating air. *Trade* was therefore entirely *prohibited* and the machinery of private trade was replaced by planned supplies for the whole people (compulsorily organised into cooperatives) with the help of the Central Union of Consumer Cooperatives (Tsentrosoyuz) and the local provincial societies subordinate to it, under the control of the Commissariat of Supply. A *state monopoly* over the most important agricultural products was introduced and all peasant enterprises were required to hand over their surpluses, above a given level of personal need, in kind. The peasants were to be compensated for these agricultural surpluses with products of the state owned industrial enterprises, and, in this way, the *capitalist commodity economy* was to be replaced by the state organised exchange of products, a *proletarian natural economy without the market*. Nationalised industry was organised in a strictly centralised manner in gigantic 'Trusts' for (roughly 50) branches of industry. Each was under a chief administration (glavk), while the function of directing, controlling and working out the economic plan for the whole country was entrusted to the *Supreme Council of National Economy*, which had already been set up on 18 December 1917. The logical consequence of the marketless natural economy was the *abolition of cash transactions* among individual branches of industry, replaced by mere accounting and book-keeping.

C   *The NEP*

Under the circumstances, the measures outlined above were a *politically necessary* prerequisite for the victory of the proletarian revolution in the Civil War and the destruction of the counter-revolutionary resistance of capital and the landowners. It was therefore mistaken to write about a 'defeat of War Communism' ([Arthur] Feiler).[73] But these measures went far beyond the limits of what was *economically* advantageous, i.e. they went beyond the degree to which previous capitalist development had prepared the domination of the *large-scale enterprise*. In particular, they affected the innumerable *small enterprises* in town and country. To extend the scope of the state-run natural economy was at the same time to increase organisational difficulties and necessarily led to the bureaucratisation of the economy. It was impossible, within the framework of the natural economy without the market, to direct hundreds of thousands of small-scale, artisanal enterprises, millions of so-called kustar (peasant) enterprises, hundreds of thousands of small trading enterprises (storehouses, warehouses, shops etc.), finally 18 million peasant farms. While large-scale enterprises were entirely incorporated into the state's natural economy, the petty bourgeoisie stubbornly resisted state control. In 1920 the peasants *concealed* a fifth of the total sown area and a third of the total harvest. But in the towns *speculators* also gained control of the products distributed by the state monopolies: instead of the legal market, which had been prohibited, an illegal capitalist market emerged; beside the official proletarian natural economy, an underground and much larger capitalist commodity economy spread out. At the beginning of 1921 it became clear that this situation was untenable. So long as the peasants were faced with the choice between the return of the landowners and the suppression of the market, they declared that they agreed with the latter. It was precisely the victory of the revolution and the removal of the counter-revolutionary threat that prompted the peasants to revolt against the prohibition of trade. The anti-feudal agrarian revolution, the distribution of the land among the peasants was, in the first instance, completed economically by the establishment of the market, the possibility of selling agricultural products. As the proletariat was the minority partner in its alliance with the peasantry, the proletarian revolution was compelled by the peasant revolution to accept a temporary retreat ('breathing-space') in the interests of the common victory over the counter-revolution. The first step in this direction was the replacement, implemented by Lenin, of the confiscation the whole of the agricultural surplus with a *tax in kind*, which left the peasants part of the harvest above what was needed for personal consumption. They were allowed to sell this on the market. In May 1921 the so-called 'New Economic Policy' (NEP) was introduced and the partial *restoration of the market* was proclaimed. For agriculture, the NEP meant that the leasing of land and the hiring of wage labourers

---

73   [Feiler 1931, p. 59.]

were allowed. But the possibility of the restoration of capitalist exploitation was limited, so long as *political power* and the 'commanding heights' of the economy, i.e. control over the basic means of production and exchange (large factories, the transport system, foreign trade, credit and the determination of prices) remained *in the hands of the proletariat*. The restoration of the power of money and the accumulation of private wealth was equally limited, so long as the working class had political power and consequently the *ability to raise taxes*.

The Soviet Union overcame many critical situations: the frightful starvation and harvest failures of 1921 and 1924, and the economic crisis of early 1923, that resulted from the so-called 'scissors', i.e. the discrepancy between industrial and agricultural prices, (a consequence of the sharper decline in industrial production than agricultural production, therefore a relative surplus of agricultural products and a fall in their prices). It subsequently entered a phase of calmer development. The New Economic Policy succeeded in overcoming the catastrophic decline in the forces of production, which touched bottom in 1921. By the end of 1926 the rebuilding of the economy was complete, almost exclusively by using domestic resources, without drawing on foreign capital, and at an unexpectedly rapid pace. In the most important areas of the economy, production reached the prewar level, in part even exceeded it. The productivity of labour and wages rose to the prewar level and one branch of large-scale industry after another was gradually transformed from making losses to making profits for the state. New tasks therefore now confronted the economic policy of Soviet power.

D   *The Five Year Plan*

The October Revolution had liquidated the classes of big landowners and big industrialists. But, so long as small-scale private industry and *private* peasant production continued to exist, the roots for the emergence of a new bourgeoisie and for *capitalism to blossom again* were still there. The foundations for a rebirth of capitalism could only really be destroyed by the liquidation of technological backwardness and the extension of the socialised sector of the economy on the basis of modern technology. 'Socialism is inconceivable without large-scale capitalist engineering based on the latest discoveries of modern science'.[74] The danger of capitalism's revival was particularly great in the countryside, where a stratum of larger capitalists developed again and again from the village bosses, the rich peasants (kulaks), who exploited the mass of the

---

74   [Lenin 1965a, p. 339.]

village poor. Any attempt to protect the village poor as the basis of the traditional small-scale enterprise – consequently, Zinoviev's programme of 'a horse
for every small peasant' too – had to remain illusory, in face of the inexorable
character of the laws of capitalist development. A successful struggle against
exploitation by the kulaks could only be conducted by *liquidating* small peasant property and transferring the village poor to new forms of *collective agricultural production* conducted with the most modern technology. This kind of
reconstruction of agriculture, however, could only be carried out on the basis of
a new and higher form of smychka, the alliance between the urban proletariat
and the poor peasants.

   This alliance had passed through various phases. It started off as a *military-
political alliance* for the conquest of power and the maintenance of the October
Revolution's achievements against the threat of a bourgeois-landlord restoration. Later on, during the NEP period, the economic content of the smychka
consisted in the effort to rebuild ruined agriculture by raising the level of
the individual peasant farming, using the *commercial aspect* of the alliance
between town and country, so that in return for the delivery of food supplies the town satisfied the village's personal consumption requirements for
the products of industry (textiles, shoes etc.). The present, higher form of the
alliance finally consists of the development of the productive forces of agriculture by overcoming the low productivity of small individual farming, i.e. by
satisfying the *productive* requirements of the village (agricultural machinery,
tractors, superior seed varieties, artificial fertiliser etc.). The organisational preconditions for this are: 1) acceleration of the tempo of industrial development;
2) transformation of peasant enterprises, which will only become possible
by using modern machinery, i.e. the creation of various forms of productive
cooperation in villages, starting with the establishment of machine tractor stations and cooperatives for the common use of the soil, and going on to the
collectivisation of farms; 3) the principal condition for the implementation of
this reconstruction is, finally, the quantitative and qualitative strengthening of
the leading social force – the proletariat – as the organiser of the whole system
of socialist reconstruction, in a predominantly peasant country. The necessity
for this reconstruction derived from the whole internal and external situation
of the Soviet Union: the danger of capitalist encirclement from outside and the
preponderance of private economic elements within the country. The working
class can only retain its power and the leading role of the proletariat can only
be secured in the long term, by such a socialist reconstruction. But it was not
just the rebirth of capitalism that had to be prevented; the crises specific to
capitalism had to be eliminated, by taking control of the market, restricting
it step by step and finally abolishing it completely. In its place, according to

the decision of All-Russian Central Executive Committee in 1920, there would
be the 'formulation of ... an *integrated production plan* for Soviet Russia as a
whole',[75] that would be of decisive significance for the further development of
the entire economy of the Soviet Union. The idea of a plan covering the whole
of the economy, prescribing and determining the direction and extent of its
development, is an old component of scientific socialism. It was also in the
minds of the Russian masses from the very first days that followed the October
Revolution. But the implementation of these plans had to be postponed initially, when [resistance to] the counter-revolution compelled the measures of
War Communism and the NEP.

For Leninism, the theoretical justification for the realisation of socialism in
an economically backward country resulted from the concrete historical situation in which it was possible to hope that the western European proletariat
would provide support for the Russian Revolution. The fact that the Russian
Revolution was isolated, however, made it necessary to consider the theoretical problem of the possibility of socialism in a *single* country. This possibitity
had already been foreseen and answered in the affirmative with great acuteness
by G.V. in Germany in 1879 in his theoretical analysis of the 'isolated socialist
state'.[76] Lenin also answered the question affirmatively, at the end of his life
(in 1923).[77] After Lenin's death the affirmative answer given by [Iosif] Stalin-
[Nikolai] Bukharin gave rise to fierce struggles and debates within the CPSU.
A resolution passed by the Fourteenth Party Conference (April 1925) affirmed
their answer to the cardinal question of socialist construction, which was subsequently confirmed by a plenum of the Central Committee. This conception
was combatted by the Mensheviks but also many Bolsheviks, in particular Trotsky as unMarxist. They argued that the construction of socialism in the Soviet
Union was impossible, owing to technological backwardness and that the ines-
capable requirement for socialist construction was the victory of the proletariat
over the bourgeoisie in all capitalist countries or at least the most important
ones.

The history of the first tentative attempts at planning the economy – its
'infancy' – can be passed over here with a refence to [Friedrich] Pollock's
groundbreaking book.[78] All that needs to be mentioned here is that, in 1920,

---

75   [Vserossiysky Centralny Ispolnitelny Komitet 1920. Grossman's emphasis. Also see Lenin
       1965c, p. 138 and Pollock 1971, pp. 233–4.]
76   Vollmar 1878.
77   [Lenin 1965b, p. 468.]
78   Pollock 1971.

Lenin asserted that the survival of the proletarian dictatorship was dependent on the electrification and industrialisation of the country, and already called for a plan for the production of energy over the next ten years. It is understandable that, during the period of Civil War and War Communism, despite all the efforts, this was not achieved. A decisive step was taken with the *establishment of the State Planning Commission* (Gosplan 22 February 1921), on Lenin's insistence. It brought previously scattered planning activities into one centre. Its first labours took place under Lenin's direct supervision. Of course, not much inital success could be expected, given the destruction wrought by the World War and Civil War. Only after the successful *reconstruction* of the industrial inheritance taken over from the bourgeoisie was the work of *new construction*, which would have started immediately after the October Revolution under more favourable historical circumstances, taken in hand in line with the decision of the Sixteenth Party Conference (October 1926). And only now did the problem of *socialist* construction arise for the Bolsheviks in all its gigantic, world historic magnitude: how and under what circumstances is such *new construction on a planned basis* possible, that is while avoiding the periodic crises so characteristic of capitalism? The fulfilment of these tasks was approached with energetic boldness and extraordinary consistency. The first *control numbers* for the year 1925–6 were already prepared by 20 August 1925. On their basis, *the possible and attainable expansion of production during the following year was calculated in advance* and *determined in advance*! For, unlike the economic research institutes of capitalist states, the control numbers do not only predict (make prognoses about) the course of future developments, independent of our wishes. Through the issue of directives to economic leaders, they also *steer* future development to the predicted outcome (Pollock).

It was soon clear, however, that a plan covering a single year was not sufficient. For large technological facilities, a construction time of five years normally has to reckoned with. To calculate the outlay of the necessary capital investment correctly, it is therefore necessary to use this period as a basis. The economic *effectiveness* of these new facilities, the full entry of their annual product into the economic process, does not occur until even later. So it was apparent that it was necessary to create a *general plan*, estimated to cover about 15 years, in order to plan the reordering of the economy, i.e. to construct a schematic model of its future structure on the basis of productive forces (material resources and available labour-power) currently at hand and expected in each successive year. Only on the basis and within the framework of such a general plan could its first part – the Five Year Plan – be calculated and determined in more detail. Its purpose was to prevent a characteristic feature of capitalism: the explosive *volatility* with which the different branches of production develop, due to concerns about profitability. It had to coordinate and sequentially determine the speed of development of the principle sectors of the economy, their connections with each other and with the overall tempo of socialist accumulation over the given period of time. But the Five Year Plan, which is first and foremost a conception of grandiose and accelerated *socialist* industrialisation, is not merely an economic document but also a programme of political class struggle within the USSR. Born in the period between 1925 and 1928, chiefly at the Fourteenth and Fifteenth Congresses of the CPSU, in the struggle against the right wing, its acceptance has determined the direction of future economic policy, in its most important aspects, on the path of social- ist construction. Its adoption marked the rejection of the so-called *theory of agrarianisation* of the bourgeois Professors [Nikolai] Kondratiev and [Nikolai] Makarov, which also met with sympathy in circles of Party right wingers ([Lev] Shanin). This theory regarded the proposed tempo of industrialisation, with its focus on attacking the village kulak, as too rapid and unrealisable. Agriculture has to be raised first, all restrictions on the growth of the individual farms of large peasants had to be removed, the export of agricultural products expan- ded, on that basis foreign trade with the capitalist world economy increased and technological equipment put in place on peasant farms, with the assist- ance of European industry. Only on this firm basis of organic development would it be possible for industry to gradually grow. According to the concep- tion of the ruling party majority (the Stalin tendency), the struggle of the Party's right against accelerated industrialisation was the expression of the influence of non-proletarian, peasant elements. Only the rapid growth of industry produ- cing means of production (heavy industry) was capable, according to the view of the party majority, of creating a basis for rapid progress in *processing indus- tries* and *agriculture*, making the Soviet Union as independent as possible from the capitalist world and finally building up branches of industry needed for the defence of the country.

On the other hand, the party majority also rejected the programme of 'hyper- industrialisation' advocated by the Party's Left, i.e. so-called 'Trotskyism'. Trot- sky regarded the tempo of the industrialisation which had been embarked on as insufficient and called for further acceleration by drawing more on the resources of the peasantry. This amounted to treating the village as a kind of colonial hinterland for the socialist town and socialist industrialisation, and would ultimately threaten the principal foundation of the proletarian dictat- orship and Soviet power: the alliance between the workers and the peasants. The ideological and organisational liquidation of Trotskyism at the Fifteenth Congress of the CPSU (1927) ensured the definitive victory of the general line of economic construction established by the Five Year Plan.

Despite the prevailing hunger for finished goods, the Five Year Plan worked out at the end of 1926 ([Stanislav] Strumilin) for the period 1926–7 to 1930–1 laid the greatest stress not on promoting the production of consumer goods destined for the broad masses (the so-called Group B) but on the development of the country's productive forces – the industries producing means of production (the so-called Group A). But it did not make use of all the possibilities offered by a planned economy. The lack of experience it displayed is noticeable in the undeveloped theory and method of planning, and also the lack of any data. After all, the experience so far garnered only covered the period of reconstructing the ruined and unutilised assets of the country under market conditions. Could these experiences (such as the growth of industry at a rate of 20 to 30 percent per annum during the period 1922/23 to 1925/26) also be applied to future socialist construction when the market was excluded? If socialism – an organised and planned economy – represents an economic principle which is superior to capitalism's anarchic mode of production, as socialist theory has always maintained, this superiority of the planned economy must be demonstrated by its successful practical application. The great practical task of the planned economy in the Soviet Union was therefore summed up in the expression: 'to overtake and outstrip the advanced capitalist countries technically and economically'[79] and thus secure the victory of the socialist system in its historic competition with the economic system of capitalism. A *dispute* of fundamental importance arose about the *tempo of future development*, over the percentage by which the gross product of large-scale industry should increase in 1926/27 and subsequent years. The percentage expansion of production is dependent on the extent of the sources of accumulation available to a country. But under capitalism a great proportion of the sources of accumulation is squandered unproductively, whether on circulation costs connected with the anarchic character of capitalist production (e.g. interest and storage costs, as a result of obstacles in circulation and lack of demand) or irrational production (e.g. inappropriate investments in factories as a result of rivalry among hostile enterprises, unutilised means of production and labour power etc.). The advantage of an organised planned economy, in contrast, lies in the extreme practicability, thus also economy in production, as shown in particular in the giant industrial complexes combining electrical, chemical and steelmaking branches (e.g. the Dnieprostroi complex or the planned unification of the coal, coke, metallurgical and chemical industries in the Donets basin). It is true that under capitalism there is also tendency to 'rationalisation', horizontal and ver-

---

79   [Stalin 1954, pp. 281–2.]

tical concentration of enterprises and the formation of cartels and giant trusts. But private property, whether in the land or in the riches beneath it, is a *barrier* to the consistent and rational operation of this tendency. Hence proposals for a planned *bourgeois* economy (Walter Rathenau and Rudolf Wissell),[80] in which private property in the means of production is essentially retained, are impossible to implement and have not withstood criticism. The nationalisation of the land and mineral resources, as well as the conversion of large-scale industry into state property, open unimagined possibilities for the planned and rational organisation of production in industrial complexes. In capitalist society there can be no question of this. And the planned economy gives rise to a similarly economical use of resources in the sphere of circulation, e.g. by eliminating superfluous circulation time and reducing it to the necessary minimum of transportation time etc. Removing the barrier of private property generalises technological progress, which is withheld from general use by private, industrial property rights under capitalism.

These and other similar advantages of the planned economy mean that there are *reserves of heightened opportunities for accumulation* in comparison with private economic accumulation. But, lacking experience, the extent of these reserves was unclear. Already in 1925/26, actual growth exceeded that proposed by 17.4 percent in large-scale industry and 17 percent in agriculture. For 1926/27 Gosplan's control numbers prescribed a growth rate of only 15.6 percent; as implemented, growth was over 21 percent. This and other experiences showed that the original Five Year Plan lagged too cautiously behind the facts; it lacked any kind of drive. It was precisely for this reason that, early in 1928, Gosplan issued a supplement to the piatiletka,[81] actually a new version of the Five Year Plan for the period 1928/29 to 1932/33. On the basis of experience gained so far, despite the introduction of the seven hour working day and the five day working week, it assumed that *growth would proceed more rapidly* than originally envisaged. The revised Plan recognised how its distinctively gigantic impetus would stimulate the interest and creative energy of the working class and the administrative apparatus in reconstructing the Soviet economy, so that they concentrated on carrying it out. The Five Year Plan thus represents a significant turning point in the economic development of the Soviet Union.

It is not possible enter into the concrete content of this process in more detail here. In order to understand the structural changes in the Soviet eco-

---

80   [Rathenau 1925; Wissell 1920.]
81   ['Piatiletka' means 'Five Year Plan'.]

nomy which aimed for and have already started, it is merely noted that, for the reasons indicated earlier, it was the *production of the means of production* and especially *sources of energy* (coal, oil, peat and electrical power) that needed to be increased initially. In terms of *raw materials*, the production of pig iron and steel, as well as copper and zinc, will be increased tremendously, and on this raw material basis, the machine building industry will quadruple over five years. The extent of the structural changes which were aimed for in the relationship between town and country and between the socialised sector and the private sector of the economy can best be seen in the extent and direction of capital investments in the economy during the previous five years (1924 to 1928) and during the five years embraced by the piatiletka:

	1924–8	1929–33
	(billion rubles)	
Total investments	26.5	64.6
including:		
a) Industry	4.4	16.4
b) Long distance electric power stations	0.8	3.1
(excluding factory based power stations)		
c) Transport system	2.7	9.9
d) Agriculture (including investment in peasant farms)	15.0	23.2

The structural transformation and the desired course of development on the path to socialist industrialisation is apparent in the increase in capital directed to industry and long distance electric power stations exceeding those in all other branches of the economy. Total capital invested should increase by 182 percent from the 1928 level but the increase in industry should be 300 percent and even 525 percent in the case of long distance power stations, while it is only 167 percent for railways and 135 percent for agriculture. The share of industry in the economy as a whole should increase from 14 percent in 1928 to 22.8 percent in 1933. The share of long distance power stations should grow from 1.4 percent to 4.1 percent, over the same period, and that of transport from 16.6 percent to 17.2 percent, while the share of agriculture should fall from 41 percent to 30.4 percent. But it is not only the shift to industrialisation that is noticeable. The rise in the share of nationalised industry signifies a *strengthening of the socialised sector* in the distribution of investment capital. According to the Five Year Plan, the proportions between the different social sectors by 1933, as compared with 1928, should change as follows. The state sector rises from 51.0 percent to 63.6 percent, the cooperative sector from 1.7 to 5.0 percent, the socialised sector as a whole from 52.7 to 68.9 percent, the private sector falls from 47.3 percent to

31.1 percent. It is not possible to go into the development of individual branches of production here. The question of how this gigantic plan is being realised is, however, interesting. Are its assumptions merely fantasies, 'expressions of desire'? In 1928 Feiler could still refer ironically to the Five Year Plan's growth figures as being 'conjugated in the future tense',[82] the first two years of the Plan immediately showed that its essential parts would not only be realised but far outstripped, that the actual tempo of accumulation was much more rapid than envisaged in the Plan.

Coal production, which rose from 28.9 million tonnes in 1913 to 36.3 million in 1927/28 (+26.6 percent), was expected to reach 75 million tonnes in 1932/33, according to the plan, i.e. more than double over five years. At the Sixteenth Party Congress (July 1930), [Valerian Vladimirovich] Kuibyshev was able to state that coal production reached 52.5 million tonnes in 1929/30 and in 1930/31 would amount to more than 72 million, so that after three years of the plan it had almost reached the total predicted for the end of the fifth year (1932/33). The same is true of the *production of oil, electrical energy* etc. According to the Five Year Plan *pig iron production* was expected to increase from 3.3 million tonnes in 1928 to 10 million tonnes in 1932/33, that is, trebled. To provide a comparative yardstick for evaluating this gigantic growth tempo, it is noted that in the United States a similar increase took 18 years (1879–97), in Germany 22 years (1883 3.4 million tonnes; 1905 10.8 million tonnes). In Great Britain 21 years were needed (1886 to 1907), to raise iron production from 7.1 million tonnes to 10.2 million tonnes, i.e. to raise it by a mere 45 percent. But even this tremendous growth tempo should be outdone. In his speech, mentioned above, Kuibyshev stated that in 1931/32 pig iron production would already reach the 10 million tonnes predicted for 1932/33. Production would reach 17 million tonnes during the last year of the plan, because the three newly constructed giants (Magnitogorsk in the Urals – the largest ironworks in Europe, with a production of 2.6 million tonnes – Zaporozhe and Kuznetsk) with a total production of 4.6 million tonnes would come on stream in 1932/33. In Germany it took 29 years (1883 to 1912) for this to happen. There are no historical analogies for such a tremendous growth tempo. With the achievement of these estimates, the Soviet Union will become the *largest pig iron producer in Europe* and the second largest in the world (after the United States of America).

Because capitalist production is for an unknown market, when it increases it meets with problems of demand and these lead to fight over markets. The purpose of increasing production in a planned economy, on the other hand,

---

82   [Feiler 1931, p. 93.]

is to satisfy needs. Individual branches of production are consumers of each other's products, because the growth of each has been coordinated and harmonised with the others in advance. The forced growth in pig iron production, for example, is a necessary prerequisite for the development of a series of industrial branches that make use of the metal: general machine construction, the construction of agricultural machinery, automobile and tractor construction, housing construction, railway construction. The value of agricultural machinery output, for example, which was 67 million rubles in 1913 and should reach 500 million rubles at the end of the Five Year Plan (1933), was already 400 million rubles in 1930 and indeed 845 million rubles in 1931, thus overtaking the annual production of agricultural machinery in the United States of America. Similar experiences in the first two years of the Five Year Plan in other industries made it possible to issue the directive embodied in the resolution of the Sixteenth Party Congress, for 'the fulfilment of the Five Year Plan in four years', in the most important branches of production.

The possibilities for realising the Five Year Plan naturally vary according to the degree to which the means of production have been brought under state control. In large-scale industry and in transport, which are entirely owned by the state, the estimates in the Five Year Plan are at the same time *directives* to perform a given amount of work. The socialist transformation of the village is much more difficult. The state cannot give binding directives to the 24 million peasant farms. All it can do is influence the direction of the natural processes taking place in the village through a series of powerful instruments of indirect 'social pressure' which it has at its disposal, e.g. by setting the prices of the products of state run industries, the provision of energy by the state, advantaging members of collective farms over private farms in the provision of industrial commodities, tax and credit policies etc. The difficulties of planning agriculture are still greater because almost a quarter of peasants farms consist of dwarf holdings, not even capable of maintaining a family and for which it was not worth keeping a horse.

Despite these difficulties, the Five Year Plan does not neglect the socialist transformation of the village and we saw that the leading idea underlying the Five Year Plan is to overcome the technological backwardness of agriculture.

One way to raise the level of peasant farming would be to allow the well-off peasants in the village (kulaks) greater freedom of manoeuvre, on the model of western European capitalist states. This would make it easier to lease land and make use of wage labour, reduce their tax burden and provide them with other assistance. It was impossible for the Soviet state to follow this path for the development of the productive forces. It is clear socialist industry in the towns cannot be developed with one hand while the path for capitalist elements in the villages is smoothed with the other. The Soviet state decided to choose a different path, the path of the final, decisive struggle against the survivals of capitalism in peasant agriculture. This is the path of the *socialist transformation of the village*, converting 24 million small, technologically primitive peasant farms into large-scale, mechanised agricultural enterprises, by socialising agricultural production. There is still a great deal of uncultivated land in the Soviet Union but the small peasant does not have the means to purchase horses, buildings and other inventory. According to the Five Year Plan, socialist industry should supply the requirements of agriculture and overcome the age-old backwardness of village life, the age-old chasm between town and country, finally allowing the transition to the classless communist society. The three forms of socialised agriculture which have existed in small numbers since the beginning of Soviet rule are the cooperative for joint cultivation, the artel[83] and the *commune*. They represent three successive stages of increasing collectivisation of peasant agriculture. In the first, only the land is handed over for common cultivation; tools, cattle and the crop remain private property. In the agricultural artel the private sphere is restricted to consumption. Finally, communes (the kolkhozy)[84] combine peasant farms into collective units, that receive support from the state in the form of machines, credit, seed, artificial fertiliser etc. In them, the last remnants of independent existence are abolished: the members of the commune live in communal houses, children are brought up communally etc. The kolkhozy free small peasants from exploitation by the kulaks but also signify a technological revolution in agriculture. As well as the kolkozy, the socialised sector includes a second group of enterprises, the gigantic state farms (sovkhozy), set up by the state, the so-called 'grain factories', on the American model. They encompass enormous areas (like, for example the 'grain factory' Gigant in the north Caucasus, with its 140,000 hectares, three times larger than the largest mechanised farms in America), devoted to the production of grain and equipped with the most modern agricultural machinery, tractors etc. In 1927/8, at the end of the period of reconstruction, the area sown in the socialised sector covered only 2.3 million hectares (the sovkhozy 400,000 hectares), i.e. just under 2 percent of the total area sown and both groups together provided roughly 7.5 percent of marketed grain. Under the Five Year Plan the size of the Soviet estates is to increase from 400,000 to five million hectares after five years and the assumed growth of collective farms from 2.3 million to 22 million hectares. The cultivated area of the socialised sector should increase

---

83   [The artel was a traditional cooperative.]
84   ['Kolkhoz', plural 'kolkhozy' is conventionally translated as 'collective farm'.]

from 2.3 million hectares in 1928 to 27 million hectares in 1933, i.e., after five years, already more than 18 percent of the cultivated area and 43 percent of the grain delivered to the market. In the course of this restructuring six million peasant households (roughly 20 million villagers) should go over from individual to collective production. The restructuring of agriculture to mechanised enterprises should be largely completed. By 1933 no less than 170,000 tractors and new machines, to a total value of 900 million rubles, should be employed in the socialised sector. Thanks to the advantages of large-scale production, the use of artificial fertiliser etc., the yield per hectare should be double that on individual peasant farms.

There is no need to particularly emphasise what a radical break with the centuries old style of village life this constitutes and what an upheaval it is in the structure of agricultural production. The 43 percent of the marketed grain which the socialised sector should provide completely transforms the situation on the grain market, making the supply of food to the towns and for export increasingly independent of the peasants' deliveries, thwarting any possibility of kulaks speculating and attempting to upset the price of grain.

A similar policy is also being pursued in relation to *livestock*. Here too the attempt is being made to guarantee the supply of meat to the towns independently of deliveries by individual peasant farms and to solve the problem of raising livestock in a socialist way by setting up huge farms specialising in cattle breeding (skotovod) and pig breeding (svinovod).

In the socialised sector of agriculture, too, the results of the first two of the five years surpassed the original estimates. In 1929/30 203 million rubles were to be invested in the *sovkhozy* and 7,000 tractors were to be placed at their disposal. The investments in fact amounted to 365 million rubles and the number of tractors available was more than twice as high. So the area of five million hectares which was expected to be under cultivation by *sovkhozy* in 1933 had already been reached by 1930. The same is true of the *kolkhozy* to a still greater degree. The amount of state support for the collective farms originally envisaged in 1929/30 was 200 million rubles. The actual figure was 320 million rubles. Likewise, the number of tractors, automobiles, agricultural machines and the quantity of artificial fertiliser placed at their disposal increased beyond the original estimate. In 1928/29 the collective farms already covered a cultivated area of 5 million hectares and in 1929/30 not less than 30 millin hectares. Thus the whole of the Five Year Plan for collectivisation had already been significantly surpassed in its second year and the sole obstacle to further growth is that young Soviet industry cannot produce enough to supply the collective farms with the tractors, machines, fertiliser etc. that they need and that there is a shortage of qualified agronomists.

Modern technology should also be introduced into individual peasant farms, by means of *contracts* they will make with the state machine tractor stations for the mechanised cultivation of the fields and harvesting. According to the supplement to the Five Year Plan, 200 such stations were set up for the first time in 1929/30 (in the Volga region, Ukraine and the north Caucasus). They have adequate numbers of tractor columns and attachments, as well as reliable permanent workers, and had five million hectares to cultivate. By 1933 1,000 such tractor stations should have been organised for 40 million hectares under cultivation. These contracts thus represent the first stage in acquainting the peasants with the most elementary form of a socialised economy and preparing them for higher forms of collectivisation.

Considering agriculture as a whole (the socialised and the private sectors), the sown area should increase from 116 to 142 million hectares, i.e. by 22 percent, during the five years between 1928 and 1933 (the cultivated area had already reached 132 million hectares by 1930). The area under grain should increase by 17 percent and industrial crops by 62 percent (particular crops, like cotton, should increase even faster, the total yield should rise rise from 718,000 tonnes to 1,907,000 tonnes, i.e. by 165 percent, which will make the Soviet Union independent of cotton imports). The grain harvest should grow by 25 percent, i.e. from 7.6 quintals per hectare to 9.5 quintals per hectare,[85] which will make the formation of a state grain reserve of almost 5 million tonnes possible and allow the amount of *grain exported* to rise again to about 8 million tonnes, by the end of the fifth year, despite the growing amount needed by the population itself (Tsarist Russia exported approximately 11 million tonnes.) The income of the agricultural population should rise by 67 percent, with the income of private farms increasing by 61 percent and that of collective farms by 84 percent, as a result of higher agricultural production and the reduction in the prices of industrial products envisaged under the Five Year Plan.

Only by taking in hand this socialist reconstruction of the village could the Bolsheviks combine into a unified Communist revolution the two revolutions, the agrarian revolution of the peasantry and the proletarian revolution in the towns, which had continued to stand unconnected side by side until the October Revolution and longer, during the periods of War Communism and the NEP.

Such a tremendous revolution in the whole of the economic life of a gigantic country inhabited by 160 million people, a revolution whose basic idea is

---

85   [A quintal, here, means 100 kilograms.]

initially to promote industries producing means of production and, for this reason, to temporarily restrict the industries only producing consumer goods, cannot occur, it is self-evident, without friction and without imposing very great sacrifices (food shortage) on the bearers the system, the workers and peasants. That such a revolutionary transformation brings about some hardship for the opponents of the system is understandable. For the historian who looks back, tracing out not the transitory phenomena that accompany a system but its essential historical core, the Five Year Plan and its underlying economic measures represent a unique attempt to replace the anarchy of the market, which has defied all previous efforts to regulate within the framework of the capitalist economy, with a mechanism of a fundamentally different type, namely an economy of socialist production on a generous scale. What now exists is still not socialism: along-side the state socialist economy, private capitalism still exists. But it is already impossible for any large-scale private activities to be undertaken in any area of the economy without permission from the State Planning Commission. Year by year, the socialist elements of the marketless economy are being strengthened, while the role of the market, of the private economy, progressively declines. The elemental compulsion of the market mechanism, inherent in the capitalist system, with its explosive booms followed by the setbacks of crises and periods of stagnation, is being overcome. Consciously planned direction, social control of the economy is replacing it. Precisely for that reason, this is the greatest socialist experiment known to history. It is of supreme significance both for economics and in practical terms. It is important for the former because economic theory, which for more than 200 years has derived all its concepts from an exchange based economy, for the first time finds here the new material of a marketless, planned economy, which will enrich the subject with new scientific concepts. In practical terms, it is important because a duel between capitalism and socialism is being fought out in the framework of the struggle over the Russian Five Year Plan, whose outcome will help to determine the fate of western European capitalism and the western European proletariat for decades to come.

Literature

In addition to the literature indicated at the end of
Schmidt, Conrad 1924, 'Bolschewismus', in *Handwörterbuch der Staatswissenschaften.* *Band 2*, edited by Ludwig Elster, Adolf Weber and Friedrich Wieser, fourth edition, Jena: Fischer, pp. 992–8.
Seraphim, Hans-Jürgen 1929, 'Bolschewismus', in *Ergänzungsband zum Handwörter-*

buch der Staatswissenschaften, edited by Ludwig Elster and Adolf Weber, fourth edition, Jena: Fischer, pp. 200–39.

Seraphim, Hans-Jürgen 1929, 'Lenin', in *Ergänzungsband zum Handwörterbuch der Staatswissenschaften*, edited by Ludwig Elster and Adolf Weber, fourth edition, Jena: Fischer, pp. 678–85.

reference should be made to the following fundamental works:

1 General Works

Hoetzsch, Otto 1917, *Russland, eine Einführung auf Grund seiner Geschichte vom Japanischen bis zum Weltkrieg*, second edition, Berlin: Reimer.

Lenin, Vladimir Ilyich 1964 [1899], *The Development of Capitalism in Russia*, in Vladimir Ilyich Lenin, *Collected Works. Volume 3*, Moscow: Progress Publishers.

Miljukov, Pavel Nikolayevich 1920, *Geschichte der zweite russischen Revolution*, Wien: Renaissance.

Miljukov, Pavel Nikolayevich 1925–6, *Russlands Zusammenbruch*, 2 volumes, Berlin: Deutsche Verlags-Anstalt.

Plekhanov, Georgii Valentinovich 1967 [1914–6], *History of Russian Social Thought*, translated by Boris M. Bekkar, New York: Fertig.

Plekhanov, Georgii Valentinovich 1939 [1914], *Introduction to the Social History of Russia*, translated by Ernest E. Beauvais, New York: Columbia University Press.

Pokrovsky, Mikhail Nikolayevich 1929 [1910–3], *Geschichte Russlands von seiner Entstehung bis zur neuesten Zeit*, translated by Alexandra Ramm, Leipzig: Hirschfeld.

Smilg-Benario, Michael 1929, *Von Kerensky zu Lenin*, Wien/Zürich: Amalthea.

2 History of the Russian Workers Movement

Balabanoff, Angelica 1969 [1926–8], *Die Zimmerwalder Bewegung 1914–1919*, Frankfurt: Neue Kritik.

Bubnov, Andrei 1930, 'V.K.P.(B)', in the *Grosse Sowjet-Enzyklopädie. Band 11*, Moskva, pp. 1–544 and the literature indicated there.

Jaroslavski, Emelian 1929, *Aus der Geschichte der kommunistischen Partei der Sowjetunion (Bolshewiki). Erster Teil: Von der Volksfreunde-bewegung bis zum imperialistischen Krieg*, Berlin: Kommunistische Internationale.

Kulczycki, Ludwig 1910–4, *Geschichte der russischen Revolution*, three volumes, Gotha: Perthes.

Martov, Julius and Dan, Theodore 1973 [1926], *Geschichte der russischen Sozialdemokratie*, Erlangen: Politladen Erlangen.

Thun, Alphons 1883, *Geschichte der revolutionären Bewegung in Russland*, Leipzig: Duncker & Humblot.

Trotsky, Leon Davidovich 1973 [1922], *1905*, Harmondsworth: Pelican.

Trotsky, Leon Davidovich 1919, *From October to Brest-Litovsk*, New York: Socialist Publication Society.

Trotsky, Leon Davidovich 1970 [1930], *My Life: An Attempt at an Autobiography*, New York: Pathfinder.

Trotsky, Leon Davidovich 1969 [1930], *The Permanent Revolution*, in Leon Trotsky, *The Permanent Revolution; and Results and Prospects*, translated by John G. Wright and Brian Pearce, New York: Pathfinder.

Zinoviev, Grigorii 1973 [1923], *History of the Bolshevik Party from the Beginnings to February 1917: A Popular Outline*, translated by R. Chappell, London: New Park.

3   Leninism

Diehl, Karl 1924, *Die Diktatur des Proletariats und das Rätesystem*, Jena: Fischer.

Gurland, Arkady 1981 [1930], *Marxismus und Diktatur*, Frankfurt am Main: Europäische Verlagsanstalt.

Kautsky, Karl 1920 [1919], *Terrorism and Communism*, London: National Labour Press.

Kelsen, Hans 1965 [1920], *Sozialismus und Staat: Eine Untersuchung der politischen Theorie des Marxismus*, third edition, Wien: Verlag der Volksbuchhandlung.

Lenin, Vladimir Ilyich 1964 [1918], *The State and Revolution*, in Vladimir Ilyich Lenin, *Collected Works. Volume 25*, Moscow: Progress, pp. 385–498.

Lenin, Vladimir Ilyich 1965 [1919], *The Proletarian Revolution and the Renegade Kautsky*, in Vladimir Ilyich Lenin, *Collected Works. Volume 28*, Moscow: Progress, pp. 227–325.

Lenin, Vladimir Ilyich 1966 [1920], *Left-Wing Communism: An Infantile Disorder*, in Vladimir Ilyich Lenin, *Collected Works. Volume 31*, Moscow: Progress, pp. 17–118.

Radek, Karl 1921, *Proletarian Dictatorship and Terrorism*, translated by Patrick Lavin, Detroit: Marxian Educational Society.

Stalin, Joseph Vissarionovich 1947 [1929], *Problems of Leninism*, Moscow: Foreign Languages Publishing House.

4   Bolshevik Economic Policy

Bauer, Otto 1920, *Bolschewismus oder Sozialdemokratie?*, Wien: Verlag der Wiener Volksbuchhandlung.

Baumeister, Mary 1930, *Die russische kommunistische Theorie und ihre Auswirkung in den Planwirtschaftsversuchen der Sowjetunion*, Jena: Fischer.

Brutzkus, Boris 1928, *Die Lehren des Marxismus im Lichte der russischen Revolution*, Berlin: Sack.

Bukharin, Nikolai 1971 [1920], *Economics of the Transformation Period*, New York: Bergman.

Choronshitzky, Jakob 1922, *Lenins ökonomische Anschauungen*, Berlin: Prager.

Dobb, Maurice 1928, *Russian Economic Development since the Revolution*, London: Routledge.

Elster, Karl 1930, *Vom Rubel zum Tscherwonjez: Zur Geschichte der Sowjetwährung*, Jena: Fischer.

Feiler, Arthur 1929, *Das Experiment des Bolschewismus*, Frankfurt am Main: Societats-Verlag.

Grinko, Grigory Thedorovich 1930, *The Five-Year Plan of the Soviet Union. A Political Interpretation*, London: Martin Lawrence (with an important table in the appendix on the geographical distribution of individual concerns).

Haensel, Paul 1930, *The Economic Policy of Soviet Russia*, London: King.

Kritsman, Lev Natanovich 1929 [1924], *Die heroische Periode der grossen Russischen Revolution: Ein Versuch der Analyse des sogenannten 'Kriegskommunismus'*, Wien/Berlin: Verlag für Literatur und Politik.

Lenin, Vladimir Ilyich 1965 [1921], *The Tax in Kind. (The Significance of the New Policy and its Conditions)*, in Vladimir Ilyich Lenin, *Collected Works. Volume 32*, Moscow: Progress, pp. 329–65

Lenin, Vladimir Ilyich 1965 [1919], *A Great Beginning: Heroism of the Workers in the Rear. 'Communist Subbotniks'*, in Vladimir Ilyich Lenin, *Collected Works. Volume 29*, Moscow: Progress, pp. 409–34.

Lenin, Vladimir Ilyich 1965 [1919], 'Resolution on the Attitude to the Middle Peasants', in Vladimir Ilyich Lenin, *Collected Works. Volume 29*, Moscow: Progress, pp. 217–20.

Page, Kirby 1930, *A New Economic Order*, New York: Harcourt, Brace.

Trotsky, Leon 1976 [1925], *Towards Socialism or Capitalism?*, translated by R.S. Townsend and Z. Vengerova, London: New Park.

Vollmar, Georg von 1878, *Der isolirte sozialistische Staat: Eine sozialökonomische Studie*, Zürich: Verlag der Volksbuchhandlung.

Yugoff, Aaron 1930 [1929], *Economic Trends in Soviet Russia*, translated by Eden Paul and Cedar Paul, London: Allen and Unwin.

The following German-language periodicals should also be mentioned:

Unter dem Banner des Marxismus (Wien-Berlin).

Osteuropa (Berlin), for its economic reports on Russia.

Also see the bibliographies in:

Grossmann, Henryk 1932, 'Internationale: Die Zweite Internationale', in *Wörterbuch der Volkswirtschaft. Zweiter Band*, edited by Ludwig Elster, fourth edition, Jena: Fischer, pp. 432–9. [See below pp. 361–376.]

Grossmann, Henryk 1932, 'Internationale: Die dritte Internationale', in *Wörterbuch der Volkswirtschaft. Zweiter Band*, edited by Ludwig Elster, fourth edition, Jena: Fischer, pp. 439–49. [See below pp. 377–402.]

Grossmann, Henryk 1932, 'Lenin, Wladimir Iljitsch', in *Wörterbuch der Volkswirtschaft, Zweiter Band*, edited by Ludwig Elster, fourth edition, Jena: Fischer, pp. 828–31. [See below pp. 410–418.]

Grossmann, Henryk 1932, 'Plechanow, Georg', in *Wörterbuch der Volkswirtschaft, Zweiter Band*, edited by Ludwig Elster, fourth edition, Jena: Fischer, pp. 1142–9. [See below pp. 419–422.]

Christian and Religious Socialism*
Carl Grünberg and Henryk Grossman
Translated from German by Ben Fowkes

1   The Concepts Defined

Werner Sombart considered socialism to be simply social rationalism, i.e. a principle of organisation according to which social life should be ordered in a fully rational way, with instinctive impulses firmly subordinated. But if socialism is understood as a *fundamental rejection of private property*, in favour of the *collective* organisation of our economic order, then 'Christian' or 'religious' socialism can be spoken of only in a broad and imprecise sense. This is because the term encompasses, in addition to Christian and religious socialists properly so called, those currents and political parties which do describe themselves as 'Christian social' but only aim at a *reform* of the dominant order, while maintaining its essential foundations, i.e. they want to replace a 'false' capitalism with a 'true', 'social' capitalism. Christianity, as such, has never spoken out in principle against private property and in favour of a collectivist social order.[1]

What lends all these Christian social parties a specific character and distinguishes them from other socialist or reformist parties, however, is their conviction that the transformation of the economic and social order they want to achieve is *dictated by and must be imbued with the spirit of Christianity or religion in general*. This is also true of other currents of religious socialism.

In our presentation of 'Christian and religious' socialism, as a programmatic demand for social transformation on a religious basis, we will accordingly exclude, on the one hand, genuine socialism and communism and other political parties with economic objectives and, on the other, activities of a purely charitable nature. It was impossible to exclude from consideration, as Sombart proposed at the Stuttgart conference of the Verein für Sozialpolitik,[2] certain

---

*   [Originally published as Grünberg and Grossmann 1931, which include substantial material from Grünberg 1911b.]
1   [See Grünberg 1933c.]
2   [Sombart 1925, p. 34. The 'Verein für Sozialpolitik' ('Association for Social Policy') was an academic society.]

activities – in truth only apparently religious – which practical life had already created and use religion merely as the means to effectively combat the 'idea of class struggle',[3] which [supposedly] grew out of atheism, and the proletarian class movement as a whole.

Christianity's split on theological grounds into rival confessions and differences in the historical development of Catholicism and Protestantism (and within the latter also between Lutheranism and Calvinism) have produced, despite common elements in their moral teachings, certain differences in the principles of their overall conceptions of material and social life. These divergences have also set the standard for the structure of the social reform movements associated with them and the way in which they act in practice. Catholicism is authoritarian and emphasises its doctrine that society is an organism, a body with its limbs. Protestantism, whose point of departure is the free individual, by contrast, has played a decisive role in shaping individualism and the emergence of capitalism, since the Renaissance. Protestantism also lacks the age-old, rigid, hierarchically enclosed organisation of the priesthood which is characteristic of Catholicism. In order to grasp these distinctive features it is necessary to examine the Catholic and Protestant social currents separately.

i   *The Catholic Social Current*

The Catholic social current aims to organise not only labour but society as a whole. Its attitude to the general social problem is determined by the view that a successful solution of the latter is only possible under the guidance of a positive ethic which stems from the hand of God himself and is therefore eternally true and supreme, as well as moral law, whose forms change in time and space and whose intermediary is the Church. Only by following this guidance for life on earth is it possible to attain the celestial destiny which is open to all human beings, despite their natural inequality and the social inequality conditioned by it. Conversely, it is just as possible to live life completely and harmoniously in the material sense if society is imbued with a common sense of religion and morality.

Society is not to be regarded as a mere collection of coexisting individuals, artificially governed by the state. It is rather a living organism, originating in humanity's natural inclination to social life. It grew out of the family, as the social cell and its parts have both particular functions and relative autonomy. The forms of socialisation start with the family and proceed upward through

---

3   [The title of Sombart's lecture, Sombart 1925.]

the local community, the province, the professional grouping to the state at the top. They are not arbitrary. Without them it is impossible for humanity to achieve its earthly goals, civilisation or morality. They flourish and stay strong as long as humanity is imbued with and dominated by religious ethical consciousness; their decline runs parallel to the weakening of the latter. And, conversely, the greater the progress made by unnatural individualistic theories, the more the moral decline worsens, selfish special interests push themselves forward at the expense of the sense of solidarity and the natural bonds of society are accordingly loosened.

It by no means follows from the above mentioned principle of the moral equality of human beings that they have a claim to equality in the material conditions of their lives. Rejection of private property, which is the origin of inequalities in the latter sense is, therefore, not at all implied. Everyone without exception does, however, have a series of inviolable rights, which are necessary for the achievement of their moral destiny. It is a sin to ignore these, because it is a contravention of God's commandments. They include the right to life, to physical integrity and the recognition of personal dignity but also, for parents, the duty and right to provide their children with well-ordered family lives and a religious, moral upbringing, and, for children, a right to receive these.

This, in itself, is a damning verdict on those phenomena of our social and economic life which modern development has produced and which, taken together, constitute the social problem. But how can these evils be managed and a new social order be brought about? The answer seems very simple: by restoring Christian moral and social doctrine. Will, however, religious sanctions, the Church's missionary activity and appeals to charity be sufficient to achieve this? Or should external compulsion be applied? In other words: should the necessary social reforms take place through *the self-help of the participants themselves*, inspired by changes in their views about the interests and needs of society or *the legislative intervention of the state*?

In the face of these questions, opinions are divided. Some remain fundamentally committed to the viewpoint of economic liberalism and think that the state's task is essentially to provide security for free individuals and associations. They view any attempt by the state to regulate economic conditions more thoroughly as a sign of social decline, even where they have to admit the need for regulation, to eliminate the most glaring abuses.

Another current emphatically rejects free competition and wants to place limits on it, not only through charitable work but through positive measures taken by the state. An improvement in the situation of those who are economically weak, in general, and the working class, in particular, cannot be expected simply as a reflexive result of Christian behaviour by the ruling classes, because their obligation is to God and they are responsible to God alone. For every individual has a direct right to a dignified human existence, according to the laws of Christian morality. The state therefore has the task and the duty of protecting this right and making it a reality, because it should not be conceived as a mechanism but as a reflection of God's will, according to which the state is the highest form of organic socialisation, below the universal community of peoples.

Both currents have this in common: their *ideal of a corporatist articulation of society* is identified, to a greater or lesser extent, with the institutions of the Middle Ages, a period when social peace prevailed more than either before or after (because it was also a period of religious unity and strength).

The principle of [state] intervention has been explicitly sanctioned by the Church. In his encyclical *Rerum Novarum* issued on 15 May 1891, Leo XIII assigned the state very broad room for manoeuvre, enabling it to intervene to maintain justice in the relations of production and distribution, in the interests of the working classes.[4] This pontifical pronouncement, which was elicited by the social democratic movement in many countries, has in turn promoted an extraordinary expansion of the Catholic democratic movement.

Precisely this development soon led the Holy See to take a step backwards. The encylical *Graves de Communi Re* of Leo XIII, on 18 January 1901, not only expressed his disapproval of the expression 'Christian democracy', which 'is offensive to many right minded people, inasmuch as there is a perilous ambiguity attaching to it', but also clearly rejected a large part of the essential content of the Christian democrats' activities.[5] Not only did Pius X subsequently adhere firmly to this conception, he gave it a sharper emphasis, in the context of his constant, systematic fight against any kind of modernist movement within the Church. And these papal declarations have certainly had a damaging effect on Christian socialism. The Catholic Church can never give entirely free rein to the desire for autonomy, the emphatic rejection of any outside authority, which resides in today's proletarian.

ii   The Protestant Social Current

The Protestant social current necessarily emanates from the same fundamental ideas as Catholic social activity. This applies both to its critical evaluation of contemporary developments in society, economics and law, and to its positive

---

4   [Leo XIII 1903, pp. 1–49. *'Rerum Novarum'* means *'Of Revolutionary Change'*. Encyclicals are
      named after the first words of their texts.]
5   [Leo XIII 1903, p. 269. *'Graves de Communi Re'* means *'Grave Discussions'*.]

attitude to the question of reform which was increasingly imposing itself. Social Protestantism lacks social Catholicism's coherence, because Protestantism has no supreme governing body which all believers – priests and lay people – feel obliged in conscience to obey. The Lutheran consistories, high councillors of the Church etc. are just *regional authorities*, whose powers and jurisdiction are territorially circumscribed, ceasing at regional boundaries. At the same time, they are also *organs of* and can be influenced by *their respective governments*, not just in fact but in theory. Moreover, their decisions are far from having the compulsory character either for lay people or priests that is the case in Catholicism, because Protestantism is based on recognition of individual freedom. In other words, in Protestantism a position on the social question can never be taken by *the Church as such* but only by *individual adherents*. If there is a common position, it results from inner agreement, not spiritual *authority*. Arising freely, it obviously cannot also be adhered to as authoritative.

The continuing distinctions between Calvinism and Lutheranism are not without interest. In contrast with Calvinism's social doctrines, Lutheranism is entirely concerned with inner spiritual life. It cannot allow its adherents to intervene actively in social struggles without exposing themselves to the reproach that they are concerned more with *material* things and good works than with saving their souls. It is otherwise with Calvinism, which does not limit itself to proclaiming 'the word' but wishes to intervene actively in daily life. Thus we also find the Christian social movements are particularly strong and appeared early in Calvinist regions and districts. Just as Calvinism was able to befriend the spirit of capitalism, for the first time it is here also trying to snuggle up to socialism.

2   History

i   *Catholic Social Activity*
a   In France

It is natural and logical that, just as in the case of socialism, we first meet with Christian social efforts in the country where the principle of individual legal equality and freedom gained its first complete victory: France. It would be going much too far to claim that they already existed during the Revolution.

The road which led to the Christian social movement was only taken much later. This occurred in connection, on the one hand, with the revival of Catholicism and of religion in general after the Restoration and, on the other, with the intellectual revolt against the industrial system, which began in France in

1804 with François-Louis-Auguste Ferrier, continued with François-Emmanuel Fodéré (1764–1835), and was classically formulated by [Simonde de] Sismondi in 1819.[6]

We encounter this religious renaissance associated with ideas of positive social reform, emancipated from church dogma for the first time, with [Henri de] Saint-Simon and the Saint-Simonianism.[7] The most significant early representative of the school of Catholic democracy, [Philippe] Buchez,[8] emerged from this background; and Saint-Simonian insights exerted no less an influence on *Christian Political Economy* by Alban de Villeneuve-Bargement (1784–1850),[9] which was unable to propose any remedy for the impoverishment of the masses by the unrestricted development of the industrial system, apart from an appeal to Christian charity. The demand for the restoration of the old guild system was most striking. In contrast, Buchez preached self-help, through cooperation, to workers. In Paris, he founded a Producers' Cooperative for Carpenters in 1831 and thus became the father of the French cooperative movement.

Hugues-Félicité Robert de Lamennais (1782–1854)[10] worked for a reconciliation between Catholicism and revolution still more energetically than Buchez, with much greater agitational force but admittedly also much less clearly. His ideas were at first purely liberal. After Gregory XVI's encyclical *Mirari Vos* of 15 August 1832,[11] condemned them, he turned in a social direction and, in his *Words of a Believer*, as well as several other eloquently inflammatory writings, demanded far-reaching reforms favouring the propertyless, popular classes.[12] He naturally broke with the Church at this point but remained entirely under the spell of the Christian-Catholic world view. And, although in a weaker form, the same is true of Constantin Pecqueur (1801–81), who asserted that only the socialisation of all means of production could create a just order of society, i.e. consistent with the will of God. François Huet (1814–69), a student of [Jean Guillaume César Alexandre Hippolyte] Colins,[13] finally, can also be assigned to this group of thinkers. In *The Social Reign of Christianity*,[14] he attempted to reconcile Christianity and socialism: society, as the sole owner of all the means

---

6   Meitzel 1933.
7   See Grünberg 1933b.
8   See Grünberg 1931b.
9   Villeneuve-Bargement 1834.
10   [Grossman did not correct Grünberg's error in the previous edition of conflating Félicité de Lamennais's name with that of his older brother, also a priest, Jean-Marie.]
11   [Gregory XVI 1833. 'Mirari Vos' means 'You Wonder'.]
12   Lamennais 1834.
13   See Grünberg 1931c.
14   [Colins 1853.]

of production, should assign them to individuals, to allow them to produce on their own, with the obvious qualification that capitals would revert to society after the demise of their owners, who in life and death would only be able to dispose of what they had themselves produced.

The intellectual movement just sketched initially took place outside the official Church, and indeed in opposition to it. But it is clear that the more socialist theories and activities became a force in French life, the more the Church had to make its influence felt. From the mid-1840s, therefore, we see increasing attempts by the clergy to familiarise themselves with the interests of the working classes and to promote them either through charitable institutions or, in some isolated cases, producers' associations. But for a long time there was no possibility of establishing a workers party on a Catholic social basis. This was because Catholic social ideas remained under the spell of economic liberalism. The most prominent, representative publicists of social Catholicism, namely Frédéric Le Play (1806–82), Claudio Jannet (1844–94) and the Belgian Charles Périn (1815–1905), never went beyond a programme of self-help: observation of the Ten Commandments, freedom of association and employers taking care of their workers (patronat).[15] Any state intervention into social life was ruled out.

Only after the Franco-German war of 1870–1 did this change. A new and strongly interventionist tendency developed in France, the Catholiques sociaux,[16] influenced, on the one hand, by the struggles of the 'Commune'[17] and, on the other, by the Catholic social movement in Germany. Its most outstanding leader was Count Albert de Mun (1841–1914), the founder of the Oeuvre des cercles catholiques [d'ouvriers], an association with a complex and hierarchical structure. Its purpose was to organise workers and artisans into professional corporations ('le régime corporatif dans l'état chrétien').[18]

The break with economic liberalism, however, met with the most determined opposition from the conservative, Catholic party of the big landowners and industrialists. They regarded the abandonment of the old ways as a dangerous innovation, suspiciously akin to socialism and they fought against it. Influential princes of the Church, bishops [Charles-Émile] Freppel and [Charles-François] Turinaz supported them, so that Count de Mun himself repeatedly

---

15   ['Patronat' means 'patronage'.]
16   ['Catholiques sociaux' means 'social Catholics'.]
17   [I.e. the Paris Commune of 1871.]
18   ['Oeuvre des cercles catholiques d'ouvriers' means 'Work of Catholic Workers Circles'. 'Le régime corporatif dans l'état chrétien' means 'the corporatist regime within the Christian state'.]

found it necessary to reject the term 'Christian socialist'. If the unwillingness of industrial workers to accept authoritarian direction from the capitalist class is also taken into consideration, it can easily be understood why Count de Mun's party was not able to achieve any lasting success. The Catholic workers circles, although spread across France, were relatively small and were never able to expand.

This failure, as well as the constant growth of social democratic trade unions hostile to the Church, called forth organisational activities with a Catholic social basis. The innovators took the view, in contrast to the old tactics, that to win over the broad masses, above all workers in large-scale industry, the Church must not concentrate only on welfare but instead offer an *autonomous* political organisation *independent of leadership by higher social strata*. This movement received exceptional support from the encylical *Rerum Novarum* of 15 May 1891. Also making use of the antisemitic current, Démokratie chrétien[19] thus emerged and established itself as a new political party with an independent programme at Rheims in 1896.

It gained a considerable number of adherents from Catholic youth circles and the lower clergy, but also benevolent assistance from the Oeuvre des cercles catholiques of Count de Mun. The more passionate the agitation of its leaders became in speeches and in print, the stronger was the opposition from the conservative side. The school of Le Play was even more hostile to Christian democracy. 'The band of democratic abbés'[20] ([Paul] Fesch, [Théodore] Garnier, [Paul] Naudet, [Jules-August] Lemire and [Hippolyte] Gayraud) were accused of playing into the hands of social democracy or at least paving the way for them. At the same time, the justification for their activities by invoking the encyclical *Rerum Novarum* was challenged. Admittedly, Pope Leo XIII did tell a delegation of French workers led by Cardinal [Benoît-Marie] Langénieux, in 1898, that 'democracy, if it is infused with a Christian spirit, will guarantee peace, welfare and happiness to the nation'. Hardly three years later, however, the encyclical *Graves de Communi Re* of 18 January 1901 opposed 'Christian democracy'.[21] The Christian democratic idea was most fully expounded in the writings of Marc Sangnier, under whose leadership a group, Sillon, which emerged from Catholic student circles, was founded in 1899.[22] Its aim was not a new theory but rather to stress the necessity for *practical*

---

19   ['Démokratie chrétien' means 'Christian Democracy'.]
20   ['Abbés' means 'priests'. The phrase is used in Sorel 1999, p. 76.]
21   [Leo XIII 1903, pp. 267–84. The encyclical was critical of the term 'Christian Democracy' but also spelt out the nature of an acceptable Christian Democracy, using the term.]
22   Sangnier 1905; Sangnier 1906. ['Sillon' means 'Furrow'.]

Christianity. It endeavoured to penetrate the working class milieu by creating study circles, popular education facilities, cooperatives and workers' gardens etc. When Pope Pius x condemned the group's fundamental views in 1910, Sillon had to change in various ways. The social Catholics responded to the activities of Sillon and launched similar activities, in competition with it, initiating the Semaines sociales (annual holiday courses, starting in 1904) and Action populaire (involving the publication of social writings, associated with an information bureau) and the Association catholique de la jeunesse française (ACJF) to organise young people.[23]

These ideas and organisations received little support outside the ranks of the clergy and the educated bourgeoisie. Likewise the *purely Catholic* and the [religiously] *mixed* trade unions, under Catholic social influence and, finally, the 'Yellows' (Jaunes) who enjoyed generous support from conservative Catholics and whose leadership the former collectivist Pierre Biétry took over.[24]

The character of the Catholic social movement changed very little after the World War, in contrast to the Protestant social movement (see below.) In 1917 a special Sillon catholique[25] was formed. The Semaines sociales were continued. The one held in Metz in 1919 was devoted in particular to social Catholicism. The last took place in Strasbourg (1922), Grenoble (1923) and Lyon (1925).

b   In Germany

Catholic socialism only started to play an important role in Germany in the 1860s, under the influence of [Ferdinand] Lassalle's agitation and theories, and in connection with the emergence of a separate workers party.[26] Freiherr Wilhelm Emanuel von Ketteler (1811–77), then a parish priest, later Bishop of Mainz, had already pointed to the importance of paying attention to the great social problems of the day in 1848, in sermons and at the first General Assembly of the Catholic Associations of Germany, in Mainz, as well as the Frankfurt National Assembly. He considered, however, that they could be solved with the old method of charity, the Christian doctrine of 'love thy neighbour'. Hence his suggestions were not given any serious consideration. It was different when he published his famous treatise *The Labour Question and Christianity*, under

---

23 ['Semaines sociales' means 'Social Weeks'. 'Action populaire' means 'Popular Action'. 'Association catholique de la jeunesse française' means 'Catholic Association of French Youth'.]
24 [The yellows were a right-wing current, which included a trade union federation and a political party.]
25 ['Sillon catholique' means 'Catholic Furrow'. This Catholic social youth organisation was under the control of the Catholic hierarchy unlike the original Sillon.]
26 [See Grünberg 1933b; Grünberg and Grossmann 1933.]

different circumstances, in 1864.[27] He borrowed extensively from Lassalle's critique of dominant economic conditions and of detested 'godless' liberalism
and, much like Lassalle, recommended producers' associations, although he
wanted these associations to be funded not by the state but by the voluntary
charitable activities of Christians. Later he went further in his demands for
state assistance. This applied even more to his faithful collaborator Christoph
Moufang (1817–90), a canon of Mainz Cathedral. They demanded not only the
raising and maintenance of religious and consequently moral awareness, and
the practical activity of the individual in all spheres of life but also state legislative barriers against the 'tyranny of capital', usury and stock-market speculation;
a just distribution of the burden of taxation and a reduction of military burdens; freedom to set up and favourable treatment of workers associations of a
beneficial character, particularly through financial support for associations of
producers; energetic protection of the working class through legal regulations,
covering the labour of women and children, hours of work, Sunday rest, compensation for people unfit for work through no fault of their own; the fixation of
wages; obliging employers to to take precautionary measures in workplaces to
maintain health and morality; state supervision of the implementation of this
legislation for the protection of the workers. Where the state did not provide
the workers with this protection and guarantee just living conditions, it was
permissible for them to fight to achieve them, even against the state. In his
speech to workers (1869),[28] Ketteler still took the view that it was possible for a
Catholic worker to be a member of the Social Democratic Workers Party. Only
later did he change his mind, as German Social Democracy increasingly came
under the influence of Karl Marx, Ketteler abandoned his initially friendly attitude to the workers movement. 'Christian socialists' took up the ideas advanced
by Moufang and, during the elections of 1871 and 1877, regarded it as advisable to cooperate with the Social Democrats, despite a warning letter from the
bishops recommending that workers should be obedient and patient. In 1877
they stood their own worker candidates, with socialist demands, against the
Centre Party.[29] When that Party realised it was in danger of losing its working
class support, it shifted position, despite the opposition of Catholic industrialists to such a step. Radical chaplains were transferred but, on 19 March 1877,
Ketteler's nephew, Count [Ferdinand Heribert] Galen, introduced proposals
for the protection of workers, restrictions on freedom of trade and freedom
of movement and support for of corporatist associations. From then on this

---

27   [Ketteler 1864.]
28   [Ketteler 1869.]
29   [The Centre Party was associated with the Catholic Church.]

counted as *the social policy programme of the Centre Party* and the back of the opposition was broken.

Before the World War, German social Catholicism did not advance intellectually or programmatically beyond Ketteler's and Moufang's proposals, formulated almost seven decades previously. It was not satisfied, however, with only taking up the question of the workers but turned its attention to policies for middle class, the organisation of artisans and peasants, for whom it sought to establish a specific agrarian law.

Ketteler and his associates worked extremely actively, from 1868, to put their programme into effect, both by publicising it and through associations. They set up numerous charitable and welfare institutions and also many Catholic workers associations, of which the most important was the Volksverein für das katholische Deutschland.[30] It was founded in 1890, with the purpose of 'combating subversive movements in the social sphere and defending the Christian social order'[31] and became the focal point of the Catholic social movement. Eventually the Christian trade unions emerged from it. At the same time, at least until the War, it was fiercely anti-socialist and worked entirely within the framework of the capitalist social order, so it does not concern us here.

Another current represented by the then chaplain Franz Hitze, is worth mentioning. Basing himself on a proposal made by Ketteler in the last year of his life (1877) and on the Catholic doctrine of the social organism, Hitze arrived at the idea of socialism introduced from above, although this would be a socialism of inequality, that would involve a structure of social estates. He wanted the whole nation to be enrolled in compulsory state guilds, which administered themselves like the guilds of the Middle Ages. Parliamentary institutions, the Reichstag and the Bundesrat,[32] were to be replaced by chambers of estates. Hitze himself later dropped these ideas but they were taken up again in 1894 by another chaplain, [Johann Peter] Oberdörffer. He published a social Catholic programme, which had the aim of organising society into autonomous professional estates on a Christian basis.[33] These would represent various social interests, in deciding on state legislation. And although the Pope himself declared, in answer to a question, that a corporatist organisation of society was entirely in line with his views, Oberdörffer's proposal was ignored. The leaders

---

30   ['Volksverein für das katholische Deutschland' means 'People's Association for Catholic Germany'.]

31   [From the first paragraph of the Volksverein's constitution, Heitzer 1979, pp. 299–300.]

32   [The Reichstag and the Bundesrat were the lower and upper houses of the German parliament, under the Empire.]

33   [Oberdörffer 1894.]

of the Centre Party were still far too caught up in the spirit of the liberal capitalist era. The current fell silent. It could not be said, either then or for many
years afterwards, that an independent Catholic workers movement existed. It
was not just that the workers associations were completely under the tutelage
of the clergy and Catholic laypeople friendly to the workers, particularly from
the ranks of the industrialists, who had befriended the workers; they were also
more interested – not least for that reason – in nurturing religiosity and the
'virtues of their social estate', moderation, contentment and industriousness,
than in promoting the workers' economic interests. In any case, they did not go
beyond the creation of benefit funds.

A transformation began after about 1885. The change was brought about
principally, on the one hand, by the rapid growth of Social Democracy and, on
the other, by Pope Leo XIII's sympathy for the workers movement, which found
expression in his encyclical *Rerum Novarum* of 1891.

Following this change, the idea that it was necessary to form *professional*
organisations also began to spread among Catholic workers themselves. Initially, under the employers' influence, all that was done was to tie *confessional
sections* for particular trades into the Catholic workers associations, so that to
belong to one organisation meant membership of the other. These sections
were still entirely dominated by the idea of the harmony of entrepreneurs' and
workers' interests.

The situation soon changed. The trade sections were unsuccessful. The
apprentices' associations did not succeed because they insisted that the masters continued to belong (honorary membership) and were deferred to. The
workers associations, however, did not succeed for the reasons already given
and because their membership was too low. But the trade union idea began
to strike deeper roots and so the need for members of the same trade to join
together in the closest possible union became ever more pressing. The thought
of satisfying it by joining the existing social democratic trade unions was abom-
inated. But the antagonism between *Catholic* and *Lutheran* workers, who also
kept their distance from Social Democracy and in fact opposed it, looked less
and less important over time, given their common economic interests and their
common Christian social world view. So it came to the establishment of *Christian trade unions on an interdenominational basis.*

In social Catholic circles, however, this development did not meet with
undivided agreement. Trade union cooperation between Catholics and Protestants threatened to weaken Catholic religious principles. There was and is
a still greater fear of the emphasis laid on material economic interests, which
repeatedly led to joint action with the social democratic trade unions in particular situations. The very distinctly democratic aspect of the movement also

gave rise to serious reservations both among the higher clergy and industrialists with Catholic social views. In the end this, naturally, had to lead it to cut
itself loose from the old authoritarian leadership. The executive of the Christian trade unions and the representatives of the Catholic workers associations
of western Germany indeed demanded that, as *a precondition for their participation* (in the Deutsche Arbeiterkongreß[34] of 1903), *only workers and officials
of the associations and organisations, who came from the workers estate*, would
able to participates as delegates, with the right to speak and vote. This demand
was justified with the argument that, although the cooperation of politicians
and social activists from outside the workers movement was valued, they must
be prevented from influencing the Congress. A non-social democratic workers
movement could only be successful if the workers took their fate in the social
sphere into their own hands. Admittedly the proceedings of the Congress itself
were marked by a spirit of fierce hostility to Social Democracy but it explicitly
rejected allowing itself 'to be used as mere battering-ram'. Similar statements,
though very much toned down, were not lacking at the second 'Arbeitekongreß'
in 1907.

This is the explanation for the pastoral letter issued by the Prussian epis-
copate on 22 August 1900, in which, just a few months before Leo XIII's encyclical *Graves de Communi Re*, the clergy were enjoined to provide undiminished
support for *Catholic* workers associations but at the same time to care for workers professional associations – within them – to demonstrate 'that no new
and religiously neutral body [is necessary] in order to defend and support the
material interests of Christian workers'.[35] So: back to *Catholic trade unions*.

This slogan was also adopted by the League of Catholic Workers Associations
of Northern and Eastern Germany, which had existed since 1896, and had its
headquarters in Berlin. The workers associations would be prevented, by their
dependence on the Church and the leadership of the clergy, from concentrating exclusively on material interests, which would be at the expense of and
would damage their ethical-religious and ideal interests.

This policy of tutelage was at first rejected by the delegated Congresses in
favour of the inter-confessional approach. But it gained the upper hand in 1902
and has been retained. This has given rise to fierce struggles between the Christian trade unions and the Catholic sections, although the bishops have by no
means adopted a unanimous position on the issue. So that, on 23 January 1909,

---

34   ['Deutsche Arbeiterkongress' ('German Workers Congress'), was a gathering of represent-
      atives from Christian and nationalist workers organisations.]
35   [Hömig 2003.]

the *L'Osservatore Romano* officially declared that the Pope's benevolence was extended equally to both sides.[36]

Developments Since 1918

After the World War, when the destructive power of capitalism was more clearly recognised, many Catholics discovered that not socialism but capitalism was the anti-Christ, which should be combatted. Whereas at the end of the last century Marxism met with the most hateful hostility from the Catholic side (the writings of Victor Cathrein),[37] after the War a current appeared that endeavoured to conduct an objective engagement with Marxism and indeed went so far as to suggest that there were affinities between it and the spirit of Christianity. The Catholic priest Wilhelm Hohoff (1848–1923), an advocate of combining socialism with Christianity, in his *The Significance of Marx's Critique of Capital* in 1908[38] and other writings, reached the conclusion that Marx was fighting against capitalism, i.e. against usury and interest, with the same arguments – proceeding from his theory of value – as the Church had used in the Middle Ages or in the encyclical *Rerum Novarum*. The materialist conception of history contains 'a very solid, justified core'. 'The views and doctrines of the great fathers of the Church' he added 'are as close to the doctrines of Marx's *Capital* as they could be and they demonstrate that not socialism and Christianity but capitalism and Christianity are related to each other as fire is to water'.[39] In 1921 Hohoff recognised that 'the organisation of the oppressed classes is the means by which Marxism proposes to get rid of the contemporary capitalist economy'. 'Class struggle', though without class hatred, 'is ... absolutely necessary'.[40] But Hohoff exhausted his efforts in purely negative polemics against the many opponents of Marxism in Catholic circles, without putting forward any positive proposals.

After the War, the idea of overcoming the evils of capitalist competition by establishing a kind of hierarchical, social estate based socialism, which was reminiscent of Hitze's earlier ideas, became popular in the Catholic camp. Some Catholic clergy believed not only that laws for the protection of workers and similar measures should be supported, as Ketteler had done, but that it is a Christian duty to fight against a social system which does not guarantee workers the position in the great Christian family that is their God-ordained

---

36   [*L'Osservatore Romano, The Roman Observer*, is still the Vatican's daily newspaper.]
37   [E.g. Cathrein 1910.]
38   Hohoff 1908.
39   [Hohoff 1921a, p. 14.]
40   [Hohoff 1928, p. 13. Hohoff emphasised the text in the second quotation.]

due. The predominantly theoretical group which advocated these ideas mainly consisted of Hohoff's pupils, the theologian Theodor Steinbüchel, Max Scheler, lastly the Protestant Johann Plenge, who gave these ideas concrete economic expression,[41] to which the others referred. Plenge did not speak directly of the organisation of the future state through social estates but his socialist organisation did proceed from the conception of the 'whole', the idea of the body and its limbs, and their organic combination, thus showing the possibility of a transition from the ideal of Catholic social teaching to a Catholic socialism. Steinbüchel inserted the doctrine of the living religious, moral community and the bond between individual members and the community as a whole into this framework,[42] with the imprimatur of the Vicar General of the Archbishopric of Cologne. Scheler's writings,[43] expressing pessimistic views about the future of Christian socialism and limiting its role to that of a temporary corrective to individualism, hindered more than promoted efforts to draw nearer to socialism.

In addition to this theoretical current, there is a more practical, political one: the Christian socialism of the radical youth movement. A 'Christian Social Party' emerged in Bavaria, with a weekly journal, *Das Neue Volk*,[44] published in Würzburg from 1919 onwards under the editorship of Vitus Heller, and a vague petty bourgeois, radical programme, issued on 5 September 1920. The supporters of this movement, who expanded their local organisation into a Christlich-Soziale Reichspartei[45] (CSRP), moved increasingly to the left. These were above all younger workers, who aimed to create a new world in a genuinely Christian spirit, fought exploitation and, finally, against the clergy's accommodation with capitalism. In June 1929, the bishops of Freiburg and Trier prohibited any kind of collaboration with *Das Neue Volk* by the priesthood. The Centre Party's press attacked Otto Kaiser,[46] a priest who advocated a Christianity of the deed on CSRP lines, sharply and the Church authorities forbade him from publishing or speaking out. At present the representatives of the CSRP, as 'Christian revolutionaries', stand on the ground of the proletariat, accepting collective ownership by all working people and the inevitability of anti-capitalist revolution. In terms of practical political activity they combatted 'Social Democracy's

---

41   [Plenge 1918.]
42   [Steinbüchel 1920; Steinbüchel 1921.]
43   [Scheler 2008; Scheler 1924.]
44   [*Das neue Volk* means *The New People*.]
45   ['The Christlich-Soziale Reichspartei' ('Christian Social Imperial Party') organised over the whole of the German state.]
46   Kaiser 1929.

betrayal of socialism', fought against fascism and for the united front of exploited proletarians, expressed great sympathy for Soviet Russia and moved towards the Communist Party, as the sole party that represented the interests of the proletariat. The proposal to rename their party the 'Christian Communist Party' (September 1930) was a characteristic move to make their political direction immediately apparent and to sharply demarcate themselves from bourgeois Christian socialist currents. In September 1929 the Christian Social youth movement held its first national conference in Koblenz.

Voices were also heard in the Volksverein (in Mönchengladbach),[47] after the War, calling for a reorientation on social questions and the replacement of previously blind hostility to socialism with full recognition of its 'fateful' necessity and the value of the ethical ideas underlying it. This is how the priest [Anton] Heinen put it in his *Mammonism and Overcoming It*.[48] The writings of the head of the movement, prelate August Pieper[49] were above all significant here. Admittedly, the way he conceived of socialism had little in common with what socialism actually is. Pieper saw socialism as the 'vehicle of a new feeling for life and a new will to live'. He saw in it the Christian ideal of a 'new and higher communal life, united by a common fate', drawing on 'selfless devotion of people to each other', which must replace the 'cold domination of person over person'. To realise the construction of socialism there must be a reaching back to 'the old pre-capitalist people's community, which was the fruit of the German spirit of cooperation'. It was clear to Pieper that 'the decisive external and internal force impelling a transformation of the capitalist economic spirit ... will either come from socialism or this transformation will not happen at all'. As these attempts at a reorientation were not continued, the *Volksverein* soon entered a period of internal crisis. The membership of this once powerful organisation shrank from 800,000 (before the War) to less than half.

Josef Kral of Munich believed that communism by no means contradicts Christian doctrine and demanded the abolition of immoral capitalism, the socialisation of both big capitalist enterprises and the land, on the basis of natural and moral law.[50] Socialism contains elements of Christian ethics. For the Church to continue to fight socialism would be 'a regrettable lapse'; on the contrary they should be reconciled.

---

47 [The headquarters of the *Volksverein für das katholische Deutschland* were in Mönchengladbach.]
48 Heinen 1919.
49 Pieper 1925.
50 Kral 1919; Kral 1920.

The writings of Professor Theodor Brauer of Cologne, the theorist of the Christian trade unions, particularly his address 'Christianity and Socialism' given at the tenth Congress of the Christian trade unions in Essen in 1920,[51] showed how far anti-capitalist views were current in the Catholic camp. This did not prevent its representatives from standing on the bourgeois side in the practical, political struggle. For Brauer rejected the socialist movement and class struggle and emphasised that the goal of Christianity is an economic system of professional estates and a corporatist state.

The 'Catholic socialists', a group of intellectuals associated with the journal *Das rote Blatt der Katholischen Sozialisten*,[52] edited by Heinrich Mertens of Cologne, can be regarded as genuine socialists. In his writings, Mertens sharply criticises individualistic capitalism from an economic and moral point of view.[53] Its private control of the means of production and over human beings is contrary to the practical needs of the social economy. Mertens therefore calls for the reconnection of workers to the means of labour, which is only possible on the basis of big, socialised enterprises. On the other hand, Mertens also criticises the sterility of contemporary official Catholic politics. Scared of actively trying to shape reality, the Church has become a defender of the existing economic order and has turned the workers into unbelievers, by its one-sidedly anti-proletarian and anti-socialist stance. Mertens demands that the Church give up this stance. Socialism is no longer atheistic; the proletariat yearns to believe. Mertens affirms the class struggle, though not in its Marxist interpretation. He conceives it rather as an ethical fight for liberation. The Church should aim for a radical reconstruction of society and it should bring about a synthesis between Catholicism and socialism, which is the bearer of the society that is coming into being. Tactically, this group stands on the ground of the Social Democratic Party but it does not, in principle, reject Communism, the possibility of an extra-parliamentary solution achieved through revolutionary violence. It is committed to revolutionary Marxism, is aware of the limits of all social policy *within* capitalism, wants *full* socialism and has made a radical break with the bourgeois world. This is why it regards the struggle against *tendencies to the bourgeoisification* of social democracy and against 'the petty bourgeois degeneration of the Party and the trade unions, which is an open secret', as one of the most important tasks. The group does not have much influence. In 1931 the *Rote Blatt* merged with the *Zeitschrift für*

---

51   [Brauer 1920.]
52   *'Das rote Blatt der Katholischen Sozialisten'* means *'The Red Journal of Catholic Socialists'*.
53   Mertens 1930.

Religion und Sozialismus,[54] which has become the joint organ of the Catholic and Protestant socialists.

We also need to refer to the most recent changes within Solidarism, founded by the Jesuit father Heinrich Pesch. The Solidarists fundamentally accept the dominant social order. They make a distinction between capitalism and 'mammonism'. It is only necessary to combat the latter. The former is a morally indifferent complex of a purely technical economic character. Nor is there any fundamental objection to capitalism, the wage system or the stock-exchange. Solidarism only wants to correct capitalism's exaggeration of the principle of individualism with the principle of Christian community. Pesch does adhere to the traditional idea of property but he wants to restrict the private, individual rights of entrepreneurs through the extension of the social rights of labour and to strengthen the position of the worker in the capitalist economy, which will lead economic actors to cooperate in solidarity. As they consider the capitalist order to be unobjectionable 'in itself', the Solidarists have to regard the class struggle as absolutely immoral and unchristian. It is a symptom of Solidarism's adaptation to the present stage of the transition from capitalism to socialism that one of Pesch's students, the Jesuit father Gustav Gundlach, while rejecting class struggle theories of a liberal or Marxist type, has created a *Catholic theory of class struggle*, combining it in the spirit of solidarist doctrine with the conceptually unclear goal of 'public welfare', while excluding any socialist objective.[55]

The essay 'The Hour of the Bourgeoisie',[56] by Karl Muth, the founder of the intellectual journal of German Catholicism, *Hochland*,[57] appeared to indicate a reorientation by the Church and attracted much attention. The confidence of socialist-inclined people in the leadership of the bourgeoisie has been greatly shaken. The fate of the bourgeoisie appears to be sealed, insofar as it is unable consolidate bourgeois forces by changing its attitude to the problem of socialisation. It was clear to Germany's most acute thinkers (Lorenz von Stein, Karl Bücher and Ferdinand Tönnies) 'that a *socialisation of our economy* can no longer be hindered or averted'. The economic hope for socialism is slowly ripening in Germany to its fulfilment and the spiritual conversion of the younger generation to religious socialism is an aspect of this. 'Socialism as a moral idea and Christianity inherently belong together.' It was therefore an omission,

---

54   ['*Zeitschrift für Religion und Sozialismus*' means '*Journal for Religion and Socialism*'.]
55   Grundlach 1929.
56   Muth 1930.
57   ['*Hochland*' means '*Highlands*'.]

with grave consequences, 'that the Christian world did not accept the socialist movement earlier and unambiguously approve of its economic ethos'.

For the the present, the official Church is fundamentally opposed to these efforts of social activation, to the idea of fulfilling the gospel of Christ on earth. This is not only because it rejects the idea of class struggle and supports class harmony, because it regards mixing religious fervour and social revolutionary posturing, 'Francis of Assisi with Lenin' ([Josef] Joos), as impossible and impermissible but also because these movements misconceive the relation of the Church to a world which is not of this world. Whatever intellectual differences there may be among various currents in the camp of Catholic socialism, they are 'ultimately movements of this world', in their innermost character, and 'to that extent they are Marxist'. 'The synthesis between contemporary socialism and Catholicism is in itself impossible and, as such, is also rejected by the highest ecclesiastical authorities' (Joos). In his reply to the Reichsverb- and katholischer Arbeitervereine, the Pope stated that, from the viewpoint of the Church's social doctrine, it is right to combat 'the *latest fallacies* of those who understand the teachings of the gospel about life on earth incorrectly and believe they can or must sympathise with the socialists or even be Catholics and socialists at the same time'.[58] An additional reason why the Church took this position could well be that no gains can be promised for the kingdom of heaven from the experiment of bringing socialist inclined workers into the movement of the Church, since the Catholic socialists have not succeeded in interesting broader proletarian circles in the Christian stance.

c   In Austria

Catholic social activity has, in all essential points, taken the same direction in Austria as in Germany. Until 1892, its most significant and influential literary champions were Carl Freiherr von Vogelsang (1818–90) and an immigrant from Germany, Rudolf Meyer. Both also succeeded in finding numerous supporters, particularly among the higher Austrian nobility. Their most prominent disciple was probably the parliamentary deputy Prince Alois Liechtenstein. In Austria, we also encountered conservative and radical-democratic currents within the Catholic social movement. The latter gave rise to the formation of the Christian Social Party, led by Prince Liechtenstein and the mayor of Vienna Karl Lueger. In Lower Austria, first of all, it became more and more entrenched,

---

58   ['Reichsverband katholischer Arbeitervereine' means 'Imperial League of Catholic Work-
      ers Associations'. The letter, written on Pope Pius's direction by Cardinal Gaspari, is quoted
      at greater length in Ragaz 1930, p. 40.]

through the clever use of popular antisemitism. After 1896 it was in control not only of the Vienna City Council but also the Lower Austrian Diet and had an extremely influential position in the Reichsrat.[59] The only serious opponent it had to reckon with was Social Democracy.

As well as the Österreichischen Katholikentag, which met six times between 1875 and 1896, the predominantly middle class Leogesellschaft, founded on the model of the Görresgesellschaft, constitute the intellectual centre of Christian social activity in general and Catholic social activity in particular.[60] Since 1907, a Katholisches-Zentralkomitee für Österreich,[61] led by Count [Ernst Emanuel] Silva-Tarouca has existed and animated organisations of women, young people, teachers and workers.

According to (approximate) official statistics at the end of 1904, the number of Catholic and Christian-social workers associations was (*approximately*) 1,168, or 13.69 percent of all workers associations in Austria; the number of members, however, was 148,698.

In Austria, too, efforts to establish independent workers organisations within the framework of the general Catholic and Christian social programme have not been lacking.

Here too, they emerged out of the need to fight Social Democracy on its own ground. Hence the Christlich-sozialer Arbeiterverein für Niederösterreich[62] was founded, on 21 November 1892, and other, similar groups soon followed. To give the movement a fixed form, it was decided to distribute a workers programme at a congress for the whole of Austria held in Vienna on 5 January 1896. The programme adopted at the fourth Congress (1901) rejected 'the class struggle as such' but, on the other hand, declared it to be 'unconditionally necessary for all Christian-minded workers in Austria to organise independently within their particular parties'. Attitudes subsequently became more radical. At the sixth Congress (1905), the new demand for independent workers political organisations was justified with the argument that 'only then would

---

59   [The Reichsrat was the lower house of the parliament of the Austrian side of the imperial Austro-Hungarian state.]
60   ['Österreichischen Katholikentag' means 'Austrian Catholic Conference'. The 'Leogesellschaft' ('Leo Society') was founded on the model of the 'Görresgesellschaft' ('Gorres Society') which is a German Catholic intellectual society that funds research and publishes material.]
61   ['Katholisches-Zentralkomitee für Österreich' means 'Catholic Central Committee for Austria'.]
62   ['Christlich-sozialer Arbeiterverein für Niederösterreich' means 'Christian Social Workers Association for Lower Austria'.]

the Christian working class receive the required consideration in the Christian parties' and only then would it be 'capable of dealing with its own affairs, of *whatever kind* which touch on workers' interests, without assistance or objections from others who are not involved'. Indeed, one speaker even said 'there is no need to be constantly scared of the term "class struggle"'. For, 'what is genuine in class struggle is the actually existing struggle of the exploited against the exploiting class'.

This work of political organisation has not yet proceeded very far at all. The organisation of trade unions goes hand in hand with it and they have taken the same course as the Christian trade unions in Germany.

After the upheaval of 1918, the previously monarchist Christian Social Party declared for the Republic. Its social character has dramatically declined. It has increasingly become a rallying point for the bourgeoisie and, most recently, has displayed strongly anti-parliamentary, fascist tendencies, as a reaction against Social Democracy, which until 1920 had played the leading role in the shrunken Austrian state.

In many respects, Anton Orel has drawn on Vogelsang.[63]

After 1918 – as in Germany – the problem of socialism was topical among Catholics and the problem of Catholicism among some socialists. In 1926 the Bund religiöser Sozialisten Österreichs was set up under Otto Bauer, an unskilled Catholic worker.[64] Bauer was joint editor with Heinrich Mertens (Cologne) of *Das rote Blatt der katholischen Sozialisten*. Another leading figure in the movement was Oskar Ewald and, in terms of world view, Wilhelm Ellenbogen, a social democratic member of the Austrian parliament, also belonged to it. Since 1 February 1930 the Bund has produced a militant journal, *Menschheitskämpfer*, every fortnight, as well as a monthly pamphlet, *Der neue Saat*.[65] Draft programmatic guidelines for this League were presented to a conference in June 1930 and, at the National Conference of Religious Socialists (3 January 1931), a resolution that it is a Christian duty to overcome capitalism and replace it with socialism was supported. Tactically the group goes along with Social Democracy. Otto Bauer, the representative of the Religious Socialists, was put forward by the official Social Democrats as a candidate at the most recent general election in Austria (9 November 1930) and the Religious Socialists were recognised as members of the Social Democratic Party with equal

---

63   Orel 1909.
64   ['*Bund religiöser Sozialisten Österreichs*' means '*League of Religious Socialists of Austria*'. Otto Bauer, 1897–1986, is not to be confused with Otto Bauer, 1881–1938, the Austrian social democratic leader.]
65   ['*Menschheitskämpfer*' means '*Fighter for Humanity*'. '*Der neue Saat*' means '*The New Sowing*'.]

rights. The well known Catholic writer Aurel Kolnai, editor of the Catholic journal *Schönere Zukunft*,[66] also joined the League very recently.

Johann Ude, Professor of Theology at the University of Graz, is not connected with this movement but has made extremely sharp criticisms of the Church in his writings,[67] which brought him into conflict with his ecclesiastical superiors. Ude considers the renewal of the world on a Christian basis to be necessary and calls for the emancipation of proletariat through the overthrow of capitalism and the interest-based economy. His positive proposals, influenced by Adolf Damaschke and Silvio Gesell, are confused and contradictory.

It should also be mentioned that a book by the Catholic priest Ángel Carbonell, issued with the imprimatur of the Bishop of Barcelona, attracted much attention in Spain. In *Collectivism and Catholic Orthodoxy*,[68] the author did reject cultural and philosophical socialism but affirmed economic socialism, the collective organisation of the economy, with the abolition of private property in the means of production.

There are no active Social Catholic movements in other countries.

In July 1928 the Catholic Workers International's founding Congress took place.

ii   *Protestant Social Activity*
a   In Germany
The coming of modern industry to Germany brought about a worsening of the economic condition of the working class. The strikes and uprisings motivated by hunger, which flared up here and there, such as the 1844 rising of the Silesian weavers, bore witness to severe distress that was not temporary. The liberal bourgeoisie, true to its *laissez-faire* principles, was passive. As far as the churches were concerned, some clergy were aware that the mass of the people were gradually slipping away from them and turning to those who promised heaven on earth. The charitable activities of church groups, Sunday schools and almshouses, which eased the distress of individuals, proved to be insufficient to win people back to the church. Hence two men, who clearly perceived the distressed conditions of the time and count as the founding fathers of Protestant socialism in Germany, arrived at the conclusion that the social evils of the time should be fought in the spirit of Christianity. In 1848, the year of revolution, Johann Hinrich Wichern (1808–81) delivered a famous speech to a Lutheran church assembly in Wittenberg on the duty of the Church to estab-

---

66   ['*Schönere Zukunft*' means '*More Beautiful Future*'.]
67   Ude 1928; Ude 1930.
68   [Carbonell 1928.]

lish an 'inner mission'. In his 1849 memorandum on the inner mission of the Lutheran Church, without proposing a social reform programme, he laid out the tasks of the mission. They were to promote Christian cooperatives among the workers estate, whose task would be to unite both landowners with day labourers on the land, as well as entrepreneurs with factory workers in the towns, on a patriarchal basis. At the same time, Wichern stressed that it was the task of the inner mission to combat revolution and strengthen respect for authority everywhere, in the spirit of the Lutheran conception of unconditional obedience to the state authorities set in place by God. Nothing came of these cooperatives, not only because workers were mistrustful but also because the entrepreneurs failed to provide any assistance.

Working Class Self Help through Economic Associations and Domestic Settlement[69] by Victor Aimé Huber (1800–1869) also appeared in 1848. Huber, who had spent many years in England in Christian socialist circles, wanted to transplant the cooperative approach, informed by the spirit of Lutheran Christian brotherhood, into all areas of economic life in Germany. To achieve this aim he did not turn to the interested parties themselves, the workers; nor did he call for state assistance – because he was an ultra-conservative and an opponent of state intervention. He appealed instead to all honourable Christian and conservative minded people of education and wealth. The achievements of 'more than twenty years of self-sacrificing activity were ... slight. Even the clergy remained cool and unsympathetic to him'.[70]

A genuine Protestant social movement only began in 1877, apparently initiated by Pastor Rudolf Todt's (1838–87) *Radical German Socialism and Christian Society*,[71] published that year. The underlying cause, however, was the rapid growth of Social Democracy and its ever greater significance in the political life of the nation. Underlying in two senses. Todt and many who shared his views attempted not only to reach an objective and clear understanding of the nature of Social Democracy and the workers' demands it advanced, so as to establish their own practical position on current struggles, they also fell into complete dependence on socialist trains of thought, leaving aside atheism and republicanism. When Todt examined German Social Democracy's programme in the light of the gospel, he wrote: 'With the exception of its atheism ... there is nothing objectionable in socialist theory, from the viewpoint of the gospel.'[72] In particular, the transformation of private property in land into collective property

---

69   Huber 1848.
70   Göhre 1896, p. 10.
71   Todt 1878.
72   [Todt 1878, p. 408.]

by no means contradicts the spirit of the gospel. Nevertheless, Todt's ideal for the future was not socialist. Under the influence of the conservative Rodbertus and after him Rudolf Meyer, Todt arrived at state socialism on a Christian basis. Here too, he went far beyond his predecessors: regarding the establishment of a political party as necessary. It 'should ... work, with all Christian means ... for state intervention and renounce the quietism of laissez-faire, laissez-passer'.[73]

In association with Professor Adolph Wagner, Rudolf Meyer and the Court Chaplain Adolf Stoecker (1835–1900), Todt set up the Zentralverein für Sozialreform auf religiöser und konstitutionellmonarchischer Grundlage,[74] in 1877. Its programme called not only for energetic Church but also state intervention in the justified interests of the working classes. It was against political activity by the Lutheran clergy and confined itself to making propaganda for policies of social reform in educated circles, by means of books, pamphlets, travelling lecturers and a journal, the *Staatssozialist*.

A year later, Stoecker and Wagner made the first attempt to go beyond educated circles and approach the working class directly, in competition with Social Democracy. On 31 January 1878 in Berlin, they founded the Christlich-soziale Arbeiterpartei.[75] Its sharply delineated state socialist programme declared that it rested, on the one hand, on a Christian, monarchical basis but, on the other, that it had arisen from 'purely political, social and moral considerations, based on economic science'. It appeared to 'completely avoid scripture as a direct point of departure'.

The attempt failed. From the very beginning the new Party received very little support from the ranks of the industrial workers. Its adherents were recruited predominantly among artisans, small merchants and officials, members of higher social estates. And so it is therefore no surprise that it rapidly took on a more and more conservative character and very soon went over completely into the antisemitic camp. Officially this was expressed in the summer of 1880, when it adopted the name Christlich-soziale Partei.[76]

Since then – leaving aside the *national social* episode which will be discussed shortly – no Lutheran social, workers party has been set up in Germany. Instead, the main emphasis has been on promoting Lutheran social aspirations and cul-

---

73 [Todt 1878, p. 390.]
74 ['Zentralverein für Sozialreform auf religiöser und konstitutionell-monarchischer Grundlage' means 'Central Association for Social Reform on a Religious and Constitutional Monarchical Basis'.]
75 ['Christlich-soziale Arbeiterpartei' means 'Christian Social Workers Party'.]
76 ['Christlich-soziale partei' means 'Christian Social Party'.]

tivating Lutheran social attitudes. This point applied as much to the 'Lutheran social workers associations' as to the Evangelisch-sozialer Kongreß.[77]

These associations arose in the Rhineland and Westphalen in 1882 and then spread across the whole of Germany. They originally had almost exclusively religious, confessional and educational aims, and did not concern themselves with social policy. Parallel with the increasing prominence of social democratic agitation including in regions of the Rhine and Westphalen, particularly after the great miners' strike of 1889, however, local associations were increasingly concerned with socio-political ideas. At first, they only adopted the conservative principles represented by Stoecker. In the other associations, however, the proletarian principle took on greater and greater life. In 1893 the old style conservatives, led by the priest Dr Ludwig Weber (2 April 1846–29 January 1922) and the younger radicals, under Pastor Friedrich Naumann (25 March 1860–24 August 1919), did agree on a compromise programme. This only superficially bridged the innate conflict. In practice and reality, it continued to rage sharply and irreconcilably. Both before and after, an aspiration for independence was apparent in Protestant similar to that in Catholic workers organisations, with whom they organised the first Deutscher Arbeiterkongreß[78] in the autumn of 1903 in Frankfurt; a second Congress convened in October 1907, in Berlin.[79]

The ability of the Lutheran workers associations to expand, nevertheless, suffered from these internal conflicts. The total number of members represented at the Deutscher Arbeiterkongreß of 1907 in Berlin was 129,000 (as against 106,000 in Frankfurt); and 92,000 of them belonged to the Gesamtverband der evangelischen Arbeitervereine[80] (as against 75,000 in 1903).

The Evangelisch-sozialen Kongreß developed in a similar fashion. It was established on Stoecker's initiative. He considered the Imperial Decrees of 4 February 1890 and the calling of the Internationale Arbeiterschutzkonferenz[81] in Berlin the moment to forcefully resume his political activities and to reconstruct the Christlich-sozialen Partei by drawing together all the social movements of a similar kind within the Lutheran Church.[82] The Evangelisch-

---

77   ['Evangelisch-soziale Kongreß' means 'Lutheran Social Congress'.]
78   ['Deutscher Arbeiterkongreß' means 'German Workers Congress'.]
79   See Grünberg and Grossmann 1931, Christian and religious socialism, above, p. 304.
80   ['Gesamtverband der evangelischen Arbeitervereine' means 'General Federation of Lutheran Workers Associations'.]
81   ['Internationale Arbeiterschutzkonferenz' means 'International Workers Protection Conference'. The Decrees expanded provisions for the protection of conditions at work and the Conference was initiated by the German government.]
82   ['Christlich-sozialen Partei' means 'Christian Social Party'.]

sozialer Kongreß was held for the first time on 27–9 May 1890 in Berlin and then took place annually.[83]

In order not to disturb the unity of the often widely divergent opinions represented at the Congress, all divisive issues had been carefully excluded from its statement of aims. The obvious result was this completely colourless, theoretical, academic formulation: 'The Congress intends to investigate the social condition of our people without preconceived ideas, measure it against the yardstick of the moral requirements of the gospel and make the gospel more fruitful and effective in contemporary economic life than previously.'[84]

Naturally, there were nevertheless ever livelier disagreements over the attitude to be taken to Social Democracy; the activity of the Church and its organs in the economic and social conflicts of the day; the question of the establishment and structure of their own Christian social party. Should the Church restrict itself exclusively to missionary tasks and only seek indirect social influence, through the revival of religious feeling? Or should it also intervene directly in contemporary socio-political conflicts? And what should its attitude to political intervention and political organisation? Should the latter have a patriarchal, conservative character or be oriented to the needs of the proletarian strata of the population?

At first it seemed as if current of the 'Young', led by Naumann and Pastor Paul Göhre (1869–1928), which wanted to answer the above questions according to their radical alternative, had the upper hand at the Congress. At the Second Annual Congress, in 1891, Professor [Wilhelm] Herrmann (Marburg) already put forward the thesis – not in fact adopted – that, notwithstanding the rejection of and very energetic fight against the materialist conception of history, 'it was unchristian to combat, in the name of the Christian church, the economic goals the workers were trying to achieve under the leadership of Social Democracy'.[85] Similarly, the fourth Congress (1893) declared itself 'in general agreement' with the guidelines put forward by Professor Kaftans (Berlin), which culminated in the conception that it was 'the duty of Christians to shape the economic order so that it offers a basis for nurturing the moral ideals of Christianity' and that this duty, 'when applied to the present economic order ... would lead both to the defence of the essential ideas that underlie it against the appetite for subversion and to demands for its reconfiguration'.[86] The idea

---

83   ['Evangelisch-soziale Kongress' means 'Protestant-social Congress'.]
84   [The first paragraph of the constitution of the Congress, adopted at the second Congress in 1891, Göhre 1896, p. 146.]
85   [Evangelisch-soziale Kongress 1891, p. 7.]
86   [Kaftan 1994, p. 153.]

of forming a *party of social reform for all ordinary people*,'[87] on a national, monarchist and Christian foundation gained ever more support and resonance. This deepened the split between the 'Old' and 'Young'. At the same time, it resulted in the Prussian Supreme Church Council's decree of 16 December 1895 prohibiting the clergy from taking part in agitation around social policy as well as Stoecker's resignation from the executive of the Congress. The resolution adopted in 1896 was a return to the viewpoint of earlier times, restricting the activities of the Congress to the promotion of Lutheran sentiments. It has remained the same to the present. The Congress established social education courses, undertook investigations into the situation of agricultural workers in Germany and, since 1904, has issued a journal, *Evangelisch-Sozial*, and a series of pamphlets, *Evangelisch-soziale Zeitfragen*.[88]

In 1896 Naumann and Göhre set up the Nationalsozialen Verein,[89] indicating that the Christian principle was being toned down. That was the end of the Christian socialism, which had initially been supported enthusiastically. The goal of the new movement was to *win the working class in large-scale industry* over to national, imperial power politics abroad, combined with encouragement of demands for social reforms, while adhering to Christianity as the 'central point of spiritual and moral life ... which must not be made a party matter but should assert itself in public life as a force for peace and the sense of community'.[90] The goal was therefore to create a national workers movement, oriented to socialism and led by educated people who were socialists, which would displace Marxist and internationalist Social Democracy. The national socialists originally propagated their ideas in a weekly newspaper, brought into existence for this purpose in Berlin, *Die Zeit: Organ für nationalen Sozialismus auf christlicher Grundlage*, which soon went under, and in the weekly *Die Hilfe*, founded by Naumann in 1894.[91]

Yet developments did not fulfil the exaggerated expectations of the National Socials. They found scarely any working class support worth mentioning. They were not even able to bring over the Lutheran workers associations and received no more than 26,500 votes, mainly from artisans, peasants, teachers and officials, at the Reichstag elections of 1898. On the other hand, a year

---

87   [Göhre 1896, p. 191.]
88   [*Evangelisch-Sozial* means 'Evangelical Social'. *Evangelisch-soziale Zeitfragen* means 'Evangelical Social Questions of the Time'. *Die Hilfe* means 'Succour'.]
89   ['Nationalsoziale Verein' means 'National Social Association'.]
90   [Nationalsozialer Verein 1896, p. 39.]
91   [*Die Zeit: Organ für nationalen Sozialismus auf christlicher Grundlage* means 'The Times: Organ for National Socialism on a Christian Basis'.]

after its foundation, internal opposition began to emerge in the bosom of the Association, no doubt partly because of disappointment, against its excessive proletarian, social emphasis. Demands were made for a 'decisive turn to the right'. In subseqent years, these become more and more pronounced. World power politics increasingly came to the forefront and social policy retreated. The National Socials, who had set out to free the industrial proletariat from the spell of international Social Democracy, now turned into liberal imperialists. After the Reichstag elections of 1903 – at which their candidates received only 30,000 votes – the majority of them finally joined the Freisinnige Vereinigung[92] which had the same objectives. Some, including the Party secretary, [Max] Maurenbrecher, found their way to Social Democracy, as Göhre already had in 1901.

Developments Since 1918

After the World War, the social activity of the Lutheran Churches grew. In Baden, the Rhineland and Westphalen, special posts were created: social pastors, familiar with social problems, who travel around to win the support of other pastors for the social idea. The constitutions of the new churches of the German federal states contain a number of old Christian social demands. The social committees of the Deutsche Evangelische Kirchenbund[93] and of a number of parishes have the task of bringing the spirit of the gospel into social life through lectures, social courses etc.

The Evangelisch-Soziale Kongreß does not have much influence; it nevertheless spreads knowledge about the facts of social life in carefully prepared lectures. The views of the Congress's leading circles are reflected in the lecture, 'The Social Pastor', delivered by its general secretary, Pastor Dr [Johannes] Herz, at its thirty-fifth annual meeting (1928).[94] Herz contrasts 'the social pastor' to the 'socialist pastor', who identifies himself with a class, the proletariat. In the struggle between two worlds, the existing, currently dominant world of capital and the socialist world in the process of emerging, Herz's 'social and non-party' viewpoint in fact means taking the side of the existing world and not the world to come. Socialist tendencies have nevertheless penetrated into some circles of the Evangelisch-Soziale Kongreß, even if they are rejected by its overwhelming majority, who dream of a 'social capitalism'. Thus the Christian labour secretary [August] Springer (Stuttgart), at the thirty-first Congress (1924), warned against attacking Marxism, which is also of value to Christian

---

92   ['Freisinnige Vereinigung' means 'Liberal Association'.]
93   ['Deutscher Evangelische Kirchenbund' means 'German Union of Lutheran Churches'.]
94   [Herz 1928.]

workers. It expressed 'a devastating indictment of violations of human dignity and it can be conceded that there are also prophetic elements in Marxism and that it has predicted a number of aspects of the contemporary worker's fate, with visionary clear sightedness'. Most recently, the critique mounted by the *religious socialists* has become more and more evident in the Congress. At its thirtieth meeting (1923) Pastor Georg Fritze (Cologne) offered a sharp critique of the Congress: the 'social questions' being discussed there were of no interest to the broad masses of the proletariat of the big cities. The previous divorce between religion and the world in the Lutheran Church must be overcome. 'Love and faith have been preached for millenia.' But lip service was not enough. 'Now belief in God must ... become a deed, a deed which will pervade the social and economic order.' In this sense, 'Karl Marx was much more religious than many defenders of religion imagine'. 'A deeply felt Christianity shines through' the ideal of socialism. The churches, despite their assurance that they stand apart from the class struggle, are actually in the middle of it but on the side of capitalism. They are 'thoroughly entangled with the system of Mammon, which forces all the true impulses of the spirit into the background. The churches will either die out, because they have cut themselves off from their great world historical task, or they will gain a new lease of life by giving dedicated assistance to the reshaping of the world in the sense of the socialist ideal.' At the thirty-fourth meeting of the Congress (1927), after speeches by Professors Robert Wilbrandt and [Friedrich] Mahling on 'Recent Developments in Socialism', a lively discussion ensued, in which Professor Eduard Heimann (Hamburg) and Pastor Georg Fritze (Cologne) advocated the conceptions and demands of the religious socialists.

The origins of the *religious socialist movement* in Germany go back to the turn of the century, when Pastor Christoph Blumhardt in Württemberg declared his support for Social Democracy, at the end of 1899. The Church authorities reacted by forcing him to give up the title of pastor. This deterred other ecclesiastics from following his example. Blumhardt, who continued his activities not by writing books but through practical work (he was a member of the Württemberg State Parliament between 1900 and 1906), initially remained a solitary figure in Germany. Only after the end of the World War did the relationship between the Church and Social Democracy change. Both emerged from the War altered. With the fall of the monarchy, the Lutheran Churches lost their Landesbischöfe.[95] In November 1918, Social Democracy, which they had combated, had become the ruling power in the state, on whose attitude their

---

95   [Until the German revolution of 1918, the hereditary Lutheran rulers of German states

fate depended. When the official representatives of the organised churches fell silent, younger forces, concerned about the Church's future, sought to bridge the gap between it and the workers, aware that the previous attitude of churches all over the world had led to a *complete dechristianisation* of the industrial workforce. (Catholics were informed of this in the essay 'The Dechristianisation of the Industrial Workforce'; Lutherans in books by Paul Piechowski and Günther Dehn.)[96] They wanted to win the mass of workers back to the Church. As a consequence of their desire to live with their proletarian parishes, the proletarian clergy sought to reform the Church and wanted to convey socialism to the centre of the Church, in the hope that the opportunist Church would adapt itself to the new situation. When the big landowners ruled 'we have a *conservative* Church ... in the period of capitalism ... we have a *liberal* Church, we will have a *socialist* Church upheld by the mass of intellectual and physical workers in town and country'.[97] At the so-called Kirchliche Woche Nürnberg[98] (25 June 1919), Pastor [Georg] Merz (Munich) made a speech about socialism to Protestant theologians: the future of the Church depends on its attitude to the workers movement. The proletariat will be the vehicle of future historical development and socialism will dominate coming decades. The mass of workers, just like official Social Democracy, are far from being religious. 'How the situation develops depends ... on the fate of the movements which are already striving to make the revival of religion and the introduction of socialism the cause of mankind, while consciously rejecting class struggle ... The Church must abandon its hostile and distrustful attitude to the workers movement.'[99]

After 1918, opposition began to grow all over Germany against the authoritarian Church, outdated and legally abolished by the revolution. The opposition favoured a 'genuine people's Church', which would be less concerned with disputes about theology and more open to considering the social needs of the broad popular masses. In the Social Democratic camp, meanwhile, the revolution's failure to achieve any practical results, the division of the Party into Majority Socialists, Independents and Communists, and the bitter factional struggles among them had undermined the confidence of the masses in the path previously taken. As the social democratic deputy Max Cohen-Reuss told the second Congress of Workers' and Soldiers' Councils in 1919, 'we issued our

---

were the heads of the Church in their states, in which capacity they were called 'Landesbischöfe', literally meaning 'state bishops'.]

96   Anonymous 1925a; Piechowski 1927; Dehn 1930.

97   Anonymous 1925b.

98   ['Kirchliche Woche Nürnberg' means 'Nürnberg Church Week'.]

99   [Cf. Merz 1919.]

supporters promissory notes on the future and now we cannot redeem them'.[100] As after every defeated revolution, a dull sense of resignation seized a section of the masses: the uncertainty and hopelessness of the proletariat's class situation led the proletariat to feel that its existence was completely meaningless. This feeling could be overcome and the suffering of the proletariat as a class take on meaning through the struggle against capitalism, as long as the hope remained that revolution could free the working class from the yoke of capitalism. With the failure of the revolution, people became sceptical about the possibility of achieving that in this world and the meaninglessness of proletarian existence really penetrated the consciousness of the masses. The religious hope for fulfilment in the next world remained the sole consolation for this disappointment. We have observed a similar renaissance of religious feelings in France after the revolution of 1848 and in Russia after the revolution of 1905.[101] Social Democracy had not kept its promises of a fundamental transformation of the existing economic order in 1918 and could not keep them after 1918, as a result of its policy of forming coalitions with bourgeois parties. It promoted the religious hopes of the disappointed masses for a better life in the next world, by stressing the *ethical* features of the socialist system of ideas, the moral improvement of the *inner* person and inner revolution, as the prerequisite and preparatory stage for the external revolution postponed, in this way, to the distant future. In this sense, Social Democracy inherited the conservative mantle of the Church.

Pastor Günther Dehn's group, the North German Bund sozialistischer Kirchenfreunde on 28 March 1919 in Berlin, was established out of this current[102] It became the Bund religiöser Sozialisten,[103] on 3 December 1919 (with numerous local groups in other cities). While these organisations were not concerned with church politics, Pastor Piechowski, in particular, raised the slogan 'conquer the Church' and the demand for the involvement of the Christian social working class in the Church's work. His group communicated the practical programme of the Bund religiöser Sozialisten to the Constituent Assembly of the Prussian Church in 1920 under the name of the *Neukölln Memorandum*.[104] In it, Piechowski proposed the establishment of free parishes within the Church's association. Piechowski saw in socialism the 'mass religion of the future', while the Church of the present is subject to the supremacy of the

---

100   [Zentralrat der Sozialistischen Republik Deutschlands 1919, p. 63.]
101   Cf. Grossmann 1931d, 'Bolshevism', above, pp. 253–255.
102   ['Bund sozialistischer Kirchenfreunde' means 'League of Socialist Friends of the Church'.]
103   ['Bund religiöser Sozialisten' means 'League of Religious Socialists'.]
104   [Piechowski 1922.]

'Church's bourgeois power-holders'. He regarded the participation of the workers in church elections as a means of class struggle within the Church. After the two groups merged, the first Congress of Religious Socialists was held in Berlin on 26 November 1921. This decided to extend the League to the whole of Germany and to issue a monthly, *Der religiöse Sozialist* (from 1 January 1922), which appeared until the end of 1923.[105]

The socialist Badische Volkskirchenbund (Dietz Group) emerged from similar activities in South Germany in 1919. This merged with the Bund evangelischer Proletarier, later called the Bund evangelischer Sozialisten,[106] founded at the start of 1920 in Pforzheim by Pastor Erwin Eckert. Its candidates received 15,000 votes at the elections to the Baden Synod in 1920. The League's organ (from 1 April 1920 the *Christliches Volksblatt* then, after 1 May 1923, the *Sonntagsblatt des arbeitenden Volkes*) was at the same time the organ of the initially radical but later very moderate, youth group Neuwerk, founded by Georg Flemmig in 1919 and named after its journal *Das neue Werk*.[107] Neuwerk group members saw possibilities for transformative Christian action in ideas about settlements and educational reform, and rejected the culture of capitalism. They lived in the settlement Habertsdorf bei Schlüchtern (in Hessen), where, at great sacrifice, they set up a *residential people's school*. They represented a purely emotional 'socialism', which for them, only meant the greatness and novelty which would transform the world, by applying the moral principles of Jesus; and also included the feeling of sympathy with workers.

All these groups joined together at a conference (Meersburg, 2 August 1924) to form an Arbeitsgemeinschaft der religiösen Sozialisten Deutschlands.[108] From 1 September 1924 the *Sonntagsblatt* was its organ. At its next meeting in Meersburg (31 July 1926) the Working Group was renamed the Bund der religiösen Sozialisten Deutschlands[109] and adopted a red flag with a black cross as its symbol. Its fifth Congress took place in Stuttgart on 3 August 1930. Since 1929 its

---

105 [*'Der religiöse Sozialist'* means *'The Religious Socialist'*.]
106 ['Badische Volkskirchenbund' means 'People's Church League of Baden'. 'Bund evangelischer Proletarier' means 'League of Lutheran Proletarians'. 'Bund evangelischer Sozialisten' means 'League of Lutheran Socialists'.]
107 [*'Christliches Volksblatt'* means *'Christian People's Newspaper'*. *'Sonntagsblatt des arbeitenden Volkes'* means *'Sunday Newspaper of Working People'*. *'Neuwerk'* means *'New Activity'*. *'Das neue Werk'* means *'The New Activity'*.]
108 ['Arbeitsgemeinschaft der religiösen Sozialisten Deutschlands' means 'Working Group of the Religious Socialists of Germany'.]
109 ['Bund der religiösen Sozialisten Deutschlands' means 'League of Religious Socialists of Germany'.]

theoretical organ, *Die Zeitschrift für Religion and Sozialismus*,[110] has appeared, edited by Professor Georg Wünsch (Marburg), as the organ linking Protestant and Catholic socialists. While other religious socialist tendencies do not accept Marxism, Professor Wünsch, who is the most familiar with Marxism and has written about it, rejects ethical justifications for socialism, such as those offered by Hendrik de Man and Leonhard Ragaz, seeing in them 'the danger of utopianism and ineffective enthusiasm which has always been the fateful accompaniment of Christian ethics'.[111] The force that would lead to socialism's victory lies in Marxism's materialist conception of history, which is not only compatible with Christianity but finds a *natural extension* in it. Wünsch proclaimed that he was a religious socialist, not because of abstract categories but because he stood on the ground of the facts. God's will can be recognised in the whole of concrete reality and its immanent contradictions, which thus sets us tasks.

Despite the ideological differences among its components, the Bund intended to be a practical, proletarian and united fighting organisation. The programme it issued raised serious accusations against the churches.[112] The churches do not serve, they want to rule. They spiritualise Christ's clear commandments, project the kingdom of God into the transcendental and comfort the suffering masses with the afterlife. As bearers of outmoded forms of religious life they become ever more reactionary. It is the task of the proletariat to renew these forms. It has to conduct this struggle within the churches and revolutionise them. The religious socialists, on the other hand, combat every attempt by the churches to cripple the class struggle of the proletariat by forming organic-estate groups of 'Christian socialists' or 'Solidarists' or to divert it from revolutionary struggle by means of reactionary forms of organisation such as Catholic and Protestant 'workers associations', social working groups including the class enemy, people's housing developments etc.

The Bund der religiösen Sozialisten, run by proletarian clergy, is an organised association which takes a practical part in the proletarian movement and tries to understand it. It celebrates May Day and commemorations of revolutions in churches, arranges proletarian celebrations and coming of age ceremonies, publishes sermons of socialist pastors (collections of the sermons of [Christoph] Blumhardt, [Leonhard] Ragaz and [Emil] Fuchs; at the end of 1929 roughly 150 Lutheran pastors were active in the social democratic camp). It

---

110   ['*Die Zeitschrift für Religion and Sozialismus*' means '*The Journal for Religion and Socialism*'.]

111   Wünsch 1927; Wünsch 1930.

112   Eckert 1976.

organises meetings of socialist theologicans (April 1930) and it fights against fascism. Standing aside from all this is another circle around the *Blätter für religiösen Sozialismus*, renamed *Neue Blätter für den Sozialismus* in 1930,[113] which is more theoretically inclined and without an organisational infrastructure. The leading intellectual figure in this circle, to which the economist Eduard Heimann (Hamburg) also belongs, is Professor Paul Tillich (Frankfurt am Main). Carl Mennicke is also active in accord with Tillich's ideas.

In his writings, Professor Tillich, who is familiar with Marxist ideas, attempts to give a new theoretical foundation for religious socialism in the sense of a philosophy of Protestant (non-ecclesiastical) existentialism.[114] Tillich developed [Armand] Bazard's doctrine of kairos,[115] describing it as the moment of 'the fullness of time'. The task of religious socialism is to proclaim the kairos of the present, to devote itself to the unconditional.[116] This philosophy of history is connected with socialism through belief in the latter's power to give meaning to an otherwise meaningless existence. Socialism is 'a social order in which a meaningful life is possible for each individual and for every group'.[117] The meaninglessness of existence is typically imposed on the proletarian life process. The class struggle that arises from this class situation of the proletariat is indissolubly linked with the nature of capitalism and should give meaning to proletarian life. Socialism is only an answer to the final, unconditioned question of meaning, that is of the 'religious' character of our existence. It is therefore 'more than only a purely proletarian movement'.[118] It raises *universal* claims and endeavours to seize hold of *every group* in society. Socialism is only indissolubly linked with the proletariat in that the proletariat, the place where the greatest degree of meaninglessness is located, is at the same time the best place in which to raise the question of the meaning of existence and to the extent that it is only through the victorious class struggle of the proletariat and by overcoming the class divisions of capitalism that the basis for a meaningful reconstruction of society will be possible. The proletariat must therefore passionately reject every attempt to suggest that its existence can be filled with meaning through transcendental existence. It 'feels that its struggle is for the kingdom of God; it senses a kind of messianic mission for itself and

---

113   ['*Blätter für religiösen Sozialismus*' means '*Journal for Religious Socialism*'. '*Neue Blätter für den Sozialismus*' means '*New Journal for Religious Socialism*'.]
114   Tillich 1926; Tillich 1930; and the programmatic essay, Tillich 1998.
115   ['Kairos' is Greek for 'right moment', Tillich uses it in the sense of a 'crucial time'.]
116   [For Tilllich the 'unconditional' is religious meaning.]
117   [Tillich 1998, p. 198.]
118   [Tillich 1998, p. 195.]

for the whole of society.'[119] On the other hand, for Tillich the socialist idea in
itself is nothing; socialism is only an external means for shaping the future. Tillich understands it as the questing spirit of the proletariat, of the 'mass'. His
entire struggle is waged against the absolute domination of rationalism. Even
so, Tillich does not reject Marxism, even in its economically materialist form.
Marxism is a reality. It has shaped the psychic being of millions and created a
community which is certain of its victory.

The socialism of this circle is too general and too abstract, too little directed
to the concrete tasks of the present to avoid ambiguity. Despite the emphasis
on the fundamental importance of class struggle, the 'universalism' of Tillich's
socialism contains within itself the danger of a diversion from the class struggle
and a return to an ascetic utopianism. This diversion was expressed very clearly
in the speech of [Henrietta] Roland-Holst at the Heppenheim conference of
religious socialists in 1928. Here the conquest of power, i.e. the overcoming of
capitalism through the class struggle, was not the task set. 'The conception that
life can only be shaped in a socialist way after "the conquest of power" and that
until this has happened all energies should be concentrated exclusively on the
class struggle is a concepticoin which must be most emphatically opposed.'[120]
All efforts should rather be directed to the inner transformation of the person,
to 'remodelling our feelings, our motives' for action, in a socialist sense – free
from any will to power – thus 'instead of making demands on others we make
demands on ourselves'. It is obvious that such a socialism has nothing to do
with real socialism.

Yet another group should not go without mention, the young Christliche
Revolutionäre in Stuttgart.[121] The group was characteristic of the chiliastic
mood of the revolutionary and post-revolutionary period. Their journal of the
same name, appeared from May 1921 as *Weltwende*.[122] It had a subtitle that said
much: 'A wakeup call ... to all those who are determined to achieve a break-
through by giving their all'. It conducted a struggle against 'the mendacity of
public affairs', against the church, the state, parties, also against the religious
socialists, because 'in the last analysis they are the bait in the Church's great
mousetrap'. In the tradition of the Anabaptists and the Levellers, they sought
the 'empire of brotherhood and peace on earth ... the purely human, classless community free from all authority built on socialism and communism ...
the thousand-year empire of peace'. They preached the necessity of revolution

119   [Tillich 1989, p. 105.]
120   [Roland-Holst 1929, pp. 177–9.]
121   ['*Christliche Revolutionäre*' means 'Christian Revolutionaries'.]
122   ['*Weltwende*' means '*World Change*'.]

because 'inner salvation and purification have been neglected'. After holding two conferences (1921 and 1922) the sect collapsed as a result of the indifference and scorn of the mass of the workers.

b   In France, Belgium and Switzerland
Young men's associations were formed among French Protestants as early as 1852. They confined themselves, almost exclusively to religious matters. Protestant social activity did not begin until after 1885. It initially aimed to reform the existing economic order in a Christian direction, without, however, leaving the terrain of this social order. Only in the first decade of the new century did a new tendency appear in the Protestant camp, which was, if not socialist – its representatives were merely 'socialisants',[123] as opposed to the genuine socialists – at least strongly anti-capitalist. It wanted a fundamental reconstruction of society on a semi-socialist, cooperative basis. In 1887 Pastor Louis Gouth, influenced by Tommy Fallot (whose most important work was *Social Christianity*)[124] and with the help of Charles Gide, the leader of the French cooperative movement, founded the Association protestante pour l'étude et l'action sociales (since 1887 this association has published a monthly journal, *Revue de christianisme social*).[125] It held its first Congress in Nîmes in 1888 and adopted its programme at its Besançon Congress (16 June 1910). Proceeding from the principle of Christian justice, it protested against 'a social order which is built on the spirit of competition and egotism'. It 'cannot regard as definitive an economic and social order which is based on perpetual war'. It therefore aimed for the 'realisation' of 'a new order' which, built on the principle of cooperation, was now already capable of 'modifying the relation between capital and labour' but at the same time 'will effectively prepare the transformation of egoistic property into collective property and the system of competition into a *system of solidarity*'. Finally, proceeding from a Christian viewpoint, it rejected both the violation of the people by capital and any violence, sabotage or class hatred on the part of the workers; it also rejected the exploitation of the so-called 'inferior races' by the civilised peoples.[126]

---

123   ['Socialisants' means 'those who have a vague affinity with socialism'.]
124   [Fallot 1911.]
125   ['Association protestante pour l'étude et l'action sociales' means 'Protestant Association for Social Study and Action'. The journal was initially called *Revue de théologie pratique et d'homilétique* (*Review of Practical and Homiletic Theology*), from 1889 *Revue du christianisme pratique*, (*Review of Practical Christianity*) and finally, from 1896, *Revue de christianisme social* (*Review of Christian Socialism*).]
126   [Conférence internationale du Christianisme social 1910. Grossman's emphasis.]

The main theorist of the movement, which was not attached to any of the political parties, was the editor of the *Revue*, Élie Gounelle.[127] After the war the Fédération française du christianisme social was set up at a congress held in Strasburg in 1922. This included, alongside the above-mentioned Association protestante, six other related organisations of practising Christians, such as Les oeuvres sociales de l'armée du salut, Le service social de 'foi et vie', Les jeunesses chrétiennes sociales, and so on.[128] Its most recent congress was held in Paris in 1928.

An eighth organisation joined the Fédération in 1928. The Union des socialistes chrétiens,[129] founded by Raoul Biville and Paul Passy in 1908 under the influence of the Americans Rufus Weeks and Edward Ellis Carr, was the left wing of the Fédération and its members were also members of the Socialist Party. Its journal is the monthly *L'espoir du monde*,[130] which has appeared since 1908. The *Union* had scarcely 600 members before the war. It derived its socialism from Christianity ('socialistes parce que chrétiens'),[131] opposed the official church's alliance with capitalism and strove for the conquest of political power by the proletariat, organised as a class and a party, with the purpose of converting the means of production into collective property. It recognised the class struggle as an unavoidable consequence of capitalism which will only disappear when capitalism itself disappears. From a confessional point of view it comprises both Protestants and Catholics, indeed even Theosophists. It is just as varied in terms of its social composition. In general, however, it rejects Marxism's stress on the state, and supports a more moderate and ethically based liberal socialism. Influenced by the agrarian legislation of the Old Testament prophet Moses, Passy in 1908 founded a *settlement*, Liéfra,[132] in the department of Aube. This social experiment was not intended to solve the social question but rather to show that collective property can prevent individual poverty. (The settlement operates on the following basis: 1 inalienable

---

127 Gounelle 1909; Gounelle 1923; Gounelle 1925. [*'Revue'* means *'Review'*.]

128 ['Fédération française du christianisme social' means 'French Federation of Social Christianity'. 'Les oeuvres sociales de l'armée du salut' means 'The Social Works of the Army of Salvation'. 'Le service social de "foi et vie"' means 'The Social Service of "Faith and Life"'. 'Les jeunesses chrétiennes sociales' means 'Christian Social Youth'.]

129 ['Union des socialistes chrétiens' means 'Union of Christian Socialists'.]

130 [*'L'espoir du monde'* means *'The Hope of the World'*.]

131 [The organisation's self-description included the observation 'we are socialists because we are Christians', e.g. *L'espoir du monde* 1914, back cover.]

132 [Liéfra is an acronym of 'liberté, égalité, fraternité', i.e. the slogan of the Great French Revolution 'liberty, equality, fraternity'.]

collective property in the land; 2 periodic redistribution of shares in property to individual families in proportion to their family size; 3 individual cultivation.) In 1927 the settlement was reorganised in line with the American [theory of the] 'enclave of economic rent' formulated by Fiske Warren (according to the principles of Henry George).[133]

As well as Paul Passy, André Philip, Professor of Economics at the University of Lyon, is a theoretician of the group.[134] According to them, Christianity and the socialist workers movement, the two forces which can renew humanity, are mutually complementary. The workers' class struggle, the fight for the improvement of the economic situation of the working class, alone will not lead to socialism. On the contrary. The improvement of the material situation of the upper layers of the working class leads everywhere to nationalism, to the bourgeoisification of these layers and their incorporation into the capitalist mechanism. This danger can only be eliminated by applying ethical and religious values. Every human being has the *right to salvation*. But the capitalist economy, with its impoverishment and oppression of the working class, creates living conditions which hinder the attainment of this goal. The conviction that the capitalist system is immoral and that everyone has the right to participate equally in the progress of civilisation therefore leads to condemnation of existing social inequality; to revolutionary struggle for socialism, for a fundamental restructuring of society, without compromises with capitalism, and for the realisation of social justice and the kingdom of God on earth. Only socialism is capable of creating a society which will correspond to the Christian ideal.

In **Belgium** too, a League of Religious Socialists was founded in mid-1930. It included Catholics, Protestants and separate groups of non-institutional Christians. While freethinking predominates in the **Walloon** (French speaking) section of Belgian Social Democracy, the **Flemish** Socialists are of a more religious temper. The leader of the religious socialists in Belgium is [Jozef] Chalmet, from Zelzate, who is also a social democratic member of parliament.

In **Switzerland**, a Protestant social movement first emerged at the end of the 1880s, prompted by developments in Germany.

Societies and conferences in Bern, Neuchâtel, Zürich, Basel and Geneva mainly confined themselves to academic discussion of social questions. The number of Protestant workers associations was very small but, in contrast to the 'workers associations' in Germany, included members from the working

---

133   [See Huntington 1921. 'Enclaves of economic rent' were utopian settlements inspired by
      Henry George's theory of a single tax on land.]
134   Passy 1909; Passy 1930; Philip 1928; Philip 1930.

class and fundamentally rejected the admission of non-workers. No attempts were ever made in Switzerland to set up political parties on a social Protestant basis.

At the beginning of the new century, in 1906, a so-called 'religious social movement' – genuinely socialist – arose in Switzerland, prompted by developments in Germany, and sought to combine Christianity and socialism. It continued the work of Christoph Blumhardt and was associated with the writings of the 'Savonarola of Zürich' Pastor Hermann Kutter and of Leonhard Ragaz, then a pastor in Basel and later a university professor. With Pastors [Jean] Matthieu, [Oskar] Pfister and others grouped around the journal *Neue Wege*,[135] which started to appear in 1906, they constituted the often cited circle of Swiss 'religious socials'.

This movement identified in Marxist historical materialism, which it regards as erroneous, biblical truths. It saw in socialism a God-given revival of the social truth of the gospel, which has been ignored and betrayed by official Christianity, despite socialism's hostility to religion. Kutter's tract *They Must*, written with prophetic verve,[136] spread very quickly in all strongly Protestant countries, particularly England and America.[137] It directed fierce criticisms against Christianity and the church of our time, which 'no longer apprehends the living God',[138] has failed to protest against great social injustice and the immorality of our class antagonisms, and has abandoned the task of recreating relations to Social Democracy.

Kutter's phrase 'they must' means that the Social Democrats drive forward, because the living God is driving them forward: 'The Social Democrats are revolutionary because God is revolutionary.'[139] According to Kutter, our whole system of production is nothing but grandiose theft. Every day it deprives the poor of their most essential rights. The goal for which Kutter strove was a kingdom of God on earth without compulsion. Ragaz, in particular, proclaimed this kingdom of God.[140] For long periods, Christianity one-sidedly placed *individual* truth, the relation of God to the individual, at the centre of its preaching and neglected the other side: the redemption of the world from social and material need, poverty, injustice, Mammon and war – the whole bounty of contemporary reality. It has imposed the division between the kingdom

---

135   [*'Neue Wege'* means *'New Paths'*.]
136   Kutter 1908, second edition 1912; French translation 1907.
137   [I.e. the United States of America.]
138   [Kutter 1908, p. 94.]
139   [Kutter 1908, p. 132.]
140   Such as Ragaz 1922; Ragaz 1928; Ragaz 1929; Ragaz 1972.

of God and the kingdom of the world. This rigidity demonstrated its static mode of thought, which regards existing social relations as a finished, unalterable and God ordained order. Religious socialism represented a dynamic mode of thought, in opposition to the rigidity of Christian doctrine. It was a corrective to the one-sidedness which projects Christ's message into a distant, other world. It is devoted to the living God and his coming kingdom on earth. On the basis of this interpretation, Ragaz expected a revolution in Christian thought and Christian practice, a re-awakening of the social and revolutionary spirit of Christianity. On the other hand, Ragaz viewed the socialist workers movement as the bursting forth – in secular form – of a truth which the Christian community should have advocated, namely the kingdom of God on earth for human beings, the kingdom which constitutes the meaning of the *Bible* and the *Old Testament*. It is the religious idea of the future transformation of the world, which only designates Social Democracy, even if it is anti-religious, as the driving force because God also dwells within the godless. 'This socialism is more radical than any other.'[141] It cannot be limited to *social reforms*. It wants a new social order, is oriented in a fundamentally different way from the existing social order. Religious socialism, that is to say, fights alongside the proletariat against capitalism for the emancipation of the proletariat and thus of the whole society. But, in relation to individual demands, it is not tied to the party dogmatism of the existing proletarian parties and is, in principle, just as accessible for Social Democrats or unattached socialists as it is to Communists and anarchists.

As far as the external shape of the future society is concerned, Ragaz wanted a 'voluntary socialism',[142] a society organised into free *cooperatives*, which makes the state as an organ of compulsion superfluous. At the international level, a great, federal community of nations will arise. It will include the whole of humanity. For by 'Christianity' Ragaz understood true religiosity, unconnected with any church, which also includes non-Christians. 'The kingdom of God stands above religions.'[143]

A religious socialism, closely associated with Social Democracy, spread rapidly in Switzerland. As early as 1909, two hundred mostly young Swiss theologians were present at the third conference of religious socialists. During the World War, when Swiss Social Democracy temporarily came under strong

---

141   [This sentiment, though not the phrase, is clearly expressed in Ragaz 1984b, particularly pp. 71–4.]

142   [Ragaz used this term as early as 1917, Ragaz 1917, p. 614.]

143   [This sentiment, though not the sentence, is clearly expressed in Ragaz 1984a, particularly p. 38.]

Bolshevik influence, the religious socialists adopted a radically pacifist and democratic attitude, conducting a struggle against the use of force. This damaged their relationship with the Party. They have recently become the main supporters of both anti-militarism in Switzerland and the free, radical people's higher education movement, which is not connected with the universities. This movement has been severely weakened by theological disputes between Kutter and Ragaz.

The Fédération romande des socialistes-religieux[144] (secretary Hélène Monastier) is an autonomous group, with its own congresses, in *French Switzerland*. Together with the French Union and the Belgian group it constitutes the Fédération des socialistes-chrétiens de la langue française.[145]

c   In England, the Netherlands, Sweden and the United States of
         America

The rise of large-scale industry immensely itensified the misery of the masses of workers in **England**, while a small group of entrepreneurs amassed wealth. In desperation, workers had recourse to self-help (trade unions). Not only did the educated and the rich remain silent about social grievances, parliament prohibited workers from organising. The official, conservative Church was also indifferent to the social misery of the workers and boycotted and even poured scorn on the efforts of the 'seditious rabble'. Only in 1848 were Christian socialist activities encountered in England. They derived directly from French influence and were not insignificantly promoted by the Chartist movement as well as the ideas and writings of Thomas Carlyle (1795–1881), an advocate of social reform on an aristocratic, conservative and ethical basis. Their first representatives were the preacher Frederic Denison Maurice (1805–72) and the lawyer John Malcolm Ludlow (1821–1911), who had been educated in France and was very familiar with the socialist theories and movements there. They were joined by Charles Kingsley (1819–75) and others followed. From November 1850 until the end of 1851 they published a weekly newspaper and, following its title,[146] they called themselves 'Christian socialists' to indicate that it was their intention to guide both unsocial Christianity and unchristian socialism onto better paths and to free society from the evils of one-sided individualism. They wanted to be more than social reformers, who merely sought to improve the

---

144   ['Fédération romande des socialistes-religieux' means 'Federation of Religious Socialists of Switzerland's French-speaking Region'.]
145   ['Fédération des socialistes-chrétiens de la langue française' means 'Federation of French-speaking Christian Socialists'.]
146   [*The Christian Socialist.*]

existing economic system. They pursued, rather, a completely rational reordering of economic life. They wanted to achieve this far-reaching goal, not at a
stroke by passing laws or using force but only gradually, through small, piecemeal activities. The first step to their goal would be the formation of voluntary
consumers' associations, so that finally the *distribution of all goods* could be
rationally regulated. Likewise, *production* would be regulated by workers combined in producers' cooperatives, which would cut out the entrepreneurs and
finally stymie the whole competitive system. Thus the great reconstruction of
society would be carried out gradually, from small centres. These considerations led them to concentrate their practical activity after 1849 chiefly on the
promotion of cooperatives in general and producers' associations in particular,
although they were unable to achieve any lasting successes with the latter.

Chartist workers were suspicious of this movement. It was, after all, the
intention of the Christian socialists to christianise socialism, i.e. to turn it away
from ideas of external revolution, wage struggles and strikes, and to direct it to
revolutionising the soul and to bridging over class conflicts with love and practical assistance. Such a tactic meant abandoning the only way in which workers
could could achieve practical successes. Even so, the Christian socialists played
no small part in promoting welfare legislation for the working classes and in
raising workers' levels of educational (foundation of a people's university, the
Working Men's College, in London). The Christian socialists in England never
managed to form an actual party. They were united in the Guild of St Matthew,
founded in 1879 by Stewart D. Headlam. This had approximately 250 members
in 1896 and conducted lively journalistic activity. The Christian Social Union
developed out of it and sought to win over clergy who supported reform. Both
societies endeavoured to win public opinion for the 'reasonable demands of
socialism'. Their activities were exclusively limited to the educated public and
particularly younger members of the clergy. The working class remained almost
entirely unaffected by this movement.

Around the turn of the century, ecclesiastical circles increasingly concerned
themselves with the social question. During the World War, Anglican archbishops established a number of committees of inquiry, whose results were presented in 1918, in a report on *Christianity and Industrial Problems*.[147] In 1919, the
Anglican Bishop of Manchester William Temple, together with the Quaker Lucy
Gardner, decided to call a large conference of all English churches to discuss
social questions. After a long period of preparation, it took place in April 1924
in Birmingham and constituted the starting-point of what was called the Copec

---

147   [Archbishops' Committees of Inquiry 1918, the report of the Fifth Committee of Inquiry.]

Movement (Conference on Christian Politics, Economics and Citizenship). The reports of commissions of specialists on twelve different subareas were presented to the 1924 conference as booklets.[148] A monthly, *The Copec News*, has appeared since November 1924. In an historical presentation to the Conference, the failure of the English churches in the face of capitalism, which led to 'the appalling catastrophe of 1914–18' and to the Peace of Versailles, which looked 'very much like a war', was conceded without further discussion.[149] The cause was identified as the gap between the doctrine and the life of the church and the elimination of this gap was called for, in the future, not indeed in the sense of church dogma but through the practical Christianity of active love. The existing social order met with sharp criticism. In the reform proposals, however, a compromise between the moderate and the more radical tendencies represented at the Conference was apparent. The foundations of the existing economic order, private property in the means of production, were retained and only mammonism, 'abundance while others starve' was combatted. Capitalism was affirmed, because 'a modern economy' is indispensable 'for supplying the mass of people with their wants and promoting science and art'. The class distinctions which are fundamental in the structure of modern society were affirmed, since every class has its special contribution to make to the life of society. Consciousness of their duty to the whole should therefore unite all classes. Only the dark sides of the capitalist system should be removed: the economic dependence of the workers, the incredible power of entrepreneurs over the masses, unemployment, class struggles and severe economic competition among nations resulting in the danger of war. On the other hand, a certain right of the whole of the people to share in private property was recognised, since this has always been obtained by the combined efforts of all. The present economic order is unchristian and requires radical, if also *step by step*, transformation. Unemployment reveals a serious defect in the capitalist system, as does the organisation of financial institutions. Legally, they are private enterprises while they perform a public function of very great importance. The following reforms were proposed: nationalisation of the banks and the conversion of important concerns into public enterprises, to be controlled by a state appointed supervisory board. The state is to become a shareholder in large enterprises. Trade is to be stabilised, in order to abolish competitive struggle. Inequality in the distribution of property and the enrichment of a small minority at the expense of the masses arising from the capitalist system, will be overcome by

---

148   Among the reports were Conference on Christian Politics 1924a, 1924b, 1924c, 1924d.
149   [Conference on Christian Politics 1924a, p. 152.]

distributing profits among the working masses. The press must be freed from the influence of capital by nationalisation.

A separate political party was not a goal. Christ should function as a 'leaven' in every party. We saw a typical, petty bourgeois programme of sham radicalism, that wanted to eliminate the 'dark sides' of a system while the foundations, on which the 'dark sides' have in fact arisen, were retained.

The group of religious socialists in English, whose organ is the monthly *The Crusader*, edited by Fred Hughes, does not have much influence. It should, however, be noted that the workers movement and its political expression, the Labour Party, is strongly religious in orientation. Many of its leaders come from the church, where they were preachers. It is true that the current Prime Minister, Ramsay MacDonald, had sharply criticised the evangelism of the official churches, in his book *Socialism and Society*:[150] from their individualist viewpoint, they deal only with the relations between a person and God and neglect social relations among people. They have regarded the gospel as metaphysics and failed to demand its application to this world and the need to transform the social organism. Even so, MacDonald assigned a great role to the church in the collective society. The solution of our social problems is impossible outside Christianity. The free churches will play a greater role in the life of the masses, the more they concern themselves not only with matters of dogma but with the needs of life.

The Copec Movement was continued internationally in the Stockholm World Conference for Practical Christianity (for Life and Work), in August 1925. In 1928, it gave rise to the International Institute for Social Christianity in Geneva and the quarterly *Stockholm*, in three languages. The programme of *Stockholm* is the 'nonpartisan' treatment of the interests of both the workers and employers. In fact, therefore, it works towards the solution of 'social questions' on the basis of the present capitalist economy. *Stockholm* carries propaganda for cooperation between employers and workers.

In the **Netherlands**, too, a religious socialist current arose quite early. It existed side by side with bourgeois, Roman Catholic socio-political organisations, under episcopal supervision, such as the Nederlandse Rooms-Katholieke Volksbond,[151] founded in 1888, with a structure of professional groups. Henri van Kol, under the pseudonym of Rienzi, published a pamphlet, *Christianity and Socialism*, in 1882.[152] In it, the later leading social democratic parliamentarian

---

150 MacDonald 1907.
151 ['Nederlandsch Roomsch-katholische Volksbond' means 'Netherlands Roman Catholic People's League'.]
152 [Kol 1888.]

upheld the interests of the proletariat, from the viewpoint of the Christian
sense of justice, and asserted that socialism and Christianity are compatible.
Subsequently, however, van Kol became completely absorbed into the socialist
movement, without establishing a specifically religious socialist group.

Pastors Willem Bax and particularly Frederik Willem Nicolaas Hugenholz
were also representatives of this trend. Hugenholz, in a periodical he edited,
Onze Kring,[153] pointed out the injustice of private ownership of means of production and the profit-based capitalist economy, demonstrated the class character of government and legislation, and stressed the need for class struggle.
But the religious element gradually disappeared from *Onze Kring*. Hugelholz
then arrived at the conviction that the proletariat must first be victorious and
the social question must be solved before any effort is made to deal with religious questions.

A religious socialist *movement* only emerged at the start of the new century.
On 31 October 1902, a new religious socialist weekly, *De Blijde Wereld*,[154] began
to appear. It still exists today. The group behind it described itself as socialist, if
not Marxist, and recognised the necessity of class struggle. But it did not create
its own organisation. Politically it was associated with the Social Democratic
Workers Party.

The Bond van Christen Socialisten (League of Christian Socialists), founded
in 1907, was the first religious socialist organisation to form an independent
political party. It was initially led in a moderate direction by [Anke] van der
Vlies, who, under the pseudonym Enka, was a well known writer. In 1912, under
the leadership of Pastor Bart de Ligt, it adopted a new, radical programme,
which proclaimed that the existing economic order, based on capitalist principles, was incompatible with the principles of Christian love, as capitalism
was the cause of the moral and physical misery of the broad masses. It therefore committed itself to the abolition of the capitalist principle and to the
struggle for the realisation of socialism. This was not a struggle for the interests
of the proletariat, but for a moral world order. In the 1918 elections, the League
succeeded in electing Pastor John William (Willy) Kruyt to the House of Representatives. He later joined the Communist caucus there. The League fell apart in
1921 as a result of internal disagreements. Its publication, *Opwaarts*, appeared
for the last time on 25 April 1921.[155] Some of its members joined the Communist
Party; another group, led by Pastor Année Rinzes de Jong, founded the Bond van

---

153   [*'Onze Kring'* means *'Our Circle'*.]
154   [*'De Blijde Wereld'* means *'The Blessed World'*.]
155   [*'Opwaarts'* means *'Upwards'*.]

Religieuse Anarcho Communisten, which advocated Tolstoyan ideas (monthly journal, *De Bevrijding*).[156]

In January 1915 the Religieus-socialistische Vereniging was set up as a federal peak organisation for the existing religious socialist organisations.[157] Its chair was Cornelis (Kees) Meijer.

During the period of ferment after the World War a religious socialist group split off from the Vereniging Woodbrookers Barchem that had existed since 1910, to form the Vereniging Arbeidersgemeenschap der Woodbrookers.[158] All these groups are numerically weak. The bulk of their members belong not to the working class but to the elite of socialist intellectuals. The first two congresses of the religious socialists of Holland (held in Amsterdam in 1927 and 1929) tried to bring these scattered forces together. Henriette Roland Holst-van der Schalk's book *The Road to Unity* endeavoured to unite the two parts of the socialist workers movement, social democratic and Communist, on a religious socialist basis.[159] A Social Democrat before the war, since 1916 in the Communist Party,[160] Henriette Roland Holst is now attempting to provide socialism with a new justification, on the basis of religious and ethical ideals.

The religious socialist movement has hardly engaged with the Catholic population of the Netherlands at all.

The only country in Northern Europe where an organisation of religious socialists has been set up is **Sweden**. Its most outstanding leaders are Dr Natanael Beskow, the head of the large People's University in Stockholm, Birkagården, and Pastor Samuel Thyssel in Nykoeping. There are, in addition, several Social Democratic pastors.

Christian socialist activities in the **United States of America** took root at the beginning of the 1880s. Their spread was facilitated by strong religious consciousness, especially among trade unionists, and the absence from American intellectual life of any sceptical traditions on the model of the European Enlightenment. Although Christian socialism did not find any organisational

---

156 ['Bond van Religieuse Anarcho Communisten' means 'League of Relgious Anarcho-Communists'. 'De Bevrijding' means 'Liberation'.]

157 ['Religieus-socialistische Vereniging' means 'Religious Socialist Association'.]

158 [The 'Vereniging Woodbrookers Barchem' ('Association of Woodbrookers Barchem') was formed by theology students from the Netherlands, who had visited the Quakers Woodbrooke study centre in Birmingham and started to offer courses at Barchem. The Barchem association gave rise to the 'Vereniging Arbeidersgemeenschap der Woodbrookers' ('Association of the Workers Community Woodbrookers').]

159 Roland Holst-van der Schalk 1928.

160 [The Sociaal-Democratische Partij, the revolutionary Marxist organisation which Roland Holst joined in 1916, renamed itself the Communistische Partij van Nederland in 1918.]

expression in the working class movement, its representatives did introduce a scientific study of workers' problems into the universities. In 1883 the religious socialist Professor Richard T. Ely published a study of the American workers movement. He also took a leading part in the American Society of Christian Socialists in Boston in 1889, organised by William Dwight Porter Bliss (1856–1926) who edited its monthly journal, *The Dawn*. In their programme, they demand that all social, political and industrial relationships should be based on the principle of 'the brotherhood of man ... according to the teachings of Jesus Christ'.[161] The aims of Christianity and socialism were therefore identical and the task of religious socialists was to make the churches aware of this great goal.

In 1893 Ely and George Davis Herron organised the American Institute of Christian Sociology, which exerted great influence and gave rise to an extensive literature, though it foundered eventually on the opposition of the clergy to Herron's radicalism. The Christian Socialist League of America (Chicago), founded by Edwin Dwight Wheelock, only had local significance. At the beginning of the twentieth century, similar activities were undertaken by Rufus Wells Weeks in New York and Edward Ellis Carr, the editor of *The Christian Socialist*, in Chicago. The ideas of Christian socialism gained a lasting influence on the public through Professor Walter Rauschenbusch, two of whose works provided an all-embracing critique of the capitalist world from the point of view of the Christian economic ethic.[162] The capitalist spirit of Mammon was incompatible with the spirit of Christianity. At the same time, social economic activities, which were especially significant in the USA, owing to the absence of any social legislation, received sustenance and support from the ideas of Christian socialism.

After the World War, the increased social activity of the Christian socialists achieved valuable practical results. The report issued by the Interchurch World Movement of North America on the big steel strike of 1919 was a happy combination of objectivity and very sharp criticism, and still contains the most objective material available today on conditions in the steel industry.[163] A whole series of religious institutions (Federal Council of Churches of Christ in America; National Catholic Welfare Conference; Institute of Social and Religious Research) have emerged directly or indirectly from the association which produced this report. They take pains to bring contemporary social problems to the attention of the religious public by reporting on them objectively.

---

161   [Bliss 1890, p. 14.]
162   Rauschenbach 1906; Rauschenbach 1912.
163   [Commission of Inquiry 1919.]

Outside the churches themselves, the propagation of Christian socialist and Christian social ideas was continued mainly by Sherwood Eddy and Kirby Page in their periodical *The World Tomorrow*. This contained extensive bibliographical material. The writings of Bishop [William Montgomery] Brown aroused great interest. He described communism as the fulfilment of Christian doctrine and accepted the political ideas of the Third International[164] (1920).

It should finally be mentioned that a Jewish religious socialist movement exists in **Poland**. For it, the *Bible* was not only the source of religion but of socialism, because it emphasised justice as the principal ethical theme of the *Old Testament* and its found confirmation of this view in the books of the prophets Isaiah, Jeremiah and Ezekiel. This movement, which had little in common with the modern theory of class struggle and had many supporters within the camp of reactionary Orthodoxy was organised in Poale Agudas Yisroel,[165] to which 20,000 Jewish workers belong.

The first international congress of religious socialists was held in Barchem (Netherlands) on 2 July 1924 and the second in Le Locle (Switzerland) on 24 August 1928. In November 1929 there was an international meeting of leaders, which set up the International League of Christian Socialists (chair Leonhard Ragaz), seated in Zürich.

Literature

In addition to the publications referred to in the text and the literature indicated in Grünberg, Carl 1906, 'Christlicher Sozialismus (christlich-soziale Bestrebungen)', in *Wörterbuch der Volkswirtschaft, Erste Band*, second edition, Jena: Fischer, pp. 612–27.

Grünberg, Carl 1911, 'Christlicher Sozialismus (christlich-soziale Bestrebungen)', in *Wörterbuch der Volkswirtschaft, Erste Band*, third edition, Jena: Fischer, pp. 623–52.

Schneemetcher, Wilhelm and W. Liese 1926, 'Christlich-soziale bestrebungen', in *Handwörterbuch der Staatswissenschaften. Dritte Band*, edited by Ludwig Elster, Adolf Weber and Friedrich Wieser, fourth edition, Jena: Fischer, pp. 174–96.

The following books and articles should also be mentioned:

---

164   See Grossmann 1932e, 'The Internationals: The Third International', below, pp. 377–402. [Brown 1923.]
165   ['Poale Agudas Yisroel' means 'Union of Jewish Workers'.]

1   General Works

Abbott, Lyman 1896, *Christianity and Social Problems*, Boston: Houghton, Mifflin.

Bliss, William Dwight Porter (ed.) 1908 [1897], *The New Encyclopaedia of Social Reform*, second edition, New York: Funk & Wagnalls.

Evangelisch-Theologische Fakultät, Universität Wien 1921, *Religion und Sozialismus. Festschrift zur 100-Jährigen Jubelfeier der evangelisch-theologischen Fakultät in Wien*, Berlin: Runge.

Gide, Charles and Charles Rist 1948 [1909], *A History of Economic Doctrines from the Time of the Physiocrats to the Present Day*, Boston: Heath.

Heitmann, Ludwig 1925-7 [1913-9], *Großstadt und Religion*, three volumes, Hamburg: Boysen.

Meyer, Rudolf 1966 [1874-5], *Der Emanzipationskampf des vierten Standes*, two volumes, Aalen: Scientia.

Rowe, Henry Kalloch 1924, *The History of Religion in the United States*, New York: Macmillan.

Soecknick, Gerda 1926, *Religiöser Sozialismus der neueren Zeit*, Jena: Fischer.

Traub, Gottfried 1909 [1904], *Ethik und Kapitalismus*, second edition, Heilbronn: Salzer.

Troeltsch, Ernst 1981 [1912], *The Social Teaching of the Christian Churches*, two volumes, Chicago: University of Chicago Press.

2   Individual Studies

Allinger, Matthias 1925, *Vom Sinn und Wesen der Gewerkschaft*, Wien: Volksbundverlag.

Althaus, Paul 1921, *Religiöser Sozialismus*, Gütersloh: Bertelsmann.

Arendt, Joseph 1926, *La nature, l'organisation et le programme des Syndicats Ouvriers Chrétiens*, Paris: Action populaire, 'Éditions Spes'.

Barbier, Emmanuel 1923-4, *Histoire du catholicisme libéral et du catholicisme social en France: du Concile du Vatican à l'avènement de S. S. Benoît XV (1870–1914)*, five volumes, Bordeaux: Cardoret.

Bebel, August 1929 [1874], *Christentum und Sozialismus: Eine religiöse Polemik zwischen Herrn Kaplan Hohoff in Hüffe und August Bebel*, Berlin: Der Freidenker.

Beer, Max 1948 [1919–20], *A History of British Socialism*, introduced by Richard Henry Tawney, two volumes, fifth edition, London: Allen & Unwin.

Beyer, Georg 1927, *Katholizismus und Sozialismus*, Berlin: Dietz.

Bliss, William Dwight Porter 1890, *What Is Christian Socialism?*, Boston: Society of Christian Socialists.

Bourgin, Georges 1923, *Les catholiques sociaux sous la monarchie de Juillet*, Paris: Rivière.

Brauer, Theodor 1927, *Ketteler: Der deutsche Bischof und Sozialreformer*, Hamburg: Hanseatische Verlagsanstalt.

Braun, Max 1912 [1905], *Adolf Stoecker*, second edition, Berlin: Verlag der Vaterländischen Verlags- und Kunstanstalt.

Brentano, Lujo 1883, *Die christlich-soziale Bewegung in England*, Leipzig: Duncker & Humblot.

Brown, William Montgomery 1923 [1920], *Communism and Christianism*, Galion, Ohio: Bradford-Brown Educational Company.

Brunstädt, Friedrich 1927, *Deutschland und der Sozialismus*, second edition, Berlin: Elsner.

Cahn, Ernst 1924, *Christentum und Wirtschaftsethik*, Gotha/Stuttgart: Perthes.

Calippe, Charles 1911–2, *L'attitude sociale des catholiques français au XIXᵉ siècle*, three volumes, Paris: Bloud.

Calippe, Charles 1918, *La vie catholique dans la France contemporaine*, Paris: Bloud et Gay.

Chenon, Emile 1921, *Le rôle social de l'Église*, Paris: Bloud & Gay.

Chouteau, Olivier 1849, *Programme de socialisme catholique*, Dôle: Brenne.

Cohen, Hermann 1919, *Die Religion der Vernunft aus den Quellen des Judentums*, Leipzig: Fock.

Cottard, Armand 1909, *Le mouvement social dans le protestantisme français (1870–1909)*, Dijon: Barbier.

Debu, Gabriel 1902, *Charles Kingsley ou le premier mouvement socialiste chrétien (1848 jusqu'à 1851)*, Lausanne: Bridel.

Dietrich, Heinrich 1927, *Wie es zum Bund der religiösen Sozialisten kam*, Karlsruhe: Verlag der religiösen Sozialisten.

Dietz, Eduard 1929, *Das religiöse Problem des Marxismus*, Karlsruhe: Verlag der religiösen Sozialisten.

Dolléans, Edouard 1906, *Le caractère religieux du socialisme*, Paris: Larose & Forcel.

Edgar, John 1915, *Socialism and the Bible*, Glasgow: Morton Edgar.

Eildermann, Heinrich 1921, *Urkommunismus und Urreligion*, Berlin: Seehof.

Ely, Richard Theodore 1889, *Social Aspects of Christianity*, New York: Crowell.

Erdmann, August1908, *Die christliche Arbeiterbewegung in Deutschland*, Stuttgart: Dietz.

Fontanelle, Henri 1926, *L'oeuvre sociale d'Albert de Mun*, Paris: Éditions Spes.

Forschner, Carl 1911, *Wilhelm Emmanuel Freiherr von Ketteler, Bischof von Mainz sein Leben und Wirken*, Mainz: Kirchheim.

Frank, Walter 1928, *Hofprediger Adolf Stoecker und die christlich-soziale Bewegung*, Berlin: Hobbing.

Franz, Albert 1914, *Der soziale Katholizismus in Deutschland bis zum Tode Kettelers*, München-Gladbach: Volksvereins-Verlag.

Gargas, Sigmund 1930, 'Der religiöse Sozialismus in den Niederlanden', *Archiv für die Geschichte des Sozialismus und der Arbeiterbewegung*, 15: 388–449.

Gerber, Max, Jean Matthieu, Clara Ragaz, Leonhard Ragaz and Dora Staudinger 1920, *Ein Sozialistisches Programm*, Olten: Trösch.

Gerhardt, Martin 1927, *Johann Hinrich Wichern. Ein Lebensbild*, Hamburg: Agentur des Rauhen Hauses.

Haessle, Johannes 1923, *Das Arbeitsethos der Kirche nach Thomas von Aquin und Leo XIII: Untersuchungen über den Wirtschaftsgeist des Katholizimus*, Freiburg im Breisgau: Herder.

Hemala, Franz 1924, *Warum christliche Gewerkschaften?*, Wien: Typographische Anstalt.

Hodges, George 1896, *Christian Socialism and the Social Union*, Boston: Church Social Union.

Hömig, Herbert (ed.) 2003, *Katholiken und Gewerkschaftsbewegung 1890–1945*, Paderborn: Schöningh.

Hübner, Paul-Gerhard 1930, *Adolf Stöckers sozialethische Anschauungen: Ein Beitrag zur christlich-sozialen Zielsetzung*, Leipzig: Deichert.

Ilgenstein, Wilhelm 1914, *Die religiöse Gedankenwelt der Sozialdemokratie*, Berlin: Verlag der Vaterländischen Verlags- und Kunstanstalt.

Joos, Josef 1920 [1914], *Der Volksverein für das katholische Deutschland*, third edition, München-Gladbach: Volksvereins-Verlag.

Die katholisch-soziale Tagung in Wien 1929, Wien: Volksbund.

Kautsky, Karl 2014 [1908], 'Christianity and Socialism', in Karl Kautsky, *Foundations of Christianity: A Study in Christian Origins*, translated by Adolf Harnack, Abingdon: Routledge, pp. 459–74.

Keeble, Samuel Eduard 1924, *Copec. An Account of the Conference on Christian Politics, Economics and Citizenship*, London: Epworth.

Ketteler, Wilhelm Emmanuel von 1924 [1911], *Schriften*, three volumes, second edition, München: Kösel & Pustet.

Koeth, Karl 1927, *Wilhelm Emmanuel Ketteler*, second edition, München-Gladbach: Volksvereins-Verlag.

Kralik, Richard von 1923, *Karl Lueger und der christliche Sozialismus*, Wien: Vogelsang-Verlag.

Latour-du-Pin-Chambly de La Charce, René de 1917 [1907], *Vers un ordre social chrétien: jalons de route, 1882–1907*, third edition, Paris: Nouvelle librairie nationale.

Laun, Justus Ferdinand 1929 [1926], *Social Christianity in England: A Study in its Origin and Nature*, London: Student Christian Movement.

Le Congrès du Christianisme social, tenu à Paris 10–13 novembre 1928 1929, Saint-Étienne: Bureau du christianisme social.

Lesowsky, Anton 1927, *Karl von Vogelsang*, Wien: Typographische Anstalt.

Lissorgues, Marcellin 1928, *Albert de Mun*, Paris: Éditions Spes.

Lugmayer, Karl 1924, *Das Linzer Programm der christlichen Arbeiter Oesterreichs*, Wien: Typographische Anstalt.

Lugmayer, Karl 1927, *Grundrisse zur neuen Gesellschaft. Berufsständische Bedarfswirtschaft*, Wien: Typographische Anstalt.

Lütgert, Wilhelm 1927, *Der christliche Sozialismus im 19. Jahrhundert*, Halle: Niemeyer.

Macfarland, Charles S. 1924, *International Christian Movements*, New York: Revell.

Mahling, Friedrich 1921, 'Das religiöse und antireligiöse Moment in der ersten deutschen Arbeiterbewegung 1840–1860', in *Festgabe von Fachgenossen und Freunden A. von Harnack*, Tübingen: Mohr, pp. 183–214.

Matthieu, Jean 1913, *Das Christentum und die soziale Krise der Gegenwart*, Basel: Helbing & Lichtenhahn.

Mennicke, Carl 1920, *Proletariat und Volkskirche*, Jena: Diederichs.

Mennicke, Carl 1926, *Der Sozialismus als Bewegung und Aufgabe*, Berlin: Becker.

Mennicke, Carl 1928, *Das Problem der sittlichen Idee in der marxistischen Diskussion der Gegenwart*, Potsdam: Protte.

Marr, Heinz 1921, *Proletarisches Verlangen: Ein Beitrag zur Psychologie der Massen*, Jena: Diederichs.

Marr, Heinz 1925, 'Die Krise im volkstümlichen Marxismus und die christliche Aufgabe', in Heinz Marr, Hinrich Knittermeyer and Paul Luther, *Marx, Kant, Kirche: Verhandlungen des Bundes für Gegenwartschristentum*, Gotha: Perthes.

Merz, Georg 1919, *Religiöse Ansätze im modernen Sozialismus*, second edition, München: Kaiser.

Mestral, Armand de 1907, *L'évolution des idées sociales du pasteur T. Fallot*, Lausanne: Bridel.

Mundwiler, Johannes 1927, *Bischof von Ketteler als Vorkämpfer der christlichen Sozialreform*, second edition, München: Buchhandlung des Verbandes Süddeutscher Katholischer Arbeitervereine.

Morny, J. 1921, *Un catholique peut-il être révolutionnaire?*, Toulouse: Imprimerie toulousiane.

Naine, Charles 1920, *Socialisme solidariste*, Genève: Forum.

Nebgen, Elfriede 1928, *Geistige Grundlagen der christlichen Arbeiterbewegung*, Berlin: Christlicher Gewerkschaftsverlag.

Neumann, Alfred 1927, *Friedrich Naumanns christlicher Sozialismus*, Leipzig: Herrmann.

Neufville, Agnès de 1927, *Le mouvement social protestant en France depuis 1880*, Paris: Les Presses universitaires de France.

Niebergall, Friedrich 1920, *Evangelischer Sozialismus*, Tübingen: Mohr.

Philip, André 1928, *Henri de Man et la crise doctrinale du socialisme*, Paris: Gamber.

Piechowski, Paul 1928, *Die Seele des Proletariats*, Karlsruhe: Verlag der Religiösen Sozialisisten Deutschlands.

Reichsverband der katholischen Arbeiter- und Arbeiterinnenvereine Deutschlands 1928, *Die katholische Arbeiter-Bewegung Deutschlands: Ziele und Aufbau*, München: Leohaus.

Schlüter, Joseph 1928, *Die katholisch-soziale Bewegung in Deutschland seit der Jahrhun-dertwende*, Freiburg im Breisgau: Caritasverlag.

Schneider, Johann 1929, *Friedrich Naumanns soziale Gedankenwelt*, Berlin: Furche.

Temple, William 1927, *Essays in Christian Politics and Kindred Subjects*, London: Long-mans, Green.

Turmann, Max 1929, *Le syndicalisme chrétien en France*, Paris: Valois.

Valdour, Jacques 1929, *La doctrine corporative*, Paris: Rousseau.

Vigener, Fritz 1924, *Ketteler*, Berlin: Oldenbourg.

Ward, Harry Frederick 1919, *The New Social Order: Order and Programs*, New York: Mac-millan.

Wenck, Martin 1920, *Friedrich Naumann: Ein Lebensbild*, Berlin: Verlag der 'Hilfe'.

Wichern, Johann Hinrich 1901–8, *Gesammelte Schriften*, six volumes, Hamburg: Agen-tur des Rauhen Hauses.

Wilke, Fritz 1920, *Der Sozialismus und das Christentum: Eine Skizze*, Berlin: Runge.

Wilkins, William George 1923, *Arbeiterschaft und Religion in England*, Solingen: Ullrich.

CHAPTER 21

Debs, Eugene*

Translated from German by Ken Todd

American union organiser and leader of the radical wing of the Socialist Party (1855–1926). Born in Terre-Haute (Indiana), attended school to the age of 14, then worked as a house-painter and locomotive fireman, became treasurer of the Brotherhood of Locomotive Firemen and editor of its monthly magazine. In 1892 he resigned from this position to become an organiser of railway workers. Here he created a new type of organisation: instead of the previous craft unions, broken up according to individual occupations, all the workers of an entire business, trust or transportation agency would form a unitary industrial union. In June 1893 Debs organised the American Railway Union, which soon numbered 150,000 members. The great popularity of Debs, who was among the best orators in America, dates to the general strike of the railway workers union of 1894, in support of the wage struggles of the workers employed by the Pullman Company in Chicago, who belonged to the union. The strike, which paralysed the entire rail traffic in large parts of the country, could only be broken by the deployment of federal troops, the declaration of martial law and the one-sided partisanship of the courts on behalf of the employers. Arrested with other strike leaders, Debs was sentenced to six months in prison. Through his experiences in union struggles, Debs became a socialist. From the remnants of the railway workers union, Debs founded the Social Democracy of America in Chicago (18 June 1897), which, following internal changes and splits, has borne the name Socialist Party of America since 1901. As its presidential candidate, Debs received almost 100,000 votes in 1900, 402,000 in 1904, 897,000 in 1912. Debs was a co-founder of the radical union organisation, the Industrial Workers of the World (IWW), in 1905, and was an opponent of the opportunistic, conservative tactics of [Samuel] Gompers in the unions, as well as of the growing reformism of the socialist parties. He fought sharply against the entry of the USA into the World War and spoke out for civil war against the war among nations, for which he was sentenced to 10 years in prison and deprivation of his civil rights.[1] As a symbol of protest, the Socialist Party nominated him as their

---

* [Originally published as Grossmann 1931e.]
1 [Debs did not, in the speech for which he was convicted, explicitly call for civil war but did

presidential candidate in 1920; he received 920,000 votes. At the end of 1921 Debs was pardoned by President Harding but never regained his civil rights.

Writings

Among his writings, the following deserve mention:

1904, *Unionism and Socialism*, Terre-Haute: Standard Publishing Company.

1905, *Revolutionary Unionism*, Chicago: Industrial Workers of the World.

1909 [1905], *Class Unionism*, Chicago: Kerr.

1918 [1906], *Industrial Unionism*, in Daniel de Leon, *Industrial Unionism*, New York: New York Labor News Company, pp. 11–22.

1948 [1914], 'A Plea for Solidarity', in Eugene V. Debs, *Writings and Speeches of Eugene V. Debs*, New York: Hermitage, pp. 366–73.

1918, 'The IWW Bogey', *International Socialist Review*, 18, no. 8 (February): 395–6.

Literature

Beer, Max 1931, *Handbuch der modernen Arbeiterbewegung*, Berlin.[2]

Brissenden, Paul Frederick 1920, *The IWW: A Study of American Syndicalism*, second edition, New York: Longman Green.

Hillquit, Morris 1906, *History of Socialism in the United States*, New York: Funk & Wagnalls.

Perlman, Selig 1923, *A History of Trade Unionism in the United States*, New York: Macmillan.

---

denounce the World War and advocated 'the war of the working class of the world against the ruling class, the capitalist class of the world', Debs 192?, pp. 22–3.]

2   [Grossman seems to have anticipated this publication, by his friend Max Beer, but it never appeared.]

CHAPTER 22

De Leon, Daniel*

Translated from German by Ken Todd

Radical leader of the socialist movement in the United States of America (1852 to 1914). Born on the island of Curaçao, studied in Europe (in Hildesheim, subsequently in Leiden). In 1873 he settled in the United States of America as a teacher of ancient languages and mathematics. Then moved to New York, where he studied law and earned his doctorate at the beginning of the 1880s while a lecturer in international law at Columbia University. At first a follower of Henry George and only later acquainted with the ideas of Marx – he translated Marx's *The Eighteenth of Brumaire*[1] into English – in 1889 he became a member of the Socialist Labor Party (SLP). He soon assumed a leading position and was the editor of the Party's weekly *People* from 1892. He sought to apply Marx's theory of class struggle to American circumstances and conducted an energetic struggle against the opportunistic, conservative tactics of the union leaders of the American Federation of Labor (AFL). Since they completely dominated union structures and made any internal opposition futile, he advocated the creation of revolutionary economic organisations of the American proletariat. Thanks to his untiring agitation, at the end of 1895 the Socialist Trade and Labor Alliance (STLA) was founded, from of a number of trade unions. This led to conflict within the SLP and to the separation of [some] socialist elements, who organised themselves into the Socialist Party in 1901, while the SLP and the STLA stagnated. In 1905, De Leon was a cofounder and leader of the Industrial workers of the World (IWW), with Eugene Debs and Bill Haywood, and conducted lively agitation for it. Its task was to prepare the working class to assume control over enterprises and of the entire process of production and thus for the construction of the new society, through the comprehensive organisation of *workers as a class* into large industrial unions. From 1900 to 1914 De Leon was editor in chief of the *Weekly People* and the daily *People*, in which he argued for the ideas and the tactics of revolutionary socialism. He was not capable, however, of grasping the significance of a political workers party. In 1912–4 he was a member of the International Socialist Bureau.

---

* [Originally published as Grossmann 1931f.]
1 [Marx 1907.]

Writings

Among De Leon's speeches and pamphlets the following deserve mention:

1905, *The Preamble of the Industrial Workers of the World*, New York: National Executive Committee, Socialist Labor Party.

1932 [1906], *Reform or Revolution*, New York: Industrial Union Party.

Literature

Brissenden, Paul Frederick 1920, *The IWW: A Study of American Syndicalism*, second edition, New York: Longman Green.

National Executive Committee, Socialist Labor Party 1920 [1919], *Daniel De Leon, the Man and His Work: A Symposium*, New York.

Haywood, William Dudley 1929, *Bill Haywood's Book: The Autobiography of William D. Haywood*, New York: International Publishers.

Katz, Rudolf 1920 [1915–6], 'With De Leon since '89', in National Executive Committee, Socialist Labor Party, *Daniel De Leon, the Man and His Work: A Symposium*, New York, pp. 1–165.

CHAPTER 23

Guesde, Jules*

Translated from German by Joseph Fraccia

The most significant figure in the socialist movement in France after 1880, born 11 November 1845 in Paris, the son of a teacher of little means, Basile. (He adopted his mother's surname Guesde.) After completing academic secondary education, he dedicated himself to journalism from 1868, and was active in the cause of republicanism during the Second Empire. In 1870 he assumed the leadership of the newspaper *Les Droits de l'homme* in Montpellier.[1] In July 1870, he was condemned to four months in prison for protesting against the Franco-German War and, in 1871, to five years in prison and a fine of 4,000 francs for supporting the Commune. He fled to Switzerland. There he associated with communist anarchists and, with them combated Marxism. In 1872, Guesde published *The Red Book of Rural Justice*,[2] which described, on the basis of documentary evidence, the atrocities committed against the Communards by the Parisian bourgeoisie. During his emigration Guesde worked as a language teacher and journalist in Geneva, later in Italy. In 1872, he drafted his anarchist-communist *Attempt at a Social Catechism* (first published in 1878).[3] In 1876, after his conviction had lapsed, he returned to France as a Marxist. He was the first to awaken the workers movement out of the lethargy into which it had sunk after the defeat of 1871. He began the struggle against Proudhonism, which was apolitical, favoured class peace was then expanding in influence. Together with Paul Lafargue (1842–1911) he became a pioneer of the revolutionary Marxist workers movement in France which, rejecting all compromise with the bourgeoisie, was built solely on the basis of the proletariat and its future leading role. In the first collectivist weekly, *Egalité*,[4] which he founded in Paris in 1877 (18 November), as in numerous lectures and speeches at meetings throughout France, Guesde – a tireless agitator and populariser, a brilliant speaker and polemicist – spread the Marxist theory of class struggle, previously little known in France, in the workers movement and accelerated its theoretical

---

* [Originally published as Grossmann 1932a.]
1 [*'Les Droits de l'homme'* means *'The Rights of Man'*.]
2 [Guesde 1872.]
3 [Guesde 1878.]
4 [*'Egalité'* means *'Equality'*.]

and organisational separation from the radical bourgeois democrats. In 1878, Guesde was condemned to a seven months in prison for his attempt, contrary to a police ban, to organise an international workers conference during the World Exposition in Paris. In prison, Guesde formulated the first socialist programme in France: *Programme and Address of the Socialist Revolutionaries*, which was adopted by several socialist groups.[5] Consequently the General Workers Congress in Marseille in 1879, in contrast to the Congresses of 1876 and 1878 (which advocated reaching *understanding* with employers) declared itself in favour of the *expropriation* of the bourgeoisie and the socialisation of the means of production in a resolution. This initiated a process of socialist clarification in the labour movement, which had previously been strongly infused with anarchist ideas. The Parti ouvrier français[6] (POF = Guesdists), whose history is intimately connected with Guesde, was founded in Marseille in 1879. At its Congress in Le Havre (16 November 1880), the Party adopted the so-called minimum programme (for electoral purposes), which Guesde formulated in collaboration with Marx, completing his final break with anarchism. Under Guesde's leadership, a struggle lasting many years against petty bourgeois anarchist and reformist elements (the Possibilists) was conducted, within and outside the Party. This ended in a split. The (Guesdist) Congress in Roanne (1882) endorsed participation in elections, however – in contrast with the reformists – only for propaganda purposes and rejected the 'parliamentarisation' of the Party, i.e. the notion of peaceful and piecemeal conquest of state power through legal, parliamentary means, as a betrayal of socialism.

Sentenced to six months in prison in 1883 for provoking civil war Guesde, in collaboration with Lafargue wrote a commentary on the Party programme, *The Programme of the Workers Party: Its History, Its Grounds and Its Provisions*, and also his text against the Possibilists, *Public Services and Socialism*.[7] In 1885, to replace *Egalité* which had folded in 1883, he established the weekly *Socialiste*, which remained the Party organ until 1898. Having failed in the elections of 1893 in Marseille, Guesde represented Roubaix in the Chamber of Deputies from 1893 to 1898 and from 1906 to1922. In his famous speeches to the Chamber on the principles of collectivism (November 1894) and also on the tendencies of economic development (June 1896), Guesde represented intransigent Marxism. But a steadily growing contradiction gradually developed between Guesde's clearly revolutionary *theoretical* position and his *tactics*, in partic-

---

5 [*Egalité* 1880, the first issue in the second series of the newspaper, which had been suppressed in July 1878.]
6 ['Parti Ouvrier Français' means 'French Workers Party'.]
7 [Guesde and Lafargue 1899; Guesde 1884.]

ular since the formulation of his Party's local government (1891) and rural programmes (1892 and 1894). This constituted the essence of Guesdism in its second phase. It was *verbally* revolutionary, a Marxism that was only orthodox in theory, which was not capable of being applied in the sphere of action and was replaced in everyday work by *reformist practice*.

In 1909 and later, Guesde did still speak about a revolutionary, forceful conquest of power but only meant elections, which were transformed from an instrument for defrauding the working class into *the* instrument for its emancipation. During the period of Boulangism[8] (1888/1889), and also during the Dreyfus Affair (1898/1900), Guesde chose the tactic of abstention, of working class inaction. By the middle of the 1890s the 'parliamentarisation' of the POF was complete. Even if Guesde did not want to draw final conclusions from it and declared himself *against ministerialism* with the words 'a socialist who goes into a bourgeois ministry ceases to be a socialist' (1899),[9] he rejected all active extraparliamentary proletarian action, like the *notion of a general strike* which swayed the masses (1890 and 1894); like the *struggle against clericalism* (1902). This tactic drove the most active sections of the proletariat to revolutionary syndicalism. The POF, which began as a Marxist, anti-reformist party, ended up merging with the reformist socialists – even though there was no intent to establish programmatic unity or convergence – to form the Parti socialiste unifié[10] (1905). Guesde was forced to support his earlier theoretical opponents and at the same time lost his previous leading role to [Jean] Jaurès.[11] The complete transformation of the POF is most clearly visible in Guesde's stance on the *question of war*. In 1885, on the occasion of the Anglo-Russian conflict in Afghanistan, Guesde greeted the war between capitalist states as the beginning of the end of capitalism, because proletarian revolution would be born of bourgeoisie's cataclysm of war. As late as the International Congress in Brussels (1891), Guesde saw *every* war as the *inevitable* result of capitalist society, built on class antagonisms. Two years later, at the Party Congress in Paris (1893), he already distinguished between offensive and defensive wars; only the former were to be combated. At that time, in relation to a 'defensive war', Guesde already developed the theory of civil peace: in case of war, the proletariat of a nation with pronounced class divisions, *must stand at the side of its bourgeoisie, in the interests of socialism*, to avoid defeat by a culturally less

---

8   [Boulangism was the short-lived anti-democratic, right-wing populist movement around the French general and politician Georges Ernest Boulanger.]

9   [Guesde used these words, citing Wilhelm Liebknecht in 1900, Guesde 1901a, p. 80.]

10   ['Parti socialiste unifié' means 'Unified Socialist Party'.]

11   See Grossmann 1932f, 'Jaurès, Jean', below, pp. 403–406.

developed nation. As a consequence, 'if France is attacked, there will be no more ardent defenders than the socialists of the Parti ouvrier français'.[12] [Gustave] Hervé's anti-militarist propaganda only strengthened Guesde in his 'patriotic' reaction. After the outbreak of the World War, the 70-year-old Guesde, former herald of intransigent class struggle, participated in the civil peace of 'défence nationale',[13] became a Minister (until the end of 1916) in the bourgeois war cabinet of the 'union sacrée'[14] and so became the visible personification of the collapse of the Second International. In February 1917 he welcomed the *bourgeois* revolution in Russia, in the expectation that Russia would now fight the War more energetically. Eight months later he declared his opposition to Lenin's *proletarian* revolution. Finally, he experienced the split in his own Party, at the Congress in Tours (December 1920), when the majority joined the Third International. He died, embittered, on 28 July 1922 near Paris.

Writings

In addition to the those mentioned above:

1878, *La République et les grèves*, Paris: Reiff.

1906 [1878], *La loi des salaires et ses conséquences*, fourth edition, Paris: Librairie du Parti socialiste.

1879, *Collectivisme et révolution*, Paris: Reiff.

1899, *Le Socialisme au jour le jour*, Paris: Giard et Brière.

1901, *Quatre ans de lutte de classe à la Chambre: 1893–1898*, two volumes, Paris: Jacques.

1901, *État, politique et moral de classe*, Paris: Giard et Brière.

1911, *En garde! Contre les contrefaçons, les mirages et la fausse monnaie des réformes bourgeoises*, Paris: Rouff.

1914, *Çà et là: De la propriété, La Commune, Le Collectivisme devant la 10e chambre, La Question des Loyers, Les Grands Magasins*, Paris: Rivière.

Literature

Bourgin, Georges 1929, 'Jules Guesde', *Archiv für die Geschichte des Sozialismus und der Arbeiterbewegung*, 14: 88–101.

Frossard, Louis-Oscar 1930, *De Jaurès à Lénine*, Paris: Nouvelle revue socialiste.

---

12   [Guesde 1901b, p. 197, quoting *Parti ouvrier français* 1893, p. 12.]

13   ['Défence nationale' means 'national defence'.]

14   ['Union sacrée' means 'sacred union'.]

Posse, Ernst Hans 1930, *Der Marxismus in Frankreich 1871–1905*, Berlin: Prager.

Weill, Georges 1924, *Histoire du movement sociale en France 1852–1924*, Paris: Alcan (with an extensive bibliography).

Zévaès, Alexandre 1911, *Les Guesdistes*, Paris: Rivière.

Zévaès, Alexandre 1923, *Le Parti Socialiste de 1904 à 1923*, Paris: Rivière.

Zévaès, Alexandre 1928, *Jules Guesde (1845–1922)*, Paris: Rivière.

CHAPTER 24

Herzen, Alexander*

Translated from German by Joseph Fraccia

Born 25 March 1812 in Moscow, the illegitimate son ('child of the heart', hence his name)[1] of former guards captain and wealthy Russian landholder [Ivan Alekseevich] Yakovlev and a German mother. As a youth he experienced the Decembrist Revolt (December 1825), whose tragic fate made a deep impression on Herzen. Together with his friend [Nikolai Platonovich] Ogarev he swore to take up the struggle against Tsarist tyranny. In 1829–33 Herzen completed his studies at the Faculty of Natural Sciences and Mathematics at the University of Moscow. After the July Revolution,[2] his world view developed in a circle of similarly inclined friends, under the influence of the Young Hegelians (the Left Hegelians) and also of the French utopian socialists. He came under political suspicion, was arrested with several comrades on 20 July 1834 and was banished to civil service in Perm and Kirov,[3] whence he was only permitted to return to Moscow in 1840. After a brief career in the Ministry of the Interior and then his second banishment to Novgorod, he was released [from the public service] in 1842 and devoted himself to literary activity in Moscow until 1847. The first stage in his thinking brought a break with the feudal slavophiles and he joined the 'western oriented'. He was on their left wing, which leaned towards democracy and socialism and struggled against the bourgeois liberal right wing ([Ivan Sergeyevich] Turgenev, [Konstantin Dmitrievich] Kavelin, [Pavel Vasilyevich] Annenkov). He succeeded in winning the right Hegelians, [Mikhail Alexandrovich] Bakunin and [Vissarion Grigoryevich] Belinsky, for the left. The study of Hegel led him to the conviction that his philosophy was the 'algebra of revolution'.[4] In 1847 Herzen travelled abroad as a materialist and, influenced by socialism, he experienced the revolution of 1848 in Paris at first-hand, in personal contact with all significant leaders of the opposition of that epoch. This period was the second stage of his thought. Herzen, aristocrat and mil-

---

* [Originally published as Grossmann 1932b.]
1 [Heart is 'Herz' in German.]
2 [The July Revolution of 1830 in France overturned the Bourbon monarchy and installed Louis-Philippe de Orléans as King.]
3 [Kirov was then called Vyatka.]
4 [Herzen 1982, p. 237. In an earlier translation 'revolutionary algebra', Herzen 1855b, p. 69.]

lionaire (he inherited a million roubles in cash from his father; his Russian landholdings were confiscated by the Tsarist regime in 1851) became a passionate critic of western European capitalism, which he labelled 'social anthropophagy'. He raised himself above the scope of utopian socialism by posing the *question of the necessity* of socialism. Expelled from Paris in 1849, he lived in Switzerland, where he gained citizenship, then, from 1852 until 1865 in London, thereafter back and forth between Geneva and Brussels. This was the third stage of his development. Deep disappointment with the [1848] French Revolution's lack of results led him intellectually from western Europe back to Russia. At first he wrote for western Europe *about* Russia, directed the foreign section of [Pierre-Joseph] Proudhon's *La voix du peuple* (for which he advanced a security guarantee of 24,000 francs),[5] published a series of books, mostly under the pseudonym Iscander. From 1853 he wrote in Europe for Russia, founded the Free Russian Press in London on 1 May 1853, with which a new epoch of Russian revolutionary activity began: the existence of *illegal Russian literature* beyond the border. After the Crimean War, Herzen expanded his publishing activity; in 1855 the publication of the *Polarnaya Zviezda* began.[6] It appeared until 1862. In a letter to [William James] Linton in 1854 Herzen posed the famous question with which, for the next half a century, the legal and illegal Russian press were occupied and constituted an important point of contention among different political parties in Russia: does Russia have to pass through all the phases of European development, especially the capitalist phase?[7] The ideas of his old opponents, the slavophiles reawoke in Herzen. In the residual socio-economic forms of Russian life, the mir (village commune), Herzen saw the source of energy for a new social order, for which the Slavs were better prepared than other peoples. He began to idealise the mir; in doing so, Herzen became one of the first 'populists'.

In 1856 Ogarev came to London and from 1 July 1857 he and Herzen began to work on the publication of *Kolokol*,[8] which had unusual success: it made its way into all the upper levels of Russian society and was even read by Tsar Aleksandr II and his wife. Next to the official government in Petersburg, Herzen became a second 'unofficial power' in London. Herzen's writings were only unable to penetrate the popular masses. He addressed himself primarily to liberal nobles, government officials and bourgeois circles. *A socialist for western*

---

5 ['*La voix du peuple*' means '*The Voice of the People*'.]
6 ['*Polarnaya zviezda*' means '*The Pole Star*'.]
7 See Grossmann 1931d, 'Bolshevism' above, pp. 239–291.
8 ['*Kolokol*' means '*The Bell*'.]

Europe, he was extremely moderate for Russia: he demanded the emancipation of the serfs, although only with compensation; the lifting of censorship; and the prohibition of corporal punishment. There was no talk of bourgeois democracy nor of *overturning* the autocracy, he did not even demand the *limitation* of absolutism through popular representation. Attacked from all sides, particularly by [Nikolai Gavrilovich] Chernyshevsky (1828–89), and disappointed by the Emancipation of the Serfs in 1861, Herzen's views became more radical in the following period, which was the last stage of his development. In so doing, he lost his previous audience and was not, however, capable of acquiring a new one in the emerging revolutionary movement. His influence ebbed. He died politically isolated in Paris on 21 January 1870.

Writings

1919–25, *Polnoe Sobranie Sochinenii i Pisem*, edited by Mikhail Konstantinovich Lemke, Moskva: Petrograd: Literaturno-Izdatelskii Otdiel.[9]

In particular, the following are mentioned:

1956 [1848–50], *From the Other Shore*, in Alexander Herzen, *Selected Philosophical Works*, Moskow: Foreign Languages Publishing House, pp. 336–469.

1956 [1848], *The Russian People and Socialism*, in Alexander Herzen, *Selected Philosophical Works*, Moskow: Foreign Languages Publishing House, pp. 470–545.

1995 [1852], *Letters from France and Italy, 1847–1851*, Pittsburgh: University of Pittsburgh Press.

1921 [1854], *Rußlands soziale Zustände*, with a postscript, edited by Antonín Stanislav Mágr, Leipzig: Reclam.

1855–9, *Aus den Memoiren eines Russen*, four volumes, Harnburg: Hoffmann und Campe.[10]

1858, *Die Russische Verschwörung und der Aufstand vom 14. December 1825*, Hamburg: Hoffmann und Campe.

1907 [1866], *Erinnerungen*, translated by Otto Buek, two volumes, Berlin: Wiegand & Grieben.

1912, *Pages choisies*, edited by Michel Delines, Paris: Mercure de France.

---

9   [There is a more recent collected works: Herzen 1954–66.]
10   [Also see Herzen 1855a and Herzen 1855b.]

Further

Kawelin, Konstantin, Iwan Turgeniews and Alexander Iwanowitsch Herzen 1894, *Konstantin Kawelins und Iwan Turgeniews sozialpolitischer Briefwechsel mit Alexander Iw. Herzen*, edited by Michail Dragomanow, Stuttgart: Cotta.

Bakunin, Mihail, Alexander Iwanowitsch Herzen and Nikolai Platonowitsch Ogarjow 1895, *Michail Bakunins sozialpolitischer Briefwechsel mit Alexander Iw. Herzen und Ogarjow*, translated by Boris Minzes, edited by Michail Dragomanow, Stuttgart: Cotta.

Literature

Bogucharsky, Vasily Yakovlevich 1920 [1911], *Aleksandr Ivanovich Gertsen*, second edition, Moskva: Gosudartstvennoe Izdatelstvo.

Kamenev, Y.V. 1916, *Ob A. I. Gerzeme o N. G. Chernyshevskom*, Petrograd: 'Zhin i Znanie'.

Labry, Raoul 1928, *Herzen et Proudhon*, Paris: Bossard.

Labry, Raoul 1928, *Alexandre Ivanovic Herzen, 1812–1870: essai sur la formation et le développement de ses idées*, Paris: Bossard.

Lenin, Vladimir Ilyich 1963 [1912], 'In Memory of Herzen', in Vladimir Ilych Lenin, *Collected Works. Volume 18*, Moscow: Progress, pp. 25–31.

Linton, William James 1892, *European Republicans*, London: Lawrence and Bullen, pp. 241–304.

Schpet, Gustav 1921, *Filosofskoe Mirovozrenie Gertsena*, Petrograd: Knigo Izdatelstvo 'Kolos'.

Sperber, Otto von 1894, *Die sozialpolitischen Ideen Alexander Herzens*, Leipzig: Duncker & Humblot.

Steklow, Georg 1920, A.J. *Herzen (Iskander). Eine Biographie*, Berlin: Seehof.

CHAPTER 25

Hyndman, Henry Mayers*

Translated from German by Ken Todd

Founder and leader of the English socialist movement, from 1880. Born on 7 March 1842 to a rich, conservative family. His father left £150,000 for the construction of churches and charitable institutions in London. After the completion of his legal studies at Cambridge University, Hyndman devoted himself to journalism and was initially active in the spirit of left-liberalism. In 1886, he participated in Garibaldi's march on the Tirol, as the war correspondent of a liberal newspaper. The following years took Hyndman to England's colonies: in 1869 he visited Australia, New Zealand, south sea islands and the United States of America. Having returned to London in 1871, he showed great sympathy for the Paris Commune. Between 1872 and 1880 he made business and study trips to California, became more and more dissatisfied with the policies of the Liberal government, particularly because of continual wars and the famine in India (1876–8). In 1878 Hyndman published a series of articles 'The Bankruptcy of India' (issued in book form in 1886),[1] in which he raised most serious charges against the English system of exploitation in India, and became a critic of capitalism. He soon (1880) found the scientific basis for his criticism in Marx's *Capital*.[2] Hyndman entered into personal contact with Marx, became a socialist and in his works *England for All* (1881) and *Economics of Socialism* (1896)[3] sought to spread Marx's ideas, without ever having properly understood them. The principal thing for him was the formation of a *political* party. When he encountered hostility to this effort from the unions, he became a bitter opponent of the union movement and oriented to the unorganised. In doing so, he closed himself off from the path to a mass party. In strikes he saw only a distraction from political struggle and was not capable of grasping the significance of the proletariat as a class. Nor could his socialism achieve true internationalism; on the contrary, it always retained a colouration dictated by English national interests. He did combat British imperialism in relation to the great peoples of

---

* [Originally published as Grossmann 1932c.]
1 [Hyndman 1886.]
2 [Marx 1976b.]
3 [Hyndman 1881; Hyndman 1896.]

Asia: China and Japan. He still did this in his *The Awakening of Asia*, written in 1917 (published in 1919).[4] The concept of the self-determination of nations oppressed by Britain, however, remained alien to him and he never went beyond the demand for Irish and Indian self-government within the limits of the British Empire.

In June 1881 he founded the Democratic Federation, which was transformed into the Social Democratic Federation (SDF) in 1884 and adopted the name British Socialist Party (BSP) in 1911. Its organ, the weekly *Justice* was published by Hyndman (from 1884) with great financial sacrifices. Despite his brilliant gifts as a speaker, agitator and publicist, over the four decades of his self-sacrificing exertions, Hyndman never succeeded in pentrating the masses. His repeated candidacies for Parliament also remained unsuccessful. Hyndman was the representative of British socialism in the International Socialist Bureau in Brussels and, from 1889 to 1907, participated in the Congresses of the Second International, for whose collapse in 1914 he shares the blame. From the start of the twentieth century, he was one of the most bitter opponents of Germany in his foreign policy and demanded the strengthening of English navy against German militarism. After the World War broke out, he immediately declared himself for 'the defence of the fatherland', for 'staying the course until victory', combatted 'pacifist traitors', and worked for the entry of Italy and other powers into the war against Germany. Expelled from his own party in 1916, he founded a small National Socialist Party, (NSP) which had no influence. He was an intractable opponent of the Bolshevik Revolution and even supported intervention in Russia. He died on the 22 November 1921 in London.

Writings

In addition to those mentioned above:
1883, *Historical Basis of Socialism*, London: Kegan Paul, Trench.
1911, *The Record of an Adventurous Life*, London: Macmillan.
1912, *Further Reminiscences*, London: Macmillan.
1915, *Future of Democracy*, London: George Allen & Unwin.
1920, *Evolution of Revolution*, London: Hyndman Literary Trust.

---

4   [Hyndman 1919.]

Literature

Gould, Frederick James 1928, *Hyndman: Prophet of Socialism (1842–1921)*, London: Allen & Unwin.

Hyndman, Rosalind Travers 1923, *Last Years of H.M. Hyndman*, London: Richards.

Longuet, Jean 1922, 'Der "große Alte" des englischen Sozialismus', *Der Kampf*, 15, no. 2: 44–8.

CHAPTER 26

The Internationals:[*]
The Second International (1889–1914)

Translated from German by Ben Fowkes

1   The Collapse of the First International

After the seat of the International was relocated to New York, an *anarcho-communist* (Bakuninist) opposition declared the decisions of the Hague Congress null and void at a Congress at St Imier in the Jura region of Switzerland (15–16 September 1872) and held further Congresses, as continuations of the International: a sixth in Geneva (September 1873), a seventh in Brussels (September 1874), an eighth in Bern (October 1876) and a ninth and final one in Verviers (September 1877).

2   The Precursors of the Second International

After the end of the 1870s, Proudhonism and Bakuninism were expiring and the Marxist ideas of the Hague Congress were again on the rise everywhere in the organised and fighting proletariat. In Germany the Social Democrats registered great successes; in France the Parti Ouvrier[1] was founded by Jules Guesde. Social democratic currents grew stronger in Belgium and the Netherlands. A series of anarchist leaders – César de Paepe, Paul Brousse and Benoît Malon – went over to Social Democracy. Under these circumstances a world congress of socialist and communist groups from almost all European countries met in Ghent on 3 September 1877. The majority voted in favour of the socialisation of the means of production and working class political activity, thereby breaking unambiguously with the anarchists. Guesde's attempt to organise an international workers congress in Paris to coincide with the World Exposition

---

[*]   [Originally published as Grossmann 1932d. The section of this article on the First International was by Carl Grünberg. Quotations from minutes of congresses are not generally referenced separately; unless otherwise indicated, their sources are listed in Grossman's bibliography at the end of 'The Internationals: The Third International', below, pp. 398–402. All emphases in these quotations are Grossman's.]
1   ['Parti Ouvrier' means 'Workers Party'.]

in 1878 failed. Only on 2–4 October 1881 was an international congress (initially intended to meet in Zürich) successfully held in Chur. The delegates, including Wilhelm Liebknecht from Germany, Malon from France and Ludwik Waryński from Poland, expressed the view that it was premature to think of setting up a new international, as most national parties were only just emerging. It was also premature to agree on a common programme. There was agreement only on several general objectives for the working class movement (socialisation of the means of production, the question of wages, provision of education).

3   The Second International's Revolutionary Period (1889 to 1904)

While the period 1848–71 had been a time of national wars (1864, 1866, 1870) and revolutions, the year 1871 opened an era of peaceful development in Europe, which lasted until 1895. During this time, in response to the long economic depression, the capitalist economy was marked by great industrial concentration and the transition from medium to large-scale enterprises. In parallel, the working class also made tremendous progress in organising *large and independent political parties* in individual capitalist countries; parties which emancipated themselves from the liberal ideas of the bourgeoisie. The long period of depression provided *an impulse to class struggle*. Everywhere the workers strove to improve their condition by acting industrially and politically, as in the case of the struggle for universal suffrage, and thought about rebuilding an international organisation. In addition to the Social Democratic Parties in Germany and France, the Emancipation of Labour group emerged in Russia (1883), the Social Democratic Federation in England (1884), the Social Democratic Workers Party in Austria (1888) and socialist workers parties in Denmark, Sweden, Italy, Belgium, Spain and Switzerland. In this way, the necessary precondition for an international association of socialist organisations was created.

Two international congresses met simultaneously in Paris on 14 July 1889, the hundredth anniversary of the storming of the Bastille: the Congress of the Possibilists,[2] which was dominated by *reformist* trade union representatives from France and England, and the Congress of *Marxists*, at which twenty important countries were represented by 407 delegates. The latter became the founding Congress of the so-called Second International, which lasted for 25 years, until it came to an end with the outbreak of the World War (1889–1914). The founding

2   [The 'Possibilitists' were members of the refomist Fédération des travailleurs socialistes de France (Federation of Socialist Workers of France), led by Paul Brousse.]

Congress was followed by a total of eight further Congresses: the second Congress took place in Brussels (August 1891), the third in Zürich (August 1893), the fourth in London (July 1896), the fifth in Paris (September 1900), the sixth in Amsterdam (August 1904), the seventh in Stuttgart (August 1907), the eighth in Copenhagen (August 1910) and the ninth, extraordinary Congress, in Basel (November 1912).

Organisationally, the Second International was never, to its end, a single united party. It was, rather, only a loose association of fully independent parties, not subject to any common discipline, which considered unity in tactics impossible and did not, therefore, regard its resolutions as binding. In 1891, when there was a proposal from the Netherlands to place the questions of tactics and alliances with bourgeois parties on the agenda, the German delegation was opposed, because only *comrades in individual countries were competent* to decide such questions. A proposal for closer cooperation among the different national organisation between Congresses, by establishing an *International Socialist Bureau* (ISB) based in Brussels, was only made at the 1896 London Congress. The Paris Congress of 1900 put the proposal into effect by allocating the necessary funds. After 1910 the ISB published a periodic *Bulletin* and also maintained a socialist archive and library. From 1904 there was also an Interparliamentary Social Democratic Commission to coordinate parliamentary actions. The ISB was never, however, more than a centre for sharing common information.

The sole and most important decision of the Second International which *obliged parties to take part in joint international proletarian action* was the resolution of the first Congress on the celebration of May Day with demonstrations for the eight hour day and the protection of labour, later also for world peace. These celebrations were particularly effective in the politically and industrially backward countries of eastern Europe, where the demonstrations, often at great sacrifice, drew the indifferent masses into the movement. In the West, on the other hand, the founding Congress's resolution on May Day was already challenged at the 1891 Brussels Congress by two of the most important delegations. The Germans and the English proposed to shift the date of the May celebrations to the first Sunday. In fact they never attempted to make the first of May a non-working day, since this might require material sacrifices. [August] Bebel and [Paul] Singer openly declared that the German Party could not recognise a decision which removed from individual parties the right to make their own decisions on the form of the May Day celebrations.

Nor was the Second International ever a *programmatically* uniform entity. It was a variegated mixture of the most diverse conceptions. Only on the left was there a clear line of demarcation, from the *anarchists*, with the division in practice completed at the first Congress. And when the anarchists nevertheless tried to attend international socialist congresses, the decision was confirmed in principle. In 1893 at Zürich acceptance of political and parliamentary action to conquer power was made a condition of admission and the definitive *exclusion of anarchists* from the Congresses of the Second International followed in 1896 in London.

In contrast, the position adopted on the right, i.e. *in relation to the reformists*, was never *fundamentally* clarified or established *organisationally* within the Second International during the entire period of its existence. This can be explained by the situation and tasks of the movement at that time: as it was, for the present, a matter of the gathering the masses together and winning them to socialism rather than to direct revolutionary action. So it was possible for different tendencies to exist side by side within the framework of a broad international organisation. The rudiments of reformism were present in the Second International from the outset. Even at the founding congress, the great majority of the delegates were in favour of *fusion* with the reformist Congress of the Possibilists, meeting in Paris at the same time. Unification did not take place only because it was rejected by the reformists, who feared being in a minority. Nevertheless, under the impact of the long economic depression, *combative class* tendencies, based on the principles and tactics of *revolutionary socialism*, predominated in the Second International during the *first period* of its existence (1889–1904). Only during the *second period* of its existence (1904–14) did the situation change. With capitalism's sudden and powerful upturn and penetration of every part of the world, particularly the great colonial regions, and the associated *structural transformation of world capitalism*, the prospects for proletarian revolution in the near future seemed to decline.[3] The tempo of revolutionary struggle slowed down and *the victory of reformism* within the parties of the Second International was stamped on the whole course of development.

The relationship between the problem of *social reform*, international labour protection and other partial working class demands to *revolution* already surfaced in discussions during the first Congress. According to the introduction to the resolution adopted on this question, the achievement of these reforms was to be supported but only as a means to an end: for the present, the development of class consciousness, later the realisation of the final goal of socialism, the revolutionary conquest of power and the expropriation of the capitalist class. In 1891 in Brussels the final goal was still more strongly emphasised in compar-

---

3   See Grossmann 1931d, 'Bolshevism' section 7 above, pp. 255–260.

ison with legislation to protect labour and the resolution adopted declared that the main objective was the *class struggle* against capitalist rule and ultimately the overthrow of capitalism and the abolition of wage slavery.

The Brussels Congress adopted a similarly revolutionary stance on the question of *militarism*, in a resolution which contained a strict dissociation from bourgeois pacifism. The ultimate reason why wars take place was declared to be capitalist society; hence attempts to get rid of militarism and bring about lasting peace without simultaneously abolishing capitalism were bound to be *ineffective*. Workers were called upon to keep protesting energetically against any appetite for military action and to prevent the catastrophe of a world war by the only effective means: the victory of socialism. The Dutch made an extensive proposal: workers were called upon not simply to protest but rather to reply to a declaration of war with a *general, mass strike*. In justification, Domela Nieuwenhuis pointed out the danger of chauvinism within socialist parties ([emobodied in the German Social Democrat Georg von] Vollmar in Germany), which might lead socialists of different countries to engage in mutual slaughter when war broke out. Workers must therefore refuse to shoot at each other. The distinction between offensive and defensive wars was an emanation of chauvinism. Diplomats portray every war as defensive. The *civil war of the proletariat* against the bourgeoisie should therefore be preferred to war between nations. Liebknecht protested against the accusation of chauvinism, *meanwhile ignoring important problems on which Nieuwenhuis had touched*, problems which eventually led to the collapse of the International in 1914! The proposal was rejected, no doubt repelling many revolutionary elements away from the socialist movement and driving them to anarchism. It is, however, noteworthy that at that time, in 1891, no-one came out in support of the defence of the fatherland, which later became the gospel of the Second International.

Two years later, at the Zürich Congress of 1893, the same question again came up for discussion, in a session on the 'attitude of social democracy *in case of war*'. While the Germans wanted to retain the resolutions of the Brussels Congress, the Dutch proposed to respond to the outbreak of war with a general strike by workers and a military strike (a refusal to follow orders) by reservists. The German proposal, said Nieuwenhuis, in practice signified complete passivity in the face of war, as it did not suggest any concrete anti-war measures. As the strength of militarism depended on the army's reservists, the task of socialists was to prevent the mobilisation of the reserves. Railway workers could disorganise mobilisation by refusing to to follow orders. Liebknecht's and [Georgii] Plekhanov's objection that, in view of the superior strength of military states, refusal to follow orders was impracticable and would require heavy sacrifices, was not convincing, he said. Precisely when war broke out, the state would not possess organs capable of coercing 'reservists in every village who were refusing to follow orders'. The Belgian [Jean] Volders objected to the German conception that it was unnecessary to carry out any *specifically anti-militarist* propaganda. The majority at the Congress nevertheless voted against the general strike, against the view that anti-militarist work was necessary and in favour of the German resolution, with a Belgian addendum obliging social-ists in parliaments *to reject military budgets*. Nor did the London Congress of 1896 go beyond these decisions. The German Social Democrats, the leading party of the Second International, at that time already showed the tendency to shy away from all struggles and means (illegal action) which would entail sacrifices, out of fear of persecution, such as they had experienced under the Anti-Socialist Law.[4]

In the resolution on *'Political tactics'*, the Zürich Congress declared *against* the opportunist tactic of making *compromises with the bourgeoisie*, which would be a betrayal of the workers' cause. It strongly emphasised that parlia-mentary action should serve only as a means to the end of the emancipation of the working class. The London Congress in 1896 designated the *establishment of an international socialist republic* as the movement's goal and demanded that workers political activity should be *independent from all bourgeois parties*. At the same time, a change in attitude to the *state* and its organs was already apparent in 1893 and 1896. In contrast to the revolutionary Marxist conception of the state,[5] the *abolition* of the state and the instruments of its power was no longer desired; rather a positive *affirmation* of the state began, which sought to *'transform* the means of capitalist rule into ones for the emancipation of the proletariat', in the spirit of fundamentally reformist-democratic conceptions.

Even so, the revolutionary conception still predominated and the London Congress of 1896 decided in favour of 'the full *right of self-determination for all nations'*. On the *colonial question* it proclaimed that colonial policy was always conducted for the purpose of extending capitalist exploitation, on the pretext of promoting civilisation or religion.

In contrast to the clear *political* line, the resolutions on the *economic policy* of the working class lacked clarity. To deal with the international monopolies, the London Congress demanded organs of international control, which should work towards the *socialisation of these enterprises through legislation*. Evidently, therefore, this 'socialisation' would be put into effect on the basis of the existing economy, without the prior overthrow of capitalism. On the *agrarian question*,

---

4   [The SPD was banned between 1878 and 1890.]
5   See Grossmann 1931d, 'Bolshevism' section 7 above, pp. 255–260.

the transfer of the land to common ownership, and the organisation of the rural proletariat was called for in 1893 and 1896. Beyond that, variations in agrarian conditions from country to country made it impossible to work out an international action programme, the resolution stated, and each nation had to be left to establish the specific demands it wanted to raise.

Factional divisions within the International began at the fifth Congress, in Paris in 1900: a right wing, a centre and a left wing emerged. This was in connection with and a result of *structural changes* in capitalism in its imperialist phase. In all capitalist countries an aristocracy of labour, an upper stratum of skilled workers organised in trade unions, had arisen. It exerted an increasingly reformist influence on parties' practice, regarding their main task as the achievement of improved working conditions for factory workers and social insurance and labour protection, through *coalitions with bourgeois parties*, rather than *class struggle against the bourgeoisie*, the revolutionary conquest of power and the overthrow of capitalism. The intellectual leaders of reformism were Eduard Bernstein in Germany, Sidney Webb in England and Jean Jaurès in France. There the Socialist Party undertook the first great reformist experiment in the 'piecemeal' conquest of power by peaceful, democratic means, with the entry of the socialist [Alexandre] Millerand into the ministry ('ministerialism').[6] Under Point 9 of the agenda ('The Conquest of State Power and Alliances with Bourgeois Parties') the [1900 Paris] Congress adopted a position of principle on the question of socialist participation in bourgeois governments. While the proposal of [Enrico] Ferri and Jules Guesde forbade the entry of socialists into bourgeois ministries under all circumstances, Kautsky – previously a representative of revolutionary Marxism – now adopted an intermediate position (the 'centre') between reformism and Marxism, for the first time. His proposal, although it contained a personal condemnation of Millerand's 'dangerous experiment', by no means ruled out the participation of socialists in a bourgeois government in principle. In fact, it declared such participation not to be one of *principle* but of *tactics*, dependent on circumstances and left the decision to the individual parties rather than the International. Composed of 'if and buts', it was *the largest concession to reformism*. As Ferri said, Kautsky's 'rubber'[7] resolution was a combination of socialist principles with bourgeois tactics. It was enthusiastically supported by the French and German reformists. The Belgian reformist [Edward] Anseele regarded '*the break with the past*' as the most significant aspect of Kautsky's resolution. Guesde opposed it: socialism

---

6   [Millerand participated in the cabinet of Prime Minister Pierre Waldeck-Rousseau, as Minister of Commerce, in 1899.]
7   [A pun: 'rubber' is 'Kautschuk' in German.]

had certainly grown but it seemed to have lost in depth and backbone what it had gained in breadth. The class situation of the proletariat would not be changed by the entry of a socialist into a cabinet. For that, the conquest of central power and the *dictatorship of the proletariat* would be necessary. Kautsky's proposal was adopted by a large majority, without ending the passionate struggle between the two approaches. This was the *first great defeat* of the revolutionary wing of the International.

On questions of *colonial policy* and *militarism*, in contrast, the radical positions of earlier Congresses were maintained. A proposal, made by Jaurès and endorsed by [Aristide] Briand, to declare the *general strike* the most effective means of social revolution was rejected. At the next Congress, in Amsterdam in 1904, this position was partially revised. An 'absolute', i.e. one hundred percent, general strike was declared impracticable and the idea of a general strike as the *sole* means of social revolution, as propagated by anarchists, was rejected. A resolution, proposed by the Dutch delegate Henrietta Roland Holst, was, however adopted. It emphasised that, *alongside* trade union and political action, a *mass strike* in a large number of economically important enterprises could also, under some circumstances, be undertaken as an 'extreme measure' to secure significant reforms or resist reactionary assaults on workers' rights.

The majority resolution at the Paris Congress concerning 'ministerialism' had not brought about any [clear] decision: both [left and right] tendencies sought to claim it for themselves. So these contradictions had to be fought out again at the *Amsterdam* Congress (1904). In the meantime, in Germany, after the Social Democrats had won enormous victories in the 1903 elections, the 1903 Dresden Congress *condemned revisionist endeavours in general*, rejected the tactic of compromising with bourgeois society and accepted a *more sharply* formulated version of Kautsky's Paris resolution of 1900 against participation in [a bourgeois] government. During the discussion of 'International Rules for Socialist Tactics' at the Amsterdam Congress, the Guesdists now presented a proposal which contained the essence of the resolution of the Dresden Party Congress. After passionate debate this was accepted. The Amsterdam Congress of 1904 was the *highpoint* of the Second International's development. But, in contrast to the Second Party Congress of Russian Social Democracy, which took place almost at the same time in London (1903),[8] it failed to draw any *organisational conclusions* from the condemnation of revisionism. On the contrary, the so-called 'Unity Resolution' declared that 'it was essential that there should be only *one* socialist party in each country'. So, in the following period, it was

---

8   See Grossmann 1931d, 'Bolshevism' section 4 above, pp. 247–249.

possible for the reformists to undermine the party from within. The narrow majority against revisionism did show the preponderance of the revolutionary wing, but also the growing strength of reformism.

This proved to be the case in the handling of the *colonial question*, since, as was correctly stated at the Congress, 'the position of social democracy on the colonial question is a reflection of its whole development'. The opportunist resolution of the English Fabians was adopted *unanimously*. It did condemn the pillage of India by England and the 'infamous colonial system' in general but it only referred to '*self-government* ... by the Indians themselves (*under British supremacy*)',[9] whereas the London Congress of 1896 had called for the *full right of self-determination* for all nations. A second resolution, justified by [Henri] van Kol, indicated positive measures to improve the situation of colonial peoples, did likewise condemn imperialist predation and impose upon socialists the duty of protecting the native peoples from attrocities and being plundered but, within the perspective of complete emancipation of the colonies, it was meanwhile their duty to 'support *the degree* of freedom and autonomy *appropriate to their stage of development*'.

4   **The Decade of Victorious Reformism in the Second International (1904–14)**

The Stuttgart Congress in 1907 marked a decisive *turn to the right, toward reformism*, in the development of the Second International, under the pressure of the increasingly tense world situation and the growing antagonisms within capitalist countries. This was underlined by the swerve to *reformism*, which Bebel and Kautsky – previously representatives of the 'centre' of German Social Democracy, the leading party of the Second International – almost suddenly made after 1905 and their unity with it against the left wing.

Imperialist antagonisms intensified around the end of the nineteenth and the beginning of the twentieth centuries and the *era of military collisions* started in 1894: the Sino-Japanese War, 1894; the Greco-Turkish War, 1896; the Spanish-American War, 1898; the British war against the Boers, 1899; the invasion of China by the Great Powers, 1900; the Russo-Japanese War, 1904; Italy's Tripolitanian War, 1911;[10] the Balkan Wars, 1912[–3]. Rising military tension was

---

9   [International Socialist Congress 1904, p. 48. Grossman's emphasis.]
10   [The Tripolitanian War was the Italian invasion of the Ottoman Turkish province which is now Libya.]

also apparent in diplomatic arrangements: the loosening of the Triple Alliance[11] through France's colonial concessions to Italy in 1902; the Anglo-French Entente Cordiale of 1904 and its extension to Russia in 1906;[12] and the military tension between Germany and France in 1905 over the Morocco question. All this gave rise to feverish preparations for war on land and at sea.

The socialists, with their vision sharpened by the Marxist historical method, recognised the significance of these events and untiringly drew the attention of the masses to the increasing threat of a world war.

Sharpening of domestic class antagonisms in all capitalist countries *paralleled* with this rising international tension: the great advances of the socialist workers movement accelerated the process by which the entrepreneurs joined together in powerful cartels. This increasingly forced workers onto the defensive in all economic struggles. Politically too, the great election victory of German Social Democracy in 1903 and the Russian Revolution of 1905 led the terrified bourgeois parties to form more solid alliances. In German government circles the removal of universal manhood suffrage at the national level was under serious consideration, as well as a narrowing of the municipal franchise. It became ever clearer that the old trade union and parliamentary methods could not achieve any further improvements for the working class, which found that it was forced to look around for *new, more intense methods of struggle* against rising economic and political pressure from the bourgeoisie. This was the meaning of discussions about the political mass strike. It was clear, however, that if the state replied to the onset of political mass strikes and mass demonstrations with armed force, this would only be the *first* step in a tactic whose *last* must lead to a decisive *struggle for power* against the class enemy. And leaders of German Social Democracy recoiled in horror from this perspective of the final revolutionary struggle for power, precisely at the decisive moment. Hence the sudden turn. The trade union bureaucracy did not want to expose its positions, organisations and finances, conquered over decades of minor skirmishes, to the risk of a revolutionary struggle. They were therefore concerned to nip any attempt to intensify methods of struggle in the bud. *The Cologne Trade Union Congress in May 1905* declared a general strike to be out of the question. In contrast, at the *Jena Party Congress* of the same year, a victory over reformism was achieved for the last time and a resolution was adopted obliging Party members to carry on a broad *mass agitation for the*

---

11   [The Triple Alliance was among Germany, Austria-Hungary and Italy.]
12   [The 'Entente Cordiale', 'Cordial Agreement' was a series of formal arrangements between Britain and France which cleared the way for joint military action.]

mass strike. If there was a desire to implement this decision, directed against the Cologne trade union resolution then the resistance of the reformist trade union bureaucracy would have to be broken and determined preparations for revolutionary struggle made. This did not happen. Bebel and the Executive of the Party did not break the resistance of the trade unions; rather the opposite occurred: Bebel and the Executive bowed to the will of the trade unions. At a secret conference between the Party Executive and the General Commission of the Trade Unions, in February 1906, the Executive completely capitulated to the trade union bureaucrats, renouncing the mass strike, despite the Jena Congress decision, with the excuse that the state of organisation was, for the time being, not mature enough for it. The *Mannheim Party Congress*, in September 1906, accepted a resolution in these terms! Kautsky gave in to Bebel and withdrew his own resolution, which dealt with the relationship between the Party and the trade unions and stressed the primacy of the former.

With the transition of Bebel and the Executive from the centre to the right wing, the revolutionary backbone of the Social Democratic Party was broken. The phraseology of revolution continues to be used but everyone knew that the Party had shrunk back from the decisive struggle for power. The right, openly reformist wing of the Party, which had been condemned in *resolutions* passed by all previous congresses, emerged victorious in *practical* terms and gained more and more influence. As the *period of imperialist wars* set in around the turn of the century, the old Party leaders, who had for decades performed the historic task of gathering the proletarian masses together, during *the period of peaceful development*, were no longer capable of grasping the *new tasks of* a new period, requiring new forms of organisation and new methods of struggle.

This change of direction within its leading party could not remain without influence on the Second International, as was apparent soon after, at the 1907 *Stuttgart Congress*. The greatest historical event involving the working class movement since the Paris Commune, the *Russian Revolution of 1905*, took place between the Amsterdam and Stuttgart Congresses of the International. But the leaders of the Second International did not consider it necessary to take a position on the lessons of the Russian Revolution. After all, Bebel had declared at Jena that it was incorrect 'to say that the Social Democrats are working towards a revolution. This idea does not even occur to us. What interest can we have in bringing about a catastrophe in which the *workers will suffer first and foremost*?'[13] It was not desirable or necessary to learn anything from the revolution, as the decision to move in the opposite direction had already been made!

---

13   [Sozialdemokratische Partei Deutschlands 1905, p. 292.]

The complete about-turn was apparent in a particularly blatant form during the discussions on the two most important points of the agenda: the questions of war and colonialism. *Support for colonial policy* was at the core of reformist policy in all countries! Van Kol, who reported the position of its Colonial Commission to the Congress, asserted that there should be more than mere negative protests against atrocities and exploitation in the colonies, there should rather be a *positive reform programme* from the viewpoint of a 'socialist colonial policy': the colonies were necessary for the present social order because of their indispensable raw materials, as destinations for the emigration of Europe's surplus population, lastly, as markets for the growing output of European industry. The immediate transition from barbarism to socialism in the colonies was impossible. They had first to undergo the process of capitalist development. The 'old twaddle about colonial atrocities' was boring. In reply to Kautsky, who opposed colonial policy and advocated the civilisation of the colonies by introducing machinery, van Kol stated, to applause from the Congress, that colonies should 'be entered *with weapons in hand*', not machines, even if his opponent called that imperialism. Bernstein declared the necessity for civilised peoples to exert a certain degree of *tutelage* over uncivilised peoples. [Eduard] David argued for the 'civilising mission' of capitalist countries in order prevent the colonies from reverting to barbarism. Only a small minority demanded that colonial policy be *rejected in principle*, along the lines of the decisions of previous Congresses – unsuccessfully. The resolution adopted by the majority signalled the *victory of revisionism in the workers movement of the imperialist countries*.

The same about-turn was apparent in the discussion of the second question which was a focus of interest at Stuttgart: the question of *militarism* and international conflicts. The majority of the French delegation, with Jaurès and [Édouard] Vaillant, demanded the prevention of war 'by national and international socialist, working class actions and the use of all means, from parliamentary action to *mass strikes and uprisings*'. In contrast, it became increasingly clear that the majority of the German delegation did not want to specify any *concrete* tactic for the prevention war. Bebel identified with the defence of the fatherland, even if the state was bourgeois. His resolution referred only in *general terms* to the prevention of war by using 'means which seem most effective'. Here too, Bebel's abandonment of his revolutionary past and his fear of the use of extra-parliamentary, illegal methods of struggle was apparent. Mentioning the methods the Party had previous used, he explained that 'We cannot allow ourselves to be pushed into methods of struggle beyond these, which could have grave consequences for Party life and even in certain circumstances for the existence of the Party'. Bebel's speech was strongly attacked from all sides. [Gustave] Hervé said that the attitude of the German Social Democrats to militarism showed that they had become bourgeois. Bebel, he said, had issued a new slogan: 'Proletarians of all countries, murder each other!'

It was almost impossible to bridge deep conflicts among the delegates. Eventually a radical amendment to Bebel's resolution, introduced by [Vladimir Ilyich] Lenin and Rosa Luxemburg, made compromise and the unanimous adoption of the resolution possible. This *amendment* contained the demand that if war did break out 'the economic and political crisis brought about by the war should be *used* to arouse the masses politically and to *hasten the overthrow of capitalist class rule*'.

At Stuttgart the parties of the Second International, above all the French and German, took up definitive positions on the question of war, which was at the forefront of worldwide working class interest. This revealed the deep divisions within the Second International and its inability to act in a unified fashion against war and militarism. In contrast, the *Copenhagen Congress*, in 1910, was a congress of 'detailed work', on unemployment, the international results of laws for the protection of labour, the relations between cooperatives and the political party, and the stuggle against capital punishment. The victorious advance of reformism was apparent everywhere. On the *cooperative question*, a resolution was adopted that, on the one hand, affirmed that the cooperative movement can never bring about the emancipation of the workers but, on the other, that consumers' associations have the task of '*helping to prepare the democratisation and socialisation of production and exchange*'. Such a mixture of revolutionary and reformist conceptions allowed anyone to read into the resolution whatever they wanted.

With bourgeois nationalism advancing in Austria, the endeavours of the Czechs to achieve national independence also coloured the attitude of Czech Social Democracy and led to the splitting of the trade unions by the Czech socialists (Separatists). The nationalism of the Czech reformists was a reaction to the attitude of the German Social Democrats of Austria, who did not campaign for the unrestricted right of self-determination for all nations, because this would threaten the survival of Austria, and *advocated mere autonomy, however only within the framework of Austria*! The Copenhagen Congress condemned the attitude of the Czech Separatists in Austria, which contradicted trade union solidarity, and prounounced *against the split in the trade unions*. The Czech reformists retorted by openly refusing to submit to the decision of the Congress.

There was an epilogue to the decision of the Stuttgart Congress on the important question of the International's *conduct if war broke out*, in a debate during the discussions over – and the title of the agenda item is already characteristic of the turn that had already been completed – 'Courts of Arbitration and Disarmament'. The danger of war had come much closer since the previous Congress. The Romanians, Serbs and Bulgarians pointed out with great clarity the immediate threat of a *storm in the Balkans*. But the reformist corruption of the Second International prevented resolution of the differences between the French and German conceptions! [Georg] Ledebour, on behalf of the resolutions committee, proposed a series of methods of avoiding the outbreak of a war, such as obligatory courts of arbitration and universal disarmament, which had long been part of the programme of bourgeois pacifism. In contrast, Vaillant and Keir Hardie, in the name of the French and English majorities, asserted that they regarded extra-parliamentary action, a general strike by munitions and transport workers, as the particularly[14] effective means of opposing war. Jaurès, profoundly displeased since the Stuttgart Congress by Bebel's attitude, did not take part in the debate. Although he regarded legal, parliamentary means as inadequate, he was, on the other hand convinced that the German Social Democrats would refuse to adopt the illegal and revolutionary methods of struggle which he advocated. In fact, the representatives of Germany, Italy and Austria declared, in Copenhagen, that a resolution in favour of a general strike would brand the party with the mark of illegality and provide [the authorities with] the opportunity to engage in the most severe persecution. So the conflict between the two groups was, as before, unbridgeable. [Émile] Vandervelde, a skilled lawyer, thought he could resolve these conflicts with a diplomatic sleight of hand: the Hardie proposal, he said, is careless and superfluous because the Stuttgart resolution already contained the same point, although expressed in a more careful form, in that it allowed the use of 'all methods' against the war, consequently a general strike and indeed even an uprising. The Congress had not wanted to 'declare openly for a general strike' to avoid giving governments any excuse for engaging in repression! So the Hardie-Vaillant proposal was rejected and a resolution in the spirit of Ledebour's remarks was adopted *unanimously*. And the deep internal conflicts were concealed from the world by veiling them.

The conduct of German Social Democracy since Stuttgart was not dictated by fear of government repression alone, as Vandervelde affirmed. Rather German Social Democracy had 'traditionally' declared itself in principle opposed general and military strikes as means to prevent war. Fifteen years later,

---

14   [Instead of 'particularly', the word in the German and English minutes of the Congress, Grossman put 'only' cf. International Socialist Congress 1910, p. 32.]

the chair of the SPD, Otto Wels testified to this during the 'stab in the back trial' in Munich (1925).[15]

The International Socialist Bureau summoned the Second International, already dying from within, riddled with reformism since Stuttgart, to an *extraordinary congress* on 24 November 1912, in Basel, which would be its last. The motive for this Congress was the immediate danger of a world war, at a time when the international situation had worsened considerably as a result of Italy's war of conquest against Turkey in 1911[16] and the Balkan War of 1912. No discussions were to take place in Basel, the Congress was to have the character of an *international demonstration* against the threat of world war.

In the *Manifesto of the International* adopted unanimously by the Basel Congress, there was a general overview of the dangerous situation in Europe, the decisive paragraphs of the Stuttgart resolution were cited and ceremoniously confirmed: to fight against war by all means, if war still occurred, to make use of the war to hasten the social revolution. That was the last word of the Second International.

5   The Collapse of the Second International under the Impact of the World War

When, after events in Sarajevo and the outbreak of war between Austria and Serbia on 28 July 1914, Germany declared war on Russia; when German troops marched into Belgium on 3 August; when the World War, which socialists had predicted for a decade, finally became a reality, the great parties of the Second International, in France and in Germany, *voted for war credits*! Despite all the anti-war resolutions of the First International in 1867 and 1868; despite the decisions of all Congresses of the Second International from 1889 to 1900; despite the resolutions in Stuttgart in 1907 and Copenhagen in 1910, obliging socialists to reply to the outbreak of war by hastening the social revolution; despite the solemn, ceremonial oath in Basel in 1912, which mobilised 'all the moral forces of the world' to 'resist the *crime* of a world war with the whole of their strength'; despite all this, the parties of the Second International and their leaders went over to the camp of the imperialist bourgeoisie, which they

---

15   [A libel case, which the author of a publication claiming that the SPD, democrats and Jews had led to Germany's defeat in World War I by stabbing it in the back brought against the editor of an SPD newspaper in Munich, for identifying this claim as a falsification of history.]

16   [That is, the invasion of Tripolitania.]

themselves regarded as responsible for the outbreak of the War.[17] Proclaiming
their 'will to victory' and their determination to 'stay the course' they placed
themselves on the side of the ruling classes and their governments, which they
had until very recently branded as criminal. They concluded a *civil truce* with
them and cooperated with them as the working classes engaged in mutual
annihilation at the front. The international organisation built up over decades
of working classes effort and the solidarity, was destroyed within a few days.
The Second International collapsed ingloriously. This collapse in practice was
soon followed by a theoretical collapse, when the theoretician of the Second
International, Kautsky, put forward the thesis in 1915 that the International was
'essentially an *instrument* for peacetime' but 'not an effective tool for use during a war'![18] Seldom in the whole history of political movements can a more
blatant contradiction between word and deed, a more open defamation of the
movement's own past, an example of a more complete failure to put into effect
principles proclaimed for a quarter of a century be found.

---

17   See Grossmann 1931a, 'Adler' above, pp. 208–209; Grossmann 1932a, 'Guesde' above, pp.
      349–353; Grossmann 1932c, 'Hyndman' above, pp. 358–360; and Grossmann 1932i, 'Plek-
      hanov', below, pp. 419–422.

18   [Kautsky 1915, p. 38. Kautsky emphasised the whole of the first quotation. This pamphlet
      was originally published as an article, Kautsky 1914.]

CHAPTER 27

The Internationals:
The Third (Communist) International (Comintern)
'The International of the Deed'*

Translated from German by Ben Fowkes

1   The Precursors of the Third International

Even in countries where the Social Democrats had decided in favour of neutrality, such as the Netherlands, the same imperialist considerations which guided the other parties of the Second International were decisive, rather than the principles of socialism and the interests of the working class. The central social democratic organ, *Het Volk*,[1] argued in favour of neutrality because a conflict with England would directly endanger the Netherlands' *colonies*!

Only a few socialist groups and parties held firm to the resolutions of the International Socialist Congresses by defending proletarian internationalism and opposing the World War. Thus the socialists of *Serbia* and *Romania*, the *Bulgarian* Party of the 'Narrow' Socialists, the small group of Dutch 'Tribunists' and the Socialist Party *of Italy*. A proletarian opposition against the war, led by Karl Liebknecht, Rosa Luxemburg, Franz Mehring and Clara Zetkin, developed slowly in Germany under the pressure of the state of siege. But only one party, the *Russian Bolsheviks*, immediately took up the struggle against the war and the Tsarist government in the Duma and started revolutionary work among the masses of workers and in the army. Moreover, as early as September 1914 they began to systematically explore the ultimate implications of their strategy and tactics in the struggle against the imperialist war.[2]

Clara Zetkin made the first attempt to organise an *international conference* during the war, when she called together an *international women's* conference

---

*   [Originally published as Grossmann 1932e. Quotations from minutes of congresses are not generally referenced separately; unless otherwise indicated, their sources are listed in Grossman's bibliography at the end of the chapter. All emphases in these quotations are Grossman's.]

1   [*'Het Volk'* means *'The People'*.]

2   See Grossmann 1931d, 'Bolshevism' section 7 above, pp. pp. 255–260.

in Bern in March 1915, which was soon followed by a *conference of socialist youth organisations*, also in Bern, in April. Only between 5 and 8 September 1915, did the first international conference of revolutionary socialists meet in Zimmerwald on the initiative of the Italian Socialist Party and with the support of the Swiss socialists. Eleven countries were represented by 31 delegates (Russia, Germany, Italy, Switzerland, France, Poland, Sweden, Norway, the Netherlands, Bulgaria and Romania). The Conference played a major role in bringing together the revolutionary elements of the defunct Second International. The so-called Zimmerwald (Leninist) Left advanced the slogan of the transformation of the imperialist war into a civil war and called for all revolutionary elements to join together in an independent organisation, a new, revolutionary proletarian international. The majority, consisting of pacifists, did not go that far *but* the *manifesto* adopted unanimously by the conference branded the War as imperialist, condemned the treason of the Social Democrats who had voted for the war credits and summoned workers to determined struggle for a peace without annexations. The next, *Kienthal* Conference, (24–30 April 1916), condemned the governmental socialists even more strongly. Its resolution on peace unanimously declared that courts of arbitration, disarmament and the democratisation of foreign policy could bring no lasting peace *on the basis of capitalism*. Lastly, it proclaimed the slogan that the *economic consequences of the war* should not be borne by the *defeated people*, i.e. the working classes, but by the *possessing* classes, through the cancellation of war debts.

2   The First Two Congresses of the Third International (1919/1920)

Only after they came to power in Russia through the October Revolution of 1917 could the Bolsheviks attempt to realise the idea of recreating an international, which they had propagated since 1914 and particularly since the 1915 'Declaration of the Zimmerwald Left'.[3] The circumstance of revolutionary ferment among the organised working class everywhere in the defeated states (Germany, Austria, Hungary, Bulgaria), at the end of 1918, and also in the victorious states (Italy and France) worked in their favour, generating much sympathy for Bolshevism. In many countries of central and western Europe, and in the Balkans, large parts of the Social Democratic Parties abandoned their previous ties and organised themselves as Communist Parties. On 24 January

---

3   See Grossmann 1931d, 'Bolshevism' section 7 above, pp. pp. 255–260. [Zimmerwald Left 1915.]

1919, in order to counter the Bern Conference,[4] the Central Committee of the Russian Communist Party issued a call for the founding of a communist international. Between 2 and 6 March 1919 the first *international communist congress* was held in Moscow, in the midst of the blockade of Soviet Russia by the Entente. Revolutionary groups and Communist Parties were only sparsely represented, owing to difficulties with passports and other obstacles. The delegates from 19 countries only represented a small minority of the proletariat organised in them. Nevertheless, they embodied the *greatest revolutionary power* the proletariat had ever possessed, as the ruling party of a gigantic country, the Russian Communist Party was in their midst. This expressed the fact that the leadership of the international revolutionary movement, which had been successively held in the nineteenth century by the English, the French and, after 1871, the Germans, had, thanks to the victory of the October Revolution, in practice passed on *formally* to the Russian proletariat, with the foundation of the Third International. The participants in the Zimmerwald and Kienthal Congresses who appeared in Moscow declared that, with the establishment of the new International, the Zimmerwald movement had been liquidated. The *organisational* form of the new International was not initially determined more precisely. In contrast, the Congress laid down *fundamental guidelines* for the movement, indicating its particular tasks in the current epoch and opposition to social democracy ('Platform of the Communist International'). The Communist International (Comintern) adopted the main slogans of the October Revolution in Russia and its methods of struggle. Following the example and learning from the experiences of the Russian Revolution, the Comintern took on the organisation and leadership of the world revolution. Lenin, in particular, presented theses on 'Bourgeois Democracy and the Dictatorship of the Proletariat' as a supplement to the point on 'The Road to Victory' in the 'Platform'. These indicated that dictatorship had played a great part in all revolutions and that the bourgeoisie, in both the English revolution of the seventeenth century and the great French revolution of the eighteenth century, were only able to break the resistance of the feudal nobility and the monarchy with the help of terror and dictatorship. At present, too, democracy is only a surface appearance; as soon as the rule of the bourgeoisie is threatened, its dictatorship becomes visible. For the working class, therefore, the choice is not democracy *or* dictatorship but the dictatorship of the *bourgeois* classes or the dictatorship of the *proletariat*. The bourgeoisie only *talks* about democracy, while in fact

---

4 [The Bern Conference of 3–9 February 1919 was the first step towards the revival of the Second International. See below, p. 387.]

it subjugates the working class in the economy, bureaucracy, justice system and education system. Genuine, proletarian democracy, can only be realised by abolishing the apparatus of the bourgeois state and power, and replacing it with workers and peasants coucils. Only the *council system*[5] can secure the participation of the broad masses in the administration of the state.

A particularly fierce struggle was declared against the conference of governmental socialists and centrists – which Lenin called the 'Yellow International' – meeting at the same time in Bern. It was the task of Communists to split the revolutionary elements off from the centre, by mercilessly criticising and exposing the centrist leaders. On the other hand, the governmental socialists, as a counter-revolutionary party, would need to be rendered harmless by means of armed force. The Congress issued a 'Manifesto of the Communist International to the Proletariat of the Entire World', which located the three internationals historically and characterised the specific task of the present epoch as the overthrow of capitalism. The First International predicted future developments and indicated the path they would take; the Second International *assembled and organised* millions of proletarians; the Third International is the international of mass action and revolutionary *realisation*, the international *of the deed*. The socialist *critique* of the deficient foundations of the bourgeois world order has already fulfilled its task. The present task of the international Communist Party is to *overthrow this order* and erect the *socialist order* in its place. The Third International regards itself as the successor and the executor of the programme originally proclaimed in the *Communist Manifesto* of 1848.[6]

The Third International and its Executive Committee, headed by Zinoviev, unleashed unusually extensive activity and propaganda over the whole world and created, in its periodical *The Communist International*,[7] issued in four languages simultaneously since August 1919, a special scientific organ for the investigation of all the problems of the international movement, an organ which has contributed greatly to increasing the profundity of thought in the sphere of international proletarian politics.

In contrast to the vacillating attitude of the Bern Conference and its conception which counted on the reconstruction of capitalism, events that followed the first Congress appeared to justify the Bolsheviks' prognosis that Europe was on the verge of a world revolution. The Spartacus Rising in Berlin (January 1919) was followed by the establishment of council republics in Budapest

5   ['Council' is 'soviet' in Russian.]
6   [Marx and Engels 1976.]
7   [*The Communist International* appeared in German, Russian, French and English. The contents of the editions in different languages were not always the same.]

(March 1919), with Béla Kun, and in Bavaria (April 1919), as well as uprisings in Dresden and other parts of Germany. Although the two council republics only survived for a short time, they were regarded as the first signs of a more general movement by many European workers. The heroic struggle of Soviet Russia against the entire Entente[8] and the counter-revolutionary revolts of [Nikolai] Yudenich, [Aleksandr] Kolchak and [Anton] Denikin supported by them aroused widespread sympathy for the Soviet Union[9] among European workers. This was expressed in the 'international strike' of 21 July 1919 against the *blockade* of the Soviet Union by the Entente. The capacity of the Third International to attract support increased rapidly. In some countries, such as Italy and Switzerland, entire socialist parties expressed their solidarity with the Third International. In Germany, Poland, Czechoslovakia, Bulgaria, Finland, Sweden, the Netherlands and the United States of America large sections of the socialist parties broke with them and formed *separate Communist Parties*. In France, Spain, Italy, the USA and Central and South America people who were previously syndicalists were on the path to abandoning their former viewpoint and joining the Comintern. The revolutionary situation became more and more acute during 1920. There were general strikes in the Balkans in February; in Germany the Communist uprising in the Ruhr (after the Kapp *putsch*) in March; mass strikes in Italy in the spring; and the general strike for the nationalisation of the railways in France in May. Finally, the victory of the Red Army over all its internal enemies, who had been supported by the Entente, and its victorious advance on Warsaw appeared to justify the perspective of an impending European social revolution, in which the workers of the west would join Soviet Russia in a general revolutionary war for the establishment of a soviet Europe.

In this revolutionary atmosphere, the *second Congress of the Communist International* assembled in Petrograd (19 July 1920) and then in Moscow, in the Kremlin (23 July to 7 August 1920). The popularity of the Communist International had grown considerably. 218 delegates from 37 countries attended. They included explicit Communists and left radicals; innumerable left socialist groups, such as Independents from Germany (Crispien and Dittmann) and representatives of the Independent Labour Party from Britain, which had left the Bern International and were requesting admittance to the Third International; radical and revolutionary trade union groups, like the British shop stewards' committees, the American Industrial Workers of the World (IWW), the French,

---

8   [The 'Entente' was the victorious alliance in World War I.]
9   [More precisely, the Russian Socialist Federal Soviet Republic, which became part of the newly constituted Soviet Union in 1922.]

Spanish and Italian Syndicalists. And, as the first swallows of a *new summer in the east*, representatives of the coloured peoples of Africa and Asia, from Turkey, Egypt, Persia, India, China, Japan and Korea, who regarded the Third International as a powerful centre in the struggle for the liberation of all the oppressed races and nations of the world. Even at the height of its success, at the time of the 1904 Amsterdam Congress, the Second International was essentially an expression of the socialist parties of *Europe*. Of 475 delegates, 460 were from nineteen European countries, eleven from the United States of America, two from Argentina and one each from Australia, Canada and Japan. At Copenhagen in 1910, of 896 delegates, 871 were from 21 European countries, 24 from the United States of America and one from Argentina. The 37 countries at the Second Comintern Congress expressed the fact that it really was a *world congress*, and a centre of attraction for the peoples of Africa and the orient. The Third International had become fashionable, so to speak. But unlike the socialists, who always regarded a mass influx of members as a success, Lenin saw in this a danger: that the Third International might be watered down by vacillating groups, which had not yet given up the ideology of the Second International. In order to prevent the Comintern from becoming a gathering point for all these indecisive elements, the Congress adopted statutes and 21 conditions, to which parties and organisations had to subscribe if they were to be accepted into the Comintern. The purpose of the conditions was to preserve the revolutionary character of the workers parties as *fighting detachments* in the epoch of impending struggles for the conquest of power. The same *conflict over organisational principles* which had been fought out between Bolshevism (Lenin) and Menshevism (Martov) within Russian Social Democracy in 1903[10] was now repeated on a world scale, in the conflict over the organisational principles of the International. These requirements did *not arise from specifically Russian conditions*: democratic *centralism* and the absolute unity of the Party; iron military discipline as a guarantee for the implementation of decisions arrived at and the maintenance of revolutionary tactics; an irreconcilable struggle against all forms opportunism, inherited from the thirty year tradition of the Second International; the combination of *legal* and parliamentary work with *illegal* revolutionary activity, particularly in the army, irrespective of all the repressive measures of the organs of the bourgeois state (martial law, states of emergency); the alliance of workers with the village proletariat and the poorest peasants. They resulted rather *from the practical task of organising the revolution*, which arose for every proletarian party in every country under the

10   See Grossmann 1931d, 'Bolshevism' section 4 above, pp. 247–249.

conditions of *civil war*. They were necessary in Russia before the 1905 Revolution, when they appeared incomprehensible in the countries of western and central Europe, which were still in a pre-revolutionary epoch. As soon as these countries moved towards revolution they became relevant. These tendencies were strengthened by the *experiences* of the War and postwar period, which demonstrated that toleration of opportunist elements in the workers parties had led to the collapse of the great socialist parties of the Second International, in 1914, and were also one of the causes of the defeat of the German and Hungarian revolutions of 1918–9. The statutes of the Communist International therefore specified its goal as the struggle to overthrow the international bourgeoisie and the creation of an international soviet republic by all means, including armed force. To achieve this goal it was necessary for the Congress to clarify the relationship between *party* and *class* ('Theses on the Role of the Communist Party in the Proletarian Revolution'). The Party, the theses stated, must not simply be the masses' advocate; as their leader, it must *be ahead of them* and show them the way forward. Organisationally it must break with the Second International's theory and practice of individual, *autonomous* national parties. There are no questions of international significance and questions of purely national significance, which can be decided by national parties without the intervention of the International. The Comintern must therefore have a centralised organisation and it must constitute a *united party for the entire world*, on the model of the First International. Individual national parties can only be *sections* of it. The same is true of the *trade unions*. The neutrality of trade unions is a bourgeois ideology. The trade unions must be subordinated to the Party. Therefore the red trade unions set up on a Communist basis must only be constituted as a particular section of the Comintern, likewise the Youth International and the women's organisation. World Congresses, the highest governing body of the Comintern, and the Executive Committee of the Communist International (ECCI), which directs the Communist International between Congresses, must be concerned with unity in international action and ensure that all sections implement the decisions adopted by the International. In order to secure *international discipline*, the statutes give these two central authorities the right to expel people and groups in breach of its decisions from the Communist International and consequently from their national sections. They therefore constitute the real centre of a gigantic world organisation, a *'general staff of the revolution'*! The 21 *conditions of admission* to the Communist International have the same purpose. They emphasise only those aspects of social democratic traditions which were the most difficult to overcome. They are intended to act like a sieve: to keep out the opportunists and only admit genuinely revolutionary elements into the Communist International and, at the same, provide a guarantee against the well-known opportunist practice of agreeing to a decision popular with the masses, in order to retain influence over them, then sabotaging its implementation.

If, on the one hand, the Communist International must be a cadre of revolutionaries, a solid, united *fighting organisation of the elite of the working class*, of its most advanced and class conscious elements, on the other it must not be *isolated from the masses*. Communists must, therefore, be active in all existing associations and organisations which include large proletarian strata that are outside the Party, *even if these organisations have no party character* or even have a reactionary characteristics, in order to influence them and to utilise them for the educational work of the Communist International. For the same reason, Communists in every country should enter *trade unions* which are under the opportunist leadership of the trade union bureaucracy, to win influence over the masses and to remove the old bureaucracy, which makes peaceful agreements with employers instead of leading the struggle *against* them. It is therefore impermissible to create *separate* trade unions artificially, without having been forced to by the terrorism of the trade union bureaucracy (e.g. the expulsion of revolutionary groups). A *Red International of Labour Unions* (RILU), also called the *Professional International* (Profintern), was set up in opposition to the Amsterdam Trade Union International, to bring together all those unions organised outside the Amsterdam framework, such as the Russian trade unions, with their many millions of members, and the trade unions founded under Communist influence in parts of Asia and Africa, which had never possessed a trade union before.

The Congress demanded an organisational break with all reformist, centrist and social pacifist elements, on the one hand, at the same time it also drew a dividing line which separated Communists from the *anarcho-syndicalists*, by imposing the obligation to make use of parliaments and *political action* for the revolutionary movement. The resolutions on the agrarian question advocated an alliance of the urban proletariat with the small and middle peasants as well as the village proletarians, without which power could not be conquered and retained in capitalist countries. These resolutions were the results of the *strategy of proletarian class struggle* based on the experiences of the Russian Revolution and also nineteenth century revolutionary struggles in Western Europe. The Second International, did not previously and does not at present have a revolutionary strategy because it never seriously posed the question of revolution and of the revolutionary conquest of power by the proletariat.

While the industrial proletariat of capitalist countries sought allies against the class enemy at home, a resolution on the *colonial question*, indicated the necessity of winning allies among colonised peoples. The Communist International would mobilise hundreds of millions of people in the colonies through the struggle for the unrestricted *right of self-determination* of *all* nations.

3   The Episode of the Two and a Half International:[11] The
       International Working Union of Socialist Parties

The centrists, under the pressure of the masses, who were demanding affiliation with Moscow, asked for admittance to the Third International at the second Congress of the Comintern. They spoke of their readiness to engage in revolution and 'recognised' the dictatorship of the proletariat, based on the council system. But in reality they had not altered their previous practice of cooperating with the bourgeois classes, as was soon apparent in the attitudes of the Unabhängige Sozialdemokratischen Partei Deutschlands (USPD), in Germany,[12] and particularly the Italian Socialists. When the Italian workers went over to the *armed occupation of factories and the latifundia*, in September 1920, when the bourgeoisie was completely disorganised and both the soldiers and the peasants were in sympathy with the proletariat, the leaders of the Italian trade unions, in return for some meaningless promises from the government, succeeded in terminating the struggle. Such conduct not only had to lead the *Comintern to break with the centrists* in Italy but everywhere. The most important centrist parties, the Independent Labour Party (ILP) in Britain, the USPD, and the Sozialdemokratische Partei der Schweiz,[13] decided at a preliminary conference in Bern (5–7 December 1920) to set up an International Working Union of Socialist Parties (IWUSP), which had left the Second International without joining the Third International. They were later joined by the Sozialdemokratische Arbeiterpartei Österreichs and the Russian Mensheviks.[14] The IWUSP declared that the Second International was dead but also that the decisions of the second Congress of the Comintern arose from specifically Russian conditions and were therefore *inapplicable* to other countries; for example, the decisions on organisational centralism, which abolished the autonomy of national parties and trade unions. An *international conference in*

---

11   [The mocking designation 'Two and a Half International' was coined by the Communist Karl Radek, Radek 1922.]
12   ['Unabhängige Sozialdemokratischen Partei Deutschlands' means 'Independent Social Democratic Party of Germany'.]
13   ['Sozialdemokratische Partei der Schweiz' means 'Social Democratic Party of Switzerland'.]
14   ['Sozialdemokratische Arbeiterpartei Österreichs' means 'Social Democratic Workers Party of Austria'. Other parties were founding members of or later joined the IWUSP.]

Vienna (22–27 February 1921) established the 'Working Union' of these parties, i.e. the international association of centrist elements. The proceedings of this, the only conference of the IWUSP, clearly demonstrated its lack of any leading political idea on which the Working Group could be based: it only endeavoured to take an intermediate position between the Second and Third Internationals, the line of 'on the one hand – on the other hand' (hence the label 'Two and a Half International'). The resolution on 'Imperialism and Social Revolution' repeated, in a watered-down form, the the Communist International's line of reasoning. It declared itself opposed to the military policies of the ruling classes, the 'defence of the fatherland' and civil peace, and in support of using the revolutionary crisis for the conquest of political power. It was decided, at the same time, that parties standing on the ground of social patriotism *could not be admitted* into the IWUSP.

The 'guidelines' on 'The Methods and Organisation of Class Struggle' adopted after Friedrich Adler's report stressed the *inadequacy* of exclusively employing the *democratic* methods of the restored Second International, because the bourgeoisie would 'break' democracy wherever there was a threat that democracy might be used against it. This was a recognition that the working class could no longer conquer power through the ballot box but 'only through direct action (mass strikes, armed rebellions etc.)' and that it could only maintain it against the conquered bourgeoisie *'through dictatorship and repression'*. Despite this recommendation of Bolshevik principles of struggle, the guidelines opposed any 'stereotyped imitation' of the Russian Revolution, without clarifying this contradiction. In relation to organisation, too, Adler endeavoured to distance himself from the traditions of the Second International: the decisions of international conferences must be binding and the autonomy of the separate national parties was thus restricted. Nevertheless, he rejected the 'centralism of the Third International'. Indeed, Richard Collingham Wallhead, of the ILP, openly declared that no international decisions would bind the ILP. As regards the Russian Revolution, the Conference regarded the possible defeat of the Soviet Union as a victory for world reaction, and therefore declared that the *defence of the Soviet republic was one of the tasks of the International*. Nevertheless, the IWUSP necessarily had to be hostile *to the proletarian state*, since it included the Russian Mensheviks. Later on, in fact, after the IWUSP merged with the Second International, an open struggle against Soviet Russia became one of the main tasks of the united International!

This contradictory attitude of the IWUSP can be explained by its *fear of a decisive fight for the conquest of power*. For, despite its revolutionary phrases, despite its recognition *'in principle'* of the main slogans of the Third International – the dictatorship of the proletariat, the council system, the necessity for social revolution and armed uprising – *in fact* it stood on the same ground of social patriotism and civil peace as the Second International, which it condemned, because it shrank back from the final struggle for power. This was despite its condemnation of the Second International and despite its verbal revolutionism. After scarcely two years, therefore, the IWUSP returned to the bosom of the International of the governmental socialists (final conference of the IASP in Hamburg, 20 May 1923). The declaration of the minority, led by Ledebour, protesting the decision to merge with an International in whose ranks there are 'malicious fascist organisations', was not even allowed to be read out! With this fusion, which in fact signified the collapse of the ideology of centrism, the brief episode of the 'Two and a Half International' came to an end.

4   The Postwar Reconstruction of the Second International: The
       Labour and Socialist International (LSI)

Attempts to rebuild the Second International began immediately after the end of the World War. Using an expression of Friedrich Adler, 'the shipwrecked survivors of the old International'[15] came together at the *conference in Bern* (3– 9 February 1919) to take a position on the discussions of the Great Powers at Versailles and to influence the Versailles peace settlement, as did the *conference in Lucerne* (2–9 August 1919). The German, French and Austrian centrists no longer participated in the next conference, in Geneva (31 July–4 August 1920), because they were in negotiations with Moscow over admission to the Comintern, whose failure led to the foundation of the Two and a Half International. The Labour and Socialist International (LSI) was only established at the Congress in Hamburg (21–25 May 1923), with the fusion of the 'Two and a Half International' with the remains of the old Second International. The Amsterdam International Federation of Trade Unions (IFTU) declared its readiness to cooperate with the LSI, while asserting its equality and full independence. The LSI held its second Congress in Marseilles in August 1925, its third in Brussels in August 1928 and its fourth in Vienna in July 1931.

It was characteristic of the political stance of the LSI that it continued prewar revisionism after the War, despite the obvious intensification of class conflicts in the meantime. In practice it sought to *cooperate with bourgeois parties* and to participate in bourgeois governments. This was already provided for in

---

15   [Quoted in Kay 1919, p. 30. The extract of Adler's speech in the original English version did not include the phrase Grossman quoted, but it is present in the longer extract in the German 'translation'.]

Article 15 of its statutes, which specifies that, in order to 'spare the LSI from the problem of ministerialism', members of its executive who become ministers immediately lost their positions on the executive, regaining it later once they are no longer in office. At the Vienna Congress Émile Vandervelde referred with pride to this 'closeness to government', to the fact that 'there are few socialist parties today which have not already spent some time in the government of their country'. This was a consequence of the LSI's fundamental conception of the tasks of socialist parties and of the *tendencies of economic development*, expressed particularly at its [1928] Brussels Congress under the influence of the long economic boom in America and the 1927 recovery in Germany. Hope in capitalist breakdown, it was said there, had turned out to be illusory: 'Capitalism has not yet played out its historical role.' It had, however, undergone a transformation 'in which elements of a socialist economy are already visible'. Owing to the growing influence exerted on the state and the economy by the working class, the new capitalism of the postwar era increasingly incorporated socialist elements. This 'organised capitalism', characterised by an ever greater degree of planning, was able to avoid crises because, thanks to unemployment insurance, it was able to shape workers' incomes according to plan and independently of the accidental fluctuations of the market. Peacefully and democratically, it was gradually 'growing into' a socialist economy through socialist parties' 'control of governments'.

In the *sphere of international politics*, too, the LSI takes on existing institutions and hopes to gradually reduce friction among nations and preserve peace through democracy and social reform, entirely in the spirit of bourgeois pacifism. The *League of Nations*, therefore, stands at the centre of the LSI's international policies, along with the questions placed on its agenda, from time to time by governments, such as reparations, international arbitration and disarmament. Admittedly, at the Hamburg Congress, Otto Bauer did state that in Austria, under the protection of the League of Nations, the reactionaries were growing stronger and that the League had degenerated into a centre of international reaction. [Henry] Brailsford pointed out that the League of Nations was a means of keeping small new states in a condition of economic and political dependence, through the military hegemony and still more through the financial strength of the great powers. Nevertheless, the resolution adopted expressed the hope that the League of Nations could be shaped into an instrument for securing peace and the rights of all nations by 'democratising its organisation'. The LSI, on the other hand, as a consequence of its *closeness to governments is beset by the same antagonisms* that divide capitalist states in the League of Nations. It protests against the 'imperialist peace' of Versailles, which it regards as a 'crime' and an 'instrument for extending war'. At the same time, its leading members include Vandervelde, one of those who drafted the dictated peace of Versailles, and Léon Blum, who affirmed that France was not imperialist and that 'the principle of reparations expressed an ideal conception'.

The LSI's open adaptation to the imperialist requirements of the colonial powers can be seen in the resolution on the *colonial question* adopted at the Brussels Congress in 1928. It did reject 'political domination over the colonial peoples *in principle*' but distinguished two groups, those from whom 'it is already possible to remove alien rule' and those who are not yet mature enough for freedom and must first be 'educated according to a plan' by their oppressors. It demanded the full right of self-determination only for China and India. For other colonies whose populations have a more progressive civilisation there is only to be a certain degree of self-government. For colonies 'without a developed civilisation', finally, there could be no self-administration at all, only a series of 'protective measures' (a code of rights of 'native people') under the control of the Permanent Mandates Commission of the League of Nations.

At the 1931 Vienna Congress, when the world economic situation had changed, the diagnosis of the tendency of capitalist development advanced in Brussels was abandoned; actually, an admission of the correctness of the economic perspectives of the Comintern at its 1921, 1922, 1924 and 1928 Congresses. Thus Otto Bauer declared that the period of postwar capitalism's 'temporary stabilisation' was now over. A period of most severe convulsions had begun (as if they had spoken at Brussels in 1928 of 'temporary stabilisation' rather than the beginning of a *rising era* of 'organised', 'new capitalism'!). [Otto] Wels asserted that 'the timbers of capitalist society were cracking' and that in Germany and Austria 'the death knell of capitalism' could be heard. This altered situation did not, however, lead to the conclusions that the breakdown of capitalism was accelerating, that a final struggle for power was necessary but that questions of tactics in the struggle for the conquest of state power must *take a back seat* 'this time' in face of the urgent task of the moment – saving democracy. In the situation of the worst economic crisis in the history of world capitalism, Otto Bauer did *not* seek to *transcend* capitalism with socialism in relation to the sector of capitalism most threatened by the world crisis – Germany. The world crisis of capitalism was rather to be *saved by the capitalists, by means of the capitalist instrument* of a big international loan and the reduction (not abolition!) of German reparation payments. In this way, capitalism or, as [Rudolf] Breitscheid expressed it, the *'economy'*, will be *saved*. Bauer as well as Breitscheid appealed to 'international capital' for solidarity, asking it to hasten to the aid of collapsing German capitalism, in its own interests, to ward off the threat of breakdown and the 'risk of civil war'. If, however, capitalism should prove incapable of mastering the crisis and the economic catastrophe and democracy nevertheless cave in, social democracy would then adopt *revolutionary* methods. Finally, the Congress called on governments to put into effect 'an immediate programme of constructive international action' to 'stem the world economic crisis'.

It is difficult to imagine a greater contradiction: they identifed the enormous world crisis as the *failure* of capitalism and, nevertheless, 'demanded' of this collapsing capitalism and its governments a programme for overcoming the crisis – a programme they did not possess themselves. Thus this *socialist Congress* in Vienna in fact turned into a *congress for the salvation of capitalism*! The opposition at the Congress – a small minority – headed by [James] Maxton (ILP) drew attention to this nonsense. He regarded the *overthrow* of capitalism, not its *salvation*, and the seizure of power by the working class as the only way out of the crisis.

[Louis] de Brouckère's report on *disarmament and the danger of war* revealed a similar contradiction and impotence. Armaments had increased in comparison with the period before the World War, he said, despite the promises enshrined in the Treaty of Versailles. The LSI must be careful not to put forward far-reaching demands for disarmament because they would not be fulfilled. It was, moreover, likely that even the modest programme of disarmament the LSI intended to propose to the League of Nations would end in failure. One should not, nevertheless, despair; again and again, after each failure, demands for disarmament should be initiated afresh.

Here too the obvious contradiction: disarmament resolutions are adopted by LSI Congresses, but where the parties of the LSI are members of or 'tolerate' governments, they vote for armaments, openly or in a disguised form! (The 'armoured cruiser Socialists' in Germany, the armaments policy of the Socialist Party of Poland (PPS) etc.) Pierre Renaudel rightly asked: 'Why work out new resolutions, when the old ones have not yet been carried out?' The opposition's declaration (from Switzerland) pointed out that the LSI, in placing its hopes in the *League of Nations*, instead of placing 'the chief burden' of the struggle against war on the *working class*, was giving rise to 'illusions and lack of clarity' in the working class, over the possibility of international disarmament carried out by capitalist governments.

5   The Comintern in the Changed World Situation (1921–8)

In 1920 the Red Army was beaten back before Warsaw. This strategic defeat was followed by a political decline in the international working class movement and a series of severe defeats in various European countries, above all the repession of the workers' rising in central Germany after the Kapp putsch (March 1921).[16] With the help of social democracy, the bourgeoisie had overcome the first revolutionary wave, the acutely revolutionary crisis of 1918–9, the struggle of the proletariat for power, and had reconstructed its state apparatus and power. Under these circumstances, the *Third Comintern Congress* met in Moscow from 22 June to 12 July 1921. Approximately 600 delegates, from 52 countries were present. The Congress had to take a position on the tasks of the international proletariat in a *completely different world situation*. The Russian proletariat could not count on immediate support from proletarian revolution in western Europe and Lenin proclaimed the transition to the New Economic Policy (NEP).[17] In the capitalist countries of Europe the workers movement also had a need for rest and bread, after so many years of hunger during the War and postwar period. Reformists were trusted anew, when they spoke of 'reconstruction'. So the Comintern had *to draw* conclusions from the *temporarily slower tempo of revolutionary development*. The *tactic* it chose depended on its diagnosis of the economic development of Europe over the next period. The ebb of the revolutionary tide led the Independent Social Democrats in Germany, like centrists everywhere, to decide that the revolution had *ended* and to complete a full swing to the right. Otto Bauer, the theoretician of the Two and a Half International, spoke of the bankruptcy of the Comintern, as the world revolution it had predicted had not come to pass. In this situation, the Communist International was faced with the question of whether its approach to revolution was correct. According to its conception, the slow-down in revolutionary development by no means signified a definitive *stabilisation* of capitalism. In his report to the third Congress on the 'The World Economic Crisis and the New Tasks of the Communist International', [Leon] Trotsky said that the collapse of capitalism was making further progress, that the recovery was only transitory

---

16   [The Kapp putsch, in March 1920, was an attempted coup, headed by former Prussian bureaucrat Wolfgang Kapp and General Walther von Lüttwitz. It was defeated by working class mobilisations, under the leadership of the social democratic trade unions. In March 1921, the Communist Party of Germany attempted to launch an uprising, known as the 'March Action', without mass support.]

17   See Grossmann 1931d, 'Bolshevism' section 9C above, pp. 272–274. [The New Economic Policy had been initiated in March 1921, before the Third Comintern Congress.]

and apparent, that the economic centre of the world had shifted from Europe to the USA and that all the previously leading economic powers had emerged economically and financially ruined from the War. A colossal level of unemployment had become a permanent phenomenon. The third Congress had absolutely no intention of abandoning the revolutionary perspective. According to Lenin's theory, the world revolution was not an event to be expected at a particular point in time but *a whole historical epoch* of declining capitalism, prevaded by civil wars and revolutions, during which *the revolutionary crisis and class antagonisms* intensify and attain ever higher forms, in spite of any temporary setbacks and defeats suffered by the proletariat. Furthermore, it was stated at the Congress, capitalism itself would soon destroy all reformism's hopes for its recovery. Capitalism everywhere had utilised the weakness of the workers movement and the proletariat's aversion to struggle by going over to the offensive, *worsening* workers' conditions of existence and imposing the cost of the World War on them. All the promises of the Second and Two and a Half Internationals that the situation would improve therefore had, inevitably, to remain unfulfilled. Thus workers would learn from *experience* that they could not improve their situation without revolutionary struggle. The mere fact of the origin and growth of mass Communist Parties in the most important countries was an expression of the intensification of class antagonisms and the maturation of the revolutionary epoch.

The *problem of tactics in the altered world situation* lay at the centre of discussions. During the first years after the war, Communists hoped the conquest of power would take place simply because the masses were revolutionary. The failure of the revolution is to be explained by the fact that the Communists who headed the movement were only a small group, that nowhere outside Russia were there well organised Communist Parties which could take over the *leadership*. The peculiarity of the present situation and the defeats of 1921 could be explained by the circumstance that, although large Communist Parties had emerged, they only constituted a vanguard, *isolated from the masses*. The conquest of power can, however, only be achieved by the masses and not by the struggles of their vanguard. The most important task of the third Congress was therefore to adapt the *tactical methods* of the Communist Parties to the new world situation, in the period of 'temporary retreat'. Not the immediate struggle for power but the slogan '*win the masses*' was now in the foreground, as the precondition for *revolution*. The Congress broke with currents, such as that represented by Paul Levi in Germany, which, despairing of revolution, went over to the camp of reformism. But it also rejected the putschist conception that the fight for power could be conducted by the vanguard alone, without the support of the broad masses. Hence it adopted the '*tactic of the proletarian united front'*, which initially led to major misunderstandings in the Communist Parties of some countries and gave rise to disagreements at several Congresses of the Communist International, but subsequently proved to be successful. When its opponents asked why, after breaking with them, it was now proposed to proceed hand in hand with the reformists, supporters of the united front tactic replied that what it did not involve reconciliation or organisational fusion, not even compromises or electoral agreements with the reformists. It was not a matter of agreements with the people 'at the top' of the reformist organisations but of 'unity from below', in the depths of the working masses. The Communist Parties should approach social democratic, syndicalist and non-party workers with the challenge to form a *common front of struggle against the bourgeoisie* in all their great and small daily struggles, over vital interests and specific demands, in order to satisfy the powerful urge of the working masses to unity in the struggle against the class enemy. Since the reformist leaders did not desire such a struggle and in fact side with the bourgeoisie, the united front tactic will expose their treacherous policies. As the masses do not learn from books and theories but from their own experiences, a gradual separation of them from their reformist leaders will result, first in daily *economic* and subsequently also *political* struggles, their mobilisation for the revolutionary struggle to achieve the seizure of power will succeed.

After the third Congress, at a Conference of the Enlarged Executive Committee of the Communist International (March 1922), the question of the *threat of a war against the Soviet Union* by the imperialist powers was raised. This never subsequently disappeared from the agenda of Congresses of the Communist International. The stronger Soviet Russia becomes, the greater the progress it makes in economic construction, the greater was the danger of an armed attack by a coalition of capitalist powers. It was therefore the task of the whole world proletariat to repel this attack with a counter-attack.

While the Comintern had its greatest difficulties in Germany and Italy in 1920 and 1921, the implementation of the united front tactic led to great friction in the French section of the International, in 1922. Similar differences arose in Italy, Norway and Czechoslovakia and led the Comintern to become divided into *factional groupings*, a right, centre and left, while at the same time a 'Workers Opposition' developed within the Russian Communist Party, which protested against the united front and 'bureaucratic' methods.[18] These internal difficulties were the main theme of the fourth Congress of the Comintern,

---

18   [The Workers Opposition existed between 1920 and 1922 and was primarily concerned with issues within Soviet Russia.]

which was held in Moscow from 5 November to 5 December 1922, immediately after the victory of fascism in Italy and during the celebrations of the fifth anniversary of the October Revolution. The Congress confirmed the 'progressive decay of the capitalist economy', without excluding the possibility of short lived periods of apparent upturn. Precisely the instability of its domination compelled the bourgeoisie to abandon the cover of legal and parliamentary methods and have recourse to open violence and to create illegal white guard[19] organisations. Fascism was not, therefore, a purely Italian phenomenon but rather *a danger with which the proletariat has to reckon in all capitalist countries.* The Congress approved the united front tactic but indicated the dangers involved in applying it. Finally, it advanced the slogan of a '*workers government*', as opposed to *coalition with the bourgeoisie*, which the social democrats advocated. Provided that there were guarantees that a 'workers government' would conduct a struggle against the bourgeoisie, such a collaboration between the Communists and the non-Communist workers parties would be a stage in the development of the united front tactic.

The Congress declared, further, that the fusion of the centrist elements (the Independents) with the open social traitors (the Majority Socialists), whether in Germany or in the international context (the merger of the Second and Two and a Half Internationals) was advantageous for the revolutionary workers movement. It would dissolve the fiction of a second revolutionary party alongside the Comintern. At a time of rapid revolutionary upsurge, under pressure from the masses, the centrists had declared themselves in favour of proletarian dictatorship and taken the road to the Third International but they had always adopted a vacillating position, obstructing revolutionary activities. Now that the wave of revolution had temporarily subsided, they had returned to the camp of the open reformists and revealed their true character to the masses.

As well as the 'Theses on Communist Action in the *Trade Unions*', the '*Theses on the Eastern Question*' and, as a supplement to the latter, '*Theses on the Black Question*' were of great significance. While the second Congress of the Communist International had only declared in principle that colonial peoples had the right of self-determination, the Comintern now proceeded to raise a *concrete tactical programme for the colonial question*, on the basis of an analysis of the real class forces in the countries of the east. Bourgeois national-revolutionary movements, which pursued national independence and unity, were to be supported by independent Communist Parties, to the extent that

---

19   ['White guard', a reference to the counter-revolutionary forces during the Russian civil
      war.]

the local bourgeoisie were conducting the struggle against imperialism and not trying to reach a compromise with it. A radical *agrarian programme* is to be raised in order to draw the broad peasant masses of the colonial countries into the struggle against imperialism, with the goal of an agrarian revolution, the expropriation of the big landowners to benefit of the peasant masses. The slogan of the *anti-imperialist united front* has the same function in the colonial countries as the tactic of the united front has in the countries of developed capitalism. The alliance with the proletariat of the west did not merely, therefore, have the task of shaking off the yoke of imperialism. The soviet system constituted, moreover, the most painless *form for the transition* of backward colonial peoples from their primitive conditions of existence to communism, the highest economic form. Marx never asserted that all nations and countries – independently of the circumstances of their historical milieu – had to pass through all economic stages (primitive economy, feudalism, capitalism, socialism) and that the only route to socialism was through capitalism. The assertion that there is no possibility for colonies to leap over the stage of capitalism was a reformist distortion of Marx's teachings.

Finally, this Congress also laid the foundation for *International Red Aid*, which was a neutral, non-party organisation devoted to providing financial and other kinds of assistance (struggle for the right of political asylum, amnesties etc.) for the growing number of casualties in the revolutionary struggle.

1923 was a year of severe defeats for the international proletariat. In Germany, after the occupation of the Ruhr by French troops and the tremendous fall in the value of the Mark in its wake, and the general strike organised by the Communists, the following uprising was bloodily suppressed by the government with the help of Social Democracy. Under different circumstances, a rising by peasants and workers in *Bulgaria* in September 1923 was also defeated by the local fascist government, headed by [Aleksandar] Tsankov, again with the active assistance of Social Democracy, whose representative Dimo Kazasov participated in the government. It was the defeat of the revolutionary workers movement in Germany, which had been the most important focus of unrest in Europe during the five years between 1918 and 1923, which created the conditions for the financial involvement of international finance capital in Europe and led to the adjustment of reparations by the acceptance of the *Dawes Plan* and the grant of international loans to Germany. This made [the resumption of] German reparation payments to the Allies as well as the *reconstruction* of Germany's finances and industry possible.

Not only the bourgeoisie but also the Social Democrats were of the opinion that the revolutionary ferment of 1919–23 was purely a sequel to the World War and was now well and truly over. Indeed, Hilferding advanced the thesis that *a*

new era of expansion of productive forces had begun for capitalism. In this situation, several hundreds of delegates from 55 countries gathered Moscow for
the *fifth Congress of the Communist International* (17 June–8 July 1924), some
months after Lenin's death. The Congress had to take positions on the defeats
mentioned above and, as a fighting organisation committed to a revolutionary seizure of power, had to carry out a severe self-criticism of Communist
Parties' mistakes in recent struggles. According to Lenin, the proletariat can
only be prepared for the revolutionary deed by carefully analysing and correct-
ing errors. After fierce debates, the Congress agreed that the Kommunistische
Partei Deutschlands (KPD)[20] had failed to take advantage of the objectively
revolutionary situation in 1923. Its rightist leaders ([Heinrich] Brandler and
[August] Thalheimer) had not freed themselves entirely from the opportunist
tendencies they had inherited from Social Democracy. They had therefore been
unable to implement the *slogan of a workers government* properly. They entered
a coalition with left Social Democrats in Saxony, participated in the formation
of a Social Democratic government and, instead of *arming the proletariat*, had
slept through the revolutionary situation, so that the bourgeoisie was able to
utilise the fateful error of the workers government by intervening rapidly to
suppress the movement. In France, too, rightist leaders had succumbed to pacifist illusions and made agreements with the right-wing socialists to cooperate
in the elections of May 1924. Communist Parties in many other countries made
similar errors. The Congress did not only condemn all these 'right deviations'
and replace the rightist leaders in Germany with a left leadership, it also adopted the *slogan of the Bolshevisation* of the Communist Parties, directed against
right, opportunist but also ultra-left currents. Bolshevisation was intended to
reinforce the adoption of Russian Communist experiences, which had an *international significance*, by the sections of the Communist International. This was
a matter of the organisational and tactical principles whose correctness had
been confirmed by the long experience of the Russian Bolshevik Party, gained
in three revolutions, those of 1905, February 1917 and October 1917, and finally
in the Civil War which followed the victory of the proletarian revolution. The
'Theses on Bolshevisation', worked out in more detail by the Enlarged ECCI
Plenum (April 1925)[21] shifted the organisational and agitational focus to the
masses. While the organisation of the social democratic parties was adapted
to parliamentary elections and constructed on the basis of members' places
of residence, for the Communist Parties the fundamental organisation was the

---

20   ['Kommunistische Partei Deutschlands' means 'Communist Party of Germany'.]
21   [Communist International 1959.]

party cell in the the factory, workshop, mine. At the same time, the statutes of the Communist International were modified to centralise the worldwide Party more strictly. Lastly, the fifth Congress countered the social democratic theory of a new period of capitalist prosperity by asserting that there was only a *relative and temporary stabilisation* of capitalism, which would not prevent its overall decline from advancing still further, as already demonstrated by the tremendous level of unemployment. The Congress also confirmed the decisions on the *united front* formulated for this period.

Resolutions on the *national and colonial question* supplemented the decisions of the second and fourth Congresses.

The *sixth Congress of the Communist International* (17 July to 1 September 1928), attended by 576 delegates representing 59 Communist Parties from all over the world, did not meet until four years after the previous Congress, following violent conflicts over political orientation within the Russian Communist Party and the Communist International, which ended with the destruction of the so-called Trotskyist opposition. In the meantime, events of great international significance had occurred. The Soviet Union was recognised de jure[22] by several great powers in 1924; English and Russian trade union representatives often met in 1925 and 1926 (the Anglo-Russian Committee); a miners strike and general strike took place in Britain in 1926, then the break in Anglo-Russian diplomatic relations [in 1927]. There was a series of revolutionary strikes and uprisings in the colonial regions: risings in Syria, Morocco and Indonesia; in India, strikes by Bombay textile workers and Calcutta railway workers; and above all the great historical event of the revolution in China. The *reports of the ECCI* on its activity and on the world situation since the third Congress thus constantly gained in significance, expressing the character of the Communist International as an international *of the deed*. They offered the Congress the opportunity to consider whether the ECCI's evaluation of the world situation and the tactics it had chosen had proved to be correct. The extensive resolution of the sixth Congress on 'The International Situation and the Tasks of the Communist International' provided a *unified picture of the world economic and political situation* from the proletarian viewpoint. It described all the more important events in international relations and within each country, the regroupment of class forces in the bourgeois and proletarian camps, and the successes and failures of proletarian tactics.

After the preliminary work of the fourth and fifth Congresses on the question of the programme, the sixth Congress adopted the final *'Program of the*

---

22   ['De jure' means 'legally'.]

Communist International,[23] one of the most significant documents in the history of the modern working class movement. It integrated the totality of the proletariat's wisdom and experience of revolutionary struggles and differed fundamentally from the programmes of the Second International. Those programmes, following the example of the 'Erfurt Program',[24] distinguished between a minimum programme for the present and a maximum programme for the distant future. In relation to the latter, they supposedly indicated tendencies of development, which capitalism must first have experienced if socialism is to eventuate in the future. The new programme of the Comintern rejects such a dichotomy. On the contrary, it proclaimed that the material conditions for the realisation of socialism *were already ripe* and that, consequently, history had placed *the revolutionary overthrow* of capitalism on the agenda. This revolutionary process could, however, be brought about by the proletariat of the *developed capitalist countries* alone. The *world system of capitalism* is not restricted to the most advanced countries of Europe and America but embraces all countries and peoples, including to the most primitive colonial territories of Asia and Africa, in its system of exploitation. So the revolutionary process also has an international character. The programme therefore distinguished different stages of the revolutionary process in different types of country, according to their level of economic development, and the specific tasks that fall to revolutionary parties at each stage. International imperialism, assailed by proletarian revolutions in the highly developed capitalist mother countries and the revolutions of millions of people in the colonies, will necessarily break down and make way for the *world system of communism*.

Literature

Adler, Friedrich 1921, '"Falls der Krieg dennoch ausbrechen sollte ...": Was trennt uns von der Zweiten Internationale?', *Der Kampf*, 14, no. 2/3: 41–4.

Adler, Friedrich 1929, 'Fünfzehn Jahre nach dem Zusammenbruch der Sozialistischen Internationale', *Der Kampf*, 22, no. 8: 349–70.

Balabanoff, Angelica 1927, *Erinnerungen und Erlebnisse*, Berlin: Laubsche Verlagsbuchhandlung.

Balabanoff, Angelica 1969 [1928], *Die Zimmerwalder Bewegung 1914–1919*, Frankfurt am Main: Neue Kritik.

---

23   [Communist International 1936.]
24   [Sozialdemokratische Partei Deutschlands 1891. The Erfurt Program was adopted by the SPD in 1891.]

Beer, Max 1924, *Krieg und Internationale*, Wien: Verlag für Literatur und Politik.

Bernstein, Eduard 1915, *Die Internationale der Arbeiterklasse und der europäische Krieg*, Tübingen: Mohr.

Braun, Adolf 1920, *Der Internationale Kongress zu Genf*, Berlin: Buchhandlung Vorwärts.

Bucharin, Nikolai 1928, *Die historische Leistung des 6. Weltkongresses der Kommunistischen Internationale*, Hamburg: Kommunistische Internationale.

Crispien, Arthur 1919, *Eine Abrechnung mit den Rechtssozialisten*, Berlin: Freiheit.

Crispien, Arthur 1920 [1919], *Die Internationale. Vom Bund der Kommunisten bis zur Internationale der Weltrevolution*, second edition, Berlin: Freiheit.

Fröhlich, Paul 1924, *Zehn Jahre Krieg und Bürgerkrieg. Band 1*, second edition, Berlin: Internationaler Verlags-Anstalten.

Grimm, Robert 1921, *Die Wiener Konferenz der Internationalen Arbeitsgemeinschaft Sozialistischer Parteien*, Bern: Unionsdruckerei.

Grünberg, Carl 1916, *Die Internationale und der Weltkrieg, Materialien*, Leipzig: Hirschfeld.

Heinz, Karl 1921, 'Was trennt uns von der Dritten Internationale?', *Der Kampf*, 14, no. 7: 239–50; no. 8: 281–6; no. 9: 326–30.

Kabakchiev, Khristo 1929, *Die Entstehung und Entwicklung der Komintern*, Hamburg: Kommunistische Internationale.

Kautsky, Karl 1920, *Die Internationale*, Wien: Wiener Volksbuchhandlung.

Kay, John Wesley de 1919, *The Spirit of the International at Berne*, Lucerne: self-published.

Lenin, Vladimir Ilyich 1964 [1915], 'The Collapse of the Second International', in Vladimir Ilyich Lenin, *Collected Works. Volume 21*, Moscow: Progress, pp. 205–59.

Lenin, Vladimir Ilyich 1965 [1919], 'The Third International, its place in history', in Vladimir Ilyich Lenin, *Collected Works. Volume 29*, Moscow: Progress, pp. 305–14.

Lenin, Vladimir Ilyich 1966 [1920], 'Theses on the Fundamental Tasks of the Second Congress of the Communist International', in Vladimir Ilyich Lenin, *Collected Works. Volume 31*, Moscow: Progress, pp. 184–201.

Lenz, Josef 1930, *Die II. Internationale und ihr Erbe 1889–1929*, Hamburg and Berlin: Kommunistische Internationale (an important work for sources).

Lorwin, Lewis Levitzki 1929, *Labor and Internationalism*, New York: Macmillan (an important source for the labour movement in America).

Milhaud, Edgar 1905, *La Tactique Socialiste et les decisions des Congrès Internationaux*, Paris: Société nouvelle de librairie et d'édition.

Müller, K.L. 1921, 'Zwischen der Ersten und der Zweiten Internationale', *Der Kampf*, 14, no. 2–3: 44–54.

Münzenberg, Willi 1919, *Die sozialistische Jugend-Internationale*, Berlin: Junge Garde.

Postgate, Raymond William 1920, *The Workers' International*, London: Swarthmore.

Radek, Karl 1922, 'Foundation of the Two and a Half International', *Communist Interna-tional*, 16/17: 31–43.

Roland Holst-Van der Schalk, Henriëtte 1906, *Generalstreik und Sozialdemokratie*, second edition, Dresden: Kaden.

Trotsky, Leon 1918 [1914], *The Bolsheviki and World Peace*,[25] New York: Boni and Liv-eright.

Trotsky, Leon 1921, *Die neue Etappe: Die Weltlage und unsere Aufgaben*, Hamburg: Kom-munistische Internationale.

Trotsky, Leon 1921 [1920], *In Defence of Terrorism (Terrorism and Communism): A Reply to Karl Kautsky*, London: George Allen & Unwin.

Trotsky, Leon 1957 [1929], *The Third International after Lenin*, translated by John G. Wright, third edition, New York, Pioneer, pp. 21–240.

Zévaès, Alexandre 1917, *La faillite de l'Internationale: faits et documents*, Paris: Renais-sance du livre.

Zévaès, Alexandre 1923, 'Les trois Internationales', appendix to *Le Parti socialiste de 1904 à 1923*, Paris: Rivière.

Zinoviev, Grigori 1970 [written 1916], *Der Krieg und die Krise des Sozialismus*, Milano: Feltrinelli.

Zinoviev, Grigori 1921, *Die Taktik der Kommunistischen Internationale: Rückblick auf die Arbeiten des III. Weltkongresses der Kommunist. Internationale*, Hamburg: Kommun-istische Internationale.

Zinoviev, Grigori 1922, *Die Kommunistische Internationale und die proletarische Ein-heitsfront*, Hamburg: Kommunistische Internationale.

Zinoviev, Grigori 1923, *Die Kommunistische Internationale auf dem Vormarsch*, Ham-burg: Kommunistische Internationale.

Zinoviev, Grigori 1924, *Die Entstehung der Kommunistischen Internationale und ihre Tätigkeit in den ersten fünf Jahren*, Hamburg: Kommunistische Internationale.

Minutes of Proceedings
A   The Second International

1889, *Protokoll des Internationalen Arbeiter-Kongresses zu Paris, abgehalten vom 14. bis 20. Juli 1889*, Nuremberg: Wörlein, 1890.

1891, *Verhandlungen und Beschlüsse des Internationalen Arbeiter-Kongresses zu Brüssel (16.–22. August 1891)*, Berlin: Vorwärts, 1893.

1893, *Protokoll des Internationalen Sozialistischen Arbeiterkongresses in der Tonhalle Zürich vom 6. bis 12. August 1893*, Zürich: Buchhandlung des Schweiz. Grütlivereins, 1894.

---

25   [The title was more accurately rendered in other translations as *War and the Interna-tional*.]

1896, *Verhandlungen und Beschlüsse des Internationalen Sozialistischen Arbeiter- und Gewerkschaftskongresses zu London vom 27. Juli bis 1. August 1896*, Berlin: Buchhandlung Vorwärts, 1896.

1900, *Verhandlungen und Beschlüsse des Internationalen Sozialistischen Kongresses zu Paris, 23. bis 27. September 1900*, Berlin: Buchhandlung Vorwärts, 1900.

1904, *Internationaler Sozialisten Kongress zu Amsterdam, 14. bis 20. August 1904*, Berlin: Buchhandlung Vorwärts, 1904.

1907, *Internationaler Sozialisten Kongress zu Stuttgart vom 18. bis 24. August 1907*, Berlin: Buchhandlung Vorwärts, 1907.

1910, *Internationaler Sozialisten-Kongress zu Kopenhagen, 28 August bis 3. September 1910*, Berlin: Buchhandlung Vorwärts, 1910.

1912, *Protokoll des Außerordentlichen Internationalen Sozialistenkongresses zu Basel am 24. und 25. November 1912*, Berlin: Buchhandlung Vorwärts, 1912.

B The Two and a Half International

1921, *Protokoll der Internationalen Sozialistischen Konferenz in Wien vom 22. bis 27. Februar 1921*, Wien: Wiener Volksbuchhandlung, 1921.

1921–3, *Nachrichten der Internationalen Arbeitsgemeinschaft Sozialistischer Parteien* [1922–3, *Bulletin of the International Working Union of Socialist Parties.*]

C The (Restored) Second International

1923, *Protokoll des Internationalen Sozialistischen Arbeiterkongresses zu Hamburg, 21. bis 25. Mai 1923*, Berlin: Dietz, 1923.

1925, *Second Congress of the Labour and Socialist International: at Marseilles, 22nd to 27th August 1925*, London: Labour and Socialist International, 1925.

1928, *Third Congress of the Labour and Socialist International, Brusseles, 5th to 11th August 1928*, three volumes, Zürich: Labour and Socialist International, 1928.

1931, *Fourth Congress of the Labour and Socialist International: Vienna, 25th July to 1st August 1931: Reports and Proceedings*, Zürich: Labour and Socialist International, 1932.

D The Third International

1919, *Founding the Communist International. Proceedings and Decisions of the First Congress*, edited by John Riddell, New York: Pathfinder, 1987 [1920–1].

1920, *Workers of the World and Oppressed Peoples, Unite! Proceedings and Documents of the Second Congress of the Communist International, 1920*, two volumes, edited by John Riddell, New York: Pathfinder, 1991 [1921].

1921, *To the Masses: Proceedings of the Third Congress of the Communist International, 1921*, edited and translated by John Riddell, Chicago: Haymarket, 2016 [1921].

1922, *Toward the United Front: Proceedings of the Fourth Congress of the Commun-*

ist International, 1922, edited and translated by John Riddell, Chicago: Haymarket, 2013.

1924, *Materialien zum Fünften Weltkongress der Kommunistischen Internationale*, Berlin: Internationaler Verlags-Anstalten, 1924.

1924, *Protokoll des Fünften Kongresses der Kommunistischen Internationale*, two volumes, Hamburg: Kommunistische Internationale, 1925.

1928, *Protokoll des Sechsten Weltkongresses der Kommunistischen Internationale*, four volumes, Hamburg: Kommunistische Internationale, 1929.

Minutes of the Enlarged Plenum of the Executive Committee of the Communist International.

[1922, *Die Taktik der Kommunistischen Internationale gegen die Offensive des Kapitals; bericht über die Konferenz der Erweiterten Exekutive der Kommunistischen Internationale. Moskau, vom 24. Februar bis 4. März, 1922*. Hamburg: Kommunistische Internationale, 1922.

[1923, *Protokoll der Konferenz der Erweiterten Exekutive der Kommunistischen Internationale, Moskau, 12.–23. Juni 1923*, Hamburg: Kommunistische Internationale, 1923.

[1925, *Protokoll der Erweiterten Exekutive der Kommunistischen Internationale Moskau 21. März–6. April 1925*, Hamburg: Kommunistische Internationale, 1925.

[1926, *Protokoll: Erweiterte Exekutive der Kommunistischen Internationale, Moskau, 17. Februar bis 15. März 1926*, Hamburg: Kommunistische Internationale, 1926.

[1926, *Protokoll der Erweiterten Exekutive der Kommunistischen Internationale, 22. November–13. Dezember, 1926*. Hamburg: Kommunistische Internationale, 1927.]

Jaurès, Jean[*]

Translated from German by Joseph Fraccia

French socialist and one of the most distinguished orators in France and the Second International. Born on 3 September 1859 in Castres in southern France, he came from a bourgeois family of little means. Thanks to the financial support from the school inspector [Félix] Deltour, he was able to attend an academic secondary school. After brilliantly completing his studies at the College of Castres, he attended the École Normale Supérieure, the nursery of French intellectual culture, where he graduated, together with [Henri] Bergson, in 1881. Jaurès became a lecturer and later Professor of Philosophy at the University of Toulouse. He spent some time in Germany. In 1885, at the age of 26, he was elected as a moderate radical to the Chamber of Deputies and moved to Paris. There he continued his philosophical studies and became well acquainted with the world of socialist thought. The fruit of his labour is a dissertation in Latin (see below under Writings) devoted to the origins of German socialism, which Jaurès traced back to [Martin] Luther, [Immanuel] Kant, [Johann Gottlieb] Fichte, and [Georg Wilhelm Friedrich] Hegel. In it, he developed his idealist conception of history, according to which history is the product of the human mind. In 1893, Jaurès declared his commitment to socialism to the Chamber, entered the socialist movement and worked with [Aristide] Briand, [Alexandre] Millerand, and [René] Viviani in the 'Indépendents' group, which in 1901 united with several smaller socialist parties to form the Parti Socialiste Français (PSF). The core of his commitment, to which he remained true for his entire life was that political democracy, established through revolutions, must be completed through economic democracy; the nation that rules sovereignly over its political institutions must also rule sovereignly over its economic institutions. Socialism is simply the logical consequence of the democratic republicanism which the great French Revolution identified as its ideal. Jaurès saw himself as the intellectual descendent and inheritor of the men who proclaimed the rights of man. As a democratic republican, Jaurès advocated the *tactic* of peaceful socialist progress, was in favour of the notion of the unity of the people and fought against the theory of class struggle, of unbridgeable con-

---

[*] [Originally published as Grossmann 1932f.]

flict between capital and labour, promulgated by the Guesdists. He also fought against their theory of the conquest of political power through force. Because the wage labour proletariat in France would scarcely ever constitute a majority of the population, it would have to seize political power as a minority and carry out the transformation of society in a dictatorial manner, which Jaurès regarded as a relapse into [Graccus] Babeuf's and [Louis Auguste] Blanqui's ideas about dictatorship. Jaurès declared himself in favour of socialists politically cooperating with bourgeois parties. Social justice can be realised in everyday reformist politics and will crown the work begun by the men of 1789–93. He was active along these lines at the parliamentary tribune, in meetings and in newspapers. In 1899 he supported Millerand's participation in a bourgeois government (Ministerialism). On the other hand, at the Bourdeaux Congress (1903) he admitted that democracy is adulterated and turned into its opposite by class antagonism and by the economic predominance of *one* class. Thus he was able, without contradicting himself, to comply with the resolution on class struggle passed by the International Socialist Congress in Amsterdam (1904) and finally to unite with the Guesdist POF to form the Parti socialiste unifié at the Paris Congress (23 April 1905).[1] During the period 1905–14, Jaurès became the real political leader of the unified Party. He possessed the ability to express the feelings that ruled the masses in convincing formulations. As the working masses were radicalised by the experience of the Millerand case, Jaurès – theoretically a reformist – became, under pressure from the masses, ready to fight the class struggle; he increasingly valued the role of the proletariat in the historical process and, shortly before his death, was inclined to centrist and leftist positions, while the orthodox Marxist [Jules] Guesde[2] underwent the opposite development and, in his practice within the Party, stood on its right wing.

In contrast to Guesde, who veiled his political abstentionism in radical formulas, Jaurès engaged in all the important political events of his time. He was extraordinarily effective in the struggle for appeals in the Dreyfus case,[3] which also gave him the opportunity to oppose *militarism*. As vice-president of the Chamber of Deputies, he influenced *foreign policy*, criticised its nationalist and imperialist tendencies and, in the spirit of pacifism, tried to dispel

---

1 ['Parti socialiste unifié' means 'Unified Socialist Party'. Its official name was 'Section française de l'internationale ouvrière', 'French Section of the Workers' International'. The POF was the Parti ouvrier français, (French Workers Party).]

2 See Grossmann 1932a, 'Guesde, Jules', above, pp. 349–353.

3 [During the 'Dreyfus Affair' of 1894–1906, French Jewish army Captain Alfred Dreyfus was falsely and repeatedly accused and convicted of being a German spy, before eventually being exonerated.]

national antagonisms, without ever having truly understood their imperialist roots. He favoured German-French understanding, international arbitration
courts, fought against colonial and armaments policies, as well as the proposed
law to prolong military service. Nevertheless, he remained committed to the
necessity of national defence and made proposals in the Chamber for the abolition of the standing army and its replacement by a democratic militia, built on
new foundations. As late as two weeks before the outbreak of the war, on 15 July
1914, he declared at the Paris Congress – in contrast to Guesde – that the *mass
strike* was the best weapon to prevent war, which he regarded as a crime of the
ruling classes. Because of his pacifist politics, Jaurès was murdered by a nationalist on the eve of the World War (31 August 1914), and became its first victim.
His murderer was found not guilty by the court. The great tribune of the people
died at the right time to avoid having to experience the political collapse of his
Party.

Writings

1899 [1886–99], *Action socialiste, premiére serie: le socialisme et l'enseignement; le socialisme et les peuples*, sixth edition, Paris: Bellais.

1891, *De primis Socialismi Germanici lineamentis apud Lutherum, Kant, Fichte et Hegel*,
Tolosae: Chauvin (1927 under the French title *Les origines du socialisme allemand
chez Luther, Kant, Fichte et Hegel*, translated by Adrien Veber, Paris: Écrivains
Réunis).

1895, *Idéalisme et matérialisme dans la conception de l'histoire: conférence de Jean Jaurès
et réponse de Paul Lafargue*, Paris: Imprimerie Spéciale.

1902, *Études socialistes*, Paris: Éditions des cahiers.[4]

1904, *Discours parlementaires. Tome premier*, with an introduction 'Le socialisme et le
radicalisme en 1885', by Jean Jaurès, edited by Edmund Claris, Paris: Cornély.

1911, *L'organisation socialiste de la France: L'armée nouvelle*, Paris: Rouff (1915, second
edition, Paris: *Humanité*).

Of the volumes of the *Histoire socialiste, 1789–1900*, published under his supervision,
Jaurès wrote

1901, *Tome I: La Constituante (1789–1791)*, Paris: Rouff.

1901, *Tome II: La Legislative (1791–1792)*, Paris: Rouff.

1901, *Tome III: La Convention I (1792)*, Paris: Rouff.

1901, *Tome IV: La Convention II (1793–1794, 9 thermidor)*, Paris: Rouff.

---

4 [Most of the content of this book is in Jaurès 1908.]

Literature

Beer, Max 1918 [1915], *Jean Jaurès: Sozialist und Staatsmann*, fourth edition, Berlin: Verlag für Sozialwissenschaft.

Blum, Oskar 1916, 'Jean Jaurès', *Archiv für die Geschichte des Sozialismus und der Arbeiterbewegung*, 7: 18–59.

Desanges, Paul and Luc Mériga 1924, *Vie de Jaurès*, fifth edition, Paris: Crès.

Gouttenoire de Toury, Fernand 1922, *Jaurès et le parti de la guerre*, introduced by Charles Gide, Paris: Éditions des Cahiers internationaux.

Herriot, Édouard 1924, *Jean Jaurès: Discours prononcé au Panthéon le 23 novembre 1924*, Paris: Payot.

Jouhaux, Léon et al. 1925, *Jaurès par ses contemporains*, introduced and with a biography by Fernand Pignatel, Paris: Chiron.

Kautsky, Karl 1919, 'Zum Gedächtnis Jean Jaurès', *Kampf*, 12, no. 18: 501–6.

Lévy-Bruhl, Lucien 1916, *Quelques pages sur Jean Jaurès*, Paris: L'Humanité; 1923, second edition under the title *Jean Jaurès: Esquisse biographique*, with unpublished letters, Paris: Rieder. This is the principal work on Jaurès.

Pease, Margaret 1917, *Jean Jaurès: Socialist and Humanitarian*, New York: Huebsch.

Rappoport, Charles 1925 [1915], *Jean Jaurès, l'homme, le penseur, le socialiste*, third edition, Paris: Rivière.

Téry, Gustave 1915 [1907], *Jaurès*, Paris: L'Œuvre.

Viviani, René and Édouard Vaillant 1927 [1914], *Un grand disparu: Jean Jaurès, extraits de ses œuvres, biographie, lettres d'Anatole France, discours prononcés à ses obsèques par René Viviani, Edouard Vaillant*, Paris: Hayard.

Zévaès, Alexandre. 1923, *Le Parti Socialiste de 1904 à 1923*, Paris: Rivière.

CHAPTER 29

Kropotkin, Peter*

Translated from German by Ken Todd

Russian, communist anarchist, of princely descent, the most significant theoretician and leader of recent anarchism in Europe,[1] born on 9 December 1842
in Moscow. At the age of 15 he entered the Corps of Pages, in which he studied mathematics, Russian literature and natural sciences. As his father wished,
he chose a military career in 1862 and spent five years as an officer with a
Cossack regiment, stationed on the Amur in Siberia. There Kropotkin had the
opportunity to study the semi-communist social organisation of primitive east
Siberian peoples (Dukhobor community).[2] During the period of intellectual
ferment after the liberation of the peasants in 1861, when there was much
talk of progress and liberal reform in intellectual circles, Kropotkin concerned
himself with the 'internal mainspring of social life'. In 1867 he left the military service, dedicated himself to mathematical and geographical studies at
Saint Petersburg University, participated in the clandestine reform movement
and affiliated himself with Nikolai Tchaikovsky and [Sergei] Stepniak (Sergei
Mikhaylovich Kravchinsky). In early 1872, he left Russia and travelled to Switzerland. Here he came in contact with members of the International and the Paris
Commune. But he showed no sympathy for Marx's historical materialism and
remained on the ground of historical idealism: he was the typical heir of the
French Enlightenment of the eighteenth century and considered reason, the
sense of moral duty and science to be the creative forces of history. Under the
influence of the anti-authoritarian clock makers of the Jura region, influenced
by Bakunin, he became an anarchist. In contrast to Bakunin, who primarily
strove for the destruction of all that existed, Kropotkin emphasised the constructive powers of the social process, rooted in 'mutual aid'.[3] In 1873, Kropotkin
returned to Russia and became a member of the Tchaikovskist secret society;
arrested in 1874, in 1876 he escaped, with Stepniak's assistance, from the Peter
and Paul Fortress to London. From 1877 he lived in Geneva, where he published

---

* [Originally published as Grossmann 1932g.]
1 See Grossmann 1931b, 'Anarchism' above, pp. 210–235.
2 [The Dukhobors were a spiritualist Russian Christian sect.]
3 [Kropotkin 1904.]

the semi-monthly journal *Le revolté*,[4] from 1879, which later became *Les temps nouveaux* (Paris).[5] Deported from Switzerland in 1881, Kropotkin lived in Lyon in 1882, where he was among those arrested after a bomb attack and in 1883 was sentenced to five years in prison. Pardoned in 1886, he took up permanent residence in London, where he collaborated actively on anarchist journals and published several works. In 1897 he gave anarchist lectures in New York. During the World War, he, like most Russian, French and Dutch anarchists, aligned himself with the imperialist bourgeoisie, signed together with a number of his comrades (Jean Grave, Charles Malato) a manifesto (28 February 1916) against a 'premature peace', for fighting on until Germany was defeated and for the defence of the 'great democracies' of the Entente.[6] Kropotkin even became a collaborator with the bourgeois *Russkie Vedomosti*.[7] In June 1917, he returned to Russia after an absence of forty years, supported the Kerensky government and the bourgeois republic. After the October Revolution, Kropotkin refrained from all political activity. In a private letter, (24 April 1919) published in 1920, 'To the workers of western Europe', Kropotkin acknowledged the historical necessity of the Bolshevik dictatorship, despite his dislike for it, and warned foreign countries against any military intervention against Soviet Russia.[8] He died on 8 February 1921.

Writings

Deserving of mention among Kropotkin's numerous writings, which appeared in many
  editions in almost all civilised languages:
1992 [1885], *Words of a Rebel*, translated by George Woodcock, Montréal: Black Rose
  Books.
1913 [1892], *The Conquest of Bread*, London: Chapman and Hall.
1901 [1899], *Fields, Factories and Workshops*, London: Swan Sonnenschein.
1899, *Memoirs of a Revolutionist*, London: Smith, Elder.
1904 [1902], *Mutual Aid*, London: Heinemann.

---

4 ['*Le revolté*' means '*The Rebel*'.]
5 ['*Les temps nouveaux*' means '*New Times*'.]
6 [Kropotkin and Grave 1964; and Kropotkin and Grave 2012. The manifesto dealt with the
   concept of 'premature peace' but did not use the phrase. Neither the words nor the concept
   of the 'great democracies' were present.]
7 ['*Russkie Vedomosti*' ('*Russian News*') was a liberal Russian newspaper, published in Moscow.]
8 [Kropotkin 1970, p. 253.]

1903, *Modern Science and Anarchism*, Philadelphia: The Social Science Club of Philadelphia.

1919 [1905], *Ideals and Realities in Russian literature*, New York: Knopf.

1909, *The Great French Revolution*, London: Heinemann.

Kropotkin's shorter writings appeared in an anthology under the title

1970 [1927], *Kropotkin's Revolutionary Pamphlets*, with an introduction, biography and bibliography by Roger N. Baldwin, New York: Dover.

Here only the following are mentioned:

1921 [1880], *An Appeal to the Young*, New York: Maisel.

1903 [1891], *Anarchist-communism: Its Basis and Principles*, London: Freedom.

1970 [1891], *Anarchist Morality*, in Peter Kropotkin, *Kropotkin's Revolutionary Pamphlets*, New York: Dover pp. 80–113.

2010 [1908], *Syndicalism and Anarchism*, libcom.org, available at: http://libcom.org/library/syndicalism-anarchism-peter-kropotkin (accessed 23 February 2017)

Literature

Ishill, Joseph (ed.) 1923, *Peter Kropotkin, the Rebel, Thinker and Humanitarian*, New Jersey: Free Spirit Press.

CHAPTER 30

Lenin (Pseudonym for Ulyanov), Vladimir Ilyich*

Translated from German by Ben Fowkes

Theoretical leader and practical organiser of the victorious proletarian revolution in Russia (1917) and the founder of the first proletarian state – the Soviet Union – was born on 10 (23 [old Russian calendar]) April 1870 in the city of Simbirsk on the Volga (now renamed after him Ulyanovsk), the son of a primary school inspector of peasant origin.[1] His oldest brother, Aleksandr, who had a lasting influence on Vladimir's development, was a member of Narodnaya Volya[2] who was executed for planning to assassinate Tsar Aleksandr III (1887). In the same year, after finishing his academic high school education, Lenin entered the Law Faculty of the University of Kazan but, after a few months, was already expelled from the university and condemned to exile in the village of Kokushkino, for participating in revolutionary student disturbances and as the brother of an executed terrorist. In Autumn 1891, he completed his law degree in Saint Petersburg as an external student and began to practice law in Samara, where he organised a Marxist circle. This was the start of his activity as a 'professional revolutionary', the first few years of which were dominated by the *struggle against Populism*. Despite his admiration for the leaders of Narodnaya Volya for their heroic struggle against Tsarism at a time when there was still no workers movement in Russia, through systematic study of Marx, Lenin came to a new conception of the tasks of the revolution and the role of the working class in it. In his first scientific work, 'New Economic Developments in Peasant Life' of 1893,[3] Lenin pointed out the growing influence of capitalism on the traditional peasant system of production, in contrast to dominant Populist theory. Another pamphlet directed against the Populists ([Nikolai Konstantinovich] Mikhailovsky), *What the 'Friends of the People' Are and How they Fight against the Social Democrats* of 1894,[4] marked the independence of the Marxist social democratic movement. Lenin's sketch 'On the so-called market question', dir-

---

* [Originally published as Grossmann 1932h.]
1 [More precisely, the Russian Socialist Federal Soviet Republic, which became part of the newly constituted Soviet Union in 1922.]
2 ['Narodnaya Volya' means 'the People's Will', a populist, terrorist organisation.]
3 [Lenin 1960f.]
4 [Lenin 1960g.]

ected against Vasilii Pavlovich Vorontsov, stemmed from the same period and was later expanded into *A Characterisation of Economic Romanticism* (second edition 1899).[5] Here, Lenin attacked a theory originated by Sismondi, advocated by the Russian Sismondists and sixteen years later placed anew in the centre of discussion by Rosa Luxemburg. This was the theory that the existence of non-capitalist *external markets* constitute the necessary prerequisite for the existence and growth of capitalism.

At the end of 1893 Lenin moved to Saint Petersburg, where he entered into contact with workers and intellectuals by giving lectures to small, illegal circles. These groups united into the illegal League of Struggle for the Emancipation of the Working Class, with Lenin's leading participation, in 1895. In the summer of the same year he established personal connections with the 'Emancipation of Labour' group ([Georgii] Plekhanov and Pavel Akselrod), during a short stay in Switzerland. Those years of direct contact with the workers of Saint Petersburg and through profound study of Marx's theory of class struggle imbued Lenin with his deep conviction in the invincible and creative strength of the proletariat, its infallible class instinct and the historic mission and leading role of the working class in the coming struggles for the liberation of all working people. In 1895, he also started to write his major work against the Populists, *The Development of Capitalism in Russia*, only published in 1899, which, together with Plekhanov's writings, delivered the intellectual death blow to Populism. His attack on [Pyotr] Struve in 1895[6] opened the *second period* in Lenin's activity, the years of struggle against 'Economism' and 'Legal Marxism',[7] although he also temporarily collaborated, in the winter of 1897–8, for example, with the left-wing organ of Legal Marxism, *Novoe Slovo*,[8] edited by Struve. On 9 December 1895 Lenin was arrested, along with many other members of his revolutionary organisation, and an issue of the illegal popular periodical, *Rabochee Delo*,[9] which he had prepared for publication, fell into the hands of the police. On 29 January 1897, after a year in prison, during which he worked on his book, and drafted a programme for a *united* social democratic party (1895),[10] Lenin was condemned to three years of exile in eastern Siberia, on the Mongolian border. He was accompanied by his co-worker and life-long companion Nadezhda Konstantinovna Krupskaya, who had also been exiled for three years.

---

5   [Lenin 1960h.]
6   [Lenin 1960i.]
7   See Grossmann 1931d, 'Bolshevism' section 3, above, pp. 245–246.
8   ['*Novoe Slovo*' means '*The New Word*'.]
9   ['*Rabochee Delo*' means '*The Workers' Cause*'.]
10   [Lenin 1960b.]

In exile Lenin remained in constant contact with the movement, engaged in economic studies and had the opportunity *to get to know the Siberian village thoroughly*. The founding Congress of the Russian Social Democratic Labour Party, in Minsk (14 March 1898), chose the exiled Lenin to be the editor of its planned central organ, *Rabochaya Gazeta*.[11] In Siberia, he organised the 1899 'Protest of the seventeen'[12] Social Democrats living in exile against 'Economism'. During his last year in exile Lenin, finally conceived the plan of organising a centralised, All-Russian, united political party of the proletariat, which he developed later in *Iskra*, in the pamphlet *What is to be Done?* (1902) and in *A Letter to a Comrade on Our Organisational Tasks* (1902).[13] By creating an all-Russian central organ *abroad*, through which all the strands of the Russian workers movement would have to operate together, the scattered circles of intellectuals and workers, working without connections with each other, would be joined together, step by step, and the path to the foundation of the Party and the calling of a Party Congress *prepared*, ideologically and organisationally. In the summer of 1900, Lenin travelled abroad, after securing correspondents and connections in all parts of Russia. Over three years, initially in Munich (from September 1900), then London and, after April 1903, Geneva, he edited *Iskra* (*The Spark*, the first issue appeared on 24 December 1900) – the 'Leninist *Iskra*'. In its pages, he provided direction by clarifying current questions of organisation, the Party programme and the tactics of the revolutionary workers movement.[14] This began the third, constructive phase in his activity, *the period of sowing the seed of his revolutionary ideas*. At that time, when the Party was still united and included Plekhanov, Akselrod, [Vera] Zasulich, [Julius] Martov and [Aleksandr] Potresov in its ranks, he became, in practice the *leader* of the Russian workers movement unlike the 'old guard', who were more interested in the theoretical organ *Zarya* (*Dawn*) and, in emigration, were isolated from the mass of Russian workers. So Lenin started to work on the task that was only completed in 1917: preparation for the great proletarian revolution in Russia. Since then, the story of Lenin's life, living as a homeless emigrant abroad for almost seventeen years, cannot be separated from the history of the Russian workers movement and, since 1917, from the history of the Russian October Revolution and the Soviet state. For a discussion of the most important stages of this history as well as Lenin's most significant *theories* (such as his theory of imperialism, his conception of the state and the theory of the dictatorship

---

11   ['*Rabochaya Gazeta*' means '*Workers' Newspaper*'.]
12   [Lenin 1960i.]
13   [Lenin 2008; Lenin 1961a.]
14   See Grossmann 1931d, 'Bolshevism' section 3, above, pp. 245–246.

of the proletariat, his theory of the leading role of the Party in its relation to the class) see the articles 'Bolshevism' and 'International'.[15] Lenin's personality and his towering leadership qualities were revealed in the decisive moments of his life: each time the movement stood at a *crossroads*, he guided it with a firm hand onto the path that led to the intended goal. Lenin's *authority* and strength as a leader did not consist in his 'authoritarian character' but in the fact that his Party comrades were convinced, again and again on the basis of their own experience, that he had shown them the historically correct path. The events of 1903 are an example. With unbending determination, through the historic split in the Russian Social Democratic Labour Party (RSDLP) and by *organisationally remoulding* it to create the necessary *instrument* for future battles and victories, he completed the break with Plekhanov and Martov, leaving the editorial board of *Iskra*. This opened the fourth phase in his activity: ruthless, decades-long *struggle against opportunism* in his own ranks, the fight against the Mensheviks, once they had abandoned the terrain of revolutionary Marxism. Struggling alone, at first against the authority of Plekhanov, the Central Committee and the whole Party apparatus, later against the authority of international social democracy ([August] Bebel) which took the side of the Mensheviks, Lenin founded a new organ, *Vpered*,[16] to combat *Iskra*. He masterfully assailed the Mensheviks in *One Step Forward, Two Steps Back* (1904),[17] a pamphlet in which he drew conclusions from the Congress at which the split took place. He was soon able to win the support of the organised masses of revolutionary Russia for his ideas.

The second decisive moment in Lenin's life occurred in 1905. In the coming revolution, Lenin saw a transformation of a new kind – *proletarian* revolution – that would move beyond the bounds of the bourgeois world in its *goal, instruments* and *tactics*. It was already clear to Lenin at that time that it would not be limited to completing the tasks of a bourgeois revolution. With clear vision, Lenin immediately recognised the essence and the future historical role of the *workers councils* (soviets) which arose in 1905. For him they were not organs of a day to day struggle, like the trade unions, but *organs of the proletarian struggle for power*, organs which would replace parliaments everywhere and be the embryo and bearers of power of a new type of state, the soviet state.

---

15   See Grossmann 1931d, 'Bolshevism' above, pp. 239–291; and Grossmann 1932e, 'The Internationals: The Third International', above, pp. 377–402.

16   ['*Vpered*' means '*Forward*'.]

17   [Lenin 1962e.]

Moreover, by advocating the *tactic of an armed uprising*, rejected by western European social democrats, and connecting it with the *political general strike*, Lenin created the tactical *methods* which were to lead to the seizure of power.

Without being in the public eye, he directed the Moscow uprising of 1905, in part from Saint Petersburg, in part from the small Finnish village of Kuokkala.[18] While Mensheviks later regarded the defeated revolution of 1905 as a 'mistake', Lenin considered that his tactics were correct and that the defeat, which happened because the peasantry became involved in the course of the revolution too late, was only temporary. The revolution of 1905 did in fact prove to be the 'dress rehearsal' which made the victorious revolution of 1917 possible, through the experience and the lessons it provided.

Finally, at that time, in 1905, Lenin laid the foundations for *revolutionary working class strategy*. As a theorist of the agrarian question, he did not deal with this from the viewpoint of the correctness or incorrectness of Marx's economic theories but first and foremost from the viewpoint of the proletariat, in its struggle for power and search for allies in this fight. Lenin *discovered the peasantry*, not as an economic category but as the ally of the revolution, without whose support the proletariat could not be victorious. Lenin, present in the gallery of the first Saint Petersburg Workers Soviet in 1905 but invisible to the public, was therefore the *principal figure in the revolution of 1905*.

Lenin had to flee to Finland in 1906/1907. While there [and then from outside the Russian Empire from late 1907], during the dismal years of the counter-revolution and internal factional struggles of 1906–10, he directed the activities of his Party, theoretically and practically conducted the *retreat* of the revolution with strategic mastery, gathered together the scattered forces of the revolution and moulded his Party into the organisational and intellectual shape which would later enable it to play a great historical role. In foreign exile again from 1907, Lenin took part in International Socialist Congresses and Conferences (Stuttgart 1907); thanks to his endeavours the illegal newspapers of the Bolsheviks, *Proletary* and *Sotsial Demokrat*,[19] were published, first in Geneva and then in Paris. Lenin also found time to write a philosophical polemic in favour of Marxist materialism and against the Machism,[20] which was widespread among Social Democrats (*Materialism and Empirio-Criticism*, 1908).[21] This period of

---

18   [Kuokkala, close to Saint Petersburg, is now in Russia and called Repino.]
19   [*'Proletary'* means *'The Proletarian'*. *'Sotsial Demokrat'* means *'The Social Democrat'*.]
20   [Machism was a positivist philosophy propounded by the physicist Ernst Mach.]
21   [Lenin 1962e.]

retreat, in which Lenin demonstrated his true leadership qualities, is 'one of the most significant of his whole career' (Zinoviev).[22]

In January 1912 the founding Congress of the Bolshevik Party and thus the definitive break with the Mensheviks took place in Prague. In July 1912 Lenin moved to Kraków, from there he directed the work of the Bolshevik caucus in the Duma[23] and participated in editing his Party's daily newspaper (*Pravda*),[24] published legally in Saint Petersburg.

When the War broke out, he was arrested by the Austrian authorities in Kraków but was soon released. He moved to Switzerland, where he was active against the imperialist war and the Second International, which had gone over to the camp of the bourgeoisie. In his slogan of turning the imperialist war into a civil war, which was attacked by social democrats everywhere as 'a fantasy of revolution' and mocked by Plekhanov as a 'farcical dream',[25] he correctly foresaw the course of events. While until 1914 Lenin was only the leader of the *Russian* proletariat, from the outbreak of the World War he also stood at the head of the international revolutionary workers movement as the War's resolute opponent and he became the intellectual leader of the Zimmerwald (left) movement and anti-imperialists in all countries. After the February Revolution broke out in Russia, while still in Switzerland, he wrote his 'Letters from afar' (March 1917),[26] already calling for the sharpest possible opposition to the Provisional Government. With a small group of Russian exiles he returned to Petrograd (3 April) via Stockholm, after an absence of ten years, having travelled through Germany in the so-called 'sealed train'. In sharp contrast to the entire leadership of his own Party, which until his arrival had a conciliatory attitude to the Provisional Government, he called for the overthrow of the Provisional Government and the *concentration of the entire power of the state into the hands of the soviets*, in his famous 'April Theses', one of the most important documents of the revolution. In his speeches, pamphlets and essays, couched in his bold, simple language, he electrified and fascinated the masses and demonstrated the need for his programme to be put into effect. In scarcely four weeks, he succeeded in completing the struggle for the *intellectual rearmament of his Party* on the path to the revolutionary seizure of power. After bloody clashes between a Bolshevik demonstration and the state power (3 to 5 July

---

22   [Sinowjew 1920, p. 20. The English translation in Zinovieff n.d., p. 27 is poor.]
23   [The Duma was the Russian parliament which had no control over the Tsarist government.]
24   ['*Pradva*' means '*Truth*'.]
25   [Quoted in Lenin 1964k, p. 118.]
26   [Lenin 1964i.]

1917), Lenin had to hide from persecution by Provisional Government. He went to Finland and from there directed preparations for the October Revolution, although he also found time to write his *The State and Revolution*, which was fundamental for the coming dictatorship [of the proletariat]. After the revolution of 25 October (7 November in the modern calendar) 1917 and the seizure of power by the workers and peasants soviets, Lenin became the Chairperson of the Council of People's Commissars and in practice guided the fate of a gigantic empire of 140 million people. As a youth, he began his political career with the question 'What is to be done?'; as a mature man he *acted* at the decisive historical moment. Bearing the banner of the victorious Russian Revolution, Lenin became the *symbol of a new epoch* in human history: a time when the *world began to be rebuilt* on socialist foundations.

At the controls of state power, Lenin concentrated all his strength on a much more difficult task: preservation of the power that had been conquered against external and internal enemies, under the most unfavourable circumstances. He combined unconditional commitment to that goal, with an unusual flexibility in the means used to attain it. He resolutely accomplished the forcible dissolution of the Constituent Assembly (18 January 1918) and its replacement by the *dictatorship of the proletariat* in the form of the soviets. In the same year, in the fiercest struggle against the opposition of the majority of his Party comrades, he insisted on the conclusion of an *immediate peace* with Germany (Treaty of Brest-Litovsk, 3 March 1918), in order to save the revolution and gain time (a 'breathing space')[27] by making unavoidable concessions to a stronger enemy. In March 1919, on Lenin's insistence, the *(Third) Communist International*, which he had called for since 1914, *was already founded*. Thus an organisation, similar to that created by Lenin at the split Congress in 1903, in preparation for the *Russian* revolution, was established on a global scale in preparation for *world revolution*.

The first years after the seizure of power were a period of the greatest economic, political and social upheavals known to history. They were a period of the expropriation of industrial and commercial capital, bold land reforms, the development of the soviet system and the new state. In this, Lenin initiated tremendous initiatives in all areas, as an organising statesperson. He not only proposed large-scale plans, pursuing their implementation in great detail but also engaged in more mundane daily work, speaking at congresses and meetings, writing numerous treatises and newspaper articles.[28] A man who never posed,

---

27   [For example, Lenin 1965d, pp. 79, 82.]
28   Such as Lenin 1965e; Lenin 1965f; Lenin 1965g; Lenin 1966.

an ascetic who demanded of himself the greatest possible effort and capacity to withstand privation, Lenin also understood how to spur the proletarian masses, suffering from the greatest austerity, on to immense exertions. Although personally gentle, Lenin was able to defeat all his opponents and keep power in the hands of the proletariat through iron severity and ruthlessness towards the class enemy (the 'red terror'), during the period of the *wars of intervention*, the *Allied blockade*, the *counter-revolution*, initiated from abroad in favour of the dispossessed classes, and the *most bitter civil war*, 1918–21 ([Aleksandr] Kolchak, [Nikolai] Yudenich, [Anton] Denikin and [Pyotr] Wrangel). In 1921 at the height of his creative powers, Lenin once again showed his superiority as a leader by recognising that the situation created in the previous period of war communism was untenable and that more remote objectives of socialist construction were for the present unrealisable. In May 1921 he accomplished a *bold change in economic policy*, pushing through the 'New Economic Policy' (NEP), which preserved the existence of the Soviet state. On 13 August 1918 the Socialist Revolutionary Fanya Kaplan attempted to assassinate Lenin, who was able to recover from the consequences for a time. He died on 22 January 1924 at Gorki, near Moscow.

As a *theorist*, Lenin rested entirely on the theories of Karl Marx; he was, nevertheless, an independent thinker, unlike those Marxists to whom Marx referred when he wrote he had 'sown dragons' teeth and harvested fleas'.[29] Lenin clarified the *true meaning* of Marx's demands, after they had been distorted by the social democrats, for the masses; reconstructed the whole polemical, class combative thrust of the original theory and discharged it in open struggles. Lenin did leave few studies devoted to general questions of Marxism behind. If the meaning of theory does not, however, consist of the construction of abstract systems and formulae but in being an intellectual tool that helps us to *grasp reality* then Lenin must be counted as one of the great theorists of socialism. His greatest theoretical achievement was that, unlike anyone before him and in contrast to epigones of Marxism like [Karl] Kautsky and [Rudolf] Hilferding, he recognised the fact that capitalism as an economic system had already passed the *high point* of its development and entered its *declining phase*, in which it was pregnant with wars and revolutions. Lenin's 'keen practicality',[30] his rare ability to foresee future developments in the essential features of the circumstances of the moment, was only the result of his theoretical superiority in assessing the total capitalist process. All his activity, his strategy and his tactics reflected this understanding.

---

29   [Marx and Engels 2010, p. 510, attributing the quote to Heinrich Heine.]
30   [Herzen applied this phrase to Francis Bacon, Herzen 1956, p. 261.]

Writings

The titles of Lenin's more important writings have already been indicated in the text.
   Complete works:
Lenin, Vladimir Ilych 1960–70, *Collected Works*, 44 volumes, Moscow: Progress.

Literature

Grossmann, Henryk 1931, 'Bolschewismus', in *Wörterbuch der Volkswirtschaft. Erster
   Band*, edited by Ludwig Elster, fourth edition, Jena: Fischer, pp. 421–44. [See above
   pp. 239–291.]
Grossmann, Henryk 1932, 'Internationale: Die dritte Internationale', in *Wörterbuch der
   Volkswirtschaft. Zweiter Band*, edited by Ludwig Elster, fourth edition, Jena: Fischer,
   pp. 439–49. [See above pp. 377–402.]
Guilbeaux, Henri 1923, *Wladimir Iljitsch Lenin: Ein treues Bild seines Wesens*, translated
   by Henri Guilbeaux and Rudolf Leonhard, Berlin: Die Schmiede.
Krupskaya, Nadezhda Konstantinovna 1970 [1929], *Memories of Lenin*, London: Pan-
   ther.
Levine, Isaac Don 1924, *The Man Lenin*, New York: Seltzer.
Lukács, Gyorgy 1970 [1924], *Lenin: A Study in the Unity of His Thought*, London: New Left
   Books.
Radek, Karl 1924, *Lenin: sein Leben, sein Werk*, Berlin: Neuer Deutscher Verlag.
Seraphim, Hans-Jürgen 1929, 'Lenin', in *Ergänzungsband zum Handwörterbuch der
   Staatswissenschaften*, edited by Ludwig Elster and Adolf Weber, fourth edition, Jena:
   Fischer, pp. 678–85.
Sorel, Georges 1999 [1919], 'In Defense of Lenin', in Georges Sorel, *Reflections on Violence*,
   translated by Thomas Ernest Hulme and Jeremy Jennings, Cambridge: Cambridge
   University Press, pp. 283–93.
Stalin, Joseph 1925 [1924], *The Theory and Practice of Leninism*, Chicago: Daily Worker.
Trotsky, Leon 1971 [1924], *On Lenin: Notes Towards a Biography*, translated by Tamara
   Deutscher, London: Harrap.
Trotsky, Leon 1965 [1931], *The History of the Russian Revolution*, translated by Max East-
   man, Chicago: Haymarket.
Wiedenfeld, Kurt 1923, *Lenin und sein Werk*, München: Wieland.
Zetkin, Clara 1934 [1924], *Reminiscences of Lenin*, New York: International Publishers.

CHAPTER 31

Plekhanov, Georgii Valentinovich*

Translated from German by Ken Todd

Leading Russian Social Democrat and outstanding Marxist theoretician, born on 25 November 1856 at Lipetsk (Tambov Governate), into a noble family. After graduating from Military Academy, he studied at the Petersburg Mining Institute, where he joined the revolutionary movement of the Narodniki (Populists) and, like all the Narodniks, was heavily influenced by the works of Bakunin. Pursued by the police, because of a speech he had made at a demonstration in Saint Petersburg, he fled abroad in 1876. He returned illegally the next year and, from 1878, worked in the Narodnik organisation Zemlya i Volya[1] as co-editor of its journal of the same name. After the Narodniks split in (1879), Plekhanov joined their non-terrorist wing, Chyornyi Peredel,[2] which continued propaganda among workers, and was the co-founder of a journal of the same name. After the production of the first issue, he had to flee abroad. There he devoted himself to comprehensive philosophical and economic studies, broke with Narodnik ideology and became a Marxist. In 1883 he published the famous polemic against the Narodniks, *Socialism and Political Struggle*, followed in 1884 by an anti-critique, *Our Differences*, against the leader of the Narodovoltsi[3] Lev Alexandrovich Tikhomirov. In that work, demonstrating the inevitability of capitalist development in Russia, which would slowly but surely undermine the old regime, Plekhanov propagandised about the necessity for the the working class to struggle *politically* for its own liberation and thus identified a new path for the defeated Narodnik movement.

In exile, with Pavel Borisovich Axelrod, Vera Zasulich, [Leo] Deutsch and [Vasily] Ignatov, he founded the first Russian Marxist social democratic organisation, Gruppa Osvobozhdenie Truda,[4] in September 1883. Its theoretical basis was contained in the two works by Plekhanov mentioned above and in two drafts of a programme, in 1883 and 1887–8. Plekhanov participated in the

---

* [Originally published as Grossmann 1932i.]
1 ['*Zemlya i Volya*' means 'Land and Freedom'.]
2 ['Chyornyi Peredel' means 'Black Redistribution'.]
3 [Plekhanov 1974a. The Narodovoltsi were the members of the populist, terrorist organisation 'Narodnaya Volya', which means 'the People's Will'.]
4 ['Gruppa Osvobozhdenie Truda' means 'Emancipation of Labor Group'.]

founding Congress of the Second International, in 1889, as the delegate of the Russian Social Democrats and outlined the tasks of the Russian proletariat before an international forum for the first time.[5] Over the following years, Plekhanov – a brilliant stylist and an extremely astute and adroit polemicist – engaged in extremely prolific activity as a writer, collaborated with *Neue Zeit*,[6] edited by Kautsky, and played a leading role in the Second International. In the era of Bernsteinian revisionism in the 1890s, Plekhanov conducted the struggle against international opportunism in the workers movement and its Russian variant ('economism', 'Struvism'),[7] as one of the most brilliant champions of dialectical materialism. In 1889 Plekhanov was temporarily expelled from Geneva and in 1895 permanently from Paris 'as an anarchist'. In 1900, together with Lenin he became an editor of *Iskra*.[8] At the same time, he was one of the principal collaborators on the theoretical monthly *Zarya*,[9] published in Geneva. At the 1903 Congress in London, which split, he initially sided but soon broke with Lenin and was inclined to the Mensheviks. During the revolution of 1905 he is a pronounced opponent of the Bolsheviks and condemned the armed uprising they led in Moscow. From 1905, he published the *Dnevnik Sotsialdemokrata* (*Diary of a Social Democrat*) in Geneva and then in Saint Petersburg. During the period of reaction 1906–12, he supported Lenin in the philosophical fight against empirio-criticism in the camp of the Russian Social Democrats, and likewise in the struggle against the 'legalism' and the 'constitutional illusions' of the Menshevik 'Liquidators'.

At the outbreak of the World War, Plekhanov placed himself on the side of defence of the fatherland against German imperialism, in alliance with the tsarism which he had previously fought for four decades. In that cause, he worked on the magazine *Prizyv* (*The Call*), published in Paris. After the February Revolution he returned to Russia, assumed the editorship of the newspaper *Yedinstvo*[10] and fiercely combatted the Bolsheviks – without success. During the last years of his life, he progressively lost influence in the Russian workers movement, from which he was now completely alienated. After the October Revolution, he regarded attempts to take violent action against the Bolsheviks as futile. In his last essay, published shortly before his death, he did regard the forcible dissolution of the Constituent Assembly as a mistake but acknow-

---

5   See Grossmann 1931d, 'Bolshevism' above, pp. 239–291.
6   ['*Neue Zeit*' means '*New Times*'.]
7   [Advocated by Petr Struve, a leading legal Marxist, hostile to revolution.]
8   ['*Iskra*' means '*The Spark*'.]
9   ['*Zarya*' means '*The Dawn*'.]
10   ['*Yedinstvo*' means '*Unity*'.]

ledged the right of the revolutionary state to defend itself by dictatorial means. Embittered by the disappointments of recent years, he died on 30 May 1918 in Terijoki, Finland.[11]

As a politician, Plekhanov vacillated on tactical questions. His estimation of the political situation during the World War and both the revolutions of 1917 proved to be mistaken. As a writer, he distinguished himself by the diversity of his scientific works. Along with numerous investigations into the problems of the Russian *workers movement*, he wrote *economic* studies of [Johann Karl] Rodbertus and [Nikolai Gavrilovich] Chernyshevsky, *philosophical* works critical of empirio-monism ([Aleksandr] Bogdanov) and the search for God ([Anatoly Vasilyevich] Lunacharsky), contributions to the history and theory of dialectical materialism, studies of utopian socialism and the development of socialism into a science.[12] The core of Plekhanov's achievements lay in his *historical* and *sociological* works. He created the materialist sociology of culture and art. His greatest, unfinished work, on which he laboured from 1909, was the posthumously published *History of Russian Social Thought*,[13] edited by David Riazanov, which was in reality a history of Russia. In it, Plekhanov succeeded in explaining the historical development of Russia in materialist terms.

Writings

Plekhanov's numerous writings were translated into almost all civilised languages. There is a complete Russian edition of his works:

1923–7, *Sochineniia*, 26 volumes, Moskva: Gosudartstvennoe Izdatelstvo.[14]

Akselrod, Pavel Borisovich and Georgii Valentinovich Plekahnov 1967 [1925], *Perepiska G.V. Plekhanova i P.B. Akselroda*, The Hague: Europe Printing.

Plekhanov's correspondence with Potresov, Martov and Lenin in:

Potresov, Aleksandr Nikolayevich and Boris Nikolayevski 1967 [1928], *Sotsial-Demokraticheskoe Dvizhenie v Rossii: Materialy*, The Hague: Europe Printing.

---

11   [Plekhanov 1921. Terijoki now in Russian and known as Zelenogorsk.]
12   [For example: Rodbertus, Plekhanov 1923; Chernyshevsky, Plekhanov 1980; Bogdanov, Plekhanov 1976b; Lunacharsky, Plekhanov 1976c; history of materialism, Plekhanov 1976a and Plekhanov 1976e; theory of materialism, Plekhanov 1974c; utopian socialism, Plekhanov 1976d; scientific socialism, Plekhanov 1976f.]
13   Plekhanov 1967.
14   [Not translated into English but see Plekhanov 1974–6.]

In addition, meriting individual mention:

1976 [1890], *N. G. Chernyshevsky*, in Georgii Valentinovich Plekhanov, *Selected Philosophical Works. Volume 4*, Moscow: Progress, pp. 45–168.

1937 [1891], 'Ibsen, Petty Bourgeois Revolutionist', in Friedrich Engels et al., *Ibsen*, edited by Angel Flores, translated by Emily Kent, Lola Sachs and Pearl Waskow, New York: Critics Group.

1976 [1893], *Essays on the History of Materialism*, in Georgii Valentinovich Plekhanov, *Selected Philosophical Works. Volume 2*, Moscow: Progress, pp. 31–182.

1894 [1895], *Anarchism and Socialism*, translated by Eleanor Marx Aveling, Minneapolis: New Times Socialist Publishing.

1976 [1908], *Fundamental Problems of Marxism*, in Georgii Valentinovich Plekhanov, *Selected Philosophical Works. Volume 3*, Moscow: Progress, pp. 117–83.

1921, *God na Rodine: Polnoe Sobranie Statei i Rechei 1917–1918*, two volumes, Paris: Povolozky.

1967 [1925], *History of Russian Social Thought*, translated by Boris M. Bekkar and others, New York: Fertig.

1926, *Introduction á l'histoire sociale de la Russie*, translated by Euginia Batault-Plékhanov, Paris: Bossard.

Lenin, Vladimir Ilyich and Georgii Valentinovich Plekahnov 1928, *L. N. Tolstoi im Spiegel des Marxismus; eine Sammlung von Aufsätzen*, Wien/Berlin: Verlag für Literatur und Politik.[15]

Literature

Deich, Lev Grigorovich 1922, *G. V. Plekhanov: Materialy Dlia Biografi*, Moskva: Novaia Moskva.

Deich, Lev Grigorovich (ed.) 1923–8, *Gruppa 'Osvobozhdenie Truda': (iz arkhivov G. V. Plekhanova, V. I. Zasulich i L. G. Deicha)*, six volumes, Moskva: Gosudarstvennoe Izdatelstvo.

Gorev, Boris Isaakovich 1925, *Georgii Valentinovich Plekhanov*, Moskva: Gosudarstvennoe Izdatelstvo.

Riazanov, David Borisovich, biographical material in *Sochineniia*, cited above.

Verow, N.E. 1918, 'G. Plechanow', *Neue Zeit*, 36, vol. 2, no. 11, 14 June: 359–64.

Volfson, Semen Yakovlevich 1924, *Plekhanov*, Minsk: Beltrestpechat.

Zaslavsky, David Yosifovich 1923, *G. V. Plekhanov*, Moskva: Raduga.

Also see the articles 'Bolshevism', above pp. 239–291; 'International', above pp. 361–402; 'Lenin' above pp. 410–418.

---

15   [Also see Plekhanov 1981a; Plekhanov 1981b.]

CHAPTER 32

Rodrigues, Olinde*

Translated from German by Ken Todd

Born in 1794 in Bordeaux, came from a family of Jewish bankers, became a teacher of mathematics at the École Polytechnique in Paris in 1812, director of the Caisse hypothécaire[1] from 1823. In the same year he became acquainted with [Henri de] Saint-Simon and supported the latter financially during the last years of his life. After the death of the master in 1825, Rodrigues founded the journal *Le Producteur* (1825–6),[2] to propagate the ideas of Saint-Simon and became the sponsor of the Saint-Simonian sect, which soon developed from being a political and social opposition into a religious community. On 31 December 1829 appointed Amand Bazard and [Barthélemy Prosper] Enfantin as the Pères suprêmes[3] of the new religion, preached class harmony and declared himself opposed to the revolutionary tactics of the revolt in Lyon.[4] After the dissolution of the sect (1832), he lived in retirement and edited the works of Saint-Simon (two volumes 1832).[5] In 1841 he published the *Poésies sociales des ouvriers*,[6] in order to show the bourgeoisie the great social thought that was alive in the proletariat. He died in 1851 in Paris.

Literature

D'Allemagne, Henry-René 1930, *Les saint-simoniens, 1827–1837*, Paris: Gründ.

Charléty, Sébastien 1896, *Histoire du saint-simonisme (1825–1864)*, Paris: Hachette.

Weill, Georges 1896, *L'École saint-simonienne*, Paris: Alcan.

---

* [Originally published as Grossmann 1933a.]
1 [A mortgage bank.]
2 [*'Le Producteur'* means 'The Producer'.]
3 ['Pères suprêmes' means 'supreme fathers'.]
4 Rodrigues 1831. [In early November 1831, silk workers in Lyon rose up and took control of the city. The uprising was suppressed by the French army on 3 December.]
5 [Saint-Simon 1832.]
6 [Rodrigues 1841.]

Social Democratic and Communist Parties[*]

Translated from German by Ben Fowkes

1   Concept

Previously, all political parties with a socialist programme, i.e. aiming to achieve a reconstruction of the legal, economic and social order on a socialist basis after gaining state power, were described as 'social democratic'. Since the War and the split in the working class movement of almost all countries between social democrats and Communists, those parties which aspire to conquer political power solely by parliamentary means, seek to *cooperate with bourgeois parties* and to participate in bourgeois governments are described as 'social democratic'. The Communist Parties, by contrast, want to conquer power in a revolutionary, extra-parliamentary way. They use the tribune of parliament essentially for purposes of propaganda, to arouse the masses and consider that it is only possible to realise socialism through the *dictatorship of the proletariat*.[1]

The preconditions for the emergence of stable mass organisations, apart from freedom in the choice of profession and of movement, are, on the one hand, a certain level of technical-economic development of the mode of production, large-scale enterprise; on the other hand, that political rights, such as the rights to organise unions, assemble, petition and vote have been conceded and are not limited to people of wealth and education. For large-scale enterprises automatically bring workers together, while at the same time economically oppressing them and constantly reinforcing their ranks, at the expense of the small enterprises through their superior competitive power. Moreover, even a minimal level of political freedom, particularly in the initial stages of the workers movement, makes it possible to organise and educate the masses politically.

---

[*]   [Originally published as Grünberg and Grossmann 1933. The text here only includes material written by Grossmann, primarily about the period after World War I, and excludes that written by Grünberg and carried over from the Grünberg 1911c.]

1   See Grossmann 1931d, 'Bolshevism' section 8, above, pp. 260–268.

2   France

After the outbreak of the World War, the Section française de l'internationale ouvrière [SFIO][2] joined the civil peace of 'défence nationale'. Jules Guesde and Marcel Sembat became Ministers of State in the bourgeois war cabinet of the 'Union sacrée'.[3] After mid-1915, however, there was a division between the social democratic majority and a minority. The majority, led by [Pierre] Renaudel, were for a fight to the finish. The minority, led by Jean Longuet, wanted a negotiated peace. Some members of the minority took part in the Zimmerwald Conference. The influence of the minority increased in 1917–18; in October 1918 it gained a majority in the Party leadership. In the elections of 1919, the still united Party received 1,615,000 votes and 68 parliamentary seats. Communist tendencies became increasingly assertive after 1918 and at the *Tours Party Congress* (December 1920) [Marcel] Cachin's and [Ludovic-Oscar] Frossard's motion to join the Third International was carried by 3,208 votes to 1,022. The Party split: the Communist majority constituted itself the French Communist Party (PCF), at the Marseilles Congress (December 1921), while the minority remained in the old SFIO. 55 socialist parliamentary deputies stayed with the old Party and only 13 went over to the PCF. The socialists replaced *L'Humanité*,[4] which the Communists had taken over, with a new central organ, *Le Populaire*,[5] edited by Léon Blum, who currently leads the socialist group [in the Chamber of Deputies]. The extraordinary [socialist] Congress held in Paris (January 1926) did reject all cooperation with the government but in fact the SFIO supported it in foreign policy (the socialist [Joseph] Paul-Boncour was the leader of the French delegation at the League of Nations) and domestic policy (Paul-Boncour also formulated the new military laws). At the elections of 1928 the [SFIO] received 1,620,000 votes and 102 seats, at the elections of 1932 they received roughly two million votes and 129 seats.

When the PCF was set up, in 1921, revolutionary elements rushed to join; many were, however, unable to accept Bolshevik tactics. A series of crises, splits and expulsions resulted. A large part of the PCF membership was lost. At the

---

2 ['Section française de l'internationale ouvrière' means 'French Section of the Workers' International'.]

3 See Grossmann 1932a, 'Guesde, Jules', above, pp. 349–353; Grossmann 1932f, 'Jaurès, Jean', above, pp. 403–406; Grossmann 1932d, 'The Internationals: The Second International', above, pp. 367–376. ['Défence nationale' means 'national defence'; 'Union sacrée' means 'Sacred Union'.]

4 [*L'Humanité* means *'Humanity'*.]

5 [*Le Populaire* literally means *'The Popular'*.]

elections of 1924 the PCF received roughly 800,000 votes and 27 seats; in 1928 1,070,000 votes and 13 seats; and in 1932 roughly 800,000 votes and 10 seats. The Parti socialiste communiste,[6] which was outside the Third International, obtained 6 seats in 1928 and 11 seats in 1932.

3   Germany

The reformist disintegration of Social Democracy became particularly apparent after the outbreak of the World War in August 1914. Both the revisionist majority and the so-called orthodox Marxists took the side of the German government, in contradiction with all the resolutions passed by Congresses of the International against war, and concluded a civil truce with the government and industrialists in the interest of the defence of the fatherland. The trade unions called off all industrial action and collaborated with the government and the military authorities in the most diverse areas. At the meeting of the SPD parliamentary caucus of 4 August 1914, just 14 out of 110 members called for the rejection of war credits but still voted in favour, with the majority. Only slowly, under the pressure of the state of siege, did a proletarian opposition to the war develop. With Karl Liebknecht, Franz Mehring, Rosa Luxemburg and Clara Zetkin at its head, it founded the journal *Die Internationale*, in March 1915 and, from 1916, distributed the illegal *Spartakusbriefe*.[7] Seventeen voted against the second round of war credits in the caucus but only Karl Liebknecht[8] in the Reichstag. His written justification for doing so was not included in the minutes. The third round of war credits (March 1915) was opposed by 32 in the caucus; by two in the Reichstag,[9] (Karl Liebknecht and Otto Rühle, which led to their expulsion from the caucus). Caucus discipline broke apart over the fourth round of war credits (August 1915), as the annexatist plans of the six large business associations had become known in the meantime. Forty-four were against in the caucus, 20 cast a negative vote in the Reichstag, giving reasons for their action and without informing the caucus beforehand. Led by Hugo Haase, the opposition to the majority socialists now came out into the open and set up the 'Social Democratic Working Group' (24 March

---

6   [The Parti socialiste communiste, Socialist Communist Party, was made up of members who had split at different times from the PCF.]

7   ['*Die Internationale*' means '*The International*'. '*Spartakusbriefe*' means '*Spartacus Letters*'.]

8   See Redaktion 1932a.

9   [The Reichstag was the lower house of the German parliament.]

1916). After the Party executive expelled the new grouping (18 January 1917) it constituted itself the Unabhängige Sozialdemokratische Partei Deutschlands (USPD),[10] at a congress in Gotha (6–8 April 1917). From now on, it worked together with the Spartakusbund,[11] founded on 1 January 1916 and active illegally, for an immediate negotiated peace, without annexations or reparations. The increasing dissatisfaction of the masses became apparent in mutinies and large strike movements (treason trial of sailors in the navy, 1917; January 1918 strike in Berlin). These were also evidence that the masses did not agree with the openly imperialist policies of the Majority Socialists, who had supported the Treaty of Brest-Litovsk (3 March 1918), imposed by force on the Bolsheviks, and later the Treaty of Bucharest. Despite its numerical weakness and lack of organisation, the Spartakusbund, in close association with the 'Zimmerwald Left',[12] exerted a strong influence on the course of the German revolution. It took the initiative in and led the revolutionary struggle and with its assistance the political idea of councils [of workers, soldiers and sailors] had temporary success (1918–19). The USPD meanwhile vacillatied indecisively between left and right. The November Revolution of 1918 was an unwelcome occurrence for the Majority Socialists ([Philipp] Scheidemann), who had already participated in the last imperial wartime government and wanted to retain the dynasty (with a parliamentary government). Only after the collapse of imperial Germany, when power had fallen into the hands of the working class and workers and soldiers councils had emerged everywhere, did they associate with the revolutionary movement, to secure its leadership for themselves and prevent its further radicalisation. They regarded the achievements of November, the democratisation of government and protection of workers, as the revolution and rejected demands that went any further. Standing on the ground of bourgeois democracy, they wanted no social revolution, no socialisation, no expropriation of the industrial and landowning capitalists, no dictatorship of the proletariat. Unlike the Independent Social Democrats, who favoured the council system, they declared support for elections to the National Assembly and immediately reached agreement with the Supreme Command of the Army to suppress the revolution (the [Friedrich] Ebert-[Karl] Groener agreement). The coalition government of the People's Representatives, made up of Major-

---

10   ['Unabhängige Sozialdemokratische Partei Deutschlands' means 'Independent Social Democratic Party of Germany'.]

11   ['Spartakusbund' means 'Spartacus League'.]

12   See Grossmann 1932e, 'The Internationals: The Third International' section 1, above, pp. 387–390.

ity Socialists (Ebert, Scheidemann and [Otto] Landsberg) and Independents (Haase, [Wilhelm] Dittmann and [Emil] Barth), formed after the 'German Socialist Republic' was proclaimed, could not be sustained. During the final weeks of December 1918 and the first weeks of January 1919, there were bloody workers' struggles for a council republic, led by the Spartakusbund and then the Kommunistische Partei,[13] which emerged from it at the end of December. The Majority Socialists ([Gustav] Noske), with the aid of mercenary soldiers from the old army, suppressed the movement of proletarian insurgents without mercy. Its leaders Karl Liebknecht, Rosa Luxemburg and Leo Jogiches were bestially murdered. The way was now open for the liquidation of the power of the workers and soldiers councils and the creation of the Weimar Constitution. The Social Democrat Ebert became president of Germany. The [Majority] Social Democrats initially assumed government alone, subsequently in coalition with bourgeois parties, and in opposition to the left wing of the workers movement. A large section of the working class left was unhappy with this turn of events and, at an extraordinary Congress of the USPD in Halle (12–17 October 1920), split the Party to go over to the KPD[14] (Unification Congress in Berlin, from 4 to 7 December 1920). The remaining right wing, which consolidated in the meantime and won 74 seats at the Reichstag elections of June 1920, returned to the bosom of Majority Socialism (1922).

The Social Democrats, in line with their altered character, replaced the Erfurt Program of 1891 with a new Party programme, adopted at their Görlitz Congress of 1921. It calls for 'the transfer of the large concentrated economic enterprises to the communal economy and further the *progressive reshaping of* the whole capitalist economy into a socialist economy', by democratic means. The only immediate demands in economic policy were for the 'Reich to supervise the means of production owned by the capitalists' and for the 'progressive extension of the enterprises owned by the Reich, states and public bodies'.[15] These demands could have been included in the programme of a bourgeois reform party. The *Heidelberg Programme*, adopted at the September 1925 Party Congress, concentrated even more on immediate demands.[16] At the Kiel Party Congress, in May 1927, an *Agrarian Program* was adopted.[17]

Social Democracy's development in the Reichstag was as follows.

---

13   ['Kommunistische Partei' means 'Communist Party'.]
14   [KPD, 'Kommunistische Partei Deutschlands' ('Communist Party of Germany').]
15   [Sozialdemokratische Partei Deutschlands 1921, pp. 3–4. Grossman's emphasis. The country was still officially called the 'Reich', i.e. 'Empire', during the interwar period.]
16   [Sozialdemokratische Partei Deutschlands 1925.]
17   [Sozialdemokratische Partei Deutschlands 1927, pp. 273–82.]

Year	Socialist votes in millions	% of all votes	Number of deputies
1919	11,509	37.7	163
1920	6,104	21.6	112
1924	6,008	20.2	100
1924	7,881	25.6	131
1928	9,150	29.3	153
1930	8,575	24.3	143

The Social Democrats in 1930 were represented in German parliaments as follows (the total number of seats in brackets): Reichstag 143 (577), Prussia 137 (450), Baveria 33 (129), Saxony 33 (96), Württemberg 21 (80), Baden 18 (88), Hamburg 61 (160), Bremen 50 (120), Lübeck 34 (80).

The Social Democrats participated repeatedly in different coalition governments, most recently, after the elections of May 1928, with Hermann Müller as Chancellor and Rudolf Hilferding[18] as Minister of Finance. When the cabinet agreed to the construction of an armoured cruiser and, at the same time, pursued dubious tax and protective tariff policies, there were fierce debates within the Social Democratic Party. After [Hermann] Müller's resignation (March 1930) the Centre Party politician, Heinrich Brüning, took over the government. Despite his reactionary economic and social policy – reductions in wages and social insurance benefits, restrictions on political rights in the constitution and policy of emergency decrees – he was supported by the Social Democrats.

The feeble opposition of the 'Left' inside the Party to this policy was a complete fiasco at the Leipzig Party Congress (May 1931). Shortly afterwards the severe measures of the Party Executive against the opposition led it to split away (October 1931).

The Kommunistische Partei Deutschlands (KPD) as a section of the Communist International is most closely connected with it, programmatically and tactically.[19] In Reichstag elections it received: June 1920 589,000 votes; May 1924 3,728,089 votes (12.7 percent) and 62 seats; December 1924 2,708,176 votes (9 percent) and 45 seats; May 1928 3,262,254 votes and 54 seats; and September 1930 4,590,160 votes and 77 seats. The recent elections to the Landtag[20] of

---

18   [Müller and Hilferding were both Social Democrats.]
19   See Grossmann 1932e, 'The Internationals: The Third International' sections 2 and 5, above, pp. 378–385, 391–398.
20   ['Landtag' means 'State Parliament'. Prussia was by far the largest German federal state.]

Prussia (April 1932) showed that the KPD has not succeeded in breaking the predominant influence of Social Democracy over the proletarian masses, despite the working class's extreme distress, as a consequence of the economic crisis, cuts in wages and social insurance benefits.

The repeated splits by left and right oppositions [from the KPD] are numerically insignificant.

4   Other Countries

a   *Switzerland*

During the war, the Social Democrats supported the Zimmerwald movement.[21] The Party's *Aarau Congress* (20 November 1915) moved still further left and called for the War to be ended by the revolutionary action of the working class, which caused the Grütli Association to split away in 1916. In line with the Zimmerwald Left, the extraordinary Party Congress in Bern (9–10 June 1917) declared its opposition to all military institutions of the bourgeois class state and for ending the War by unleashing a revolution. The *workers congress* in Basel (27–29 July 1918) adopted a similar resolution. Workers' disappointment, as a consequence the failure of a *general strike* (11–14 November 1918), led by the so-called Olten Action Committee,[22] and an attempted general strike in August 1919 closed the revolutionary period. The extraordinary Party Congress in Basel (16–17 August 1919) resolved by 318 to 147 votes to adhere unconditionally to the Third International; this resolution was overturned by a vote of the whole membership. When the Party Congress in Bern (10–12 December 1920) voted by 315 to 213 to reject the Third International's 21 conditions,[23] the left wing withdrew from the Party and established the Kommunistische Partei der Schweiz[24] (5–6 March 1921). Both parties acted together in the autumn of 1922 to defeat the 'subversion referendum'.[25] In 1919 the Social Democrats received 175,000 votes

---

21   See Grossmann 1932e, 'The Internationals: The Third International' section 1, above, pp. 377–378.

22   [The Olten Action Committee was established to lead workers' struggles and was made up of seven representatives of the trade unions and Social Democratic Party. It first met in the town of Olten.]

23   See Grossmann 1932e, 'The Internationals: The Third International', above, p. 392.

24   ['Kommunistische Partei der Schweiz' means 'Communist Party of Switzerland'.]

25   [A law against sedition, the 'Federal Law on the Amendment of the Federal Criminal Law of 4 February 1853 Concerning Crimes against Constitutional Order and Internal Security and Concerning the Introduction of Conditional Imprisonment', was forced to a referendum, on 24 September 1922, and defeated.]

and 41 seats in elections for the Nationalrat,[26] in 1922 171,000 votes and 43 seats, in 1925 192,000 votes and 49 seats (of 198), and at the elections of October 1928 220,000 votes and 50 seats. At the Basel Party Congress (30 November 1929) the main subject of discussion was the question of participation in government. At the Basel Party Congress of 1928, an *agrarian programme* was adopted, raising demands which would benefit small peasants. The Social Democrats made great progress in communal elections. In Zürich they obtained an absolute majority (1931); in Geneva 42 percent of the votes.

After the Party split of 1920 the Swiss Social Democrats joined the so-called Two and a Half International,[27] although at the beginning of 1927 they finally returned to the Second International they had once fought against.

The Communist Party received 14,387 votes (two percent) and three seats in the elections of 1925; in 1928 it received 14,818 votes and two seats.

b   *Austria*

During the World War, the Austrian Social Democrats, led by Victor Adler, supported the government's war policy. After the fall of the Austrian Empire they took part in the government and, until 1920, played the leading role in the new, much smaller Austrian republic. Since then, in opposition again, they have been happy to use revolutionary phraseology, as there was no way out of the Austrian crisis and, given the intensification of class antagonisms, not least as a consequence of the 'reconstruction' of the state's finances under the aegis of the League of Nations (September 1922). The Linz Party Congress of 1926 adopted a new *general programme* for the Party, which included the *agrarian programme*, proposed at the Vienna Congress (November 1925), and even flirted with the idea of the dictatorship of the proletariat. Of course, in practice the Party is always ready to pursue a policy of compromise with and toleration of bourgeois reaction, just like the Social Democratic Party of Germany. This contradiction between verbal radicalism and practical opportunism is most apparent in the report presented by Otto Bauer, the intellectual leader of Austrian Social Democracy, to the most recent Congress of the Second International, in Vienna (1931).[28] Austrian Social Democracy is one of the best organised parties of the Second International. It has achieved its greatest influence in Vienna,

---

26   [The Nationalrat is the Swiss federal parliament.]

27   [See 'The Internationals: The Third International', section 3, above, pp. 385–387.]

28   See 'The Internationals: The Third International', section 4, above, pp. 387–390. [For Bauer's verbal report to the Congress on the situation in Germany and central Europe, see Bauer 1931.]

where it completely dominates the City Council and has engaged in brisk activity in the spheres of education, training, welfare and housing policy, as well as municipal enterprises. The Party obtained 41 percent of the vote in the 1919 elections to the Nationalrat,[29] 36 percent in 1920, 40 percent in 1923, 42 percent in 1927 and 41 percent in 1930. Its number of parliamentary seats rose from 68 in 1923 to 71 in 1927 and 72 (of 165) in 1930. In recent years the Social Democrats have led a so far successful defensive struggle against Heimwehr[30] fascism, which has gained strength with the open support of the bourgeoisie, particularly since the events of July 1927 (the demonstration by workers in Vienna, who stormed the Palace of Justice in reaction to the not guilty verdict in the Schattendorf murder trial, and the subsequent massacre by the police – 90 dead and almost 1,000 wounded).

The Party has seven daily newspapers, the most important of which is the *Arbeiter-Zeitung* in Vienna, and over 18 monthlies. Its monthly theoretical journal is *Der Kampf* (Vienna).[31] The trade union movement, with 896,000 members in 1923 and 737,300 members in 1930 (a year of crisis), is most intimately connected with the Social Democratic Party.

The Communist Party of Austria has no great significance. In the elections of 1923 it received 22,164 votes (0.7 percent), 1927 16,119 votes (0.4 percent), 1930 20,951 votes (0.6 percent). It has seats neither in the Austrian parliament nor in the City Council of Vienna.

c   *Belgium*

During the World War the Parti ouvrier belge[32] (POB) stood on the side of the bourgeois government. [Emile] Vandervelde became a Minister. After the end of the War universal suffrage was introduced and the parliamentary elections of November 1919 brought the Party 70 seats. Four members of the POB were Ministers in the coalition government of 1919–21. In the 1921 elections the Party won 68 seats; in the 1925 elections it obtained 820,116 votes (39.4 percent) and had the strongest caucus in the parliament, with 78 of 187 seats. In the Senate it had 39 of 93 seats. It participated twice, each time with four Ministers, in coalition governments between 1925 and 1927. The parliamentary elections of May 1929 brought the Party only 803,347 votes (36 percent) and the loss of eight seats. The

---

29   [The Nationalrat is the lower house of the Austrian federal parliament.]
30   [The 'Heimwehr' ('Home Guard'), was a far-right Austrian nationalist, paramilitary organisation, with links to the Christian Social Party.]
31   [*'Arbeiter-Zeitung'* means *'Workers' Newspaper'*. *'Der Kampf'* means *'The Struggle'*.]
32   [*'Parti ouvrier belge'* means 'Belgian Workers Party'.]

Party Congress in Brussels, 4–7 April 1931, adopted a new programme. The Party has six daily newspapers (among them *Le Peuple*,[33] published in Brussels).

The Communist Party of Belgium emerged from a split in opposition to the POB's patriotic line during the war. In the elections of 1925, it won 29,422 votes (0.4 percent) and two seats. In the 1929 elections the pro-Stalin tendency won 43,237 votes and one seat, the Communist opposition (the pro-Trotsky tendency) won 7,237 votes.

d The Netherlands

During the World War the Sociaal-Democratische Arbeiderspartij supported a policy of neutrality but for imperialist reasons.[34] After the war the Party conducted a campaign for disarmament and put a bill to this effect before the parliament but it was rejected (8 March 1927). Among its other demands, the call for the workers to be granted the right of co-determination in factories should be mentioned. In the first post-War elections of 1922, in which women could vote, the Party obtained 567,769 votes and 20 seats. In the elections of July 1925, 706,689 votes (22.9 percent) and 24 of the 100 seats. In the elections of July 1929 the number of votes rose to 804,714 but the number of seats remained the same. A special *Agrarian Congress*, in Wageningen (October 1928), called for a law to protect tenant farmers and set the socialisation of the land as the final goal, in the interests of 400,000 Dutch agricultural workers and roughly 100,000 proletarianised tenant farmers. The demands of the Party with regard to the *colonial question* were originally adapted to the imperialist requirements of the colonial powers, in line with the resolution of the Brussels Congress of the Second International.[35] It called for 'a system of reforms to alleviate the economic distress of the indigenous people'. Only at a special *Party Congress on Colonial Questions* in Utrecht (January 1930), in response to revolutionary disturbances in the Netherlands East Indies, was a new colonial programme, disavowing colonial imperialism and 'unconditionally recognising the right to national independence' adopted.[36]

The Party's left wing, which had existed for several years (with its own newspaper, *De Socialist*), split away at the Party Congress of Easter 1932, in Haarlem,

---

33   [*'Le Peuple'* means *'The People'*.]
34   See Grossmann 1932e, 'The Internationals: The Third International' section 1, above, pp. 377–392. ['The Sociaal-Democratische Arbeiderspartij' means 'Social Democratic Workers Party'.]
35   See Grossmann 1932d, 'The Internationals: The Second International', above, p. 389.
36   [Sociaal-Democratische Arbeiderspartij in Nederland 1930, pp. 45–9.]

and set up the Onafhankelijke Socialistische Partij[37] (OSP) under the leadership of Edo Fimmen.

The Communist Party received 53,664 votes (1.8 percent) and two seats at the elections of 1922, 36,786 votes and one seat in 1925, and 37,770 votes and one seat in 1929. There were repeated splits in the Communist Party. The [David] Wijnkoop group obtained 29,860 votes and one seat at the 1929 elections; it subsequently rejoined the official Communist Party. The 'Communist Workers Party' (the group of Herman Gorter) remains outside the Communist Party.

e   *The Scandinavian Countries: Denmark, Sweden and Norway*
        Denmark

At the end of April 1924, the Social Democrats won 55 of 148 seats in the Folketh-ing, 25 of 76 in the upper house and 36.6 percent of the votes.[38] With the support of the 20 Left Liberals, the Social Democrats formed the government and Thorvald Stauning became Prime Minister. After 19 months (December 1926), the coalition fell apart over the Social Democrats' proposals for unemployment relief and lower taxes on the less well off. The [following] conservative government limited social legislation, reduced support for the unemployed, restricted the municipal franchise and lightened the tax burden on the wealthy. At the elections of May 1929, the Social Democrats received 41.8 percent of votes and 61 seats, while the Left Liberals only returned with 16 seats. The two left parties then again formed a government (of nine Social Democrats and three Left Liberals) under Stauning. Its programme was primarily the reversal of the Conservatives' restrictions. In 1928, about 310,000 workers were organised in trade unions.

The Communist Party obtained 6,219 votes at the 1924 elections; 3,656 votes in 1929.

        Sweden

In the postwar period, as a result of the electoral reform of 1919 which introduced universal suffrage with proportional representation, the number of Social Democratic deputies who sat in the Second Chamber rose to 99.[39]

---

37 ['Onafhankelijke Socialistische Partij' means 'Independent Socialist Party'.]
38 [The Folkething was the lower house, while the Landsting was the upper house of the Danish parliament.]
39 [The Social Democrats had 93 seats after first elections under universal suffrage in 1921; the Social Democratic Left Party, formed by those expelled from the Communist Party for their opposition to the Comintern's 21 conditions, had six seats and merged with the Social Democratic Party in 1923.]

[Hjalmar] Branting [had already] formed the first purely Social Democratic government (March 1920), which survived until October. Branting's second government, formed after the Party's victory in the 1921 elections, lasted until April 1923. In the September 1924 elections the Social Democrats won 725,407 votes (41.1 percent) and 104 seats. The third Social Democratic minority government, from January 1925 to June 1926, was overthrown by a coalition of bourgeois parties, which feared that the workers parties (including the Communists) would eventually gain a majority, which required only seven more seats. At the elections of September 1928, the Social Democrats only won 90 seats, although their vote increased to 873,931. In order to win over layers of small peasants, the Party Congress of 3–9 June 1928, passed resolutions for an agrarian programme, which called for land reforms involving the abolition of ground rent, the protection of tenant farmers and the promotion of agricultural settlement. The other demands concerned old age and unemployment insurance, as well as disarmament. The Swedish Social Democratic Party is among the best organised parties in the Second International. It is strongly represented in the municipal councils of many cities, in Malmö, Göteborg and, since 1931, Stockholm it has had absolute majorities. The socialist trade unions had 39,000 members in 1900 and 313,000 in 1924. The total number of workers organised in trade unions in 1924 was 350,000.

Half of the left socialists, who had split from the Social Democrats in 1917, went over to the Communists in 1919 and founded the Swedish Communist Party in 1921. In elections to the Second Chamber, it won 7 seats in 1921, 5 seats and 65,283 votes in 1924, and 8 seats and 151,567 votes in 1928. This Party of so-called National Communists was expelled from the Third International in 1929.[40] The official Party of the 'Moscow' Communists has no parliamentary seats.

Norway

After the war, in 1921, the Norwegian Labour Party joined the Third International. This led the Social Democrats, under Magnus Nilssen, to split away and form the Social Democratic Party of Norway. When the Labour Party, however, refused to unconditionally accept the Comintern's 21 conditions from Moscow it was expelled from the Third International in 1923. The supporters of Moscow, in consequence, left the Labour Party and set up the Communist Party. At the elections of October 1924 to the Storting,[41] the Labour Party received 179,567

---

40   [Formally, most leaders and members of the Party were expelled by the Comintern, rather than the Party as a whole.]

41   [The Storting is the Norwegian parliament.]

votes and 24 seats, the Social Democrats 85,743 votes and 8 seats, the Communist Party 59,401 votes and 6 seats. In 1927 the Labour and Social Democratic Parties united. Their united parliamentary group had 34 members. The Party received 368,106 votes (36.8 percent) and won 59 (of 150) seats, in the Storting elections of autumn 1927. The workers government formed in January 1928 only lasted 14 days, overturned by the State Bank.

The Communist Party received 40,074 votes (4 percent) in the elections of 1927 and its representation in the Storting fell from the previous 6 to 3 seats.

f   *Italy*

In 1914, the Italian Socialist Party took a decisive position against intervening in the World War. [Benito] Mussolini, who was then the editor of the Socialists' central organ, *Avanti*,[42] did go over to the interventionists and leave the Party (November 1914) but the Party itself remained true to its anti-war policy and participated in the Zimmerwald and Kienthal Conferences. After the end of the War, the Socialist Party benefitted from this stance, when demobilised soldiers returned home disappointed. A wave of revolutionary strikes and local uprisings flooded over the country. The Socialist Party became more radical: the *Bologna Congress* of October 1919 proclaimed its entry into the Third International but did not expel the opportunist right wing and did not understand how to lead the revolutionary masses. At the November 1919 elections it received 1,840,000 votes and 156 seats (of 850), which made it the strongest party in the country. But the indecisive attitude of the divided Party leadership in the midst of revolutionary ferment, as the working masses move *to the armed occupation of factories and large landed estates* (August–September 1920), disappointed the masses and allowed the reformists, who made a pact with [Giovanni] Giolitti behind the scenes, to throttle the movement. At the *Livorno Congress* in January 1921 the Communists vainly tried to push through acceptance of the 21 conditions for admission to the Third International. This would have resulted in the expulsion of the reformists. When the Congress rejected the 21 conditions, the Communists left and organised themselves as a separate Communist Party of Italy. But cleavages continued to open within the workers movement. After the reformists were expelled from the Party at the Rome Congress (beginning of October 1922) there were two social democratic parties side by side: the openly reformist Partito Socialista Unitario Italiano (supporters of Turati) and the centrist Partito Socialista Italiano (Maximalists).[43] Weakened

---

42   ['*Avanti*' means '*Forwards*'.]

43   ['Partito Socialista Unitario Italiano' means 'United Italian Socialist Party'. 'Partito Socialista Italiano' means 'Italian Socialist Party'.]

and fragmented, the socialist workers movement was unable to successfully resist Fascism, which was supported by the terrified bourgeois classes on the quiet. The Fascists' 'March on Rome' and Mussolini's seizure of power already took place on 28 October 1922.

The elections of 6 April 1924 were held on the basis of a fascist electoral law. Despite fascist terror, the Maximalists (who had kept hold of the Party's central press organ, *Avanti*) obtained 360,694 votes (5 percent) and 22 seats; the Reformists (who had founded the newspaper *Giustizia* as their central organ) obtained 422,957 votes (5.9 percent) and 25 seats; the Communist Party obtained 268,191 votes (3.7 percent) and 19 seats. After the government dissolved the Partito Socialista Unitario in (November 1925) it was immediately refounded under the name Partito Socialista Unitario dei Lavoratori Italiani.[44] Again forcibly dissolved by the government (November 1926), it transferred its headquarters to Paris (7 November 1926), where its *first Congress abroad* was held (18–19 December 1927). Its Action Program sets as its task the restoration of the unity of Italian socialism and the overthrow of fascism. A *unification congress* of the Maximalists and Reformists did in fact take place in Paris (19–20 July 1930), the old Party name Partito Socialista Italiano was again adopted and the *Avenire del Lavoratore*, which had appeared for the previous 34 years in Switzerland, was converted into the new organ of the united Party under the name *Avanti*.

g The Balkan Countries: Bulgaria, Yugoslavia and Romania
α Bulgaria
The Bulgarian Social Democratic Workers Party was formed in 1893 and in 1894 adopted a declaration of principles modelled on the Erfurt Program. It split in 1903 into a revolutionary, or 'Narrow' (orthodox Marxist) tendency and an opportunist or 'Broad' tendency. The latter took part in the imperialist policies of the bourgeoisie, justified the Balkan War of 1912 and the World War, and voted for war credits. The Narrows was one of the few socialist groups which, like the Serbian and Romanian socialists, defended proletarian internationalism and fought against the World War. The Bulgarian Broad Social Democrats emerged compromised from the lost War; the working masses followed the Communists (the former Narrows). In 1919 the Social Democrats joined with the bourgeoisie in the coalition government of [Teodor] Todorov in the hope that once the Communist Party had been smashed up the masses would follow

---

44   ['Partito Socialista Unitario dei Lavoratori Italiani' means 'Unitary Socialist Party of Italian Workers'.]

them. They took part in the coup against [Aleksandar] Stambulisky's government (June 1923) and sent a Social Democrat, Dimo Kazasov, into the newly formed fascist government of [Aleksandar] Tsankov. They also took part in the elections of November 1923 in coalition with the fascist government block and voted for the first 'Law for the Protection of the State', which dissolved the Communist Party and made it illegal. The rising of peasants and workers against government terror was defeated with the active assistance of the Social Democrats.[45] Two Communist deputies were murdered and the remainder were expelled from parliament (early in 1925). A fresh rising, in April 1925, was also bloodily suppressed. Not until the Party Congress of January 1926 were the co-conspirators in the fascist coup of June 1923, Kazasov and Arsen Tsankov (the brother of Prime Minister Tsankov), expelled from the Party! At the elections of March 1927 to the Sobranie,[46] the compromised Social Democrats could only obtain 10 seats, while the illegal Communist Party, under the name 'Workers Party', received 29,210 votes and 4 seats. In the elections of 21 June 1931, the Social Democrats only obtained 27,323 votes and 5 seats, the illegal Communist Party ('Workers Party') gained 168,281 votes and 31 parliamentary seats.

β   Yugoslavia

After the collapse of Austria-Hungary, the Socialist Workers Party of Yugoslavia was formed from fragments of the old Austrian and Hungarian Social Democratic Parties.[47] In 1918–19 the social democratic leaders took part twice in coalition governments. At the Socialist Congress in Vukovar (20 June 1920), the Party as a whole joined the Third International, though the Social Democrats remained within it as a right wing. In the first elections after the war (1921) the Communist Party gained 58 seats. Only after the government had imposed an emergency law 'for the protection of the state', which expelled the Communist deputies from the Skupstina[48] and outlawed the Communist Party, did the Social Democrats set up a United Social Democratic Party (December 1921).

---

45   [An ill-timed Communist uprising took place on September 1923, after the Communist Party had been inactive during the coup against Stambulisky's elected and popular government in June 1923.]

46   [The Sobranie is the Bulgarian parliament.]

47   [In addition to Bosnian, Slovenian and Croation Social Democratic Parties, which had existed on the former Austrian and Hungarian territories of Yugoslavia, and the Montenegran Social Democrats, the Social Democratic Party of Serbia not only fused itself into the new organisation but also provided its two most prominent leaders.]

48   [The Skupstina was the Yugoslav parliament.]

In the elections to the Sobranie of September 1927,[49] the Social Democrats received 25,000 votes and won one seat, the Communists ('Independent Party') also received 25,000 but no seats. After the coup of January 1929 the Social Democratic Party was dissolved by the dictatorship and all political activity was forbidden.

The free trade unions did continue to function. At the beginning of 1930 they had approximately 40,000 members. The Chambers of Labour, consultative bodies which represent the interests of the working class, have so far been spared by the dictatorship.

γ Romania

Immediately after the end of the War, the workers movement in Romania experienced a tremendous upsurge, under the leadership of Communists. As a result of the failure of the *general strike* (October 1920), which the government defeated by militarising the railways, the movement collapsed. There was ruthless repression. In June 1921 the Federation of Socialist Parties was founded at the Ploeşti Congress. This combined the socialist parties of old Romania and the newly acquired parts of Austria and Hungary. It received 25,000 votes and one seat (of 369) in the elections of March 1922. In December 1924 the government imposed an emergency law, directed against the workers movement. At the Congress of May 1927, the previously federal organisation was unified under the name Partidul Social Democrat din România (Social Democratic Party of Romania). In the elections of July 1927 the Social Democrats received 50,059 votes (1.8 percent), as against 40,594 (1.6 percent) the previous year, but did not win a seat. After the resignation of the Liberal government in November 1928, the Social Democrats concluded an electoral alliance with the governing National-Peasant Party, in order to make use of the semi-fascist electoral law which favoured whichever party was in power. They won 9 seats. In the elections of June 1931 (after the resignation of the National-Peasants from the government) they received 94,957 votes (3.3 percent) and 6 seats.

The illegal Communist Party received 38,851 votes (1.4 percent) and no seats in the 1928 elections. It received 73,716 votes and five seats in the elections of 1931 but the Chamber annulled this result. The membership of the trade unions amounts to roughly 41,400.

---

49 [Sobranie is the Bulgarian/Macedonian equivalent of the Croation/Serbian Skupstina, the Yugoslav parliament.]

h   *England*

In 1918 universal suffrage was introduced in Great Britain and the number of members of the House of Commons was fixed at 615. In the same year, the Labour Party adopted a *socialist programme* (common ownership of the means of production). It was extended in 1928. At the elections of 1918 it received 2,171,230 votes and 57 seats; in 1924 5,281,626 votes and 151 seats; in 1929 8,048,968 votes and 287 seats.

After its victory in the 1924 elections, the Labour Party formed its first minority government, with [Ramsay] MacDonald as Prime Minister. It lasted from January until the end of October and was overturned when it decided to enter into closer commercial and financial relations with the Soviet Union. In the summer of 1929 the Labour Party again formed a government and restored diplomatic relations with the Soviet Union, which had been broken off by the Conservative government in 1925. It did not implement any socialist measures and its policy on the question of unemployment was essentially to provide charity. It nevertheless collapsed after two years because, in the Empire's critical financial condition, industrial and banking circles demanded reductions in unemployment benefits. The overwhelming majority of the Labour Party opposed this anti-working class policy but the cabinet and the Party caucus were split. MacDonald and [Philip] Snowden openly went over to the idea of forming a National Government and MacDonald became the Prime Minister of a conservative cabinet of 'national concentration'.[50] At the elections of 27 October 1931 the Labour Party received a mere 6,081,826 votes and 46 seats. The experiences of this period have contributed to the radicalisation of the English working class movement.

The Communist Party of England (CPE)[51] has no influence worth mentioning. It received about 70,000 votes at the last elections.

i   *The United States of America*

The Socialist Party fought fiercely against the entry of the United States into the World War. Its leader, Eugene Debs, called for a civil war against the war between the nations, for which he was sentenced to ten years in prison.[52] The

---

50   [More accurately, MacDonald presided over a coalition government of Labour rats, Conservatives and Liberals. The term 'national concentration', meaning a government of the right, was advocated by the German conservative Centre Party politician and chancellor in 1932, Franz von Papen. This approach led to Hitler's appointment as Chancellor in 1933. The term was not current in Britain at the time Grossman wrote.]

51   [The Party's name was in fact the 'Communist Party of Great Britain'.]

52   [Debs did not, in the speech for which he was convicted, explicitly call for civil war but did

Socialist Party suffered severe losses as a result of government terror during the last years of the War and because the Communists split away (1921). The courts took advantage of the political indifference of workers, a consequence of the long period of prosperity, to cancel a number of important labour laws. At the congressional elections of November 1924, the Socialist Party won 2 seats (in New York and Milwaukee) of 531. It did not stand a candidate of its own, in the presidential election of 1924, and supported the candidature of Robert La Follette. The Socialist Party has been more active since 1926 when, as a consequence of extreme rationalisation, 3 to 5 million workers were already unemployed. This led to wage reductions and strikes (the year long strike of coal miners). The Socialist Party won 40,536 votes at the congressional elections of 1928 but no seats. Its candidate, Norman Thomas, received a mere 267,478 votes in the presidential election of 1928. In the congressional elections of 1930 the Socialist Party received 238,797 votes. Almost half the Party is organised in foreign language sections (Finnish, Yugoslav, Italian, Lithuanian, Jewish).

The Farmer-Labor Party, founded in 1919, received 277,540 votes in the congressional elections of 1930. The Communist Party (Workers Party), founded in 1921, received 60,385 votes at the same elections. The Socialist Labor Party belongs to the past (30,532 votes in 1930).

k   *Russia*

For the development of socialism in Russia, see the article 'Bolshevism'.

Literature

In addition to the literature mentioned in

Grünberg, Carl 1907, 'Sozialdemokratie', in *Wörterbuch der Volkswirtschaft. Zweite Band 2*, edited by Ludwig Elster, second edition, Jena: Fischer, pp. 851–74.

Grünberg, Carl 1911, 'Sozialdemokratie', in *Wörterbuch der Volkswirtschaftslehre. Zweite Band*, edited by Ludwig Elster, third edition, Jena: Fischer, pp. 799–827.

Drahn, Ernst 1926, 'Sozialdemokratie', in *Handwörterbuch der Staatswissenschaften. Band 7*, edited by Ludwig Elster, Adolf Weber and Friedrich Wieser, fourth edition, Jena: Fischer, pp. 510–66.

we refer to the following publications:

---

denounce the World War and advocate 'the war of the working class of the world against the ruling class, the capitalist class of the world', Debs 192?, pp. 22–3.]

1 General Works

The following periodicals contain rich material on the history of the socialist and Communist movements in all countries:

Archiv für die Geschichte des Sozialismus und der Arbeiterbewegung, volumes 1 to 15, Leipzig, 1910–30.
Die Gesellschaft, Berlin.
Der Kampf, Wien.
Die Kommunistische Internationale, Berlin.
Internationale Presse-Korrespondenz, Berlin.
Jahrbuch für Politik, Wirtschaft, Arbeiterbewegung, 1922/23, 1923/24, 1924/25, Berlin.
Sozialistische Monatshefte, Berlin.
Reports of the parties to party congresses.
Minutes of the International Congresses of the Second and Third Internationals (see 'The Internationals' above, pp. 361–402).

Beer, Max 1957 [1919–25], *The General History of Socialism and Social Struggles*, New York: Russell & Russell.
Davis, Jerome 1930, *Contemporary Social Movements*, New York: Century.
Grigaut, Maurice 1931, *Histoire du travail et des travailleurs*, Paris: Delagrave.
Herkner, Heinrich 1921 [1894], *Die Arbeiterfrage: Eine Einführung*, two volumes, seventh edition, Berlin: de Gruyter.
Rappoport, Angelo S. 1924, *Dictionary of Socialism*, London: Unwin.
Sombart, Werner 1924, *Der proletarische Sozialismus: ('Marxismus')*, tenth edition, two volumes, Jena: Fischer.
Zimand, Savel 1921, *Modern Social Movements: Descriptive Summaries and Bibliographies*, New York: Wilson.

2 Individual Studies

Austria

Austerlitz, Friedrich 1931, *Ausgewählte Aufsätze und Reden*, Wien: Wiener Volksbuchhandlung.
Bauer, Otto 1970 [1923], *The Austrian Revolution*, New York: Franklin.
Bauer, Otto 1930, 'Die Bourgeois-Republik in Oesterreich', *Kampf*, 23, no. 5: 193–202.
Brügel, Ludwig 1922–5, *Geschichte der Oesterreichischen Sozialdemokratie*, five volumes, Wien: Wiener Volksbuchhandlung.
Danneberg, Robert 1931 [1924], *The New Vienna*, translated by Henry James Stenning, London: Labour Party.
Trotsky, Leon 1975 [1929], 'The Austrian Crisis and Communism', in *Writings of Leon Trotsky (1929)*, New York: Pathfinder, pp. 383–96.

Belgium

Bertrand, Louis 1906–7, *Histoire de la démocratie et du socialisme en Belgique depuis 1830*, two volumes, preface by Emile Vandervelde, Bruxelles: Dechenne.

Bertrand, Louis 1927, *Souvenirs d'un meneur socialiste*, two volumes, Bruxelles: L'Églantine.

Bologne, Maurice 2005 [1930], *De proletarische opstand von 1830 in Belgie*, Bruxelles: Aden.

Troclet, Léon-Eli 1931, *Les Partis Politiques en Belgique*, Bruxelles: L'Églantine.

Vandervelde, Emile 1925, *Le Parti Ouvrier Belge 1885–1925*, Bruxelles: L'Églantine.

Wasnair, Emile 1930, *Histoire ouvrière et paysanne de Belgique*, Bruxelles: L'Églantine.

Bulgaria

Pettkoff, G. 1928, 'Die bulgarische Sozialdemokratie und die Bauern', *Der Kampf*, 21, no. 3: 113–7.

Denmark

Wijnblad, Emil and Alsing Andersen 1921, *Det danske Socialdemokratis Historie fra 1871 til 1921*, two volumes, København: Fremad.

England

Bardoux, Jacques 1924, *J. Ramsay Macdonald*, Paris: Plon.

Beer, Max 1948 [1919–20], *A History of British Socialism*, introduced by Richard Henry Tawney, two volumes, fifth edition, London: Allen & Unwin.

Clayton, Joseph 1926, *The Rise and Decline of Socialism in Great Britain, 1884–1924*, London: Faber & Gwyer.

Cole, George Douglas Howard 2011 [1929], *The Next Ten Years in British Social and Economic Policy*, London: Routledge.

Cole, George Douglas Howard 1921, *Workers' Control in the Mining Industry*, London: Labour Publishing Company.

Communist International 1928, *Communist Policy in Great Britain: The Report of the British Commision of the Ninth plenum of the Comintern*, London: Communist Party of Great Britain.

Communist Party of Great Britain 1929, *The New Line. Documents of the 10th Congress of the Communist Party of Great Britain, held at Bermondsey, London, on 19th–22nd January 1929*, London: Communist Party of Great Britain.

Greenwood, Arthur 1929, *The Labour Outlook*, London: Chapman & Hall.

Gruyter, Jan de 1929 [1924], *Macdonald et le Labour Party*, Bruxelles: L'Églantine.

Haden-Guest, Leslie 1926, *The Labour Party and the Empire*, London: Labour Publishing Company.

Labour Party 1930, *What the Labour Government Has Done*, London: Labour Party.

Lees-Smith, Hastings Bertrand (ed.) 1971 [1928], *Encyclopaedia of the Labour Movement*, three volumes, Detroit: Gale.

Leubuscher, Charlotte 1921, *Sozialismus und Sozialisierung in England*, Jena: Fischer.

MacDonald, James Ramsay 1923, *The Foreign Policy of the Labour Party*, London: Palmer.

Pollak, Oskar 1931, 'Zwei Jahre englische Arbeiterregierung', *Der Kampf*, 24, no. 5: 201–13.

Rothstein, Theodore 1983 [1929], *From Chartism to Labourism: Historical Sketches of the English Working Class Movement*, London: Lawrence and Wishart.

Rutherford, Vickerman Henzell 1928, *India and the Labour Party*, London: Labour Publishing Company.

Shaw, George Bernard 1930, *Fabianism*, London: Fabian Society.

Slater, Gilbert 1925, 'Die englische Arbeiterbewegung seit 1914', *Archiv für die Geschichte des Sozialismus und der Arbeiterbewegung*, 11: 368–84.

Tracey, Herbert (ed.) 1925, *The Book of the Labour Party: Its History, Growth, Policy and Leaders*, three volumes, London: Caxton.

Wertheimer, Egon 1929, *Das Antlitz der britischen Arbeiterpartei*, introduced by George Douglas Howard Cole, Berlin: Dietz.

Wertheimer, Egon 1930, *Das Birminghamer Programm der britischen Arbeiterpartei*, Hamburg: Bildungsausschuss.

Also see

Grossman, Henryk 1932, 'Hyndman, Henry Mayers', in *Wörterbuch der Volkswirtschaft. Zweiter Band*, edited by Ludwig Elster, fourth edition, Jena: Fischer, pp. 369–70. [See above pp. 358–360.]

Grünberg, Carl 1931, 'Chartismus', in *Wörterbuch der Volkswirtschaft. Erster Band*, edited by Ludwig Elster, fourth edition, Jena: Fischer, pp. 525–8.

Grünberg, Carl 1932, 'Owen, Robert', in *Wörterbuch der Volkswirtschaft. Zweite Band*, edited by Ludwig Elster, fourth edition, Jena: Fischer, p. 1103.

Grünberg, Carl and Henryk Grossmann 1931, 'Christlicher und religiöser Sozialismus', in *Wörterbuch der Volkswirtschaft. Erster Band*, edited by Ludwig Elster, fourth edition, Jena: Fischer, pp. 538–59. [See above pp. 292–344.]

France

Clark, Marjorie Ruth 1966 [1930], *A History of the French Labor Movement (1910–1928)*, New York: Johnson Reprint.

Compère-Morel, Constant Adolphe 1920, *Le socialisme agraire*, Paris: Rivière.

Delevsky, Jacques 1930, *Les Antinomies socialistes et l'évolution du socialisme français*, Paris: Giard.

Déslinières, Lucien 1929, *L'organisation socialiste*, Paris: France-édition.

Grossmann, Henryk 1932, 'Guesde, Jules', in *Wörterbuch der Volkswirtschaft. Zweiter Band*, edited by Ludwig Elster, fourth edition, Jena: Fischer, pp. 256–8. [See above pp. 349–353.]

Grossmann, Henryk 1932, 'Jaurès, Jean', in *Wörterbuch der Volkswirtschaft. Zweiter Band*, edited by Ludwig Elster, fourth edition, Jena: Fischer, pp. 382–3. [See above pp. 354–357.]

Grünberg, Carl 1932, 'Kommune (Paris)', in *Wörterbuch der Volkswirtschaft, Zweiter Band*, edited by Ludwig Elster, fourth edition, Jena: Fischer, pp. 597–9.

Levasseur, Emile 1903–4 [1859], *Histoire des classes ouvrières en France, 1789 à 1870*, second edition, two volumes, Paris: Rousseau.

Lichtenberger, André 1895, *Le socialisme au XVIIIe siècle: étude sur les idées socialistes dans les écrivains francais du XVIIIe siècle avant la révolution*, Paris: Alcan.

Louis, Paul 1927, *Histoire de la class ouvrière en France de la révolution jusqu'à nos jours*, Paris: Rivière.

Louis, Paul 1925, *Histoire du socialisme en France*, Paris: Rivière.

Maritch, Sreten 1930, *Histoire du mouvement social sous le second empire à Lyon*, Paris: Rousseau.

Posse, Enst H. 1930, *Der Marxismus in Frankreich, 1871–1905: die proletarische Klassen-kampflehre des Marxismus und die parteipolitische Arbeiterbewegung bis zur Grün-dung des Parti socialiste*, Berlin: Prager.

Weill, Georges 1924, *Histoire du mouvement social en France 1852–1924*, third edition, Paris: Alcan.

Weill, Georges 1929, 'Die sozialistische Partei in Frankreich 1920–1928', *Archiv für die Geschichte des Sozialismus und der Arbeiterbewegung*, 14: 67–87.

Zévaès, Alexandre 1919, *Le Parti socialiste unifie et la guerre*, Paris: L' Effort.

Zévaès, Alexandre 1923, *Le Parti socialiste de 1904 à 1923*, Paris: Rivière.

Germany

Bernstein, Eduard (ed.) 1907–10, *Die Geschichte der Berliner Arbeiterbewegung*, three volumes, Berlin: Buchhandlung Vorwärts.

Brandis, Hirschfeld 1931, *Die deutsche Sozialdemokratie bis zum Fall des Sozialistenge-setzes*, Leipzig: Hirschfeld.

Drahn, Ernst and Susanne Leonhardt 1920, *Unterirdische Literatur im revolutionären Deutschland während des Krieges*, Berlin: Gesellschaft und Erziehung.

Fabian, Walter 1930, *Klassenkampf in Sachsen: Ein Stück Geschichte 1918–1930*, Berlin: Arbeitswelt.

Grossmann, Henryk 1931, 'Bebel, August', in *Wörterbuch der Volkswirtschaft. Erster Band*, edited by Ludwig Elster, fourth edition, Jena: Fischer, pp. 301–2. [See above pp. 236–238.]

Grossmann, Henryk 1932, 'Internationale: Die Zweite Internationale', in *Wörterbuch der Volkswirtschaft. Zweiter Band*, edited by Ludwig Elster, fourth edition, Jena: Fischer, pp. 432–9. [See above pp. 361–376.]

Grossmann, Henryk 1932, 'Internationale: Die Dritte Internationale', in *Wörterbuch der*

Volkswirtschaft. Zweiter Band, edited by Ludwig Elster, fourth edition, Jena: Fischer, pp. 439–49. [See above pp. 377–402.]

Grünberg, Carl 1932, 'Die Erste Internationale (Internationale Arbeiterassociation– IAA)', in *Wörterbuch der Volkswirtschaft. Zweiter Band*, edited by Ludwig Elster, fourth edition, Jena: Fischer, pp. 430–2.

Grünberg, Carl 1932, 'Lassalle, Ferdinand', in *Wörterbuch der Volkswirtschaft. Zweiter Band*, edited by Ludwig Elster, fourth edition, Jena: Fischer, pp. 803–4.

Grünberg, Carl 1932, 'Marx, Karl', in *Wörterbuch der Volkswirtschaft. Zweiter Band*, edited by Ludwig Elster, fourth edition, Jena: Fischer, pp. 899–901.

Haase, Ernst 1929, *Hugo Haase: Sein Leben und Wirken*, Berlin: Otten.

Kampffmeyer, Paul 1930, *Georg von Vollmar*, München: Birk.

Kommunistische Partei Deutschlands 1928, *Der Reichstag 1924–1928: 4 Jahre kapitalistische Klassenpolitik, Handbuch der Kommunistischen Reichstagsfraktion*, Berlin: Internationaler Arbeiter-Verlag.

Kommunistische Partei Deutschlands 1928, *Richtlinien für die Parlamentspolitik der KPD in den Ländern und Gemeinden*, Berlin: Internationaler Arbeiter-Verlag.

Krüger, Hans and Fritz Baade 1927, *Sozialdemokratische Agrarpolitik*, Berlin: Dietz.

Lipinski, Richard 1927–8, *Die Sozialdemokratie von ihren Anfängen bis zur Gegenwart*, two volumes, Berlin: Dietz.

Marck, Siegfried 1927, *Reformismus und Radikalismus in der deutschen Sozialdemokratie*, Berlin: Laub.

Marck, Siegfried 1931, *Sozialdemokratie*, Berlin: Pan-Verlag.

Mehring, Franz 1921 [1897], *Geschichte der deutschen Sozialdemokratie*, eleventh edition, four volumes, Berlin: Dietz.

Prager, Eugen 1970 [1921], *Geschichte der USPD: Entstehung und Entwicklung der unabhängigen Sozialdemokratischen Partei Deutschlands*, Glashütten: Auvermann.

Quarck, Max 1970 [1924], *Die erste deutsche Arbeiterbewegung: Geschichte der Arbeiterverbrüderung 1848/49*, Glashütten: Auvermann.

Radek, Karl 1925, *Die Barmat-Sozialdemokratie*, Hamburg: Hoym.

Renner, Karl 1929, *Karl Kautsky: Skizze zur Geschichte der geistigen und politischen Entwicklung der deutschen Arbeiterklasse, ihrem Lehrmeister Kautsky zum fünfundsiebzigsten Geburtstag*, Berlin: Dietz.

Scheidemann, Philipp 1923, *Memoiren eines Sozialdemokraten*, two volumes, Hamburg: Severus.

Schroeder, Wilhelm 1912, *Geschichte der sozialdemokratischen Parteiorganisation in Deutschland*, Dresden: Kader.

Italy

Angiolini, Alfredo 1908 [1900], *Cinquant'anni di socialismo in Italia*, third edition, Firenze: Nerbini.

Bonomi, Ivanoe 1945 [1928], *Leonida Bissolati e il movimento socialista in Italia*, Roma: Sesante.

Croce, Benedetto 1963 [1928], *A History of Italy, 1871–1915*, translated by Cecilia M. Ady, New York: Russell & Russell.

Michels, Robert 1911, 'Die exklusive Arbeiterpartei in Norditalien 1882–1892', *Archiv für die Geschichte des Sozialismus und der Arbeiterbewegung*, 1: 285–316.

Michels, Robert 1925, *Sozialismus in Italien*, München: Meyer und Jessen.

Nenni, Pietro 1987 [1930], *La lutte de classe en Italie*, preface by Filippo Turati, Milano: SugarCo, 1987.

Partito Socialista Italiano 1966 [1930], *Il Congresso dell'Unità Socialista, Parigi, 19–20 Luglio 1930*, Milano: Capellini.

Salvemini, Gaetano 1930, *La terreur fasciste 1922–1926*, sixth edition, Paris: Gallimard.

Netherlands

Troelstra, Pieter Jelles 1950 [1927], *Gedenkschriften*, four volumes, Amsterdam: Querido.

Vliegen, Wilhelmus Hubertus 1928, 'Die Niederlande und ihre Kolonien', *Der Kampf*, 21, no. 8: 400–46.

Norway

Meyer, Håkon 1927, *Veier, mål og midler: betragtninger over arbeiderbevegelsen*, Oslo: Eget.

Meyer, Håkon 1928, 'Die Entwicklung der Arbeiterbewegung in Norwegen', *Der Kampf*, 21, no. 3: 118–22.

Romania

Sozialdemokratische Partei Rumäniens 1930, *Aktionsprogramm und Organisationsstatut der Sozialdemokratischen Partei Rumäniens*, Cernăuţi: Sozialdemokratische Partei Rumäniens.

Dumas, Charles and Khristian Rakovski 1915, *Les Socialistes et la Guerre*, Bucureşti: Cercul de editură.

Gabriel, Josef 1928, *Fünfzigjährige Geschichte der Banater Arbeiterbewegung*, Temesvar: Schwäbische Verlag.

Pistiner, Jakob 1925, 'Der Imperialismus der Randstaaten', *Der Kampf*, 19, no. 10: 375–80.

Radacenau, Lothar 1928, 'Zur neuen Politik der rumänischen Sozialdemokratie', *Der Kampf*, 21, no. 10: 423–9.

Voinea, Şerban 1928, 'Die Arbeiterbewegung in Rumänien', *Der Kampf*.[53]

---

53   [There is no such article in *Der Kampf* between 1924 and 1932.]

Voinea, Şerban 1924, 'Der Sozialismus in rückständigen Ländern', *Der Kampf*, 18, no. 12: 500–8.

Sweden

Bull, Edvard 1922, 'Die Entwicklung der Arbeiterbewegung in den drei skandinavischen Ländern', *Archiv für die Geschichte des Sozialismus und der Arbeiterbewegung*, 10: 329–61.

Heberle, Rudolf 1925, *Zur Geschichte der Arbeiterbewegung in Schweden*, Jena: Fischer.

Henriksson-Holmberg, Gustaf 1916, 'Die Entwicklungsgeschichte der Arbeiterbewegung in Schweden', *Archiv für die Geschichte des Sozialismus*, 6: 32–83.

Switzerland

Bretscher, Willy and Ernst Steinmann (eds) 1923, *Die sozialistische Bewegung in der Schweiz 1848–1920*, Bern: Iseli.

Grimm, Robert 1925, *Das sozialdemokratische Arbeitsprogramm: eine Vortragsreihe*, Bern: Sozialdemokratische Partei der Schweiz.

Heeb, Friedrich (ed.) 1930, *Der Schweizerische Gewerkschaftsbund 1880–1930*, Bern: Schweizerischer Gewerkschaftsbund.

Schenker, Ernst 1926, *Die sozialdemokratische Bewegung in der Schweiz, von ihren Anfängen bis zur Gegenwart*, Appenzell: Jakober.

Sozialdemokratische Partei der Schweiz 1928, *Die Sozialdemokratische Partei der Schweiz: Historische Notizen über ihre Entstehung, ihr Wachstum und ihre Aktion*, Bern: Schweitzerische Sozialdemokratische Parteisekretariat.

United States

Rand School of Social Science 1929, 1930, 1931, *American Labor Year Book*, New York: Rand School of Social Science.

Beard, Mary 1920, *A Short History of the American Labor Movement*, New York: Harcourt, Brace, Howe.

Bimba, Anthony 1927, *The History of the American Working Class*, New York: International Publishers.

Commons, John Rogers 1918, *History of Labour in the United States*, two volumes, New York: Macmillan.

Dubreuil, Hyacinthe 1930 [1929], *Arbeiter in USA*, translated by Hans Kauders, Leipzig: Bibliographisches Institut.

Harnack, Arvid 1931, *Die vormarxistische Arbeiterbewegung in den Vereinigten Staaten*, Jena: Fischer.

Haywood, William Dudley 1966 [1930], *Bill Haywood's Book: The Autobiography of William D. Haywood*, New York.

Hillquit, Morris 1910 [1903], *History of Socialism in the United States*, fifth edition New York: Funk & Wagnalls.

Lauck, William Jett 1929, *The New Industrial Revolution and Wages: A Survey of the Radical Changes in American Theory and Practice Which Have Come in since the Present Era of Prosperity*, New York: Funk & Wagnalls.

Lufft, Hermann 1928, *Samuel Gompers: Arbeiterschaft und Volksgemeinschaft in den Vereinigten Staaten von Amerika*, Berlin: Hobbing.

Perlman, Selig 1923, *A History of Trade Unionism in the United States*, New York: Macmillan.

Ware, Norman J. 1964 [1929], *The Labor Movement in the United States 1860–1895: A Study in Democracy*, New York: Vintage.

Yugoslavia

Lapčević, Dragiša 1979 [1922], *Istorija socijalisma u Srbiji: Rat i Srpska socijalna demokratija: Okupacija*, Beograd: Slovo Ljubve.

Topalowitsch, Zivko 1928, 'Politik der Grossmächte am Balkan', *Der Kampf*, 21, no. 8: 369–76.

CHAPTER 34

Sorel, Georges

Translated from German by Joseph Fraccia

French socialist, anti-democratic thinker and theoretician of revolutionary syndicalism, born on 2 November 1847 in Cherbourg, into a pious Catholic family. After completion of an academic secondary education, Sorel attended the École polytechnique in Paris,[1] became an engineer and was employed by the state in 'bridge and road construction'. Having been named a chief engineer in 1892, Sorel departed from state service, renouncing his pension in order to be able to devote himself to his studies with complete independence. He had already begun his literary activity in 1889 as a Proudhonist moralist, with a short essay, 'The trial of Socrates'.[2] In the following years, he immersed himself in Marx and joined the socialist movement (1893). From then on he devoted himself to the cause of the proletariat. Armed with an encyclopaedic knowledge, he researched proletarian struggles, sensibilities and daily life, and engaged in extraordinarily fruitful intellectual activity for 30 years. No leader and always outside the workers movement, he lived first in Paris and then, after the death of his wife, whose origins were humble, in complete isolation in Boulogne-sur-Seine.

Sorel begins his first stage as a reformist, when he is a principal contributor to two Marxist reviews *L'ère nouvelle* (1893–4) and *Le devenir social* (1895–7);[3] he hopes that cooperation between the proletariat and other classes will lead to the realisation of socialism which he called the 'workers movement in democracy'. When, however, it became apparent after the victory of [Alfred] Dreyfus's appeal, that the sublime struggle for morality and justice had become a political business, a trade in ministerial posts and also that the rising wave of reformism in other countries similarly resulted in a parliamentary morass, Sorel saw democracy as a threat to the future of the proletariat and socialism. In his period of greatest creativity 1900–10, he turned to *revolutionary syndicalism*, to which he remained loyal until his death. In this spontaneous movement of workers in France, its ruthless disavowal of state action and parliamentarism, its appeal for 'direct action', for violence and the general strike, its bitter

---

1 ['École polytechnique' means 'Polytechnic University'.]
2 [Sorel 1889; an extract in English: Sorel 1976a.]
3 [*L'ère nouvelle* means '*The New Era*'. *Le devenir social* means '*The Social Future*'.]

struggle against intellectuals, Sorel believed he had found the correct path for the proletarian struggle for emancipation and set himself the task of providing it with a deeper theoretical foundation. During this period his major works appeared: *Reflections on Violence, The Illusions of Progress* and 'The Decomposition of Marxism'.[4] Together with Hubert Lagardelle, [Victor] Griffuelhes and Édouard Berth, he was at the same time also a principal contributor to *Le mouvement socialiste* (1899–1910).[5]

Early on, Sorel recognised the weakness of social democracy, whose theoretical leaders (Jules Guesde, Karl Kautsky) were, in the pre-war period, regarded as the recognised representatives of exemplary Marxism. With bitter mockery he began to combat the dominant ideologies of social democracy and to work out a theory of revolutionary syndicalism, in which he attempted to unify, in a very original fusion, the influences of Marx and Proudhon. Sorel's historical significance consists in having understood that, at a time when, in the ranks of the Marxists themselves, Marxism had generally become superficial, at a time of reformist abandonment of original goals, it was necessary to crystallise, with intelligence, courage and energy, the *revolutionary core* of Marxism; to return the *class struggle* in all of its sharpness to the primary position, to fiercely combat parliamentary socialists' accommodation with bourgeois democracy and to emphasise again and again the *catastrophic aspect* of the social revolution. Drawing on the fundamental Marxist idea of social revolution and on [Giambattista] Vico's theory of revolutionary leaps (*ricorsi*), Sorel emphasised the impulsively volatile character of the social movement. He combated the shallow application of the *evolutionary idea*, which the reformist socialists had taken over from bourgeois democracy, that was socially reactionary, despite all the radical 'progressive' phrases.

Influenced by [Henri] Bergson's anti-intellectual philosophy, Sorel turned against the *overestimation of the intellectual factor* in the workers movement and against the Marxist simplifiers of historical materialism, according to whom progressive capitalist development will automatically be accompanied by a corresponding growth of the class consciousness and revolutionary will of the proletariat. In contrast, Sorel emphasised that the broad masses' revolutionary will to fight is not a question of appropriating Marxist ideas but rather of *instinct*, which is formed through experience of the class struggle in daily life and which drives the spirit of the masses forward. Starting with the fact that the ideas and party programmes, formulated in a comprehensible man-

---

4   Sorel 1999, with an appendix, 'In defence of Lenin' from the fourth edition of 1920; Sorel 1969; Sorel 1961.

5   [*Le mouvement socialiste* means '*The Socialist Movement*'.]

ner by a handful of intellectuals, only influenced the proletarian masses to a very small degree, Sorel attempted to complete the Marxist *epistemology* of the class struggle through the analysis of the *psychological* mechanism of the class struggle. From this viewpoint, Sorel delivered a principled *critique of democracy* as a system and of its political form: the state and parties.

Sorel saw the cause of the weakness of the workers movement in its inability to adapt to the unique characteristics of the proletarian soul, in order to be able to comprehend workers as *producers*, in the context of their activity in the labour process. Among socialists of all countries the organisation of the *party* has stepped into the place of the organisation of the proletarian *class*. The mechanism of the political party has a corrupting effect: it is open not only to proletarian elements but to members of all classes, that is, also to bourgeois elements, on the basis of which a cleavage emerges between programme and practice and the proletarian character of the workers movement is weakened. The 'party' is the old grouping from Greek antiquity into the nineteenth century; it replaces the rule of one clique of intellectual leaders with that of another, without preparing for the end of rule itself. The true organisational form of workers *as a class* is, on the contrary, the *trade union* (*syndicat*), the embryo of social renewal, which encompasses workers as producers and can therefore emotionally influence them. The true form of working class struggle is therefore not the ballot paper but rather the *strike* and the *general strike*, as revolt of the producers on the field of production itself. So Sorel arrives at his theory of 'myths' as guiding ideas in the formation of revolutionary proletarian class consciousness. One such great idea is the general strike as the means to the revolutionary transformation of society.

In order, however, to be able to carry out this transformation, the working class must achieve confidence in itself and in its historical mission: the construction of a new economic order. It must generate its own cultural elements, and – in contradiction with the solely consumer culture of the bourgeoisie – develop a pure producer morality that strengthens its proletarian consciousness and will to act.

Sorel provided no self-contained theory of the proletariat, constructed on an historical and economic foundation – as Marx did – which gives rise to proletarian tactics. He concentrated his entire theory on a single point: the realisation of socialism by the determined proletarian elite, which is resolutely prepared for the decisive battle (bataille napoléonienne), encompassed in organisations of producers.[6]

---

6   ['Bataille napoléonienne' means 'Napoléonic battle'.]

When French syndicalism, despite its healthy revolutionary core, strayed along opportunistic detours, after 1910, and was just as little able to preserve the momentum of the French proletariat as the Second International of reformist socialists, which fell apart at the beginning of the World War despite its decades of educational work, Sorel descended into the blackest pessimism and despaired over the future of the proletariat. He saw in the 'Great War' the struggle of plutocratic interests in democratic disguise. As Lenin unleashed the Russian Revolution and the Bolsheviks seized power, Sorel gained new hope for the future of the proletariat. Seventy-three years old and near death, he defended the proletarian Soviet Republic with touching boldness. While Kautsky, Guesde, [Rudolf] Hilferding and other representatives of official Marxism conducted the most bitter vendetta against the proletarian Russian state, the anarcho-syndicalist Sorel wrote his famous 'In Defence of Lenin' (1920),[7] for Lenin the Marxist. He died on 28 August 1922.

Writings

Apart from the writings mentioned in the text, also see

1976 [1898], *The Socialist Future of the Syndicates*, in Georges Sorel, *From Georges Sorel: Essays in Socialism and Philosophy*, translated by John Stanley and Charlotte Stanley, New York: Oxford University Press, pp. 71–93.

1925 [1898], *La ruine du monde antique: Conception matérialiste de l'histoire*, second edition, Paris: Rivière.

1903, *Saggi di critica del marxismo*, Milano/Palermo/Napoli: Sandron.

1922 [1903], *Introduction à l'économie moderne*, second edition, Paris: Jacques.

1984 [1906], *Social Foundations of Contemporary Economics*, translated by John L. Stanley, New Brunswick: Transaction.

1909, *La revolution dreyfusienne*, Paris: Rivière.

1919, *Matériaux d'une théorie du prolétariat*, Paris: Rivière.

1920, 'Advance towards Socialism', in Georges Sorel, *The Illusions of Progress*, translated by John Stanley and Charlotte Stanley, Berkeley: University of California Press, pp. 187–214.

---

7 [Sorel 1999, pp. 283–92.]

Literature

Berth, Edouard 1928, 'Nachwort', in Georges Sorel, *Über die Gewalt*, translated by Ludwig Oppenheimer, Innsbruck: Universitäts-Verlag Wagner.

Bouglé, Célestin Charles Alfred 1908, *Syndicalisme et démocratie*, Paris: Cornély.

Cazalis, Emile 1923, *Les positions sociales du syndicalisme ouvrier en France*, Paris: Les Presses universitaires de France.

Lanzillo, Agostino 1910, *Giorgio Sorel*, Roma: Libreria editrice romana.

Maletzki, Alexander 1923, 'Georges Sorel', *Die Kommunistische Internationale*, 24: 125–51 (a good, short presentation).

Pirou, Gaëtan 1927, *Georges Sorel: 1847–1922*, Paris: Rivière (with bibliographical information).

Pirou, Gaëtan 1910, *Proudhonisme et syndicalisme révolutionnaire*, Paris: Rousseau.

Posse, Ernst H. 1978 [1930], 'Der Antidemokratische Denker', introduction to Georges Sorel, *Die Auflösung des Marxismus*, translated by Ernst H. Posse, Hamburg: Edition Nautilus.

Posse, Ernst H. 1930, 'Sorels "Faschismus" und sein Sozialismus', *Archiv für die Geschichte des Sozialismus und der Arbeiterbewegung*, 15: 161–93.

Serbos, Gaston 1913, *Une philosophie de la production: le néo-marxisme syndicaliste*, Paris: Rousseau.

On revolutionary syndicalism also see:

Grossmann, Henryk 1931, 'Anarchism', section 4, in *Wörterbuch der Volkswirtschaft. Erster Band*, edited by Ludwig Elster, fourth edition, Jena: Fischer, pp. 97–109. [See above pp. 210–235.]

References

Adler, Georg 1891, 'Die Entwicklung des sozialistischen Programms in Deutschland, 1863–1890', *Jahrbuch für Nationalökonomie und Statistik*, 56, 1.

'Advocatus' (Paul Vogt) 1895, 'Das Proportionalwahlsystem und die deutschen Reichstagswahle', *Neue Zeit*, 13, no. 29: 68–73; 13, no. 30: 100–8; 31: 142–9.

Anonymous 1892, *Jakim być powinien program młodzieży żydowskiej?*, Lwów: Wydawnictwo Członków Towarzystwa 'Syon'.

Anonymous 1900, *Di geshikhte fun der yidisher arbeyter bevegung in Russland un Poylen*, Genève: Algemeyner yidisher arbeyterbund in Lita, Poylen un Rusland.

Anonymous 1902, *Historya żydowskiego ruchu robotniczego na Litwie w Polsce i Rosyi*, London: Wydawnictwo ogólno-żydowskiego związku robotniczego na Litwie, w Polsce i Rosyi.

Anonynous 1925a, 'Die Entchristlichung der Industriearbeiterschaft', *Mitteilungen an die Arbeiterpräsides der Diözese Paderborn*, 2.

Anonymous 1925b, *Neuwerk*, February.

Anonymous 2007 [1907], *The International Anarchist Congress: Amsterdam, 1907*, Federazione dei Comunisti Anarchici, http://www.fdca.it/fdcaen/press/pamphlets/sla-5/sla-5.pdf, accessed 3 October 2016.

Arbeiter-Zeitung 1897, 'Sechste Parteitag der österreichischen Sozialdemokratie', 9 June: 2–4.

Arbeytershtime 1892, 3.

Archbishops' Committees of Inquiry 1918, *Christianity and Industrial Problems*, London: Society for Promoting Christian Knowledge.

Aschkenaze, Tobiasz 1904, 'W kwestyi żydowskiej', *Krytyka*, 6, vol. 1, no. 6: 438–46; and 6, vol. 2, no. 1: 45–53.

Bacon, Francis 1905 [1620], *Novum Organum. Book 1*, translated by R. Ellis and James Spedding, London: George Routledge and Sons.

Bakounine, Michel 1873 [1868], 'Discours de Bakounine au Congrès de Berne', in Comité Fédéral Jurassien, *Mémoire présenté par la fédération jurassienne de l'Association internationale des travailleurs à toutes les fédérations de l'Internationale*, Sonvillier: Comité Fédéral Jurassien, pp. 20–38.

Bakounine, Michel 1895 [written 1871], 'Dieu et l'état', in Michel Bakounine, *Oeuvres. Tom 1*, Paris: Stock, pp. 261–326.

Bakunin, Mikhail 1953 [1870], 'Ethics: Morality of the State' [an extract from *The Bears of Bern and the Bear of Petersburg*], in Mikhail Bakunin, *The Political Philosophy of Bakunin: Scientific Anarchism*, edited by Grigori Petrovitch Maximoff, New York: Free Press, pp. 136–45.

Bakunin, Mikhail 1971a [1867], *Federalism, Socialism, Anti-Theologism*, in Mikhail Bakunin, *Bakunin on Anarchy: Selected Works by the Activist-Founder of World Anarch-ism*, translated by Sam Dolgoff, New York: Vintage, pp. 102–47.

Bakunin, Mikhail 1971b [1869], 'The Policy of the International', in Mikhail Bakunin, *Bakunin on Anarchy: Selected Works by the Activist-Founder of World Anarchism*, translated by Sam Dolgoff, New York: Vintage, pp. 160–74.

Bakunin, Mikhail 1971c [1871], *God and the State*, in Mikhail Bakunin, *Bakunin on Anarchy: Selected Works by the Activist-Founder of World Anarchism*, translated by Sam Dolgoff, New York: Vintage, pp. 225–42.

Bauer, Helene 1929, 'Ein neuer Zusammenbruchstheoretiker', *Der Kampf*, 22, no. 6: 270–80.

Bauer, Otto 1931, 'Bauers rede', *Arbeiter-Zeitung*, 31 July: 2–3.

Bauer, Otto 2000 [1907], *The Question of Nationalities and Social Democracy*, translated by Joseph O'Donnell, Minneapolis: University of Minnesota Press.

Becker, Bernhard 1875, *Geschichte der Revolutionären Pariser Kommune in den Jahren 1789 bis 1794*, Braunschweig: Bracke.

Biliński, Leon 1883, *O istocie, rozwoju i obecnym stanie socjalizmu*, Kraków: Przeglądu Polskiego.

Biro-Jakubowicz, Henryk 1905, '"Bund" Ogólno-żydowski związek robotniczy na Litwie, w Polsci i w Rosyi', *Krytyka*, 7, vol. 1, no. 1: 37–45; and 7, vol. 1 no. 2: 140–50.

Bliss, William Dwight Porter 1890, *What is Christian Socialism?*, Boston: Society of Christian Socialists.

Bramble, Tom 2012, 'Is there a Labour Aristocracy in Australia?', *Marxist Left Review* 4, Winter: 103–51.

Brauer, Theodor 1920, *Christentum und Sozialismus: Vortrag gehalten auf dem 10. Kon-greß der christlichen Gewerkschaften Deutschlands am 23. November 1920 in Essen*, Köln: Christlicher Gewerkschaftsverlag.

Braunthal, Alfred 1929, 'Der Zusammenbruch der Zusammenbruchstheorie', *Die Gesell-schaft*, 6, vol. 2, no. 10: 280–304.

Brown, William Montgomery 1923 [1920], *Communism and Christianism*, Galion, Ohio: Bradford-Brown Educational Company.

Buonarroti, Philippe 1836 [1828], *Babeuf's Conspiracy for Equality*, London: H. Hether-ington.

Buschman, Marten and Tessel Pollmann 1987, 'Een goed bewaard sociaal-democratisch geheim: apostel Van Kol en Domela Nieuwenhuis en hun koffieplantage op Java', *Vrij Nederland*, 7 February.

Carbonell, Ángel 1928, *El Colectivismo y la ortodoxia católica: estudio religioso social*, Bar-celona: Subirana.

Cathrein, Victor 1910 [1890], *Der Sozialismus: Eine Untersuchung seiner Grundlagen und seiner Durchführbarkeit*, tenth edition, Freiburg: Herdersche Buchhandlung.

Cliff, Tony 1957, 'The Economic Roots of Reformism', *Socialist Review*, 6, no. 9, available at: https://www.marxists.org/archive/cliff/works/1957/06/rootsref.htm.

Cliff, Tony 1974 [1955], *State Capitalism in Russia*, London: Pluto.

Cliff, Tony 1975, *Lenin. Volume 1: Building the Party*, London: Pluto.

Cliff, Tony 1989, *Trotsky: Towards October 1879–1917*, London: Bookmarks.

Colins, Jean Guillaume César Alexandre Hippolyte 1853, *Règne social du christianisme*, Paris: Didot Frères.

Commission of Inquiry, Interchurch World Movement of North America 1919, *Report on the Steel Strike of 1919*, New York: Harcourt, Brace and Howe.

Communist International 1936 [1928], *Program of the Communist International, Together with Its Constitution*, New York: Workers Library.

Communist International, Executive Committee 1959 [1925], 'Bolshevization and Questions of Organisation', in *The Communist International: 1919–1943 Documents. Volume 2, 1923–1928*, edited, abridged and translated by Jane Degras, London: Royal Institute of International Affairs, pp. 197–9.

Conference on Christian Politics, Economics and Citizenship 1924a, *Historical Illustrations of the Social Effects of Christianity*, London: Longmans Green.

Conference on Christian Politics, Economics and Citizenship 1924b, *Industry and Property*, London: Longmans Green.

Conference on Christian Politics, Economics and Citizenship 1924c, *Christianity and War*, London: Longmans Green.

Conference on Christian Politics, Economics and Citizenship 1924d, *The Social Function of the Church*, London: Longmans Green.

Conférence internationale du christianisme social 1910, 'Déclaration de principes', *Le Christianisme social*, 23, no. 6 (20 June): 382–4.

Daszyński, Ignacy 1902, 'Nationalität und Socialismus', *Socialistische Monatshefte*, 6, no. 9, September: 733–7.

David, Eduard 1903, *Socialismus und Landwirtschaft*, Berlin: Verlag der Socialistischen Monatshefte.

Day, Richard 1972, *Leon Trotsky and the Politics of Economic Isolation*, Cambridge: Cambridge University Press.

Debs, Eugene Victor 192?, *Eugene V. Deb's* [sic] *Canton Speech*, Chicago: Socialist Party of the United States.

Dehn, Günther 1929, *Proletarische Jugend: Lebensgestaltung und Gedankenwelt der grossstädtischen Proletarierjugend*, Berlin: Furche.

Diehl, Karl 1922, *Ueber Sozialismus, Kommunismus und Anarchismus*, fifth edition, Jena: Gustav Fischer.

Draper, Hal 1953/1954, 'The Myth of Lenin's "Revolutionary Defeatism"', *New International*, 19, no. 5, September–October: 255–82; no. 6, November–December: 313–51; and 20, no. 1, January–February: 39–59.

Ebner, Mayer 1907, 'Der jüdische Klub im österreich. Parlament', *Die Welt*, July: 9–10.

Eckert, Erwin 1976 [1927], *Was wollen die religiösen Sozialisten?*, Würzburg: JAL-Reprint.

Egalité 1880, 'Programme et adresse des collectivists-révolutionnaires Français', 21 September: 1.

Elster, Ludwig 1933, 'Smith's Lehre und die Lehren der sog. "Klassiker" der Volkswirtschaftslehre', in *Wörterbuch der Volkswirtschaft. Band 3*, edited by Ludwig Elster, fourth edition, Jena: Fischer, pp. 211–34.

Eltzbacher, Paul 1908, *Anarchism*, translated by Steven T. Byington New York: Tucker.

Engels, Frederick 1975 [1845], *The Condition of the Working Class in England*, in *Marx and Engels Collected Works. Volume 4*, New York: International Publishers, pp. 295–596.

Engels, Frederick 1975b, 'Rapid Progress of Communism in Germany', in *Marx and Engels Collected Works. Volume 4*, New York: International Publishers, pp. 229–33.

Engels, Frederick 1979a [1852], 'Poles, Tschechs and Germans', in *Marx and Engels Collected Works. Volume 11*, New York: International Publishers, pp. 43–6.

Engels, Frederick 1979b [1851], 'Revolution and Counter-revolution in Germany', in *Marx and Engels Collected Works. Volume 11*, New York: International Publishers, pp. 3–96.

Engels, Frederick 1990a [1888], 'Preface to the 1888 English edition of the *Manifesto of the Communist Party*', in *Marx and Engels Collected Works. Volume 26*, New York: International Publishers, pp. 512–18.

Engels, Frederick 1990b [1901–2, written 1891], 'A Critique of the Draft Social Democratic Programme of 1891', in *Marx and Engels Collected Works. Volume 27*, New York: International Publishers, pp. 217–32.

Engels, Frederick 1990c [1895], 'Introduction to Karl Marx's *The Class Struggles in France, 1848 to 1850*', in *Marx and Engels Collected Works. Volume 27*, New York: International Publishers, pp. 506–24.

L'espoir du monde 1914, 7, nos. 7–8 (August).

Estreicher, Stanisław 1896, *Rozwój organizacji socjalistycznych w krajach polskich*, Kraków: Spółka Wydawnictwo Polska.

Evangelisch-soziale Kongress 1891, *Verhandlungen des 2. evangelisch-soziale Kongresses*, Göttingen: Vandenhoeck & Ruprecht.

Eyneygler, Karol 1906, 'Vegn unzere agitatsie un propaganda', *Sotsial-Demokrat*, 28 September: 2–3.

Fallot, Tommy 1911, *Christianisme social: études et fragments*, Paris: Fischbacher.

Feiler, Arthur 1931 [1929], *Das Experiment des Bolschewismus*, sixth edition, Frankfurt am Main: Frankfurter Societäts-Druckerei.

Feldman, Wilhelm 1893, *Asymilatorzy, syoniści i polacy*, Kraków: Barański.

Feyner, Leon 1948, 'Di bundishe prese in Krake fun 1905 bis 1930', in *Historisher samlbuch: materialn un dokumentn tsushtayer tsu der geshikhte fun algemainer yidishn arbeter-bund* Warsaw: Farlag 'Ringen'.

Foster, John Bellamy and Robert W. McChesney 2010, 'Listen Keynesians, It's the System! Response to Palley', *Monthly Review*, 61, no. 11, April: 44–56.

Fritsche, Gustav 1966 [1927], *William Morris' Sozialismus und anarchistischer Kommunismus*, Leipzig: Tauchnitz.

Gechtman, Roni 2005, *Yidisher Sotsializm: The Origin and Contexts of the Jewish Labor Bund's National Program*, PhD thesis, New York: New York University.

Gesamtparteivertretung, Sozialdemokratische Arbeiterpartei Österreichs 1905, 'Bericht der Gesamt Parteivertretung an den Parteitag', *Arbeiter-Zeitung*, 22 October: 8–9.

Godwin, William 1842 [1793], *Enquiry Concerning Political Justice, and its Influence on Morals and Happiness*, two volumes, fourteenth edition, London: Watson.

Goethe, Johann Wolfgang von 1869 [1808], *Faust: Eine Tragödie*, Leipzig: Brockhaus.

Goethe, Johann Wolfgang von 2014 [1808], *Faust: A Tragedy*, in Johann Wolfgang von Goethe, *Faust I & II*, translated by Stuart Atkins, Princeton: Princeton University Press, pp. 1–119.

Göhre, Paul 1896, *Die evangelisch-soziale Bewegung, ihre Geschichte und ihre Ziele*, Leipzig: Grunow.

Gounelle, Élie 1909, *Pourquoi sommes nous chrétien-sociaux?*, Saint-Blaise: Roubaix, Foyer solidariste.

Gounelle, Élie 1923, *L'inspiration fondamentale du christianisme social*, Saint-Etienne: Bureau du christianisme social.

Gounelle, Élie 1925, *L'église et les problèmes économiques, industriels et sociaux: rapport présenté à la Conférence chrétienne universelle du christianisme pratique de Stockholm*, Alençon: Corbière et Jugain.

Graetz, Heinrich 1895 [1870], *History of the Jews. Volume 5, From the Chmielmicki Persecutiom of the Jews in Poland (1648 C.E.) to the Present Time (1870 C.E.)*, Philadelphia: Jewish Publication Society of America.

Gregory XVI 1833 [1832], *The Encyclical Letter of Pope Gregory XVI*, Dublin: Richard Moore Tims.

Grossman, Henryk 1905a, *Proletariat wobec kwestii żydowskiej z powodu niedyskutowanej dyskusyi w Krytyce*, Kraków: Drukani Wladyslawa Teodorczuka.

Grossman, Henryk 1905b, 'Dem proletariat benegeye tsu der yidenfrage', in *Yudisher Sotsial-Demokrat* 1, April, pp. 6–13, and 3, June, pp. 7–11.

Grossman, Henryk 1905c, 'Od redakcyi', *Zjednoczenie*, 1, February: 1–3.

Grossman, Henryk 1905d, Letters to the Foreign Committee of the Bund, Bund MG2 f107, YIVO Archive, New York.

Grossman, Henryk (Jindřich) 1906a, 'Židovská strana sociálně demokratická v Haliči', *Akademie: Socialistická Revue*, 10, no. 1: 13–18.

Grossman, Henryk 1906b, 'Der II oyserordentlikhe kongress fun der Jud. Sots. Dem. Partey, II fortsetsung', *Sotsial-Demokrat*, 15 June: 2–4.

Grossman, Henryk 1906c, 'Vegn unzere agitatsie un propaganda', *Sotsial-Demokrat*, 24 August: 2–3 and 14 September: 2–3.

Grossman, Henryk ('H. G'., in Roman letters) 1906d, 'Poylenklub, yudenklub, un der tsionistisher sharlatanizmus', *Sotsial-Demokrat*, 28 September: 1–2.

Grossman, Henryk 1907a, *Der Bundizm in Galitzien: a beytrag tsu der geshikhte fun der yudisher arbeyter-bevegung in Galitsien*, Kraków: Ferlag der 'Sotsial-Demokrat'.

Grossman, Henryk 1907b, Speech in 'A breyte vehler versamlung fun der Yudisher Sostialdemokratie in Krakau', *Sotsial-Demokrat*, 19 April: 4.

Grossman, Henryk 1911, 'Polityka przemysłowa i handlowa rządu Terezyańsko-Józefińskiego w Galicyi 1772–1790 (Referat na V. Zjazd Prawnikow i Ekonomistów Polskich)', *Przegład prawa i administracyi*, 36: 1045–87; also an off-print.

Grossman, Henryk 1912, Letter to Karl Radek, 17 September 1912, Henke Nachlass, Archiv der sozialen Demokratie der Friedrich-Ebert-Stiftung, Bonn.

Grossman, Henryk 1913, Letter to Józef Dománski, 17 September 1912, in Kark Radek, *Meine Abrechnung*, Bremen: Karl Radek, pp. 23–4.

Grossman, Henryk 1914, *Österreichs Handelspolitik mit Bezug auf Galizien in der Reformperiode 1772–1790*, Vienna: Konegen.

Grossman, Henryk 1923, 'Przycznek do historji socjalizmu w Polsce przed laty czterdziestu', in Karol Marks, *Karol Marks: Pisma niewydane, 1 Listy Marksa do Kugelmana, 2 Przyczynek do Krytyki socjaldemokratycznego programu partyjnego. Przełożył, wstępem i uwagami zaopatrzył*, translated by Henryk Grossman, Warsaw: Książka, 1923, pp. iii–xxvii.

Grossman, Henryk 1948, Letter from Henryk Grossman to Walter Braeuer, January 13, Braeuer Collection, Johann-Heinrich von Thünen Museum, Tellow, Mecklenburg-Vorpommern.

Grossman, Henryk 2017a, *Essays and Letters on Economic Theory*, edited by Rick Kuhn, Leiden: Brill.

Grossman, Henryk 2017b [1933], 'Fifty Years of Struggle over Marxism', translated by Rick Kuhn and Einde O'Callaghan, in Henryk Grossman, *Essays and Letters on Economic Theory*, edited by Rick Kuhn, Leiden: Brill, pp. 332–88.

Grossman, Henryk 2017c [1929], 'The Change in the Original Plan for Marx's *Capital* and its Causes', translated by Geoffrey McCormack, in Henryk Grossman, *Essays and Letters on Economic Theory*, edited by Rick Kuhn, Leiden: Brill, pp. 183–209.

Grossman, Henryk 2017d [1922], 'The Theory of Economic Crisis', in Henryk Grossman, *Essays and Letters on Economic Theory*, edited by Rick Kuhn, Leiden: Brill, pp. 44–9.

Grossman, Henryk 2017e [1928], 'A New Theory of Imperialism and the Social Revolution', translated by Geoffrey McCormack and Julian Germann, in Henryk Grossman, *Essays and Letters on Economic Theory*, edited by Rick Kuhn, Leiden: Brill, pp. 120–76.

Grossman, Henryk 2017f, Letter to Paul Mattick, 16 September 1931, translated by Tom O'Lincoln, in Henryk Grossman, *Essays and Letters on Economic Theory*, edited by Rick Kuhn, Leiden: Brill, pp. 233–8.

Grossman, Henryk 2017g, Letter to Paul Mattick, 30 June 1932, translated by Ben Fowkes, in Henryk Grossman, *Essays and Letters on Economic Theory*, edited by Rick Kuhn, Leiden: Brill, pp. 238–9.

Grossman, Henryk 2017h, Letter to Paul Mattick, 6 March 1933, translated by Ben Fowkes, in Henryk Grossman, *Essays and Letters on Economic Theory*, edited by Rick Kuhn, Leiden: Brill, pp. 239–42.

Grossman, Henryk 2017i, Letter to Paul Mattick, 7 May 1933, translated by Tom O'Lincoln, in Henryk Grossman, *Essays and Letters on Economic Theory*, edited by Rick Kuhn, Leiden: Brill, pp. 243–6.

Grossman, Henryk 2017j, Letter to Paul Mattick, 17 June 1933, translated by Tom O'Lincoln, in Henryk Grossman, *Essays and Letters on Economic Theory*, edited by Rick Kuhn, Leiden: Brill, pp. 247–51.

Grossman, Henryk 2017k [1934], 'Sismondi, Jean Charles Leonard Simonde de (1773–1842)', in Henryk Grossman, *Essays and Letters on Economic Theory*, edited by Rick Kuhn, Leiden: Brill, pp. 55–119.

Grossman, Henryk 2017l [1932], 'The Evolutionist Revolt Against Classical Economics', in Henryk Grossman, *Essays and Letters on Economic Theory*, edited by Rick Kuhn, Leiden: Brill, pp. 556–99.

Grossman, Henryk 2017m [1941], *Marx, Classical Political Economy and the Problem of Dynamics*, translated by Rick Kuhn, in Henryk Grossman, *Essays and Letters on Economic Theory*, edited by Rick Kuhn, Leiden: Brill, pp. 469–534.

Grossmann, Henryk 1913, Letters to Józef Dománski, 12 May 1911 and 17 September 1912, in Kark Radek, *Meine Abrechnung*, Bremen: Karl Radek, pp. 22–4.

Grossmann, Henryk 1929, *Das Akkumulations- und Zusammenbruchsgesetz des kapitalistischen Systems (zugleich eine Krisentheorie)*, Leipzig: Hirschfeld.

Grossmann, Henryk 1931a, 'Adler, Victor', in *Wörterbuch der Volkswirtschaft. Erster Band*, edited by Ludwig Elster, fourth edition, Jena: Fischer, pp. 21–2.

Grossmann, Henryk 1931b, 'Anarchismus', in *Wörterbuch der Volkswirtschaft. Erster Band*, edited by Ludwig Elster, fourth edition, Jena: Fischer, pp. 97–109.

Grossmann, Henryk 1931c, 'Bebel, August', in *Wörterbuch der Volkswirtschaft. Erster Band*, edited by Ludwig Elster, fourth edition, Jena: Fischer, pp. 301–2.

Grossmann, Henryk 1931d, 'Bolschewismus', in *Wörterbuch der Volkswirtschaft. Erster Band*, edited by Ludwig Elster, fourth edition, Jena: Fischer, pp. 421–44.

Grossmann, Henryk 1931e, 'Debs, Eugene', in *Wörterbuch der Volkswirtschaft. Erster Band*, edited by Ludwig Elster, fourth edition, Jena: Fischer, p. 564.

Grossmann, Henryk 1931f, 'Leon, Daniel de', in *Wörterbuch der Volkswirtschaft. Erster Band*, edited by Ludwig Elster, fourth edition, Jena: Fischer, pp. 564–5.

Grossmann, Henryk 1932a, 'Guesde, Jules', in *Wörterbuch der Volkswirtschaft. Zweiter Band*, edited by Ludwig Elster, fourth edition, Jena: Fischer, pp. 256–258.

Grossmann, Henryk 1932b, 'Herzen, Alexander', in *Wörterbuch der Volkswirtschaft. Zweiter Band*, edited by Ludwig Elster, fourth edition, Jena: Fischer, pp. 360–1.

Grossmann, Henryk 1932c, 'Hyndman, Henry Mayers', in *Wörterbuch der Volkswirtschaft. Zweiter Band*, edited by Ludwig Elster, fourth edition, Jena: Fischer, pp. 369–70.

Grossmann, Henryk 1932d, 'Internationale: Die Zweite Internationale', in *Wörterbuch der Volkswirtschaft. Zweiter Band*, edited by Ludwig Elster, fourth edition, Jena: Fischer, pp. 432–9.

Grossmann, Henryk 1932e, 'Internationale: Die dritte Internationale', in *Wörterbuch der Volkswirtschaft. Zweiter Band* fourth edition, Jena: Fischer, pp. 439–49.

Grossmann, Henryk 1932f, 'Jaurès, Jean', in *Wörterbuch der Volkswirtschaft. Zweiter Band*, edited by Ludwig Elster, fourth edition, Jena: Fischer, pp. 382–3.

Grossmann, Henryk 1932g, 'Kropotkin, Peter', in *Wörterbuch der Volkswirtschaft. Zweiter Band*, edited by Ludwig Elster, fourth edition, Jena: Fischer, pp. 696–7.

Grossmann, Henryk 1932h, 'Lenin (Pseud. für Uljanow), Wladimir Iljitsch', in *Wörterbuch der Volkswirtschaft. Zweiter Band*, edited by Ludwig Elster, fourth edition, Jena: Fischer, pp. 828–31.

Grossmann, Henryk 1932i, 'Plechanow, Georg', in *Wörterbuch der Volkswirtschaft. Zweiter Band*, edited by Ludwig Elster, fourth edition, Jena: Fischer, pp. 1140–1.

Grossmann, Henryk 1932j, *Fünfzig Jahre Kampf um den Marxismus 1883–1932*, Jena: Fischer.

Grossmann, Henryk 1933a, 'Rodrigues, Olinde', in *Wörterbuch der Volkswirtschaft. Dritte Band*, edited by Ludwig Elster, fourth edition, Jena: Fischer, p. 99.

Grossmann, Henryk 1933b, 'Sorel, Georges', in *Wörterbuch der Volkswirtschaft. Dritte Band*, edited by Ludwig Elster, fourth edition, Jena: Fischer, pp. 236–8.

Grossmann, Henryk 1933c, '7 Die Fortentwicklung des Marxismus bis zur Gegenwart', in *Wörterbuch der Volkswirtschaft. Dritte Band*, edited by Ludwig Elster, fourth edition, Jena: Fischer, pp. 313–41.

Grossmann, Henryk 1992 [1929], *The Law of Accumulation and Breakdown of the Capitalist System: Being also a Theory of Crises*, abridged English translation by Jairus Banaji, London: Pluto Press.

Grossmann, Henryk 2009a [1935], 'The Social Foundations of Mechanistic Philosophy and Manufacture', translated by Gabriella Shalit, in *The Social and Economic Roots of the Scientific Revolution: Texts by Boris Hessen and Henryk Grossmann*, edited by Gideon Freudenthal and Peter McLaughlin, Dordrecht: Springer, pp. 103–56.

Grossmann, Henryk 2009b [written 1930s and 1940s], 'Descartes and the Social Origins of the Mechanistic Concept of the World', in *The Social and Economic Roots of the*

Scientific Revolution: Texts by Boris Hessen and Henryk Grossmann, edited by Gideon Freudenthal and Peter McLaughlin, Dordrecht: Springer, pp. 157–229.

Grossmann, Henryk and Carl Grünberg 1971, *Anarchismus, Bolschevismus, Sozialismus: Aufsätze aus dem Wörterbuch der Volkswirtschaft*, edited by Claudio Pozzoli, Frankfurt am Main: Europäische Verlagsanstalt.

Grünberg, Carl 1911a, 'Anarchismus', in *Wörterbuch der Volkswirtschaft. Erste Band*, edited by Ludwig Elster, third edition, Jena: Fischer, pp. 92–7.

Grünberg, Carl 1911b, 'Christliche Sozialismus', in *Wörterbuch der Volkswirtschaft. Erste Band*, edited by Ludwig Elster, third edition, Jena: Fischer, pp. 638–52.

Grünberg, Carl 1911c, 'Sozialdemokratie', in *Wörterbuch der Volkswirtschaft. Zweite Band*, edited by Ludwig Elster, third edition, Jena: Fischer, pp. 799–827.

Grünberg, Carl 1911d, 'Herzen, Alexander', in *Wörterbuch der Volkswirtschaft. Zweite Band*, edited by Ludwig Elster, third edition, Jena: Fischer, p. 1318.

Grünberg, Carl 1931a, 'Bakunin, Michael', in *Wörterbuch der Volkswirtschaft. Erster Band*, edited by Ludwig Elster, fourth edition, Jena: Fischer, p. 235.

Grünberg, Carl 1931b, 'Buchez, Philippe-Joseph-Benjamin', in *Wörterbuch der Volkswirtschaft. Zweiter Band*, edited by Ludwig Elster, fourth edition, Jena: Fischer, p. 513.

Grünberg, Carl 1931c, 'Colins Jean-Guillaume-César-Alexandre-Hippolyte, Baron de', in *Wörterbuch der Volkswirtschaft. Zweiter Band*, edited by Ludwig Elster, fourth edition, Jena: Fischer, p. 560.

Grünberg, Carl 1931d, 'Babeuf, François-Noël', in *Wörterbuch der Volkswirtschaft. Zweiter Band*, edited by Ludwig Elster, fourth edition, Jena: Fischer, p. 233.

Grünberg, Carl 1932a, 'Godwin, William', in *Wörterbuch der Volkswirtschaft. Zweiter Band*, edited by Ludwig Elster, fourth edition, Jena: Fischer, p. 207.

Grünberg, Carl 1932b, 'Internationale: Die Erste Internationale (Internationale Arbeiterassociation–IAA)', in *Wörterbuch der Volkswirtschaft. Zweiter Band*, edited by Ludwig Elster, fourth edition, Jena: Fischer, pp. 430–2.

Grünberg, Carl 1932c, 'Proudhon, Pierre Joseph', in *Wörterbuch der Volkswirtschaft. Zweiter Band*, edited by Ludwig Elster, fourth edition, Jena: Fischer, pp. 1186–7.

Grünberg, Carl 1933a, 'Stirner, Max', *Wörterbuch der Volkswirtschaft. Dritte Band*, edited by Ludwig Elster, fourth edition, Jena: Fischer, pp. 547–8.

Grünberg, Carl 1933b, 'Sozialistische Ideen und Lehren I (Sozialismus und Kommunismus)', *Wörterbuch der Volkswirtschaft. Dritte Band*, edited by Ludwig Elster, fourth edition, Jena: Fischer, pp. 272–313.

Grünberg, Carl and Henryk Grossmann 1931, 'Christlicher und religiöser Sozialismus', in *Wörterbuch der Volkswirtschaft. Erster Band*, edited by Ludwig Elster, fourth edition, Jena: Fischer, pp. 538–59.

Grünberg, Carl and Henryk Grossmann 1933, 'Sozialdemokratische und kommunistische Parteien', in *Wörterbuch der Volkswirtschaft. Dritte Band* fourth edition, edited by Ludwig Elster, Jena: Fischer, pp. 238–57.

Grundlach, Gustav 1929, 'Klassenkampf', *Staatslexikon der Görres-Gesellschaft. Band 3*, fifth edition, edited by Hermann Sacher, Freiburg: Herder, pp. 394–9.

Guesde, Jules 1872, *Le livre rouge de la justice rurale*, Genève: Blanchard.

Guesde, Jules 1878, *Essai de catéchisme socialiste*, Bruxelles: Kistemaechers.

Guesde, Jules 1884, *Services publics et socialisme*, Paris: Oriol.

Guesde, Jules 1901a, *Cinquième Congrès socialiste international tenu à Paris du 23 au 27 Septembre 1900: compte rendu analytique*, Paris: Société nouvelle de librarie et d'édition.

Guesde, Jules 1901b, *Quatre ans de lutte de classe à la Chambre: 1893–1898*. 2, Paris: Jacques.

Guesde, Jules and Paul Lafargue 1899 [1881, 1883], *Le Programme de Parti Ouvrier: ses considérants & ses aricles*, fifth edition, Lille: Parti ouvrier français.

Hallas, Duncan 1985, *The Comintern*, London: Bookmarks.

Hammacher, Emil 1909, *Das philosophisch-ökonomische System des Marxismus*, Leipzig: Duncker & Humblot.

Harding, Neil 1983, *Lenin's Political Thought Theory and Practice in the Democratic and Socialist Revolutions*, London: Macmillan.

Hautmann, Hans 1970, *Die Anfänge der Linksradikalen Bewegung und der Kommunistische Partei Deutschöstereichs*, Wien: Europa Verlag.

Heinen, Anton 1919, *Der Mammonismus und seine Überwindung*, Mönchengladbach: Volksvereins-Verlag.

Heitzer, Horstwalter 1979, *Der Volksverein für das katholische Deutschland im Kaiserreich 1890–1918*, Mainz: Schöningh.

Hélvetius, Claude Adrien 1773, *De l'homme II* 135, London.

Hélvetius, Claude Adrien 1969 [1773], *A Treatise on Man: His Intellectual Faculties and His Education. Volume 2*, New York: Burt Franklin.

Herz, Johannes 1928, *Der soziale Pfarrer: aus Georg Liebsters Lebensarbeit*, Göttingen: Bandenhoeck & Ruprecht.

Herzen, Aleksander 1954–66, *Sobranie Sochinenii*, Moskva: Nauka.

Herzen, Alexander 1855a, *My Exile in Siberia. Volume 1*, London: Hurst and Blackett.

Herzen, Alexander 1855b, *My Exile in Siberia. Volume 2*, London: Hurst and Blackett.

Herzen, Alexander 1956 [1845–6], *Letters on the Study of Nature*, in Alexander Herzen, *Selected Philosophical Works*, translated by L. Navrozov, Moscow: Foreign Languages Publishing House, pp. 97–305.

Herzen, Alexander 1982 [1870], *My Past and Thoughts: The Memoirs of Alexander Herzen*, abridged by Dwight Macdonald, translated by Constance Garnett, Berkeley: University of California Press.

Hohoff, Wilhelm 1908, *Die Bedeutung der Marxschen Kapitalkritik: Eine Apologie des Christentums vom Standpukte der Volkswirtschaftslehre und Rechtswissenschaft*, Paderborn: Bonifacius.

Hohoff, Wilhelm 1921, *Die wissenschaftliche und kulturhistorische Bedeutung der Karl Marx'schen Lehren*, Braunschweig: Rieke.

Hohoff, Wilhelm 1928 [written 1921], Letter of 13 February 1921, in *Wilhelm Hohoff und der Bund Katholischer Sozialisten*, edited by Eduard Dietz, Karlsruhe-Rüppur: Verlag der Religiösen Sozialisten.

Huber, Victor Aimé 1848, *Die Selbsthülfe der arbeitenden Klassen durch Wirtschaftsvereine und innere Ansiedlung*, published anonymously, Berlin: Bessersche Buchhandlung.

Huntington, Charles White 1921, *Enclaves of Single Tax*, Harvard: Fiske Warren.

Hyndman, Henry Mayers 1881, *England for All*, London: Gilbert & Rivington.

Hyndman, Henry Mayers 1886, *The Bankruptcy of India*, London: Swan Sonnenschein, Lowrey.

Hyndman, Henry Mayers 1896, *Economics of Socialism*, London: Twentieth Century Press.

Hyndman, Henry Mayers 1919, *The Awakening of Asia*, London: Cassell.

International Socialist Congress 1904, *Internationales Sozialistisches Kongress/Congrès socialiste international/International Socialist Congress, Amsterdam 1904: Resolutionen/Résolutions/Resolutions*, Bruxelles: Gand.

International Socialist Congress 1910, *Internationaler Sozialisten-Kongress zu Kopenhagen, 28 August bis 3. September 1910*, Berlin: Buchhandlung Vorwärts

Jaurès, Jean 1908, *Studies in Socialism*, translated by Mildred Minturn, second edition, London: Independent Labor Party.

Jüdishe sozial-demokratishe Partei in Galitsien 1905a, *Bericht zum Gesamt-Parteitage der Oesterreichischen Sozialdemokratie in Wien 1905 (1. Mai–3. Oktober 1905)*, Kraków: Verlag des jüdischen Wochenblattes 'Der Sozialdemokrat'.

Jüdishe sozial-demokratishe Partei in Galitsien 1905b, *An die Sozialdemokraten in Oesterreich!*, Kraków: Verlag des jüdischen Wochenblattes 'Der Sozialdemokrat'.

Kaftan, Julius 1994 [1893], 'Christentum und Wirtschaftsordnung', in *Die protestantischen Wurzeln der Sozialen Marktwirtschaft: ein Quellenband*, edited by Günter Brakelmann und Traugott Jähnichen, Gütersloh: Gütersloher Verlagshaus, pp. 152–7.

Kaiser, Otto 1929, *Vom Ringen einer Priesterseele*, Würzburg: Das neue Volk.

Kamenev, Y.V. 1916, *Ob A. I. Gerzeme o N. G. Chernyshevskom*, Petrograd: 'Zhin i Znanie'.

Kant, Immanuel 1998 [1781], *Critique of Pure Reason*, translated by Paul Guyer and Allen W. Wood, Cambridge: Cambridge University Press.

Kant, Immanuel 2004 [1783], *Prolegomena to Any Future Metaphysics That Will Be Able to Come Forward as Science*, translated by Gary Hatfield, Cambridge: Cambridge University Press.

Kautsky, Karl 1893, *Der Parlamentarismus, die Volksgesetzgebung und die Sozialdemokratie*, Stuttgart: Dietz.

Kautsky, Karl 1903 [1902], *The Social Revolution*, translated by A.B. Askew, Clerkenwell Green: Twentieth Century Press.

Kautsky, Karl 1904, 'On the Problems of the Jewish Proletariat in England', *Justice*, 23 April: 4.

Kautsky, Karl 1909, *The Road to Power*, Chicago: Bloch.

Kautsky, Karl 1914, 'Die Internationalität und der Krieg', *Neue Zeit*, 33, vol. 1, no. 8, 27 November: 225–50.

Kautsky, Karl 1915, *Die Internationalität und der Krieg*, Berlin: Buchhandlung Vorwärts.

Kautsky, Karl 1916 [1902], *The Social Revolution*, Chicago: Kerr.

Kay, John de 1919, *Der Geist der Internationale in Bern, zusammen mit dem Kerne der charakteristischsten Reden und dem Wortlaute der Resolutionen*, Luzern: John de Kaye.

Kelsen, Hans 1965 [1920], *Sozialismus und Staat: Eine Untersuchung der politischen Theorie des Marxismus*, third edition, Wien: Verlag der Volksbuchhandlung.

Ketteler, Wilhelm Emanuel von 1864, *Die Arbeiterfrage und das Christenthum*, Mainz: Kirchheim.

Ketteler, Wilhelm Emanuel von 1869, *Die Arbeiterbewegung und ihr Streben im Verhältniß zu Religion und Sittlichkeit Eine Ansprache, gehalten auf der Liebfrauen-Haide am 25. Juli 1869*, Mainz: Kirchheim.

Knies, Karl 1883, *Die politische Oekonomie vom geschichtlichen Standpunkte*, second edition, Braunschweig: Schwetschke.

Kol, Henri van (Rienzi) 1888 [1882], *Christendom en socialisme*, Gravenhage: Liebers.

Komitet Organizacyjny Żydowskiej Partyi Socyalno-demokraticyczney w Galicyi 1905, *Czego chcemy?*, Kraków.

Komornicki, Kazimierz Jaksa 1850, 'Znakomitszych ekonomistów', *Atheneum* (Wilno), 4: 91–119.

Konopnicka, Marya 1915 [1905], 'Im więcej śmiem pożądać', *Piezye. Tom 6*, Warszawa: Gebethner i Wolff.

Kral, Josef 1919, *Sind Christentum und Sozialismus unvereinbar?*, München: Verlag der Katholiken- und Kirchenzeitung.

Kral, Josef 1920 [1919], *Der christliche Sozialismus: Die Versöhnung von Christentum und Sozialismus; System einer Gesellschaftsreform nach Naturrecht und Sittengesetz*, second edition, Dillingen: Keller.

Krasiński, Zygmunt 1975 [1836], *Iridion*, translated by Florence Noyes, Westport, CT: Greenwood Press.

Kremer, Arkadi and Julius Martov 1983 [1893], *On Agitation*, in *Marxism in Russia: Key Documents, 1879–1906*, translated by Richard Taylor, edited by Neil Harding, Cambridge: Cambridge University Press, pp. 192–205.

Kropotkin, Peter 1904 [1902], *Mutual Aid: A Factor of Evolution*, London: Heinemann.

Kropotkin, Peter 1970 [1919], 'To the Workers of Western Europe', in Peter Kropotkin, *Kropotkin's Revolutionary Pamphlets*, New York: Dover, pp. 252–6.

Kropotkin, Peter 1992 [1885], *Words of a Rebel*, translated by George Woodcock, Montréal: Black Rose Books.

Kropotkin, Peter and Jean Grave 1964 [1916], 'Le Manifeste des Seize', available at: https://web.archive.org/web/20010121223100/http://www.users.skynet.be/AL/LIBRAIRIE/increva/vol3/1418.htm, accessed 24 February 2017.

Kropotkin, Peter and Jean Grave 2012 [1916], 'The Manifesto of the Sixteen', translated by Shawn P. Wilbur, available at: http://libertarian-labyrinth.blogspot.com.au/2011/05/manifesto-of-sixteen-1916.html, accessed 24 February 2017.

Kuhn, Rick 2007, *Henryk Grossman and the Recovery of Marxism*, Urbana and Chicago: University of Illinois Press.

Kurjer Lwówski 1905, 'Rewolucja partyjna', *Kurjer Lwówski*, 30 June: 2.

Kuskova, Yekaterina 1970 [1899], 'Credo', in Vladimir Ilych Lenin, *Collected Works. Volume 4*, Moscow: Progress, pp. 171–4.

Kutter, Herman 1908 [1904], *They Must; or God and the Social Democracy: A Frank Word to Christian Men And Women*, Chicago: Co-operative Printing Company.

La Rochefoucauld, François de 2003, *Maxims of Duc de La Rochefoucauld*, Boston: International Pocket Library.

Lamennais, Hugues-Félicité Robert de 1897 [1834], *Paroles d'un croyant*, Paris: Bibliothèque nationale.

Landau, Saul Raphael 1897, 'Syonizm: po kongresie w Bazylei w sierpniu r. 1897', *Przegląd polski z list*, 32, 2, no. 126, October, November, December: 290–304.

Laveley, Émile de 1881, *Le socialisme contemprain*, Paris: Baillière.

Leo XIII 1903, *The Pope and the People: Select Letters and Addresses on Social Questions*, London: Catholic Truth Society.

Lenin, Vladimir Ilyich 1960a [1895], *Explanation of the Law on Fines Imposed on Factory Workers*, in Vladimir Ilych Lenin, *Collected Works. Volume 2*, Moscow: Progress, pp. 29–72.

Lenin, Vladimir Ilyich 1960b [1924, written 1895–6], *Draft and Explanation of a Programme for the Social Democratic Party*, in Vladimir Ilych Lenin, *Collected Works. Volume 2*, Moscow: Progress, pp. 93–121.

Lenin, Vladimir Ilyich 1960c [1895], 'The Economic Content of Narodism and the Criticism of it in Mr. Struve's Book (the Reflection of Marxism in Bourgeois Literature)', in Vladimir Ilych Lenin, *Collected Works. Volume 1*, Moscow: Progress, pp. 333–507.

Lenin, Vladimir Ilyich 1960d [1899], *A Protest by Russian Social Democrats*, in Vladimir Ilych Lenin, *Collected Works. Volume 4*, Moscow: Progress, pp. 167–82.

Lenin, Vladimir Ilyich 1960f [written 1893, 1923], 'New Economic Developments in Peasant Life', in Vladimir Ilych Lenin, *Collected Works. Volume 1*, Moscow: Progress, pp. 11–124.

Lenin, Vladimir Ilyich 1960g [1894], *What the 'Friends of the People' Are and How they Fight against the Social Democrats*, in Vladimir Ilych Lenin, *Collected Works. Volume 1*, Moscow: Progress, pp. 129–332.

Lenin, Vladimir Ilyich 1960h [1897], *A Characterisation of Economic Romanticism (Sismondi and our Native Sismondists)*, in Vladimir Ilych Lenin, *Collected Works. Volume 2*, Moscow: Progress, pp. 129–265.

Lenin, Vladimir Ilyich 1960i [1899], *A Protest by Russian Social Democrats*, in Vladimir Ilych Lenin, *Collected Works. Volume 4*, Moscow: Progress, pp. 167–82.

Lenin, Vladimir Ilyich 1961a [1902], *A Letter to a Comrade on Our Organisational Tasks*, in Vladimir Ilych Lenin, *Collected Works. Volume 6*, Moscow: Progress, pp. 229–50.

Lenin, Vladimir Ilyich 1961b [1904, written 1903], 'Draft Rules of the RSDLP', in Vladimir Ilych Lenin, *Collected Works. Volume 6*, Moscow: Progress, pp. 474–6.

Lenin, Vladimir Ilyich 1962a [1905], 'Two Tactics', in Vladimir Ilych Lenin, *Collected Works. Volume 8*, Moscow: Progress, pp. 148–57.

Lenin, Vladimir Ilyich 1962b [1905], articles in *Vperyod, Collected Works. Volume 8*, Moscow: Progress.

Lenin, Vladimir Ilyich 1962c [1905], 'Social-democracy and the Provisional Revolutionary Government', in Vladimir Ilych Lenin, *Collected Works. Volume 8*, Moscow: Progress, pp. 275–92.

Lenin, Vladimir Ilyich 1962d [1905], 'Should We Organise the Revolution?', in Vladimir Ilyich Lenin, *Collected Works. Volume 8*, Moscow: Progress, pp. 167–76.

Lenin, Vladimir Ilyich 1962e [1908], *Materialism and Empirio-Criticism: Critical Comments on a Reactionary Philosophy*, in Vladimir Ilyich Lenin, *Collected Works. Volume 14*, Moscow: Progress, pp. 17–361.

Lenin, Vladimir Ilyich 1962f [1907], 'The International Socialist Congress in Stuttgart', in Vladimir Ilyich Lenin, *Collected Works. Volume 13*, Moscow: Progress, pp. 82–93.

Lenin, Vladimir Ilyich 1962g [1905], *Two Tactics of Social-Democracy in the Democratic Revolution*, in Vladimir Ilych Lenin, *Collected Works. Volume 9*, Moscow: Progress, pp. 15–140.

Lenin, Vladimir Ilyich 1962h [written 1905, published 1940], 'Our Tasks and the Soviet of Workers' Deputies: A Letter to the Editor', in Vladimir Ilych Lenin, *Collected Works. Volume 10*, Moscow: Progress, pp. 17–28.

Lenin, Vladimir Ilyich 1962i [1906], 'Tactical Platform for the Unity Congress of the RSDLP: Draft Resolutions', in Vladimir Ilych Lenin, *Collected Works. Volume 10*, Moscow: Progress, pp. 147–63.

Lenin, Vladimir Ilyich 1963 [1912], 'In Memory of Herzen', in Vladimir Ilych Lenin, *Collected Works. Volume 18*, Moscow: Progress, pp. 25–31.

Lenin, Vladimir Ilyich 1964a [written 1916, published 1917], *Imperialism, the Highest Stage of Capitalism: A Popular Outline*, in Vladimir Ilyich Lenin, *Collected Works. Volume 22*, Moscow: Progress, pp. 185–304.

Lenin, Vladimir Ilyich 1964b [1918], *The State and Revolution*, in Vladimir Ilyich Lenin, *Collected Works. Volume 25*, Moscow: Progress, pp. 385–498.

Lenin, Vladimir Ilyich 1964c [1916], 'Imperialism and the Split in Socialism', in Vladimir Ilyich Lenin, *Collected Works. Volume 23*, Moscow: Progress, pp. 105–20.

Lenin, Vladimir Ilyich 1964d [1914], 'The Tasks of Revolutionary Social-Democracy in the European War', in Vladimir Ilyich Lenin, *Collected Works. Volume 21* Moscow: Progress, pp. 15–19.

Lenin, Vladimir Ilyich 1964e [1914], 'The War and Russian Social-Democracy', in Vladimir Ilyich Lenin, *Collected Works. Volume 21*, Moscow: Progress, pp. 25–34.

Lenin, Vladimir Ilyich 1964f [1915], 'The Conference of the RSDLP Groups Abroad', in Vladimir Ilyich Lenin, *Collected Works. Volume 21*, Moscow: Progress, pp. 158–64.

Lenin, Vladimir Ilyich 1964g [1930, written 1915], 'The Draft Resolution Proposed by the Left Wing at Zimmerwald', in Vladimir Ilyich Lenin, *Collected Works. Volume 21*, Moscow: Progress, pp. 345–8.

Lenin, Vladimir Ilyich 1964h [1916], 'Proposals Submitted by the Central Committee of the RSDLP to the Second Socialist Conference', in Vladimir Ilyich Lenin, *Collected Works. Volume 22*, Moscow: Progress, pp. 169–79.

Lenin, Vladimir Ilyich 1964i [1917], 'Letters from Afar', in Vladimir Ilyich Lenin, *Collected Works. Volume 23*, Moscow: Progress, pp. 295–342.

Lenin, Vladimir Ilyich 1964j [1917], 'The Tasks of the Proletariat in the Present Revolution', in Vladimir Ilyich Lenin, *Collected Works. Volume 24*, Moscow: Progress, pp. 19–26.

Lenin, Vladimir Ilyich 1964k [1916], 'Opportunism and the Collapse of the Second International', in Vladimir Ilyich Lenin, *Collected Works. Volume 22*, Moscow: Progress, pp. 108–20.

Lenin, Vladimir Ilyich 1964f [1915], 'The Conference of the RSDLP Groups Abroad', in Vladimir Ilyich Lenin, *Collected Works. Volume 21*, Moscow: Progress, pp. 158–64.

Lenin, Vladimir Ilyich 1964i [1917], 'Appeal to the Soldiers of all the Belligerent Countries', in Vladimir Ilyich Lenin, *Collected Works. Volume 24*, Moscow: Progress, pp. 186–8.

Lenin, Vladimir Ilyich 1964 [1903], 'The National Question in Our Programme', in Vladimir Ilyich Lenin, *Collected Works. Volume 6*, Moscow: Progress, pp. 452–61.

Lenin, Vladimir Ilyich 1965a [1918], 'The Conference of the RSDLP Groups Abroad', in Vladimir Ilyich Lenin, *Collected Works. Volume 27*, Moscow: Progress, pp. 323–54.

Lenin, Vladimir Ilyich 1965b [1923], 'On Co-operation', in Vladimir Ilyich Lenin, *Collected Works. Volume 3*, Moscow: Progress, pp. 467–75.

Lenin, Vladimir Ilyich 1965c [1921], 'Integrated Economic Plan', in Vladimir Ilyich Lenin, *Collected Works. Volume 32*, Moscow: Progress, pp. 137–45.

Lenin, Vladimir Ilyich 1965d [1918], 'A Serious Lesson and a Serious Responsibility', in Vladimir Ilyich Lenin, *Collected Works. Volume 27*, pp. 79–84.

Lenin, Vladimir Ilyich 1965e [1918], 'The Immediate Tasks of the Soviet Government', in Vladimir Ilyich Lenin, *Collected Works. Volume 27*, Moscow: Progress, pp. 235–77.

Lenin, Vladimir Ilyich 1965f [1919], *The Proletarian Revolution and the Renegade Kautsky*, in Vladimir Ilyich Lenin, *Collected Works. Volume 28*, Moscow: Progress, pp. 227–325.

Lenin, Vladimir Ilyich 1965g [1919], *A Great Beginning: Heroism of the Workers in the Rear. 'Communist Subbotniks'*, in Vladimir Ilyich Lenin, *Collected Works. Volume 29*, Moscow: Progress, pp. 309–34.

Lenin, Vladimir Ilyich 1966 [1920], *'Left-Wing' Communism, An Infantile Disorder*, in Vladimir Ilyich Lenin, *Collected Works. Volume 31*, Moscow: Progress, pp. 17–118.

Lenin, Vladimir Ilyich 2008 [1902], *What Is To Be Done?*, in Lars Lih, *Lenin Rediscovered: What Is To Be Done? in Context*, Chicago: Haymarket, pp. 673–840.

Liebknecht, Wilhelm 1876, *Zur Grund und Bodenfrage*, second edition, Leipzig: Genossenschaftsbuchdruckerei.

Lonu 1903, *Der tsienizm*, London: Algemeyner yidisher arbeyterbund in Lita, Poylen un Rusland.

Luśnia, Michał [pseudonym of Kazimierz Kelles-Kraus] 1904, 'W kwestii narodowsci zydowskiej', *Krytyka* 6, vol. 1, no. 1: 52–61; and 6, vol. 1, no. 2: 120–30.

Luxemburg, Rosa 1973 [1893], 'Bericht an den III. Internationalen Sozialistischen Arbeiterkongress in Zürich 1893 über den Stand und Verlauf der sozialdemokratischen Bewegung in Russisch-Polen 1889–1893', in Rosa Luxemburg, *Gesammelte Werke. Band 1/1*, Berlin: Dietz, pp. 5–13.

Luxemburg, Rosa 1976 [1896–1918], *The National Question: Selected Writings by Rosa Luxemburg*, translated by Horace B. Davis et al., edited by Horace B. Davis, New York: Monthly Review Press.

MacDonald, James Ramsay 1908 [1905], *Socialism and Society*, London: Independent Labour Party.

Machiavelli, Niccolò 1882 [1532], *The History of Florence*, in Niccolò Machiavelli, *The Historical, Political, and Diplomatic Writings. Volume 1*, translated by Christian E. Detmold, Boston: Osgood.

Martynov, Aleksandr 1905, *Dvie diktatury*, Genève: Rossiyskaya sotsial-demokraticheskaya rabochaya partiya.

Marx, Karl 1907 [1852], *The Eighteenth Brumaire of Louis Bonaparte*, translated and prefaced by Daniel de Leon, second edition, Chicago: Kerr.

Marx, Karl 1975 [1844], 'On the Jewish Question', in Karl Marx and Frederick Engels, *Marx and Engels Collected Works. Volume 13*, New York: International Publishers, pp. 146–74.

Marx, Karl 1976a [1847], *The Poverty of Philosophy: Answer to the Philosophy of Poverty by*

M. Proudhon, in Karl Marx and Frederick Engels, *Marx and Engels Collected Works. Volume 6*, New York: International Publishers.

Marx, Karl 1976b [1867], *Capital: A Critique of Political Economy. Volume 1*, translated by Ben Fowkes, Harmondsworth: Penguin.

Marx, Karl 1979 [1852], *The Eighteenth Brumaire of Louis Bonaparte*, in Karl Marx and Frederick Engels, *Marx and Engels Collected Works. Volume 11*, New York: International Publishers.

Marx, Karl 1982 [1844], 'Zur Judenfrage', in Karl Marx and Friedrich Engels, *Marx-Engels-Gesamtausgabe, Ökonomische Manuskripte und Schriften. Abteilung 1. Band 2*, Berlin: Dietz, pp. 141–69.

Marx, Karl 1985 [1864], 'Provisional Rules of the Association', in *Marx and Engels Collected Works. Volume 20*, New York: International Publishers, pp. 14–16.

Marx, Karl 1986a [1871], *The Civil War in France*, in Karl Marx and Frederick Engels, *Marx and Engels Collected Works. Volume 22*, New York: International Publishers, pp. 307–60.

Marx, Karl 1986b [1964, written 1868], 'Remarks on the Programme and Rules of the International Alliance of Socialist Democracy', in *Marx and Engels Collected Works. Volume 21*, New York: International Publishers, pp. 207–11.

Marx, Karl 1989 [1891, written and circulated 1875], *Critique of the Gotha Program*, in *Marx and Engels Collected Works. Volume 24*, New York: International Publishers, pp. 75–100.

Marx, Karl 1991 [1877], Letter to Frederick Engels, 23 July 1877, in Karl Marx and Frederick Engels, *Marx and Engels Collected Works. Volume 45*, New York: International Publishers, pp. 244–8.

Marx, Karl 1979 [1852], *The Eighteenth Brumaire of Louis Bonaparte*, in Karl Marx and Frederick Engels, *Marx and Engels Collected Works. Volume 11*, New York: International Publishers.

Marx, Karl and Friedrich Engels 1976 [1848], *Manifesto of the Communist Party*, in Karl Marx and Frederick Engels, *Marx and Engels Collected Works. Volume 6*, New York: International Publishers, pp. 477–519.

Marx, Karl and Friedrich Engels 2010, *The German Ideology*, in Karl Marx and Frederick Engels, *Marx and Engels Collected Works. Volume 5*, New York: International Publishers, pp. 15–539.

Medem, Vladimir 1943 [1904], 'Di sotsialdemokratie un di natsionale frage', in Vladimir Medem, *Vladimir Medem: tsum tsvantsikstn yortsayt*, New York: Amerikaner Reprezentants fun Algemaynem Yidishn Arbeter-bund, pp. 173–219.

Meitzel, Carl 1933, 'Sismondi', in *Wörterbuch der Volkswirtschaft. Band 3*, edited by Ludwig Elster, fourth edition, Jena: Fischer, pp. 210–11.

Mertens, Heinrich 1930, *Katholische Sozialisten: Programmatische Aufsätze*, Mannheim: Verlag der religiösen Sozialisten.

Merz, Georg 1919, *Religiöse Ansätze im modernen Sozialismus*, München: Kaiser.

Meyer, Rudolf 1873, *Die bedrohliche Entwickelung des Sozialismus und die Lehre Lassalles*, Berlin.

Mickiewicz, Adam 1917 [1834], *Pan Tadeusz or The Last Foray in Lithuania: A Story of Life among Polish Gentlefolk in the Years 1811 and 1812*, translated by George Noyes Rapall, London: Dent.

Mirabeau, Honoré-Gabriel Riqueti 1834 [1789], 'Discours prononcé à la Tribune Nationale, États de Provence. Aix, 30 janvier 1789', in Honoré-Gabriel Riqueti Mirabeau, *Oeuvres de Mirabeau. Tome 1*, Paris: Lecointe et Pougin, pp. 3–21.

Młot, Franciszek 1901, *Kalendarz robotniczy*, Lwów: Robotnika.

Morris, William 1892 [1890], *News from Nowhere: Or an Epoch of Rest*, Hammersmith: Kelmscott Press.

Morris, William 1893 [1887], *True and False Society*, Hammersmith: Hammersmith Socialist Society.

Morris, William 1896 [1888], *Signs of Change: Seven Lectures Delivered on Various Occasions*, London: Longmans, Green and Co.

M R 1905, 'Die Juden-frage in Galitsien', *Dos yidishe Wort*, Kraków, 1–2: 13–15.

Muth, Karl 1930, 'Die Stunde des Bürgertums', *Hochland*, 28, no. 1, October: 1–14.

Naprzód 1892a 'Pierwszy kongres socyalno-demokratycznej partyi w Galicyi', 15 May: 1–3.

Naprzód 1892b, 'Kronika', 1 August: 4.

Naprzód 1892c, 'Ze stowarzyszeń i zgromadzeń', 15 August: 4.

Naprzód 1892d, 'Strejk tkaczy żydowskich w Kołomyi', 15 August: 4.

Naprzód 1892e, 'Strejk tkaczy w Kołomyi', 1 September: 4.

Naprzód 1892f, 'Ruch robotniczy', 1 December: 3.

Naprzód 1893a, 'II, Zjaza socyalno-demokratycznej partyi w Galicyi', 7 April: 1–4.

Naprzód 1893b, 'Ze stowarzyszeń i zgromadzeń', *Naprzód*, 19 May: 2.

Naprzód 1893c, 'Ruch żydowski', 2 June: 2–3.

Naprzód 1903, 'Konferencya socyalistów żydowskich', 13 May: 1–2.

Naprzód 1905, 'Sprawy partyjne' 127, 11 May: 1.

Naprzód 1907, '1 Maj w Galicyi', 5 May: 5.

Nationalsozialer Verein 1896, *Protokoll über die Vertreter-Versammlung aller National-Sozialen in Erfurt vom 23. bis 25 November 1896*, Berlin: Verlag der 'Zeit'.

Nemours, Pierre Samuel Dupont de 1833 [written 1815], Letter to Jean-Baptiste Say, 22 April 1815, in Jean-Baptiste Say, *Mélanges et correspondance d'économie politique*, Paris: Chamerot.

Oberdörffer, Johann Peter 1894, 'Kathoische-sociales Programm', *Kölner Correspondenz für die geistlichen Präsides katholischer Vereinigungen der arbeitenden Stände*, 7, 8–11: 113–65.

Orel, Anton 1909, *Kapitalismus, Bodenreform und christlicher Sozialismus*, Wien: Opitz.

Organizatsions Komite fun der Yudisher Sotsial-Demokratisher Partey in Galitsien 1905, 'Vos viln mir?', *Yudisher Sotsial-Demokrat*, 2, May: 1–9.

Parti ouvrier français 1893, *Onziéme congrès national du Parti Ouvrier*, Lille: Delory.

Pascal, Blaise 1869 [written around 1656–7], 'Of the Geometrical Spirit', in Blaise Pascal, *The Thoughts, Letters, and Opuscules of Blaise Pascal*, New York: Hurd and Houghton.

Passy, Paul 1909, *Christianisme et socialisme*, Paris: Société des Traités.

Passy, Paul 1930, *Souvenirs d'un socialiste chrétien*, Issy-les-Moulineaux: 'Je sers'.

Philip, André 1928, 'Le Chrétien et l'Action Sociale', *Stockholm*, 1: 198–209.

Philip, André 1930, *Socialisme et christianisme*, Paris: Christianisme social.

Piechowski, Paul 1922, *Denkschrift des Bundes religiöser Sozialisten (Abt. Neukölln) über die kirchliche Lage der Gegenwart*, Berlin-Neukölln: Kasper.

Piechowski, Paul 1927, *Proletarischer Glaube: Die religiöse Gedankenwelt der organisierten deutschen Arbeiterschaft*, Berlin: Furche.

Pieper, August 1925 [1924], *Kapitalismus und Sozialismus als seelisches Problem*, second edition, München-Gladbach: Volksverein-Verlag.

Pilat, Tadeusz 1893, 'Własność tabularna w Galicyi', *Wiadomości statystyczne o stosunkach krajowych*, 39.

Plekhanov, Georgii Valentinovich 1921 [1918], 'Buki az-ba', in Georgii Valentinovich Plekhanov, *God na rodine: polnoe sobranie statei i rechei 1917–1918 g. Tom 2*, Paris: Povolozky, pp. 216–364.

Plekhanov, Georgii Valentinovich 1923 [1883], 'Ekonomicheskaya teoriya Karla Rodbertusa-Yagetsova', in Georgii Valentinovich Plekhanov, *Sochineniia. Tom 1*, Moskva: Gosudartstvennoe Izdatelstvo.

Plekhanov, Georgii Valentinovich 1967 [1925], *History of Russian Social Thought*, translated by Boris M. Bekkar and others, New York: Fertig.

Plekhanov, Georgii Valentinovich 1974a [1885], *Our Differences*, in Georgii Valentinovich Plekhanov, *Selected Philosophical Works. Volume 1*, translated by Richard Dixon, Moscow: Foreign Languages Publishing House, pp. 107–352.

Plekhanov, Georgii Valentinovich 1974b [1889], 'Speech at the International Workers' Socialist Congress in Paris', translated by Richard Dixon, in Georgii Valentinovich Plekhanov, *Selected Philosophical Works. Volume 1*, Moscow: Foreign Languages Publishing House, pp. 398–400.

Plekhanov, Georgii Valentinovich 1974c [1895], *The Development of the Monist View of History*, translated by Andrew Rothstein, in Georgii Valentinovich Plekhanov, *Selected Philosophical Works. Volume 1*, Moscow: Foreign Languages Publishing House, pp. 480–697.

Plekhanov, Georgii Valentinovich 1974–81, *Selected Philosophical Works*, five volumes, Moscow: Progress.

Plekhanov, Georgii Valentinovich 1976a [1908], *Fundamental Problems of Marxism*, in Georgii Valentinovich Plekhanov, *Selected Philosophical Works. Volume 3*, Moscow: Progress, pp. 117–83.

Plekhanov, Georgii Valentinovich 1976b [1908, 1910], *Materialismus Militans: Reply to Mr Bogdanov*, in Georgii Valentinovich Plekhanov, *Selected Philosophical Works. Volume 3*, Moscow: Progress, pp. 188–283.

Plekhanov, Georgii Valentinovich 1976c [1909], 'On the So-called Religious Seekings in Russia', in Georgii Valentinovich Plekhanov, *Selected Philosophical Works. Volume 3*, Moscow: Progress, pp. 306–413.

Plekhanov, Georgii Valentinovich 1976d [1913], 'Utopian Socialism in the Nineteenth Century', in Georgii Valentinovich Plekhanov, *Selected Philosophical Works. Volume 3*, Moscow: Progress, pp. 534–76.

Plekhanov, Georgii Valentinovich 1976e [1893], *Essays on the History of Materialism*, in Georgii Valentinovich Plekhanov, *Selected Philosophical Works. Volume 2*, Moscow: Progress, pp. 31–182.

Plekhanov, Georgii Valentinovich 1976f [1893], 'Preface to the Third Edition of Engels' *Socialism: Utopian and Scientific*', in Georgii Valentinovich Plekhanov, *Selected Philosophical Works. Volume 3*, Moscow: Progress, pp. 31–55.

Plekhanov, Georgii Valentinovich 1980 [1909], *N. G. Chernyshevsky*, in Georgii Valentinovich Plekhanov, *Selected Philosophical Works. Volume 4*, Moscow: Progress, pp. 169–367.

Plekhanov, Georgii Valentinovich 1981a [1908], 'Tolstoy and Nature', in Georgii Valentinovich Plekhanov, *Selected Philosophical Works. Volume 4*, Moscow: Progress, pp. 559–82.

Plekhanov, Georgii Valentinovich 1981b [1908], 'Karl Marx and Lev Tolstoy', in Georgii Valentinovich Plekhanov, *Selected Philosophical Works. Volume 5*, Moscow: Progress, pp. 672–89.

Plenge, Johann 1918, *Die Revolutionierung der Revolutionäre*, Leipzig: Neue Geist.

Pollock, Friedrich 1971 [1929], *Die planwirtschaftlichen Versuche in der Sowjetunion 1917–1927*, Frankfurt am Main: Verlag Neue Kritik.

Polska Partia Socjalno-Demokratyczna Galicji i Śląska Cieszyńskiego 1904, *Z uchwały IX kongresu Polskiej Partyi socyalno-demokratycznej dla Galicyi i Śląska*, Kraków.

Post, Charles 2010, 'Exploring Working-class Consciousness: A Critique of the Theory of the "Labour Aristocracy"', *Historical Materialism*, 18: 3–38.

Proudhon, Pierre-Joseph 1851a, *Idée générale de la révolution au XIXe siècle, (choix d'études sur la pratique révolutionnaire et industrielle)*, Paris: Garnier freres.

Proudhon, Pierre-Joseph 1851b, *Les Confessions d'un révolutionnaire, pour servir à l'histoire de la révolution de février*, third edition, Paris: Garnier Frères.

Proudhon, Pierre-Joseph 1869 [1861], *La guerre et la paix*, two volumes, second edition, Paris: Librairie internationale.

Proudhon, Pierre-Joseph 1921 [1863], *Principe fédératif*, Paris: Bossard.

Proudhon, Pierre-Joseph 1865, *La capacité politique des classes ouvrières*, Paris: Dentu.

Radek, Karl 1922, *Meine Abrechnung*, Bremen: Karl Radek.

Radek, Karl 1922, 'Foundation of the Two and a Half International', *Communist International*, 16/17: 31–43.

Ragaz Leonhard 1917, 'Unser Sozialismus', *Neue Wege*, 11: 583–619.

Ragaz Leonhard 1922, *Weltreich, Religion und Gottesherrschaft*, 2 volumes, Erlenbach-Zürich: Rotapfel.

Ragaz Leonhard 1928, 'Die Kirchen und der Klassenkampf', *Stockholm*, 1: 49–60.

Ragaz Leonhard 1929, 'Was ist religiöser Sozialismus?', *Zeitschrift für Religion und Sozialismus*, 1: 7–21.

Ragaz Leonhard 1930, 'Religiöses und Kirchliches', *Neue Weg*, 24, no. 1: 39–41.

Ragaz Leonhard 1972 [1930], *Von Christus zu Marx – von Marx zu Christus*, Hamburg: Furche.

Ragaz Leonhard 1984a [1917], 'Not Religion but the Kingdom of God', in Leonhard Ragaz, *A Ragaz Reader: Signs of the Kingdom*, translated by Paul Bock, Grand Rapids: Eerdmans, pp. 27–38.

Ragaz Leonhard 1984b [1929], 'Which World View Belongs to Socialism', in Leonhard Ragaz, *A Ragaz Reader: Signs of the Kingdom*, translated by Paul Bock, Grand Rapids: Eerdmans, pp. 75–96.

Rathenau, Walter 1925 [1918] *Die neue Wirtschaft*, in Walter Rathenau, *Gesammelte Werke, Band 5*, Berlin: Fischer, pp. 179–261.

Rauschenbusch, Walter 1907, *Christianity and the Social Crisis*, New York: Macmillan.

Rauschenbusch, Walter 1912, *Christianizing the Social Order*, New York: Macmillan.

Redaktion 1932a, 'Liebknecht, Karl', in *Wörterbuch der Volkswirtschaft. Zweiter Band*, edited by Ludwig Elster, fourth edition, Jena: Fischer, p. 875.

Redaktion 1932b, 'Luxemburg, Rosa', in *Wörterbuch der Volkswirtschaft. Zweiter Band*, edited by Ludwig Elster, fourth edition, Jena: Fischer, p. 874.

Reiman, Michal 1987, *The Birth of Stalinism: The USSR on the Eve of the 'Second Revolution'*, Bloomington: Indiana University Press.

Renner, Karl 1899, *Staat und Nation: staatsrechtliche Untersuchung über die möglichen Principien einer Lösung und die juristischen Voraussetzungen eines Nationalitäten-Gesetzes*, Wien: Dietl.

Reyzen, Solomon 1927 [1914], *Leksikon fun der yidisher literatur, prese un filologie. Band 1*, second edition, Vilno: B. Kletskin.

Rezawa 1894, 'Die Juden-Ausweisung in Rußland und die polnische Frage', *Neue Zeit*, 12, vol. 2, no. 37: 324–33.

Rodrigues, Olinde 1831, in *Le globe*, 12 December.

Rodrigues, Olinde 1841, *Poésies sociales des ouvriers*, Paris: Paulin.

Roland-Holst, Henriette 1929, 'Sozialismus und persönliche Lebensgestaltung', in Sozialistische Tagung, *Sozialismus aus dem Glauben: Verhandlungen der sozialistische Tagung in Heppenheim a. B. Pfingstwoche 1928*, Zürich: Rotapfel, pp. 152–79.

Roland Holst-van der Schalk, Henriëtte 1928, *De weg tot eenheid*, Amsterdam: Querido.

Rousseau, Jean-Jacques 1923 [1762], *Rousseau's Social Contract, etc.*, translated by G.D.H. Cole, London: Dent.

Russian Social Democratic Labour Party 1978 [1904], 'Organisational Rules of the Russian Social Democratic Labour Party', in *1903 – Second Congress of the Russian Social Democratic Labour Party*, translated by Brian Pearce, London: New Park.

Saint-Simon, Henri de 1832, *Oeuvres complètes*, two volumes, edited by Olinde Rodrigues, Paris: Librairie saint-simonienne.

Sangnier, Marc 1905, *Le Sillon, esprit et méthode*, Paris: Au sillon.

Sangnier, Marc 1906, *La vie profonde: éveils et visions*, Paris: Perrin.

Scheler, Max 1924, *Christentum und Gesellschaft*, Leipzig: Neue Geist-Verlag.

Scheler, Max 2008 [1919], 'Prophetischer oder marxistischer Sozialismus?', in Max Scheler, *Gesammelte Werke. Band 6*, fourth edition, Bonn: Bouvier, pp. 259–72.

Schorske, Carl E. 1983 [1955], *German Social Democracy, 1905–1917: The Development of the Great Schism*, Cambridge, Massachusetts: Harvard University Press.

Second International, 1896, *Verhandlungen und Beschlüsse des Internationalen Sozialistischen Arbeiter- und Gewerkschaftskongresses zu London vom 27. Juli bis 1. August 1896*, Berlin: Buchhandlung Vorwärts.

Second International, 1900, *Verhandlungen und Beschlüsse des Internationalen Sozialistischen Kongresses zu Paris, 23. bis 27. September 1900*, Berlin: Buchhandlung Vorwärts.

Second International, 1904, *Internationaler Sozialisten Kongress zu Amsterdam, 14. bis 20. August 1904*, Berlin: Buchhandlung Vorwärts.

Second International, 1907, *Internationaler Sozialisten Kongress zu Stuttgart vom 18. bis 24. August 1907*, Berlin: Buchhandlung Vorwärts.

Sejm Krajowy Królestwa Galicyi i Lodomeryi wraz z Wielkiem Księstwem Krakowskiem 1866, [*Kadencja I, sesja IV*] *Stenograficzne Sprawozdania z Czwartej Sesyi Sejmu Krajowego Królestwa Galicyi i Lodomeryi wraz z Wielkiem Księstwem Krakowskiem w roku 1866* [*całość*], 12 posiedzenie, 7 December, available at: http://jbc.bj.uj.edu.pl/dlibra/docmetadata?id=10444&from=publication, accessed 30 August 2016.

Semler, Heinrich 1880, *Geschichte des Socialismus und Communismus in Nordamerika*, Leipzig: Brockhaus.

Sinowjew, Georg 1920 [1918], *N. Lenin: Sein Leben und seine Tätigkeit*, translated by Julian Gumperz, Berlin: Malik.

Słowo Polskie 1905, 'Znamienny separatyzm', afternoon edition, 8 May: 1–2.

Słowacki, Juliusz 2010 [1834], *Kordian*, translated by Gerard T. Kapolka, Chicago: Green Lantern Press.

Snyder, Timothy 1997, 'Kazimierz Kelles-Krauz (1872–1905): A Pioneering Scholar of Modern Nationalism', *Nations and Nationalism*, 3, no. 2: 231–50.

Sobelman, Michael 1990, 'Polish Socialism and Jewish Nationality: The Views of Kazimierz Kelles-Krauz', *Soviet Jewish Affairs*, 20, no. 1: 47–55.

Sociaal-Democratische Arbeiderspartij in Nederland, 1930 *Verslag van het koloniaal congres der Sociaal-Democratische Arbeiderspartij in Nederland, gehouden op 11 en 12 Januari 1930 te Utrecht*, Amsterdam: Arbeiderspers.

Social Democratic Workers Party 1869, *Social Democratic Workers' Party, Eisenach Program (August 8, 1869)*, translated by Erwin Fink, available at: https://archive.org/details/EisenachProgram, accessed 20 February 2017.

Sozialdemokratische Partei Deutschlands 1906, *Protokoll über die Verhandlungen des Parteitages der Sozialdemokratisches Partei Deutschlands, abgehalten zu Mannheim vom 23. bis 29 September 1906*, Berlin: Buchhandlung Vorwärts.

Sombart, Werner 1925, 'Die Idee des Klassenkampfes', *Weltwirtschaftliches Archiv*, 21: 22–36.

Sophocles 2007, *Ajax*, in Sophocles, *Four Tragedies*, translated by Peter Meineck and Paul Woodruff, Indianapolis: Hackett, pp. 1–61.

Sorel, Georges 1889, *Le procès de Socrate. Examen critique des thèses socratiques*, Paris: Alcan.

Sorel, Georges 1961 [1908], 'The Decomposition of Marxism', in Irving Louis Horowitz, *Radicalism and the Revolt Against Reason: The Social Theories of Georges Sorel*, New York: The Humanities Press.

Sorel, Georges 1969 [1908], *The Illusions of Progress*, translated by John Stanley and Charlotte Stanley, Berkeley and Los Angeles: University of California Press.

Sorel, Georges 1976, 'The Trial of Socrates', extract in Georges Sorel, *From Georges Sorel: Essays in Socialism and Philosophy*, translated by John Stanley and Charlotte Stanley, New Brunswick: Transaction, pp. 62–70.

Sorel, Georges 1999 [1908], *Reflections on Violence*, translated by Thomas Ernest Hulme and Jeremy Jennings, Cambridge: Cambridge University Press.

Sotsial-demokrat, Kraków.

Sozialdemokratische Arbeiterpartei Österreichs 1896, *Verhandlungen des fünften österreichischen Sozialdemokratischen Parteitages abgehalten zu Prag vom 5. bis einschließlich 11. April 1896 auf der Schützen-Insel*, Wien: Brand.

Sozialdemokratische Arbeiterpartei Österreichs 1897, *Verhandlungen des sechsten österreichischen sozialdemokratischen Parteitages abgehalten zu Wien vom 6. bis einschließlich 2. Juni 1897 im Saale des Hotel Wimberger*, Wien: Brand.

Sozialdemokratische Arbeiterpartei Österreichs 1899, *Verhandlungen des Gesamtparteitages des Sozialdemokratie in abgehalten zu Brünn vom 24. bis 29. September 1899 im 'Arbeiterheim'*, Wien: Brand.

Sozialdemokratische Arbeiterpartei Österreichs 1903, 'Bericht der Gesamtvertretung der Sozialdemokratie in Oesterreich', *Verhandlungen des Gesamtparteitages des Sozialdemokratie abgehalten zu Wien vom 9. bis 13. November 1903*, Wien: Brand, pp. 11–15.

Sozialdemokratische Partei Deutschlands 1891, *The Erfurt Program*, translated by Thomas Dunlap, available at: https://www.marxists.org/history/international/social-democracy/1891/erfurt-program.htm, accessed 20 February 2017.

Sozialdemokratische Partei Deutschlands 1905, *Protokoll über die Verhandlungen des Parteitages der Sozialdemokratisches Partei Deutschlands, abgehalten zu Jena vom 17. bis 23 September 1905*, Berlin: Buchhandlung Vorwärts.

Sozialdemokratische Partei Deutschlands 1921, *Das Programm der Sozialdemokratischen Partei Deutschlands, betroffen am 23. September 1921 zu Görlitz*, Kiel: Haase.

Sozialdemokratische Partei Deutschlands 1925, *Das Heidelberger Programm: Grundsätze und Forderungen der Sozialdemokratie*, Berlin: Vorstand der Sozialdemokratischen Partei Deutschlands.

Sozialdemokratische Partei Deutschlands 1927, *Sozialdemokratischer Parteitag 1927 in Kiel: Protokoll*, Berlin: Dietz.

Spinoza, Benedict 1954 [1677, written 1664–5], *Ethics, Preceded by On the Improvement of the Understanding*, translated by William Hale White, Amelia Hutchinson Stirling and R.H.M. Elwes, New York: Hafner.

Stalin, Iosif Vissarionovich 1954a [1924], *Foundations of Leninism*, in Joseph Vissarionovich Stalin, *Problems of Leninism*, Moscow: Foreign Languages Publishing House.

Stalin, Iosif Vissarionovich 1954b [1930], 'Political Report of the Central Committee to the Sixteenth Congress of the c.p.s.u.(b.), June 27, 1930', in *J. V. Stalin Works. Volume 12 April 1929–June 1930*, Moscow: Foreign Languages Publishing House.

Stein, Ludwig 1897, *Die soziale Frage im Lichte der Philosophie*, Stuttgart: Enke.

Steinbüchel, Theodor 1920, 'Die Idee eines christlichen Sozialismus', *Deutsche Arbeit*, 1: 4–13.

Steinbüchel, Theodor 1921 [1920], *Der Sozialismus als sittliche Idee: Ein Beitrag zur christlichen Sozialethik*, Düsseldorf: Schwann.

Stirner, Max 1907 [1845], *The Ego and His Own*, translated by J.L. Walker, New York: Tucker.

Strasser, Josef 1982 [1912], *Der Arbeiter und die Nation*, Wien: Junius Verlag.

Strobel, Georg W. 1974, *Die Partei Rosa Luxemburgs, Lenin und die SPD: Der polnische 'europaische' Internationalismus in der russischen Sozialdemokratie*, Wiesbaden: Steiner.

Sweezy, Paul 1942, *The Theory of Capitalist Development*, London: Dobson.

Świętochowski, Aleksander 1878, 'Socjalizm i jego błędy', *Nowiny*, 110, 18 October: 1; 112, 20 October: 1; 115, 23 October: 1; 117, 25 October: 1; 119, 27 October: 1.

Świętochowski, Aleksander 1910, *Utopje w Rozwoju Historycznym*, Warszawa: Gebethner i Wolff.

Swift, Jonathan 1894 [1742], *Travels into Several Remote Nations of the World by Lemuel Gulliver*, London: Macmillan.

Thompson, Edward Palmer 1976 [1955], *William Morris: From Romantic to Revolutionary*, New York: Pantheon.

Tillich, Paul 1926 *Kairos*, Darmstadt: Reichl.

Tillich, Paul 1930, *Religiöse Verwirklichung*, Berlin: Furche.

Tillich, Paul 1989, 'Class Struggle and Religious Socialism', in Jacquelyne Anne K. Kegley (ed.), *Paul Tillich on Creativity*, Lanham, MD: University Press of America, pp. 95–118.

Tillich, Paul 1998 [1930], 'Sozialismus', in Paul Tillich, *Main Works/Hauptwerke. Volume 3*, Berlin: de Gruyter, pp. 189–204.

Tobias, Henry J. 1972, *The Jewish Bund: From Its Origins to 1905*, Stanford: Stanford University Press.

Todt, Rudolf 1878, *Der radikale deutsche Sozialismus und die christliche Gesellschaft*, second edition, Wittenberg: Herrosé.

Trotsky, Leon 1924, 'Rech na zasedanii petrogradskogo soveta po voprosu o demokraticheskom soveshhanii', in Leon Trotsky, *Sochineniya*, Moskva: Gosudartstvennoe Izdatelstvo, pp. 283–5.

Trotsky, Leon 1969 [1930], *The Permanent Revolution*, in Leon Trotsky, *The Permanent Revolution; and Results and Prospects*, translated by John G. Wright and Brian Pearce, New York: Pathfinder.

Trotsky, Leon 1972, *The Stalin School of Falsification*, translated by John G. Wright, New York: Pathfinder Press.

Trotsky, Leon 1975 [1933], 'The German Catastrophe: The Responsibility of the Leadership', in Leon Trotsky, *The Struggle Against Fascism in Germany*, Harmondsworth: Penguin, pp. 397–404.

Tucker, John Henry 1891, *The Anarchists: A Picture of Civilization at the Close of the Nineteenth Century*, translated by George Schumm, New York: Tucker.

Ude, Johann 1928, *Der ideale Staatsbürger und seine Wirtschaftsethik*, Klagenfurt: Merkel.

Ude, Johann 1930, *Eigentum, Kapitalismus, Christentum*, Graz: Stocker.

Untersuchungskommission im Angelegenheit des Mitgliedes der Sozial-Demokratie Russisch-Polens und Littauens Karl Radek 1914, 'Bericht der Untersuchungskommission im Angelegenheit des Mitgliedes der Sozial-Demokratie Russisch-Polens und Littauens Karl Radek', Item G689–136, Karl Kautsky Papers 2979, International Institute of Social History, Amsterdam.

Varga, Eugen 1930, 'Akkumulation und Zusammenbruch des Kapitalismus', *Unter dem Banner des Marxismus*, 4, no. 1: 60–95.

Villeneuve-Bargement, Alban de 1834, *Économie politique chrétienne*, three volumes, Paris: Paulin.

Vollmar, Georg von 1878, *Der isolirte sozialistische Staat: Eine sozialökonomische Studie*, Zürich: Verlag der Volksbuchhandlung.

Vserossiysky Centralny Ispolnitelny Komitet 1920, 'Rezoliutsiia ob elektrifikatsii Rossii', *Biulleten GOELRO*, 1: 2.

Wileński, Tadeusz 1904, *Kwestya żydowska*, Kraków: Latarnia.

Winterer, Landelin 1891, *Der internationale Sozialismus von 1885 bis 1890*, Köln: Bachem.

Wissel, Rudolf 1920, *Die Planwirtschaft*, Hamburg: Auer.

Wundt, Wilhelm Maximilien 1889 [1880], *Logika: rozbiór zasad poznania oraz metod naukowego badania. Tom 1 Teorya poznania*, Warszawska: Gebethner i Wolff.

Wundt, Wilhelm Maximilien 1893, *Logik: Eine Untersuchung der principien der Erkenntniss und der Methoden wissenschaftlicher Forschung. Band 1, Erkenntnisslehre*, Stuttgart: Ferdinand Enke.

Wünsch, Georg 1927, *Evangelische Wirtschaftsethik*, Tübingen: Mohr.

Wünsch, Georg 1930, 'Materialistische Geschichtsauffassung und christliche Wahrheit', *Die Zeitschrift für Religion and Sozialismus*, 2.

Yudisher Sotsial-Demokrat 1905, 'Nakh dem kongress', 3 June: 1–6.

Zarząd polskiej partyi socyalno-demokratycznej w Austryi 1905, 'Sprawy partyjne', *Naprzód*, 11 May: 1.

Zentralrat der Sozialistischen Republik Deutschlands 1975 [1919], *11. Kongress der Arbeiter-, Bauern- und Soldatenräte Deutschlands vom 8.–14. April 1919 im Herrenhaus zu Berlin: stenographisches Protokoll*, Glashütten, Auvermann.

Zetterbaum, Max 1900, 'Probleme der jüdisch-proletarischen Bewegung', *Neue Zeit*, 19, vol. 1, no. 11, 12 December: 324–30.

Zetterbaum, Max 1901, *Przedświt*, 1.

Zimmerwald Left 1915, 'Two Declarations', in *The Bolsheviks and the World War: The Origin of the Third International*, edited by Olga Hess Gankin and Harold Henry Fisher, translated by Olga Hess Gankin, Stanford: Stanford University Press, pp. 333–4.

Zinovieff, G. n.d. [1918], *Nikolai Lenin: His Life and Work*: Cleveland: Toiler Publishing Association.

Żydowska Partya Socyalno-Demokratyczna Galicyi 1905a, *Przed Kongresem*, Kraków, 2 June.

Żydowska Partya Socyalno-Demokratyczna Galicyi 1905b, 'Odpowiedzi Polskiej Partyi Soc.-Dem. Galicyi', in Żydowska Partya socyalno-demokratyczna Galicyi, *Przed Kongresem*, Kraków, 2 June, pp. 1–6.

Index, Including Abbreviations and Micro Biographies

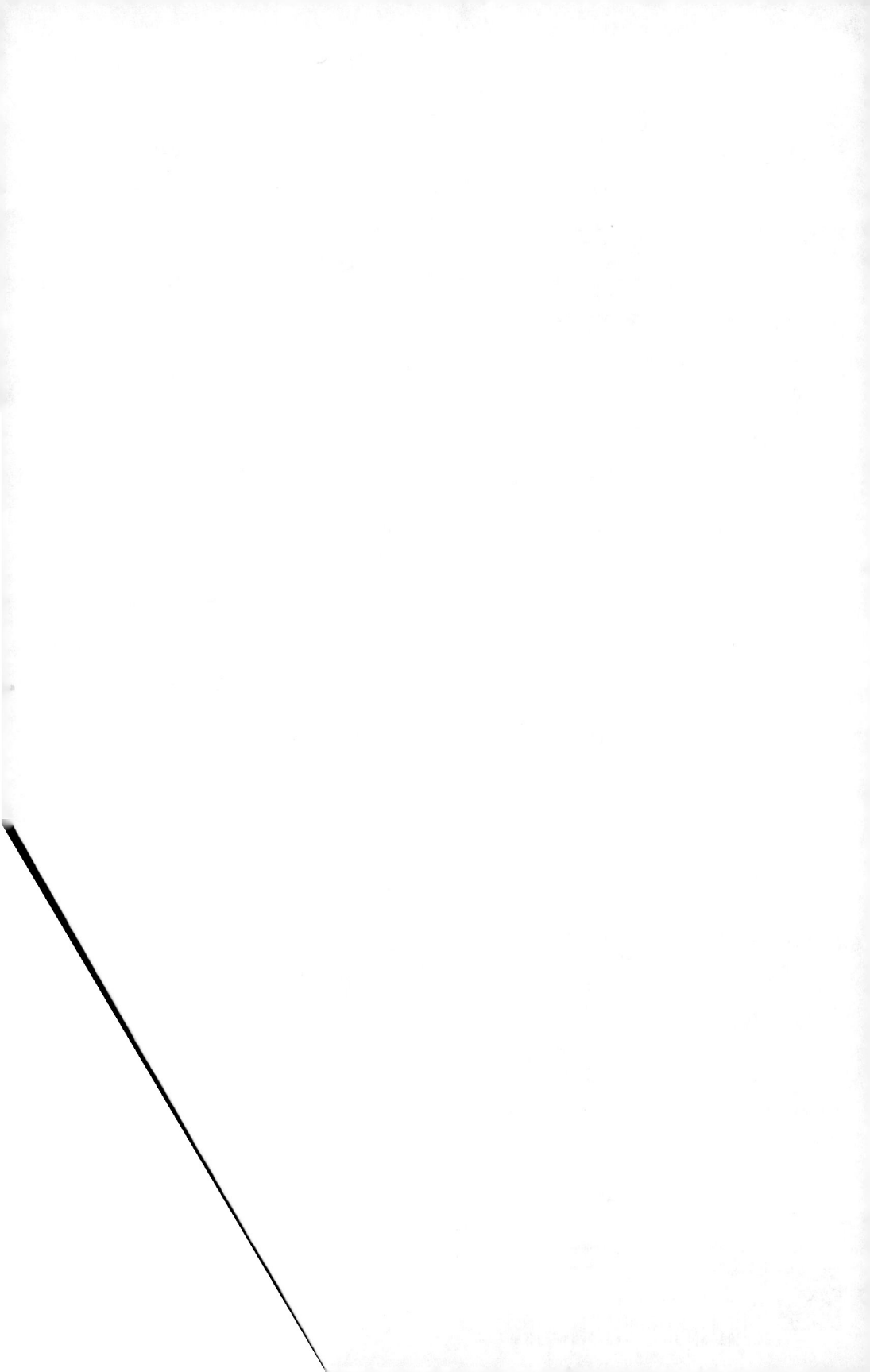

www.ingramcontent.com/pod-product-compliance
Lightning Source LLC
Chambersburg PA
CBHW070857030426
42336CB00014BA/2240